D0990642

PERCEPTUAL COHERENCE

Perceptual Coherence

Hearing and Seeing

STEPHEN HANDEL

OXFORD
UNIVERSITY PRESS
2006

OXFORD
UNIVERSITY PRESS

Oxford University Press, Inc., publishes works that further
Oxford University's objective of excellence
in research, scholarship, and education.

Oxford New York
Auckland Cape Town Dar es Salaam Hong Kong Karachi
Kuala Lumpur Madrid Melbourne Mexico City Nairobi
New Delhi Shanghai Taipei Toronto

With offices in
Argentina Austria Brazil Chile Czech Republic France Greece
Guatemala Hungary Italy Japan Poland Portugal Singapore
South Korea Switzerland Thailand Turkey Ukraine Vietnam

Published by Oxford University Press, Inc.
198 Madison Avenue, New York, New York 10016

www.oup.com

Library of Congress Cataloging-in-Publication Data
Handel, Stephen.
Perceptual coherence : hearing and seeing / Stephen Handel.
p. cm.
Includes bibliographical references and index.
ISBN-13 978-0-19-516964-5
ISBN 0-19-516964-6
1. Sensory receptors. 2. Auditory perception. 3. Visual perception. I. Title.
QP447.H36 2005
152.1—dc21 2005013750

9 8 7 6 5 4 3 2 1

Printed in the United States of America
on acid-free paper

To My Family, My Parents,
and the Bowling Ball Cat,
once again

Preface

The purpose of this book is to describe and explain some of the similarities and differences between hearing and seeing. It is written as an intermediate-level text. It is not mathematical, although it depends on mathematical and analytical thinking. I have tried to walk a line between an overly simplified and an over-the-top presentation of the material.

I think of this text as a "bridge" book in two ways.

The first bridge is between hearing and seeing. It used to be that individuals who studied hearing and seeing thought of themselves as studying perception. Perceiving, with only rare exceptions, involves making inferences and decisions based on information coming from several modalities simultaneously. The choice of using auditory, visual, or tactile input (or combinations) would be based on the particular problem studied. Audition and vision would be model systems, to be employed according to the research question. Currently, the technical expertise required to do research with either sense, and the enormous amount of information about both, have led to a distinct intellectual fissure, with separate journals and professional meetings. The research literature often makes passing references to similar outcomes in other senses, but there is little follow-up.

On top of these experimental issues, I think there is a general belief that hearing and seeing are fundamentally different. I have enumerated many of these differences in table 1.1. Nonetheless, I have always thought that beneath these differences are fundamental similarities in the ways that all modalities make sense of the external world. All events and objects (and perceivers) exist in a common space and time, and all events and objects have a sensory structure that can be picked up by the perceiver. Taken together, I believe that this implies that the internal structures for hearing and seeing are at least qualitatively the same.

There is no single way of connecting the different aspects of hearing to corresponding aspects of seeing. For example, here I connect color to timbre, but another compelling connection would be visual texture to timbre, or color to pitch. Hopefully, the material here will lead readers to consider other possibilities.

Without exception, all chapters contain information about both hearing and seeing. The two chapters that are more exclusively concerned with one sense, chapter 7 about color and chapter 8 about timbre, should be considered as a matched pair. I wrote the chapter about color thinking about timbre and vice versa.

The second bridge is between the introductory materials found in undergraduate sensation and perception, sensory physiology, or basic neuroscience courses and advanced courses covering audition or vision as well as the published literature. I have assumed that readers are not complete novices and that they have had an introductory course, so that many preliminary concepts are not explained fully. I have tried to simplify the figures to emphasize the important points.

There are many excellent introductory textbooks and many excellent advanced texts, and this is designed to slot between the two. Among the advanced texts that I have found particularly useful are Dayan and Abbott (2001), De Valois and De Valois (1988), Gegenfurtner and Sharpe (1999), C. D. Geisler (1998), Kaiser and Boynton (1996), Hartmann (1998), Palmer (1999), Rieke, Warland, de Ruyter van Steveninck, and Bialek (1997), Shevell (2003), and Wandell (1995). These are all more mathematical, and focus on either hearing or vision. My hope is that this book will make the transition to these texts and the professional literature easier.

One of the pleasures of writing a book is the ability to take time to reread books that now are considered passé. I have thoroughly enjoyed Floyd Allport's (1955) treatment of perceptual theories, Georg von Bekesy's (1967) book on sensory inhibition, Julian Hochberg's (1964) slim paperback on perception, and Wolfgang Kohler's (1969) summary of Gestalt psychology. I have also rediscovered the work of Rock (1997), which is discussed at length in chapter 9. I suggest that everyone should read these classics; they are exceptional.

On the whole, each chapter is relatively self-contained. Chapters 1, 2, and 3 cover the basic material and probably should be read first. The remaining chapters can be covered in any order, depending on the interests of the reader.

Many people have contributed to the writing of this book, often unbeknownst to themselves. I would like to thank Dr. Roy D. Patterson for allowing me to spend a sabbatical in his laboratory. Roy's ideas have been the germ for many of the themes in this book: his ideas have become so intertwined with my own that I am afraid that I have not given him appropriate credit. I am deeply grateful to Dr. Howard Pollio, my colleague in the Psychology Department at the University of Tennessee for 30 years. Howard always has challenged my "mechanistic" explanations and he has forced me to accept the essential intentionality and creativity of perceiving. I am afraid that I will not have satisfied him or myself with what I have been able to write here about either issue. I am also deeply grateful to Dr. Molly L. Erickson and Dr. Sam Burchfield in the Audiology and Speech Pathology Department at the University of Tennessee. Molly has taught me much about acoustic analysis and voice timbre, and has good-naturedly squelched all of my outrageous analogies between hearing and seeing. Sam has been a constant support throughout.

This book has been a tremendous stretch for me and I would like to thank Drs. David Brainard, Rhodri Cusack, David Field, Jeremy Marozeau, and Mark Schmuckler for supplying data, and particularly Drs. Albert Bregman, Peter Cariani, C. D. Geisler, and Paris Smaragdis for patiently answering questions and improving the text. Hopefully they have pushed the book back from the precipice of the Peter Principle. Finally, I would like to thank the staff at the Jackson Laboratory. Doug McBeth and Ann Jordan have processed my reference needs with unfailing good humor and Jennifer Torrance and Sarah Williamson have patiently taught me the finer points of figure preparation in a fraction of the time it would have taken me to figure it out myself.

Contents

PERCEPTUAL COHERENCE

1

Basic Concepts

In the beginning God created the heavens and the earth
Now the earth had been wild and waste
Darkness over the face of Ocean . . .
God said: Let there be light! And there was light . . .
God separated the light from the darkness
Let there be lights in the dome of the heavens to separate the day from the night
And let them be for lights in the dome of the heavens, to provide light upon the earth
God made the two great lights,
The greater light for ruling the day and the smaller light for ruling the night, and the stars.

The beginning of Genesis is perfectly delimited; nothing missing, nothing extra. What consistently intrigues me is the second line, "Now the earth had been wild and waste, darkness over the face of Ocean" (Fox, 1983, p. 4). In the text that follows, God brings order out of chaos. God did not create order from nothingness. It is along the continuum between chaos and randomness to order and structure that our perceptual world forms. Our phenomenal world is not based on the overall level of randomness or order. Rather, our phenomenal world is created by the difference or ratio between randomness and order. Following the initial creation, God made things different: To separate the night from the day God made the greater light and the smaller light. The night is not dark; it is a lesser light. Here again, the phenomenal world is not based on the overall magnitude of light (or sound), but on the difference or ratio between the lightest and darkest or between the loudest and softest. In general terms, this contrast allows us to make sense of a physical world that varies by orders of magnitudes greater than any single cell of our sensory systems can encode. This contrast allows us to partition the perceptual world into the objects and events that we react to. Moreover, this contrast allows us place objects and events into equivalence categories that are necessary to make sense of the world.

From this perspective and that of Genesis, the opposite of looking at, listening to, or grasping is not blackness, silence, or lack of pressure, but unstructured energy, energy that does not afford the perceiving of things or events in the world. The energy in the physical world and the energy coded by the receptors at the periphery are neutral. Perceiving is not merely attending to parts of the incoming energy, but is the abstraction of the structured energy out of the ongoing flux. It is the interpretation of the physical properties of objects and events. Hoffman (1998) described vision as an intelligent process of active construction; the world is not recovered or reconstructed. The act of looking or listening constructs objects. This is as true for seeing a tree in a snowstorm as it is for hearing a word in a thunderstorm. Perceiving is creative and not passive.

The purpose of this book is to match up auditory and visual perception. Throughout, I take the position that perception is active and that we attend to the structured parts of the world. Therefore, I do not think of *perception* as a noun, but as a gerund, *perceiving*. Looking, listening, searching, overhearing, grasping, touching, manipulating, and so on are the processes of perceiving. These processes are multifaceted. There is no doubt that biological processes exist that transform and code the firings from the peripheral receptors. But, there is no general agreement about how those firings construct the world. On the one hand, the sensory data, if taken over time and space, may have sufficient information to create unambiguous percepts (Gibson, 1966). On the other hand, sensory data may be inherently ambiguous, so that there are necessary inferential and heuristic processes to make sense of every firing pattern. The best strategy would be to make use of cues that are most likely to be correct and have the least variability (Jacobs, 2002). Following Helmholtz (1867), we would perceive what in the past would have most likely generated the sensory data (Purves, Lotto, & Nundy, 2002). It is not necessary or even appropriate to claim a predominant role for any level of processing. Rather, we make use of all levels to create the appearance of things.

All Sensations Belong to Things and Are Understood With Respect to Those Things

As a first guess, visual stimulation is assumed to come from one or more reflecting surfaces of rigid objects moving in three dimensions, and auditory stimulation is assumed to come from one or more continuously vibrating sources moving in three dimensions. It may be that the visual world consists of light waves passing through transparent surfaces, or that the auditory world consists of pressure waves reflecting off passive objects, but that is not the usual way sensations arise and not the usual way we understand and integrate those sensations. We make use of these usual properties to integrate independent local excitations at the receptors (e.g., the motion of lighted dots, the variation in sound pressure, the brightness patterning of textures) into one or more coherent surfaces and objects. Visual information is "shaped" by the object: the parallel beams of light from a distant source (e.g., the sun) are reflected and shaped into a pattern that signifies the surface and shape of the object. In similar fashion, auditory information is shaped by the object: Air particles are mechanically "pushed around" and shaped into a pattern that signifies the physical properties (e.g., shape, size, material) of the vibrating surface.

Thus, I believe that the usual distinction that vision gives us objects and audition gives us events is a trap. It misleads us into thinking about vision as a spatial sense and about audition as a temporal sense. According to the *Oxford English Dictionary*, the original definition of object is "something thrown in the way," or "to stand in the way so as to obstruct or obscure." Objects are typically opaque, so they block the recognition of other objects that are behind them. In contrast, the definition of events is "to emerge out of a temporal flow." But all perceiving concerns the appearance of things, and things exist in space and time simultaneously. To Griffiths and Warren (2004), object analysis is the analysis of information that corresponds to things and their separation from the rest of the sensory world. To put it differently, all sensory input is interpreted in terms of familiar causative agents or events and not in terms of the manner and nature of sensory stimulation (R. M. Warren, 1999). Raymond (2000, p. 48) makes a similar claim: "the idea is that the brain deals in the currency of object representations, not disembodied stimulus features."

One example of our inclination to perceive sensations as bound to objects occurs with random dot kinematograms, as shown in figure 1.1. Dots are programmed to move as if each were attached to the surface of a transparent cylinder. Even though the cylinder is rotating at a constant speed (A), the observer does not see the dots moving at a constant speed. Instead the observer sees the dots slow down as they reach the edge of the cylinder, stop, and then speed up in the reverse direction as they near the center line of the cylinder (the dots also change size as they move from the front to the back of the cylinder) (B). If the dots did not change velocity or size and simply reversed direction, the perception would be that of a flat surface. Observers effortlessly see the dots moving coherently, and attached to the front or back surface of a rigid cylinder consistent with their direction of movement. What is important is that the observers infer the presence of a cylinder even if

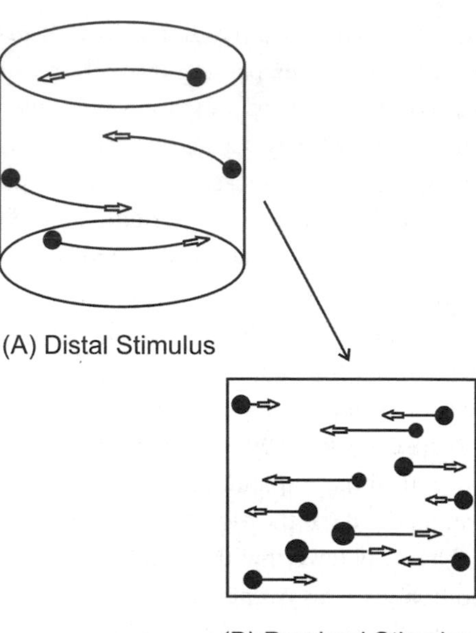

Figure 1.1. Dots are programmed to move as if each was attached to the surface of a transparent cylinder. The cylinder is rotating at a constant speed, so that each dot moves at a constant speed, the distal stimulus depicted in (A). However, the the observer sees the dots change speed and direction as indicated by the arrows attached to each dot. The observer also sees the dots change size as indicated by the size of the dots in the proximal stimulus diagrammed in (B).

individual dots disappear and new ones come into existence. Thus, the perceptual stability and existence of the cylinder surface is created and maintained by the pattern of movement of the dots, yet the temporal properties of individual dots has little effect on perception of surface; the cylinder has a perceptual existence that is independent of any single dot.

Another example of our inherent tendency to perceive elements as part of a three-dimensional object is the classic demonstration of the perception of human figures due to movements created by small lights placed on the joints (e.g., wrists, knees, angles, shoulders). Johansson (1973) dressed the actors in black so that only the lights were visible. When the lights are stationary, they appear to be randomly placed and no form is seen, but as soon as the lights begin to move it is easy to tell whether the actor is running or walking, and even the gender of the actor (Cutting, 1978). It is interesting to note that it is much harder to see the human action if the film is presented upside down (Dittrich, 1993). For both the rotating cylinder and the running person, the three-dimensionality of the immediate percept is based on the pattern of movement of the dots. If the movement stops (or does not resemble plausible biological actions), the percept collapses into a flat random collection of moving dots.

It is worthwhile to point out that the perception of a rotating cylinder or walking dots is based on at least two other implicit assumptions about the world: (1) there is only one light source and (2) it is a single rigid object even though its appearance changes. The same sort of implicit assumptions occur for the auditory world: (1) there is a single sound source and (2) it is the same source even though its acoustical properties change. The most useful heuristic is to accept the default assumption of one source because in the natural course of time, its properties change due to a slightly different location, orientation, movement, or excitation. Pizlo (2001) argued that all perceiving should be considered as the inverse problem of going from the proximal stimulation at the receptor to the distal object in the world and that all perceiving depends on the operation of a priori probabilities and constraints such as smoothness and good continuation. In Pizlo's view, without constraints, perceptual interpretations (what the proximal stimulation tells us about the world) are not well-posed problems: There may not be a solution, or there may be several solutions. Regardless of whether you believe that the proximal stimulation is interpreted according to evolutionary tuning of the senses to the environment or according to empirical probabilities discovered with experience, or both, the interpretation is that of objects.

The Perceptual World Emerges From Processes at Many Levels

Although our auditory and visual phenomenal world is one of unified objects and happenings, the convergent and divergent auditory and visual pathways (as well as feedback loops from higher brain centers) suggest that the processing of sensory information occurs both simultaneously, in parallel at different neural locations, and successively, serially, as firing patterns converge from these locations. Furthermore, for both hearing and seeing, the initial processing of the physical energy occurs at a local level, not globally. For hearing, the acoustic wave is broken down into frequency components and the receptive cells in the inner ear fire maximally to intensity variation at specific frequencies. For seeing, cells fire to the intensity variation in small regions of the retina and moreover fire maximally to intensity variation that occurs along specific directions (i.e., black-white variation horizontally as opposed to vertically). What this means is that many mechanisms, modules, processing units, or channels (many different words are used to describe these neural "calculators") make use of the same sensory firing pattern to calculate different properties of the object and event.

Although it appears that some properties (e.g., color) are constructed in specific cortical regions, it would be a mistake, however, to think of these mechanisms as being encapsulated and strictly independent. Nakayama (1985) argues that there are several subsystems underlying the perception of motion and that one or many could be utilized depending on the perceptual demands. Thus, the puzzle is how the various mechanisms are integrated; the problem of analysis is "solved" in terms of the neural circuitry. Each such property enters into the perceiving of many qualities. For example, a motion detection system would enter into the perception of the third dimension, the sense of one's own movement, the detection of impending collisions, and so on. For a second example, the relative intensities of the different frequencies give us pitch, instrumental and voice quality, the sense of an approaching object due to the Doppler effect, speech vowels, and so on. Moreover, there are interactions between vision and audition (see Shimojo & Shams, 2001, for a short review; see also material in chapter 9).

Still another issue is the creative intentionality in perceiving. The organization of light and sound into meaning can usually be done in several ways. The sections below describe some of the heuristics people use to make sense of stimuli. Yet, we all know of instances in which we seem to will ourselves to see or hear something differently. For example, we can make the Necker cube reverse in depth or even force it down into two dimensions; we can listen to an orchestra as a whole or pick out particular instruments; and we can listen to singing phonetically or melodically.

Perceiving Occurs at Several Spatial and Temporal Scales Simultaneously

The first theme stated above explicitly links the perception of bits and pieces of objects to the overall properties of the objects themselves. All of the scales or grains are interdependent due to the fact that they are inherent in the same object or in the same scene. Wandell (1995) argued that we perceive motion with respect to broader "ideas" concerning "dense" surfaces and objects. Julesz (1971, p. 121) made the same argument that the visual system tries to find a global solution in the form of a dense surface instead of localizing points in depth and will disregard, within limits, differences in the disparity values from the two eyes that signify different depths. Bregman (1993) made an analogous assertion for hearing: The auditory system tries to find a global solution in terms of a single source. Namely, we will try to hear a single sound or sequence of sounds as coming from one object. We will break the sound wave into different sound sources only if the expected harmonic and temporal relationships among frequency components that would be created by a single source (e.g., all components should start and stop at the same time) are continuously violated. In the same way that the entire visual scene creates the percept, the rhythmic relationships among frequency components found in longer sequences of sounds will also determine our decision of whether there are one or more sound sources. A single sound source is the default solution, and the auditory system accumulates evidence before shifting to a multiple-source global solution. Thus, both what we see and what we hear are created at several levels of perceiving. All perception occurs within such a broad context.

Simple examples that illustrate the levels of perceiving are found in photomosaic pictures. Large-scale objects are created by means of arrays of smaller photographs that have the appropriate overall color and brightness to represent features of the larger object. I have a 45 × 60 cm poster of the Statue of Liberty on my wall constructed from more than 1,000 little photographs. It is possible to focus on the overall shape of the head or on the individual photographs at nearly all reasonable distances from the poster. I am always overwhelmed by the creative possibilities available in perceiving.

The Aperture Problem

Although I have argued above that perceiving depends on multiple stimulus properties that can span spatial and temporal scales, typically we cannot make use of all the available properties at once due to sensory limitations, memory limitations, or even environmental obstacles. For example, cells that code orientation, motion, and shape in the vision system have small receptive fields so that each cell responds as if looking at a very small part of the visual field, and cells that code frequency in the auditory system respond to only a limited set of frequencies so that each cell responds as if hearing only a small part of the signal. It is the convergence of cells at the higher visual and auditory centers that yields cells that respond to larger parts of the field, but the success of that convergence must be due to combining corresponding parts of the field. Moreover, auditory and visual sensations occur across time, and the visual glimpse or auditory snippet at a particular instant must be interpreted by what has preceded it and what will follow it.

The aperture problem is exemplified when looking at the motion of a uniform line through a rectangular opening, as shown in figure 1.2. The problem is that one cannot determine the direction or speed of motion of the line. It could be moving along its own length at any speed, but the restriction of information through the opening makes movement in that direction ambiguous. There are no unique points on the line that allow unambiguous matching from instant to instant. Without some kind of mark on the line, it is impossible to determine if any in-line movement occurred. Regardless of the actual movement of the line, observers simply report the line as moving perpendicular to its orientation without mention of any other motion. That percept minimizes the speed and distance the line seems to move.

What we want to do is represent all possible movements of the line. We start with a straight diagonal line shown in figure 1.2(A). We can represent

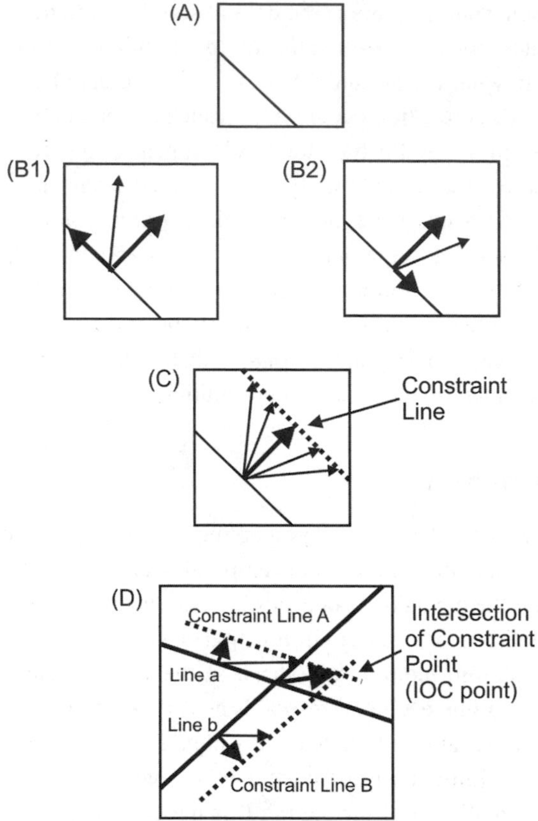

Figure 1.2. The movement of a uniform line (in A) seen through an aperture is ambiguous because it is impossible to see any in-line movement. Two possible in-line movements are shown in (B1) and (B2) and the vector sum of the perpendicular and in-line movement is depicted by the lighter vector. The sum of every possible in-line movements combined with the known perpendicular motion creates a set of vectors that will fall along the constraint line. Four such vectors are shown in (C) as well as the "pure" perpendicular movement. If two lines move simultaneously, the lines are often perceived to move together toward the intersection of the two constraint lines (abbreviated IOC point) (D). The light arrows represent the movement of each line.

any motion by the sum of two vectors at 90° in (B1 and B2): One vector is perpendicular to the line (seen) and the other is along the line (unseen). The length of each vector represents the speed along that direction, but of course, we cannot know the in-line speed. Two possible in-line movements are shown in B1 and B2 (darker lines) and the resulting sum of each of the two movements with the (known) perpendicular movement by the lighter line (a vector). All of the vectors combining the seen perpendicular movements with the possible, but unknown in-line motions, end on a single straight line parallel to the actual line termed the *constraint line,* the dotted line shown in figure 1.2(C).[1]

Suppose that more than one line is moving within the opening. A downward-sloping line (line a in D) moving to the right would appear to move diagonally up to the right, creating the constraint line A. An upward-sloping line (line b in D) moving to the right would appear to move diagonally down to the right, creating the constraint line B. Observers report that the perceived motion of the two lines together is toward the intersection of the two constraint lines (the IOC point), directly to the right.

I want to argue that the aperture problem is ubiquitous in all perceiving. Our ability to extract the relevant information is always being obstructed in one form or another. In audition, the aperture is not spatial but temporal. In the sense of seeing a visual scene through a slit that allows viewing the scene only as a series of overlapping spatial segments, so too we hear an auditory stimulus only through a temporal slit that allows a series of overlapping temporal segments. In both hearing and seeing, we perceive things by putting together the ongoing overlapping signal. If the aperture is unduly restrictive and reduces the contrast between order and disorder, the perception changes. For example, viewing a uniformly colored surface through an aperture changes the appearance of the color. The aperture reduces the contextual information from the entire scene to brightness and hue information from small spatial areas. The color takes on a filmy appearance and does not appear to be attached to a surface.

The Correspondence Problem

The aperture problem is the cause and complement of the correspondence problem. The visual and auditory sensory worlds are in constant flux (as well as the flux due to eye movements) so that the sensations at any moment cannot unambiguously signify objects or events, and yet we perceive a stable phenomenal world by matching successive visual glimpses and successive auditory segments into stable objects. I have come to believe that the correspondence problem lies at the heart of perception.

The correspondence problem originally referred to the problem of fusing the slightly different visual images in each eye by matching their features. But in the same fashion as argued for the aperture problem, the correspondence problem can be found in nearly all instances of perceiving. Take, for example, exploring a single object using both hands. Here it is

1. If one point on the line is marked, or if one end point is shown, the actual movement can be perceived unambiguously. What happens is the movement of that point is assumed to be true of all the unmarked points on the same line (a rigidity assumption). Palmer (1999) termed this the *unique-point heuristic*.

obvious that the surfaces uncovered by each hand must be placed in registration in order to create a solid object. I can identify five types of problems.

Correspondence Between Binaural and Binocular Inputs

Due to the positioning of the two eyes, the retinal images are slightly displaced spatially with respect to each other, and similarly due to the positioning of the two ears, auditory images are slightly displaced temporally with respect to each other. Thus the problem is to match the visual features in each eye and to match the auditory features in each ear.

The traditional solution for vision was to assume that the image in each eye was analyzed first, so that the correspondence problem was reduced to matching the shapes found in each eye. However, Julesz (1971) demonstrated that binocular correspondence could occur for a wide variety of random-dot stereograms that precluded classic shape matching. The correspondence was achieved by identifying that part of the random array that was common to both eyes. Thus, shape matching is not necessary, although it may occur normally. In the natural world, the correspondence problem can be simplified by making use of the normal properties of real surfaces. Namely, continuous surfaces change slowly and gradually, while discontinuities between surfaces create sharp contrasts.

The traditional solution for hearing is to assume that there are cells sensitive to various time delays created by the outputs from the two ears. Imagine that the neural signal from the near ear is transmitted along parallel neurons so that the signal in each neuron is delayed by an increasing amount of time. Then, each delayed signal is matched against the far ear signal. The match (i.e., the coincidence of the firings) will be maximized at one delay and that delay will signify a direction in space based on head size. Simultaneously, the two firings will become fused into a unified percept.

Correspondence Between Patterns Repeated in Space or Time

Imagine a sequence in which a set of identical but randomly placed dots changes position. We can think of this as a sequence of images, such as the frames of a motion picture. If the motion is rigid, the relative positions of the dots do not change and the correspondence problem becomes matching the dots in one image with those in a later image that represents the same pattern that could have been rotated or translated. If the motion is nonrigid, then the correspondence problem becomes finding the match that represents the most likely transformation. Similarly, imagine a segment of a random sound that is repeated without interruption so that the listener hears a continuous sound. The correspondence problem is to isolate the repeating segments so that the amplitudes at corresponding time points in each segment are perfectly correlated.

As found for the binaural and binocular correspondences discussed above, the proposed explanations make use of heuristics that reflect the highly probable characteristics of the environment to reduce and simplify the matching problem. For example, one such visual heuristic is that most objects are rigid so that correspondences requiring deformations are given low probabilities, and one such auditory heuristic is that most sounds come from a single sound source that changes frequency and amplitude slowly so that correspondences requiring large changes are given low probabilities. One unresolved issue is what units are being matched. The match could be based on simple elements such as lines, blobs, and individual sounds, or based on geometric figures and rhythmic or melodic phrases.

Correspondences Within One Interrupted Visual Image or Auditory Segment

In our cluttered environment, one visual object is often partially occluded by other objects, yielding a set of disconnected parts, and a single sound is often masked by partially overlapping competing sounds, yielding a sequence of interrupted parts. Here the correspondence problem is whether the parts are separate objects themselves or come from one auditory or visual object.

Correspondences Between Auditory and Visual Information

We see and hear a ball bounce, a person speaking, or a violinist playing. In all such cases, the energy in each modality must be kept in correspondence in space and time. If the information is deliberately misaligned in space (ventriloquism) or time (flashing lights that are not synchronous with sound rhythms), sometimes the information in one modality dominates (we "listen" to the visual dummy and see the lights as synchronous with the auditory rhythm) and sometimes there is a compromise. On the whole, observers are biased toward the more reliable information, irrespective of modality.

Correspondences Between Objects and Events at Different Orientations, Intensities, Pitches, Rhythms, and So On

It is extremely rare that any object or event reoccurs in exactly the same way. The perceptual problem is to decide whether the new stimulus is the reoccurrence of the previous one or a new stimulus. Sometimes, an observer must judge whether two shapes can be matched by simple rigid rotations or reflections. But often the new stimulus is a more complex transformation of the original one, such as matching baby to adult pictures or matching an instrument or singer at one pitch to an instrument or singer at a different pitch. In both of these cases, the perception of whether the two pictures or two sounds came from the same source must depend on the creation of a trajectory that allows the observer to predict how people age or how a novel note would sound. I would argue that the correspondence problem is harder for listening because sounds at different pitches and loudness often change in nonmonotonic ways due to simultaneous variation in the excitation and resonant filters. The transformation simultaneously defines inclusion and exclusion: the set of pictures and sounds that come from one object and those that come from other objects.

Inherent Limitations on Certainty

Heisenberg's uncertainty principle states that there is an inevitable trade-off between precision in the knowledge of a particle's position and precision in the knowledge of the momentum of the same particle. Niels Bohr broadened this concept by arguing that two perspectives may be necessary to understand a phenomenon, and yet the measurement of those two perspectives may require fundamentally incompatible experimental procedures (Greenspan, 2001). These ideas can be understood to set limits on the resolution of sensory systems. For vision, there is a reciprocal limitation for space and time (and, as illustrated in chapter 2, a reciprocal limitation between spatial frequency and spatial orientation). Resolution is equivalent to the reliability or uncertainty of the measurement; increasing the resolution reduces the "blur" of the property. The resolution can be defined as the square root of the variance of repeated measurements.[2]

For audition, there is a reciprocal limitation between resolution in frequency and in time. To simultaneously measure the duration and frequency of a short segment, the resolution of duration restricts the resolution of the spectral components and vice versa. Suppose we define the resolution of frequency and time so that $(\Delta F)(\Delta T) = 1$.[3] Thus, a temporal resolution of 1/100 s restricts our frequency resolution to 100 Hz so that it would be impossible to distinguish between two sounds that differ by less than 100 Hz. Gabor (1946) has discussed how to achieve an optimal balance between frequency and space or time uncertainty in the sense of minimizing the

2. In chapter 9, we will see that resolution also determines the optimal way to combine auditory and visual information.

3. In general, $(\Delta F)(\Delta T) = \text{constant}$, and the value of the constant is determined by the shape of the distributions and the definitions of the width (i.e., the resolution) of the frequency and time distributions.

overall uncertainty. Gabor argued that Gaussian (sinusoidal) distributions of frequency and time are optimal because the product of their uncertainties is a minimum: $(\Delta F)(\Delta T) \geq .07$. Actually, human performance can be a bit better than this physical limit (Hartmann, 1998).

One way to conceptualize inherent uncertainty is to imagine a simple *x-y* coordinate system in which the *x* axis represents frequency and the *y* axis represents duration. If there was no uncertainty, then any tone could be represented by a single point in the *x-y* space. But because there is uncertainty, the best we can do is create a minimum rectangular area in the space so that the width along the *x* axis represents the frequency resolution with the height along the *y* axis representing the duration resolution. If we want to measure both frequency and duration with equal resolution, then the area becomes a square. The receptor will not be able to resolve combinations of tones within that square. If we want to measure frequency with greater resolution, then the square becomes a vertical rectangle so that the *x* width gets smaller, but the *y* height (i.e., resolution) must increase to maintain the same area. Similarly, if we want to increase the resolution for duration by making the *y* height smaller, we must necessarily decrease the resolution for frequency by making the *x* width longer to maintain the same rectangular area (Daugman, 1985).

Figure 1.3A illustrates the joint uncertainty arising from spatial frequency and spatial orientation as discussed in chapter 2. Figure 1.3B illustrates that to increase frequency resolution by elongating the frequency axis to encompass more cycles, it is necessary to reduce the length of the orientation axis, thereby decreasing orientation resolution. Figure 1.3C illustrates that to increase spatial orientation resolution by elongating the orientation axis, it is necessary to reduce the length of the frequency axis.

The solution to the resolution problem is to construct a perceptual system with multiple levels so that there is a distribution of resolution trade-offs at each level and so that there is also a trade-off of resolutions between lower and higher levels. This solution returns us to the second theme: Perceiving is the interplay of several levels at once. For the visual system, we can imagine an initial level composed of receptors with small receptive fields, some optimized for frequency resolution and some optimized for orientation resolution. Each receptor is sensitive to changes in a tiny part of the visual scene. The problem is to convert this local information into coherent global percepts. We can further imagine that this first level feeds into a second level that integrates sets of spatially adjacent receptors so that the receptive field is larger but the resolution is less. The second level feeds into a third level that integrates sets of adjacent second-level receptors and so on. By combining all lower and higher levels in parallel, the perceptual system gets the best of two worlds: spatial detail from the initial level embedded in the global shapes from the higher levels. For the auditory system, the initial level would respond to individual frequencies; the next level would integrate the firings

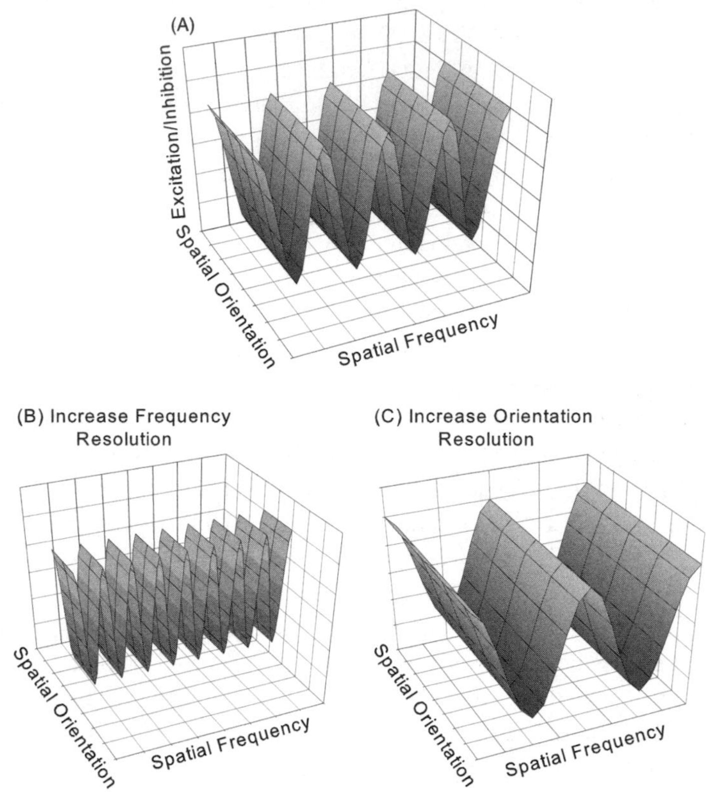

Figure 1.3. The joint uncertainty arises from spatial frequency and spatial orientation resolution, as discussed in chapter 2. Panel (B) illustrates that increasing frequency resolution by elongating the frequency axis necessarily reduces the orientation resolution. Conversely, panel (C) illustrates that increasing spatial orientation resolution by elongating the orientation axis necessarily reduces the spatial frequency resolution.

of adjacent frequencies. Still higher levels would integrate lower levels to create tone quality (i.e., timbre and pitch), and temporal organizations such as rhythm that extend over longer time spans.

Aperture, Correspondence, and Inherent Uncertainty

The aperture, correspondence, and inherent uncertainty issues are all interrelated. The inherent trade-offs in resolution force us to create "tight" apertures in space and time to capture the rapidly changing light and sound energy that signify the boundaries of objects and events. The necessity for apertures to maintain the fine-grain information in turn creates the correspondence problem. The "snapshots" in space and time must be fused to create a useful perceptual world.

What will emerge in the following chapters is that the correspondence problem is solved in two ways. The first may be termed *effortless and passive*. Here the correspondences are found without conscious effort, before higher-order processes involved with shape analysis or figure-ground segmentation occur. The second may be termed *effortful and attentive*. In this second case, the correspondences are found by actively searching the stimuli to seek out the matches. As a first approximation, the first type of correspondence occurs in the short range, across small displacements in space or time, while the second type occurs in the long range, across large displacements. Perhaps the best strategy is to choose the process that minimizes the correspondence uncertainty.

Perceiving the World Occurs in Real Time

Given the immediacy and transparency of perceiving, it is easy to forget that perceiving is based on the patterning of neural spikes (Rieke et al., 1997). The spike train is not a static image; it is a running commentary or simultaneous translation of the objects and contrasts in the world. Here is yet another trade-off hinging on temporal integration: between combining the spike trains in time to average out inherent errors or maintaining correspondence with the ongoing changes. As I will argue throughout the book, the solution entails a continuum of neural mechanisms that cover the range from short temporal periods necessary for responding to rapid changes to long temporal periods necessary for averaging responses.

Rieke et al. (1997) persuasively argued that the neural spike code must be understood in the context of the natural timing of external events and in the context of what alternative events could occur. In many natural environments, stimulus variation may occur within intervals of 100 ms (e.g., speech sounds) so that given typical neuron firing rates from 10/s to 50/s, the stimulus change may be signaled by as few as one to five spikes. Thus, there may be sparse coding in the temporal domain in which there is but one spike for each change in the environment. (I return to the issue of sparse coding in chapters 2 and 3.) The interpretation of such a neural code cannot be made without some a priori knowledge of the possible stimulus changes, and our interpretation of the information and redundancy of the signals cannot be done without defining such alternatives. The auditory and visual worlds are not random, and there should be strong internal correlations in the neural spike train that match the internal structure of objects and events.

Rieke et al. (1997) went on to point out that the classic dichotomy between neural coding based on spike rate and that based on the timing between spikes (e.g., phase-locking to specific parts of the signal) should be understood in terms of the rate of change of the stimulus. If the stimulus is not varying (e.g., a static visual image), rate coding provides the usable information, and the timing information is nonexistent. If the stimulus is constantly changing, then the timing between spikes provides the useful information and the average firing rate may be unimportant. But if the stimulus is changing very rapidly, then the neural system may not be able to fire rapidly enough to synchronize to each change, and then only rate coding would be possible. In sum, the interpretation and usability of the neural code can be investigated only in terms of the intentionality of the perceiver, be it a fly, bat, or human, in a probabilistic environment.

Perceptions Evolve Over Time

Previously I argued that perception is the construction of the distal world from the proximal stimulation. What we often find is that perception of an event evolves over time. Initially, the percept is based purely on the proximal stimulus, but over time that percept is superceded by one that takes into account the overall context, previous stimuli, prior knowledge, and so on that result in a more accurate rendition of the distal world.

One example of this occurs if two lines with slightly different orientations are viewed through an aperture. Suppose the two lines are moving perpendicularly at very different velocities that are represented by the lengths of the two vectors. There are two possible perceptions here. The first, shown in figure 1.4A, which I term the *proximal motion*, is simply the vector sum of the two line vectors and therefore is an upward motion that is between the two individual motions, a sum. The second, shown in figure 1.4B, which I term the *distal motion*, is in the direction of the intersection of the two lines of constraint. That motion is up to the right, outside the individual motions. Observers report that the initial perception is that of the vector sum (less than 90 ms of presentation), but that percept soon gives way to motion toward the intersection of constraints (Yo & Wilson, 1992). The vector sum motion will still bias the perceived motion, pulling it toward the sum direction and away from the constraints' motion. I discuss other examples of this in chapter 9.

Pack and Born (2001) have shown that the response of individual cells of alert monkeys in the middle temporal visual area (MT or V5) of the visual pathway, which has been shown to integrate directional motion from lower levels, mirrors this perceptual transition. Early in the visual pathways, direction-sensitive neurons have only small receptive fields, so that they can respond to but a small region of a moving object. Thus they are likely to "send up" the visual pathways incorrect or conflicting information about motion. The stimuli used by Pack and Born were short parallel line

(A)

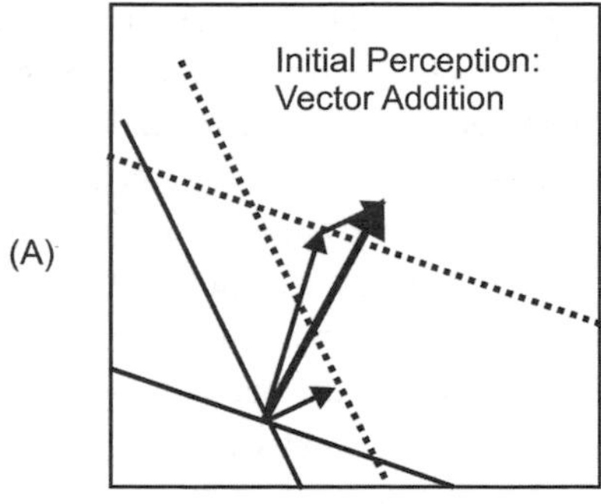

(B)

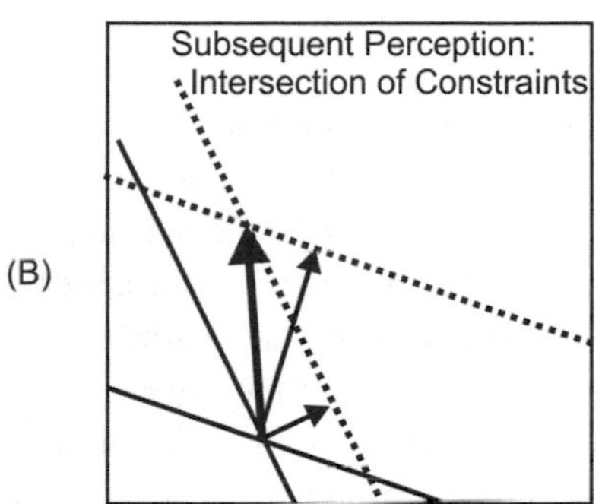

Figure 1.4. If two lines (or two gratings) move at different speeds, the initial percept is that both lines move together in a direction between the perpendicular movements of the two lines, as pictured in (A). Within a short time, the percept switches and now the two lines appear to move toward the intersection of constraints. As shown in (B), paradoxically that motion can be outside the angle formed by the two individual movements.

segments at different orientations. The lines moved either strictly perpendicular or 45° off from perpendicular. They found that the initial direction-specific responses (70 ms after movement onset) were affected by the original orientation of the bar, with the majority of responses perpendicular to orientation. But over time, the effect of the orientation decreased and the MT cells began to encode only the actual stimulus direction. Thus, by integrating responses that individually are spatially limited, the MT region can derive a relatively accurate picture of motion.

Perceptual Variables Are Those of Contrast and Change

The fundamental problem in beginning to understand perceiving is to isolate the important physical variables that create our perceptual world and to discover how to measure those variables to create simple relationships. We need to know which properties affect our construction of objects and events in the world, and which properties provide background and context. We could precede either empirically by manipulating the levels of the properties to determine their effects on perception, or we could proceed rationally by considering how such properties could affect perception in natural conditions.

From the latter perspective, we are asking a joint question about the ecology of the environment, the organism's goals in that environment, and the properties of the sensory systems. Consider overall intensity and the resulting perception of brightness and loudness. For both hearing and seeing, the range of intensities from the lowest (e.g., dim evening, whispers) to highest (e.g., sunny noon, rock music concerts) values can exceed the ratio of 1,000,000:1. However, individual neurons can only signal changes of intensity across the much smaller range of 100:1 or 1,000:1 because the firing rate saturates and cannot increase beyond that range. Yet we need to optimize our sensitivities at all light levels.

Clearly we need sensory energy in order to perceive at all, and overall intensity can provide information about such things as the size and distance of objects. But opaque solid or vibrating objects are characterized by their contrast to the overall level of energy. What is important for seeing is the ability to take the neutral mosaic of different light intensities reaching the retina and assign the bits to opaque objects interspersed and overlapped in space and time. What is important for hearing is taking the neutral pattern of air pressure variation and assigning parts to one or more vibrating objects interleaved in time and space. What characterizes all such objects is that the variation in intensity (i.e., their contrast) at the boundaries occurs more rapidly across time and space than variation in the background environment. Thus, we should expect the auditory and visual neural systems to maintain the correct response to contrast variation and to sacrifice an accurate response to overall illumination and loudness. In fact, the majority of cortical visual cells do not respond to blank scenes of any illumination. Moreover, the firing rates of many neurons in the auditory and visual pathways have a sort of gain control. As the background intensity increases, the average firing rate remains constant (instead of increasing) so that the neuron still can increase its firing rate to increases in intensity above the background. Without such a gain control, the firing rate would saturate at even modest background intensity levels.

There are many ways to demonstrate that contrast determines our perceptual world. Imagine a scene in which a black piece of paper is situated in a region of bright sunlight while a white piece of paper is situated in a region of dim light created by shadows. The black piece of paper would reflect more light energy overall. However, the black paper is seen as black while the white paper is seen as white. Thus, the amount of light energy per se does not determine brightness. The brightness is based on the ratio of the reflectance from the paper to the reflectance from the background. The visual system partials out the overall level of illumination (possibly to avoid saturation). The ratios are calculated in terms of the light in the local areas surrounding each piece of paper, and not in terms of the overall light across the entire scene. For hearing, we can construct a tone that oscillates in amplitude across time (analogous to a visual stimulus that oscillates in brightness across space). The threshold for detecting the amplitude changes is nearly identical across a 100-fold change in overall intensity. In similar fashion, we can construct a complex tone by summing together a set of frequency components such that each component has a different amplitude. The threshold for detecting a change in amplitude of just one of the components also is relatively constant across a wide range of overall amplitudes (D. M. Green, 1988). Thus, the important auditory properties are those that signify changes in the relative vibration patterning that characterizes objects.

If we proceed empirically, then we would look for dependent variables that change smoothly, optimally in linear fashion, to changes in independent variables. Given the ecological properties described above, we should not expect a linear function. In fact, simple relationships are not found; the functional relationships change smoothly but not in linear fashion. At lower intensities, it appears that all the energy is integrated to detect the object at the cost of perceiving fine details. But at higher intensities, inhibitory processes emerge that limit the neural response in order to achieve a sharper auditory or visual image. Thus, auditory and visual adaptation at higher intensities maximizes object detection based on contrast. This makes intensity a nonlinear property that is not scalable. The functional relationships that exist for small changes in intensity at lower magnitudes are not the same ones that exist for the identical changes at higher magnitudes.

Perception Is the Balance of Structure and Noise

Above I have argued that the perceptual variables are those of change. But obviously that is just one part of the answer. The change must be predictable and that predictability must be able to be derived by the observer. Barlow (1990) put it differently: Perception converts possibly hidden statistical regularities into explicit recognizable forms to prepare for the figure-ground segregation necessary for learning. Perception is the construction of a representation that enables us to make reliable inferences about associations among sensations in the world around us.

At one end, there is noise in which there is no predictability among elements. For auditory noise, the pressure amplitudes are not predictable from one instant to another. For visual noise, the brightness of elements (e.g., points of different grayness levels) is not predictable from one spatial location to another. At the other end are periodic auditory and visual events in which there is perfect predictability between elements separated by a specific time interval or spatial distance. We might say that the combination of the predictable and nonpredictable parts is the "stuff," and that the abstraction of the predictable parts yields the "things" of perceiving. (The stuff is really defined in terms of the things that result from the stuff.)

When there is a mixture of unpredictable and predictable elements, there is a normally irresistible perceptual segregation that isolates the predictable parts. If we mix a predictable tonal component together with a nonpredictable noise component, the perception is that of listening through the noise to hear the tone. Similarly, if we look at an object through a snowstorm, the perception is that of looking at an object whose parts are being covered and uncovered. I find it impossible to put the noise back into the tone to hear an integrated sound or to put the snowflakes back onto the object. I believe that the auditory and visual segregation is obligatory and represents the first step in achieving the objects of perceiving. Bregman (1990) has termed this process *primitive segregation*.

As argued above for single properties, it is the contrast or ratio between the amount of structure and amount of noise that is the important perceptual variable. For auditory stimuli that can be conceptualized as lying on the continuum between tone and noise, listeners reliably can judge the perceptual tone:noise ratio even when the overall levels of the stimuli are varied randomly (Patterson, Handel, Yost, & Datta, 1996). Perceiving is contextual and relativistic.

Rules of Perceiving Should Be True for All Senses

All of the above implies that listening, seeing, grasping, smelling, and tasting are fundamentally the same. Although the sensory inputs and sensory receptors are quite different in structure and operation, and the actual contrasts may be different, all function by partitioning and contrasting structure and noise. All senses have been optimized through evolution to provide animals with information about survival: predators, conspecifics, and food and water. But all senses must simultaneously be general-purpose systems that can respond to an ever-changing environment.

Often it is difficult to find the best way to illustrate correspondences between the senses. It is possible to attempt to match the basic dimensions of auditory and visual experience and then compare their psychophysical properties. I have implicitly compared loudness to brightness above, and pointed out that the range of perceptible physical energy is relatively equivalent. At this level, the comparisons would tend to focus on the parity of discrimination (e.g., ranges of discriminability, difference thresholds and Weber ratios, time and space integration windows). It is also possible to match the gestalt (for lack of a better word) properties of auditory experience (such as timbre, pitch, noise, roughness, texture, vibrato, location, motion, consonance, repetition, melody, and rhythm) to the gestalt properties of visual experience (such as shape, motion, color, brightness, texture, symmetry, transparency, opacity, and location in three-dimensional space). For example, is the perception of temporal auditory noise equivalent to the perception of spatial visual noise? Finally, it is possible to compare the segregation of auditory scenes into sound-producing objects to the partitioning of a visual scene into light-reflecting objects. Figure-ground visual organization assigns a contour line to one and only one object. Does figure-ground auditory organization similarly assign a frequency component to one and only one object? Is there a generalized time-space representation into which all sensory experience is intertwined?

At first, the differences between hearing and seeing seem huge. Is it possible to use the same conceptualizations for listening and looking, given the vast differences in their normal functioning? Light energy is electromagnetic. Light waves travel nearly instantaneously, so that interocular temporal differences cannot exist. The wavelengths are miniscule (400–700 nm), which allows excellent spatial resolution, while the frequency is very high, which disallows phase-locking of the neurons to individual cycles. Sound energy is mechanical pressure. Pressure waves travel slowly, so that interaural temporal differences can be used for localization. The wavelengths can be body size, which minimizes the ability to determine object size and shape, while the frequency is relatively low, so that neurons can phase-lock to individual cycles. The physiological differences reflect these differences. The visual system has 120 million spatial sensors per eye (every rod and cone in each eye can be thought to represent one spatial point), while the auditory system has but 2,000 inner hair cells per ear that cannot represent spatial direction. However, the 2,000 auditory inner hair cells have different frequency sensitivities, whereas the visual system has but three different cone sensitivities and just one rod sensitivity. These differences are summarized in table 1.1.

On this basis, Kubovy and Van Valkenburg (2001) claimed that audition and vision serve very different spatial functions: "listening to" serves to orient "looking at." Caelli (1981) suggested that it is impossible to meaningfully compare the different kinds of perception, and Julesz and Hirsh (1972) argued that analogies between vision and audition might, at best, not be very deep because visual perception has to do with spatial objects while auditory perception has to do with temporal events.

Nonetheless, I would argue that perceiving in all sensory domains is finding structure in the energy flux and that deriving equivalences among the domains can deepen our understanding of how we create the external world. For example, one kind of equivalence is that the cortical representation of all senses tends to be arranged into discrete processing areas. Nearly always, adjacent cells represent slightly different values of the same feature (e.g., acoustic frequencies or spatial orientations). In each of these cortical

Table 1.1 Comparison of Hearing and Seeing

Property	Hearing	Seeing
Type of Energy	Mechanical Pressure Waves	Electromagnetic Waves
Speed of transmission	a. Relatively slow—(340 m/s) b. Allows for interaural temporal differences to judge direction	a. Nearly instantaneous—(3×10^8 m/s) b. No interocular temporal differences
Wavelength	a. Relatively long—(.02–10 m) b. Poor spatial discrimination	a. Very short—(400–700 nm) b. Excellent spatial resolution (light shadows)
Frequency	a. Relatively slow—(30–20000 Hz) b. Allows phase-locking to individual cycles c. Excellent temporal resolution	a. Very high—($4.3–7.5 \times 10^{14}$ Hz) b. Phase-locking impossible c. Poorer temporal resolution
Physiological sensors	a. Mechanical process b. Rapid regeneration c. Rapid adaptation	a. Chemical process b. Slow regeneration c. Slow adaptation
Number of receptors	Relatively small number—(2,000 hair cells/ear)	Large number—(120,000,000/eye)
Cerebral cortical area	8%	20–30%
Sensitivity	Distributed across frequency range	Three types of cones plus one type of rod
Object properties	Tend to be intermittent	Tend to be stable
Additivity	Sound pressure waves are transparent and add together	Light waves reflect off opaque objects and usually block each other

zones, an environmental stimulus or movement becomes represented by an isomorphic pattern of firing in the cortex (DeCharms & Zador, 2000). There is no necessity for this type of organization and yet all systems have evolved to this arrangement.

To represent the auditory and visual worlds, I make use of the concept of autocorrelation in space for vision (co-occurrences of brightness or color patterns separated by a fixed distance) and autocorrelation in time for audition (co-occurrences of intensity patterns separated by a fixed interval). By thinking in terms of autocorrelation to find order, I shift the explanation for perception to the global space-time properties of the ongoing stimulus array (Uttal, 1975). It is in same tradition as the efforts of J. J. Gibson to describe what there is to perceive in the world.

To represent the correspondences between the physical world, neurological codes, and perceptual experience, I will again use the correlation. Here, we would expect the correlation to be between stimulus contrasts and neurological contrasts (differences in rate or timing of the spikes). Both experimental data and mathematical simulations (Panzei & Schultz, 2001) indicate that the nature of the correlation depends on the timing of the stimulus contrasts, the presumed time in which the nervous system integrates the firings, and the variability in the noise of the neurons (this is the same argument made by Rieke et al., 1997, described previously). The correlation should not make use of a simple physical description of the stimulus. The nervous system does not create a perfect recording or photograph of the stimulus, and may exaggerate or disregard certain physical correlations and properties. Moreover, the perceptual representation is malleable as the person shifts attention. Julian Hochberg (1982, p. 214) argued, "the attributes that we perceive do not in general exist in some internal model of the object waiting to be retrieved. They are the results of our intention to perceive, and they appear in the context of the perceptual task that calls upon them." Thus, there may be no single kind of correlation that always is used, but we might expect that the auditory and visual systems will use the same neural contrasts when faced with equivalent stimulus contrasts (DeCharms & Zador, 2000).

Summary

The many interrelated concepts discussed in this chapter shape the intent of this book. Namely, I search for correspondences in the construction of the external world achieved by abstracting the structure of auditory and visual sensations across space and time. This is not to argue that there is consensus as to how sensory systems create a percept. There is not such a consensus and I would suspect that this lack is due to the diverse ways in which a percept could be constructed. Formulating the correspondences is slippery, and the bases for the correspondence can change from instance to instance. Nonetheless, the consistent goal is to compare the textures of the auditory and visual phenomenal worlds.

2

Transformation of Sensory Information Into Perceptual Information

If we take the reasonable position that perceptual systems evolved to perceive the spatial and temporal properties of objects in the world, then the place to begin is with an analysis of the characteristics of that physical world.[1] For some species, the perceptual world may consist of specific objects necessary for survival, and therefore we might look for physiological mechanisms that uniquely detect those objects (e.g., specific cells in the frog's tectum, colloquially termed *bug detectors* by Lettvin, Maturana, McCulloch, and Pitts (1959) that fire to small dark convex objects moving relative to the background). For other species including humans, the perceptual world is ever expanding in terms of novelty and complexity and therefore we might look for physiological mechanisms that detect statistical regularities and relationships, rather than specific things. This suggestion is analogous to Shepard's (1981) theory of psychophysical complementarity that physiological mechanisms and perceptual heuristics evolved in response to physical regularities. It may be possible to predict the characteristics of peripheral and central processes by figuring out how such regularities could be coded optimally.

We should ask a variety of questions:

1. Are there physical regularities in the scenes we normally encounter (excluding man-made objects that produce sounds at particular frequencies or that are made up of vertical and horizontal straight lines meeting at right angles)?

1. It is possible to take a different theoretical stance and argue that the function of sensory systems is to enable appropriate behavior with or without a conscious percept.

2. Are the sensitivities and functioning of the physiological mechanisms and perceptual systems optimally constructed to encode physical regularities in the world? Do these systems make use of the prior probabilities of objects and events?
3. Do the perceptual organizations mirror the physical properties of the world in terms of the physical actions necessary to survive (breaking through the camouflage of predators and prey)?

There are many reasons for an optimal code:

1. An optimal code will compensate for the rather limited range of firing rates for individual cells in the retina and inner ear in the face of much wider variation of physical properties in the world.
2. In the vertebrate visual system, the number of optic nerve fibers creates a bottleneck for the transmission of retinal signals to the brain. The human eye contains about 5 times more cones, and 100 times more rods, than optic nerve fibers (Thibos, 2000). For each eye, there are approximately 100 million receptor cells in the retina but only 1 million fibers in the optic nerves so that the retinal signal must be compressed to achieve the necessary transmission rate (the number of cells does increase again to more than 500 million cells in the cortex). The purely spatial retinal information of the rods and cones is transformed into a localized receptor-based analysis based on frequency and orientation that can sacrifice the part of the retinal information that is redundant and that does not help capture the object causing the sensations.
3. An optimal code at the receptor level will minimize the propagation and amplification of intrinsic error as the signal progresses through the nervous system.
4. An optimal code will match the output of the perceptual mechanism to the distribution of the independent energy in the external world. An important fact about natural time-varying auditory and visual scenes is that they do not change randomly across time or space. Due to the physical properties of objects, the brightness and color of any single visual object and the frequency and loudness of any single sound object change very gradually across space and time. Nonpredictable, sharp, and abrupt changes signify different visual and different sound-producing objects (Dong & Atick, 1995). Therefore, removing the predictable parts or making them explicit (Barlow, 2001) can lead to a concise and nonpredictable description.

We need to be cautious about embracing any optimality argument because it is impossible to state definitively just what should be optimized. As stated in chapter 1, perceptual systems need to be optimized in two conflicting ways: (1) for those relatively static properties involved in specific tasks and contexts (e.g., identification of mating calls and displays); and (2) for those emergent properties that identify auditory and visual objects in changing situations. A fixed set of feature detectors would be best for the former but unable to encode novel properties, while a dynamic nervous system that can pick up correlated neural responses would be best for the latter but unable to rapidly encode fixed properties. As described in this chapter, the auditory and visual systems are organized into tracts that are selective to particular stimulus dimensions, but there is an immense amount of interconnection among the tracts. What you hear or see has been modified by those interactions among the neural tracts.

In what follows, I consider two interrelated issues. The first issue is the neurological transformations that convert the sensory excitations that result only in increases in firing rate at the receptors into excitatory or inhibitory codes that represent objects in the world. Every neuron in the auditory and visual pathways is maximally sensitive (selective) to combinations of stimulus dimensions. For example, an auditory neuron might respond to particular combinations of frequency and amplitude, while a visual neuron might respond to particular combinations of frequency and spatial position. In general, farther up the pathways, the neurons become more diverse and selective and respond only to particular combinations of stimulus dimensions. It does not seem to be that perception occurs only at the end of the auditory or visual pathways; rather, the brain selects and alters the neural firings throughout the pathways.

The second issue is the match between the above transformations and the structured energy in the auditory and visual worlds. This entire book is predicated on the assumption that there is a close match between the two. It is more logical to proceed from stimulus energy to neurological transformation to reflect the role of evolution. However, I have found it easier to work in the reverse direction, first understanding the neural transformations and then matching those transformations to the properties of stimulus energy.

Neurological Transformations: The Concept of Receptive Fields

The receptive field of a neuron is the physical energy that affects the activity of that neuron. The receptive fields of nearly all cells past the receptor level contain both excitatory and inhibitory regions. The receptive field concept was first used in vision by Hartline (1940) to describe the ganglion retinal cells in the frog's retina, but it is so general that it has been used for all modalities and at all levels of the nervous system. Once the receptive field is known, it becomes a description of the transformation of some property of the sensory energy into a sequence of neural firings. Colloquially, we think of that property as being a feature of the visual and auditory stimulus and imagine that the identification of an object is based on the collection of such features. But we should not be trapped by that metaphor; the neurons really are filters, not feature detectors.

In vision, the receptive field is defined as the retinal area in which an increase or decrease in illumination changes the firing rate of the ganglion neuron (or cortical neuron) above or below the average rate of firing found in the absence of stimulation (Kuffler, 1953). The receptive field of the ganglion or cortical cell will be determined by the sensory receptors to which it is connected. To determine the retinal location and the spatial and temporal properties of the receptive field, flashing small lights, moving bars, or more complex configurations are presented at different retinal locations to identify the retinal positions and the light/dark patterns that maximally excite and inhibit the cell. In audition, the receptive field is defined as the frequencies, intensities, and durations of the acoustical wave that increase or decrease the firing rate of the neuron (identical to that for vision) and it is identified in the same way as in vision. Receptive fields imply specialization in firing. For vision, the receptive field of a neuron is localized at a particular retinal location and differentiated in terms of the spatial and temporal pattern of the light energy that fires that cell. For audition, the receptive field is localized at a position on the basilar membrane and is differentiated in terms of the temporal pattern of the acoustic energy that fires the cell.

Intuitively, the way to identify the receptive field is to present a wide array of visual and auditory stimuli and pick out those stimuli that increase the firing rate of the cell and those stimuli that decrease the firing rate. If you are smart (and lucky), then it will be possible to construct such a set. However, given the innumerable configurations in space, white-and-black contrast, frequency, intensity, and frequency and intensity oscillations that might uniquely trigger an auditory or visual cell, a more formalized procedure often is necessary.

The procedure that has evolved has been termed *reverse* or *inverse correlation.* In essence, the experimenter presents a sequence of randomly varying stimuli and then averages the stimulus energy that precedes a neural spike. Imagine a very short duration, very small pinpoint of light that is either brighter or darker than the surround. Furthermore, imagine that any response immediately following the presentation of the pinpoint simply increases the firing rate by one spike. Next, the experimenter presents the lighter and darker light many times at each spatial position and counts the number of spikes for each light (clearly the responses will not be identical at a single point to either light due to chance factors in the nervous system or in the light emitted). After measuring the probability of firing to each light at every position, the experimenter can identify excitatory regions where an increase in intensity generates a spike, inhibitory regions where a decrease in intensity generates a spike, and neutral regions where neither an increase nor decrease in intensity change generates a spike. In effect, he or she is correlating the input (light intensity) to the output (spike probability). The responses of the neuron define its own receptive field.

Now consider a more complex case in which the relevant stimuli are unknown. We might try using natural stimuli. However, it can be difficult to describe the characteristics of a neuron using natural stimuli because natural stimuli have internal correlations of energy, so that it may be impossible to link the spikes to a specific feature of the stimulus. For this reason, white noise has often been used as the stimulus to identify the receptive field. White noise can be simply understood as a pattern or sequence of light or sound stimuli such that the amplitudes vary randomly so that no correlation or prediction is possible between any two amplitudes separated in space or time.

We present the random white noise continuously. The intensity of the stimulus prior to each spike is measured and cumulated in say 100 sequential 1 ms time bins. Then, the intensities in each bin are averaged separately. The stimulus feature (intensity pattern) that triggers the spike will occur consistently in the time bins prior to the spike and therefore create high average amplitudes (or high probabilities), while the nonrelevant features will vary randomly (being essentially error) and average toward zero. This outcome is termed the *spike-triggered average stimulus* (Dayan & Abbott, 2001). The spike-triggered average stimulus is mathematically equivalent to calculating the correlation between the stimulus amplitude at each prior time point and the probability of a spike. It also has been termed the *fast Weiner kernel*, or the *reverse correlation function*. It is the receptive field of the cell.

In table 2.1, I generated a series of 60 random numbers (0–9 with an average of 4.5) and indicated the 18 spikes by the symbol *. I then averaged the intensities in the five time periods preceding the spike and plotted the averages in figure 2.1.

We could classify the receptive field of this hypothetical cell as an "on" cell that fires when the intensity at –20 ms and 0 ms is high. (I constructed the sequence so that spikes occurred if the sum of two successive intensities was 12 or greater.)

A more complex case occurs when the stimuli consist of multiple frequencies and the problem is to induce the receptive field, which may consist of several excitatory and inhibitory regions. I constructed a simplified example in table 2.2 in which four frequencies were presented (16 possibilities). As above, there were 60 presentations, spikes are indicated by *, and the probability that each frequency occurred in the four time bins preceding the spike is shown in table 2.3. The probabilities for F_1 and F_4 are close to the expected value; the probabilities for F_3 are above the expected value (excitation) particularly for –20 ms; and the probabilities for F_2 are below the expected value (inhibition), particularly for –20 ms.

Table 2.1 Derivation of the Receptive Field

(A) Stimulus Sequence and Resulting Spikes

Stimulus	4	6	7	0	3	2	1	2	4	0	5	1	5	9	5	4	1	6	6	8	4	5	9	6	3	3	8	3	7	7	9
Spike		*												*	*				*	*	*		*	*						*	*

Stimulus	0	5	1	5	4	0	4	3	3	4	4	4	8	9	2	0	6	9	3	1	9	7	0	5	5	9	0	2	3	5	9
Spike													*	*				*	*			*				*					*

(B) Derivation of Reception Field (Assume Stimuli Are Presented at 20 ms Intervals)

	Time Before Spike				
Spikes	80	60	40	20	Spike
1			4	6	7
2	0	5	1	5	9
3	5	1	5	9	5
4	5	4	1	6	6
5	4	1	6	6	8
6	1	6	6	8	4
7	6	8	4	5	9
8	8	4	5	9	6
9	3	8	3	7	7
10	8	3	7	7	9
11	3	4	4	4	8
12	4	4	4	8	9
13	9	2	0	6	9
14	2	0	6	9	3
15	9	3	1	9	7
17	7	0	5	5	9
18	0	2	3	5	9
Mean	4.6	3.4	3.8	6.7	7.2
SD	3.0	2.5	2.1	1.7	1.9

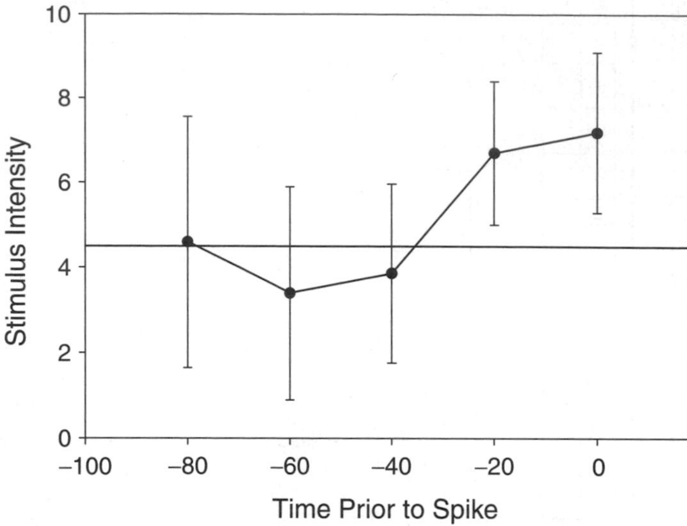

Figure 2.1. Average and standard deviation of the stimulus intensity before a spike (derived from table 2.1).

We can represent this cell from two perspectives. The response is depicted in figure 2.2A, measured from the tone onset at time 0. It portrays the receptive field as a filter. This simplified representation illustrates that 20 ms after the presentation of F_3 the firing rate decreases (shown in black), that 20 ms after the presentation of F_2 the firing rate increases (shown in white), and that the presentation of other frequencies does not change the baseline rate. If both F_2 and F_3 were presented, the resulting firing rate would be the difference between the two effects. The response is depicted in figure 2.2B, measured backward from the spike at time 0, as for reverse correlation. The frequency response of the cell can be found by drawing a vertical line through the region of maximum excitation (shown to the right). The temporal response can be determined by drawing a horizontal line through the region of maximum excitation, shown below the receptive field. This cell will fire with the highest probability 20–40 ms following the F_2 stimulus. It "detects" F_2.

It is useful to conceptualize the receptive field as a linear filter. As the auditory or visual stimulus energy evolves over time, the receptive field allows certain energy configurations through. An auditory receptive field could fire only when a specific range of frequencies occurs (a band-pass filter), or it could respond only to an upward (or downward) frequency glide within a set time period. We can test how well we have characterized the receptive field by simulating the receptive field mathematically, presenting

Table 2.2 Spikes Resulting From the Presentation of Tones Composed of One to Four Frequency Components

	Time														
Frequency	1	2	3	4	5	6	7	8	9	10	11	12	13	14	15
F_1		X	X				X	X	X	X					
F_2	X	X	X		X	X			X				X		
F_3	X		X	X	X	X				X	X	X	X		X
F_4			X		X		X				X			X	X
Spike					*						*	*	*		
	16	17	18	19	20	21	22	23	24	25	26	27	28	29	30
F_1	X		X	X	X			X	X			X	X	X	
F_2			X		X		X			X	X	X	X		
F_3	X	X	X	X	X							X	X		
F_4		X	X	X	X			X		X			X		
Spike	*	*	*		*										
	31	32	33	34	35	36	37	38	39	40	41	42	43	44	45
F_1		X		X	X						X			X	X
F_2		X			X	X	X		X		X				
F_3	X			X			X	X	X	X	X	X		X	
F_4	X		X		X	X		X	X				X	X	
Spike		*			*				*		*		*		*
	46	47	48	49	50	51	52	53	54	55	56	57	58	59	60
F_1	X		X	X			X		X	X		X	X		X
F_2						X		X	X	X			X		X
F_3	X	X	X	X		X		X				X			
F_4		X	X		X		X	X		X					X
Spike		*	*	*	*								*		

a realistic stimulus input, and then calculating the output of the simulated receptive field. We then correlate the simulated response to that of the actual neural receptive field using the identical input.

Suppose we manipulate the receptive field, moving the inhibitory region relative to the excitatory region, as shown in figure 2.3 by 20 ms. Assume that only the F_2 and F_3 frequencies are presented, each at 100 units. In the gray region, the probability of response is .25 (resting rate); in the black inhibitory region the probability is 0.1; and in the white excitatory region the probability is .9. Now imagine that we are measuring the output of the cell starting at the onset of the tones. The response rates are shown in table 2.4.

At the tones onset, the cell fires at its base rate to any frequency. Then from 10 ms to 20 ms, F_2 hits the excitation region before F_3 hits the

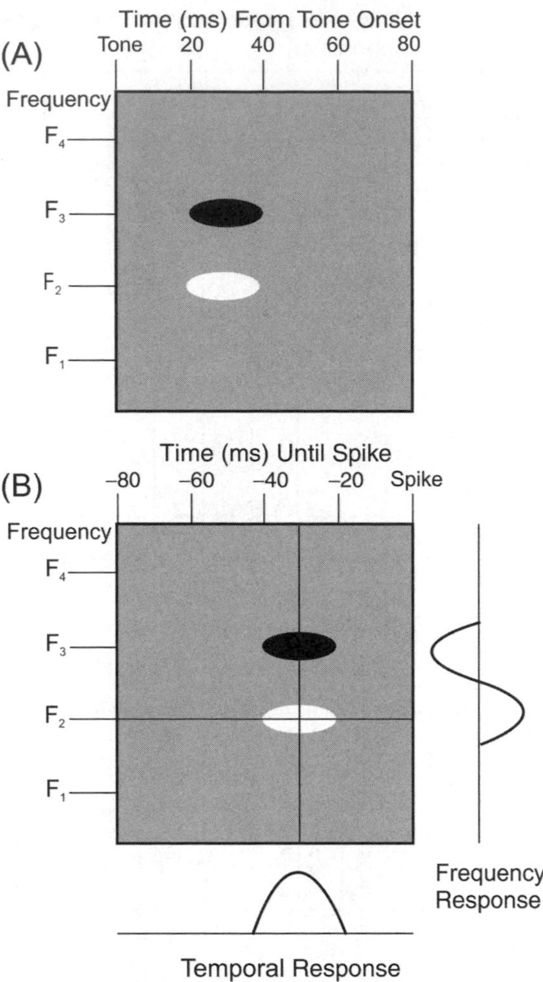

Figure 2.2. The receptive field for a cell. The gray area represents the baseline firing rate; the white area represents the excitation region; and the black area is the inhibition region. In (A), the response is portrayed in terms of the stimulus onset at time 0; in (B), the receptive field is portrayed in terms of the spike. Here, the excitation and inhibition areas can be thought of as features that trigger (or inhibit) a spike.

Table 2.3 Probability of Firing Based on Table 2.2

	Time Before Spike (ms)				
Frequency	80	60	40	20	0 (Spike)
F_1	.61	.56	.50	.50	.50
F_2	.50	.28	.33	**0**	.44
F_3	.56	.44	.61	**1.00**	**.67**
F_4	.44	.44	.50	.44	.61

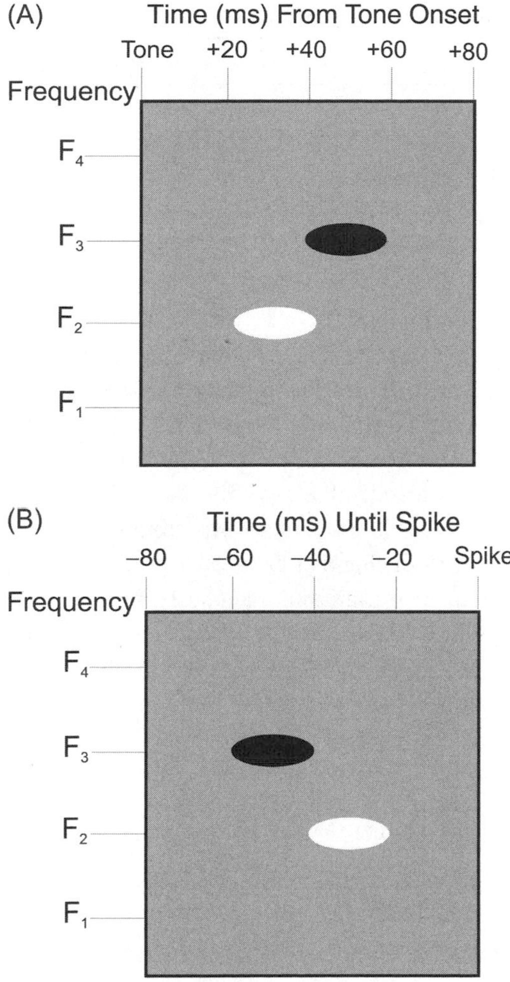

Figure 2.3. The receptive field for the cell in figure 2.2 in which the inhibitory region is offset by 20 ms. The maximum increase in firing rate occurs 20 ms after the tone onset, while the maximum decrease in firing rate occurs 40 ms after tone onset.

inhibition area and the rate increases. As the tones reach the F_3 inhibitory region, the firing rate decreases, particularly beyond 40 ms. Finally the firing rate returns to the resting level.

A more complicated case is shown in figure 2.4 for a cell that is most likely to fire for frequencies around 2000 Hz, but the principle is exactly the same.

This procedure does not completely solve the problem of generating the receptive field for three reasons. First, the choice of the stimuli still limits what you can find out. For example, experiments that use white

Table 2.4 Firing Rate From Time of Onset of Tones

	Time From Onset of Tones (ms)							
Frequency	Onset	+10	+20	+30	+40	+50	+60	+70
F_3	.25 × 100	.25 × 100	.25 × 100	.25 × 100	.10 × 100	.10 × 100	.10 × 100	.25 × 100
F_2	.25 × 100	.25 × 100	.90 × 100	.90 × 100	.90 × 100	.25 × 100	.25 × 100	.25 × 100
Sum	50	50	115	115	100	35	35	50

noise should theoretically be able to induce the features that make up the receptive field of any cell. But such random noise stimuli have not worked out well for neurons in the auditory cortex that are not sensitive to or even inhibited by broadband white noise. Thus, the initial choice of stimuli will affect the ability to identify the receptive field. Second, because the reverse correlation procedure averages the stimuli that create a spike, it would be difficult to distinguish between a neuron that fires only when two different frequencies are simultaneously present and a neuron that fires simply to either of the two frequencies (unless combination stimuli are presented). Third, the majority of real stimuli have internal correlations, so that it is necessary to partial out those correlations to derive the receptive field.

Receptive Fields in Vision

At the Retinal Ganglion Cells and Optic Nerve

The visual system transforms the retinal mosaic into a set of pathways that encode different properties of the visual stimulus. Much of this transformation occurs in the eye itself. The excitation from each retinal point diverges and connects to a set of ganglion cells such that each cell is selective for one property. (I am using the term *property* simply to mean a particular spatial configuration of brightness.) Every retinal point becomes represented by a set of equivalent ganglion cells. Thus, combining the analogous ganglion cells across the retinal points creates a retinal map of that property, and the convergence of all the ganglion cells in the optic nerve creates a parallel set of retinal property maps. The single-excitation map is transformed into multiple-property maps.

Briefly, the eye can be conceptualized as being composed of three layers. Light entering the retina first passes through the ganglion cells, then through the inner and outer plexiform layers that contain the amacrine cells, the bipolar cells, and the horizontal cells, and finally reaches the rod and cone receptors. The light energy always causes an increase in firing

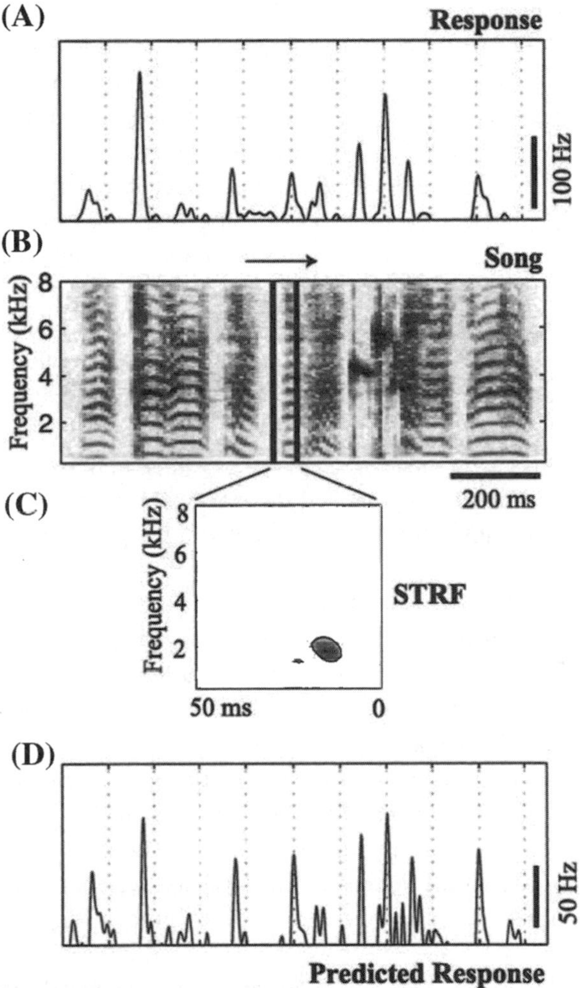

Figure 2.4. The illustration of a receptive field as a linear filter. The actual response is shown in (A). A spectrogram representation of a conspecific song is shown in (B). A window containing the spectral-temporal receptive field pictured in (C) is drawn across the song (0 represents the spike). The overlapping parts of the song and the spectral-temporal receptive field are multiplied point by point and summed together to get the predicted response rate. The predicted response, represented in (D), can be compared to the actual response in (A). From "Feature Analysis of Natural Sounds in the Songbird Auditory Forebrain," by K. Sen, F. E. Theunissen, and A. J. Doupe, 2001, *Journal of Neurophysiology, 86*, pp. 1445–1458. Copyright 2001 by the American Physiological Society. Reprinted with permission.

rate of the rods and cones. The signal passes back through the horizontal and bipolar cells, where synaptic connections alter the firing patterns. The final cellular stage consists of the retinal ganglion cells. Basically, the ganglion cells digitize the chemical signals in the retina, and our perceptual world is limited by the outputs of the ganglion cells.

Kuffler (1953) was the first person to characterize the receptive fields for ganglion cells near the optic nerve using small points of light flashed at different retinal positions. The majority of retinal ganglion cells have a bull's-eye-like receptive field. Either the receptive field contains an on-center in which a point of light above the background increases the rate of firing and an off-surround in which a point of light below the background increases the rate of firing (often simply termed an *on-off cell*), or the reverse, with an off-center and an on-surround (an *off-on cell*). We can imagine that the center region of the receptive field is based on direct connections from the receptors and the surround region is based on indirect connections through intermediate cells in the plexiform layer of the retina.

Rodieck (1965) postulated that the on- and off-regions could be explained by the difference in spatial integration for the on and off mechanisms. The probability of a spike for each mechanism was assumed to resemble a Gaussian or normal curve with respect to the position within the receptive field. The spatial extent (i.e., variance) of the center response was assumed to be smaller than the extent of the surround response by a factor of three due to the different integrations of the bipolar and horizontal cells. The area for center response was slightly greater than the area for the surround response to represent the dominance of the center region, and the output of the ganglion cell was simply the difference between the two sensitivity functions.

A two- and three-dimensional representation of an on-off receptive field based on the Difference of Gaussian model (termed DOG) is shown in figure 2.5. The three-dimensional representation is simply the rotated two-dimensional representation. This representation is for increments of light. If we measure the response to decrements of light, the changes in firing rates reverse. A decrease of light intensity in the center generates a reduction in the firing rate, while a reduction in the surrounding circular area produces an increase in the firing rate. Thus, the responses to increments and decrements of light are mirror images.

In general, there is always a matching on-center and off-center ganglion cell to represent each retinal point. The bipolar and horizontal cells work in tandem to create the center-surround field. The bipolar cells receive inputs from a small number of cones and create the center on- or off-response (whether the response is on or off depends on the type of chemical receptor on the cell surface). The horizontal cells receive input from many more

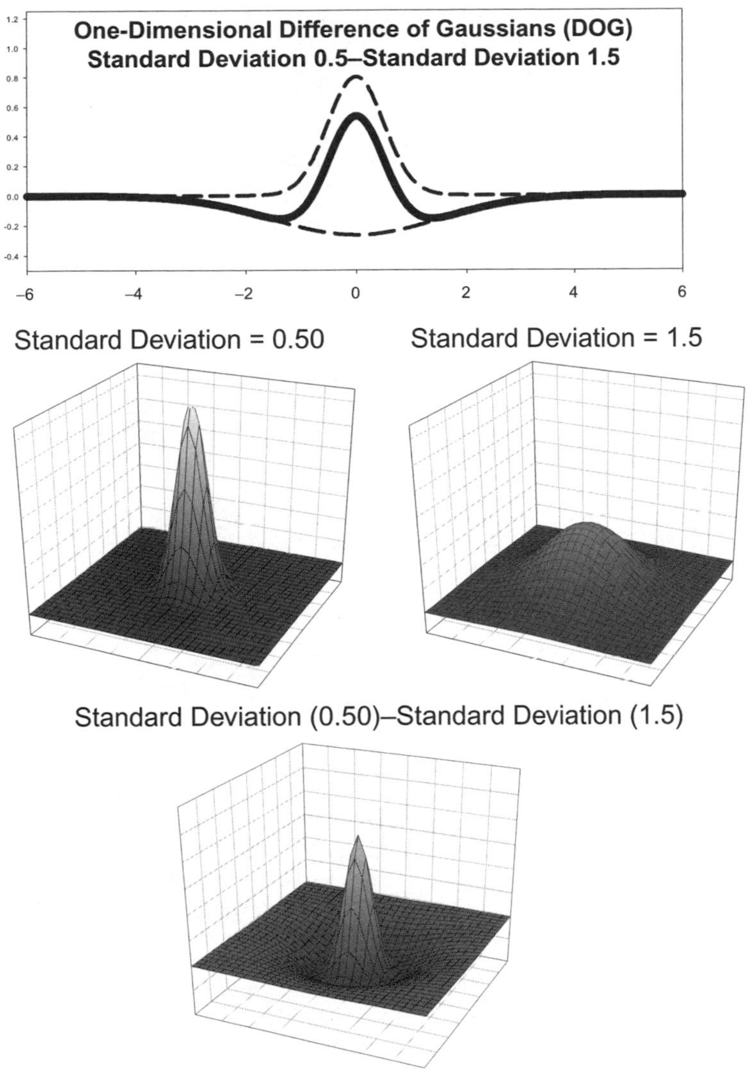

Figure 2.5. Two- and three-dimensional Difference of Gaussians. The standard deviation of the center is 0.5 and the standard deviation of the surround is 1.5.

cones and add the surround on- or off-response by directly stimulating the bipolar cells or by feedback to the cones themselves.

Because the spatial resolution of the narrower center region exceeds that of the broader surround (i.e., the variance is lower), the difference between the center and surround regions creates a band-pass filter that maximizes the firing rate to a narrow range of grating frequencies. The width of the center and surround regions will depend on the number of receptors that

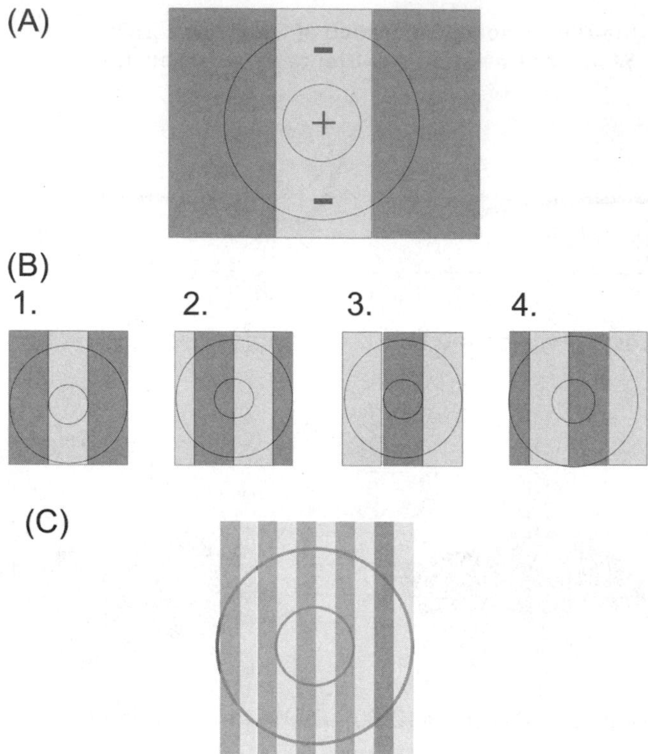

Figure 2.6. Representation of a simple on-off cell. The maximum excitation would occur if the white bar of the grating falls completely on the on-center and the black bars fall completely on the off-surrounds, as shown in (B). Simple on-off cells are phase sensitive, as illustrated in (B). The excitation would be maximum in (B1), close to baseline in (B2), maximally inhibited in (B3), and equal to baseline in (B4). If the frequency of the grating decreases as in (A) or triples as in (C), the firing would be close to baseline because the white and black bars fall in the on- and off-regions.

are integrated by the bipolar and horizontal cells (the orientation of the bars does not matter because the receptive fields are circular).[2] The optimal grating frequencies will be those in which the widths of the black-and-white bars equal the widths of the center and surround. As shown figure 2.6, the maximum increase in firing shown in (B1) will occur when the width of a white bar (representing an increase in intensity) completely falls within the center on-region and the flanking black bars (representing a decrease in intensity) fall in the surround off-regions. By the same reasoning, the maximum

2. Typically, spatial gratings are described in terms of frequency: the number of black-and-white cycles per degree of visual angle. This provides a convenient metric that is independent of the distance from the viewer. For a constant frequency, the black-and-white bars must increase in width as the grating moves away from the viewer.

decrease in firing will occur for the identical widths of the white-and-black bars if the phase of the grating is changed 180° by moving it laterally so that a black bar falls on the entire on-region and the flanking white bars fall on the entire off-regions (B3). There will be little change in firing rate if the grating is moved 90° or 270°, shown in (B2) and (B4), because the white-and-black bars fall equally into the on- and off-regions. At the lower spatial frequencies (wider white and black bars) shown in (A), the on-center and off-surround subtract from each other because all of the black-and-white grating bars fall in both regions. At higher frequencies shown in (C), the on-center and off-surround again subtract from each other because both white and black grating bars fall within the excitation areas. The on- and off-regions cannot resolve the spatial variation.

The ganglion cells appear to form two classes, midget and parasol cells, which encode bands of spatial frequencies at localized regions of the retina. The midget cells make up the majority of retinal ganglion cells; at every location the receptive field of the midget cells is smaller (approximately 3×) than those of the parasol cells. In the fovea, midget cells are connected to a single cone while the parasol cells always receive inputs from many retinal cells. Based on the narrower receptive field, the midget pathway encodes a higher band of frequencies than the parasol pathway. Another difference between the midget and parasol pathways is that the midget pathways encode color while the parasol pathways encode brightness. For most midget cells, the center is dominated by one range of wavelengths while another dominates the surround. For the parasol cells, the same frequency range dominates both the center and surround regions. The parasol cells tend to respond to any change in illumination and often respond only if the stimulus is moving in one direction.

Why should there be parallel on-center and off-center channels? I think the answer goes back to the fact that the perceptual world depends on fine-grain contrasts between objects and backgrounds. For both on-off and off-on cells, the surround excitation is subtracted from the excitation of the central image point. This inhibition will be highest (and the response rate lowest) for regions of equal intensity, and inhibition will be lowest at points where intensity changes. As argued above, auditory and visual objects change slowly, so that points close in time and space tend to have similar intensities. The on-off ganglion cells therefore decorrelate the image, isolating changes in brightness and removing the redundancies due to adjacent regions of equal brightness. A second effect of the subtraction is that the firing rates are reduced, so that neural firing rates do not reach their maximum and asymptote (discussed further in chapter 6).

Hosoya, Baccus, and Meister (2005) made the stronger claim that the spatial-temporal receptive fields of the retinal ganglion cells change in just a few seconds in a new environment to optimize the detection of subsequent environmental changes. The ganglion cells adapt to the statistics of the new environment and become more responsive to the statistics of a different environment. For example, after presentations of a uniform light intensity pattern, the cell becomes more responsive to a checkerboard pattern and conversely, after presentations of a checkerboard pattern, the cell is more responsive to a uniform intensity pattern.

A basic issue in understanding ganglion cells is the degree to which these cells display the property of superposition (linearity) of firing rate. A neuron is said to be linear if the change in firing rate in response to several stimuli presented together simply is the sum of the changes in firing rate generated by each stimulus presented individually. Thus, if one point of brighter light falls in the on-region, increasing the rate of firing, and a second point of brighter light falls in the off-region, decreasing the rate of firing, the predicted change in firing rate for both lights is the difference in the individual changes. Most important, if neurons are linear, then it is possible to predict the response to any arbitrary stimulus by simply summing the response to every point in the stimulus.

Our interpretation of whether linearity holds depends crucially on how we measure any change in light intensity. If we simply define the change in intensity directly, then linearity fails. However, if we define the change in intensity as a ratio based on the background illumination, then linearity often occurs. To give a simple example: suppose the background level is 50 and we create one stimulus at 150 (contrast = [150 – 50]/50 = 2) and a second stimulus at 200 (contrast = 3). If contrast linearity holds, then the neural response to the sum of those two lights should equal that to a stimulus of 300 (and not 350). But if the background level is 100 instead of 50, then the neural response to the sum of those two lights should equal that to a stimulus of 250. Linearity does hold at constant levels of background illumination, although it does not hold across levels. The physical variables for perceiving are contrasts, referenced to steady-state backgrounds.

The receptive field varies with stimulus size, intensity, color, and any other property that affects the firing of the receptors. This lack of invariance argues that the whole idea of a receptive field should be reconceptualized (Shapley, 2000). However, what is critically important for what follows is that multiple cells represent each retinal location. The receptive field of each of these cells is most sensitive to a different, but narrow range of spatial frequencies and orientations. Taken together, the receptive fields form an overlapping distribution of frequency and orientation sensitivity. From each location in the retinal array, there will be parallel sets of outputs with different resolutions that abstract certain characteristics of the brightness contrast. It is the contrast in energy and not the amount of energy that determines our perceptual world.

At the Primary Visual Cortex

The next point in the visual pathways at which the receptive fields have changed qualitatively is the primary visual cortex (area V1; the lateral geniculate physically is the next step in the pathway, but the receptive fields are similar to those at the retinal ganglion cells). Almost all the visual input to higher visual cortical areas passes through V1. The number of neurons in the primary visual cortex is 200 to 500 times greater than the number in the lateral geniculate, demonstrating the remarkable explosion in the number of visual cells. The receptive fields of cells in V1 typically respond to a narrower range of stimuli than those in the retina and lateral geniculate and often are simultaneously selective with respect to spatial position, orientation, spatial and temporal frequency, contrast, direction of movement, and color. There is a retinotopic map with the cells locked to eye movements. Much of this pioneering work was performed by Hubel and Weisel (1962, 1968), which resulted in their receiving the Nobel Prize in 1981.

Most cells in the primary visual cortex respond strongly to flashing and moving bars and gratings, but not to static patterns. Hubel and Weisel, using flashing dots, identified two types of cells. For *simple* cells, one spatial region responds either to the onset or offset of light. For *complex* cells, all spatial regions respond both to the onset or offset of light; complex cells signal change. In the past 10 years it has become clear that a complete description of both simple and complex cortical cells must involve the analysis of the receptive field over time. The simple and complex cells can be split into two major classes. For *separable* cells, the spatial organization of the receptive field can be analyzed into independent x and y orientations. The receptive field may be static, but if it does transform, the on- and off-regions do not shift spatially over time (although the on- and off-regions may reverse). Approximately 50–70% of cells in the primary visual cortex are separable; the response is unaffected by the velocity and direction of movement of the stimulus. For *nonseparable* cells, the spatial organization of the receptive field cannot be analyzed into independent x and y orientations because the receptive field transforms over time; the response is affected by the velocity and direction of movement of the stimulus (e.g., a bar of light or black-and-white grating). To represent both separable and nonseparable cells, the x axis will depict the receptive field along the dimension perpendicular to the preferred orientation (i.e., the horizontal dimension for cells with a vertical orientation). If the receptive field does not transform over time, the y axis will depict the receptive field parallel to the preferred orientation. If the receptive field does transform over time, the y axis will depict the time from a spike. (The receptive field parallel to the preferred orientation is not displayed.)

Static Spatial-Temporal Receptive Fields: Simple Cells The receptive fields of simple cells are elongated and orientation specific and respond at their highest rates for white-and-black patterns at one frequency and at one orientation. These cells are phase-specific, much like the ganglion cells described previously.

The receptive fields of simple cortical cells were determined by Jones and Palmer (1987b) using reverse correlation. Bright and dark spots were presented randomly, and the spatial field was calculated by subtracting the regions where the darker stimuli (i.e., off-responses) evoked spikes from the regions where brighter stimuli (i.e., on-responses) evoked spikes. The regions of the receptive field that respond to dark and bright are shown in figure 2.7A as increases in firing rates, and then the dark regions are subtracted in figure 2.7B. An example of the response to bright and dark stimuli at different times before a spike is shown in figure 2.7C.

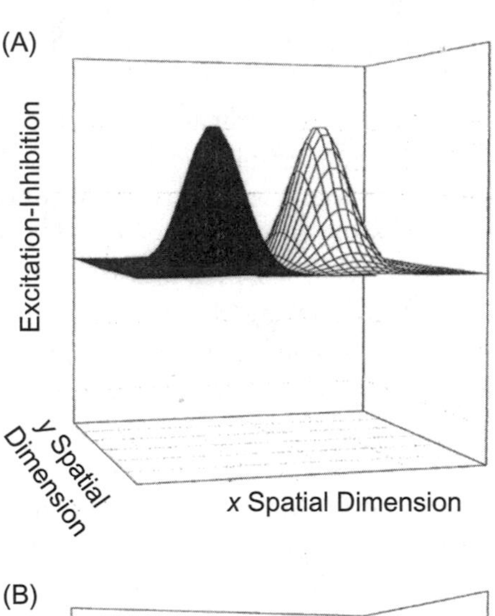

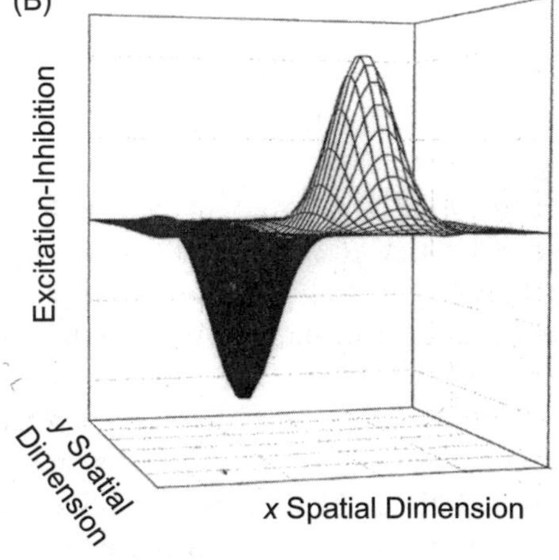

Figure 2.7. Derivation of simple cortical cells. The first step is to isolate the retinal areas that affect the firing rate. Both excitation and inhibition areas are plotted as positives in (A). The inhibitory areas are subtracted in (B). An example of the response to bright and dark stimuli at three times before the spike is depicted in (C). The strongest response occurs 50 ms before the spike. From "The two dimensional spatial structure of simple receptive fields in cat striate cortex," by J. P. Jones and L. A. Palmer, 1987b, *Journal of Neurophysiology, 58*, 1187–1911. Copyright 1987 by the American Physiological Society. Reprinted with permission.

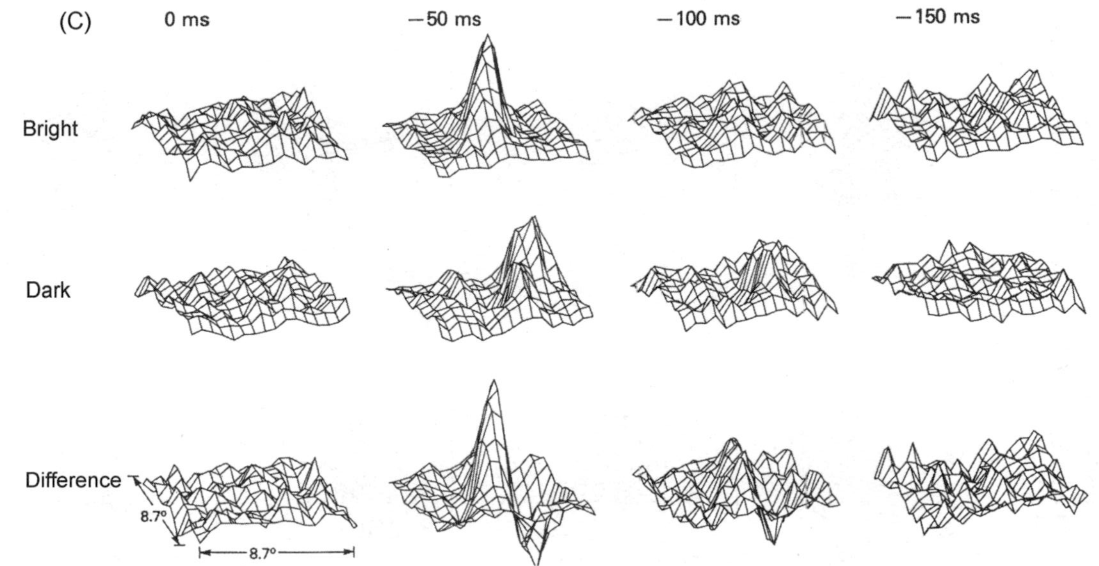

Figure 2.7. Continued

Four typical simple cortical cells are shown in figure 2.8 (Jones & Palmer, 1987b). The three-dimensional spatial representations as well as the contour plots are shown. Cells A, B, and C are termed odd-symmetric (as is figure 2.7) and cell D is termed even-symmetric due to organization of the excitatory and inhibitory fields.

If the receptive fields are separable, then the on-off regions do not shift in space. This is most easily seen using the contour plots. For separable fields, lines drawn along the receptive field zero crossings would be perpendicular

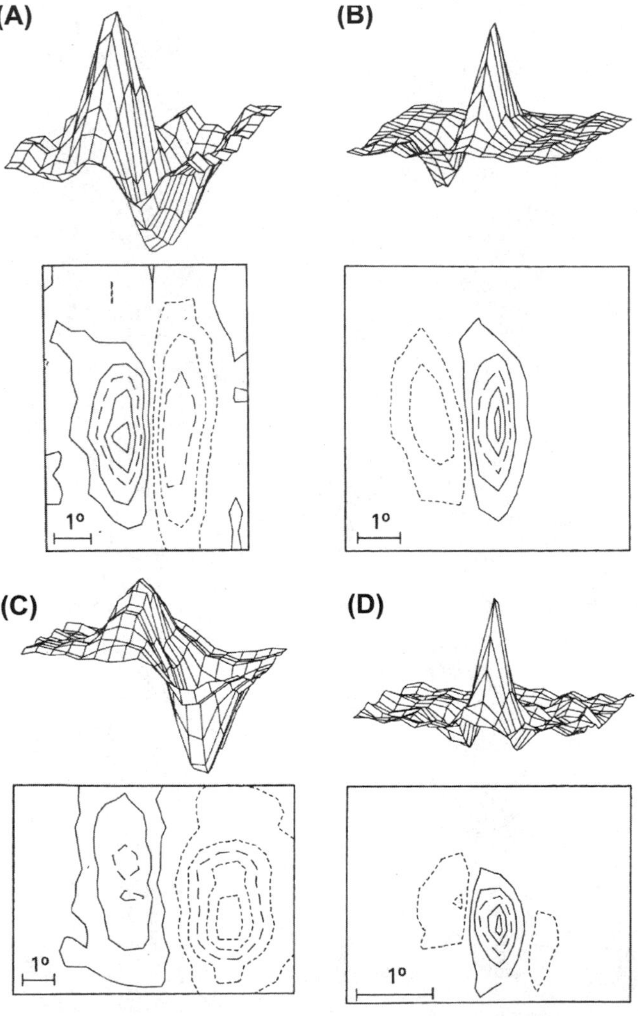

Figure 2.8. Illustration of four representative cortical cells. Cells A and B are separable, and cells C and D are nonseparable. From "The two dimensional spatial structure of simple receptive fields in cat striate cortex," by J. P. Jones and L. A. Palmer, 1987b, *Journal of Neurophysiology, 58*, 1187–1911. Copyright 1987 by the American Physiological Society. Reprinted with permission.

to lines connecting the receptive field maximums. The receptive field generated in figure 2.7 is separable, as are cells A and B in figure 2.8. In contrast, cells C and D, in particular, are not separable because their on-off regions shift across the receptive field.

We easily can see how different black-and-white gratings affect the firing rate. Suppose the on-off regions are assumed to be oriented vertically, as shown in figure 2.9. The on-region is shown in white and the off-region is shown in black. The firing rate will be highest when the lighter and darker bars of the grating line up with the on and off receptive fields as in B1. The firing rate will not change from baseline if the grating is shifted one-half bar right or left (B2), or if the grating is rotated so that both the light and dark stripes overlap the on-off regions (B3 and B4), or if the frequency of the bars (i.e., width) increases as in (A) or decreases as in (C), so that again the light/dark stripes of the grating overlap the on-off regions. These cells will respond identically if the grating moves in either direction. This is the same analysis used for the circular on-off ganglion cells in the retina. What is different is that the firing rate of cells in V1 is determined by the orientation of the grating as well as by the frequency of the grating, while the firing rate of the retinal cells is determined by frequency only. (A second difference is that cortical cells have very low spontaneous rates so that we can detect inhibition only indirectly.)

Hubel and Weisel (1962) presented the working hypothesis that simple cells with a specific orientation in V1 could be created by summing the outputs of on-off and off-on cells in the lateral geniculate that lie along that same angular direction (i.e., linear-orientation receptive fields). This has been termed a *feed-forward model* by Ferster and Miller (2000). As shown in figure 2.10, it is possible to construct several different horizontal line or edge detectors with different spatial orientation and frequency resolutions by summing varying numbers of on-off cells and off-on cells (see Derrington & Webb, 2004). The same cells also can be combined vertically to produce simple cortical cells with a different orientation. What this means is that every on-off and off-on cell contributes its output to several cortical cells. Ferster and Miller (2000) argued that Hubel and Weisel's model is to a large degree correct; the outputs from the lateral geniculate do determine the orientation specificity. Sharon and Grinvold (2002) suggested that in addition to the input from the lateral geniculate, recurrent inhibition in V1 acts to accentuate the response to the preferred orientation by suppressing responses to orthogonal orientations.

The feed-forward model cannot account for all of the properties of the simple cortical cells. One issue, to which I return in chapter 6, is that the orientation response is relatively independent of the contrast of the black-and-white grating. We need contrast invariance to identify boundaries between objects at different light levels. But at high contrasts, the on-response would

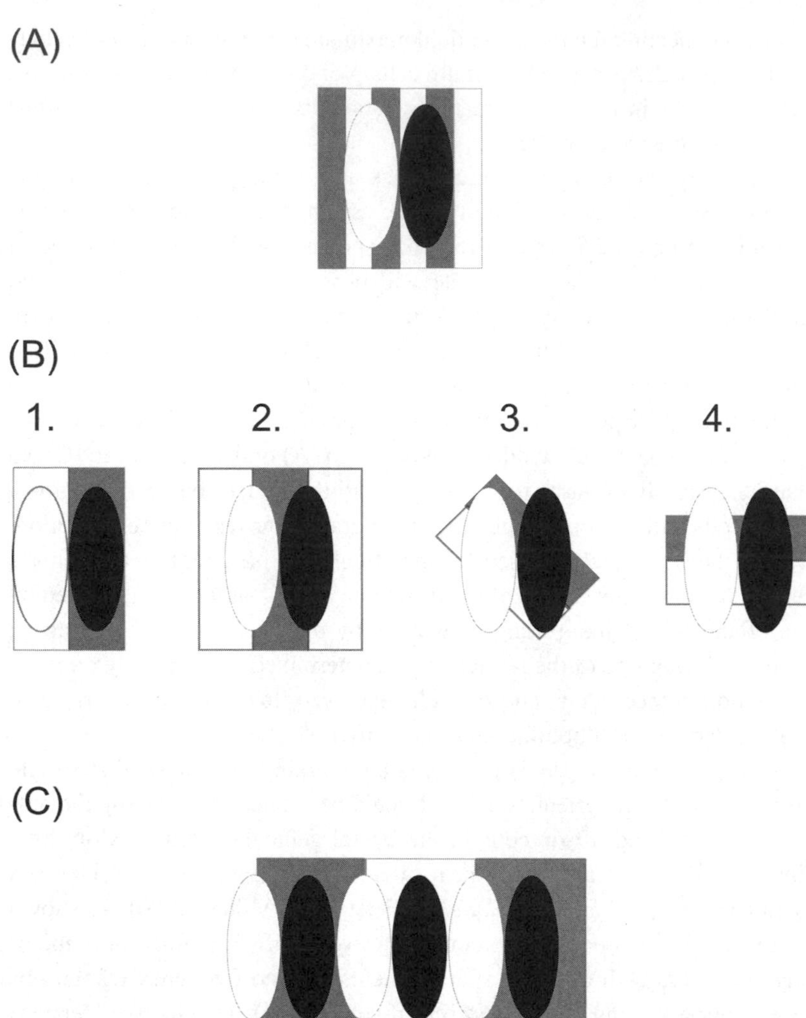

Figure 2.9. The effect of spatial frequency and orientation on the firing rate of simple cortical cells. The maximum firing rate occurs when the black-and-white bars of the grating exactly match the oriented cell as in (B1). The firing rate will return to baseline if the grating moves laterally (i.e., changes phase) as in (B2) or changes orientation as in (B3) and (B4). In the same way, the firing rate will not change if the spatial frequency of the grating does not match the frequency of the cell as in (A) and (C).

dominate the off-response because the off-on cells cannot reduce their firing rate below the average rate as much as on-off cells can increase their rate above the average. Thus, there will be high levels of excitation to all grating orientations. Therefore, the linearity of the simple cortical cells (as shown by the response to single and multiple points of light) cannot be understood

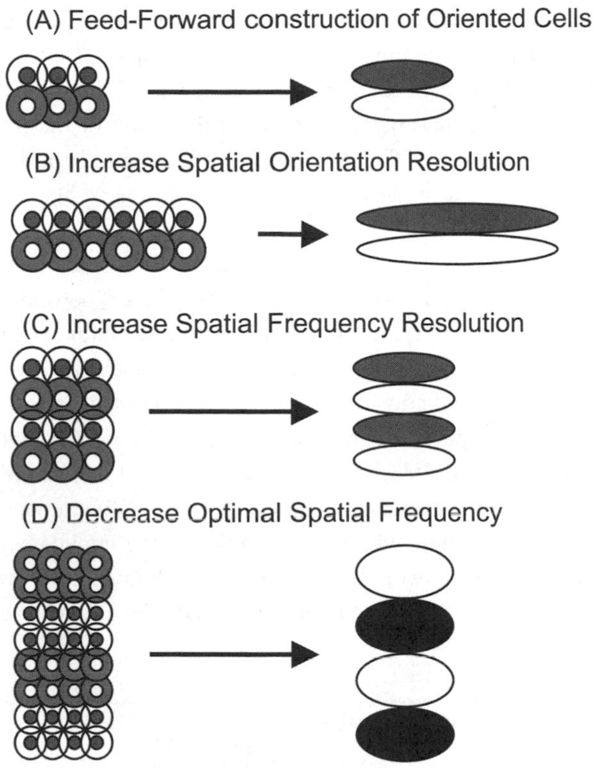

(A) Feed-Forward construction of Oriented Cells

(B) Increase Spatial Orientation Resolution

(C) Increase Spatial Frequency Resolution

(D) Decrease Optimal Spatial Frequency

Figure 2.10. Feed-forward models can help explain the origin of oriented cortical cells. To increase the spatial orientation resolution, the length of the on- and off-regions would be lengthened by combining a greater number of circular on-off cells along the horizontal axis (B). To increase the frequency resolution, the number of on- and off-regions would be incremented by combining cells along the vertical axis (C). To vary the optimal spatial frequency, the number of circular cells that compose each on- and off-region would be varied along the vertical axis (D). Adapted from *Foundations of Vision* by B. Wandell, 1995, Sunderland, MA: Sinauer.

simply in terms of the summation of the excitation and inhibition from many lateral geniculate cells.

The receptive fields of these cells are highly structured. They represent a restricted retinal area, and they respond to a range of spatial frequencies and orientations. We can imagine the receptive field to be a filter, or effectively a multiplier. We take the illumination falling on the receptive field and multiply it by the receptive field pattern to measure the effect of the illumination on the spike rate of the cortical cell.

There are always processing limitations so that the transmitted information must be constrained to some maximum value; improving the frequency resolution must necessitate the reduction in orientation resolution as described in chapter 1. A two-dimensional envelope with a Gaussian fall-off (in both frequency and position) multiplied by a sine or cosine wave filter would minimize the overall uncertainty (Daugman, 1985; Gabor, 1946).

We can start with representative one-dimensional functions, depicted in figure 2.11. Changing either the standard deviation or the phase of the Gaussian envelope changes the pattern of the function. It is possible to produce even-symmetric or odd-symmetric receptive fields (figure 2.11A and 2.11B respectively).

For the two-dimensional receptive fields of simple cortical cells, the choice of the Gaussian envelope will change the trade-off between the uncertainty with respect to the spatial frequency of the stimulus pattern and the uncertainty with respect to spatial orientation, illustrated in figure 2.12. In (A), the number of oscillations along the *x*-axis determines the frequency resolution and the length of the oscillations along the *y*-axis determines the orientation resolution. If the Gaussian surface falls away more slowly along the *x* axis due to a larger standard deviation (in B), then the frequency resolution would decrease slightly while the resolution of the spatial position along the *y* spatial dimension would decrease more dramatically because the length of the oscillations is much shorter (in D). The opposite changes in

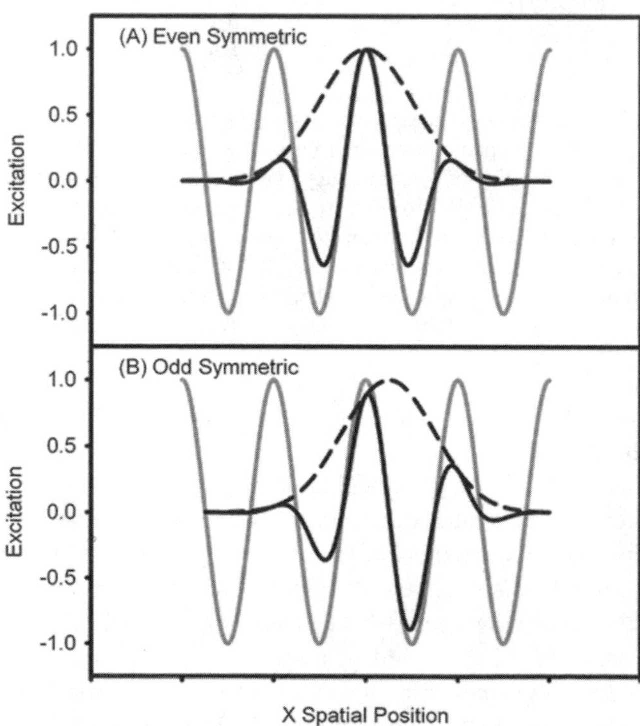

Figure 2.11. The phase of the Gaussian envelope can yield even and odd symmetric Gabor functions from the same cosine carrier function.

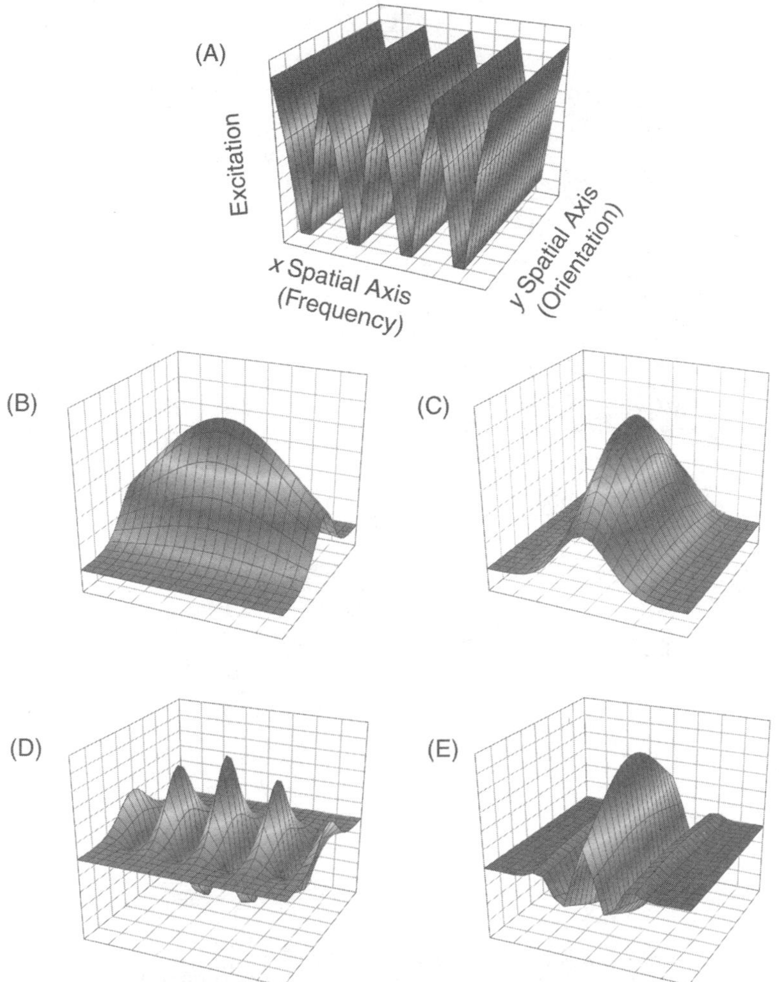

Figure 2.12. Two-dimensional Gaussian envelopes with different standard deviations change the resolution along the x and y spatial dimensions. In (B), the standard deviation along the x-axis equals 3 and the standard deviation along the y-axis equals 1. In (C), the values of the standard deviations are reversed.

resolution would occur if the Gaussian surface falls away more slowly along the y-axis (C). The orientation resolution would decrease slightly (still a long length) while the frequency resolution would decrease dramatically because there is just one large oscillation (E). This change in resolution is illustrated in figure 2.12 using Gaussian envelopes with standard deviations of 1 and 3.

Jones and Palmer (1987a), following the analyses of two-dimensional Gabor functions by Daugman (1985), were able to fit 97% of the variance in the experimental receptive fields with Gabor functions. Three examples are shown in figure 2.13. Gabor functions were unable to fit only 3 of the

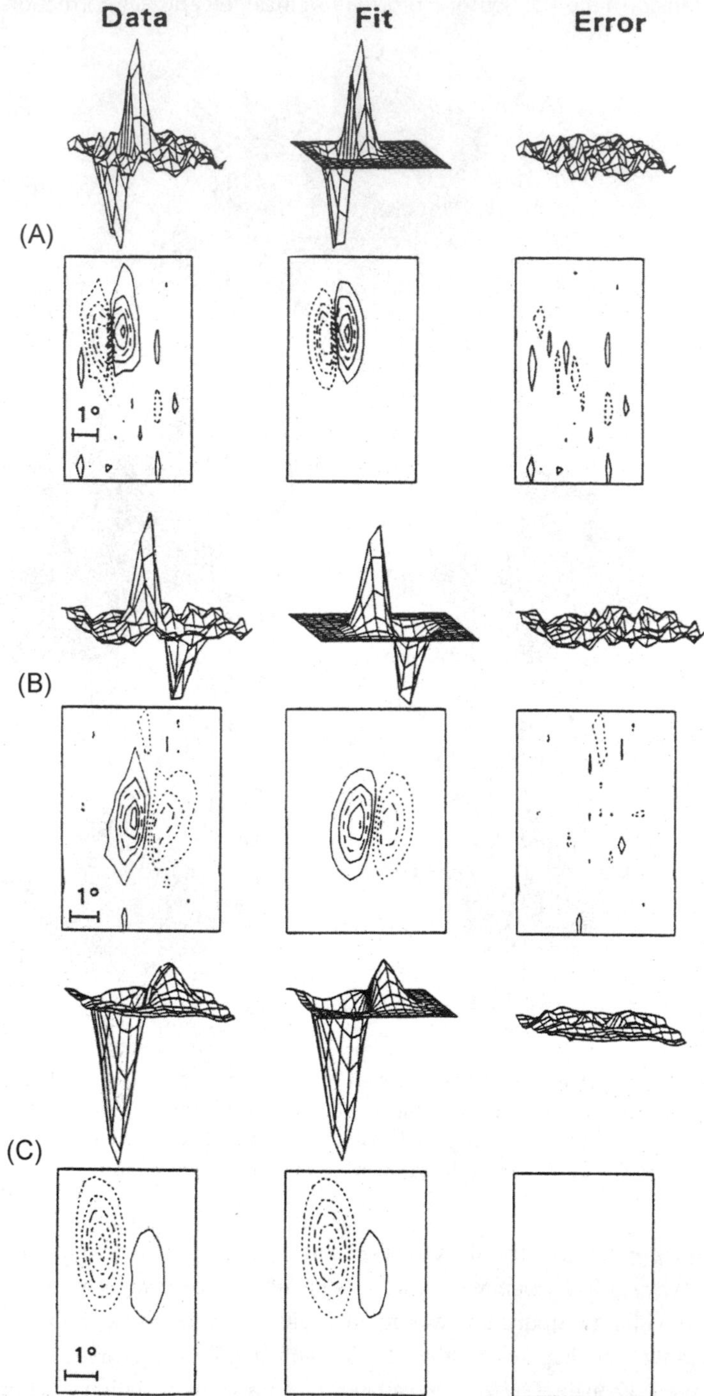

Figure 2.13. The fit of Gabor functions to simple cortical cells. From "An evaluation of the 2D Gabor filter model of simple receptive fields in cat striate cortex," by J. P. Jones and L. A. Palmer, 1987a, *Journal of Neurophysiology, 58*, 1233–1258. Copyright 1987 by the American Physiological Society. Reprinted with permission.

36 receptive fields. The ability to model the receptive fields using Gabor functions does not necessarily mean that the nervous system optimizes the uncertainty. Other functions will fit the receptive field data as well. By using the Gabor functions, the authors made a theoretical, not an empirical, decision. Research attempting to use Gabor functions to represent the more complex receptive fields of cells further up the visual tract has been relatively unsuccessful.

I have argued that the role of the visual system is to decompose the visual image into localized regions and to analyze those regions at different resolution levels. We can measure the resolution of a cell in terms of its bandwidth. The bandwidth is defined in terms of the frequency or orientation that brings about the peak response rate. It is the range between the two frequencies or orientations flanking the best frequency or orientation that still yields a 50% response rate. (The bandwidth for frequency is defined in terms of octaves, the $\log_2$ of the ratio of the high to low frequency. For example, if the best frequency was 3 cycles per degree, the bandwidth would be 1 if the high and low frequencies were 4 and 2 cycles per degree, and the bandwidth would be 2.3 if the frequencies were 5 and 1 cycle per degree respectively.) Cortical cells with the same bandwidth have the same resolution regardless of the frequency at which the maximum response occurs. The average frequency bandwidth is about 1.2 octaves; the majority of cells have bandwidths between 0.8 and 1.2 octaves, and a range between 0.7 and 3.0 octaves. These values reflect rather sharp frequency tuning. Bandwidths of about 1 octave may be optimal due to the intensity variation in natural visual scenes, as discussed in chapter 3. The average orientation bandwidth is about 45°.

Why should there be such diversity in the shapes of the receptive fields? Elder and Sachs (2004) suggested that one function of such diversity is to improve the detection of luminous edges in natural environments. Given the inherent variability of visual scenes in terms of competing edges, it is an advantage to have a variety of shapes to best encode the scene. Elder and Sachs illustrated how different odd-symmetric filters could be used to detect a variety of edges in figure 2.14.

Static Spatial-Temporal Receptive Fields: Complex Cells One way to model complex cells is to imagine paired simple cells, either with the same phase or shifted by 180°, as shown in figure 2.15. Even if the grating shifts laterally, then a complex cell will continue to fire due to the other simple cell.

Time-Varying Spatial Receptive Fields: Separable The receptive fields of many cells change over time. Conceptually, we could present a randomly varying white noise image and then average the images at different time points before the occurrence of a spike (e.g., 80, 60, 40, 20 ms) to derive the receptive fields at each time point. The receptive fields are then

Figure 2.14. The detection of edges requires detectors at differing frequencies and orientations. Adapted from "Psychophysical Receptive Fields of Edge Detection Mechanisms," by J. H. Elder and A. J. Sachs, 2004, *Vision Research, 44*, 795–813.

spliced together to generate an *x-t* plot. Two simple examples show the *x-y* receptive field at five different time points and then spliced together to create *x-t* receptive fields, as shown in figure 2.16. In the first example, the receptive field does not shift spatially, although it reverses phase. Nonetheless, it is a separable receptive field because the *x-t* field can be recreated using a vertical *t* axis and a horizontal *x* axis that reverses polarity between –40 ms and –60 ms. In the second example, the receptive field shifts spatially so that the *x* axis and *t* axis are not perpendicular; it is a nonseparable receptive field.

For separable receptive fields, the *x* (frequency), *y* (orientation), and *z* (time) axes are independent. It is possible to construct the *x-y* receptive field by multiplying the *x* field by the *y* field, and similarly it is possible to construct a space-time field by "multiplying the *x-y* spatial field by the *t*-temporal field" (DeAngelis, Ohzawa, & Freeman, 1995, p. 452).

The firing pattern of a V1 cell in an awake monkey to spatial gratings with different orientations and frequencies (Mazer, Vinje, McDermott, Schiller, & Gallant, 2002) is a clear example of a separable receptive field, shown in figure 2.17. The two-dimensional plots for pairs of variables averaged across the third variable are sketched. Both frequency and orientation

(A)

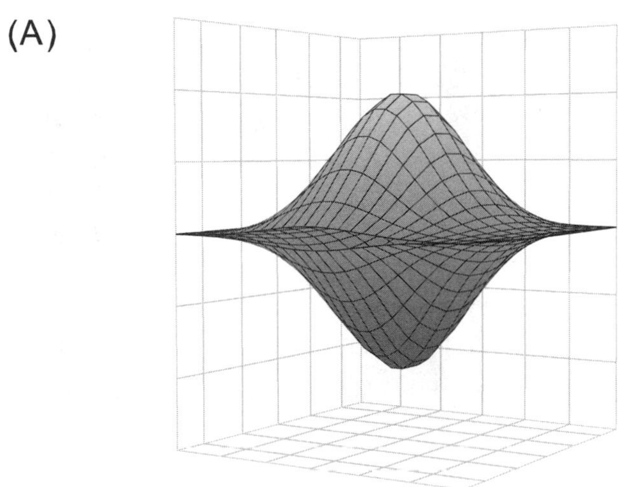

(B)

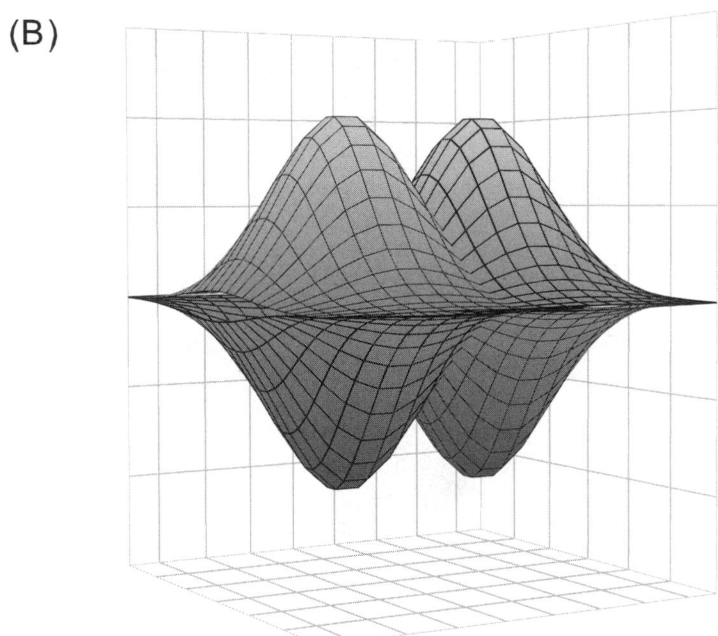

Figure 2.15. Complex cells can be hypothesized as being created by a feed-forward mechanism that combines simple cells with differing phase relationships. (A) Complex cell from the sum of two simple cells; (B) complex cell from the sum of two odd-symmetric simple cells with a 180° phase shift.

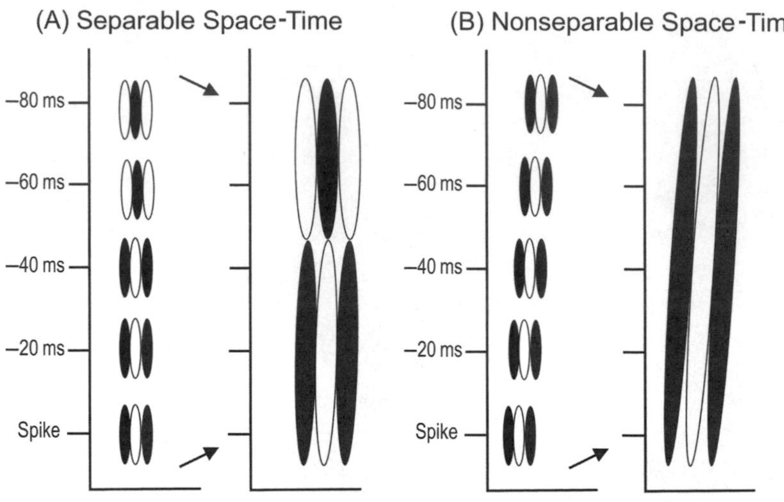

Figure 2.16. The derivation of separable and nonseparable spatial-temporal receptive fields. Combining the spatial receptive fields on the left side of (A) and (B) at time points before a spike derives space-time receptive fields on the right side. The retinal spatial position does not shift for separable cells, although the on- and off-regions may reverse, as shown in (A). In contrast, the retinal spatial position shifts for nonseparable space-time cells, as shown in (B).

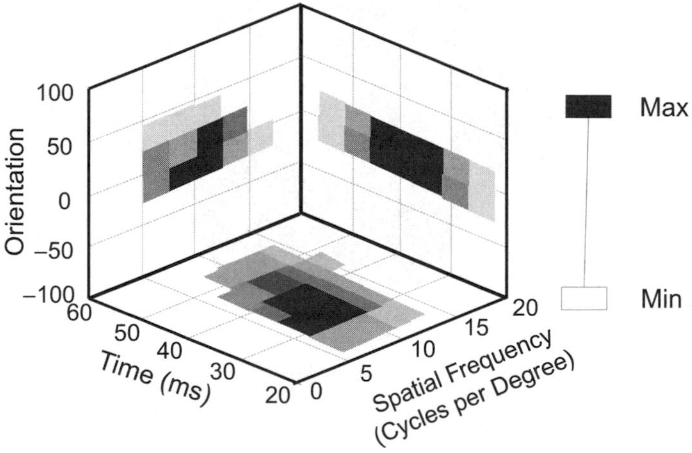

Figure 2.17. A separable frequency-orientation cell found in V1 in an awake monkey. In this example, the frequency × orientation response can be predicted by multiplying the frequency × time plane by the orientation × time plane. The maximum firing rate is depicted in black. Adapted from "Spatial Frequency Tuning and Orientation Tuning Dynamics in Area V1," by J. A. Mazer, W. E. Vinje, J. McDermott, P. H. Schiller, and J. L. Gallant, 2002, *Proceedings of the National Academy of Science, 99*, 1645–1650.

are time separable because neither variable shifts over time. Because both frequency and orientation are time separable, it is possible to predict the frequency × orientation plot from the multiplication of the overall frequency and orientation responses.

Another example of a separable receptive field is shown in figure 2.18A. Both pairs of receptive fields reverse in polarity over time. But the regions of zero crossing between the on and off fields at different time points before a spike lie along a vertical line that is perpendicular to the horizontal line between the regions of maximum response. The receptive field is "attached" to one retinal point.

Time-Varying Spatial Receptive Fields: Nonseparable For nonseparable cells, the receptive field shifts across the retina over time. For *x-t* plots, the receptive fields appear to slope to the left or right as you go down the temporal *y* axis (toward the spike at 0). Notice in figure 2.18B that for nonseparable fields the on- and off-regions shift but do not reverse over time.

Most simple nonseparable cortical cells are quite selective for the direction and velocity of the light onset and offset. These cells will fire most strongly if a white-and-black grating moves laterally in the same direction as the slope of the space-time field, but not if the grating is stationary or

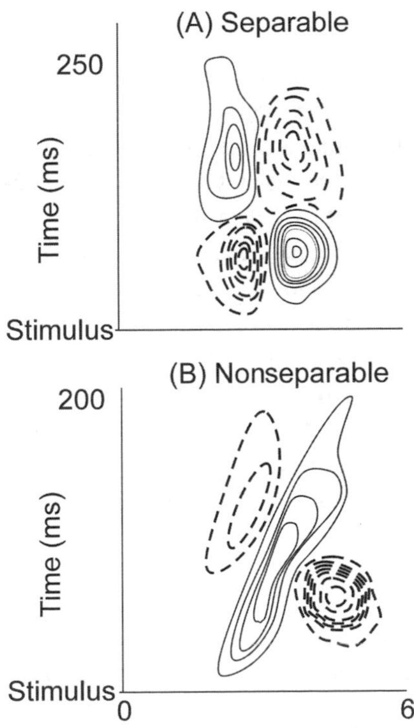

Figure 2.18. Separable and nonseparable space-time receptive fields. For the temporal *y* dimension, the 0 value is the stimulus onset. Adapted from "Receptive-Field Dynamics in the Central Visual Pathways," by G. C. DeAngelis, I. Ohzawa, and R. D. Freeman, 1995, *Trends in Neuroscience, 18*, 451–458.

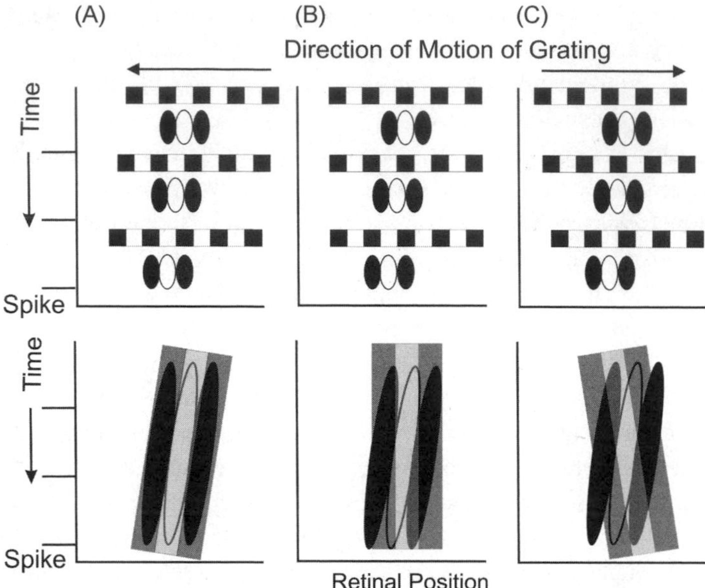

Figure 2.19. Nonseparable cells respond to only one movement direction. In (A), the movement direction matches the spatial shift of the receptive field so that the response is strong throughout. If the grating is stationary as in (B) or the movement direction is opposite to the spatial shift (C), the response is weak.

moves in the opposite direction. In the simplified figure 2.19, the nonseparable spatial-temporal receptive field slopes to the left prior to the spike. If the grating is moving to the left, then the grating and the spatial-temporal receptive field stay in registration and the response is high. If the grating does not move or moves to the right, then the white and dark regions of the grating pass over the on-off regions of the cell, and the response is much less.

The shift in the position of the receptive field and the movement of the grating stimulus are often portrayed overlaid in an *x-t* plot, as shown in the bottom row of figure 2.19. In this representation, the leftward movement of the grating lines up with the space-time shift of the receptive field, while the rightward movement crosses the receptive field at an angle in the rightmost column. This differential response to direction of movement found for nonseparable cells does not occur for separable cells. Separable cells respond equally to movement in both directions.

Classical and Nonclassical Receptive Fields: Effect of Surrounds One additional complexity is that the neural response due to excitation within the receptive field can be affected by excitation of the areas surrounding the receptive field (Fitzpatrick, 2000). (Excitation of the surround area by itself does not result in a neural response.) Inhibition occurs most frequently, albeit in idiosyncratic ways, and reduces the firing between 0% and 100%. The inhibitory areas are localized and tend to be asymmetric, located to one side of the retinal cells generating the receptive field. Facilitation occurs only if gratings are presented at the preferred orientation at the receptive fields' "end zones." In effect, the simple cell sums the excitation along the increased length: the summation area can be two to four times longer than the classical field. The facilitation is highest at low contrast levels and disappears (or even produces inhibition) at high contrast levels. This facilitation can be understood as a mechanism to improve the detection of extended contours, corners, or local curvature when the detection is difficult due to a weak signal (low contrast).

The original mapping of area V1 suggested that there is a very specific column organization. There is a set of cells representing one retinal location and then a set of cells representing an adjacent retinal location. Within each set, the spatial frequencies are postulated to be in a polar arrangement, the preferred orientation of the cells smoothly rotates around 180°, and there is a regular progression of orientations for each eye separately. Subsequent work has shown that there are local discontinuities in the V1 orientation map; Das and Gilbert (1997, 1999) showed that there are regions where the orientation of the receptive fields changes relatively slowly and smoothly, but interspersed between these regions of local change are fractures or discontinuities where the orientations of the receptive fields change rapidly. Even at the discontinuity boundaries, there is a precise architecture in terms of orientation and direction preferences (Ohki, Chung, Ch'ng, Kara, & Reid, 2005). (Surprisingly, although the visual cortexes of rats contain direction-sensitive cells, those cells are scattered randomly. The regular progressions in the cat's cortex may yield greater resolution by combining the responses of cells with similar directional sensitivities).

Das and Gilbert (1990, p. 660) suggested that receptive fields at opposite sides of the discontinuity act to "compute features that are maximally dissimilar (e.g., two perpendicular bars) while cells with receptive fields within a smooth region compute features that are maximally similar."

What this all means is that by the first cortical region the retinal input has been dramatically changed from a photograph at the retinal cells to a representation of intensity contrast. Moreover, this representation occurs at multiple levels of spatial frequency and orientation that would allow for the segregation and identification of objects in natural scenes that occur regardless of the scale of the object. De Valois and De Valois (1988) argued persuasively that this representation is not to one of bars or edges. Rather, the representation is to one of frequency and orientation and this transformation is local. The periodicities in visual images are found at small regions and scales, not across large areas.

Multiresolution Theories

The organization of V1 is in terms of simple and complex cells with specific orientations and spatial resolutions due to the number and width of the on-off regions. Each cell is in effect a linear filter that generates an output based on the match between the stimulus and the receptive field. This physiological organization has led to describing and conceptualizing this organization as reflecting a multiresolution solution to the uncertainty problems described previously. Specifically, simple cells with one narrow on-off region can yield precise position information, while simple cells with multiple on-off regions yield precise frequency information, as illustrated in chapter 1. Computational theories have utilized models of simple cells as the input filters (four to eight orientations × four to eight spatial scales) to represent each point in the image (e.g., Bergen & Landy, 1991).

However, the inhibitory effects described above, both among cells with receptive fields at similar and dissimilar orientations, create a much more complex picture. The responses of individual cells must be understood in terms of large-scale firing distributions in the visual cortex. Multiresolution theories combining linear filters (albeit with nonlinear components) may provide the framework for both auditory and visual theories, but it may be the local inhibitory effects that generate the stuff of perception.

Receptive Fields in the Auditory System

If we use the visual system as a guide, the representation of auditory objects (e.g., speakers, instruments, dripping faucets, wind, guns) would progress from the physical sound pressure wave to sets of cortical cells that respond to unique combinations of frequency and intensity across time. The initial step would be to decompose the complex acoustic wave into the component frequencies. These components would then be coded in terms of their temporal onsets and offsets, as well as their frequency and intensity variations across time. These are the features that distinguish environmental, animal, musical, and speech sounds. Furthermore, the uncertainty constraints found in accurately computing visual-spatial orientation and frequency simultaneously also would arise in the auditory system but now would be transformed into the difficulty of computing frequency and time simultaneously. Here too we might expect the solution to be in terms of multiple auditory images with differing spatial and temporal resolutions (i.e., a multiresolution representation). In some ways, the task of listening is harder: Visual objects usually are opaque, so that the illumination of each spatial point comes from one object. But the acoustic signal is transparent, so that the air pressure intensity at each temporal point may come from more than one sound-producing object. One of the premises of this book is that perceptual systems "want to" attribute energy to objects so that one goal of the auditory system is to decompose the acoustic wave into a set of frequency components, and then meld together sets of the component frequencies to create objects. Each set of frequencies creates the pitch and sound quality (i.e., timbre) of the sound. This process is discussed in chapter 9.

The auditory system encodes information in two parallel ways. Due to the physical construction of the inner ear, different cells in the auditory nerve and auditory cortex will fire at higher rates to specific ranges of frequencies. As discussed in chapter 1, Rieke et al. (1997) argued that the type of neural coding would depend on the temporal properties of the stimulus. The frequencies of the pressure waves used for hearing are relatively low, so that the auditory neurons can phase-lock and generate a spike at the identical point on successive cycles of the pressure waves. If phase-locking does occur, then the properties of the sound could be signified by the timing between spikes within one or a group of neurons or by the timing between spikes from different neurons. Such a temporal pattern code would be crucial to encode periodicities such as the rhythm of short clicks. These regularities can be derived using the autocorrelations within a spike train or the cross-correlations between spike trains.[3] Alternatively, we could follow the implicit model used for the visual system in which each cell in V1 is conceptualized as a specific filter (i.e., frequency × orientation × location) and the average rate of firing is the relevant dependent variable. The properties of sounds would be based on the firing rates of cells tuned to overlapping frequency ranges. This model has been termed a rate-place code because it is the firing rate of a particular cell (i.e., its place) that is critical.

At the Inner Ear and Auditory Nerve

The neurons coming out of the cochlea in the inner ear divide the acoustic signal into overlapping frequency bands. A set of tuning curves spanning a wide range of frequencies is shown in figure 2.20. Once the neuron fires, there is no designation of which particular frequency or intensity combination triggered the cell. (The lack of history is typical for all sensory systems.) Retinal ganglion cells also divide the visual image into frequency bands (by means of the width of the on-off regions) at different retinal locations.

3. The autocorrelation and cross-correlation can be understood in terms of frequency distributions of the timing between successive spikes. For the autocorrelation, we would tabulate the distribution of time intervals between successive spikes for individual neurons (a first-order autocorrelation). If a strong autocorrelation exists, the majority of intervals should be nearly identical, and the frequency distribution would be peaky. For the cross-correlation, we would consider one spike train as the reference and tabulate distribution of the time intervals between each spike in the reference spike train and the nearest spike in the comparison train. If the reference train is related to the comparison, then the majority of intervals should be found at one positive interval. If the two trains are unrelated, then the distribution should be random.

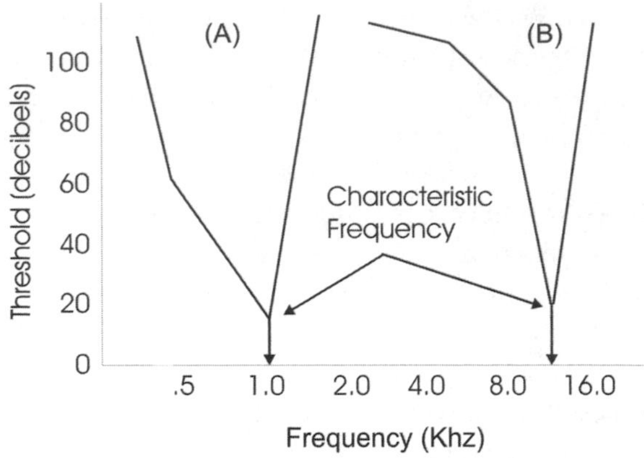

Figure 2.20. Frequency-intensity response areas of single auditory fibers. The response area represents all combinations of frequency and intensity that yield firing rates significantly above the resting rate Response areas for two cells are shown. The characteristic frequency (F_{cf}) is the frequency at the lowest threshold. Cells with high characteristic frequencies can have low frequency "shelves" as shown for (B).

Each tuning curve could be roughly described as being V-shaped. The lower tip defines the characteristic frequency at which the cell is most sensitive and the V bounds different combinations of frequency and amplitude that trigger the cell. It is possible to fire the cell at a relatively wide range of frequencies by increasing the intensity of the tone. In contrast to the symmetrical retinal ganglion cells, the tails are not symmetric, and that is the result of the propagation of the pressure wave along the basilar membrane. The propagation wave travels from the high-frequency region of the basilar membrane at the oval window to the low-frequency region at the base. Each point on the basilar membrane captures a high-frequency component, and only the lower-frequency components travel onward. Thus, the intense high-frequency components do not affect the physical displacement of the lower-frequency end of the basilar membrane. In contrast, the intense lower frequencies will affect the motion of the entire membrane.

The width of the tuning function roughly equals the selectivity of the neuron. While it might appear that the neurons ought to be highly selective to provide the most accurate frequency information, frequency resolution necessarily creates timing uncertainty. In the cat, frequency selectivity increases with characteristic frequency; the tuning curves become narrower (less damped). At frequencies around 1 kHz, the damping is high and the selectivity is low, so that the response to a click may last only for one cycle (low frequency resolution/high time resolution). At frequencies around 10 kHz, the damping is lower and the selectivity is high, so the response to a click may last for 10 cycles or more (high frequency resolution/low temporal resolution). This is another example of the frequency × time trade-off, which may be compared to the frequency × orientation trade-off in vision.

The physical construction of the basilar membrane creates a frequency analyzer, so that the composite sound wave is broken into its components—high frequencies stimulate hair cells at the narrow stiff membrane right next to the oval window apex and low frequencies stimulate hair cells at the broader, looser base. It is a tonotopic representation—there is a smooth monotonic change in frequency selectivity along the membrane (analogous to a retinotopic representation of spatial positions in the retina). For the cat, there is a simple logarithmic relationship between frequency and location: each octave (a 2:1 ratio of frequencies) takes about the same 3.5 mm distance on the membrane. This physical construction creates a fractal scale ($1/f$) that, as we find in chapter 3, is matched by the physical sound and light power in natural environments. Equal lengths on the basilar membrane match the octave bands that have equal power in the environment. The logarithmic relationship is not perfect: the low frequency end is compressed. LePage (2003) suggests that this warping optimizes higher-frequency resolution and that the longer basilar membranes found in larger mammals act to improve low-frequency resolution that is degraded due to compression.

Phase-locking occurs when the neuron fires at a specific point in the stimulus cycle. To measure the degree of phase-locking, the probability of firing is calculated at specific times within the cycle. A classic example of phase-locking is shown in figure 2.21. Three points are important. First, the phase-locking begins at relatively low intensities at which the rate of responding has not increased. By 10-18 dB, there are clearly more responses around 0.6 ms, although the overall response rate has not increased. Second, phase-locking results in the suppression of firing at other points in the cycle. Third, degree of phase-locking does not decrease at the highest intensities. Any single neuron does not fire on every cycle. In fact, measurements indicate that the probability of firing on any given cycle is independent of the previous firing pattern. But if the cell does fire, it will tend to be at the same point in the stimulus cycle.

Phase-locking is limited to lower frequencies, roughly up to 4000 Hz at the auditory nerve. The degree of phase-locking diminishes up the auditory pathway so that effectively there is no phase-locking (less than 100 Hz) at the auditory cortex. Why, then, should there be phase-locking at all? One possibility is that it represents a strategy to reduce the redundancy of the neural signal. If the auditory system is attempting to provide both temporal (onset, offset, intensity envelope) and frequency information about the signal, then phase-locking is very efficient. The repetitive stimulus cycle is converted into firing at specific time intervals for each neuron, and that stability will create a set of cross-correlations among neurons with the same or different characteristic frequencies. Even if the precise timing is

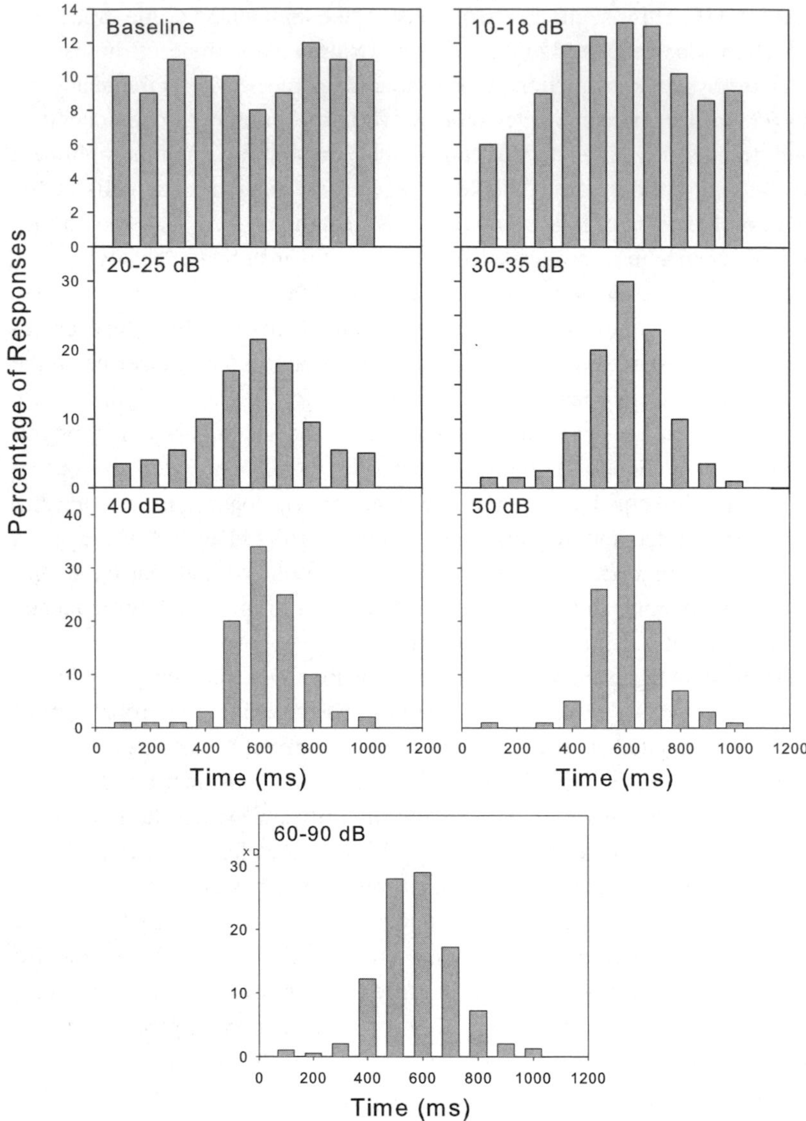

Figure 2.21. Phase-locking in the auditory nerve to a 1000 Hz tone. As phase-locking comes to dominate at the higher-intensity levels (30 to 90 dB), there is little change in the response rate or degree of synchrony. Adapted from "Phase-Locked Response to Low-Frequency Tones in Single Auditory Nerve Fibers of the Squirrel Monkey," by J. E. Rose, J. F. Brugge, D. J. Anderson, and J. E. Hind, 1967, *Journal of Neurophysiology, 30*, 769–793.

lost going up the pathway, the representation of the stimulus has been reduced to the correlated firing of specific neurons, and has been transformed into an efficient sparse code (described in chapter 3).[4]

Sounds are constantly evolving in frequency and intensity, and speech is characterized by low-frequency modulations in amplitude. The firing rates of the auditory neurons tend to accurately track those changes, even to the point that they overshoot. In the typical stimulus presentation, a sine wave (or white noise) is modulated in amplitude or frequency by a different sine wave. In figure 2.22, a tone burst at the cell's best frequency is amplitude modulated by a 120 Hz sinusoidal wave (each cycle is shown by an arrow). All the fibers tracked the occurrence of the modulation at low tone-burst intensities quite well, but did not track as well at higher tone-burst intensities. At the auditory nerve, fibers can track modulation frequencies up to 500–1000 Hz by synchronizing to the amplitude variation, a form of phase-locking. But, further along the auditory pathways, the rate decreases to 50–400 Hz.

All theories about the encoding of auditory information (particularly those for pitch) start by conceptualizing the inner hair cells of the cochlea as a set of overlapping band-pass filters such that the output of each hair cell filter reflects the energy within that frequency range. There is a one-to-many connection between the hair cells that encode frequency and the cells in the auditory nerve. As many as 10 auditory nerve cells are connected to a single hair cell, but each auditory neuron is connected to only one hair cell. The characteristic frequency of each cell in the auditory nerve therefore is determined by the location of that hair cell along the basilar membrane. The spikes along any nerve can be interpreted in two ways: (a) in terms of the rate of firing based on the location of the hair cell, that is, a rate-place code; and (b) in terms of the degree of phase-locked timing between spikes.

Firing Rate × Place Models For rate models, the output of each hair cell filter (as measured by the rate of firing in an auditory nerve cell) is averaged over time. The patterning of the firing rates across filters with different characteristic frequencies is assumed to determine the perceived sound. Rate models do not make use of phase-locked responding in any filter channel—all that is used is the average firing rate. Although such a rate model should work theoretically, there are two difficulties. The first difficulty is that at higher intensities, more and more neurons begin to fire, so that in the extreme, all of the hair cells respond equally and the original firing pattern is lost (see figure 2.20). The second difficulty is that the firing rates of auditory neurons saturate at relatively low intensities, so that it is difficult to understand how the auditory system could code intensity differences between intense sounds based only on average rates.

4. Musical tonality is nearly always associated with phase-locked spike information.

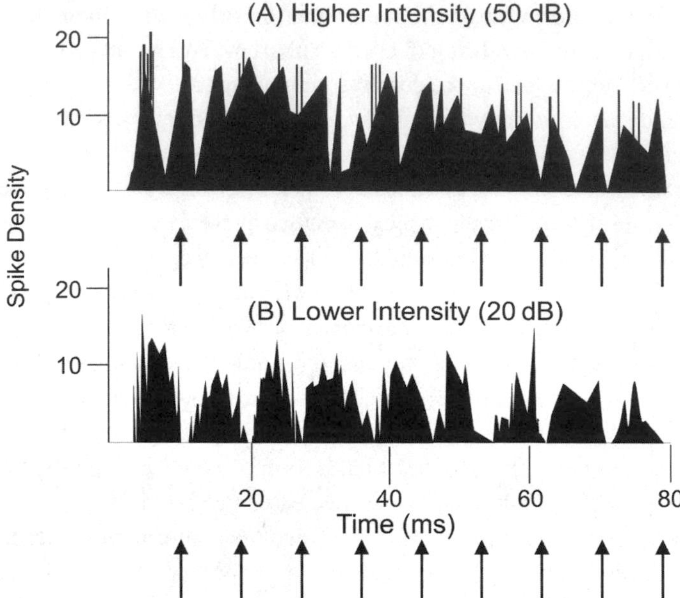

Figure 2.22. Neural synchronization of the medium spontaneous-rate-firing fibers to amplitude-modulated tones. An arrow indicates each cycle of the 120 Hz amplitude-modulating tone. There is an obvious suppression of firing rate at the lower intensities in synchrony with the modulating tone. There is practically no suppression at the higher intensity level. There is less inhibition for the low and high spontaneous-rate fibers, even at the lower intensity. Adapted from "Subcortical Neural Coding Mechanisms for Auditory Temporal Processing," by R. D. Frisina, 2001, *Hearing Research, 158*, 1–27.

Temporal × Place Models For temporal models, the actual firing patterns of each filter are used to isolate consistent interspike intervals or periodicities that can encode frequency. As the firing pattern of each filter becomes phase-locked to one frequency, all of the intervals between successive spikes will become identical to the period of that frequency (or multiples of the period if the cell does not fire on every cycle). Licklider (1951) proposed that the auditory system performed an autocorrelation between the spike train and progressively delayed versions to isolate those regularities. The peak values of the autocorrelation would occur at the period and multiples of that period.

For pure temporal models, the regularities are combined in some way, but without making use of the frequency tuning of the neurons. Thus, pure temporal models are the antithesis of rate models—temporal models retain the interspike intervals due to phase-locking, but lose the frequency information due to the place of the neuron filters, while rate models retain that frequency information but lose the interspike intervals.

We can start by constructing the frequency distribution of the interspike intervals for each cell. The repeating stimulus wave is illustrated in figure 2.23A. The resulting spikes and many of the interspike intervals for one cell are shown in figure 2.23B. These intervals are plotted as a function of the stimulus onset in figure 2.23C: The *x* axis represents time, and the *y* axis represents the interspike intervals in milliseconds.

The phase-locking of the spikes of auditory cells with different characteristic frequencies to a sound is shown in the two columns below the single cell representation. Each row represents one cell, and the spikes to repetitions of the stimulus waveform are shown as black "blips." The degree of phase-locking is expressed by the tightness and regularity of the blips. The number of spikes at each time point is combined across all the cells to generate the population histogram. The overall phase-locking is clear: The peaks in the number of spikes occur once per waveform repetition (roughly every 6.5 ms, 150 Hz).

Corresponding to the phase-locking in the firing of each cell are the all-order interval distributions shown in the right panel at the bottom of figure 2.23. Here, the blips represent the number of occurrences of every interspike interval separately for each characteristic frequency. Summing the number of intervals across the cells generates the population-interval histogram. The peaks of this histogram represent the fundamental frequency of the sound ($1/F_0$) plus the weaker harmonics.

Place × Timing Place × timing models represent the strength of the phase-locked response of each hair cell filter by the autocorrelation among the spikes. The *y* axis becomes the characteristic frequency of the hair cell filter; the *x* axis becomes the intervals between spikes; and the *z* axis becomes the strength of the autocorrelation (phase-locked responses) among spikes at each time interval. The autocorrelation at each characteristic frequency is calculated separately, in contrast to pure rate models in which the intervals are summed together. Figure 2.24A illustrates a schematic calculation of the autocorrelation at each frequency to a complex sound. The amplitudes of the autocorrelations are summed across fibers to derive the summary histogram. The stimulus shown in figure 2.24B consists of the first 10 harmonics of a 100 Hz complex tone. The phase-locked response for cells with a characteristic frequency of 200 Hz should occur at periods of the 200 Hz 2nd harmonic (5, 10, 15 ms . . .) while the phase-locked response for cells with a characteristic frequency of 1000 Hz should occur at the period of the 1000 Hz 10th harmonic (1, 2, 3 ms . . .). Because the phase-locking is not perfect, the response and autocorrelation look like a series of normal curves centered at the periods of the component frequencies. The autocorrelations at the characteristic frequencies of the receptors are summed to create a *summary correlogram* that isolates the 10 ms period of

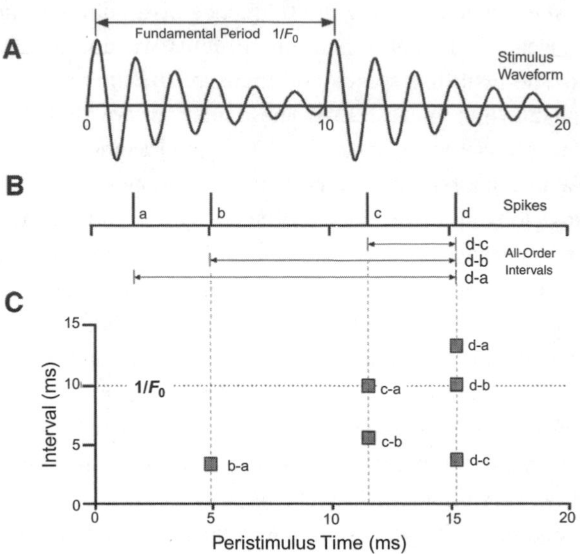
A
Fundamental Period $1/F_0$
Stimulus Waveform
0
10
20
B
a
b
c
d
Spikes
d-c
d-b
d-a
All-Order Intervals
C
Interval (ms)
$1/F_0$
d-a
c-a
d-b
c-b
d-c
b-a
Peristimulus Time (ms)

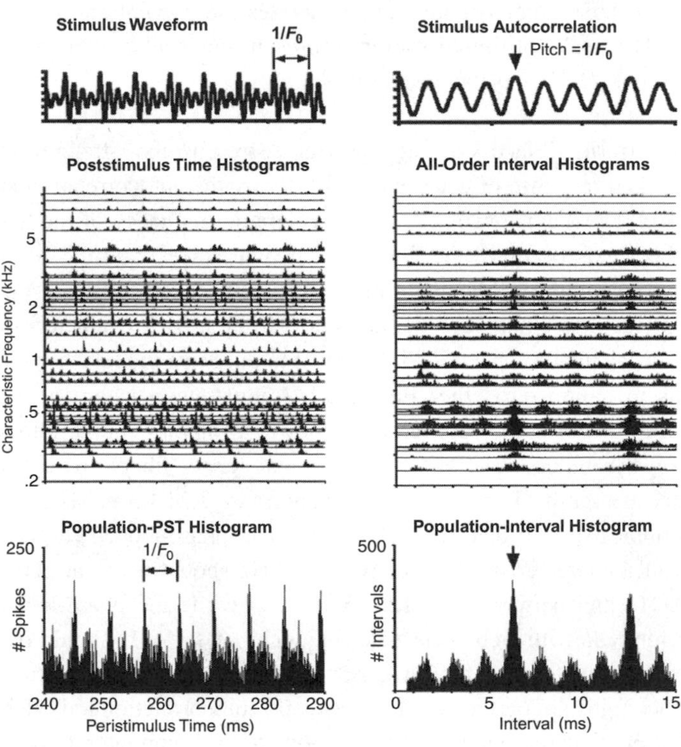
Phase-Locking of Discharges in the Auditory Nerve
Stimulus Waveform
$1/F_0$
Stimulus Autocorrelation
Pitch $=1/F_0$
Poststimulus Time Histograms
All-Order Interval Histograms
Characteristic Frequency (kHz)
Population-PST Histogram
Population-Interval Histogram
Spikes
Intervals
Peristimulus Time (ms)
Interval (ms)

the 100 Hz fundamental. Correlogram representations, and timing models in general, have been rather successful in matching results from human pitch judgment experiments.

Given the frequency limitations to phase-locking, it is best to hypothesize that both rate and timing are used by the auditory system: Timing coding occurs up to the frequency determined by the phase-locking limit, and rate coding occurs at frequencies beyond that. As you go up the auditory system, the phase-locking limit decreases so that by the primary auditory cortex, that limit may be only 40 to 50 Hz (T. Lu, Liang, & Wang, 2001). T. Lu and Wang (2004) argued that rate and timing coding may encode different properties of the auditory input or encode the same property by means of different populations of neurons. In that work, roughly 40% of the cortical neurons synchronized to the onsets of rapidly occurring clicks (down to a 30 ms interval between clicks), while the remaining 60% of the cells did not have any timing information. T. Lu and Wang (2004) argued that the latter cells are a transformed representation of the stimulus that could encode other properties.

At the Auditory Brainstem and Midbrain

One strong similarity between the spatial receptive fields in vision and the frequency receptive fields in audition is that both occur at different resolutions. Spatial receptive fields and critical bands vary in bandwidth and are densely distributed along the frequency dimension. There is local coding in both. A second similarity is the spatial overlap of receptive fields in vision and the frequency overlap of critical bands in audition.

This firing pattern is carried by the auditory nerve to the cochlear nucleus. Here, parallel processing channels are created that abstract certain acoustic features. One such enhanced feature is the degree of amplitude

---

Figure 2.23. Derivation of a population peristimulus histogram and population all-order interval histogram. The population peristimulus histogram sums the number of spikes across fibers with different characteristic frequencies at time points after stimulus onset. The derivation of an all-order peristimulus histogram for a single fiber is shown schematically in (A), (B), and (C). The stimulus waveform is shown in (A), the spikes are shown in (B), and all of the intervals between spikes are shown in (C). An example of a population all-order interval histogram is shown below. The histogram covers a 50 ms interval beginning 240 ms after stimulus onset. At the top of the left column is the stimulus waveform, below that the spikes for fibers with different characteristic frequencies, and at the bottom the total number of spikes at each time point. At the top of the right column is the autocorrelation for the stimulus waveform, below that is the intervals between spikes for fibers with different characteristic frequencies, and at the bottom is the frequencies of the intervals between spikes. Figure courtesy of Dr. Peter Cariani.

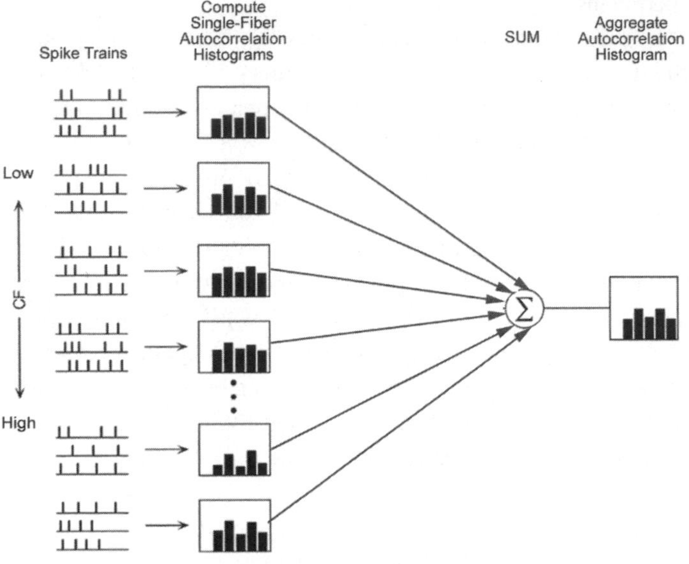
(A) Aggregate Autocorrelation Histograms
Spike Trains
Compute Single-Fiber Autocorrelation Histograms
SUM
Aggregate Autocorrelation Histogram
Low
CF
High
Σ

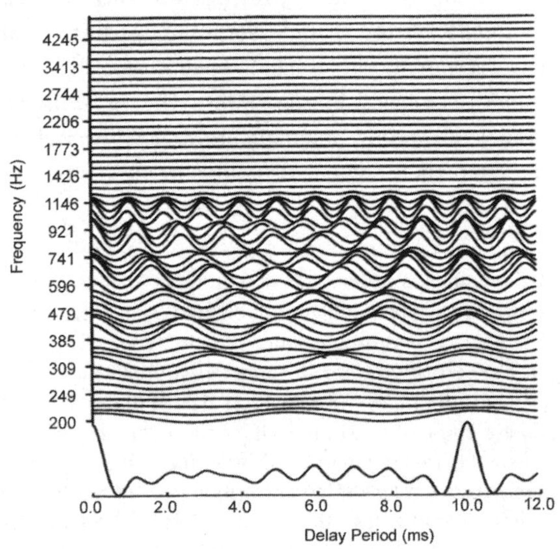
(B) Summary Correlogram of the First 10 Harmonics of a 100 Hz Tone
Frequency (Hz)
4245
3413
2744
2206
1773
1426
1146
921
741
596
479
385
309
249
200
0.0
2.0
4.0
6.0
8.0
10.0
12.0
Delay Period (ms)

modulation that characterizes speech, animal communication, and music. Neurons in the cochlear nucleus can amplify the depth of the amplitude modulation over a wide range of sound levels. Moreover, the effect of background noise is small, and there are neurons in which the response to the amplitude modulation actually is enhanced in background noise. The rate of amplitude modulation is coded by the synchronous responses (i.e., the phase-locked responses) to the modulation.

The inferior colliculus integrates almost all the ascending acoustic information and determines the form in which information is conveyed to the auditory cortex. The receptive fields of many neurons match those from lower nuclei in the auditory pathways and also match the results from psychophysical experiments using the same paradigms. The frequency bandwidths are similar and the receptive fields are relatively constant across changes in intensity.

This differs from the receptive fields found at the auditory brainstem. There, the bandwidth greatly increases at higher intensities. This suggests that the ability to resolve frequencies should decrease at higher intensities because the bandwidths of the tuning curves measure the ability to resolve differences between frequencies, but that is not the case. We can measure the behavioral ability to resolve and integrate frequencies by determining the frequency range of a noise that masks the detection of a tone at the middle frequency of the noise. This range has been termed the *critical band.* Noise energy outside this frequency range does not affect the detectability of the tone. This experimental procedure yields bandwidths that are roughly one third of an octave wide and are basically constant across a wide range of intensities. Frequencies that fall within one critical band are not resolved (into distinguishable frequencies) and are summed. It is critically important to understand that there are many critical bands, and there is a great deal of

---

Figure 2.24. Panel (A) is a schematic drawing of place × timing models. The cochlea performs an initial frequency analysis and then the outputs at the different frequencies are analyzed separately, the place component. The timings between the spikes of each such output are autocorrelated (equivalent to measuring the frequency distribution of the intervals), and the excitation is assumed to be proportional to the size of the autocorrelation at each delay interval. The summary autocorrelation histogram is calculated by adding the autocorrelations across receptors, as illustrated at the right. Figure courtesy of Dr. Peter Cariani. Panel (B) is an example of a summary correlogram based on the first ten harmonics of a 100 Hz sound. The evenly spaced peaks at each frequency are due to the autocorrelations at multiples of the period. The summary correlogram isolates the 10 ms period of the 100 Hz fundamental. From "Virtual Pitch and Phase Sensitivity of a Computer Model of the Auditory Periphery. I. Pitch Identification," by R. Meddis and M. J. Hewitt, 1991, *Journal of the Acoustical Society of America, 89*, 2866-2882. Copyright 1991 by the American Institute of Physics. Reprinted with permission.

overlap in the frequency range of different bands: One band may extend from 1000 to 1050 Hz, while a second band may extend from 1005 to 1055 Hz, and so on. Only at the inferior colliculus in the auditory midbrain, where the bandwidth does not change with intensity, do the correspondences between the physiological and perceptual bandwidths emerge.

Any single cochlear frequency band is represented physically as a two-dimensional plane or lamina. The typical connection between cells is within a single-frequency lamina. There is a topographical gradient of the bandwidths at each isofrequency lamina: Neurons with broader bandwidths, many beyond the measured critical band, are located more peripherally, while neurons with narrower bandwidths are located more centrally.

Many cells in the inferior colliculus (as well as in lower nuclei) are excited by the stimulation of one ear and inhibited by the stimulation of the other ear. Pollak, Burger, and Klug (2003) suggested that due to excitatory and inhibitory inputs from lower centers, trailing sounds can be inhibited by the leading sound, yielding the precedence effect, or the law of the first wavefront. Here, the locations of the successive echoes in a reverberant room are suppressed and do not contribute to the perceived location of the sound. All of the echoes, however, do combine to create the volume and timbre of the sound.

At the Primary Auditory Cortex

The auditory pathway has a tortuous path passing through several brain nuclei before reaching the auditory cortex. We might expect dramatic changes in the receptive fields, given the many opportunities for neural convergence. Yet if we assume that there will be homologies between the organization of the visual and auditory systems, we would expect that organization according to frequency would be the dominant factor (termed *tonotopic*) and that there would be a primary auditory cortex (that may be subdivided) and subsequent subregions. In these other regions of the auditory cortex, the cells will have different properties, may not be tonotopic, and may mainly have nonseparable frequency-time receptive fields (i.e., responsive to frequency glides). However, in all regions, tonotopic frequency organization would still be the overarching physiological concept. In what follows, I first consider the overall properties of the organization of the auditory cortex. Then I consider the characteristics of spectral-temporal receptive fields and question whether these are auditory feature detectors that are tuned to the unique requirements of a species.

Organization of the Primary Auditory Cortex

The tonotopic organization coming out of the cochlea is maintained along the entire auditory pathway and results in a two-dimensional representation in the cortex. In the primary auditory cortex (A1), cells with the identical characteristic frequency are arrayed in roughly parallel lines, with the highest frequency closest to the suprasylvian fissure. A tonotopic dimension has been found in every mammalian species studied, and regions representing biologically significant frequencies often are enlarged, analogous to the magnification for foveal vision in V1. Cells with the same characteristic frequency form a two-dimensional sheet.

One way of describing the organization of each characteristic frequency sheet is in terms of the bandwidth of the receptive field. Each sheet runs vertically (dorsal-ventral), and the distribution of bandwidths can be divided into roughly three regions. On the whole, the neurons in the central region are characterized by narrow bandwidths that are constant across variations in intensity. The neurons in the ventral region are characterized by wider bandwidths, and the effect of intensity on the bandwidth is weak. The dorsal region is more complex, and the bandwidths tend to oscillate in width toward the end of the dorsal region. Many neurons in the dorsal region have multiple excitatory regions and may have one or more inhibitory regions. There is a striking alternation in the bandwidths of clusters of cells from the central to the extreme dorsal region that is found even for responses to single frequencies (Schreiner, Read, & Sutter, 2000). In addition to encoding characteristics of the frequency spectrum, other cells in A1 encode binaural properties such as interaural time and intensity differences. The binaural properties vary periodically along the isofrequency axis, but the relationship to the bandwidth is unclear (Read, Winer, & Schreiner, 2002).

Shamma and Klein (2000) and colleagues have suggested another organizing principle for an isofrequency sheet based on the symmetry and scale (bandwidth) of the receptive fields. At the center of the sheet, the two inhibition regions are symmetrical around the center excitation region. Moving out from the center along the symmetry axis, the three regions combine into two, one excitatory and one inhibitory. At one end, the inhibitory region occurs at the lower frequencies, while at the other end the inhibitory region occurs at the higher frequencies, as shown in figure 2.25. (Recall that there are asymmetric receptive fields in V1 consisting of single excitatory and inhibitory regions.) The local symmetry axis is perpendicular to the scale axis that encodes the bandwidths of the receptive fields.

The symmetry and scale axes are presumed to underlie the perception of the direction and rate of frequency glides. To understand the response for frequency glides, we need to include the physiological finding that the inhibitory response takes longer to develop than the excitatory response (this is the same assumption about the time course of inhibition found in the difference of the Difference of Gaussians model for visual on-off cells). Thus, if an upward frequency glide first passes through a lower-frequency inhibitory region, the delayed inhibitory response will occur at the same time

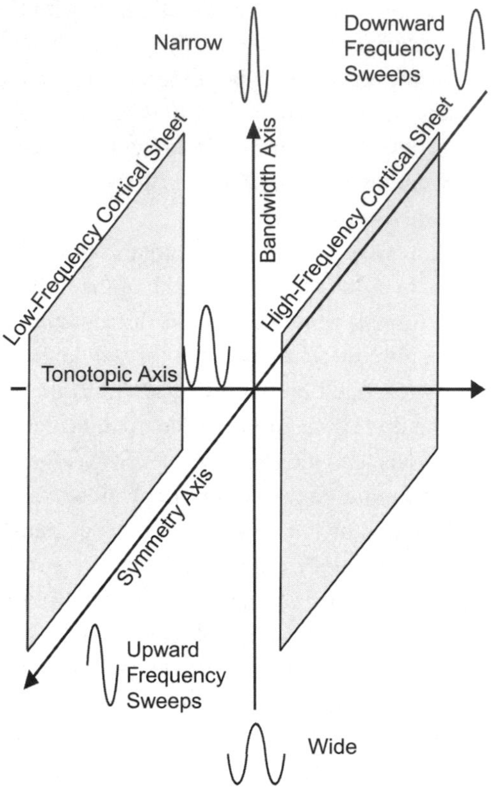

Figure 2.25. The proposed three-dimensional organization of A1. The first axis is tonotopic frequency, the second axis is symmetry, and the third axis is bandwidth. Adapted from "Auditory Representations of Timbre and Pitch," by R. Lyon and S. Shamma, 1996, in H. L. Hawkins, T. A. McMullen, A. N. Popper, and R. R. Fay (Eds.), *Auditory computation* (Vol. 6, pp. 221–270). New York: Springer-Verlag.

as the subsequent response from the higher-frequency excitation region, and the overall firing rate will not change to any degree. However, if an upward glide first passes through a lower-frequency excitation region, then the excitatory response will beat the inhibitory response from the higher-frequency inhibitory region and there will be a large change in the firing rate. On this basis, these "symmetry" cells can distinguish the direction of the frequency glide. The majority of cells respond to downward sweeps, and generally glides toward the characteristic frequency generate stronger responses than glides away from that frequency (Weisz, Wienbach, Hoffmeister, & Elbert, 2004). Along the scale axis, neurons with narrow bandwidths will respond to rapid glides, and cells with wide bandwidths will respond to slower glides.

M. L. Sutter, Schreiner, McLean, O'Connor, and Loftus (1999) directly investigated the types and distributions of cells with complex receptive fields in the cat. For each cell, they first characterized the excitatory receptive field—the combinations of frequency and intensity that excited the cell. Following this, they presented a low-intensity tone at the characteristic frequency on every trial, along with a second tone at differering frequencies

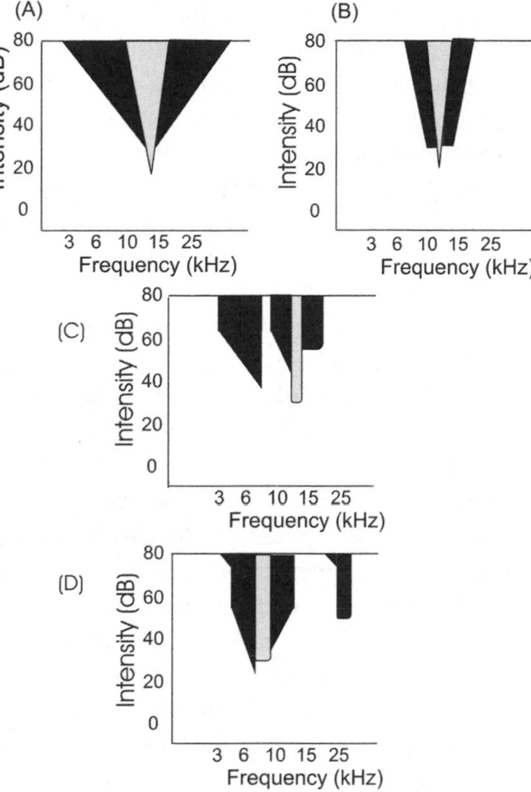

Figure 2.26. Simplified examples of the three most common inhibitory band structures. The most common type has one excitatory band and two surrounding inhibitory bands. Two examples that vary bandwidth are illustrated in (A) and (B). Neurons with one excitatory and two bounding inhibitory regions account for 35% of the total. The two remaining structures have one excitatory band and three inhibitory bands, two inhibitory bands on one side of the excitatory band and one on the other (C and D). Adapted from "Organization of Inhibitory Frequency Receptive Fields in Cat Primary Auditory Cortex," by M. L. Sutter, C. E. Schreiner, M. McLean, K. N. O'Connor, and W. C. Loftus, 1999, *Journal of Neurophysiology, 82*, 2358–2371.

and intensities. The combinations of frequency and intensity of the second tone that inhibited the firing of the target cell by 50% defined the inhibitory areas for that cell.

M. L. Sutter et al. (1999) created a typology of the different inhibitory receptive field structures based on the number and position of inhibitory regions. Simplified versions of the three most common patterns are shown in figure 2.26. The distribution differs between the ventral and dorsal regions. In the ventral region, over 50% of the cells have one inhibitory region above and one inhibitory region below its excitation region; the inhibitory bands are symmetrical. In contrast, in the dorsal region, the majority of cells have three or more inhibitory bands asymmetrically surrounding the excitation region. These appear to be the asymmetric cells found by Shamma and Klein (2000).

These results support the contention that cells in the dorsal region with multiple inhibitory regions are more suited to analyzing sounds such as speech and music with multiple spectral components that undergo slow and fast frequency changes. The multiple inhibitory regions alter the firing rate of these cells when other frequencies are present (e.g., different vowels) and can respond differentially to frequency glides. The cells in the ventral region respond poorly to broadband sounds; they are more suited to signal the presence of individual frequencies. They hear the world through a narrower aperture. Again, our representation of auditory objects depends on the patterning of firings in both the ventral and dorsal regions; it is not either-or. A sound with a single frequency would excite cells in both regions; the introduction of other sounds would change the firing of the cell in the dorsal region due to the inhibitory bands but would not affect the firing of the cell in the ventral region. If the ventral firing did not continue, we could not determine if the original frequency had terminated or not.

Read, Winer, and Schreiner (2001) have traced the interconnections between cells in the primary auditory cortex. Although it would be logical for the narrow and broadband neurons with the same best excitatory characteristic frequency to be interconnected, that is not the case. Instead, the connections are between neurons with the same characteristic frequency that share a common bandwidth: narrow-bandwidth cells connect to other narrow-bandwidth cells and broad-bandwidth cells connect to broad-bandwidth cells. Thus, there is a functional and physiological separation between the two classes of cells. It may be that the narrow and broadband cells have different spectral-temporal properties due to the excitation and inhibition regions that maintain this segregation.

It is interesting that there are not many interconnections among cells in different isofrequency sheets. This is in contrast to the visual cortex, where there are many interconnections between cells representing adjacent retinal points. One possible explanation for this difference is that many important sound objects are made up of roughly harmonic frequency components (multiples of the fundamental) as opposed to background noise, which is likely to be composed of a continuous range of frequencies. Visual objects are connected in space so that adjacent retinal points are very likely to represent the same object. Thus, it makes sense to connect adjacent cells in the visual cortex because one object usually causes the firing of those cells, but it does not make sense to connect adjacent cells in the isofrequency sheets because one sound object is unlikely to cause the firing of those cells. In fact, such a pattern of interconnections enhances sound segmentation, as discussed in chapter 9.

We can conceptualize these spectral organizational schemes in terms of static and frequency glide sounds. For static sounds, cells with wide excitation regions would be best driven by sounds with high-amplitude, broad frequency bands (e.g., instruments with many close partials), while the frequency components of those same sounds would fall in both the excitation and inhibition regions of cells with narrow response regions and not affect their firing rate. In contrast, cells with narrow response regions would be driven best by sounds with high-amplitude discrete harmonics. For sounds with frequency glides, cells with broad response regions will respond to wider frequency swings, while cells with narrow response regions will respond to narrower frequency swings. What this all means is that cells with different bandwidths create a means to encode the acoustic signal at different levels of resolution or, to put it in another way, to encode it in terms of both coarse, slowly changing physical variables and fine, rapidly changing physical variables. The spectral organization results in topographically distinct areas that are maximally responsive to different types of information in the acoustic wave (see T. Lu & Wang, 2004). This concept of multiresolution in frequency and time is exactly analogous to the multiresolution in frequency and orientation found in the primary visual cortex. Nelken (2002), in an insightful review, cautioned that these results can vary widely as a function of species and stimulus amplitude, as well as the method of anesthesia.

Receptive Fields: Spectral-Temporal Properties The stimuli used to determine receptive fields experimentally are of two sorts. The first uses basic stimuli, amplitude- or frequency-modulated sine waves, to derive receptive fields that should be found in a variety of species. The disadvantage of these stimuli is that cells may be responsive to correlated acoustic components that would not be isolated with independent auditory inputs. The second uses natural calls (e.g., mating or warning signals) of the species being studied to uncover receptive fields that may illustrate nonlinear higher-level receptive fields. The disadvantage here is that because most species-specific calls have correlated stimulus components, it is necessary to remove those correlations before determining the receptive field.

Independent Frequency Component Stimuli L. Li, Lu, and Wang (2002) investigated the response to frequency and amplitude-modulated sinusoidal waves in awake marmoset monkeys. Nearly all neurons responded to amplitude modulation and about 70% responded to frequency modulation. The response was stronger to these modulated sounds than to pure tones. The discharge rates of five representative neurons are shown in figure 2.27. Each neuron shows a distinct peak at the same frequency for the amplitude and frequency modulation. L. Li et al. (2002) suggested that the similarity

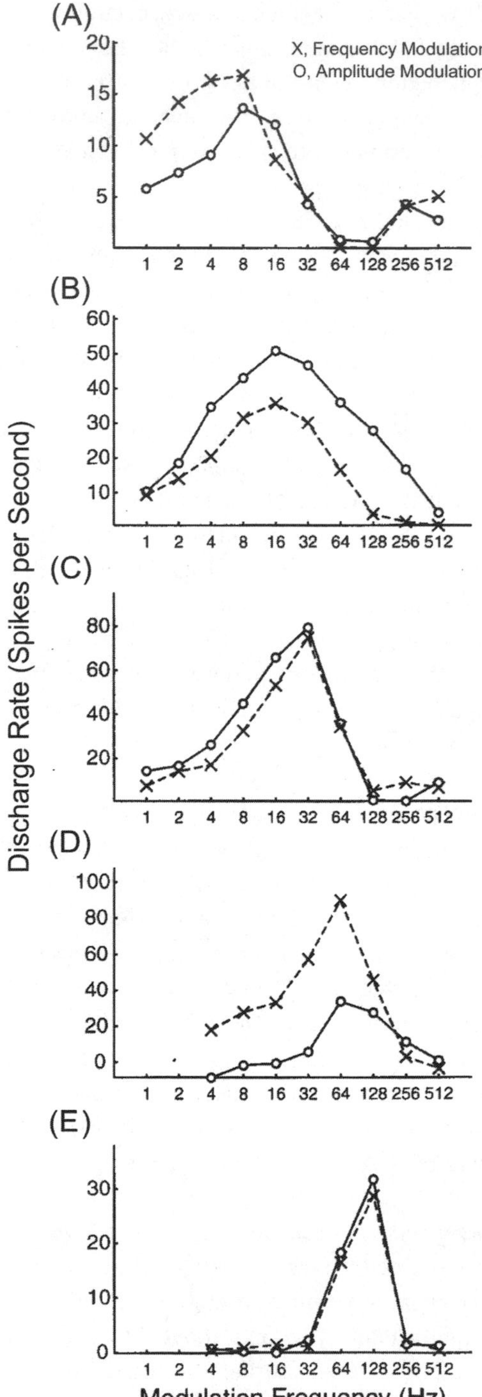

Figure 2.27. The response of five different neurons in awake monkeys to amplitude and frequency modulation. Most neurons had similar response patterns to amplitude and frequency modulation. From "Neural Representations of Sinusoidal Amplitude and Frequency Modulations in the Primary Auditory Cortex of Awake Primates," by L. Li, T. Lu, and X. Wang, 2002, *Journal of Neurophysiology, 87*, 2237–2261. Copyright 2002 by the American Physiological Society. Reprinted with permission.

in the discharge pattern between amplitude and frequency modulation results from a common temporal modulation mechanism that extracts all types of change from a complex acoustic environment.

Wang, Lu, Snider, and Liang (2005) found many cells in awake monkeys that show high-rate sustained firing to steady-state tones at their characteristic or best frequencies and high-rate sustained firing to amplitude-modulated tones at the best modulation frequency. The same cells show only onset responses if the tone and amplitude modulation frequencies differ from their optimal values. This means that when a sound is first heard, there is an onset response across a large population of cells with a wide range of best frequencies. Then, as the signal continues, only those cells whose preferred frequencies match the sound keep on firing, although at a slower rate than the onset rate. The onset response has a short latency and therefore can provide precise information about onsets and transitions in the environment, while the sustained responses can provide precise information about the frequency composition of the sound.

DeCharms, Blake, and Merzenich (1998) used the reverse correlation technique to derive spectral-temporal receptive fields in awake owl monkeys. The stimuli were auditory chords typically composed of one note from each of seven octaves. The notes were chosen randomly so that any single chord could be composed of a variable number of notes in one or more octave ranges. Each chord was only 20 ms in duration, and about 30,000 chords were used to characterize each spectral-temporal receptive field. Simplified but typical spectral-temporal receptive fields are shown in figure 2.28.

Only a small number of cells had spectral-temporal receptive fields with a single region of excitation and no inhibition. The spectral-temporal receptive fields shown in figure 2.28 illustrate diverse response patterns. The neuron in (A) has a narrow frequency region of excitation flanked by inhibitory frequencies, presumably tuned to pick up a continuous frequency edge at a precise tonal frequency. The neuron in (B) fires to an alternating off-on pattern at a specific frequency, presumably tuned to pick up successive stimulus pulses. The neuron in (C) has a downward excitation frequency glide, while the neuron in (D) has a complex set of multiple excitatory and inhibitory subregions. In fact, the vast majority of cells did have multiple subregions. Overall, the bandwidth of the response areas was 1.8 octaves (about 1.5 times that for visual fields) and the duration of the response ranged from 20 to 100 ms.

What this means is that the auditory cortical cells respond to local features of the stimulus, in much the same way argued for the visual cortical cells. As DeCharms et al. (1998, p. 1443) stated, "In decomposing visual forms or auditory scenes, the cortex uses detectors with similar characteristics for finding the position of stimulus edges along the sensory receptor

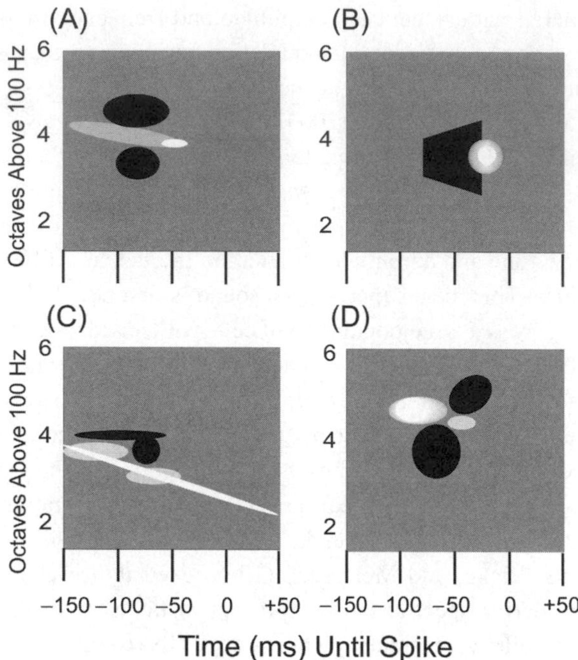

Figure 2.28. The spectral-temporal receptive fields of four representative auditory cells. Nearly all neurons had multiple excitation and inhibitory regions and seem tuned to auditory characteristics that define objects. Adapted from "Optimizing Sound Features for Cortical Neurons," by R. C. DeCharms, D. T. Blake, and M. M. Merzenich, 1998, *Science, 280*, 1439–1444.

surface, finding stimulus edges (onsets) in time, finding stimulus movements, and finding feature conjunctions."

Shamma (2001) and Shamma and Klein (2000) measured the receptive fields in A1 using sounds made up of many harmonics across a five-octave frequency range. The amplitudes of the harmonics are modulated across the logarithmic frequency axis by a sine wave that drifts either up or down in frequency. The sine wave creates an amplitude envelope across the frequency range that gradually shifts in frequency, as shown in figure 2.29. By varying the frequency, rate of drift, and amplitude (depth of modulation) of the sine wave, it is possible to measure the spectral-temporal response field from the resulting firing pattern. Examples of rippled spectra are shown in figure 2.29.[5]

Researchers (Depireaux, Simon, Klein, & Shamma, 2001; Kowalski, Depireaux, & Shamma, 1996) investigated whether the spectral and temporal components of the neural response were separable and independent. In

5. The ripple stimuli are modeled after drifting sinusoidal gratings, discussed in chapter 5, used to investigate second-order motion.

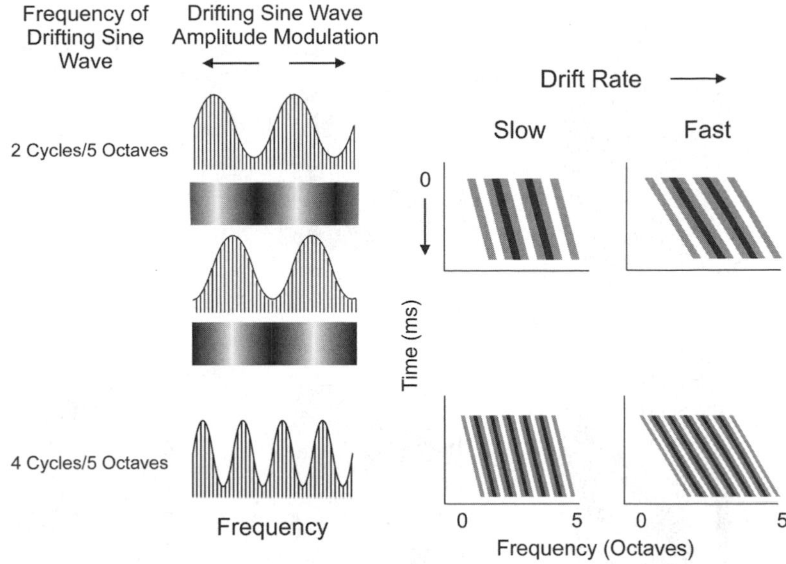

Figure 2.29. Dynamic ripple stimuli consist of many simultaneously presented tones that are equally spaced along the logarithmic frequency scale (i.e., equal frequency ratios). A sinusoidal envelope that sweeps up or down the frequency axis across time modulates the amplitude of the tones. Two time points are shown as the envelope drifts to the right. The sinusoidal envelope can vary in frequency and rate of drift. The envelope across time can be depicted as a frequency × time graph: The frequency becomes represented by the width of the intensity bars and the rate by the slope. Adapted from "On the Role of Space and Time in Auditory Processing," by S. Shamma, 2001, *Trends in Cognitive Science, 5*, 340–348.

practice, this means measuring the response to several modulation frequencies at one drift rate, measuring the response to several velocities (both upward and downward in this research) at one modulation frequency, and then being able to predict the response for all combinations of frequency and velocity. Depireaux et al. (2001) found that there was a distribution of separability. Some cells were completely separable and the response to both upward and downward ripples was independent of the velocity of the ripples; other cells were separable to either upward or downward ripples so that they would respond differentially to upward and downward frequency glides.

Using more natural stimuli, Sen, Theunissen, and Doupe (2001) also derived a separability index (essentially a measure of the error between the actual and predicted) and found that there is a wide distribution in the degree of separability. The frequency × time receptive fields for two auditory cells in the zebra finch is shown in figure 2.30. For the cell shown in (A), the frequency selectivity is relatively constant across time so that the response of this cell is separable. The predicted response, assuming independence between time and frequency, is nearly indistinguishable from the actual

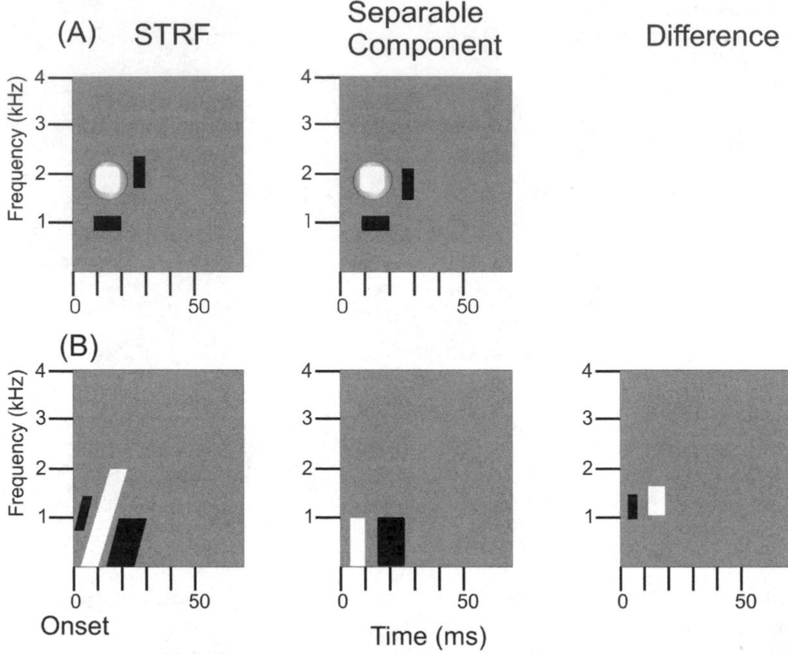

Figure 2.30. The spectral-temporal receptive fields, the separable components, and the difference between the spectral-temporal receptive field and separable part are shown for two auditory cells in the finch. In (A), the frequency response does not shift over time, so that there is no difference between the actual receptive field and the estimate based on separability. In (B), the frequency response does shift; the separable components do not capture that shift, so that there is a residual component. The separable plus the residual would reproduce the frequency-time response. The stimulus onset occurs at time 0. Adapted from "Feature Analysis of Natural Sounds in the Songbird Auditory Forebrain," by K. Sen, F. E. Theunissen, and A. J. Doupe, 2001, *Journal of Neurophysiology, 86*, 1445–1458.

receptive field, and the difference is not shown. For the cell shown in (B), the frequency selectivity shifts across time, so that the response is nonseparable. The predicted response based on separability shown in the second column makes the frequency selectivity constant across time (the strictly constant [vertical] frequency response), so that there is a large difference between the separable (linear) prediction and the actual response.

Species-Specific Stimuli Wang, Merzenich, Beitel, and Schreiner (1995) used species-specific calls of marmoset monkeys to determine if there were neurons in A1 with spectral-temporal receptive fields tuned to those calls. The twitter calls were short broadband sounds (6000-12000 Hz) that repeated every 100 ms. There were no unique call detectors. On the whole, the receptive fields of neurons reflected the basic spectral-temporal properties of the acoustic wave but were phase-locked to the onset and offset envelope of each twitter at the cell's characteristic frequency, but not phase-locked to the temporal fine structure within each twitter (also found by L. Li et al., 2002, described previously). However, there were subpopulations of neurons that tended to respond more strongly to exact replicas of the calls than to synthetic variations with the identical spectral characteristics but slower or faster temporal rhythms. The phase-locking in the neural code to a simplification of the stimulus led to a higher degree of synchronization across populations of neurons scattered across the cortex surface. Thus, Wang et al. (1995) concluded that the neural representation is spatially distributed across the cortex in terms of characteristic frequency but at the same time temporally synchronized so that there is a coherent representation of the spectral-temporal characteristics of each call. Any single neuron is probably associated with several subpopulations, meaning that every neuron undoubtedly is involved in the representation of more than one call. This is a characteristic of sparse coding, discussed in chapter 3.

Barbour and Wang (2003) pointed out that acoustic calls have wide irregular spectrums. They found two kinds of cells in the auditory cortex of awake marmoset monkeys. The first responded preferentially to these sorts of sounds with high contrast between the frequency regions. The second responded preferentially to sounds with low-contrast spectra. The high contrast cells seem to correspond to the cells described by Sutter, Schreiner, McLean, O'Connor, & Loftus (1999) with many excitatory and inhibitory regions, while the low contrast cells would correspond to cells with only a small number of excitatory and inhibitory areas.

Wang et al. (1995) speculated that the subpopulations of neurons distributed across the cortical field most sensitive to a particular call come about by means of plasticity of the neural connections that can be modified by learning and experience. To demonstrate that the responses to natural twitter calls was not simply due to the acoustic properties, Wang and Kadia (2001) created natural and reversed twitter calls and presented both to marmosets and cats. Only the neurons in A1 of the marmosets discriminated between the natural and reversed calls; there was no difference in the response of neurons in A1 of the cat. In fact, the responsiveness of the marmosets to the reversed calls equaled that of both the natural and reversed calls for the cat. Wang and Kadia speculated that it was early experiences that led to the differential response for the marmosets.

Fritz, Shamma, Elhilali, and Klein (2003) found that attending to specific target tones generated rapid changes to the spectral-temporal receptive fields of roughly 70% of the A1 neurons in the ferret. If the target tone was centered on an excitatory region, the excitatory response in that region was enhanced (effectively increasing the contrast), and if the target tone was centered on an inhibitory region, the inhibitory response in that region was decreased, effectively decreasing the contrast (see figure 2.31). The changes were exceedingly rapid, occurring within minutes. A minority of cells (33%) immediately returned to their initial receptive fields, while the remaining cells maintained their changes for hours. The changes only occurred if the ferrets performed a task dependent on the target tone; passive listening did not change the spectral-temporal receptive fields. The authors suggested that cortical cells are never fixed and constantly evolve due to top-down and bottom-up influences controlled by the context.

Work by Theunissen, Sen, and Doupe (2000) illustrates the complexities in trying to uncover higher-order aspects of the spectral-temporal receptive

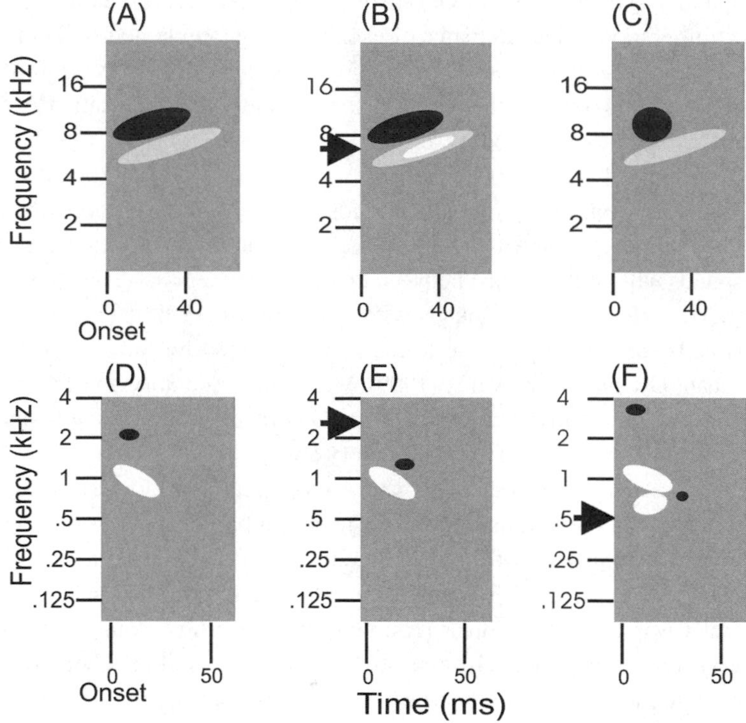

Figure 2.31. The effect of attending to target tones can be rapid. The response of a cell before training is shown in (A). The target tone was 6000 Hz, and the initial effect was to increase the excitation around 6000 Hz, shown in (B). After a short period of time, the spectral-temporal receptive field evolved so that although the initial increase in excitation disappeared, the inhibitory area slightly higher than the target tone decreased. A similar effect is illustrated in (D), (E), and (F). The response before training is shown in (D). After training with a 3000 Hz tone, the inhibitory region around 2000 Hz shifted to a lower frequency (E). After a second training session with a 500 Hz tone (F), an excitation region emerges at a frequency slightly higher than 500 Hz. Adapted from "Rapid Task-Related Plasticity of Spectrotemporal Receptive Fields in Primary Auditory Cortex," by J. Fritz, S. Shamma, M. Elhilali, and D. Klein, 2003, *Nature Neuroscience, 6*(11), 1216–1223.

fields. The authors pointed out that for natural stimuli such as the zebra finch songs used here, there are strong spectral and temporal correlations. For example, the overall amplitude envelopes of a set of frequency bands (neglecting the fine variations within the envelope) are correlated over time so that the onsets and offsets of one band can predict the corresponding timing of another band. This suggests that the optimal stimulus representation should remove such correlations in order to reduce the redundancies.

However, Theunissen et al. (2000) found that the correlations between frequency bands did affect the spectral-temporal receptive fields because simulated versions of songs that balanced the average frequency distribution and rhythmic distribution did not yield firing patterns identical to those of the actual sounds that contained the correlations. Two typical neurons of this sort are shown in figure 2.32. Neuron (A) appears to be tuned to a downward-moving frequency edge, while neuron (B) appears to be tuned to a nonoverlapping combination of frequencies between 1500 and 2500 Hz, followed by frequencies between 4000 and 6500 Hz.

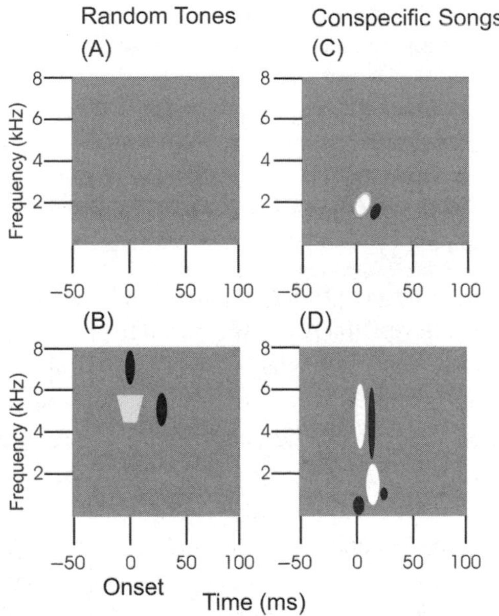

Figure 2.32. The response of two auditory neurons to real conspecific songs shows a distinct receptive field structure (C and D). The response, however, is very weak to a sequence of tones that has the same frequency distribution as the real conspecific songs, but a different sequence and rhythm (A and B). From "Spectral-Temporal Receptive Fields of Nonlinear Auditory Neurons Obtained Using Natural Sounds," by F. E. Theunissen, K. Sen, and A. J. Doupe, 2000, *Journal of Neuroscience, 20*, 2315–2331.Copyright 2000 by the Society for Neuroscience. Reprinted with permission.

Theunissen et al. (2000) also pointed out that the spectral-temporal receptive fields calculated for a single cell may dramatically shift if the stimulus is varied, indicating that the measured receptive field is sensitive to the entire song context. Nonetheless, in spite of the apparent shift in the spectral-temporal receptive fields, it is still possible to use the spectral-temporal receptive fields found for one stimulus to predict the response to a second stimulus if the two stimuli are of the same sort. Thus, the response to one natural calling song can be predicted from a different calling song but not from a random sequence of tones, and vice versa.

Machens, Wehr, and Zador (2004) added another cautionary conclusion about the generality of spectral-temporal receptive fields. At the beginning of this chapter, I pointed out that spectral-temporal receptive fields could be thought of as linear filters. We can pull the spectral-temporal receptive fields through sound and predict the spike pattern by essentially multiplying the sound spectrogram by the spectral-temporal receptive fields. Machens et al. (2004) found that although they could derive the spectral-temporal receptive fields of a cell to a specific natural stimulus, those derived spectral-temporal receptive fields could not predict the response pattern to a different stimulus. Only 11% of the response power could be predicted by the linear component, leading the authors to conclude that the response properties of auditory cortical cells were due to nonlinear interactions between sound frequencies and time-varying properties of the auditory system.

Summary of Receptive Fields in the Primary Auditory and Visual Cortex

The neural encoding by the primary auditory and visual cortex is roughly the same: Sensory information is transformed into general perceptual information. The pressure wave at the ear is locally analyzed in the cochlea into frequency components that vary over time and possibly space (although auditory localization depends on the comparison between the neural signal from the two ears). The lightness array at the eye is locally analyzed at the retina into circular on-off regions and is further analyzed in the visual cortex into local frequencies and orientations. Thus, at both the auditory and visual cortex, any stimulus is represented by the excitation at spatially distributed locations and the equally important inhibition at other locations. At every cortical location, there is representation at different resolutions. For both senses, there is a distribution of separable and nonseparable frequency × space × time neurons. It does not appear that the auditory or visual transformations create spectral-temporal and spatial-orientation temporal receptive fields that are tuned to specific features in an animal's environment (this is discussed further in chapter 3). Both the auditory and visual systems act to code general properties in sound and light, although there is strong evidence that early experience can lead to tuning of properties that have biological significance. Our phenomenal perception is achieved by synthesis, by combining the coincident or temporally correlated neural firings.

Higher Auditory and Visual Regions

The organization of the brain appears to be based on the complementary principles of functional integration and functional specialization. The overriding principle is segregation: Cells with common functions are grouped together. Such a spatial constraint means that there is a convergence of fibers going into the specialized regions and a divergence of fibers coming out of the region. The convergent fibers are patchy forward-driving connections (i.e., bottom-up) between cortical regions that create the greater selectivity at higher levels, and the divergent fibers are the more numerous backward connections (top-down) that modulate and shape the specialization of the cortical regions. Friston (2002) made a compelling argument that the backward connections metaphorically tell the cells in A1 and V1 what to expect in the near future and change the receptive fields of those cells to be more tuned to these expected sound and light configurations. Therefore, the specialization implied by one specific receptive field is not an intrinsic property of a region in the cortex, but depends on the overall activity of the forward and backward connections.

Why should the auditory and visual regions be organized into specialized regions? Van Essen, Anderson, and Felleman (1992) suggested several reasons:

1. Auditory and visual objects are immensely complicated, and it would be extremely difficult to design circuitry to compute all of the features at once. It makes sense to break the problem into small manageable parts.
2. By breaking up the processing into smaller units, it becomes possible to employ specific neural circuits for each part. Inhibition is used to sharpen various auditory and visual attributes. But it is critical that the inhibitory circuits for one attribute do not affect the circuits for a different attribute, and that is most easily accomplished by computing each attribute in a separate region.
3. Within a specialized region, the identical circuitry (e.g., frequency/orientation filters in V1) may be replicated many times so that computations can be done quickly in parallel fashion.
4. Specialization allows for top-down attending to particular attributes.
5. Specialization allows for unique integration pathways. Perceiving the world depends on the ability of a specialized region to influence computation within another region and the subsequent integration of the outcomes of all regions.

Although the hierarchies proposed for the auditory and visual systems seem to imply serial processing—a step-by-step progression from lower to higher areas—this is not the case as argued by Friston (2002) above and by Paradiso (2002). Perception relies on a division of labor and dynamic interactions among areas. Due to the latencies in firings, neurons in lower and higher regions will be active at the same time. As Paradiso noted, there are many instances in which firing patterns in V1 are more closely correlated to the percept than firing patterns in higher regions. Kanwisher and Wojiciulik (2000) reviewed evidence which indicates that feedback can affect processing as early as V1 (and we would expect the same for the primary auditory cortex). Moreover, Kanwisher and Wojiciulik pointed out that attention can lead to selection based on object features or on spatial location.

Visual Pathways

There have been several attempts to represent the hierarchical organization of the pathways in the visual system. The possible hierarchies based on the known feed-forward and feedback connections among the 30 or so known visual areas are incredibly complex, and, as Hilgetag, O'Neill, and Young (2000) pointed out, there is no single optimal hierarchy, merely a very large set of possible hierarchies (in the millions, according to the authors) that have the same number of inconsistencies. A simplified version that isolates the hierarchical levels found in all solutions is shown in figure 2.33.

There are several essential features. First, the visual areas V1 and V2 lie at the base of the hierarchies, and all of the neural pathways pass first through these two areas. In V2, cells can respond to contours created by changes in luminance (black-and-white differences) as found in V1, but cells also can respond to contours based on nonluminance cues such as textures, patterns, and binocular depth. In addition, many cells are selective for curved contours (selectivity for curvature is enhanced in higher visual centers, as described below). Furthermore, the cells in V2 tend to be insensitive to the phase, losing the particular location of the stimulus, due to nonlinearity in response. The cells respond to stimulus movement, not to eye movement.

Second, the pathways tend to break into two parts after V1 and V2, and this split can be traced back to the differences between the midget and parasol cells in the retina.

What Pathways

The "what" pathways respond to higher spatial frequencies, have a slower latency, and sacrifice temporal resolution for high spatial resolution. The midget cells that seem best suited to encode spatial detail project to the parvocellular layers of the lateral geniculate, pass through V1 and V2, and then on to V4 and along the ventral pathway to the inferotemporal cortex.

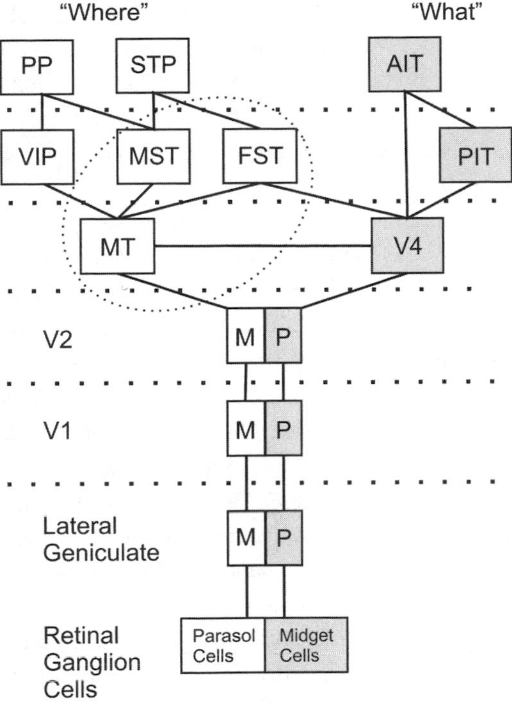

Figure 2.33. The organization of the visual system. The parasol cells in the retinal and lateral geniculate underlie the location-movement (M) cortical regions while the midget cells underlie the what-shape regions (P). All of the proposed hierarchies begin with separate levels for V1 and V2. Following V2, there is a hypothesized split in which the medial temporal area is specialized for location and movement, and V4 and the inferior temporal region are specialized for shape. As can be seen in the figure, there are many interconnections, so that the proposed split must be quantitative rather than being a complete dichotomous split. Any percept must be the result of the integration of many visual areas. Abbreviations: M, magnocellular layer; P, parvocellular layer; MT, middle temporal; VIP, ventral intraparietal; MST, medial superior temporal; FST, fundus superior temporal; PP, posterior parietal; STP, superior temporal parietal; PIT, posterior inferotemporal; AIT anterior inferotemporal. Adapted from "Seeing the Big Picture: Integrating of Image Cues in the Primate Visual System," by L. J. Croner and T. D. Albright, 1999, *Neuron, 24*, 777–789.

The transformations found in response patterns in going from V1 to V2 are enhanced from V2 to V4. The receptive fields get larger, so that the same feature can excite the cell over a larger retinal area (not that the features get larger themselves). The receptive fields of many cells are tuned for curved contours with specific radii of curvature (e.g., concentric and spiral gratings). Gallant, Braun, and Van Essen (1993) found V4 cells that responded only to sinusoidal gratings in Cartesian, polar, or hyperbolic coordinate systems and only to a narrow range of those gratings. Zetzsche, Krieger, and Wegmann

(1999) argued that, in fact, visual encoding based on polar organization would yield the optimal representation of the statistical redundancies of natural scenes, and Gallant et al. (1993) suggested that such non-Cartesian cells could respond to regions of symmetry or regions of high information. Gallant (2000) summed this up by stating that these cells are sensitive to shape, size, and configuration, but not to spatial position.

Cells in the inferotemporal cortex have large receptive fields, and individual cells respond to complex configurations of simple shapes. The configurations are not random but are selective to ethological patterns such as faces and hands (patterns made of distinct parts). These cells are responding to the coincidence of features that appear and disappear together (eye shapes, noses, and mouth shapes). Cells may respond regardless of cue defining the boundaries of the shape (Sary, Vogels, Kovacs, & Orban, 1995) and often will not respond to one part of a configuration, demonstrating the nonlinearity of the cell (Kobatake & Tanaka, 1994). Overall, inferotemporal cortex cells are excited by specific configurations of shape attributes but are insensitive to the cues for shape and the absolute position of the shape because the receptive fields are so large.

Sigala and Logothetics (2002) demonstrated that training can affect the selectivity of neurons in the anterior inferotemporal cortex. They trained two monkeys to distinguish schematic faces that differed in eye height, eye separation, nose length, and mouth height. The 10 faces were placed into two categories based on unique combinations of eye height and eye separation, so that the monkeys could not perform the task based on only one cue. Roughly 50% of 100 neurons increased their firing rate to one of the four facial features, and of these cells, 72% were selective to the two diagnostic eye variables and not to the nondiagnostic nose and mouth variables. These results therefore show that neurons can come to respond to features of complex stimuli that denote different categories. This outcome suggests a way that monkeys (and humans) can learn to interpret visual objects.

Where (Movement) Pathways The "where" pathways respond to low spatial frequencies, have shorter latencies, and sacrifice spatial resolution (i.e., bigger integration areas) for higher temporal resolution. The parasol cells that seem best suited to encode temporal detail project to the magnocellular layers of the lateral geniculate, and also pass through V1 and V2, and then along the dorsal pathway to the medial temporal, the medial superior temporal cortex, and the parietal region. Many cells are tuned to complex movements such as expansion and contraction and are influenced by stimuli in the nonclassical receptive fields. The response of cells in the medial superior temporal cortex is suppressed when the motion of the background is identical to that in the middle of the field. Effectively, then, these cells respond to relative motion.

Auditory Pathways

The auditory system is faced with exactly the same problem as that of the visual system: Identifying the object based on the proximal spectral components and localizing that object based on the time of arrival or intensity differences between the two ears.

In the core auditory region, there are two or three fields including A1 that are organized according to frequency. The A1 core area projects to a narrow surrounding belt area composed of at least seven fields, and in turn the belt area projects to the parabelt area, as shown in figure 2.34. Finally, the parabelt area projects to the temporal, frontal, and parietal cortex for additional processing.

Rauschecker and Tian (2000) and others have proposed that the auditory pathways, like those of the visual pathways, are organized into a what stream devoted to object identification and a where stream devoted to object localization. The caudal-lateral belt region receives information about object location (the where stream) that is relayed via the dorsal pathway to the posterior parietal cortex and the dorsolateral prefrontal cortex. The anterior-lateral regions of the belt and parabelt receive information for object perception (the what stream) that is projected via the ventral pathway to the temporal cortex.

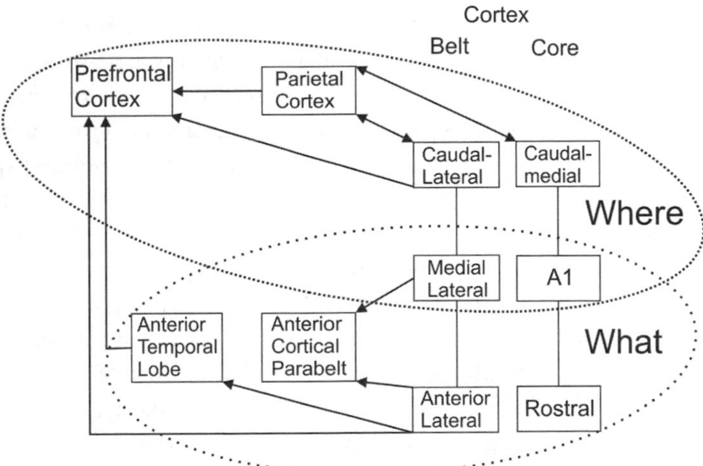

Figure 2.34. The hypothesized organization of the auditory system that parallels the what and where split found in the visual system. The dorsal medial geniculate nucleus (thalamus) feeds A1 and the caudal-medial cortical areas while the ventral medial geniculate (thalamus) feeds A1 and the rostral cortical areas. Again, survival requires an integrated percept combining auditory what and where information with visual what and where information. Adapted from "Mechanisms and Streams for Processing of 'What' and 'Where' in Auditory Cortex," by J. P. Rauschecker and B. Tian, 2000, *Proceedings of the National Academy of Science, 97*, 11800–11806.

What and Where Pathways

I would suggest that if the what-where division is fundamental, then it can be understood in terms of the uncertainty principle discussed in chapter 1. If there is an inherent inverse relationship between spatial and temporal resolution, then the only way to achieve maximum resolution along both dimensions is to use different measuring instruments for each (or possibly to make two measurements using one instrument). Given that it is implausible to try to alternate between optimizing the spatial and temporal resolution using one pathway, the auditory and visual systems evolved two pathways.

It should be noted that the hypothesized what and where pathways for the auditory and visual systems differ physiologically. For the auditory system, the two systems arise from fundamentally different kinds of excitation: the what system arises from the spectral components typically encoded identically in both ears, while the where system arises from the differences in timing and intensity between the two ears. In contrast, for vision the what (high-frequency) and where (low-frequency) systems arise from a split in the same frequency components in the entire scene (typically encoded nearly identically in both eyes). Therefore, frequency and time may not be separable due to the convergence of two neural streams (Mazer et al., 2002).

However, I find myself somewhat skeptical about conceptualizing the auditory and visual systems in terms of two relatively independent and parallel pathways. Anatomically, there is a great deal of interconnection between the two pathways, so there must be considerable cross-talk between the pathways. Moreover, single-cell and multicell recording experiments often do not find differences in the coding properties of cells in the two regions (summarized by Griffiths, Warren, Scott, Nelken, & King, 2004). For example, Zatorre, Bouffard, Ahad, and Belin (2002), using positron emission tomography imaging, found that auditory spatial processing was not localized in the temporal cortex but that certain posterior regions (the where stream) did integrate the location of events with the spectral or temporal features used to identify objects. The where stream becomes engaged only if there are distinguishing acoustic properties.

Perceptually, it is impossible to determine the "where and motion" without determining the "what and form." To resolve visual motion requires the detection of changes in the surface properties of objects (e.g., texture, brightness) across time; motion is not perceived directly (discussed in chapter 5). But these same properties are used to determine form. Consider the problem of perceiving a deflating balloon flying through the air. There needs to be a constant updating of both motion and shape based on the value of the other property, and that would be impossible without extensive feedback among the pathways. To resolve auditory localization and motion requires the detection of the timing and intensity differences among the frequency components in each ear. But in most natural situations, there are multiple sound sources with overlapping frequency components that are heard in both ears (discussed in chapter 9). What this means is that the frequency components in each must be allocated to sources before the locations of those sources can be determined, and the imaging results of Zatorre et al. (2002) support that the spectral-temporal acoustic properties are prior to location. Yet the timing and intensity differences between the ears for each component affect the allocation of the components to objects. On top of these problems, we experience stationary or moving objects at locations; we do not experience movements of stimulus features. I expect that future research will give a clearer description of the joint operation of the anatomical pathways.

What Could a Neural Code Be?

Eggermont (2001) singled out five principles that are the hallmarks of the change in the neural code from receptor to cortex. Eggermont's review is exclusively about the auditory system, but the hallmarks he identified are equally compelling for the visual system.

Transformations Create Intensity Independence

At the level of the auditory nerve, fibers respond to a range of frequencies that broadens as the intensity is increased. For this reason, at normal conversational levels, all of the fibers would be continuously active so that no single fiber could unambiguously signal either frequency or intensity. Yet pitch, the critical bandwidth, frequency discrimination, sound localization, and speech perception do not change as a function of intensity. The transformation of the visual code also creates intensity independence and contrast independence. Proposed mechanisms for auditory and visual gain controls are discussed in chapter 6.

Transformations Sharpen Tuning

Many transformations maximize the responsiveness to discontinuities in the proximal stimulus (e.g., auditory and visual edges), and those discontinuities are critical for detecting ecologically important stimuli (e.g., mating and warning auditory calls, and visual identification of predators, prey, and conspecifics).

Tuning Is Due to Populations of Cells

Eggermont (2001) argued that the sharpening of individual cells due to various forms of inhibition can never be sufficient, so that groups of neurons are necessary to achieve the accuracy required to code environmental information. He estimated that 40 neurons would be sufficient to achieve neural accuracy for sound localization, and that 95 sites could discriminate among nine actual and simulated cat meows (Gehr, Komiya, & Eggermont, 2000). The number of neuron sites increases dramatically when there are more events to be discriminated. For example, for 90 different cat meows, roughly 10,000 neural sites would be necessary (Gehr et al., 2000). Population coding is discussed further in chapter 3.

Transformations Accentuate Dynamic Changes

Usually we can take an auditory or visual scene and describe it in terms of the changes in its objects. Sounds and lights may go on or off, oscillate in loudness or brightness, or change in terms of their temporal and frequency components. Eggermont likened the frequency components to the texture of the scenes and the oscillations to the contours of the scenes. The texture of the scene is coded in terms of the spatial distribution of the firings along isofrequency auditory cortex slices or iso-orientation and isofrequency visual cortex columns. The contour or rhythm of the scene is coded in terms of the changes in rates of firings of the texture regions. This creates a distinction between continuity (texture) and change (contour) coded in different ways in the cortex. There would be relatively independent neural representations for continuity and change, albeit using the identical neural elements. This, in principle, is equivalent to the what and where pathways described above.

Elhilali, Fritz, Klein, Simon, and Shamma (2004) found that cells in the A1 region of ferrets were able to simultaneously encode the contour and fine structure of modulated sounds. In previous work, cells in A1 were unable to phase-lock to continuous sounds with frequencies beyond 20 Hz, and yet they were able to accurately synchronize to stimulus onsets and transients. Elhilali et al. were able to make sense of this paradoxical finding using a type of dynamic ripple stimuli (see figure 2.31). They discovered that the slow amplitude modulation envelope acted as a gate that allowed cells to phase-lock to the fine structure (up to 200 Hz) of the sounds. Without such a modulation, the cells did not respond to the repetitive frequencies found in environmental sounds or speech. Thus, the auditory system is preserving two time frames: The slowly changing envelopes that reflect changes in the resonant properties of objects and the frequencies that excite those resonances.

At one level, this dichotomy works as an organizing metaphor. But there are many ambiguous cases where temporal or frequency changes could signal the contour of one object or could signal the transition between two different objects. The contour of one object could be the texture of another object and vice versa.

Transformations Create Synchronized Topographic Maps

Everything I have said to this point argues that our world emerges from the patterning of firings in the auditory and visual cortex. There are no "grandmother" cells that uniquely fire to a picture of your grandmother. The synchronization of the firings is assumed to solve the correspondence problem described in chapter 1: which firings go with each object. Rarely do different objects appear and disappear at the same time. As long as the nervous system preserves the timings of the onsets and offsets of objects relatively well, the synchronization of the firings will create the correct objects at the correct locations.

Receptive Fields Are Labile and Not Invariant

I would add that due to the diverse kinds of feedback, receptive fields will change their response profiles and could even create receptive fields that respond to specific combinations of auditory or visual contours.

Summary

I believe that auditory and visual encoding are perceptually identical. The goal of both modalities is to capture the physical properties and movements of objects in the world given inherent physical uncertainties. Even at the level of single cells in the primary auditory and visual cortex, there are striking similarities in receptive fields. Moreover, both cortical regions are organized into somewhat specialized modules that are highly interactive. There is little evidence for encapsulated processing within either sense and, as described in chapter 9, little evidence for encapsulated processing between senses. The organization is remarkably plastic, and changes in responsiveness occur over both short and long time scales. Fast adaptation to specific stimulus properties acts simultaneously with slower plastic reorganizations to constantly tune the neural response to the objects in the world.

The issue to be discussed in chapter 3 is whether auditory and visual coding is adapted to the statistics of the environment. As mentioned previously, it is always risky to presume that the evolutionary goal was to maximize information transfer.

3

Characteristics of Auditory and Visual Scenes

Up to this point, we have been implicitly taking the viewpoint of the external experimenter: We create a known stimulus of varying complexity and then try to discover the resulting neural response. However, here we take the viewpoint of the organism: Given the neural response, what can the animal deduce about the object that produced that neural pattern? The excitation of the retinal photoreceptors or the inner ear hair cells does not yield objects. The ability to pull out objects must depend on the discovery of the spike patterns across receptors that specify objects. Barlow (1981) speculated that the role of the sensory systems was to remove the redundant and therefore uninformative spike patterns, leaving a set of independent neural units that signify the properties of those objects (e.g., contour lines of faces, voice quality of singers). More recently, Barlow (2001) has argued that the reduction in redundancy is not as important as the detection of the redundancies (the nonrandom probabilities) that signify structure and statistical regularity in the environment. The neural representations become hypotheses about the current environment. The discussion in chapter 2 suggests that at the level of the primary auditory and visual cortexes, any object would be represented by the patterning and synchrony of firing across many neural units. Levy, Hasson, and Malach (2004) argued that at least 30 million cells in the visual system are used to represent one image. The auditory and visual problem is to segment the environment into likely objects, and it may be the inherent redundancies that are necessary to do that.

Information, Redundancy, and Prior Probabilities

Information Theory and Redundancy

We can use the framework of information theory (Shannon & Weaver, 1949) to quantify how much the neural response tells us about the stimulus. Our interest lies in the mutual information between stimuli and neural responses. Given the neural response, how much is the uncertainty reduced about which stimulus actually occurred (which is the same reduction in uncertainty about the resulting neural response given the stimulus, hence mutual)? I frame all of these questions in terms of conditional probabilities: Given the neural response, what are the probabilities of the possible stimuli as compared to the probabilities of the same stimuli before observing the response?

In defining *information*, Shannon (1948) was guided by several commonsense guidelines.[1] The first was that the uncertainty due to several independent variables would be equal to the sum of the uncertainty due to each variable individually. Independence means that knowing the values of one variable does not allow you to predict the value of any other variable. The probability of any joint outcome of two or more independent variables becomes equal to the multiplication of the probabilities of each of the variables:

$$\Pr(w, x, y, z, \ldots) = \Pr(w)\Pr(x)\Pr(y)\Pr(z) \ldots \tag{3.1}$$

To make the information from each variable add, we need to add the probabilities, which can be accomplished by converting the probabilities into the logarithms of the probabilities.

The second consideration was that the information of a single stimulus should be proportional to its "surprise," that is, its probability of occurrence. Thus, events that occur with probability close to 1 should have no information content, while events that occur with a low probability should have high information content.

Shannon (1948) demonstrated that defining the information in terms of the negative logarithm is the only function that satisfies both considerations.[2]

$$\text{Information} = -\log_2 \Pr(x). \tag{3.2}$$

If there are several possible outcomes, then the information from each outcome should be equal to its surprise value multiplied by the probability of that event. This leads to the averaged information for a stimulus distribution or a response distribution:

1. I use the terms *information* and *uncertainty* interchangeably. The uncertainty of an event equals its information value.

2. Traditionally, the logarithm is set to base 2 to make the information measure equivalent to the number of bits. In fact, the choice of base is completely arbitrary because simply multiplying by a constant converts between any two bases.

$$\text{Information} = -\sum \Pr(x_i) \log_2 \Pr(x_i). \tag{3.3}$$

Therefore, events with low probabilities contribute little to the overall information in spite of their high surprise value. The maximum information and uncertainty occur when each stimulus has equal probability, and in that case the information reduces to $\log_2 N$, where N refers to the number of stimuli. As the probability distribution becomes more unequal, the overall information progressively decreases. If one stimulus occurs all of the time, the information goes to 0. The measure of information is bits if using $\log_2$—it is only a number, like a percentage, without a physical dimension.

If we want to define the information for combinations of two variables (x_i, y_j), then the information summed over all *x*s and *y*s becomes

$$\text{Information} = -\sum\sum \Pr(x_i, y_j) \log_2 \Pr(x_i, y_j). \tag{3.4}$$

If the two variables are independent, then

$$\text{Information} = -\sum\sum \Pr(x_i) \Pr(y_j) \log_2 \Pr(x_i) \Pr(y_j) \tag{3.5}$$

$$\text{Information} = -\sum \Pr(x_i) \log_2 \Pr(x_i) - \sum \Pr(y_j) \log_2 \Pr(y_j) \tag{3.6}$$

$$\text{Information} = I(x) + I(y). \tag{3.7}$$

But natural stimuli are never made up of independent (or random) variables, and natural messages are never composed of independent random sequences of elements. For example, the letter *q* is nearly always followed by the letter *u*. After identifying a *q*, knowing that *u* occurs next rarely gives us any information (or conversely, that letter position does not create any uncertainty). We measure the actual information in terms of conditional probabilities; that is, given the letter *q*, what is the probability of *u* in the following letter slot? The difference between the information based on independent variables and that actually measured is the constraint or structure in the stimulus or the mutual information between stimulus and response.

There are several important points about this measure of information:

1. The information measure can be generalized to variables that have continuous distributions that often involve integrating over the range of the values. Moreover, the information measure can be further generalized to random functions such as sound pressure waveforms over time.
2. The information does not depend on the central tendency (i.e., mean) of the (stimulus or response) distribution. The information does depend on the number of possible states. If all states are equally probable, increasing the number of states twofold increases the information by 1 bit.
3. As Rieke et al. (1997) pointed out, the number of states for continuous variables is infinite. To make the measure valid for continuous variables, we need to create discrete bins in which we cumulate the values of the variable at discrete time points. Thus, our measurements will always

have a finite precision due to the size of each bin. A concrete example occurs when measuring the information in a spike train. Here we create bins that are so narrow that only a single spike could occur in a bin, so that the information is calculated from a string of zeros and ones.

4. The information of a single spike train is undefined. The uncertainty that the organism faces in determining the external world from one spike train comes from the ensemble of possible spike trains, not the arrangement of zeros and ones in that single train. In fact, we assume that the organism knows the entire set of possibilities. Information is not an absolute quantity, but describes how much we can learn from a stimulus relative to what we know about the stimulus ensemble. Garner (1962) argued that the difficulty of all cognitive processes (e.g., learning) should be understood in terms of the number of possible alternatives.
5. From the information measure, we can attempt to find a distribution that yields the maximum uncertainty given a set of constraints such as the mean firing rate or the maximum variability of the response (Rieke et al., 1997). The solutions usually are not the same.

We can now consider mutual information, or the information that a neural signal can convey about the external stimulus. The above discussion tells us that mutual information can be defined only for a known set of stimuli (e.g., a set of 10 different brightness values). In the simplest of terms, a neural signal (a set of 10 different firing rates) can convey information about the stimulus only if it changes in a reliable way in response to changes in the stimulus. The variability in the response to different stimuli must be greater than the variability in the response to repeated presentations of the same stimulus. (This is equivalent to the ratio of between variance to within variance used for all statistical tests.) One end point occurs if each stimulus gives rise to one unique response, and the mutual information is at a maximum and is equal to the information in the stimulus distribution. The other end point occurs if each stimulus gives rise to the same distribution of responses, and the mutual information equals 0.

We use the conditional probability $\Pr(r \mid s)$ to represent the probability that response r (e.g., firing rate) was given if stimulus s (e.g., brightness level) was presented and $\Pr(s \mid r)$ to represent the probability that stimulus s was presented given the response r. To calculate the mutual information, we have to sum the information due to each possible stimulus exactly as we did for the information of single events. The conditional information for each stimulus is $\Sigma \Pr(r \mid s) \log_2 \Pr(r \mid s)$. In effect, we are measuring the uncertainty of the responses for that stimulus. To create the measure of information across all possible stimuli, we weight the conditional information for each stimulus by the probability of that stimulus:

$$\Sigma \Pr(s)[\Sigma \Pr(r \mid s) \log_2 \Pr(r \mid s)]. \qquad (3.8)$$

This measure is effectively the noise or uncertainty found for the repeated presentation of a single stimulus averaged across stimuli.

To calculate the mutual information $I(R{:}S)$, we start with the information in the spike train response. It is the upper limit of the mutual information that occurs if each response is made to only one stimulus. The actual mutual information is lower because of the conditional information of each stimulus (equation 3.4), that is, the variability in the response for each stimulus. We must subtract the variability of the response for each stimulus from the overall response variability to give the amount of information in the response distribution that is contingent on the stimulus. This gives us:

$$I(R{:}S) = \Sigma \Pr(r) \log_2 \Pr(r) - \Sigma \Pr(s)[\Sigma \Pr(r \mid s) \log_2 \Pr(r \mid s)]. \qquad (3.9)$$

The mutual information is symmetric: The information about the set of stimuli from the set of responses is exactly the same amount of information about the set of responses from the set of stimuli. Thus, we can write the equation for the mutual information from the perspective of the stimulus:

$$I(R{:}S) = \Sigma \Pr(s) \log_2 \Pr(s) - \Sigma \Pr(r)[\Sigma \Pr(s \mid r) \log_2 \Pr(s \mid r)]. \qquad (3.10)$$

This symmetry is analogous to that found for the correlation coefficient squared: The variance in x predicts the variance in y to the same extent that the variance in y predicts the variance in x.

We can define mutual information in still another way:

$$I(R{:}S) = I(R) + I(S) - I(R,S). \qquad (3.11)$$

From this perspective, we can think of the responses and stimuli as the rows and columns of a matrix. Then the mutual information is the sum of the information of the marginal probabilities of the rows and columns (i.e., the marginal probabilities in each row are obtained by summing the probabilities across the columns for that row, and the marginal sums for columns are gotten in analogous fashion) minus the information of the probabilities of the individual cells in the matrix.[3] If the row and columns are independent, then the probability of each cell will be equal to the row probability multiplied by the column probability: The mutual information is 0. If the rows and columns are completely dependent, then there will be only one entry per row or column: The information across the cells equals the information in the rows, or equivalently the columns, and the mutual information is equal to the identical row or column information. (In this form, the mutual information is identical to chi-square contingency measures.)

3. Here I am talking about random samples, not population values.

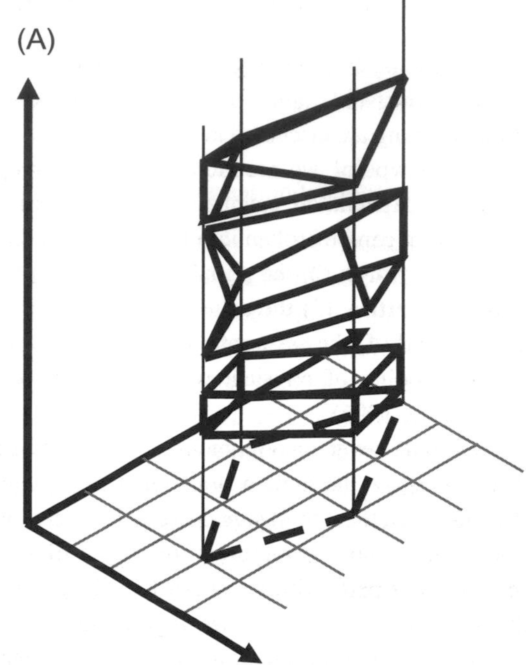
(A)

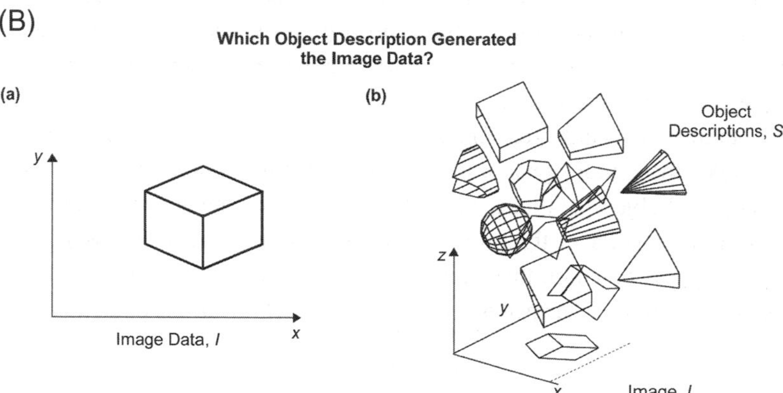
(B)
Which Object Description Generated
the Image Data?
(a)
y
Image Data, I
x
(b)
Object
Descriptions, S
z
y
x
Image, I

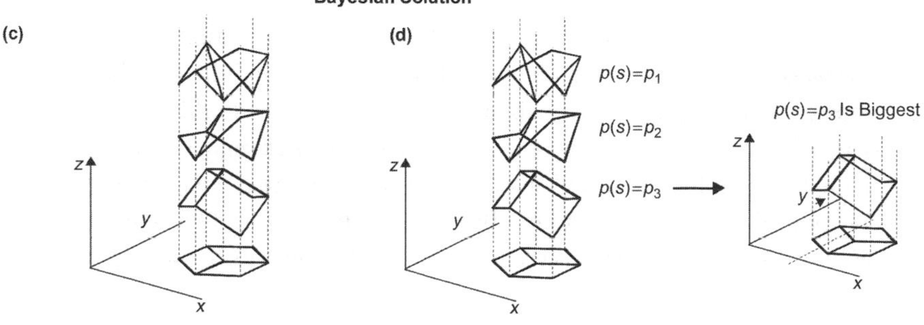
Bayesian Solution
(c)
z
y
x
Likelihood, p(I/S), Narrows Selection
Consistent With Projection
(d)
z
y
x
p(s)=p1
p(s)=p2
p(s)=p3
p(s)=p3 Is Biggest
z
y
x
Prior, p(S), Further Narrows Selection

Paradoxically, to get to the posterior probabilities above, we start by assuming a source object, and then estimate the probability of the source producing that signal. (This is analogous to classical inferential statistics: We assume that the null hypothesis is correct and then calculate the probability of obtaining the sample mean based on the null hypothesis). For example, to decide whether a sound came from a trumpet or clarinet, we start by assuming it was a clarinet (or trumpet) and estimate the probability that each instrument could have produced that sound. These are termed *likelihood probabilities*:

$$\begin{gathered} \Pr(\text{sound} \mid \text{clarinet}) \\ \Pr(\text{sound} \mid \text{trumpet}). \end{gathered} \tag{3.14}$$

The likelihood function reflects the degree of regularity in the environment. If there were a high degree of regularity, no information loss, no noise, then the likelihood would be 1 for one object and 0 for the other possible objects. Lack of regularity and noise flattens the likelihood functions, decreasing those near 1 and increasing those near 0. To put it another way, these are reliability estimates.

We also need to use our prior assumptions about the probability of objects (termed *a priori probabilities*) in a context. We would be likely to judge that the sound came from a trumpet if we are listening to a brass instrument group. In general, though, the prior probabilities are another set of assumptions about the properties of objects. For example, suppose we hear a rapid set of clicks that randomly seem next to the left ear, right ear, or straight ahead. One possible object would be a single rapidly flying cricket, but we would probably assign that a low probability because in our world model, crickets do not fly that quickly. We would assign a higher probability to three crickets at different positions, chirping at random. In probabilities:

$$\begin{gathered} \Pr(\text{object}_A) \\ \Pr(\text{object}_B) \\ \Pr(\text{object}_C). \end{gathered} \tag{3.15}$$

Figure 3.1. The Bayesian approach to the indeterminacy between the proximal image and the distal object. Any image (dashed diamond) could have been caused by many objects, as illustrated in (A). The likelihood ratios and prior probabilities are used to derive the best guess as to the distal object shown in (B). From "Bayesian Models of Object Perception," by D. Kersten and A. Yuille, 2003, *Current Opinion in Neurobiology, 13*, 150–158. Copyright 2003 by Elsevier Science Ltd. Reprinted with permission.

Now it is possible to make use of Bayes's formula to calculate the posterior probabilities:

$$\Pr(\text{object}_A \mid \text{signal}) = [\Pr(\text{signal} \mid \text{object}_A) \times \Pr(\text{object}_A)]/\Pr(\text{signal})$$
$$\Pr(\text{object}_B \mid \text{signal}) = [\Pr(\text{signal} \mid \text{object}_B) \times \Pr(\text{object}_B)]/\Pr(\text{signal}) \qquad (3.16)$$
$$\Pr(\text{object}_C \mid \text{signal}) = [\Pr(\text{signal} \mid \text{object}_C) \times \Pr(\text{object}_C)]/\Pr(\text{signal}).$$

Our interest is in the perceptual decision, and since the signal probability is constant for each object, we can simplify the formulas by omitting that probability. Now the formula becomes:

$$\Pr(\text{object}_A \mid \text{signal}) = \Pr(\text{signal} \mid \text{object}_A) \times \Pr(\text{object}_A)$$
$$\Pr(\text{object}_B \mid \text{signal}) = \Pr(\text{signal} \mid \text{object}_B) \times \Pr(\text{object}_B) \qquad (3.17)$$
$$\Pr(\text{object}_C \mid \text{signal}) = \Pr(\text{signal} \mid \text{object}_C) \times \Pr(\text{object}_C).$$

A gain–loss function can be associated with each posterior probability, namely, the costs of selecting each possible object. There are several possible decision rules based on the expectation (posterior probability × gain or loss) such as maximizing the minimum gain (maximin criterion).

To summarize, perceptual decisions are contingent on the estimated conditional probabilities (the likelihood functions) and the estimated prior structure (a priori probabilities) of the environment. These conditional probabilities will be accurate to the extent that we have constructed an accurate physical and perceptual model of those instruments. The prior structure reflects the perceiver's expectations about the regularities in the environment. It normalizes the conditional probabilities (e.g., $\Pr(\text{signal} \mid \text{object}_A)$ by the probability of occurrence of object A in that environment. Although Bayesian methods are often maligned because they are "subjective," the probabilities are objective in the sense that they do represent environmental probabilities. It may be that the perceiver has evolved highly biased estimates of those probabilities leading to wild distortions, but theoretically the probabilities can be objective.

Connecting Bayesian Probabilities to Information Redundancy

Both information and Bayesian theory can be thought of as modeling communication between stimulus and object. This parallel is reinforced because the terms in each theory appear equivalent. For information theory we had:

$$\Pr(s)[\Sigma \Pr(r \mid s) \log_2 \Pr(r \mid s)] \text{ from (3.8).}$$

For Bayesian theory we had:

$$\Pr(\text{object}_A \mid \text{signal}) = \Pr(\text{object}_A) \times \Pr(\text{signal} \mid \text{object}_A) \text{ from (3.13).}$$

In the second part of equation 3.8, we multiply the contingent information of response (r) given stimulus (s) by the probability of stimulus (s). This is essentially the same term as that found in equation 3.13: We multiply the conditional probability of the response given the stimulus (s) by the probability of stimulus (s). Both multiplications create posterior probabilities: likelihood functions × prior probabilities.

In spite of this similarity, information theory and Bayesian theory get used for different purposes. Information theory measures a capacity (sometimes termed bandwidth) while Bayesian theory ranks decision alternatives. But Bayesian methods provide a mechanism to evolve the probabilities that are necessary to calculate information. Information theory is basically silent about how the perceiver derives those probabilities.

Statistical Regularities in the Environment

If the evolutionary goal of perceptual systems was to maximize the rate of information transfer, then information theory provides a metric to measure and compare the maximum possible to that actually achieved (i.e., the mutual information). More important, information theory provides a way of understanding some physiological mechanisms that appear to maximize information transmission. This provides a means to determine how well perceptual systems are matched to the statistical structure of the environment.

The maximum information occurs when each element has an equal probability and there is complete independence in the temporal sequence or spatial position of the elements. It is obvious that neither of these conditions is true for auditory and visual scenes, so that the actual information in a message will be less than the maximum possible. But Atick (1992) suggested that the transformations in the nervous system can be understood as attempts to increase the actual transmitted information and thereby minimize the difference between the maximum information and the mutual information.

The first transformation would act to make the response probabilities to sensory magnitudes (e.g., auditory frequency, visual brightness) more equal. The distribution of the firing rates would be matched to the probability of different intensity levels.

The second transformation would reduce the correlation among the sensory elements. For natural visual scenes, elements close in space within one object are likely to be equally bright so that there is no need to transmit the stimulus energy at all points. Elements close in space, but in different objects, are likely to be equally different in brightness, so again there is no need to transmit all of the differences. As described below, by transforming the energy into different spatial resolutions, it is possible to reduce those correlations. For natural auditory scenes, the vibrations from any object are likely to start and end at the same time, to change slowly in loudness and pitch, and for animal and human sounds to be composed of harmonic frequencies (multiples of the fundamental frequency). By analogy to vision, transforming the sound energy into different temporal and frequency resolutions will reduce that redundancy.

In what follows, I will juxtapose theoretical models based on information theory with actual experimental data. The goal is to discover the degree to which theory and data match each other and to determine whether such a match is similar for audition and vision.

Autocorrelation and Fourier Analysis

On the whole, identical bits of energy that occur closely in frequency (or multiples of frequencies), intensity, space, and time that undergo the same physical changes probably come from the same process. (Echoes are an example of highly correlated data that come from different processes.) There are several ways of representing these statistical contingencies. The simplest would be in terms of the autocorrelations in energy between adjacent spatial points in visual scenes and adjacent temporal points in auditory scenes. Figure 3.2A illustrates that the correlation is very high between the relative intensity of pixels one position apart and that the correlation gradually declines between pixels two and four positions apart. Figure 3.2B illustrates that the correlation in brightness between 2 pixels separated by 40 pixels in a natural scene still equals about 0.35. By the same token, the autocorrelation in the ratio between note frequencies found in a simple melody would gradually decrease as the notes become further apart in time.[5]

There is another kind of internal autocorrelation due to common changes among parts of an object or common changes in sounds. The Gestalt psychologists illustrated that points of light that undergo the same direction of movement are perceived as forming one coherent object; this organizational principle was termed *common fate* and the illustration of a random dot kinematogram in chapter 1 demonstrates the power of such organization (in chapter 5, I discuss experiments showing that even a small fraction of light points moving in the same direction yield coherent motion). In the auditory environment, virtually every sound is composed of several frequency components. Nelken, Rotman, and Yosef (1999) argued that the frequency components of background noise (as in a flock of crows) undergo correlated increases and decreases in amplitude. It is those correlated

5. I will make use of frequency ratios because of the logarithmic spacing of frequencies along the basilar membrane (chapter 2) and because the relationship among pitches is best represented by the ratios between frequencies.

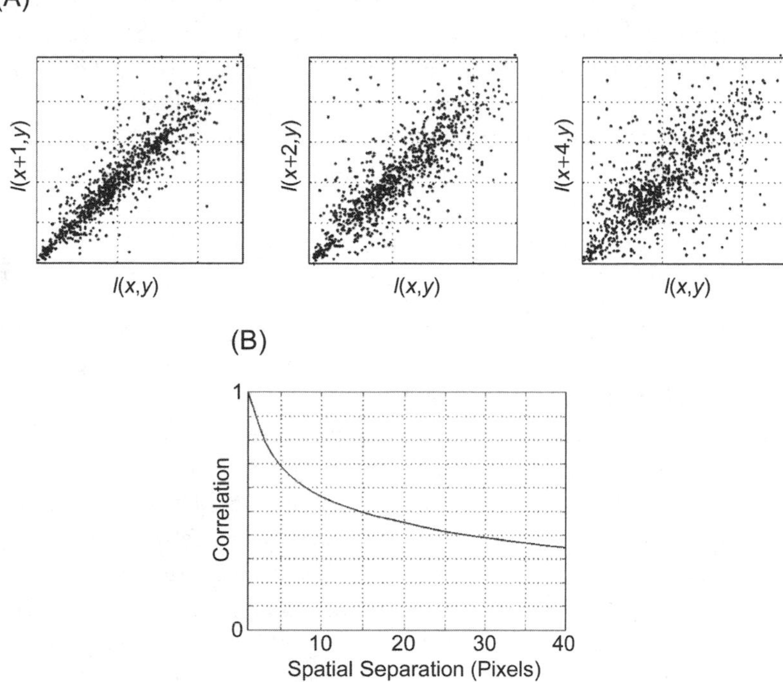

Figure 3.2. The redundancy in visual scenes is quite high. The correlation between the brightness of pixels [*I*(*x*,*y*)] slowly decreases as the distance between the pixels increases. The scatterplots of the brightness values of pixels 1, 2, and 4 apart are shown in (A). The size of the correlation in brightness as a function of distance is expressed in (B). From "Natural Image Statistics and Neural Representation," by E. P. Simoncelli and B. A. Olshausen, 2001, *Annual Review of Neuroscience, 24*, 1193–1216. Copyright 2001 by Annual Reviews. Reprinted with permission.

fluctuations that help segment the noise from the signal (this has been termed *comodulation release* and is covered in chapter 6).

An alternate representation of the regularity makes use of the Fourier analysis of a visual or auditory scene. The Fourier analysis (for both auditory and visual scenes) represents the variation in brightness across space or the variation in pressure across time by the sum of a series of sine and cosine waves of different frequencies and phases. The Fourier decomposition is frequency only; the sine or cosine waves do not vary across time or space. Each scene can be characterized (and recreated) by the sum of those waves. A sine or cosine wave with 0 Hz frequency would not change across space or time and thereby indicate overall brightness or loudness. A wave with 1 unit of frequency would go through one cycle in a specified distance or time unit. Similar arguments hold for waves of higher frequency. Low-frequency waves represent slow changes in intensity, such as a shadow along a whitewashed wall or speech rhythms. Higher-frequency waves represent more rapid changes (e.g., tree trunks in a sunny forest, picket fences, or a rapid musical trill), and even higher frequencies are seen and heard as uniform and continuous (e.g., musical tones) due to limitations in neural resolution. The Fourier representation is most appropriate for repeating scenes that do not vary across space or time. Each component sine or cosine wave is invariant.

If the amplitudes of the Fourier waves are plotted against their frequencies, there are several prototypical outcomes:

1. The amplitudes of each component sine wave are equal, and the phases are random.[6] The amplitude of one point in the scene does not predict the brightness of another point.
2. There is a nonmonotonic relationship between frequency and amplitude. For example, the sound of a musical instrument or the sound of a vowel can be portrayed by the amplitude of two or more frequency components. In most cases, the frequencies of the components are multiples of the lowest fundamental frequency, and to some degree the differences between instrumental sounds or spoken vowels are due to the pattern of the amplitudes of those harmonic frequencies. For example, the amplitudes of the odd harmonics of a clarinet note are high, but the amplitudes of the even harmonics are low due to the resonances of an open tube. If the instrument note or vowel is recorded at one speed (or sampling rate) and replayed at another, the note or vowel will sound different.
3. There are monotonic relationships between amplitude and frequency such that amplitude is proportional to $\sim 1/f^c$ where the exponent c can range from 0 to 3 or 4. These functions are termed power laws and have the important property of being self-similar. They are termed *fractal processes*: The same power law relationship holds on all scales. The relationship between amplitude and frequency would be identical whether a camera is zoomed in on a small location or zoomed out to encompass the entire field. When viewing a mountain range, the pattern of altitude variation within one peak is similar to the pattern of variation across peaks. As one zooms in, the same level of complexity emerges; the global and local contours are similar in the geometric sense. When listening to sounds that obey a power law function, the pitch of the sound would not change if the speed of playback was increased or decreased. There are no inherent time or frequency scales—whatever happens in one time or frequency range

6. The Fourier representation of a narrow edge or sound click also contains equal amplitudes, but the phases are also equal.

happens on all time and frequency scales. The relationship between amplitude and frequency is invariant.[7]

For a random walk process, the amplitudes of the Fourier waves decrease at the rate of $1/f^2$ so that for each doubling of frequency (an octave), the amplitude of the wave decreases fourfold. The brightness or pressure of any next point is equal to the value of the first point plus a random increment. Thus, there will be just slow changes in the amplitudes and there will be high correlations between the values of adjacent points. As the distance between the two points increases, the correlation gradually decreases due to summing more and more random increments. The autocorrelation between points separated by a constant distance will always be the same. The difference between successive values is a series of random values and therefore creates white noise ($1/f^0$).

The most interesting outcomes occur when the amplitudes decrease at the rate of $1/f$. Every time frequency is doubled the amplitude is decreased by one half, so that the energy in each octave remains identical. Many physical processes follow this $1/f$ relationship, including nerve membrane potentials, traffic flow, sunspot activity, and flood levels of the Nile River. Schroder (1991) pointed out that $1/f$ functions can be conceptualized as the combination of several processes with different distances and timings and that the end result is that there is a varying correlation among the fluctuating levels across the frequency range. Consider a simple simulation suggested by Voss (Gardner, 1978) based on the sum of three dice. We start by throwing all three and recording the sum. Then only one die is selected, rethrown, and the new sum recorded. On the next trial two dice are selected, both are rethrown, and the new sum recorded. On the third trial, only one die is selected, rethrown, and the sum recorded. On the fourth trial, all three dice are selected and thrown and the sum recorded. All the following trials follow the identical sequence. In this simulation, the correlation between adjacent points is not constant. The correlation between points in which one die changed will be 2/3 because two of the three dice remain the same; the correlation between adjacent points in which two dice changed will be 1/3; and the correlation between adjacent points in which all three dice changed will be zero. Thus, there will be regions in time or space of correlated sums. The number of independent processes (i.e., the number of dice) will determine the size of the correlated regions. All $1/f$ processes can be represented by the linear sum of short-range processes that have different time scales (Wagenmakers, Farrell, & Ratcliff, 2004). For example, heart

7. Power laws have been used to describe an extraordinary range of phenomena: the frequency of earthquakes of different magnitudes, the distribution of income among individuals, the energy for metabolism for animals with different body masses, and the density of animals with different body masses (Marquet, 2002).

rate fluctuations are regulated in the short run by the autonomic nervous system and regulated in the long run by circadian rhythms due to hormonal variation.

In figure 3.3, a series of amplitude by time sequences with different fractal organizations are illustrated. All the sequences start with the same "seed," so the gradual smoothing is due to the change in the exponent of the power law. The white noise ($1/f^0$), in which all frequencies have equal amplitude, is characterized by random fluctuations, while the brown noise ($1/f^2$) is characterized by low-frequency slowly undulating "hills and

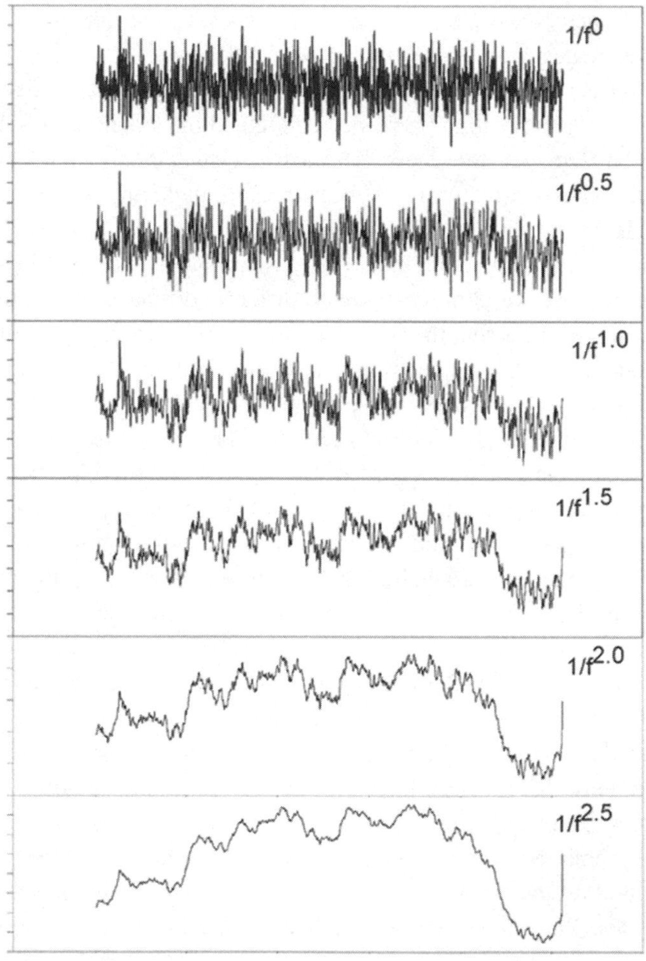

Figure 3.3. Representative examples of power laws. Sequences of amplitudes (*y*-axis) generated by different fractal exponents are shown in the six panels (there are 1,024 values on the *x*-axis for each panel). The contour clearly smooths out as the exponent increases. Data courtesy of Dr. Mark Schmuckler.

valleys" that support the high-frequency jagged variations. The $1/f$ noise combines the random $1/f^0$ noise with the highly constrained $1/f^2$ noise. There are amplitude variations at all frequencies, with the majority of the energy at the lower frequencies.

Power Laws in Natural Scenes

The $1/f$ power law function is important because it fits many natural auditory and visual scenes. One question is whether sensory systems have evolved to optimally code this energy distribution.

Auditory Scenes

The $1/f$ dependence is usually not obtained for spectra of natural sounds. For example, Nabelek, Tucker, and Letwoski (1991) calculated the sound pressure averaged over 15–30 s for six types of sounds. None followed the $1/f$ relationship. There was a broad frequency region of roughly equal pressure, and then a gradual decrease at higher frequencies. However, noise such as that found in classrooms (Hodgson, Rempel, & Kennedy, 1999) does appear to decline above 1000 Hz according to a $1/f$ function.

The $1/f$ relationship is found for the spectrum of the distribution of intensity (power) and frequency fluctuations across time in environments and in music. The six panels in figure 3.3 should be interpreted in this way: If the fluctuations follow a $1/f^{2.0}$ relationship, then the power or frequency at time $t + 1$ equals the value at time t plus a random increment generating the slow oscillation found in the next to bottom panel.[8] To determine the type of relationship, the sound amplitude at each time point is squared to produce a measure of power, and then the Fourier spectrum is calculated on the fluctuations in power. Alternately, the frequency (the number of zero crossings per time unit) is measured at successive time points, and the Fourier spectrum is calculated on the fluctuations in frequency across time. DeCoensel, Botteldooren, and De Muer (2003) found the $1/f$ relationship for fluctuations in loudness and pitch for rural and urban soundscapes. The $1/f$ relationship was strongest in time intervals up to 5 s where the fluctuations are due to the source itself. Beyond 5 s, the fluctuations were greater than predicted by the $1/f$ function and seemed to be due to isolated events. Remember that the construction of a $1/f$ sequence by throwing three dice led to the conclusion that $1/f$ power laws were based on correlations on different scales. Nearly all examples of $1/f$ scales can be understood in terms of short-term processes within one event and long-term processes between different events.

8. The temporal auditory power fluctuations are equivalent to the fluctuations in the spatial visual contrasts used to derive the $1/f^2$ power scales.

Voss and Clarke (1978) calculated the spectral density of audio power and frequency fluctuations for a variety of musical selections and for different types of radio stations averaged over 12 hours. The regions where the $1/f$ relationship held true could be understood in terms of the type of music played. For example, the $1/f$ relationship of the audio power fluctuations for classical music stations extended for greater lengths of time than that for a rock station, where the length approximates a single tune. An identical result was found for the frequency fluctuations. Namely, the $1/f$ relationship for classical music stations playing long pieces was greater than that for jazz and rock stations playing shorter selections. Hsu and Hsu (1990) further demonstrated that the distribution of the frequency intervals in classical music follows a $1/f^c$ relationship. The logarithm of the frequency of the size of the interval between successive notes is inversely related to the logarithm of the interval size, creating a $1/f^c$ relationship. Schroder (1991, p. 109) included van der Pol's quote about Bach, "it is great because it is inevitable (not white noise) and yet surprising (not brown noise)." Perhaps modern music veers too much toward the randomness of white noise.

As a tour de force, Voss and Clarke (1978) constructed music according to the $1/f$ rule. Thus, small variations in frequency and duration were more frequent than large variations, and yet larger variations occurred periodically to reset or restate the theme. They found that listeners preferred those melodic sequences constructed according to the $1/f$ relationship; sequences in which successive notes were randomly selected ($1/f^0$) were judged to be too chaotic, and sequences constructed according to the $1/f^2$ relationship were too boring and predictable. Musical sequences following different fractal organizations constructed by Voss and Clarke are shown in figure 3.4.

Visual Scenes

The analysis of visual scenes also has demonstrated the $1/f$ relationship between the amplitude of the brightness contrast and frequency. This relationship often is presented in terms of the power of the brightness contrast and frequency, and because power is the square of amplitude, the relationship between power and frequency is $1/f^2$, as found above for sounds (Burton & Moorhead, 1987). What I am trying to do is represent the brightness along one axis (say along the x axis) by a series of sinusoidal waves so that the first one would undergo one cycle per image, the second one would undergo two cycles per image, and so on. Conceptually, one simply takes pictures of natural scenes and measures the brightness contrast at each point: The brightness contrast is defined as the ratio between the brightness at that spatial location and the average brightness across the entire scene. Then the Fourier analysis is used to calculate the amplitude of the frequency components

Figure 3.4. Musical sequences constructed according to power laws. For $1/f^0$ sequences, each note is chosen randomly. For $1/f^2$ sequences, each successive note is determined by a random increment to the previous note. For $1/f$ sequences, the intervals between notes are determined according to the $1/f$ power law (i.e., small increments are more likely than large ones). From "$1/f$ Noise in Music: Music From $1/f$ Noise," by R. F. Voss and J. Clarke, 1978, *Journal of the Acoustical Society of America, 63*, 258–263. Copyright 1987 by the American Institute of Physics. Reprinted with permission.

necessary to reproduce the fluctuations in brightness along one orientation. Field (1987) presented several pictures of widely different characteristics, calculated the amplitude of the frequency components along several axes, and then averaged the amplitudes. The brightness contrast of all six pictures followed the $1/f$ relationship.

Field argued that a $1/f$ amplitude relationship would occur if the relative contrasts were independent of viewing distance. Imagine taking a simple picture of a black-and-white grating and moving it twice the distance away. Now the black-and-white bars are half as wide, so that the frequency of the grating is twice the original frequency. If the amplitude falls off at $1/f$, each octave will still have equal energy, so that the relative power in each doubled frequency will not change. Moreover, each octave will have the same variance (i.e., the same amount of information), so that if each neural unit has the same bandwidth, each will transmit an equal amount of information. Ruderman (1997) pointed out that the $1/f$ relationship for natural scenes is remarkably constant even for striking changes in the brightness of individual pixels. A strong test of the $1/f$ relationship can be done by first averaging small blocks of pixels, say all 2×2 blocks, and then demonstrating that the $1/f$ relationship still holds for the averaged signal. (Since mixing pixels reduces the total contrast, the contrast would need to be renormalized.) As an extreme case of blocking, Ruderman converted all pixels below the average brightness to black and all pixels above average brightness to white. All such conversions did not affect the $1/f$ scaling, demonstrating that whatever statistical structure exists at one spatial (i.e., angular) grain exists at all levels of the grain.

Up to this point, the $1/f$ amplitude-scaling factor was calculated by measuring the correlations among the pixels in one static image, although it is clear that images change gradually in time just as they change in space. Dong and Atick (1995) argued that in general it is impossible to separate the spatial and temporal variation. However, in cases in which the spatial and temporal regularities can be separated, the temporal power scaling factor is $1/w^2$ (in Hz) and the amplitude scaling factor is $1/f$ (also see Hateren, 1993). Thus the spatial and temporal scaling factors are roughly the same. To explain this outcome, Dong and Atick suggested that there is a distribution of static images at different distances and also that there is a distribution of relative motions at different velocities (essentially the same type of distribution found for relative contrast levels).

Implications of $1/f^c$ Power Laws

Why is this important? Remember the basic argument in chapter 1 that contrast provides the critical information for audition and vision. If the amplitude falls off at $1/f$, then there will be roughly equal contrast auditory and visual energy in all octave bandwidths. If the visual system or the auditory system is organized into sensors with octave bandwidths, which seemed to be true for the visual and auditory space-time receptive fields described in chapter 2, then each sensor will encode and transmit an equal amount of information about the contrast in terms of the variance in its firing rate. As is argued below, an equal distribution of energy is an optimal code, and a bandwidth of one octave allows a relatively small number of sensors to encode the contrast information. The on-off and off-on surround cells found in the initial stages of the visual system will produce firing outputs that are invariant to the scale of the receptive field.

We can speculate that the $1/f$ relationship that holds for typical visual environments (e.g., fields, forests) influenced the evolution of visual sensitivity functions. But it is much harder to figure out what auditory environments could have driven the evolution of the auditory system. We can imagine the sounds of predators, prey, storms, fire, wind, and so on that would have been important for survival, but those sounds are highly variable and intermittent, and most animal species function quite well in environments ranging from seaside to windy plains to noisy cities that would have different patterns of energy. Moreover, I have not argued that the acoustic energy at different frequencies follows a power law. The acoustic energy for any single sound occurs at discrete frequencies and as the loudness increases, the amplitudes of the higher frequencies increase more rapidly those of than the lower frequencies. Any $1/f$ power laws for sounds are probably restricted to a very artificial world. The $1/f$ scale emerged only for the fluctuations (i.e., correlations) of the power over long time periods that may not be important for survival.

We might ask why the $1/f$ relationship occurs in music. Voss and Clarke (1978) argued that $1/f$ sequences represent an intermediate level of predictability. Serial and atonal music that approaches white noise ($1/f^0$) in its lack of predictability has never been popular. In $1/f$ music, the majority of pitch changes are small (one note) and there are few large pitch changes that can lead listeners to segregate the notes into two different sound sources, breaking the coherence of the sequence, as discussed in chapter 9 (Bregman, 1990). Thus, this rationale does not make use of the statistics of natural sounds but depends on intuitions about the cognitive interpretation of music.

To understand why the $1/f$ power law is found for nearly all visual scenes, we need to go behind the commonsense view that the visual world is made up of edges and delimited rigid objects. Two explanations have been offered. Olshausen and Field (2000) argued that the brightness distribution of most natural scenes spans a range of 600–1,000 to 1 due to variations in the reflectance of the different materials and lighting in the scene. If we consider the frequency distribution of pixel brightness, typically there is a narrow peak at the lower intensities along with a flatter, wider distribution at higher intensities. The reflectance within any object will tend to be somewhat constant, but different parts of the object may be illuminated more strongly than others due to the angle of the sun, shading by other objects, and so on. The regions of low reflectance generate the narrow peak at low brightness regardless of illumination, and the regions of high reflectance, coupled with changes in illumination, generate the more spread-out distribution of higher brightness values. The variation of high illumination due to lighting would create the high-frequency but low-amplitude components, while the lack of variation in the low-illumination regions would create the higher-amplitude low-frequency components. Attias and Schreiner (1998) found a similar result for music, speech, and environmental sounds. There are more extremely soft sounds than extremely loud sounds in all three types of sounds, so that the large dynamic range of naturally occurring sounds is due more to the abundance of soft sounds than the infrequent loud sounds.

Ruderman (1997) proposed a different but not necessarily competing explanation. Ruderman started by assuming that the reflection within objects is basically constant but that the reflection from different objects varies randomly. Thus the correlation in brightness between points within an object must be high, but the correlation between points in different objects must be zero. Furthermore, Ruderman argued that visual images are made up of independent occluding objects and that the sizes of the objects in the visual images follow a power law (a function in the form of $1/f^c$). If this is the case, then the correlation in brightness between pixels will follow a power law function given the constant reflection within objects and power law function of object size. Balboa, Tyler, and Grzywacz (2001) argued that the power law spectra will emerge for nearly all scenes simply due to the fact that objects have different sizes: The sizes of the objects do not have to follow a power law. The authors claimed that small objects create exponents close to −3 and big objects create exponents close to 0, so that in a natural scene the exponent will be close to −1 due simply to the averaging of the exponents. Balboa et al. made an interesting point about underwater vision. Underwater blur tends to predominantly reduce the energy at higher frequencies and thereby make the exponent more negative. Thus, if the visual system evolved to match the energy distribution in the environment, then we might expect slightly different sensitivities in underwater animals.

The variation in illumination across the image can have two opposite effects. First, if the illumination within one object varies, that variation can increase the difference between the brightness of two pixels within that object, which would make the distinction between objects weaker. Second, if the illumination between objects changes, that variation can increase the difference in brightness of the pixels in the different objects, which would make the distinction between objects greater. Depending on the image, variation in illumination can lead to stronger or weaker object formation. Overall, variation in illumination tends to reduce the correlation among pixels, making the exponent closer to 0 (i.e., white noise) for nearly all configurations of objects.

Phase Relationships and Power Laws

Natural visual scenes contain edges and lines that are object boundaries or arise from occluding objects, while natural auditory scenes contain intermittent impulse sounds along with several simultaneous ongoing complex harmonic and inharmonic sounds. These edges, lines, and impulses cannot be represented by simple correlations because they arise due to the phase relationships among the Fourier components. For example, if we have a continuous set of frequency components, those components will create a click sound or a visual edge if they are in phase (start at the same point in the wave) but will create a noisy static-like sound or a homogeneous texture if they are out of phase.

The phase relationships are critical for vision. Thomson (1999) found that natural visual scenes do have higher-order statistical structure due to localized nonperiodic features such as bars, lines, or contours at different positions in the scene. If the phase relationships are maintained but the amplitudes of the components are randomized, the image is still recognizable. But if we remove the phase information, the image comes to resemble noise. It is likely that the formation of such edges is due to the higher-frequency spatial components because it seems improbable that the low-frequency components could simultaneously be in phase with multiple edges in a scene.

Now consider a "square" wave sound constructed by summing in phase one sine wave representing the fundamental frequency, with additional sine waves representing the odd harmonics. The amplitudes of the odd harmonics are inversely proportional to their number (e.g., fundamental/1 + 3rd harmonic/3 + 5th harmonic/5 + 7th harmonic/7 and so on). Each additional harmonic further squares off the wave. If the harmonics composing the square wave are not in phase, the resulting pressure wave no longer looks like a square wave. The pressure wave still obviously repeats and the period of the wave is still the same, being based on the fundamental frequency. In most instances, listeners report that the in-phase and out-of-phase square waves have the same pitch. However, the timbre or sound quality does seem to change between the two, because the intensity of one or two of the harmonics may have been increased due to the linear summation of the out-of-phase harmonics.

The ear has been described as being phase-deaf because the pitch does not change. The simplest explanation is that the ear performs a frequency analysis and encodes each frequency separately. The phase relationships among the frequencies are lost, and pitch and timbre become based on the amplitudes of the harmonics. But the discrimination of pitch for nonchanging sounds is only one aspect of hearing, and is, in my opinion, not a very important one. Phase differences do affect the formation of auditory objects.

For example, Kubovy and Jordan (1979) built up a set of sounds, each composed of 12 harmonically related sine waves (e.g., 600, 800, 1000, . . . 2800 Hz). They created 12 different tones, in which 11 of the 12 sine waves were in phase and 1 was out of phase. Kubovy and Jordan (1979) then presented sequences of the tones (at a presentation rate of about 3 tones per second) so that the out-of-phase wave either increased or decreased in frequency and listeners had to judge which direction occurred (a simple example of upward movement using four components would be: −+++, +−++, ++−+, +++−). Listeners were able to judge the direction for sets of higher-frequency harmonics (e.g., 2200–2800 Hz) but were unable to judge direction for sets of lower-frequency harmonics (600–1200 Hz). It is not clear why this difference occurred. If the 12 stimuli were presented one at a time, no matter which sine wave was out of phase, the pitch did not change. Listeners matched the pitch of the complex tone to the same pure tone. The effects of phase were found only in sequences in which the phase shift moved across the frequency components of the complex sounds.

Moreover, changing phase relationships among components of complex sounds led listeners to segment the sounds into sets of frequency components with constant phase relationships. Suppose we had two overlapping complex sounds with similar but not identical fundamental frequencies. Why should the two sounds separate? One possible answer is that the phase relationships within each sound would be invariant, but the phase relationships between the two sounds would shift over time because the fundamental frequencies were not identical, and that shift could be encoded by the phase-locked response to each sound. Similar to the work of Kubovy and Jordan (1979), it would be the changing phase relationships that are the perceptual information.[9]

I would argue that the effect of phase is identical for hearing and seeing. For static objects, the phase relationships do not affect periodicity but do affect quality, while for changing objects the phase relationships create stability and movement. (In chapter 5, I consider motion created by phase changes.) The ear is not phase-deaf and the eye is not phase-blind.

Physiological Transformations That Maximize Information Transmission

Given the statistical structure of the environment, what should be the optimal transformation of the proximal stimulus at the retina or at the cochlea into a neural signal? The answer depends on what we imagine the goals of sensory

9. Listeners can make use of phase differences to localize sounds. If we present one tone to each ear by means of headphones and then gradually increase the phase difference between the tones, listeners report that the sound is circling their head.

systems to be. One possibility would be to use a code that maximizes information transmission but decreases redundancy. A second possibility would be to use a code that increases redundancy to maximize reliability but reduces the rate of information transmission, for example by encoding each stimulus twice. There needs to be a balance between these goals.

If the goal is to maximize information transmission, one mechanism is to equalize the use of response categories or firing rates: Each firing rate should be equally probable. A second mechanism would be to create a factorial code: The probability of any joint outcome is simply the probabilities of the individual parts multiplied together; that is, the parts are made independent. Taken together, we shape the input-output function, the inputs being the set of possible stimulus values, the outputs being the set of possible neural responses, and the function being the coupling of one or more inputs to a single output. The goal is to make the probability of each outcome equal and independent.

At the Receptor Level

Here the goal would be to use each output level equally often. Such a response distribution, being uniform, would convey the maximum amount of information. In nearly all instances, the number of possible inputs will be greater than the number of response rates, due to limitations in neural firing rates. This can be done by shaping the input-output function so that there are large differences in response rates (i.e., spikes per second) among inputs that occur with high probability and small differences in response rates among inputs that occur with low probability. Consider a simple example in which there are 10 possible states but only five different response rates. If each of the 10 inputs were equally likely, one output code would pair adjacent inputs to one response rate: (1,2), (3,4), (5,6), (7,8), (9,10).[10] But if inputs 4, 5, and 6 each occurred 20% of the time and the remaining inputs were equally probable, an output code that nearly equalized outputs would be: (1,2,3), (4), (5), (6), (7,8,9,10).

These types of response functions were first found in the large monopolar cells of blowfly compound eyes (Laughlin, 1981), but similar functions have been found for vertebrate eyes. The monopolar cells respond to contrast levels but, like all other neurons, face a coding problem because their dynamic range of firing rates is much less than the range of physical variation. Laughlin first measured the probability of different contrast levels in the natural woodland environment. This distribution is shown at the bottom of figure 3.5, and the cumulative probability is shown in the upper right

10. I have created functions that combine adjacent inputs because that seems most realistic, but functions such as (1,10), (2,9), (3,8), (4,7), and (5,6) would also equalize probabilities.

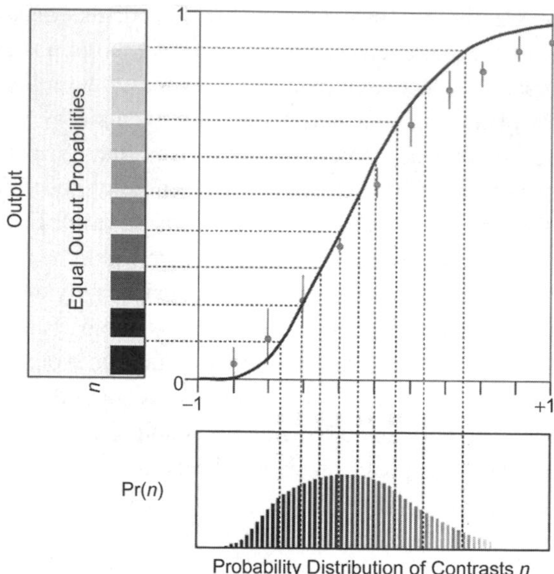

Figure 3.5. Transformation of an input distribution so that the outputs of the sensory cells have a flat probability distribution. This transformation maximizes the possible mutual information. From "Vision and the Coding of Natural Images," by B. A. Olshausen and D. J. Field, 2000, *American Scientist, 88*, 238–245. Copyright 2000 by *American Scientist*). Reprinted with permission.

panel. The optimal coding strategy to make the probability of each response rate more equal is simply to split the cumulative curve into equal sections, one for each possible output level. Each output level will signal a different range of contrasts. For regions of high probability contrasts (i.e., where the cumulative probability curve is steepest), each response output level will represent just a small range of contrasts. For regions of low probability contrasts (i.e., where the cumulative curve is flat), each response output level will represent a wide range of contrasts. As can be seen in figure 3.5, the actual response of monopolar cells to sudden increments of light around the steady background level closely matches the theoretical response rates based on equalizing the probability of the output response rates (Laughlin, 1981).

Even if each and every cell optimally encodes the stimulus variation, we still have three problems: (1) each cell will respond to a range of stimuli due to its bandwidth; (2) each cell will respond differently to the same stimulus due to the cell's inherent variability; and (3) the reliability of the response code must be ensured in the face of cell death and damage. These problems can be minimized if information is encoded by clusters of cells and not by single cells. This has been termed *population coding*. Pouget, Dayan, and Zemel (2000) illustrated population coding by means of cells that are tuned to slightly different directions of movement, and the same sort of analysis could extend to any sensory property (e.g., auditory localization or frequency identification). The overall firing rate of each cell is assumed to arise from the sum of the deterministic component due to the direction of movement and the noisy random component that is assumed to vary independently from instance to instance. A Gaussian distribution models the deterministic component of the cell's response, so that each cell will respond maximally to one direction and fire at lower rates in response to other directions. Across the population of cells, all directions would be represented roughly equally. Harper and McAlpine (2004) pointed out that for auditory localization, the optimal population distribution depends on head size and sound frequency; it may not be uniform.

If there were no noise in the firing rate, then the output of every cell would provide an error-free estimate of the movement direction (actually two directions, because the firing rate is assumed to be a symmetric Gaussian curve; see figure 3.6). But given the inherent noise and variability in the firing rate of a single cell, it is impossible to separate the true direction part from the noise part. Any movement direction will yield a distribution of responses, one from each receptor. However, using the firing pattern across the population of cells can minimize the error. There are several alternative ways to estimate the direction:

1. Choose the receptor with the highest firing rate. In Bayesian theory, this is equivalent to finding the maximum likelihood function, Pr(response | stimulus direction). However, picking the direction based on the receptor with the highest firing rate would be prone to error, given the variability of the responses.
2. Choose the direction with the highest posterior probability, Pr(stimulus direction | response). In Bayesian theory, this is equivalent to multiplying the likelihood function by the prior probability of that direction. The posterior probabilities would be calculated for each receptor separately. If all directions are equally probable, then the maximum likelihood and posterior probabilities are equal. This solution would still be prone to error.
3. Derive a function based on the firing rates of all the individual cells, and then shift the function laterally to find the best fit. Two solutions are shown in figure 3.6C and 3.6D. The first is to fit a cosine function (population vector coding) at the peak of the response distribution, (C); the second is to find the template derived from the noiseless tuning functions shown in (A) that best fit the response distribution, for example, at the peak of the response distribution as in (D). The peak position corresponds to the maximum likehood estimate (Pouget et al., 2000).

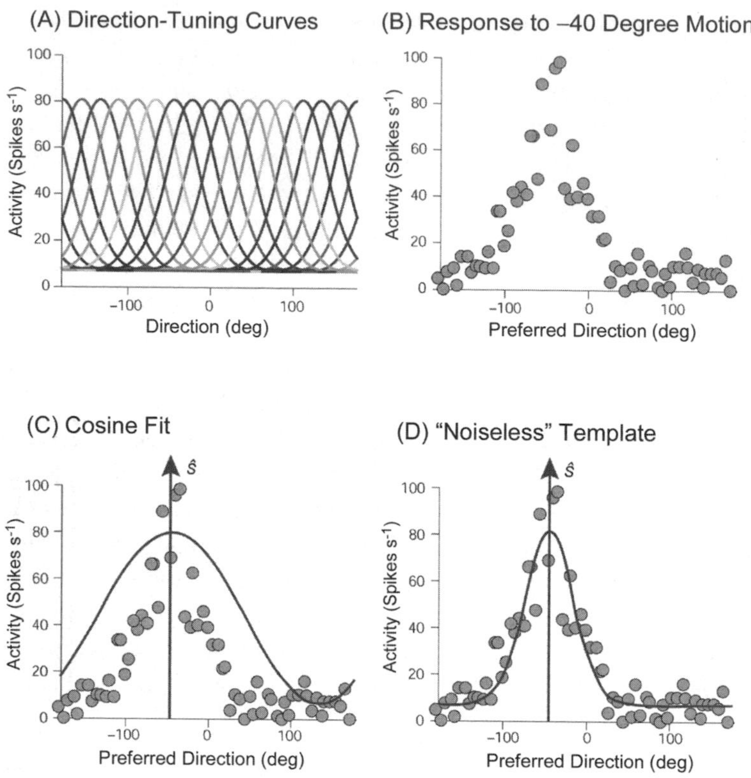

Figure 3.6. Population coding: The responses from a set of sensory cells with slightly different sensitivities are combined to yield a response distribution. Panel (A) illustrates direction-tuning curves for a set of 15 bell-shaped symmetric neurons. The outputs of 64 such cells to an object moving at –40° are shown in (B). This output is composed of two parts: the deterministic component shown in (A) and an independent error for each neuron. This distribution in turn is used in some way to calculate the most probable input. In Panel (C), the best fitting cosine function is fitted to the output distribution. The peak of the cosine is the estimate of the motion direction. In Panel (D), the predicted response distribution based on the individual error-free tuning curves in (A) is calculated for the set of possible directions. The predicted distribution that best fits the obtained neural response pattern is assumed to be the estimate of the movement direction. This is the maximum likelihood estimate, Pr(response | stimulus direction). From "Information Processing With Population Codes," by A. Pouget, P. Dayan, and R. Zemel, 2000, *Nature Reviews: Neuroscience, 1*, 125–132. Copyright 2000 by the Nature Publishing Group. Reprinted with permission.

There is an interesting parallel between the coding in the individual monopole cells and the coding in populations. In both cases, information mainly is carried by the steep part of the response curve where there is a large change in the firing rate for small changes in the stimulus value (i.e., the highest derivative). At the peaks of the response curves where the receptors are most active, relatively large changes in the stimulus (e.g., brightness or direction) create only small variations in the firing rates.

At the Ganglion Cells in the Retina

The goal at the ganglion cells would be to make the outputs of the cells as independent as possible. Adjacent retinal cells will have highly correlated temporal and spatial firing patterns because the brightness of neighboring points in the visual scene is likely to be similar, as in figure 3.2. The same is true for sound: The loudness, the set of frequency components, and amplitude or frequency oscillations are likely to be similar across successive time points (Nelken et al., 1999). To the degree that the outputs are correlated, there is redundancy and a reduction in information transmission.

Optimizing the response patterns of individual cells may not yield maximum information transmission across a population of cells. To do that, each neuron should have a response distribution (in terms of probability of response) that is independent of all other neurons. If this can be achieved, then each neuron would convey information about independent components of the objects in the world, and such a factorial code would yield the maximum amount of information. In the retina, pairs of nearby ganglion cells do indeed convey independent information (Nirenberg, Carcieri, Jacobs, & Latham, 2001). Nirenberg et al. (2001) estimated that 90% of the information could be derived by assuming that the ganglion cells fire independently. Given the bottleneck at the optic nerve, such independence would minimize any information loss. Combining the concept of response equalization with the concept of response independence gives us a set of tools to analyze actual response distributions.

Returning to the notion that adjacent auditory and visual elements are not independent, we need to minimize that lack of independence in order to create a code that transmits the maximum information (given the constraint that there is a fixed signal variance). If we use the outcome for the optimal code for single receptors as a model, we might expect that here the optimal code also will have equal power at all frequencies. In essence, the way to do this is to make the power at each spatial or auditory frequency equal and independent, exactly like white noise. In general, the power spectrum of the signal should be linked to the power spectrum of the internal noise so that the total power at each frequency—signal plus noise—is equal. Rieke et al. (1997) depicted this process as the "water filling analogy" such that the total power is a flat line as illustrated in figure 3.7.

In natural scenes, the high spatial frequency components are relatively rare due to the $1/f$ power function. As described above, the optimal way to create the maximum information transmission is to reverse the correlation inherent in the $1/f$ images by making the power equal at all frequencies: attenuating

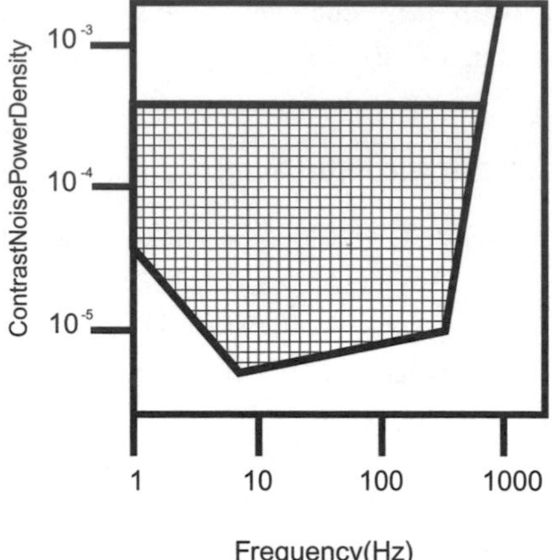

Figure 3.7. To maximize information transmission, the power at each frequency should be equal (similar to the concept in figure 3.5). The dark line at the base shows the noise in the sensory system. Therefore, to equalize the power at all frequencies, the useful sensory power should have the frequency distribution shown by the cross-hatching. Then the sum of the input and noise will be constant across frequency. Adapted from *Spikes: Exploring the Neural Code*, by F. Rieke, D. Warland, R. de Ruyter van Steveninck, and W. Bialek, 1997, Cambridge, MA: MIT Press.

the low spatial frequencies and boosting the high spatial frequencies in proportion to the original amplitudes (Atick, 1992). The term *whitening* refers to the equal distribution of energy across frequency bands; whitening removes the autocorrelations of brightness within objects but retains the boundaries. This procedure undoes the lack of independence in the firing patterns among sets of two neurons. All spatial frequencies therefore will have the same power or variance (creating white noise). Each frequency acts independently, which maximizes information transmission.

The concentric excitation and inhibition areas of the on-off and off-on ganglion cells serve to decorrelate the spatial frequencies and to optimize information transmission. These cells act as whitening filters by attenuating the strong low spatial frequency component where the signal-to-noise ratio is high (see figure 2.3). But as the frequency increases the signal-to-noise ratio is reduced, and eventually the signal gets lost in the noise. Given the limited dynamic range in firing rates of individual neurons, it makes no sense to attempt to encode those frequencies. Thus the optimal strategy would be to combine a high-pass filter to reduce redundancy at the lower frequencies (i.e., whitening) with a low-pass filter to separate signal from noise by attenuating the noisy high-frequency components. Together, the two filters create a band-pass filter that has a spatial organization similar to that of the on-off and off-on cells found in the retina and lateral geniculate (see figure 2.2 based on the Difference of Gaussians model). Dan, Atick, and Reid (1996) recorded the responses of individual neurons in the lateral geniculate nucleus of the cat to natural time-varying movies and to white-noise stimuli. They found that the neuron firing rates became uncorrelated to the natural movies but were correlated to the white noise stimuli. The filtering properties of those neurons seem to have evolved in response to the statistical regularities in the change of brightness over time for natural scenes (i.e., $1/f^c$ functions), so that to a degree they are unsuitable for random variations in brightness. Such neurons do not fire to spatially uniform arrays since those stimuli carry no information.

At the Cortical Level

The goal at the cortex would be to represent the spatial position and orientation, frequency, and temporal occurrence of parts of the auditory and visual objects. These properties cannot be optimized simultaneously due to Heisenberg's reciprocal uncertainty principle.

As described previously, Gabor (1946) showed that the best function to represent time and frequency uncertainty was a sinusoidal wave with a Gaussian (normal bell shape) drop-off. Examples were shown in figures 2.11 and 2.12. Although Gabor initially discussed the time × frequency trade-off, his approach is equally suited to minimize the spatial orientation × spatial frequency trade-off necessary for visual images. The concept of a Gabor function can be generalized to two spatial dimensions by creating a Gaussian fall-off along the second dimension and can be generalized to time by creating a Gaussian fall-off that extends in time.

We can imagine that each visual cortical receptor operates as a filter that transforms the brightness pattern at a particular retinal location into a firing pattern. The receptive field resembles a Gabor function that selectively codes for a specific spatial frequency at a particular orientation. Each retinal location would be represented by several cortical receptors, each one being maximally sensitive to a different mix of frequency, orientation, and phase resolution. In fact, we might expect that the uncertainty trade-off would vary with frequency: At the lower frequencies the frequency resolution would increase at the expense of the spatial orientation resolution and at higher frequencies the reverse would occur. The area of each filter (see figure 1.3) would be equal to match the statistical properties of the visual environment, that is, the equal power in each octave due to the $1/f^2$ function of the image. In fact, the receptive fields of neurons in the cortex closely do resemble Gabor functions of space and frequency, as illustrated in figure 2.7 by Jones and Palmer (1987a). This outcome suggests that the visual system attempts to optimally represent the reciprocal properties of orientation and frequency in coding the image.

We can also imagine that each auditory cortical receptor operates as a filter that transforms the frequency × intensity × time input into a firing pattern. Here the receptive fields would resemble Gabor functions that selectively code for frequency, intensity, and timing. Each frequency would be represented by several receptors with different bandwidths that trade frequency selectivity for temporal selectivity, as illustrated in chapter 2. Moreover, the different patterns of excitation and inhibitory bands found by M. L. Sutter et al. (1999) shown in figure 2.26 would suggest that these bands are decorrelating the sound image. I am somewhat hesitant to make this argument because sounds are rarely composed of adjacent frequency components. Nonetheless, I feel confident that the auditory and visual systems have evolved similar solutions to the trade-offs in resolution and redundancy/reliability, as described later in this chapter.

Neurons with similar receptive fields are located near each other and yet, as described above, Nirenberg et al. (2001) found that the responses in terms of rate in the retinal ganglion cells were largely independent. Reich, Mechler, and Victor (2001) investigated the independence of neurons in the primary visual cortex in terms of the timings between spikes. The question is whether it is better to sum the spikes across the neurons to average out the effect of noise, or whether it is better to keep the firings from each neuron separate to maximize the information transmission. Clearly, if the pattern of spike timings for each cell is regular and correlated in some way to the stimulus, summing the response to create a rate code will reduce the internal regularity found in the individual spike trains. This, in turn, would reduce information transmission. Reich et al. (2001) found that the timing within each spike train did convey independent information, so that combining spike trains led to a loss of information. The neural problem then becomes keeping the differences in the spike trains accessible to later stages of visual processing.

Does Cortical Organization Maximize Information Transmission?

The final question is the connection between the coding strategy and the statistical properties of the image, namely the $1/f$ power function. Why have the cortical receptors come to have Gabor-like functions? More generally, why are cortical receptors broadly tuned, so that the firing of a large number of cells is required to represent any external stimulus? What is the advantage of a population coding mechanism involving many receptors relative to one in which individual cortical receptors are tuned to rather precise stimuli (e.g., the infamous cell that pictures your grandmother)? The objects in the environment in the former case would be represented by a global firing pattern across a large percentage of the cell population (termed *dense representations*), while in the latter case the objects would be represented by the firing pattern of single cells (termed *local representations*). Both dense and local representations have fatal flaws. Dense representations, while able to represent a nearly unlimited number of objects, are highly redundant, using many cells to represent every single object. Because of the large number of cells firing at any instant, learning is very slow, it is difficult to calculate the probability of an object, and there is a limit on the ability to associate different objects to each other. Local representations, in contrast, will represent only as many object as there are cells, will lose a representation if a single cell dies, and will be unable to recognize and categorize similar but not identical objects.

Because dense and local representations appear unlikely, theoretical analyses and experimental outcomes have led to the acceptance of a compromise solution termed *sparse coding* as the most likely way objects are represented (Field, 1994). Sparse distributed coding does not reduce redundancy by using a smaller number of cells. In fact, the number of cells may increase. But the number of cells responding to any given input is minimized. For any given input, only a small number of cells will fire, and each input will be represented by a small, but unique, set of cells. Across the entire population of likely events, every cell will have the same but low probability of firing, but the probabilities will be concentrated at specific inputs. Suppose there are eight cortical cells. If there are 56 possible inputs, we could construct a sparse code by using combinations of three of the eight cells to represent each input. Each cell therefore would fire to 21 of the 56 inputs. The simple redundancy among adjacent spatial and temporal inputs is transformed into a complex output code so that each output represents a noncontingent set of inputs. An illustration of sparse distributed coding is shown in figure 3.8.

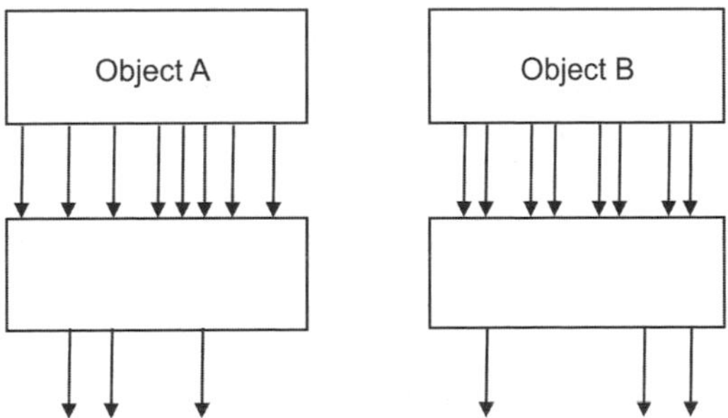

Figure 3.8. Sparse coding: Each output neuron will fire for only a small number of inputs. Sparse outputs composed of three neurons represent different inputs formed by eight neurons.

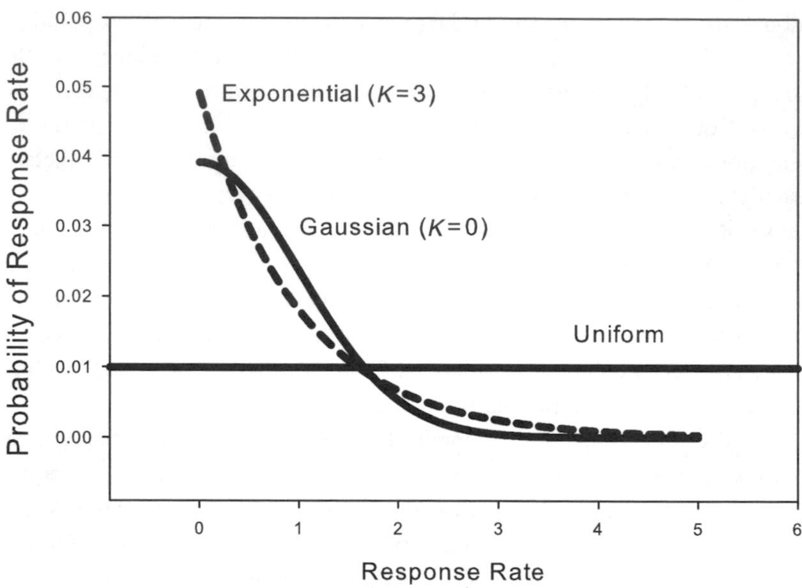

Figure 3.9. Kurtosis increases for sparse coding. Essentially, each output neuron is either on or off; the cells rarely fire at an intermediate rate. Compared to a Gaussian function (kurtosis = 0), the exponential function (kurtosis = 3) has a higher probability of not firing at all, a lower probability of firing at low rates, and a higher probability of firing at high rates.

The consequence of such sparse distributed coding is to change the activity of individual cells from a theoretical normal distribution. Within any time interval, a cell will fire at very high rates only for a small number of inputs; the cell will not fire at all or will fire at a low rate for the vast majority of inputs. Field and coworkers described this change in terms of *kurtosis*, the peakedness (fourth moment) around the mean value. A comparison between a uniform distribution, a normal distribution, and an exponential distribution with a high value of kurtosis is shown in figure 3.9. As the kurtosis increases, the uncertainty decreases and the redundancy increases because the no-response output becomes more and more probable (the maximum information transmission occurs when all outputs are equally likely, the uniform distribution).

Sparse coding representations have several appealing features:

1. Sparse representations can be made relatively resistant to neurological damage simply by duplicating the set of units responding to each input (Foldiak & Young, 1995).
2. Sparse representations seem to match the appearance of natural images in terms of a set of independent features such as edges that contain correlations among sets of points (Barlow, 2001). By explicitly

representing these naturally occurring features, the visual and auditory systems become tuned to object discrimination (at the cost of becoming relatively poor at discriminating random noise patterns). Sparse representations can capture phase relationships that determine edges and impulse sounds and thus are able to represent the essential parts of images.

3. Any object would be represented by the unique firing pattern of a small number of available cells. Each cell has a relatively low probability of firing overall, so that any interference between different stimulus features is unlikely. But the small number of firing cells should make it easy to detect the correspondence of a spatial property such as an edge across two images separated in space or time. By the same token, it should be easier to detect the correspondence between a present stimulus and a memory, because the number of neurons firing is small (Perez-Orive et al., 2002).

In a more general framework, Laughlin (2001) argued that the energy requirements for neural functioning have acted as a constraint that has influenced the coding and processing of sensory information. Although the brain consists of just 2% of body mass, the mammalian brain uses about 20% of total body energy, and 50–80% of that energy is used for neural signaling. The remaining energy is used to maintain the brain—it is a fixed cost. The huge energy load due to the creation of neural signals appears to have led to cortical localization that places highly interactive subunits physically close to each other in order to create the most economical wiring.

Laughlin (2001) hypothesized that the degree of sparse coding is a reflection of the limited amount of energy available to the organism, and that the degree of sparseness reflects the severity of that limitation. The way to minimize energy usage would be to reduce the number of neurons, even though each neuron must therefore fire more frequently. It would be more efficient to construct a coding system composed of 8 neurons such that 4 neurons fire per event (encoding 70 events uniquely) than one composed of 70 neurons such that 1 neuron fires per event (encoding 70 events uniquely). Overall, the neural system will minimize the energy requirements to "get the job done just right enough."

Sparse Coding

Visual Naturalistic Modeling

The basic strategy of the simulations described below is to start with a set of black-and-white pictures of natural scenes presented one after another to a set of theoretical receptors. Each receptor is made up of a 12 × 12 array of light-sensitive units. The receptors learn not by being right or wrong, but by maximizing mutual information under the sparseness constraint. What we are mathematically trying to find is a set of independent basis functions that when added together reproduce the image of the natural scene.[11]

We impose the sparse-coding restriction that the output of each basis function is zero for most inputs but strongly excitatory or inhibitory for a small number of inputs. In terms of the mathematical analysis (principal components), the basis functions are the causes of the visual scenes so that if added together they will reproduce the natural scenes. If the causal basis functions resemble the space-time receptive fields of retinal or cortical receptor cells that decode the brightness patterning of visual scenes, then it is possible to argue, somewhat indirectly, that the physiological receptive fields have evolved to maximize mutual information by matching the causes.

Field (1987), following such a strategy, found that the basis functions indeed resembled Gabor functions similar to the receptive fields of cortical neurons (see figures 2.7 and 2.14 for cortical receptive fields). Compared to normal (Gaussian) probability distributions, the Gabor-like functions had sharper probability peaks at zero response and higher probabilities of extreme response rates. Field (1987) further demonstrated that by maximizing the sparseness of the distribution, he was able to match the bandwidth (approximately 0.8–1.5 octaves) and vertical-horizontal aspect ratio (2 to1) of cortical cells. This outcome supported the notion of a sparse code: Individual neurons would be active only when a particular brightness pattern (i.e., a causal basis) occurred at a specific location and orientation. Any single scene would stimulate only a small set of these receptors, but each possible scene would activate a different set of receptors.

Olshausen and Field (1996, 1998) "trained" a set of basis functions using image patches randomly selected from natural scenes to minimize the difference between the image patch and the reconstruction using the addition of basis functions. Minimizing the number of basis functions by adding a cost for each additional basis function imposed sparseness. The resulting set of basis functions was *overcomplete*, so that there were more basis functions than the dimensionality of the input.[12] The theoretical advantage of an overcomplete basis set is that the visual (and auditory) worlds

11. The set of sine and cosine functions for the Fourier analysis is one basis set. A set of Gaussian functions, as illustrated in figure 3.6, is another basis set. We can produce any arbitrary curve by multiplying the height of each Gaussian by a constant and then summing the resulting Gaussian functions together point by point.

12. For example, an overcomplete set might have 200 basis functions to describe a 12 pixel × 12 pixel image that contains only 144 independent points. Because the set is overcomplete, there are an infinite number of solutions to describing the 144 image points. The sparseness criterion is necessary to force a single solution.

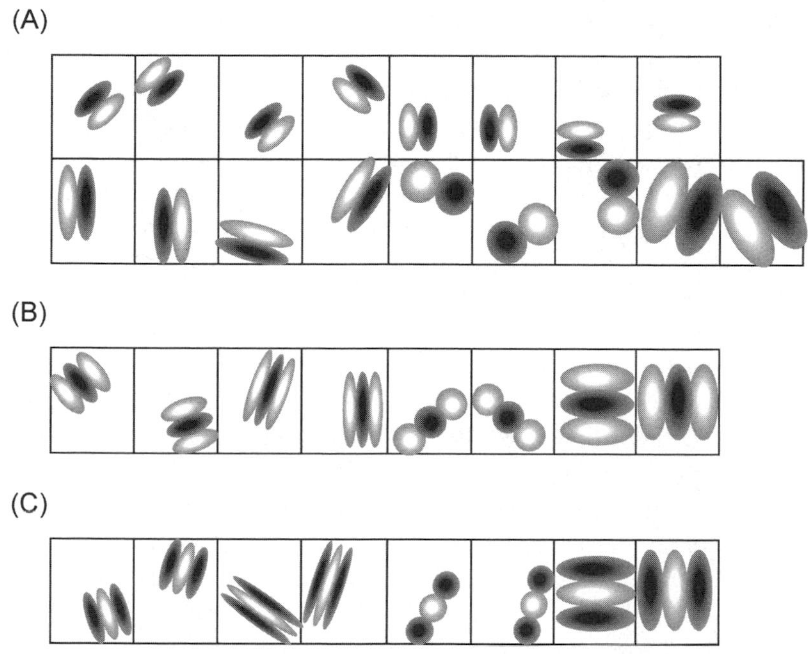

Figure 3.10. Basis functions trained from natural images. Each basis function resembles a simple spatial frequency × spatial orientation cortical cell. The derived functions can be roughly categorized into three categories: (A) odd symmetric with one on- and one off-region; (B) even symmetric with an on-off-on configuration; and (C) even symmetric with an off-on-off configuration. Each type of function occurs at different frequencies, orientations, and positions within the 12 × 12 image patch. Adapted from Olshausen, 2002.

contain objects at many different scales, frequencies, and locations, so that it is highly unlikely that there is a minimum set of basis functions that could encode such variability. Simoncelli, Freeman, Adelson, and Heeger (1992) demonstrated that such an overcomplete set makes each basis function represent a specific interpretation—the amount of structure at a particular location, orientation, and scale. Moreover, it creates smooth changes in the activities of the individual basis functions as a result of small changes in the input, an obviously desirable outcome. The outcome of this simulation is a set of basis functions that closely resemble the receptive field properties of cells in V1, although these basis functions were derived only from the properties of the images (see figure 3.10).

Bell and Sejnowski (1997) derived a solution similar to that of Olshausen and Field (1996) using the information theory concept of maximizing information by making the individual receptive field filters and basis functions as independent as possible (independent component analysis). Conceptually, each filter represents the receptive field of one cortical cell as portrayed in figure 3.10 and the corresponding basis function represents the input that maximally stimulates that filter. Passing an image through any filter yields the strength of the corresponding basis function.

Given that primary cells have spatial-temporal receptive fields (see figures 2.18 and 2.19), Hateren and Ruderman (1998) utilized sequences of natural images to more closely simulate normal vision. They performed independent component analyses on sequences of 12 images (roughly 0.5 s total) taken from television shows. The basis functions resembled bars or edges that moved as a unit perpendicular to their orientation. The majority respond to edges moving in one direction only, exactly what would occur with nonseparable spatial-temporal receptive fields (also found by Olshausen, 2002). Generally speaking, there is a negative correlation between spatial and temporal tuning; filters centered at higher spatial frequencies are more likely to be tuned to lower temporal frequencies and vice versa.

Hateren and Ruderman (1998) suggested that the space-time properties of the filters explain the sparse response distribution. The visual world consists of rigid homogeneous objects moving at different speeds that occlude one another. A localized space-time filter would typically measure small brightness differences within a single homogeneous object and therefore would have a high probability of not responding at all (i.e., peaky at zero). Such a space-time filter would respond strongly to the brightness contrasts found at edges that move into or out of the receptive field, and those responses make up the long, low probability but high firing rate tails of the response distribution.

Up to this point, the analyses have not made use of any properties of the nervous system. All of the outcomes have been based on an analysis of sets of images (although physiological considerations act to impose constraints). A second strategy begins with a hypothetical but naive nervous system. It is hypothetical because, based on current knowledge, you build in a plausible set of interconnections and cortical units, a model of how the interconnections combine, a model of how the outputs of the cortical cells are integrated, a model of learning, a measure of error to drive the learning procedure, and so on. It is naive because at the beginning of the simulation all of the interconnections and units have equal strength (although the procedural "software" is in place). Then you present a series of images and measure the difference between the original image and the reproduction of the image by the hypothetical model.[13] On the basis of the learning and error models, the strengths of the connections and units are changed across the set of images to yield the closest matches. The resulting structure of the interconnections and units is then thought to be a model for how the actual

13. The term *reproduction* is used in a least-squares error sense. The visual system obviously does not create a replica of the image.

nervous system is organized. These outputs, when combined, would optimally reproduce the original image.

Hyvärinen and Hoyer (2001) followed this strategy to derive the receptive spatial fields and spatial arrangement of the complex cells found in the primary visual cortex V1. Simple cells will increase their firing rate above baseline if a white band falls on the excitation region and a black band falls on the inhibition region but reduce their firing rate below baseline for the reverse arrangement. Complex cells, in contrast, will increase their firing rate for either arrangement; they are phase insensitive. Intuitively, the simple cells feed forward to the complex cells such that either an increase or decrease in firing rate of simple cells increases the firing rate of the complex cell. Hyvärinen and Hoyer (2001) modeled this process by assuming that (1) the outputs of the simple cells (the difference between the firing rate and the baseline-firing rate) are squared so that all changes in the light pattern due to movements of edges increase the firing rate, and (2) the outputs from nearby simple cells (a 5×5 grid of cells) converge on every complex cell. They then use independent component analysis to maximize the sparseness or independence of the complex cell responses. To maximize the sparseness of the complex cells means that the simple cells that converge on a complex cell should have as similar a filter response as possible. The authors argued that if the responses of the convergent simple cells were independent, then the response of the complex cell would be more normal and less peaky (an outcome predicted from the central limit theorem).

The results can be considered in terms of the simple cells and in terms of how the activations of the simple cells create the complex cells. Each retinal region is represented by a set of adjacent overlapping simple cells. The receptive fields of the simple cells in figure 3.11 differ in retinal location and orientation of the brightness contrast, and respond to a narrow range of spatial frequencies. The topographic map of each set of simple cells shows that the cells are smoothly arranged spatially in terms of orientation and position. The majority of the receptive fields are simply scaled versions of another field. Thus the receptive fields possess differing spatial and temporal scales that create the multiresolution characteristics of perceptual systems described in chapter 1. The simple cells that are pooled to create complex cells have similar receptive fields.

The results of Hyvärinen and Hoyer (2001) provide a model to explain the retinal topographic organization of the visual cortex. Starting with a simple feed-forward model in which simple cells converge on complex cells and invoking a criterion of maximal independence creates the spatial arrangement of receptive fields found in all species.

Körding, Käyser, Einhouser, and König (2004) followed a different route to derive the properties of complex cells. They argued that nearly all visual objects and higher-level variables change slowly or not at all over time, even

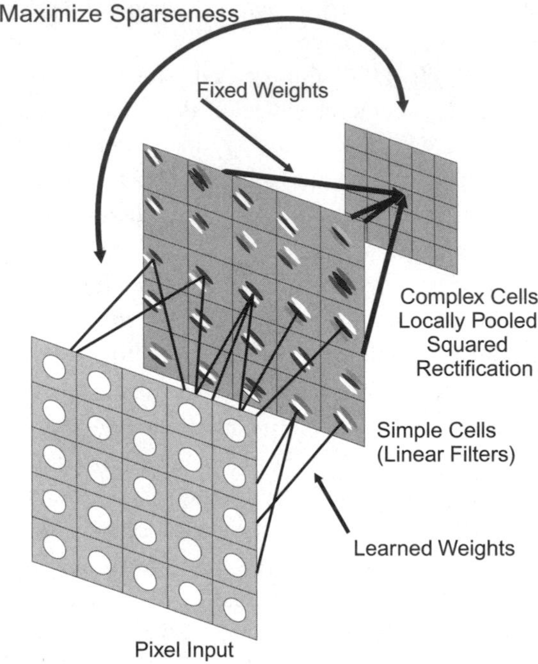

Figure 3.11. Derivation of the receptive fields of complex cells. The derived receptive fields of the simple cells (linear filters) resemble those in figure 3.10 and also illustrate the smooth transition in spatial position necessary to construct complex cells. The sparseness constraint derives from the convergence of the 5 × 5 set of simple derived cells onto each complex cell. The simple derived cells that converge are similar in frequency, orientation, and position, but have random phases. Adapted from "A Two-Layer Sparse Coding Model Learns Simple and Complex Cell Receptive Fields and Topography From Natural Images," by A. Hyvärinen and P. O. Hoyer, 2001, *Vision Research, 41*, 2413–2423.

though lower-level variables may change more rapidly. They use the example of a tiger's stripes, which may oscillate back and forth due to small muscle movements even though the tiger does not change position. On this basis, Körding et al. used a learning procedure to derive the simulated responses of cells that were maximally coherent over two successive views of a scene (but being maximally different from each other). The resulting simulated cells resembled complex cells. Each simulated complex cell was the sum of the squared firing rates of pairs of simple cells that had the same Gabor-like orientation and frequency response but were shifted 90° laterally with respect to each other. Such cells are translation and contrast-reversing invariant. The authors concluded that complex cells in the primary visual cortex can be understood as being an optimal way to encode the stability of natural objects.

To summarize, the independent components analysis of natural images yield filters that closely resemble the space × orientation receptive fields found in V1. Even though the filters could have resembled the circular on-off receptive fields found in the retina and lateral geniculate, they did not. Olshausen and O'Connor (2002) suggested that the independent components analysis will derive filters at the point where the number of sensory neurons greatly increases. In the visual system, that occurs after the constriction due to the optic nerve, discussed in chapter 2.

Auditory Naturalistic Modeling

Cusack and Carlyon (2004) constructed a set of 10 s sequences composed of four different kinds of sounds: (a) a pure tone; (b) a three-component harmonic sound; (c) an eight-component harmonic sound; and (d) a noise. The sounds were randomly distributed across the 10 s duration. Each sound usually overlapped with at least one other sound. Cusack and Carlyon used the independent components analysis procedure to derive basis functions that would encode the auditory input. The authors restricted the number of functions to six to simplify the results. An example of a test sequence and the derived basis functions are shown in figure 3.12.

The six basis functions (receptive fields) shown in (d) are tuned to the particular sounds presented. The second basis function responds when the eight-component harmonic tone occurs; the fourth function responds when the pure tone occurs; and the fifth and sixth functions respond when the noise occurs. The firing of each basis function is context independent: each fires only if its stimulus is presented. The basis functions effectively segregated the sequences into the different sounds.

The derived basis functions can recover only the characteristics of the presented sounds (the visual simulations used more than 100,000 images). If the presented sounds were composed only of noises, then the basis functions also would be noise segments. Here, because the inputs were limited, the independent component functions were in fact the input sounds themselves.

Lewicki (2002) and Smaragdis (2001) derived independent component bases for short segments (8–9 ms) of (a) environmental sounds (e.g., rustling brush, crunching twigs, rain, fire) that typically have short duration, composed of a broadband of nonharmonic frequencies; (b) animal vocalizations that are typically of longer duration, composed of narrow harmonic frequencies; and (c) speech sounds, composed of longer-duration harmonic vowels and shorter-duration nonharmonic consonants. Differences between voiced [ba] and [da] and voiceless [pa] and [ta] stop consonants depend on voice-onset differences as small as 10 ms. Each component base was limited to 128 sample points.

The trade-off between frequency and time localization resulting from the Heisenberg uncertainty principle implies that the independent components ought to differ among the three stimulus classes. For the environmental

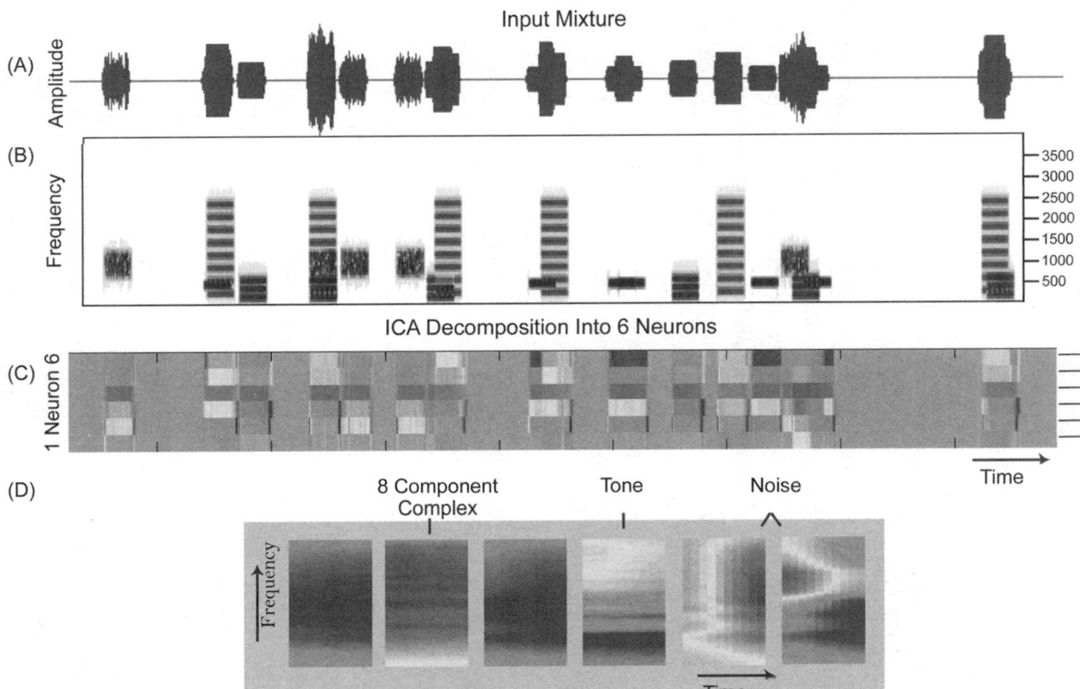

Figure 3.12. Independent components analysis (ICA) of the sequence of four sounds. The amplitude and frequency components of one 10 s sequence are shown in (a) and (b). Six basis functions (i.e., neurons) were derived. The firing of each neuron is shown in (c) and the frequency by time receptive fields are shown in (d). The recovered components tend to match the input sounds. Figure courtesy of Dr. Rhodi Cusack.

sounds, the independent components ought to be accurately localized in time, at the expense of frequency resolution. In contrast, for the animal vocalizations the independent components ought to accurately resolve the harmonic frequencies at the expense of temporal resolution (the animal calls hardly changed in the 8 ms). For speech, both frequency and temporal resolution are important, so that the independent components ought to be a composite of components that resolve frequency best and those that resolve time best.

As can be seen in figure 3.13A, the independent components that maximize the efficient coding do differ among the three types of stimuli. For

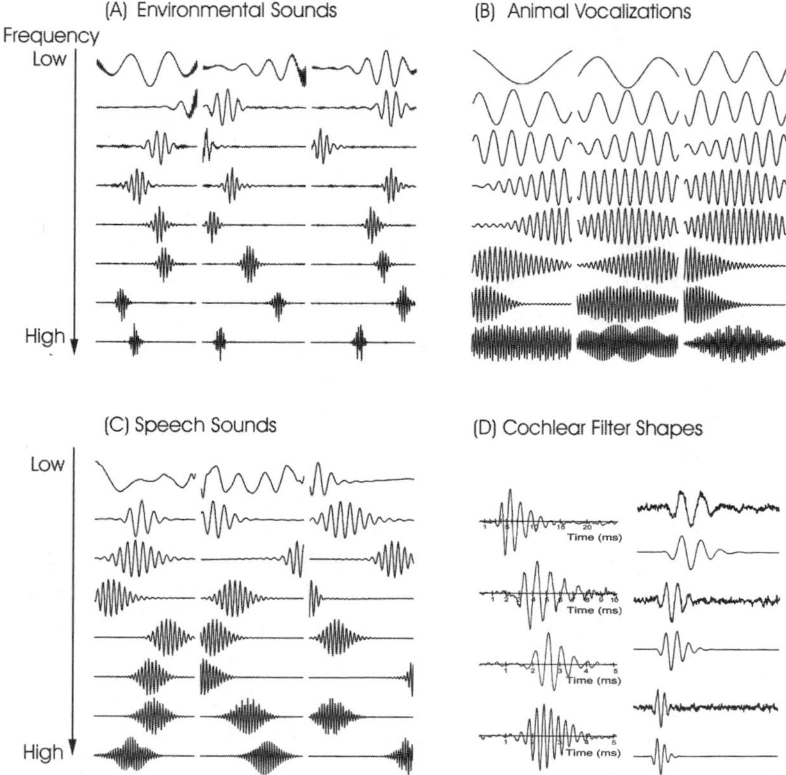

Figure 3.13. Independent component analysis of (A) environmental sounds, (B) animal vocalizations, and (C) speech sounds. The independent components for environmental and speech sounds are localized in frequency and time and illustrate the frequency × time trade-off. At the lower frequencies, the frequency resolution is maximized, and at the higher frequencies, the time resolution is maximized. The independent components for the animal vocalizations are mainly the Fourier components. The responses of auditory fibers are shown in (D). These responses, with the exception of being asymmetrical, are close to the independent components. Adapted from "Efficient Coding of Natural Sounds," by M. S. Lewicki, 2002, *Nature Neuroscience, 5*, 356–363.

the environmental sounds shown in (A), the components have a dominant resonance frequency, and the higher-frequency bases are localized in time. For the animal vocalizations, the independent components resemble Fourier components that extend across the entire window to maximize the frequency resolution. For speech sounds, the lower-frequency components tend to extend across the entire duration of the segment, while the higher-frequency bases are localized to maximize the temporal resolution.

It is possible to organize these results in terms of the trade-off between frequency resolution and temporal resolution first discussed in chapter 1. At one extreme, the frequency × time space can be organized to maximize temporal resolution (figure 3.14A). At the other extreme, using the same number of rectangular blocks, it is possible to maximize frequency resolution (figure 3.14C), and this matches the independent components found for the animal vocalizations. In between are wavelet representations (figure 3.14B), in which the kind of resolution trade-off varies across frequency. Typically, frequency resolution is maximized at the lower frequencies and temporal resolution is maximized at the higher frequencies, and that matches the independent components found for speech. Alternately, the frequency resolution could be maintained until a higher frequency, and that seems to match the independent components found for speech.

Lewicki (2002) argued that the independent components found for speech most closely resemble the responses of cochlear hair cells measured at the auditory nerve to similar stimuli. These responses are shown in figure 3.13D. We can speculate that the choice of speech sounds was based on the previous evolution of coding mechanisms for environmental and animal sounds that were important for survival.

Let me try to sum all of this up. What the visual system appears to do is recode the dense distribution of firings of the retinal cells into a sparse distribution of firings of the oriented cells in the V1 cortex. To do this, the visual system has evolved coding mechanisms that create representations of the edges and boundaries that signify objects in the environment. There is a series of steps from the retina to the cortex that makes use of the statistical regularities both within and between objects at differing frequency and orientation resolutions to create cells tuned to object properties. The explosion in the number of visual cells past the optic nerve bottleneck allows the cortical representation to be overcomplete, to be perceptually continuous. The work of Cusack and Carlyon (2004), Smaragdis (2001), and Lewicki (2002) shows that it is possible to hypothesize that the same type of efficient recoding occurs at the cochlea. The derived independent component filters show the same relationship between characteristic frequency and bandwidth found at the auditory nerve. The derived bases for both auditory and visual inputs reflect the multiresolution solution to the aperture and correspondence problems. The bases are localized in

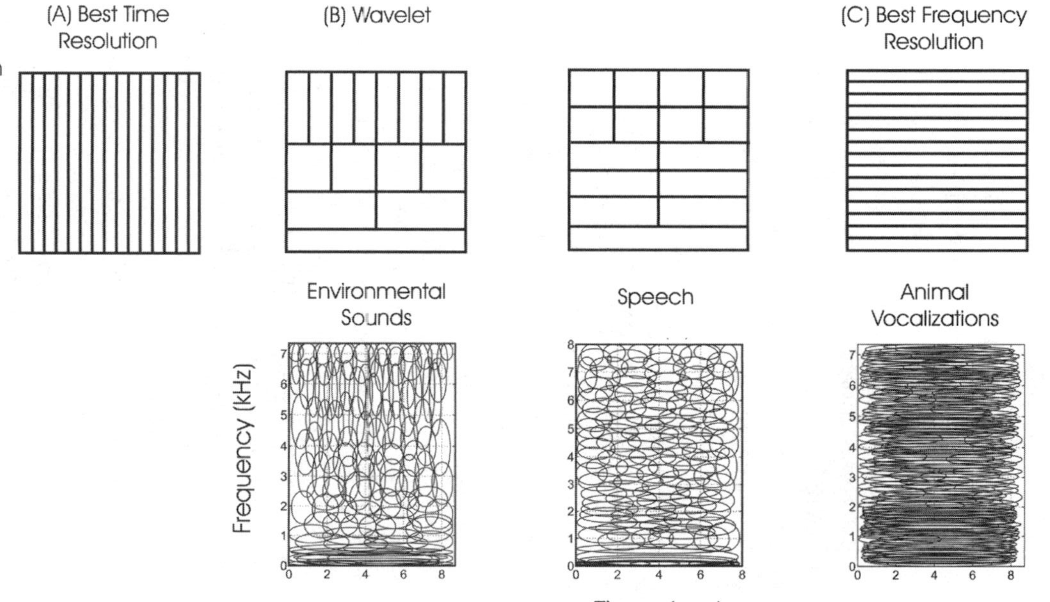

Figure 3.14. The independent components can be understood in terms of the frequency × time resolution trade-off. The frequency × time space can be "tiled" in different ways. The animal vocalizations are tiled to maximize frequency resolution, while the speech and environmental sounds are tiled to maximize frequency resolution at the lower frequencies and to maximize temporal resolution at the higher frequencies Adapted from "Efficient Coding of Natural Sounds," by M. S. Lewicki, 2002, *Nature Neuroscience, 5*, 356–363. and "A New Window on Sound," by B. A. Olshausen and K. N. O'Connor, 2002, *Nature Neuroscience, 5*, 292–294.

frequency and spatial orientation or by frequency and time. For both there are trade-offs between the frequency resolution and the time or orientation resolution.

Experimental Physiological and Perceptual Outcomes Using Natural Stimuli

Even though the environment may be made up of many processes that can be modeled in terms of $1/f^c$ power laws and models of cortical cells display a sparse firing distribution, that does not mean that (1) the neural cells actually are organized to yield sparse coding, and (2) people are sensitive to the self-similarity of the processes. Moreover, although it may be true that people can distinguish between auditory and visual fractal representations based on different values of the frequency exponent, that still does not necessarily imply that people perceive the fractal structure itself.

Experimental Physiological Outcomes

Vinje and Gallant (2000, 2002) created a sequence of visual images that simulated what a monkey would see if it scanned a static natural scene and recorded from neurons located in area V1 of two awake macaque monkeys. Vinje and Gallant were particularly interested in how the firing of a classical receptive area is influenced by stimulation of the surrounding area (the nonclassical receptive field described in chapter 2). The theoretical and computation approaches described above hypothesize that area V1 uses a sparse code to efficiently represent natural scenes (remember, natural scenes have a great deal of built-in redundancy, so that sparse codes would be effective). Vinje and Gallant hypothesized that stimulation of the nonclassical response field increased the degree of sparseness. The results demonstrated that indeed a sparse code best represented the firing patterns found in the roughly 60 neurons. Moreover, as the nonclassical receptive field increased in size, the sparseness of the firing increased due to the nonlinear receptive field interactions (compare figure 3.15C to figure 3.15B). Individual neurons became more selective in responding to complex stimuli, so that the kurtosis of the firing distribution increased. Stimulation of the nonclassical receptive fields reduces the response to noise more than it reduces the firing to stimulus properties, and that increases the efficiency of the coding. Vinje and Gallant found that the degree of sparseness was the same for sequences of black-and-white gratings and natural movies, suggesting that it is the correlated energy at different orientations in both types of images that created the sparse coding.

Perez-Orive et al. (2002) presented a particularly compelling example of sparse coding in the olfactory system of locusts. Roughly 90,000 receptor neurons converge on about 1,000 excitatory projection neurons in the ol-

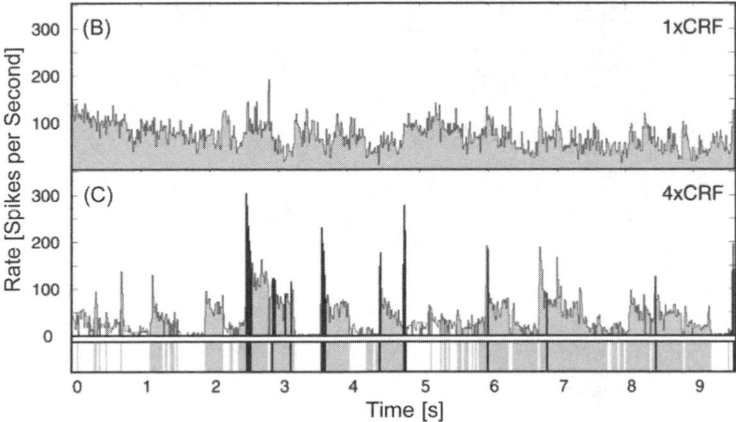

Figure 3.15. Sparse coding in V1. The white line in (A) represents the simulated visual scan path. The small white circle portrays the classical receptive field (CRF) size, while the larger white circle is four times the CRF diameter. The response of one V1 neuron to a presentation of the movie confined to the CRF is pictured in (B). The responses were summed in 13.8 ms bins. The selectivity index of these data is only 13%, which implies a dense distribution of responses across the stimulus set. (The selectivity will equal 0 if the cell responds to every stimulus and will equal 1 if it responds to only one stimulus.) The response distribution to 20 presentations of the movie using a stimulus size four times the CRF diameter is shown in (C). Stimulation of the nonclassical receptive field increases the selectivity to 51%. Increases in the firing rate are indicated in black. The underbar highlights increases in rates (black) and decreases in rates (white). Increases occur at onset transients. From "Natural Stimulation of the Nonclassical Receptive Field Increases Information Transmission Efficiency in V1," by W. E. Vinje and J. L. Gallant, 2002, *Journal of Neuroscience, 22*, 2904–2915. Copyright 2002 by the Society for Neuroscience. Reprinted with permission.

factory bulb. The bulb projects to the mushroom body, which is a memory area containing about 50,000 neurons. Each projection neuron connects to about 600 Kenyon cells in the mushroom body, so that each mushroom body Kenyon cell receives between 10 and 20 convergent inputs.

Each cell in the olfactory bulb responds to a large fraction of the possible odors with a sustained response. Thus, the sparseness is very low (like that of auditory hair cells and retinal cells). For some odors, the firing of the projection neurons becomes synchronized, producing an oscillating evoked neural response. In contrast, in the mushroom body the same odors activate only a small proportion of the cells, and the activity of each cell may consist of only

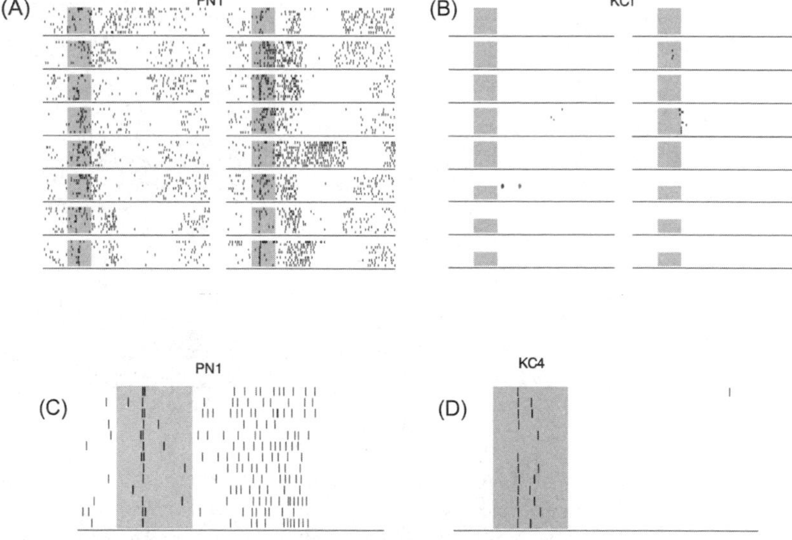

Figure 3.16. Sparse coding in the mushroom body of the locust. The presentation of the odor is portrayed by the grayish rectangle. The response of one projection neuron and one Kenyon cell to 16 different odors is depicted in (A) and (B). Each row represents one trial (the smaller gray rectangles for KC1 in (B) are due to a smaller number of presentation trials). The projection neuron is active prior to the presentation of the odor (PN1 in A). The response to all of the 16 odors is characterized by sustained responses. Although the timing and synchrony to the different odors vary slightly, it appears nearly impossible to distinguish among the odors. In contrast, the responses of the Kenyon cells occur to only 4 of the odors, and consist of only a small number of spikes (KC1 in B). A more detailed picture of the response to one odor is shown in (C) and (D). Each odor presentation is drawn as a single row. The response of PN1 is quite variable, but the initial response of the Kenyon cell is precisely aligned to the onset of the odor and there is only one or two spikes per presentation. From "Oscillations and Sparsening of the Odor Representations in the Mushroom Body," by J. Perez-Orive, O. Mazor, G. C. Turner, S. Cassenaer, R. Wilson, and G. Laurent, 2002, *Science, 297*, 359–365. Copyright 2002 by the American Association for the Advancement of Science. Reprinted with permission.

one or two action potential responses (see the responses to different odors for a projection neuron and for a Kenyon cell in figure 3.16). The authors propose that the cells in the mushroom body act as coincidence detectors of phase-locked convergent firings from the projection neurons in the olfactory bulb. It is the correlations among spike trains that are of primary importance, not the rate. (The neural information about which odor occurred is conveyed by only one or two spikes, in line with the position of Rieke et al. [1997].)

Laurent (2002) pointed out that most odors consist of possibly hundreds of volatile components and that odor perception tends to bind those components together. An odor is therefore a pattern that exists at several levels of resolution, for example, aromatic-minty-spearmint. The odor space is enormous and there will be huge empty regions. Laurent (2002) suggested that the coincidence detection proposed by Perez-Orive et al. (2002) is somewhat transient; two cells may synchronize at one time and yet not synchronize at another time. Over time, the firing rates of projection neurons rise and fall so that different groups of cells are active at different times and that patterning differs for particular odors. The mushroom body cells therefore will fire only when the oscillations in firing rates create highly synchronized firings among the 10 to 20 inputs. On top of this constraint to high firing levels due to the variability in firing rates of the projection neurons, there is a consistent inhibitory response that follows each mushroom body cell response. Both factors create the sparse code. Because each odor has a distinct sparse code, it should be relatively easy to identify each odor and separate them if they occur together.

The consistent inhibitory response described by Laurent (2002) has been found in the rat's auditory cortex and also contributes to the formation of a sparse code (Wehr & Zador, 2003). The excitatory and inhibitory receptive fields are tuned to the same frequency × intensity values, termed *cotuned*, with the inhibitory response delayed relative to the excitatory response by 1–5 ms (this is analogous to complex visual cells with the same frequency × orientation receptive fields). The inhibitory component does not appear to sharpen the frequency tuning. But the inhibitory component blocks the firing from the excitatory component after the delay interval (1–5 ms). Thus, the inhibitory response creates a transient, sparse firing pattern within the delay, in which only one or two spikes signal the tone onset.

When neurons are firing at the high rates characteristic of sparse coding, the timing of spikes is particularly regular, and the trial-to-trial variance in the number of spikes to a given stimulus is minimum (Reinagel, 2001). After a spike, a neuron enters into an absolute refractory period before another spike can occur. Following the absolute period, there is a relative refractory period in which a larger stimulus input is required to fire the cell. The probability of the next spike is determined by two somewhat opposing factors—the time elapsed since the last spike and the strength of the input. With a stronger

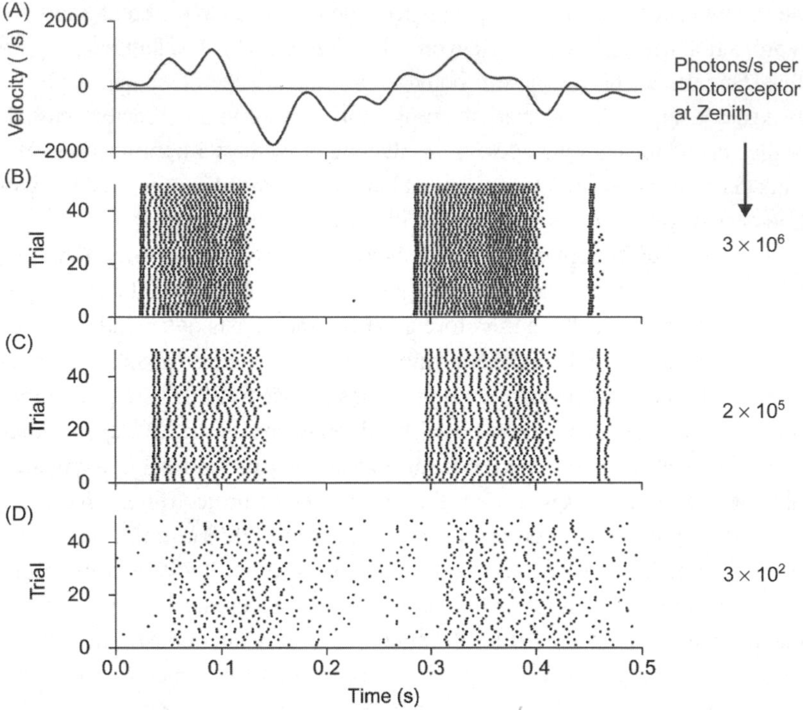

Figure 3.17. Firing rates become more regular as the response rate increases due to greater light energy. The responses are evoked from yawing motions in captive insects. (A) depicts the flight path, and (B) through (D) portray the change in the firing pattern as the light energy decreases. Within the three panels, each row represents one repetition of the flight pattern. From "Neural Coding of Natural Motion Stimuli," by G. Lewen, W. Bialek, and R. de Ruyter van Steveninck, 2001, *Network, 12*, 317–329. Copyright 2001 by the Institute of Physics. Reprinted with permission.

input, the majority of spikes will occur directly after the fixed absolute refractory period and therefore the number of spikes on successive presentation is likely to be similar. Reinagel (2001) summarized experimental work by Lewen, Bialek, and de Ruyter van Steveninck (2001) illustrating that neural responses alternate between periods of very high responding rates and periods of very low responding rates. At higher illuminations where presumably more cells would be firing, the alternations are sharpest, as pictured in figure 3.17.

Quiroga, Reddy, Kreiman, Koch, and Fried (2005) found an invariant, sparse, and explicit code for pictures of individuals, landmarks, and objects when recording from individual neurons in the medial temporal lobe of human epileptic patients. The medial temporal lobe is assumed to underlie late-stage visual processing and long-term memory. In these individuals, specific cells only would respond to varying images (i.e., different views and sizes) of specific persons or objects (e.g., Sydney, Australia, opera house). However, these cells also respond to the names of those persons and objects, so that they may be related more to the long-term abstract memory representation than to the visual input. Nonetheless, the visual representation near the end of visual processing is remarkably sparse and invariant and approaches the one-to-one coding assumed to occur for grandmother cells.

Perception of Fractal Processes

Gilden, Schmuckler, and Clayton (1993) contrasted a fractal model of roughness to an intuitive signal + noise model of roughness. Visual roughness was portrayed by a line graph (similar to the $1/f^c$ functions shown in figure 3.3) with different degrees of jaggedness (reversals in contour) and auditory roughness by a sequence of pitches, loudnesses, or durations with different numbers of random reversals in contour (Schmuckler & Gilden, 1993).

The theoretical issue is whether a fractal description or a signal + noise description is a better model of how people perceive these sorts of patterns. First, for an auditory or visual fractal model, the roughness is found at all levels of the scale, so that we could say that the roughness pervades and is inherent in the stimulus. Gilden et al. (1993, p. 462) put it clearly: "Natural contours are to be conceived as nothing but roughness." No piece of the contour can be analyzed separately; the contour cannot be decomposed into separate parts.

Second, in contrast, a signal + noise model is assumed to consist of two parts. The first part is *intrinsic*, an invariant component that does not change across occasions; it is equivalent to a true score in linear models. In terms of roughness, it is a smooth undulating low-frequency component, the visual or auditory contour. The second part can be said to be extrinsic, a temporal or spatial variability that is added to the intrinsic part. The high-frequency extrinsic noise acts to mask the intrinsic part. To return to roughness, the noise component is an add-on; it creates the roughness or jaggedness of the surface. From this perspective, the act of perceiving is to penetrate through the noise to perceive the invariant. In natural visual settings, Gilden et al. (1993) described it as perceiving through the camouflage. The signal + noise model is not a physical model for any process nor for the way in which the stimuli were actually constructed (the fractal model is the correct one). Instead, the signal + noise model is a principle of perceptual organization and, to the extent that perceivers use such a principle, they misunderstand the principle underlying the fractal physical process.

There were two experimental questions. The first was simply whether people could discriminate between stimuli with different values of the fractal constant c. The second (if indeed people could make that discrimination) was the internal perceptual model that people used to make the discrimination.

First, Schmuckler and Gilden (1993) investigated the ability of listeners to discriminate between different fractal noises using variations in pitch, loudness, and duration. Stimuli were constructed for $1/f^0$, $1/f^1$, and $1/f^2$. The results demonstrated that listeners could discriminate among the three fractal processes using variations in pitch and loudness but not duration. Moreover, the overall range of variation (one octave versus three octaves) and the number of steps (13 versus 37) within the range did not affect the discrimination. To generalize these results to a wider range of fractal values, Schmuckler and Gilden (1993) constructed sequences with values of the exponent ranging from 0 to +3.9. Here the maximum sensitivity was in the range between 2 and 3, curiously, outside the value where most auditory sequences and visual scenes occur.

Second, given that people could discriminate among different fractal exponents, Gilden et al. (1993) attempted to model the perceptual process underlying that discrimination. They found that a signal + noise model best predicted the discriminations, even though the stimuli were not constructed according to a two-part structure. When people look at contours, they perceive an overall trend and superimposed noise. Moreover, people perceive the trend and noise as being independent, as two separate types of information. Now if the individuals must discriminate between two fractal representations, they can make use of the difference in the ranges of either the trend or the noise. The fractal structure that connects all levels of the roughness contour is not used to make the discrimination. People perceive as if there is a smooth contour that carries the noise even though the smooth contour and noise are one and the same.

Perhaps the reason that the perceptual model does not match the physical model is the close ecological connection between perception and action. There is no need to be able to specify the hierarchical structure of surfaces, but there is a great need to be able to traverse a rocky surface, and perhaps our sense of balance is best achieved by making "noisy" adjustments to smooth slopes.

All of the above strongly suggests that the coding in the auditory and visual systems is sparse and is based on a minimum population code. We should be hesitant, however, to argue that perceptual systems evolved in accordance with that principle. What is controversial is whether perception is most accurate for natural scenes which preserve the power law and in which the phase relationships that create edges and lines are maintained. Gilden et al. (1993) did not find this to be true, but the stimuli used were quite simple and not representative of natural environments.

To investigate whether detection is most accurate for power law scenes, Parraga, Troscianko, and Tolhurst (1999) followed a different procedure. They created a set of pictures that morphed between a car and a cow or between a man's face and a woman's face. They measured the Fourier spatial amplitudes of each picture and found that all followed the $1/f^c$ function. The authors then changed the $1/f^c$ function by either increasing the constant c to further reduce the higher-frequency components, creating blur, or decreased the constant c to whiten the image (i.e., to equalize the energy at higher frequencies). Both variations reduce the viewers' ability to distinguish between two morphs. On this basis, Parraga et al. argued that the visual system is optimized for the statistics of natural scenes.

Billock, Cunningham, Havig, and Tsou (2001) investigated the perception and discrimination of textures that varied in both the temporal and spatial power exponent. They constructed textures that could be represented as:

$$\text{Amplitude } (F_s, F_t) = K/F_s^{\beta}F_t^{\alpha}. \tag{3.14}$$

When both the temporal and spatial exponents were small (.2–.4), the textures seemed like fine dynamic noise. If the temporal exponent increased with a small fixed spatial exponent, the textures appeared to resemble waves in a viscous fluid. If the spatial exponent increased with a small fixed temporal exponent, the textures seemed to be composed of diffuse blobs that jittered rapidly. When both exponents increased together, the texture resembled coherent large masses that undulated very slowly. Interestingly, the authors commented that when the spatial and temporal exponents were within values found naturally, subjects tended to give real-world descriptions. Overall, the ability to discriminate between different temporal exponents decreased as the spatial exponent increased. That is, the movement of the large global blobs tended to mask small differences in the movements.

Summary

The basic question of this chapter is whether there are general design principles that underlie all the sensory systems and that yield efficient information transmission. There are several reasons for suspecting that such principles do not exist. First, there are the diverse properties of sensory stimulation, ranging from electromagnetic light energy to mechanical sound vibrations to odor molecules. The research discussed in this chapter makes use of sets of "naturalistic" stimuli, but the properties of those stimuli are not made explicit. Second, there are different kinds of redundancies, ranging from visual-spatial proximity to auditory harmonic relationships. Third, there are different scene properties, ranging from spatially or temporally bounded objects to unchanging or low-frequency smoothly changing surfaces or sounds. We might speculate that phase relationships are critical when the visual and auditory scenes contain spatially or temporally bounded objects or things, while they are unimportant for unchanging or low-frequency smoothly changing surfaces or sounds (A. Li & Zaidi, 2001). Moreover, occluding opaque visual objects hide each other, as opposed to multiple sound objects, which sum their frequency components when they occur simultaneously (multiple odors also sum). Fourth, there are context effects that can alter the perceptual qualities in all the sensory systems. Fifth, there are conflicting design objectives, ranging from maximizing information transmission to maximizing reliability.

Yet I come away with the sense that there is a coherent set of design principles that can unify perceptual processing and experience. First, there is the tuning of sensory receptors to sensory energy. Second, there is the hierarchical transformation of local processing to global percepts. Third, there are lateral circuits that remove redundancies. Fourth, there are feedforward and feedback circuits that tune sensory systems to the environmental context. Fifth, there are convergent and divergent circuits that seem to generate sparse coding that balances the need for maximizing transmission, reliability, and stability. These principles seem to complement the coding principles put forth by Eggermont (2001), discussed at the end of chapter 2. In a summary review, Simoncelli (2003) argued that the theory of efficient coding has served as a heuristic to motivate the investigation of the influence of the statistics of the natural environment on the statistics of the neural response. However, the principle of efficient coding cannot, by itself, explain the organization of sensory systems.

4

The Transition Between Noise (Disorder) and Structure (Order)

Let us start with the problem of defining texture. The word *texture* has the same Latin root as the word *textile*, and originally both words referred to the character of a fabric due to the quality and weaving of the threads. Texture was later generalized to refer to the surface characteristics of an object resulting from the quality and arrangement of the particles or constituent parts (Bergen & Landy, 1991). The surface characteristics have often been termed the visible grain, determined by variations in dimensions such as brightness, color, and shape. In common use, these parts or grain must be small compared to the object as a whole. Otherwise, the particles would determine the object's shape and not its texture. Two textures are different if they do not share the same grain (i.e., surface variation) or if they do not have the same statistical distribution (i.e., pattern of the grain). The difficulty is that all surfaces, however different from one another, can be said to have a texture, so that any inclusive definition becomes implausible. Moreover, the texture of any real object can be understood in terms of the object or surface that generated that texture (tree bark), or as an abstract visual design with a uniform or variable pattern. The lack of a comprehensive definition applicable to all qualities of texture is widely acknowledged (Gorea, 1995).

This chapter is broken into two broad areas. The first concerns the segmentation of visual scenes that are composed of arrays of discrete elements. The initial research made use of achromatic dots of differing brightness, while subsequent work made use of different micropatterns. For both types of stimuli, the goal was to develop statistical and physiological models that would predict the perceived segmentation. The second concerns the perception of surface characteristics. The term *surface characteristic* is used in its broadest sense to include visual contour and flow lines, auditory timbre, and visual symmetry.

Visual Texture Segmentation

Texture segmentation refers to the process by which a visual scene is broken into discrete enclosed areas or an auditory sound is broken into discrete sources. Each area or source is perceived against a background. This segmentation is based on differences in the grains, or in the distribution of the grains across space. It is assumed that such segmentation represents an early or even the initial stage in perceptual processing. Adelson put it elegantly: "vision is still stuff, rather than things" (quoted in Bergen, 1991, p. 121). Texture segmentation is presumed to take place at levels of representation preceding the construction of even simple objects (I reconsider this assumption in chapter 9).[1]

It is possible to identify two approaches. The first approach has been to attempt to identify textural features that lead to segmentation. The goal of initial experiments using random dot arrays by Julesz (1962) and subsequent experiments by Beck (1966) and Julesz using discrete elements (e.g., T, L, +) was to define the statistical properties that lead to the segmentation of the array. These experiments were attempting to create not a catalog of textures but a catalog of segmentation elements. These segmentation elements may not have any simple relationship to the textural features that underlie our perception of real objects.

The second approach has been to develop models of segmentation based on the conceptualization of visual cortical cells as localized spatial filters at differing frequencies and orientations (colloquially called *back-pocket models*). These filters process the visual input in parallel; the output of each filter is transformed in some nonlinear way (e.g., squaring), and then differences in the outputs are used to detect different regions (i.e., discontinuities in the arrays). There are many variants of these models: two or more levels of filters with differing spatial extents, mutual inhibition among adjacent filters, nonlinear transformations among levels, and local and global integration.

The two approaches are complementary. The feature extraction approach does not utilize the known properties of the auditory and visual systems to construct stimuli, but the features found inductively in traditional perceptual experiments would presumably be implemented in some fashion at one or

1. Chapter 9 also concerns grouping and segmentation. The difference is that this chapter is mainly concerned with the properties of discrete elements that are grouped together in nonoverlapping regions of the scene.

more cortical levels. For example, the spatial-temporal receptive fields of individual neurons or combinations of neurons might resemble those features. In contrast, the filter approach does not consider the statistical nor configural properties of objects in the environment, but the stimulus arrays that are clearly segmented by the proposed neural models would presumably be composed of the extracted features discovered in the segmentation experiments.

Features: From Visual Random Dot Spatial Arrays to Segmentation Elements (Textons)

To the Gestalt psychologists, the basic perceptual problem was that of segmentation, the process by which the entire visual field was broken into subunits (or alternately perceived as a whole). The Gestalt psychologists were not against analysis as commonly portrayed; in fact, they believed that the visual system segmented the field. What they rejected was the level of analysis based on elementary sensations. Experiments on segmentation still revolve around isolating the appropriate level of analysis. As described below, the search for that correct level led to a shift from studying the statistical properties of arrays of dots varying in brightness to studying the statistical properties of simple geometric forms.

Spatial Arrays of Dots

In one of the first experiments, B. F. J. Green, Wolf, and White (1957) constructed random dot matrices to investigate the discrimination of differences in dot density. They utilized a matrix with 128 × 128 dot positions and filled each position with either a white dot or a black dot based on a fixed probability. In a typical trial, two probabilities were selected (say .55 and .50). Then, either the 128 columns were partitioned into 8 blocks of 16 columns apiece and alternate blocks were filled in with dots at .55 and .50 probabilities, or the 128 rows were broken into 8 blocks of 16 rows and filled in with the same probabilities. The subjects simply judged whether the distribution of white and black elements varied in the columns or rows.

B. F. J. Green et al. (1957) found that the minimum difference in probability needed to achieve 75% correct judgments was about 8% for a duration of one-quarter s or less the difference, but only 5% for a duration of 1 s or more. Surprisingly, there was little difference in discrimination between the 1 s and the 4 s duration. One of the more interesting findings concerned the effect of the number of blocks on discrimination. There were five conditions with 2, 4, 8, 16, and 32 blocks with 64, 32, 16, 8, or 4 rows or columns respectively. For both experienced and inexperienced subjects, the best discrimination occurred for 8 blocks with 16 rows or columns apiece; performance decreased for 4 and 16 blocks, and decreased further for 2 and

32 blocks. Phenomenally, discrimination occurs by attending to the contours at the changes in probability. With 2 or 4 blocks, there are too few contour changes, while with 16 or 32 blocks there are not enough rows or columns to establish the contours. B. F. J. Green et al. pointed out that these results preclude an explanation purely based on brightness (luminance), because the identical brightness differences occur for each condition. Rather, the participants were responding to the emergence of consistent statistical differences between the blocks.[2]

Within a few years, Julesz (1962) began an extensive set of investigations aimed at discovering texture properties leading to segmentation. The majority of this work used an interesting amalgam of qualitative perceptual outcomes along with local and global quantitative statistical specifications of the stimulus properties. To measure perceptual segmentation, Julesz typically used a simple dichotomous go/no-go measure. Imagine that a simple geometric form like an X is repeated many times to form a rectangular array. This rectangular array is embedded at a random position within a bigger rectangular region created by repeating a different texture element like a +, and the observer's task is to judge whether the two regions defined by the texture elements spontaneously and effortlessly segregate (see example in figure 4.5). To Julesz, texture segmentation is necessarily characterized by the rapid "pop-out" (within 100 ms) of the region defined by the embedded texture element and therefore can be assumed to be preattentive, prior to focal attention and object or shape identification. If the identification of the region of the embedded texture element takes active search and scrutiny of all the texture elements, Julesz concluded that the two texture elements are not discriminable as operationally defined by segmentation. It is very important to note that the two elements taken in isolation are easy to discriminate. It is the regions defined by the elements that are not discriminable; that is, the figural contrast between elements does not create segmentation. I make use of this distinction between effortless direct perceiving and attentive cognitive perception throughout this chapter and the next one. It will prove relevant to a wide variety of perceptual outcomes, although it may not simply map onto physiological mechanisms.

To specify the properties of the stimulus array, Julesz and coworkers first made use of *k*-order statistics. Each *k*-order represents a different property of the array and can be understood in either conditional probability or geometric terms. These statistics are not restricted to any particular type of texture element.

2. MacKay (1965) pointed out an interesting illusion for random-dot patterns. After fixating on a single point for 10 to 20 s, the array comes to appear more regular and uniform. It is as if higher-level networks determining long-range form perception adapt and thereby lose the complex patterning.

$K = 1$: The first-order statistic is the probability that any dot in the array will have a certain brightness or luminance. In B. F. J. Green et al. (1957), there were only two levels of brightness (i.e., white or black) so that Pr(white) = 1 – Pr(black). Julesz (1962) used two to four levels of brightness (black, dark gray, light gray, white). Different probability distributions vary the overall brightness and contrast of the array, and this variable has been termed *spatial density* or *tonal quality*. Three random textures based on different probability distributions of 10 different gray levels are shown in figure 4.1. Different probability distributions create textures that yield easy segregation.

$K = 2$: The second-order statistic is the conditional probability between pairs of dots. Simply put, given the brightness of one dot, is the probability of the brightness of a second dot different than its probability of occurrence according to the $K = 1$ statistic? In figure 4.2, three examples of $K = 2$

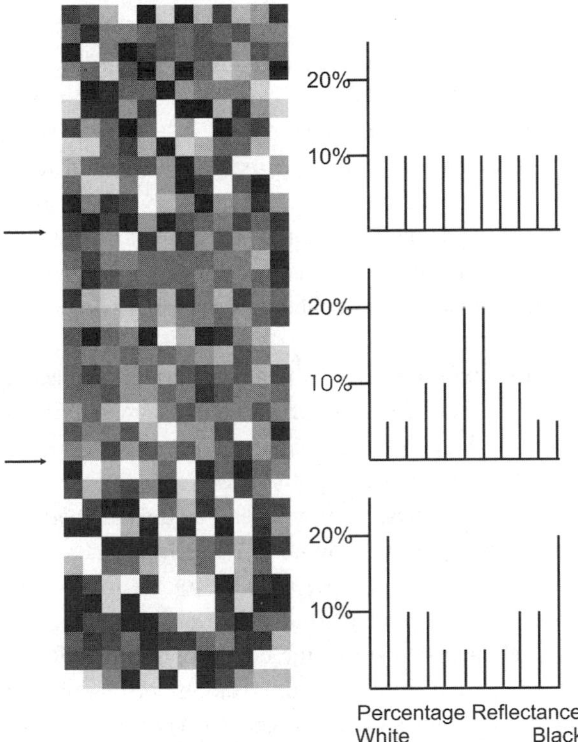

Figure 4.1. Texture differences due to $K = 1$ statistics of the reflectance of the individual squares in each 12×12 matrix. The y axis gives the percentages of each of the 10 different reflectance values. Differences in the $K = 1$ statistic generate rapid segmentation between the three matrices arrayed vertically, although the boundary is soft.

Figure 4.2. Differences in sequences due to the $K = 2$ statistic. In all sequences, the $K = 1$ statistic is identical. (A) $K = 2$: $\Pr(w \mid w) = \Pr(b \mid b) = 0.5$; $K = 1$: $\Pr(w) = \Pr(b) = 0.5$. (B) $K = 2$: $\Pr(w \mid w) = \Pr(b \mid b) = 0.6$; $K = 1$: $\Pr(w) = \Pr(b) = 0.5$. (C) $K = 2$: $\Pr(w \mid w) = \Pr(b \mid b) = 0.75$; $K = 1$: $\Pr(w) = \Pr(b) = 0.5$.

sequences are shown. In (A), the conditional probabilities equal the probability of occurrence (e.g., $\Pr[w \mid b] = \Pr[w]$), so that there is no predictability beyond the probability of occurrence, that is, $K = 1$. The texture would be random throughout, and by analogy to sound we would term it white noise ($1/f^0$). In (B) and (C), the conditional probabilities progressively differ from $K = 1$, and these particular second-order statistics will tend to generate short horizontal line segments of equal brightness due to the higher probability of dots of equal brightness following each other.

It is natural to think of the conditional probabilities referring to adjacent dots in the array, and in that case the second-order statistics create differences in what may be termed the granularity of the texture. To the degree that the second-order statistics predict the brightness levels among the dots beyond that of the first-order statistics, they will lead to distinct regions within the overall texture. The patterns in figure 4.2 clearly segment into regions.

However, it is not necessary to think of the second-order statistics as referring only to adjacent elements. Instead, the conditional probabilities could refer to dots separated by any number of intervening dots and in any number of possible directions. Julesz and coworkers (1984) captured these possibilities by methods of integral geometry. Imagine a line of specific length, a dipole. Two textures will have identical second-order statistics if random "throwing" of such lines on the two textures results in equal probabilities of falling on two dots with the identical brightness. (For $K = 1$, the analogous procedure is random throwing of one dot on two textures. Those textures will have the same first-order statistics if the probabilities of falling on a particular texture element are identical.)

Second-order statistics are identical to autocorrelation statistics, and thus to the frequency spectrum. This identity allows us to compare results from visual texture patterns to auditory noise patterns. For example, in a following section on repeated noise segments, we will show that the auditory system can pick up the predictability between individual amplitudes in ongoing noise generated by repeating noise segments up to 1 s in duration. For both the auditory and visual systems, there is a temporal separation or spatial separation limit to the ability to make use of the second-order predictability. Below these limits, perception is effortless and spontaneous; above these limits, perception requires scrutiny and calculation.

$K = 3$ and higher: The higher-order statistics involve the predictability of one dot based on the combination of the values of two or more other dots. In conditional probability terms, for $K = 3$ using adjacent dots at positions $i - 1$, i, and $i + 1$: $\Pr(X_{i+1}|X_i, X_{i-1})$. We can argue that third-order predictability occurs to the extent that this probability differs from $\Pr(X_{i+1} \mid X_i)$. For example, $\Pr(w|w) = 0.60$ and $\Pr(w|w,w) = 0.75$. As for $K = 2$, the third-order statistics can refer to the geometry of dots at different orientations and distances. Here, the appropriate geometric figure is a triangle with specific lengths of sides. By analogy, two textures have identical third-order statistics if the vertices of such randomly thrown triangles have the identical probability of all three vertices falling on dots with identical brightness levels. Higher-order statistics incrementally increase the number of dots used for prediction. For $K = 4$, three dots are used to predict a fourth, and the geometric figure is a rectangle; for $K = 5$, four dots are used, and the geometric figure is a pentagon, and so on.

Julesz began with random dot patterns to eliminate all familiar cues and constructed textures in terms of the hierarchy of k-order statistics. If the $K = 1$ statistics are equal, will two textures with different $K = 2$ statistics effortlessly break apart; if the $K = 1$ and $K = 2$ statistics are equal, will textures with different $K = 3$ statistics effortlessly break apart, and so on. The experiments were constructed so that only the highest-level *k*statistic differed to ensure that it was the higher-order statistic that created the segmentation.

From the start, it was clear that differences in the first-order statistic (i.e., the dot density) lead to segmentation, as illustrated in figure 4.1, and thus confirmed the results of B. F. J. Green et al. (1957). The perceived edge between the two textures is "soft" and "winding" because the brightness difference between the textures at the edge would be subject to chance variation in the lightness levels. It also was obvious that differences in the second-order statistic, the granularity, would lead to segmentation (see figure 4.2). But at that point, examples of segmentation between two textures that had identical first- and second-order statistics, but different higher-order statistics, could not be found.

These outcomes led to Julesz's conjecture that the visual system could not make use of third-order contingencies and that any two textures that had identical lower-order statistics could not create effortless segmentation. What this means is that the visual system does not detect differences in the phase spectra of the two textures. This conjecture did not seem likely to be correct because visual edges are due to the in-phase relationship of the spatial frequency components, as shown in chapter 3. Moreover, even at this point, there were many counterexamples to this conjecture that were explained away in terms of unique clusters of points that might form extended lines or equal brightness triangles or geometric shapes. For example, changes in the texture that lead to different clusters of bright dots will lead to segmentation, regardless of the order statistics. Metaphorically, the visual system acts like a slicer; it creates clusters from dots of similar brightness, but it does not create clusters based on predictable sequences of brightness that interleave values. Thus, if we describe brightness levels going from 1 to 5, the visual system will split apart a linear sequence like 13233123124554544555 but not the sequence 64144614615232253253 as illustrated in figure 4.3, even though both have identical statistical properties in terms of *k*-order statistics.[3]

Segregation Micropatterns

These outcomes forced the realization that effortless texture discrimination is not based on the statistical analyses of brightness distributions of individual points, but involves a kind of preprocessing that extracts and connects neighboring points with similar brightness values. It is the spatial arrangement of the correlations, and not merely their statistical strength, that is crucial for the detection of texture differences (Victor & Conte, 2004). As a result, Julesz and colleagues moved from random dot textures and began to create micropatterns that consisted of 4 to 12 black dots or short lines that could be specified in terms of their second- and higher-order statistics. The

3. Yellot (1993) and Victor (1994) provided contrasting interpretations of the *k* statistics. Yellot argued that the statistics refer to specific textures, so that any two textures that have identical $k = 3$ statistics are by definition equal. In contrast, Victor (1994) argued that the statistics refer to an ensemble of textures (as in information theory) so that two specific textures, while coming from ensembles with identical statistics, might in fact be easily discriminable. From this latter perspective, it does make sense to investigate whether observers can detect higher-order textural differences. However, in most tasks the observer must distinguish between two textures, each defined by ensemble statistics. Thus, the perceptual difficulty is determining the ensemble statistics from a single sample. Tyler (2004) suggested that observers intuitively employ a roving sampling window to measure the properties at different regions and then employ a decision rule to judge whether the two regions come from the same ensemble.

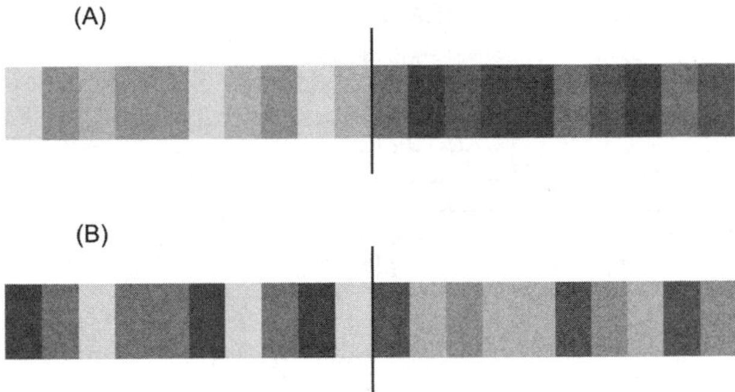

Figure 4.3. The visual system will segment predictable sequences that "slice" brightness levels but cannot segment the identical predictable sequences that interleave brightness levels. (A) Segmentation based on brightness (slicer); (B) segmentation that cannot be based on brightness.

experiments were analogous to those using the random dot textures. A small area created by repeating one micropattern replaced the equivalent area in a larger area based on a different micropattern. The subjects still judged if the small area effortlessly popped out of the larger area. Examples are drawn in figure 4.4.

As found for the random dot textures, the *k*-order statistics were unable to predict which pairs of textures would break up into regions and which ones would not. Even though all of the micropatterns could be easily discriminated apart if presented two at a time in isolation, the majority of pairs could be separated in arrays only by carefully attending to each micropattern in turn. To put it differently, discriminability did not predict segmentation. The conclusion was that it was the local gestalt configuration of the micropatterns that generated the effortless segmentation.

If a generalizable statistical representation does not work, then the only remaining strategy is to catalog those configurations that produce segmentation, and later attempt to relate them to known physiological mechanisms. Julesz termed each of these configurations *textons* (these have been termed *textels* or *texels* by other authors) and defined them in terms of conspicuous local features. The most important static texton is elongated "blobs" (rectangles, ellipses, lines), with features defined by color, angular orientation, length, and width. Less clearly defined textons are based on the number of line ends or terminators, and on concepts like corner, closure, and three-dimensional orientation (see figure 4.4). For dynamic visual stimuli, texton features include flicker and motion. Julesz (1995, p. 134) admitted, "what these textons are is hard to define" and went further to argue that it is only the density of the texton features that matters for segmentation. It is the difference in the first-order statistic that draws attention,

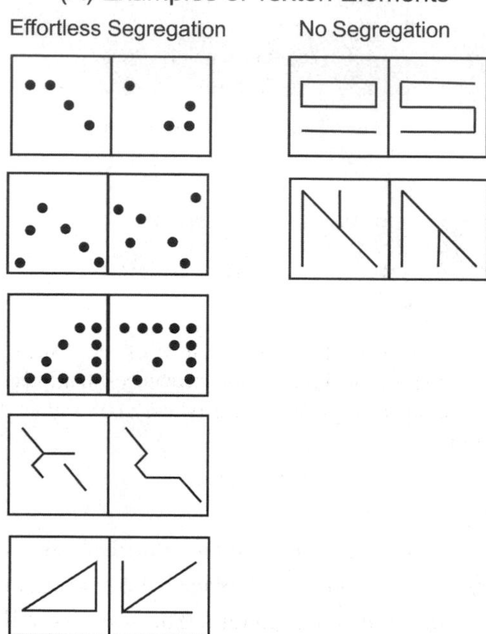

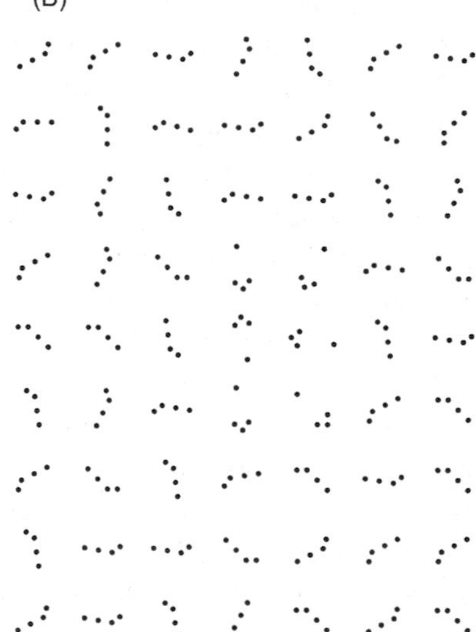

Figure 4.4. (A) Five examples of micropatterns that support segregation and two micropatterns that do not. (B) An example of a stimulus in which a small rectangular array of one type of micropattern (a corner texton) is embedded within a larger array of another type of micropattern (a linear texton). The textons are randomly rotated within each array. Adapted from "Toward an Axiomatic Theory of Preattentive Vision," by B. Julesz, 1984, in G. Edelman, W. E. Gall, and W. M. Cowan (Eds.), *Dynamic Aspects of Neocortical Function* (pp. 585-612). New York: Neurosciences Institute.

but it is focal attention that generates the actual spatial position (unknowable from preattentive processes only) and it is also focal attention that provides the glue to connect adjacent or distant configurations.

To summarize at this point, differences in the densities of local texton features draw attention to those areas. But, to make use of Adelson's

Figure 4.5. Texture segmentation of simple geometric shapes is determined by orientation, and not by the perceived similarity of the shapes. The Ts are judged to be more similar to each other than to the L-like corner. The 45° Ts segregate although Ts and Ls are judged most dissimilar. Adapted from "Textural Segmentation," by J. Beck, 1982, in J. Beck (Ed.), *Organization and Representation in Perception* (pp. 285-317). Hillsdale, NJ: Erlbaum.

distinction once again, it is still stuff. Large changes in the positions of adjacent features are not noticed. To convert stuff to things requires focal attention. The focal attention binds dots and lines into the micropatterns and the micropatterns into figural regions. Local features segment textures, not global-order statistics

In moving away from a statistical to a geometrical explanation, this work converged on parallel research done by Beck (1982) that started from a classical Gestalt perspective. Beck began with the working hypothesis that the similarity between distinct geometric shapes determins the grouping into discrete regions. Thus, Beck's arrays were composed of shapes like lines, angles, Ts, and crosses because it was assumed that the differences in the local geometrical properties of the shapes determine segmentation (these shapes are analogous to the later textons of Julesz). In one clear example, Beck made use of upright Ts, 45° Ts, and upright Ls (figure 4.5). Based on the concept of effortless grouping, the 45° Ts strongly split off from the other figures even though the two Ts were judged most similar in shape; orientation was more important than similarity. What is common to the work of both Julesz and Beck is the conclusion that texture segmentation is based on simple physically defined properties that do not necessarily reflect the similarity between the elements.

Nothdurft (1997) showed that segmentation is not based simply on local first-order densities. Instead, perceptual segmentation occurs when there is a sufficiently large difference between regions in terms of luminance, texton,

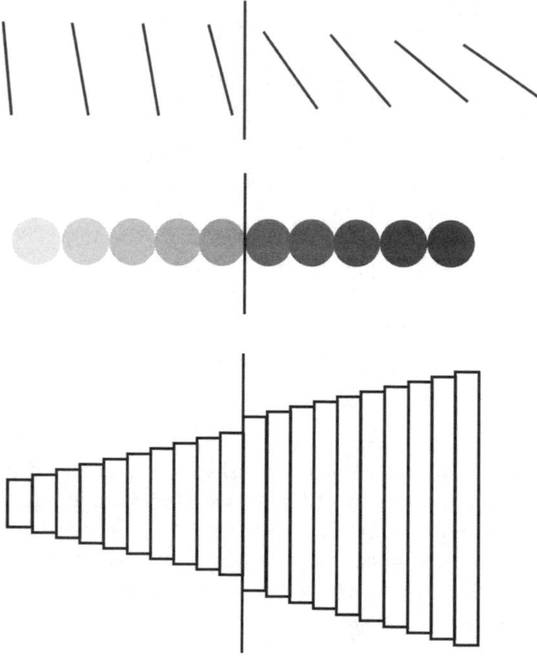

Figure 4.6. Segregation occurs when there is a discontinuity in a feature gradient. Discontinuities produce segregation for a variety of features.

size, orientation, or any other feature that could yield segmentation. It is the degree of contrast that is critical. As shown in figure 4.6, segmentation into perceptually coherent regions will occur where the orientation, brightness, and vertical size gradients undergo rapid change. The ratio of the change between elements at the perceptual boundaries must be significantly greater than the change between elements within each coherent texture region. Thus, the differences required for segmentation are relative to the variations within each texture region. Moreover, there are configural effects based on the orientation of the elements at the texture boundary (Ben Shahar & Zucker, 2004).

Nothdurft (1997) also demonstrated that the features can reinforce or interfere with segmentation based on the spatial arrangements. For example, orientation segmentation is made much harder if luminance contrast would lead to segmentation of partially overlapping areas (see figure 4.7). In similar results, Snowden (1998) found that irrelevant variations such as those due to color can interfere with segmentation tasks based on area defined by the elements. The reaction times increased by 33% due to irrelevant variations. In contrast, irrelevant dimensions do not increase reaction time (less than 10%) when searching for a single element (e.g., a vertical line in an array of 45° lines) so that it appears that the irrelevant dimensions bring

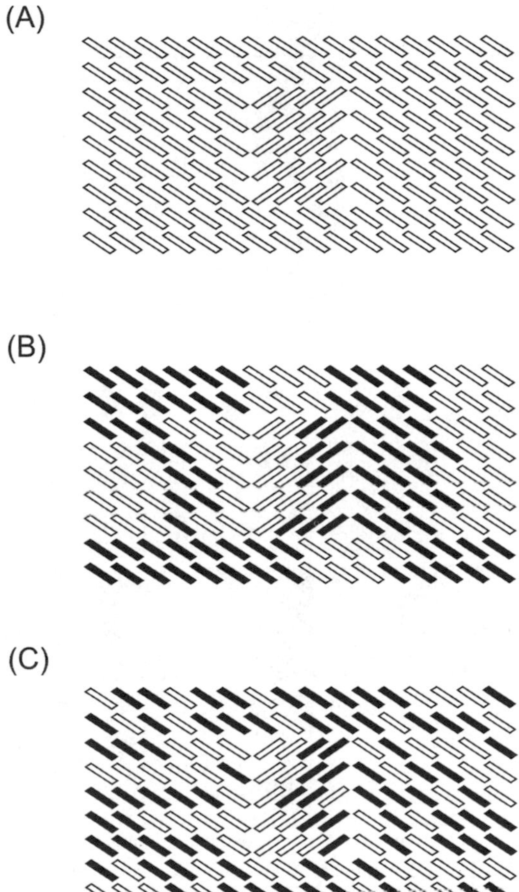

Figure 4.7. Incompatible combinations of orientation and brightness make segregation ambiguous. In (A), segregation due to orientation is effortless. In (B), segregation by orientation is pitted against segregation by brightness and is difficult to perceive. However, in (C) the random variation in brightness does not interfere with segmentation by orientation to the same degree because the random variation does not create an alternative grouping. Adapted from "Different Approaches to the Coding of Visual Segmentation," by H.-C. Nothdurft, 1997, in M. Jenkin and L. Harris (Eds.), *Computational and Psychophysical Mechanisms of Visual Coding* (pp. 20–43). Cambridge, UK: Cambridge University Press.

about poorer performance by creating alternative grouping arrangements that would not affect searching for a single item.

Filter Models: Back-Pocket Models

The above research making use of line segments at differing orientations seems to call for an explanatory model in terms of the simple and complex

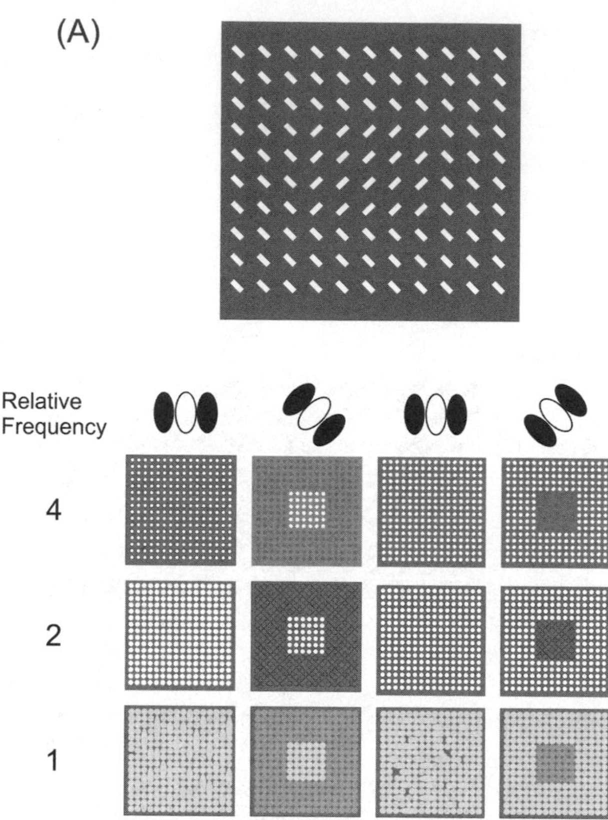

Figure 4.8. Back-pocket models of segregation can isolate differences in orientation (A) and shape (B). Each dot in every response matrix represents the response of one frequency × orientation receptor at that location. In (A), receptors oriented at 45^0 and 135^0 segment the short lines. In (B), the middle frequency x orientation receptors segment the "+'s" from the "L's" and "T's", but do not segment the "L's" from the "T's." Adapted from "Computational Modeling of Visual Texture Segregation," by J. R. Bergen and M. S. Landy, 1991, in M. S. Landy and J. A. Movshon (Eds.), *Computational Models of Visual Processing* (pp. 253-271). Cambridge, MA: MIT Press.

cells found in the visual cortex (V1). These kinds of models, the so-called back-pocket models of texture segregation, share a common form.[4] All start by assuming that the visual array is filtered by a parallel set of oriented linear cortical cells. To represent each retinal location, the models use anywhere from 16 individual cortical cells that vary in orientation and spatial frequency (4 orientations × 4 spatial frequencies) to 180 cortical cells (18 orientations × 10 frequencies). The output of each orientation × frequency filter is squared to produce an energy measure and then, in the

4. These are termed *back pocket* because researchers pull the basic form out of their back pockets to make sense of new examples of texture segregation.

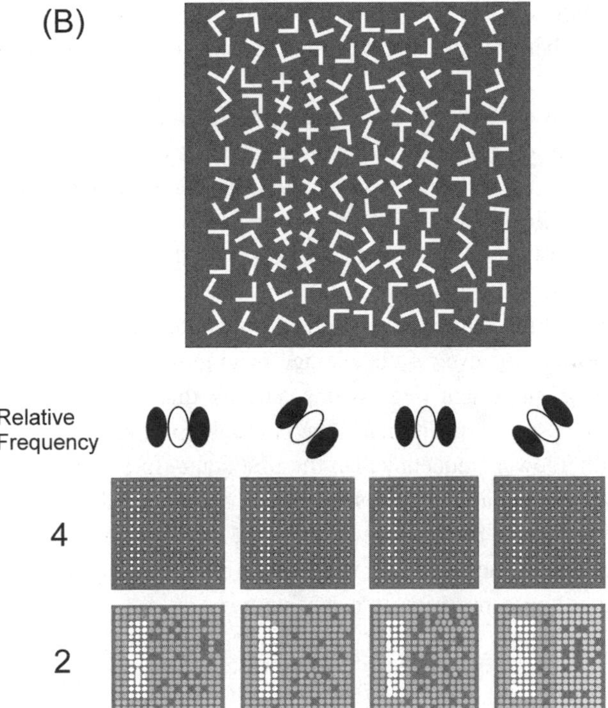

Figure 4.8. Continued

simplest versions, the outputs from cells with the same spatial frequency and orientation are summed together in local areas. The visual field is broken into nonoverlapping enclosed regions at places where large differences in the outputs exist; the outputs within regions are relatively equal. Two examples of this process using a simple model with 4 orientations × 4 spatial frequency filters per location are shown in figure 4.8. In the first example, the outputs of the filters oriented at 45° and 135° appear to represent the perceived segregation, particularly at higher spatial frequencies. In the second example, the outputs of the filters at the middle spatial frequencies at all orientations appear to represent the perceived segregation. The texture model does not differentiate between the characters L and T in figure 4.8B.

These models that make use of one filter stage are limited to texture patterns in which the different orientations occur in nonoverlapping spatial areas. They cannot predict segregation if the basis for segregation is the contrast or the patterning of the orientations within spatial areas (A. Sutter & Hwang, 1999). For example, consider the texture pattern in figure 4.9. In this pattern, each 2 × 2 unit contains two vertical orientations and two horizontal orientations, although in two different arrangements. Because the elements are the same, the outputs of vertically and horizontally oriented filters within any 2 × 2 region would be identical, and yet there is a clear segregation between the regions with the different arrangements of the elements.[5]

To account for this sort of segregation, the simple version of the back-pocket model incorporates two additional stages. The first of these additional stages (the second in the model) transforms the outputs so that decreases in firing rates below the baseline level are made equal to the baseline (rectifying), or the decrease is squared so that decreases and increases in firing rate are made equal. The effect is to make the output from regions with high contrast variability greater than from regions with low contrast variability, even if the average brightness is the same (e.g., black-and-white gratings generate greater outputs than a dark gray/light gray grating). The second additional stage is made up of another set of oriented filters with a lower frequency than the first stage. In essence, the first-stage filters pick up the rapid variation within a region, and the third-stage filters pick up the slower brightness variation (i.e., the carrier frequency). These linear-nonlinear-linear (LNL) models are able to predict how hard it is for observers to segment various types of textures.

Summary

What makes this work problematic is the nagging question of whether any of it really taps into texture perception. Textures of real surfaces do not consist of arrays of discrete patterns that appear to be embossed on a flat background. Instead, such textures are composed of elements that appear to represent interleaved edges and continuous surfaces that tend to change shape smoothly. As described in chapter 3, the edges arise due to in-phase spatial frequencies, and smooth surfaces arise due to changes in the patterning and density of the elements. What makes the work on micropattern segregation important is the impetus it gave to attempts to create realistic neural models to simulate why certain pairs of features led to segmentation while other pairs did not. Yet even here I am skeptical that there is a definable set of primitives that create segmentation. Nothdurft (1997) and Ben Shahar and Zucker (2004) have demonstrated that segmentation is a function of the overall context, so that segmentation is based on contrast, the argument made in chapter 1.

5. These sorts of textures have been termed *non-Fourier* or *second-order patterns* because perceptual discrimination cannot be due to brightness differences encoded by the simple cortical cells. The outputs of the simple cortical cells are hypothesized to be transformed by a nonlinear function, and that output is further filtered by oriented cells with a lower spatial frequency. If the nonlinear transformation squares the outputs, the result resembles a complex cortical cell in which brightness levels above and below the background produce the same firing rate increase. Second-order patterns are discussed further in chapter 5.

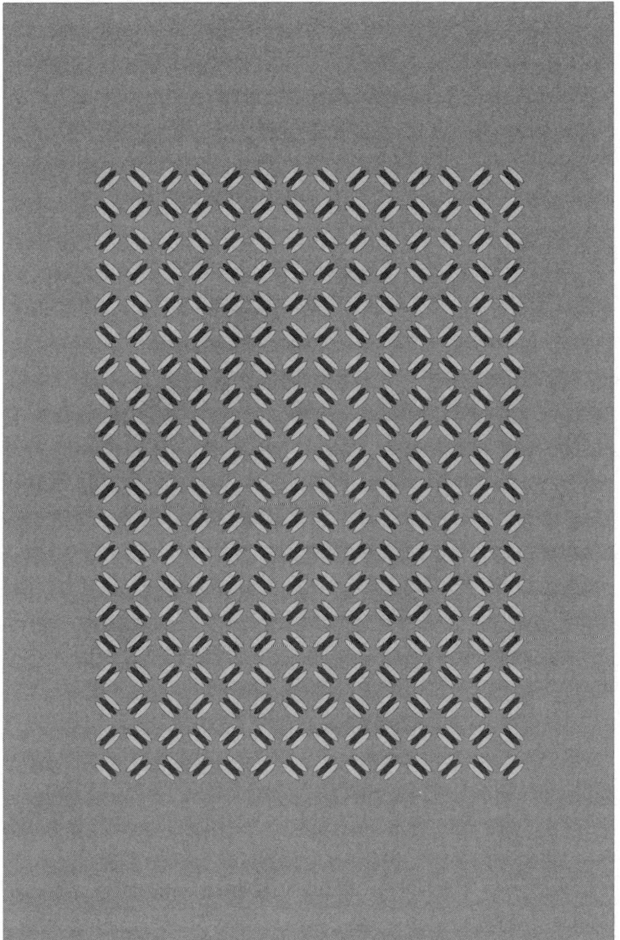

Figure 4.9. An array that cannot be segregated based simply on brightness differences (termed *non-Fourier textures*). Segregation requires a nonlinear transformation of firing rates that effectively encodes contrast and not brightness along with a second linear filter tuned to a lower spatial frequency. Adapted from "A Comparison of the Dynamics of Simple (Fourier) and Complex (Non-Fourier) Mechanisms in Texture Segregation," by A. Sutter and D. Hwang, 1999, *Vision Research, 39*, 1943–1962.

Surface Textures

Visual Glass Patterns

Glass (1969) introduced a class of texture patterns in which a random dot pattern is duplicated; the duplication is transformed by rotation, magnification, or translation and then superimposed onto the original random pattern. If this process is done over and over again, the superposition of the original and all the duplicates generates a global "streaky" percept in which flow lines appear to connect the corresponding points in the original and transformed duplicates. If the duplicates are rotated a small amount, then a concentric pattern emerges. If the duplicates are expanded, then a starlike radial pattern emerges, and if the duplicates are moved horizontally or vertically, then horizontal or vertical lines emerge. You perceive the global structure created by the flow lines, not the original or duplicated random arrays. Several examples are shown in figure 4.10.

The perception of the patterning is global, based on finding the correspondences between "matched" dots. Dots become matched when there are

(A) Four 12° Counterclockwise Rotations

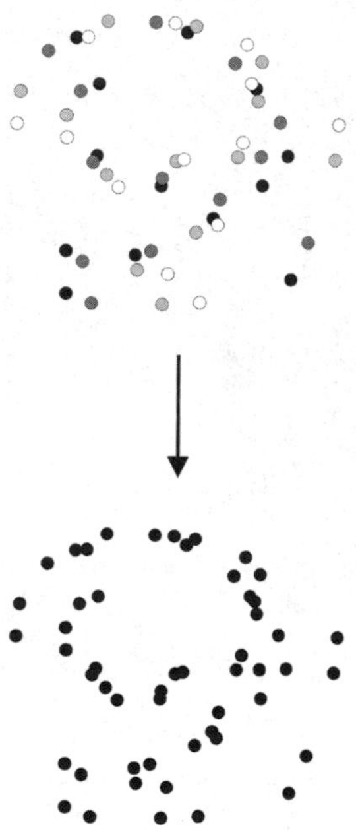

(B) Linear *x-y* Glass Pattern

Figure 4.10. The construction of a rotation Glass pattern is shown in (A). The initial pattern is black; the first rotation is dark gray; the second rotation is light gray; and the third rotation is white. Even with different brightness levels, the rotation flow lines are easy to see. If all the dots are made black, the rotation is more obvious. Another type of Glass pattern based a linear *x-y* shift is shown in (B).

consistent orientations within subregions of the field. Matched dots rarely are the closest ones. Looking at any small area through an aperture destroys the pattern, because the global correspondences are lost. All that remains are inconsistent accidental pairings. The individual features and the global pattern are independent, because the pattern emerges even if short line segments at different orientations replace the dots. Glass patterns resemble continuous, global natural textures. Both the perception of Glass patterns and segmented texture regions from different micropatterns occur very rapidly (about 100 ms) without eye movements, and thus classify as effortless and preattentive.[6]

R. K. Maloney, Mitchison, and Barlow (1987) measured the strength of the perceived global pattern by adding unpaired random dots to the dot configuration until that pattern disappeared and the dot texture began to look random. They found that Glass patterns were remarkably stable. Consider a dot and its match, generated by a small rotation. Concentric patterns were visible even if there were 6 to 10 random dots lying closer to an original dot than its real match. Several examples are shown in figure 4.11. Thus, the visual system does not depend on a nearest neighbor analysis; instead, it pools local orientations over an extended region. Variable-orientation pairings that emerge by chance in small regions must be disregarded. The important unresolved problem is the scale of that integration.

Theoretically, each type of Glass pattern should be equally discriminable because the autocorrelation between matched points will be identical no matter how the patterns are duplicated and superimposed: the local statistics are identical. However, this is not the case because rotation (concentric) and magnification (radial) transformations are easier to perceive than translation (parallel) transformations, and vertical translations are easier than horizontal translations (Jenkins, 1985; see figure 4.10). In addition, although the autocorrelation is still the same, the Glass pattern does not emerge if the pattern and its duplicate are opposite contrasts to the background (e.g., gray background, black [original] and white [duplicate] dots; Glass & Switkes, 1976), if the elements of a pattern and its duplicate differ strongly in energy

6. Glass patterns are similar to auditory iterated rippled noise stimuli (Yost, Patterson, & Sheft, 1996). To construct these stimuli, a segment of random noise is delayed by *d* ms and added back to the same noise. If this process is repeated *n* times, the autocorrelation of the amplitudes at the delay *d* equals $n/n + 1$. The resulting sound has two components: a tonal component with a buzzy timbre sounding like an airplane propeller with a pitch at $1/d$ ms and a noise component sounding like a hiss. The strength of the tone component is proportional to the autocorrelation, and after 16 iterations the sound is nearly completely tonal. The parsing of the sound into tone and noise is effortless and irresistible, and another example of preattentive figure-ground organization. Thus, for both Glass patterns and iterated rippled noise, the original stimulus is duplicated at a fixed distance or time interval and then added to the original. The strength of the tonal percept increases with the number of iterations and the strength of the global visual pattern would also increase with the number of spatial shift and superimposed iterations.

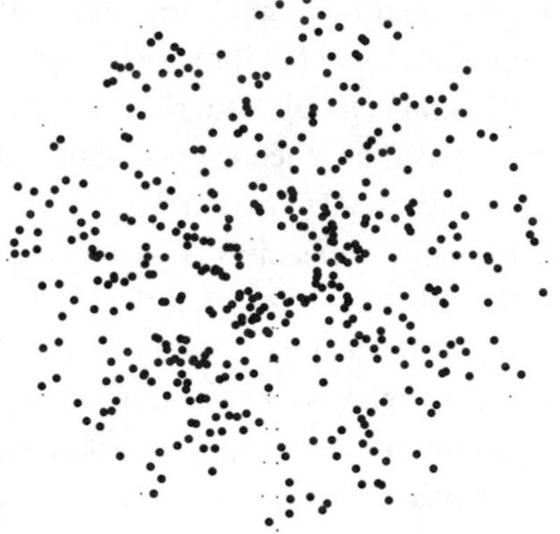

Figure 4.11. Camouflaging circular Glass patterns based on 75 pairs of points by adding 300 randomly placed elements (A). A similar example of camouflaging a radial Glass pattern is sketched in (B). The ability to detect the circular and radial patterns demonstrates that observers must integrate orientation over a wide region and not rely on a nearest neighbor heuristic. Adapted from "Limit to the Detection of Glass Patterns in the Presence of Noise," by R. K. Maloney, G. J. Mitchison, and H. B. Barlow, 1987, *Journal of the Optical Society of America, A, 4*, 2336–2341.

(J. A. Wilson, Switkes, & De Valois, 2004), or if the duplicate is shifted beyond a maximum value specific to each type of transformation. Thus, the visual system does not merely calculate the autocorrelation across the entire field, because none of these three limitations would affect the value of the autocorrelation. This is another argument for a localized integration area and demonstrates that all types of pattern pickup are constrained by space, time, and energy limitations as described in this chapter and in chapter 1.

Prazdny (1986) has generated interesting cases in which two Glass patterns are superimposed and presented at the same time. For example, one

Figure 4.11. Continued

pattern could be generated by rotation, creating concentric flow lines, and the second by expansion, generating radial flow lines. If the dots in both patterns have identical energy (i.e., roughly size × contrast), then it is impossible to see both patterns. If the energy of one pattern is reduced, then the more energetic pattern is perceived easily while the weaker pattern can be perceived by focused attention.[7]

The most interesting outcomes occur when comparing single Glass patterns composed of dots with different energy levels to superimposed Glass

7. A similar breakdown of the perceived structure occurs if two iterated rippled noise stimuli with different delays are added together. For example, if one stimulus is constructed with a delay of 10 ms (a pitch of 100 Hz) and a second is constructed with a delay of 8 ms (a pitch of 125 Hz), the tonal percept is destroyed. The tonal percept is maintained only when the delays are multiples (2/4/8 ms) so that the pitches would be harmonically related (Handel & Patterson, 2000).

patterns in which each pattern is composed of dots with different energy levels as above. Consider the former case: we start with a random dot array, create a duplicate in which each dot is reduced in size and contrast, rotate the duplicate, and then superimpose the two. Even though the dots are different, the concentric lines appear, so that the patterning is achieved by integrating across energy levels. Now consider the latter case: One Glass pattern is defined by the stronger dots and a different one is defined by the weaker dots. In this case, the pattern segregates; there is no integration across energy levels (see figure 4.12). This first outcome does not support the notion of a lightness "slicer" suggested by Julesz (1962) above to account for texture segmentation. Instead, the effects of the energy differences depend on the overall patterning among the dots.

The perception of the Glass patterns is a second-order effect ($K = 2$); the observer must detect conditional probabilities that may involve different separations and orientations. For example, with a rotation, the separation between matched dots, signifying the consistent change in orientation around the circumference, varies as a function of the distance from the center. Pairs of points with the same separation and distribution of orientations that are randomly placed around a circle do not lead to the perception of concentric circles.

Researchers (H.R. Wilson & Wilkerson, 1998; H.R. Wilson, Wilkerson, & Assad, 1997; Seu & Ferrera, 2001) have compared the discriminability of concentric, radial, hyperbolic, parallel, and spiral Glass patterns. Their results indicate, as found previously, that concentric and radial patterns are easier to find in embedded random noise than parallel or spiral patterns in the equivalent amount of noise. Concentric and radial patterns contain paired dots at all orientations, and the authors argue that the greater sensitivity to concentric and radial patterns is due to the global pooling of the information at all orientations necessary to perceive those transformations. In contrast, parallel patterns contain matched dot pairs at only one orientation, so that there is only local pooling. (However, Dakin & Bex, 2002, demonstrated that with experience, viewers are able to learn to integrate parallel translation patterns over a wider spatial area.)

Their proposed model is envisioned to consist of three stages, each stage being localized in a higher-level visual cortical area. The first step occurs in V1, the initial processing region. Here each region of the stimulus configuration is analyzed by a set of discrete orientation filters that measure contrast at different visual angles. The second step occurs in V2. Here the outputs from V1 are rectified to produce a positive neural response, and that is followed by a second stage of orientation filtering to create a more localized orientation response (LNL model). Finally, the third step occurs in V4, where the orientation information at all angles from a localized retinal area

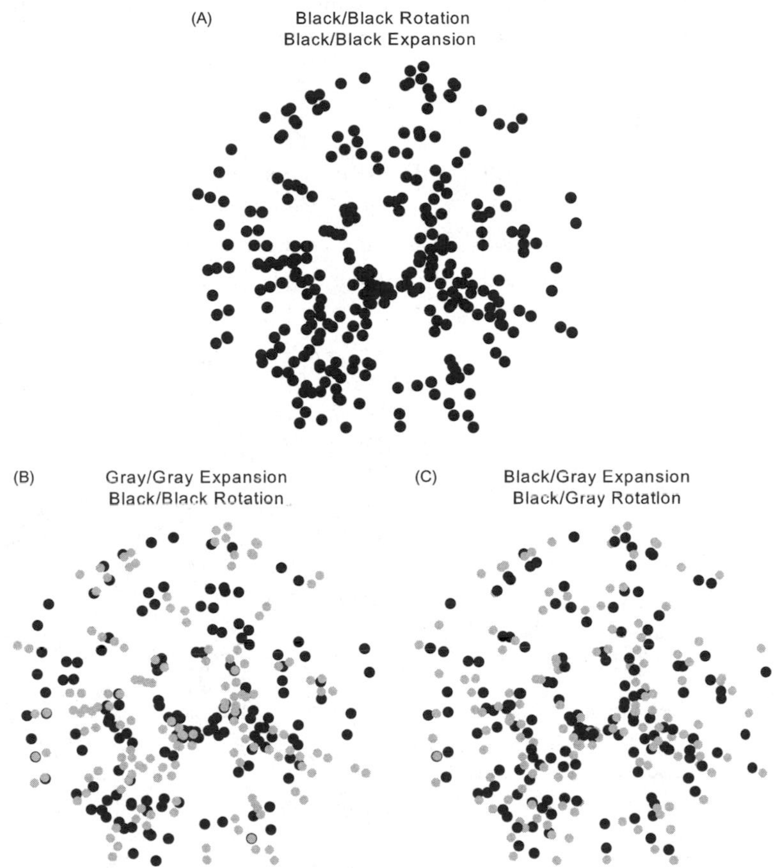

Figure 4.12. Glass patterns can be perceived if the elements are different brightness levels (figure 4.10) or dot sizes so that there is integration across energy levels. All of the Glass patterns here were constructed with one transformation of the original random pattern. If the original and transformed pattern have the same brightness, it is very difficult to perceive the two different Glass patterns (A). If the two patterns have different brightness levels, it is relatively easy to perceive the two patterns separately (B). However, if both patterns have two corresponding levels (i.e., original in black, transformation in gray), again it is almost impossible to perceive the two patterns (C). Adapted from "Some New Phenomena in the Perception of Glass Patterns," by Prazdny, 1986, *Biological Cybernetics, 53*, 153–158.

found in V2 is summed. In this model, the inputs from different orientations are weighted differentially. The weighting function in figure 4.13 is optimized to detect + shapes. Other weighting functions could be optimized to detect other shapes, such as crosses. As described in chapter 2, neural units in V4 respond to concentric and radial patterns, and Wilson and coworkers hypothesized that it is this three-stage process that sums orientation information to create those cells, as illustrated in figure 4.13.[8]

Visual Contours

The perception of Glass patterns illustrates the sophisticated ability of the visual system to find statistical regularities that exist within a noisy image. The extraction of the structure, although seemingly instantaneous, must involve complex feed-forward and feedback processes among many neural

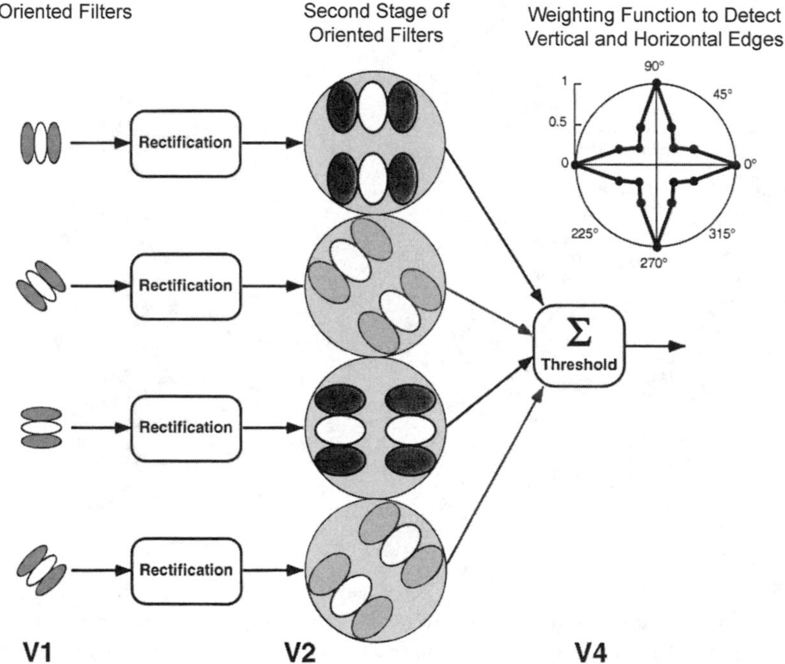

Figure 4.13. A neural model for the detection of Glass patterns. The sensory excitation at each retinal region is filtered by a set of differently oriented filters. The four pathways shown differ by 45°. The output of each pathway is rectified, and then the nonlinear rectified output is further filtered at the same orientation but a lower frequency. The excitation from all the pathways is weighted, shown by the contrast of the even symmetric filters, and summed. Different weighting functions could be optimized to detect circular, radial, and linear patterns. From "Detection of Global Structure in Glass Patterns: Implications for Form Vision," by H. R. Wilson and F. Wilkerson, 1998, *Vision Research, 38*, 2933–2947. Copyright 1998 by Elsevier Science Ltd. Reprinted with permission.

8. There is an obvious similarity between the back-pocket models for texture segmentation and the H. R. Wilson and Wilkerson (1998) model to account for the perception of the Glass flow lines. Moreover, both are similar to the models shown in chapter 5 to account for the perception of second-order motion.

regions. The process must have many false starts and dead ends where the initial segmentations of the elements to form edges do not yield the contours of coherent objects. There are many interpretations of any image, so that the open question is why some interpretations of the image are preferred over others.

As described earlier, the Gestalt psychologist's answer was in terms of electrical force fields in the cortex that acted to integrate the elements. The forces minimized energy so that the resulting percept maximized regularity, but that does not necessarily imply maximizing simplicity.[9] One of the minimizing energy rules was termed *good continuation*, the perceptual tendency to continue a smooth line at an intersection with another line (Pizlo, Salach-Golyska, & Rosenfeld, 1997). An alternative answer to the prevalence of good-continuation perceptual judgments is in terms of the regularities found in natural scenes. Do smooth lines that continue at intersections actually bound single objects? Do perceptual contour judgments match those regularities? If so, then good continuation, and the Gestalt laws in general, can be understood and predicted from the properties of auditory and visual objects.

W. S. Geisler, Perry, Super, and Gallogly (2001) measured the co-occurrence of edges in natural scenes. They first identified each edge in a photograph and then calculated the separation distance and the difference in orientation between every pair of edges. The most probable co-occurrence occurred between two nearby edges that were approximately parallel. The two edges often formed a continuous edge (for a curving edge, the most probable edge continued the curve). W. S. Geisler et al. (2001) argued that this outcome makes good sense because physical processes such as erosion, shading, and perspective would create continuous or parallel edges. The next step was to categorize the edge elements as belonging to one object or to different objects. If the concept of good continuation has any value in segmenting a natural scene, then any two nearby and parallel edge elements should more likely be part of one object than parts of two different objects. If this is true, and it was, then the best perceptual bet would be to assume that a smoothly changing edge bounds a single physical object. What this analysis does is provide a likelihood ratio explanation to good continuation: Good continuation works because that is the way objects are.

Several experiments have investigated the detection of contours in noisy scenes (W. S. Geisler et al., 2001; Hess & Field, 1999; Pizlo, 2001). In

9. Originally, the dynamics of the field forces were used to explain why things looked the way they did, essentially without reference to the external world. Then, in what I think is a brilliant book, Kohler (1969) argued that there is no difference between the dynamics of cortical field forces and the dynamics of physical processes in the world. This in a sense closed the circle and created an isomorphism between the perceptual world and the physical world.

nearly all of the individual experiments, the viewer must judge which of two images contains a contour. As might be expected, detection improves when the number and density of the contour elements increases, and detection becomes poorer as the change in angle among the elements increases. If the path angle is greater than about 30°, detection approaches chance levels. For those contours, observers cannot find a smooth continuation connecting the two legs of the path.

The conceptual models for contour detection begin by assigning local associative strengths among adjacent elements based on distance and orientation. These local strengths become the seeds for "growing" the contour, combining pairs of elements into one elongated contour. For example, W. S. Geisler et al. (2001) assumed transitivity: If A is grouped with B, and if B is grouped with C, then A and C are assumed to be on the same contour. Altmann, Bulthoff, and Kourtzi (2003), using human brain imaging techniques, found that both early retinotopic cortical areas (V1, V2) and the later occipitotemporal area are involved in the detection of contours created by discrete elements. The temporal pattern of activation suggested that feedback from higher cortical areas might modulate the processing in the early areas.

Has the visual system evolved to make use of good continuation as an organizing principle because it maximizes the probability of detecting physical objects?[10] This is exactly the same logic used in chapter 3 to argue that the visual system evolved to maximize mutual information. In that case, I was reluctant to conclude that the auditory and visual pathways evolved to maximize information transmission by matching power law frequency distributions, and I am similarly reluctant here.

Auditory Texture: From Auditory Noise to Pitch

Auditory noise refers to a nonrepetitive signal in which the amplitude varies randomly. In terms of the frequency spectrum, the amplitudes and the phases of the frequency components are randomly distributed. The power across the frequency components may be flat, creating white noise, or may vary, creating pink or brown noise (see chapter 3). Auditory noise and visual random dot arrays are equivalent: the $K = 1$ statistic (in terms of amplitude or luminance) may vary from example to example, but the $K = 2$ statistic always equals the $K = 1$ statistic. In other words, there is no predictability between time points or between spatial points. Each auditory

10. Good continuation of pitch, intensity, spatial location, and so on are also important organizing principles for hearing. The same ecological argument can be made. This is discussed further in chapter 9.

and visual noise example does have a specific quality, and Pollack (1975) demonstrated that listeners can learn to identify individual auditory random noise segments.[11] All of the segments had identical long-term frequency spectra, so that the listeners must have been picking up unique short-term sound qualities in each segment.

In the work described below, I generate a short segment of noise that does not create the perception of any pitch, and then investigate the outcomes when that single noise segment is repeated or when different noise segments are interleaved and repeated. The analogous visual presentation would be to create a random dot array with a specified $K = 1$ statistic, and then place repetitions next to each across a page (or to create two arrays with the same $K = 1$ statistic and alternate them across a page). The perceptual problem, then, is to discover the repeating units by abstracting the duration or the spacing of the repetitions.[12]

If we generate a sound by concatenating or butting together short segments of noise, there are many interesting possibilities. At one extreme, we could repeat the exactly same segment from two to many times. (Using letters to represent different segments, this would create AA to AAAAA. . . .) At the other extreme, we could make each segment different, to create ABCDEF. . . . Between these extremes, we could present one segment twice, present a different segment twice, and then either revert back to the original segments (e.g., AABBAABB . . .) or continue to present novel segments (e.g., AABBCCDDEE . . .). The naive view would be that the particular noise segments, the duration of the segments, and the sequence order did not matter. Each segment contains only a random order of amplitudes, and butting such segments together should generate only a longer but still noisy sound. However, this view misses the essential point. Repeating the identical noise segment does create an internal structure: The amplitude variation in each noise segment is identical and, as the outcomes presented below illustrate, the hearing system is exquisitely tuned to pick up that predictability. The degree of predictability does of course depend on the particular noise segments and the way that those segments are combined. The ability of listeners to pick up that predictability must depend in part on the characteristics of the auditory system, in part on general cognitive limitations such as the duration of memory, and in part on the skills and training of the listener.

Consider one extreme, the repetition of the same noise segment: AAAAAA. We can depict each noise segment by a series of 10 random

11. The ability to distinguish among random noises is discussed again in chapter 6.

12. I do not know of any auditory research that has attempted to discover auditory textons. If I attempted to use the strategy employed in creating the back-pocket model, I would make use of the findings about auditory spectral-temporal receptive fields described in chapter 2. For example, A1 cells that respond to frequency glides or amplitude and frequency modulations would make up the first-stage linear filters.

numbers, say 7652013586, with each digit representing the amplitude for 1 ms. Thus, in this instance each segment is 10 ms, or equivalently 100 segments per second. When these 10 are repeated six times, it generates the sequence:

765201358676520135867652013586765201358676520135867652013586.

Knowing how we constructed the order, it is easy to pick out the repetitions and perceive the sequence as six repetitions of 10 numbers. The autocorrelation function is zero for all time delays (i.e., time lags) except for the delay equal to the 10 ms length of the segment. The autocorrelation is perfect if correlating time n to time $n + 10$: 1 with 11, 5 with 15, and so on. (It is also true that the autocorrelation is perfect between n and $n + 20$, but that longer span is usually not reported perceptually.)

Now consider the other extreme, a sequence of different noises: ABCDEF. Here, the autocorrelation will be zero for all time lags. (It is true that there probably will be positive autocorrelations at some delays in short sequences, but these are simply due to the characteristics of the particular noise segments, and the autocorrelation will go to zero as the sequence is lengthened with new random noise segments.)

The interesting cases, as usual, lie between the two extremes. To move one step up from a random sequence, we could repeat each noise twice to create AABBCC. Again using 10 random numbers to depict each segment, we would get something like:

765201358676520135863754204805375420480508422689530842268953.

Now the autocorrelation function flip-flops. At the 10 unit delay, there is perfect predictability as you step through the sequence from element 1 to 10: 1 is the same as 11, 2 is the same as 12, and so on, until you hit element 11. Elements 11 through 20 are uncorrelated to elements 21 through 30 because they are different noises. The autocorrelation snaps back to 1 starting with element 21 and going through 30, and then reverts back to zero from 31 to 40. Thus the overall autocorrelation is going to be +0.50, the average of 1.00 and 0.00.

A more complex case occurs if we alternate doubled noise segments of different durations. Suppose we alternate two identical 10 ms segments (labeled by letters) with two identical 8 ms segments (labeled by numbers) and continue this process using different samples of noise. Such a sequence would be labeled AA11BB22CC33. . . . In this case, the predictability oscillates between a 10 ms and an 8 ms delay, interspersed with regions of no predictability that continue throughout the sequence.

The perceptual question is whether listeners can pick up the internal structure and resulting predictability and, if they can, what are the limits? In all of the examples given above, the essential problem is that of correspondence.

Conceptually it is as if the listener must try different delays or offsets of the sequence relative to itself to maximize the predictability of corresponding elements.

As mentioned above, the $K = 2$ statistic is equivalent to the autocorrelation statistic. Using autocorrelation to explain the pickup of temporal (or spatial) information is useful for all types of sound waves that repeat over time or spatial arrays that repeat over space. For both listening and looking, there is a spatial or temporal separation that maximizes the conditional probability and the autocorrelation. As described in this chapter, the pickup of these probabilities is bounded in time or space; any predictability that exists beyond a temporal duration or spatial separation is not perceived effortlessly.

Before starting, it is useful to review some traditional views about tonal and nontonal pitch perception. Normally, tonal pitch occurs between the frequencies of 20 and 20000 Hz. Within this region, the sound is continuous and has an obvious low-to-high attribute. However, there is a distinct difference in the quality of the sound (i.e., timbre) between tones in the 20–6000 Hz range and tones in the 6000-20000 Hz range. The tones in the lower frequency range have a much fuller, richer musical sound. (However, at the lower end of this range, 20–60 Hz, complex sounds from instruments like the piano often have a weak pitch.) Tones in the higher range have a much thinner sound. This difference in quality may be due to a shift in the neural coding of frequency. In the lower range, individual neurons phase-lock to distinct points in the sound wave. In the higher range, the ability to phase-lock disappears, and frequency would be encoded only by position on the basilar membrane.

At frequencies less than 20 Hz, the perception becomes one of a series of discrete clicklike sounds, even though the sinusoidal wave is still continuous. The clicks appear to go together to form a coherent rhythm down to rates of 0.5 Hz, or one click every two seconds. At slower rates, each click seems separate from the rest, and the perception of a rhythm disappears. At frequencies greater than 20000 Hz, the mechanical properties of the ear limit the ability to track or follow the rapid vibrations, and those frequencies are not heard.

What this means is that we will need to consider at least three frequency regions. The first two are within the tonal region, and the empirical question is whether there is a difference in the perception of repeated noise in the range where phase-locking is possible and in the range where phase-locking is impossible. The third is in the frequency range below tonal perception where discrete sounds are heard. R. M. Warren (1999) termed this frequency region *infrapitch*.

Because we do not have any direct understanding of how the auditory system picks up the repeating structure, it makes more sense to describe some outcomes and see how these might delimit possible neural mechanisms based on the timings between spikes. I will start with the continuous repetition of a single noise segment and then consider the perceptual outcomes for complex sequences constructed by combining different noise segments.

Sequences Created by Repeating the Identical Noise Segment

To repeat: we generate one random noise segment and then recycle that segment so that there is no separation between the end of one and the beginning of the next repetition. Even though each of the segments sounds like a random noise, *shhh*, the surprising outcome about such sequences is that for a wide range of segment durations, we hear a buzzy tone with a distinct pitch. The pitch is determined by the duration of one noise segment (e.g., if the duration is 2 ms, the pitch comes from the 500 Hz fundamental frequency). The tonal quality of the buzzy tone is determined by the amplitude of each harmonic that occurs at a multiple of the fundamental frequency (e.g., the amplitude at 1000, 1500, 2000 Hz, etc.). Remarkably, the tonal percept is relatively immediate, and there is little or no time lag to the tonal perception.

Consider first the tonal perception range. If the segment duration is less than 0.0125 ms, so that the fundamental frequency is greater than 8000 Hz, the repeating noise sounds much like a pure sinusoidal wave, because the first harmonic (16000 Hz) is nearly at the frequency limit of the auditory system. This means that any sample of noise will sound identical when repeated at that rate. If the segment duration is between 0.0125 and 10 ms (i.e., durations that yield frequencies from 100 to 8000 Hz), the repeated noise segments produce richer tones due to the perceivable harmonics. Due to the harmonics, different repeated noise segments can create quite diverse sounds. For durations greater than 10 ms (less than 100 Hz), the sounds undergo several transitions. From 10 to 15 msec (100-70 Hz), the repeated noise generates a noisy pitch that sounds continuous or smooth. At longer durations up to 50 ms (70–20 Hz), the noisy pitch appears pulsed or accented; it is not continuous. For durations between 50 and 250 ms (20–4 Hz), the repeated noise is heard as motorboating (Guttman & Julesz, 1963). There is a regular beat at the repetition rate, much like a low-frequency staccato whoomp-whoomp. It is a noisy repetition, not a continuous noise. At even longer durations of 250–1000 ms (4–1 Hz), it is possible to hear the sequence as a noisy global percept described as a whooshing sound, or it is possible to detect repetitive features such as clanks and thumps that seem to occur in discrete parts of the segment. This latter possibility is in contrast to the motorboating range, in which component features are not heard.

Up to these durations, perceiving is direct and effortless, much like the visual texture segregation described previously. The percepts are global even for motorboating and whooshing sounds, based on the entire waveform of the noise segment. As stated above, different noises yield distinct timbres and features, and this demonstrates that while the autocorrelation can give a measure of the possible predictability, by itself it does not provide a complete description of the perception because the autocorrelation would be identical in all cases, and yet very different phenomena occur.

For tonal durations greater than 1000 ms (1 Hz), the nature of perceiving changes. Perceiving becomes constructive. Initially, all one hears is continuous noise, and the listener must search for distinct repeating sound bits that reoccur regularly to create a simple rhythm (Limbert, 1984). These rhythmic features may be labeled (e.g., bonk, old dishwasher) or may not. Such features can disappear and then reappear or new features can begin to be heard, but the essence of the percept is that of continuous noise with superimposed rhythmic features. There is a fair degree of variability across subjects in the choice of feature and resulting recycling point, although subjects tend to make the same choice on repetitions of the same repeated noise (Kaernbach, 1992). As could be expected, longer durations lead to a wider choice of features. Although we might describe the identification of a repeating feature as cognitive, listeners did not verbally label the features; they insisted that they did better by remembering the rhythm of the noise and the overall sound quality of the features. For very long repeating noise segments at durations of 10, 15, and 20 s, R.M. Warren, Bashford, Cooley, and Brubaker (2001) argued that the listeners are not really picking up the periodicity of the repetition but are really engaged in a vigilance-type task in which they are trying to detect each reoccurrence of the selected feature.

I come away with the impression that perceiving is sensibly continuous and yet it yields qualitatively different phenomena. The critical factor is the duration of each noise segment. At durations that normally lead to tonal perception (50 ms or shorter), the repeating noise segments take on a tonal quality with a pitch equal to the inverse of the duration. At any duration, the repetition of a different noise segment will create the same pitch, but a different timbre. At longer durations up to 1 s, the perception gradually transforms into an atonal rhythmic pulsing that may contain discrete sound features. Beyond the 1 s duration, the noisy aspect predominates, and the listener must actively hunt for repeating sound features that mark the repetition.

I do not think that this transition from the effortless perception of repetition to the active detection of repetition merely represents a memory limitation, because we find the analogous transition in a variety of situations. One way to think about this transition is that it represents a limitation on coherence or connectedness. In part, I am basing this on rhythmic perception: Discrete tones separated by 1.5 s or less are heard as a unified rhythm, while discrete tones separated by a greater interval are usually heard as disconnected tones. Another way to think about this transition is that it represents a limitation on the detection of correspondences. Up to durations of 1 s, the auditory system seems to automatically find the best time separation to match elements so as to maximize the predictability of the sequence. Beyond that duration, the automatic matching fails, and the listener must create the matches from derived features. The identical correspondence problem occurred for the visual Glass patterns described above, and we will see in chapter 5 that the same correspondence problem occurs for visual spatial movement. Within a distance range, the visual system automatically matches parts of objects, but beyond that distance the perceiver must derive the matches.

Sequences Created From All Different Noise Segments

A sequence created from different noise segments (e.g., ABCDEF, where each letter represents a different segment) does not produce a pitch, regardless of the length of the segments. However, two such sequences based on different segments of noise can sound different due to the individual segments and the serendipitous correlations that are created between the end of one segment and the beginning of another. Needless to say, perceptually there are no segments. In my informal listening, the only time I can hear a difference between sequences such as ABCDEF and FDBECA is when a feature pops up in one order and not the other.

If the two sequences are made up of the same segments but played in different orders (ABCABC versus ACBACB), as R.M. Warren and Bashford (1981) reported, it is easy to discriminate between the two. In this work, each segment was 50 ms so that the repeating units in each sequence (e.g., ABC or ACB) would be 150 ms (6.67 Hz). The ability to discriminate between such sequences may require some explanation. The differences in the sound quality among noise segments are due to the random variation in the sound pressure amplitudes across their duration. This variation yields different magnitudes and phases of the harmonics (from the Fourier analyses) that compose the segment, and this variation creates the different sound quality. But given that the sound is continuous and changing, where does a listener break up the ongoing pressure variation into segments? In these sequences, there is a repeating unit of 150 ms, either ABC or ACB. For such sequences, I hear the same motorboating reported by Guttman and Julesz (1963). There is a noisy sound with a beat corresponding to the repeating unit, which suggests listeners are breaking up the sequence into temporal units of 150 ms (notice that there are three ways of constructing the 150 ms units) and deriving a running average harmonic structure within those units. If the two sequences sound differently, then these differences would be due to serendipitous correlations that are created between the end of one unit (composed of three segments) and the beginning of another. In general, for different orderings of a fixed set of segments, such correlations would change erratically, and we would expect that discrimination would be quite variable across the different orderings and across different sets of noise segments.

Sequences Created by Repeating and Alternating Different Noise Segments

Sequences made up of the identical noise segment (e.g., AAAAAA) maximize the internal predictability, so that they yield the strongest perception of a complex tone. Sequences made up of different segments (e.g., random noises ABCDEF . . .) minimize the internal predictability so that they yield only the perception of continuously varying noise. Between these end points are more complex sequences constructed by joining together different noise segments, each of which is repeated a set number of times. I will describe some preliminary work using naive listeners that illustrates the perceptual change from noise to tone as a result of varying the number of repetitions of the noise segments.

The first case to consider is constructed by repeating one noise segment a number of times, then repeating a different noise segment with the identical duration the same number of times, and continuing this process, choosing a different noise segment each time. At one extreme, we get 2 repetitions per segment, AABBCCDDEE . . . , and at the other end we get 10 or more repetitions:

AAAAAAAAAABBBBBBBBBBCCCCCCCCC . . .

which approaches the repetition of one identical segment.

R. M. Warren, Bashford, and Wrightson (1980) and Wiegrebe, Patterson, Demany, and Carlyon (1998) have investigated the two-repetition case: AABBCC. Their results were very consistent in finding a noisy tonal perception that does not change its sound very much across different samples of noise. With two repetitions, the autocorrelation oscillates between 1 within the repetition of one noise and 0.0 between noise segments, so that overall the autocorrelation equals 0.50. At this level of internal structure, the timbre differences that arise from different segments are not perceived.

In preliminary work, I explored the perceptual effects created by increasing the number of repetitions. For two repetitions, the tonal strength was weak but roughly equal for segment durations from 0.125 ms (8000 Hz) to 32 ms (31 Hz). There were no timbre differences between the different noise segments at any duration. As the number of repetitions increased, the tonal percept strengthened, the noisy percept weakened, and differences between durations (i.e., frequencies) emerged. By four repetitions per segment (AAAABBBBCCCCDDDD . . .), the autocorrelation equaled 0.80 due to the correlation of 1.0 within the four repetitions and 0.0 between the different noise segments. There still was a noisy component, and the overall sequence sounded gritty and rough. At this point, the different timbre associated with each noise segment became apparent, and the sequence seemed to vary in quality at the same pitch as the segments changed. However, the gain in tonal strength and the increase in the perceived variation in timbre for four repetitions were much less for segment durations below 0.5 ms (frequencies above 2000 Hz). By eight repetitions per segment (the autocorrelation equaled 8/9), the noisy component disappeared, except for the 0.125 ms durations (8000 Hz). For this segment duration, at which the second harmonic at 16000 Hz was presumed not to affect perception, the tonal strength did not grow at all up to 12 repetitions and the segments did not appear to change quality. The pitch strength for sequences of identical noises also reached its maximum at eight repetitions, so that there was no difference between changing the noise segment every eight repetitions and continuously repeating the same noise segment.

It is interesting to contrast these results with those from sequences of alternating noise segments (e.g., AAAABBBBAAAABBBB . . .). If we start with the simplest case, ABABAB . . . , listeners perceived the sequence as being made up of the repeating unit AB, not of alternating A and B segments. Thus the pitch was one half the pitch that would have resulted from A or B. The entire sequence was heard as completely tonal, and the tonal quality did not change. As the number of repetitions increased (e.g., from AABBAABB to AAAABBBBAAAABBBB), the percept changed as the perceived repeating unit shifted back to the individual segments. The buzzy noise changed quality due to the different noises and seemed to warble back and forth. This shift had two effects, as illustrated in figure 4.14.

First, initially the AABBAABB construction was more tonal than the AABBCCDD construction. The tonal component decreased in strength as the number of repetitions increased due to a shift from perceiving the repeating unit as [AB] or [AABB] to perceiving the individual segments [A] in [AAAA] and [B] in [BBBB] as repeating. In contrast, for the AABBCCDD construction, the tonal component consistently increased as the number of repetitions increased, so that by 8 to 12 repetitions there was no difference in the tonal strength between the two kinds of sequences.

Second, I asked listeners to judge the warble in the sound, and that is shown in figure 4.14B. For the longer-duration segments (e.g., 8 ms segments), there was a strong sense of timbre alternation at even 2 or 4 repetitions, and any difference between ABAB and ABCD sequences in the strength of alternation disappeared after about 8 to 12 repetitions. For the

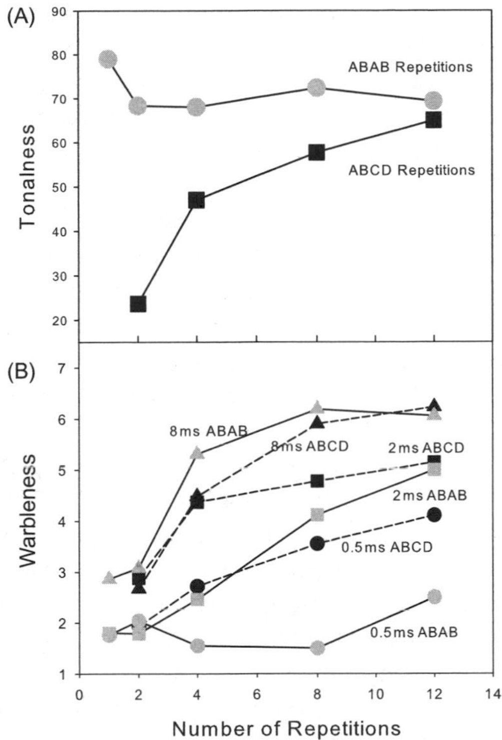

Figure 4.14. The tonal strength (A) and degree of warble (B) for repeating random noise segments.

shorter-duration segments, the reverse was true. Listeners were more likely to maintain the combined AB segment as the repeating unit, so that the timbre did not vary (e.g., the sequence AAAABBBBAAAABBBB was perceived as the repetition of [AAAABBBB]). For example, for 2 ms segments (500 Hz), the strong perception of alternating timbres for ABAB sequences occurred only for 12 or more repetitions (e.g., in shorthand notation 12A, 12B, 12A, 12B) but the perception of timbre changes for ABCD sequences occurred for 4 or more repetitions (e.g., 4A, 4B, 4C, 4D). There was a perceptual tendency to hang onto the perception of one repeating segment until it produced such long-duration segments that the perception of a strong pitch became problematic. At that point, the perception of warble began, and its strength grew as the number of repetitions increased further. A more extreme example occurred for the .5 ms segments (2000 Hz). If the segments alternated, it took more than 48 repetitions (48A, 48B, 48A, 48B) before the perception of warble occurred. Thus, it appears that the fundamental factor in determining the tonal perception for ABAB sequences is the number of repetitions × the duration of each segment: roughly, if the number of repetitions × the duration of each segment is greater than 24, then the perception of timbre warble occurs.

In chapter 5, I discuss visual random dot kinematograms (RDK) that closely correspond to the repeated noise sequences described here. RDKs are typically constructed by first generating a random two-dimensional array of dots (either white dots on a black surround or vice versa). This array becomes the first frame presented to the subject. In the second frame, a subset of the dots is moved laterally the identical short distance (the empty space left behind is filled in with another random array of dots). If the timing between the two frames is correct, observers report seeing the subset of dots move coherently. As soon as the second frame remains constant, the subset of dots fades back into the entire array and essentially becomes invisible.

Let's make the correspondences clear. For both repeated noise and RDKs, we start with a randomly generated stimulus: a random sequence of amplitudes for the repeated noise stimulus and a random array of dots for the RDK stimulus. Then we repeat the entire noise segment in time or repeat a subset of dots in time and space. In both cases, the perceptual system isolates the repeating unit and creates an object, a tonal percept, or an organized subgroup of moving dots. What differs between the two is that the entire noise segment is repeated, while only subsets of the dots are moved.

We can make the two stimuli even closer by adding a random noise to the repeated noise stimulus. Now any segment consists of the repeating segment plus a random segment of noise, so that across the entire sequence each segment is different (e.g., the first segment would be A + N1, the second segment would be A + N2, and so on, where N1, N2 . . . represent the added random noise; of course this is logically equivalent to simply adding continuous noise). The added random noise should mask the tonal percept by weakening the perception of the autocorrelation between segments. Thus, the listener must pick up the identical segments embedded in the segments + noise sequence in the same way the observer must pick up the identical subset in the subset + random dot array. It should come as no surprise that listeners have no trouble in hearing the tonal percept embedded in the noise. In fact, it is almost impossible to simply hear the sound as continuous noise (remember that it is very difficult to mask Glass patterns).

Sequences Made Up of Repeating Segments With Different Durations

We can create more complex sequences if we alternate the duration of the repeated segments. If we represent the segments based on one duration by letters and the segments of the second duration by numbers, a typical sequence with four repetitions per segment would be:

AAAA1111BBBB2222CCCC3333.

As found above, there is a gradual perceptual change as the number of repetitions increases. For two repetitions (e.g., AA11BB22CC33), there is a slight sense of a complex tone created by the two durations. For four repetitions, the two pitches become more apparent, although both seem to occur at the same time. You can shift attention to either pitch, but there is no perception of alternation. However, by eight repetitions, the two pitches appear to alternate, and it is quite easy to anticipate the changes. It is interesting to note that the perceptual changes occur at about the same number of repetitions found for sequences in which all segments had the identical duration. It may be that the tonal strength is weaker for the minimum case of two repetitions, but beyond this there is little evidence that the perception is any more difficult.

A similar effect was found by Whitfield (1979) using discrete pulses to create the perception of pitch. Whitfield created two pulses with interelement intervals of 4.7 ms (termed A) and 5.3 ms (termed B). If the former is repeated continuously the resulting frequency is 214 Hz, and if the latter is repeated consistently the frequency is 187 Hz. Whitfield created alternating sequences ranging from ABABAB . . . to 10A, 10B, 10A, 10B. . . . The perceptions were identical to those found for the random noise segments. For ABABAB or AABBAABB . . . , listeners perceived a steady tone at the average frequency of 200 Hz. For 4 to 6 repetitions of A and B, listeners perceived a steady tone with a flutter, and only at 10 repetitions and beyond did listeners hear two alternating tones.

Sequences Made Up of Repeating Identical Segments Alternating With Random Segments

We can further weaken the internal structure by alternating repeating identical segments with random segments. (Here I restrict the discussion to segments of identical length. For example, one such sequence could be AAAABCDEFFFFGHIJ. . . .) For these sequences, the autocorrelation is equal to $(N - 1)/2N$, where N is the number of repetitions. The autocorrelation can only approach 0.5 as the number of repetitions increases, so that we would expect a weaker tonal strength.

In fact, the tonal strength is weaker for these sequences. With 4 repetitions as shown above, there is only a weak perception of pitch and noise that seems to extend throughout the sequence. By 8 repetitions, the perception is of an alternation between the tonal repeated identical segments and the random noise segments. But the tonal part is still noisy and rough.

It is clearly not as tonal as the above sequences that contain strings of identical noise segments. By 12 repetitions, the tonal part no longer sounds noisy, and the tonal strength matches a sequence of identical noise segments. This is about a 50% increase in the number of repetitions necessary to generate a nonnoisy tonal repetition.

Repetition and Symmetry

In terms of picking up the correlated structure found in pattern repetition (translation in space or time) and pattern reflection, hearing and seeing are complementary. As described above, the emergence of pitch from pattern repetition is nearly always effortless and rapid. But it is extremely difficult to perceive temporal symmetry. We could take a segment of random noise (A), reverse it (A^r), and then construct the sequence A A^r A A^r A A^r . . . or the sequence AAAA A^r A^r A^r A^r. The symmetry of A and A^r would not be perceived. Instead, the A A^r A A^r A A^r sequence would have a pitch determined by the sum of A and A^r (i.e., twice the duration of A) and a timbre based on [AA^r]. Composers have written music in which a melody is played forward and backward, but listeners do not perceive that reversal (although the symmetry is seen easily in the written score).

In contrast, the perception of spatial repetition is extremely difficult for random dot patterns. As can be seen in figure 4.15, it is very hard to perceive that the four quadrants are identical. It is possible to discover the identity by focusing on serendipitous micropatterns and testing whether those micropatterns are found in all quadrants. This clearly resembles listeners trying to find distinctive sounds and then listening for them to repeat when the period is very long.

But the visual perception of bilateral symmetry is rapid and effortless for random dot patterns. As is clear from figure 4.15, symmetry about the vertical axis is easier to detect than symmetry about the horizontal axis, and it is much easier to detect symmetry in central viewing (foveal) than in peripheral viewing. The extent to which the symmetry is perceivable from the centerline will depend on the particular stimulus. Corrupting the symmetry only along the vertical axis can disrupt the perception of symmetry even though the rest of the pattern is symmetrical and, conversely, inserting a symmetrical vertical axis can lead to the illusion that the entire pattern is symmetrical.

However, the detection of bilateral symmetry can be difficult for arrays using elements of different colors, sizes, orientations, or spatial frequencies. Huang and Pashler (2002) suggested that observers judge whether each value of one dimension is symmetric one by one. For color, observers would first judge whether the red squares are symmetric, then judge whether the blue squares are symmetric, and so on. Thus, the time required

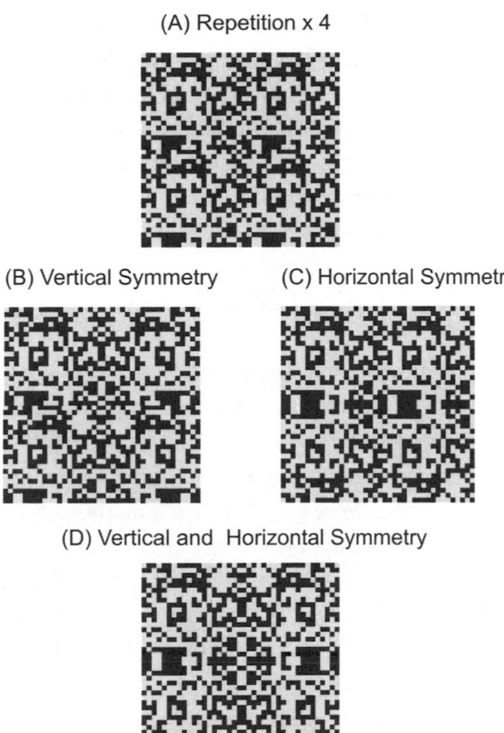

Figure 4.15. The perception of visual repetition is very difficult. It is possible to see the fourfold repetition in (A) by identifying unique configurations in each quadrant. Vertical (B), horizontal (C), and vertical and horizontal (D) symmetry are perceived effortlessly.

for symmetry detection will depend on the number of different values that must be individually tested.

Consider a way to determine the axis of symmetry. To simplify, assume that the axis of symmetry is vertical. Suppose there are six columns composed of dots of differing brightness (ABCCBA) so that the symmetry axis lies between columns 3 and 4. Then, for every pair of columns, correlate the brightness levels across rows. For random dot patterns, each column will be perfectly correlated to only one other column: 3-4, 2-5, and 1-6. All the other correlations should be low or zero because the arrays are generated randomly. Notice how this process resembles discovering repetition symmetry. Again, suppose there are six columns (ABCABC) so that the repetition axis lies between columns 3 and 4. Then, for every pair of columns, correlate the brightness levels across rows. In this case, the correlated columns would be 1-4, 2-5, and 3-6.

The important point here is that statistical structure in the stimulus does not necessarily mean that it can be picked up by the perceptual system. The auditory system is tuned to repetition symmetry (ABCABC), while the visual system is tuned to reflection symmetry (ABCCBA). We need to be hesitant in assuming that because information exists in the stimulus array it is usable perceptual information. Moreover, real objects do not have perfect spatial or temporal symmetries (such as faces or rhythms), so that there must some way to combine the distributions of correlations into a criterion value in order to judge whether symmetry exists.

Can an Autocorrelation Model Explain Texture Perception?

When I think about how people solve repeated noise sequences to derive repeating segments, I imagine that people somehow create two parallel strings and slide them relative to each other. At one offset, the numbers coincide, and that temporal interval yields the repeating unit and ultimately the pitch of the sequence. When I try to imagine how people solve Glass patterns, I come up with a similar strategy: People select different subsets of the dots and somehow try to find equivalent spatial patterns in the remaining dots. How such a matching procedure could be implemented in the auditory or visual system is not well understood, so my explanation can only be an informed hypothesis.

It is interesting to note that similar computational problems arise in several places. First, for audition, there is the problem of spatial localization. For a source located on one side of the head, the sound will reach the near ear before it reaches the far ear, and the temporal difference (termed the *interaural delay*) will vary systematically with the spatial location. The time difference reaches its maximum when the source is directly opposite one ear and gradually decreases to zero as the source moves directly in front of or behind the head. The physiological problem, then, is to calculate the time delay between the sound reaching the near ear and the far ear. It is easy to recast this problem in terms of autocorrelation: Namely, the problem becomes finding the time delay that produces the maximum correlation between the two excitations. Conceptually, the first output from one ear is delayed progressively in time, and the interaural delay is taken to be that shift which maximizes the correlation between the near and far ear excitations. More than 50 years ago, Jeffress (1948) suggested that there was a set of delay lines coming from each ear. Every delay line from one ear was crossed with every delay line from the second ear (e.g., t and $t + .002$ ms), and the excitations from the two signals fed into one coincidence detector that was assumed to calculate the correlation between the two signals. Every coincidence detector thus calculated onc interaural delay. Although this type of model is conceptually simple and there are cells that respond maximally to specific interaural delays, the continuing problem is that there is little evidence that delay lines actually exist in either the auditory or visual system. The lack of such delay lines has led Shamma (2001) to suggest that there is direct spatial comparison of the movement of the sound wave along the basilar membranes of the near and far ears because, that can directly represent the interaural delay.

Second, for vision, there is the problem of tracking the movement of objects in space. Starting with Reichardt (1961), models for the perception of movement are based on delay lines feeding into coincident detectors. Imagine an edge that moves spatially. The outputs from every receptor would be a set of delay lines (including one with zero delay), and those would be paired one-to-one with delay lines from other receptors at different spatial positions. Each such pair of delay lines would converge on one coincidence detector. The speed and direction of movement would be calculated by the cross-correlations of the spike patterns between pairs of delay lines by the coincidence detectors (this is covered more completely in chapter 5).

I have conceptualized the conversion of auditory or visual excitation into separate, but overlapping sensory channels. Each channel is most sensitive to a particular auditory or spatial frequency, and the excitation of each channel is a function of the stimulus energy at that frequency. As described in chapter 2, the excitation can be conceptualized in terms of the firing rate of each channel or in terms of the timing between the spikes of the neurons. There need not be only one mechanism.[13]

To the extent that the neurons are phase-locked to the excitation, then each repetition should generate the identical distribution of intervals between the spikes. There are several possible mechanisms that we could postulate that maintain the neural spike sequence so that matches can be found among the repeating units. Cariani (1999) hypothesized that there are sets of recurrent delay lines that detect the repetition. Any signal creates a set of memory traces that encode the spike timings. Each trace is delayed by a different time interval. The new incoming signal is compared to every delayed version of the current memory trace and for each delay, a coincidence detector passes on those spikes that occur in the same time bins from the circulating trace and the present signal. There would be many coincident spikes for the delay lines that match the repetition rate of the signal, but only a small number of coincident spikes for the delay lines that do not.

13. Given that organisms need different kinds of information about the external world, we would expect that there would be several ways in which neural excitation could and would code that information. Victor (2000) presented an information theory method for estimating whether using the coincidence in the timing of the spikes improves the information transmission above that obtained by simply counting the number of spikes. He estimated that the gain is roughly 20-30%. Using a similar method, Victor (2000) argued that when several neurons signal the identical stimulus property (i.e., neurons that have the same best frequency), transmission is better if the spike trains of each such neuron are kept separate, rather than summing all together. The gain here is smaller, about 10%. This is the same conclusion as Reich et al. (2001).

This process creates a new set of delayed traces that in turn are compared to the next signal. Over time, the relative signal strength of the delay line at the period of the signal would increase due to a high number of coincidence spikes, and the strength of the other delay lines would decrease.

These sorts of models seem to capture our implicit understanding of how we make sense of repeating patterns. To provide an equivalent sort of visual stimulus, we could construct a random dot kinematogram similar to the ones shown in figure 1.1. The observer would see a streaming pattern of dots and would have to judge each time the pattern recycled. A similar two-dimensional recurrent delay line model would work.

Moreover, it seems that models based on the timings among the spikes can also account for the change in perceived periodicity and pitch for alternating random noise segments. As described above, a sequence such as ABABAB is perceived as repeating AB units. But, as the number of repeats is increased from

AABBAABB to AAAAAAAABBBBBBBBAAAAAAAABBBBBBBB

the perception shifts to repeating A and B units. The perceived pitch doubles and the timbre of the noise shifts back and forth from As to Bs. The sequence is not perceived as repeating AAAAAAAABBBBBBBB units, even though this 16-segment unit is a perfect repeat. We can speculate that there are limits to the ability to find periodicities at long intervals, so that perceptual strength would decrease for the repeating units based on 16 noise segments. If the noise segment were 2 ms (a frequency of 500 Hz), the duration of 8 As followed by 8 Bs would be 32 ms (31 Hz), close to the lower limit for tonal perception.

All of these models depend on the existence of neurons capable of detecting the coincidence of incoming excitations. In the auditory pathway, octopus cells fit the requirements for a coincidence detector (Oertel, Bal, Gardner, Smith, & Joris, 2000). The octopus cells are found in the mammalian cochlear nucleus and cross the bundle of auditory fibers. Several features of the octopus cells make them superbly suited to detecting spike coincidences. First, each octopus cell spans about one third of the frequency array of the auditory fibers and therefore can integrate the firings across a wide range of frequencies. In mice, a single octopus cell could be expected to receive inputs from auditory nerve cells that span two to three octaves. Anywhere from 60 to 240 fibers would converge on a single cell, and roughly one tenth to one third of the fibers seem to be necessary to trigger the octopus cell. Second, the summation of synaptic potentials from many fibers within 1 ms is required to cause a firing. Third, octopus cells can fire rapidly with exceptionally well-timed spikes to periodic broadband sounds like clicks. Fourth, octopus cells can phase-lock at very high rates, between 800 and 1,000 spikes per second and respond to tones above

2000 Hz with a single action potential at the onset of the tone. Moreover, the octopus cells show the strongest synchronization of all cells in the cochlear nucleus to amplitude-modulated (AM) stimuli. All of these factors point to octopus cells as the cell type that could detect synchrony in the firing of auditory nerve fibers between a delayed representation and a present stimulation. The properties of these auditory octopus cells are nearly identical to those of the odor-detecting coincidence cells described in chapter 3 (Laurent, 2002; Perez-Orive et al., 2002).

Summary

If there is one thread running through this chapter (and the entire book), it is the concept that perceiving is essentially identifying correspondences across time and space that segment the auditory and visual field, but that there are striking limitations in our ability to find those correspondences. There are limitations due to the grain of the correspondences, the resolution of the nervous system, the organization of the pathways, and cognitive limitations in the ability to match the physical properties or even levels of a single property. These correspondences may be abstract or may even transform across the auditory or visual scene. The perception of circular Glass patterns depends on correspondences that change as a function of distance from the center and as a function of orientation.

In chapter 5, I consider still another correspondence problem: creating matches between objects that change position or orientation across time. Such matches can be based on changes in brightness, or contrast, or abstract properties like rotation direction or vibration frequency. The perceptual properties that underlie correspondence are extremely diverse; again there is a tension between general-purpose and specific tuned processes.

5

Perception of Motion

It is early August in Tennessee, and I am enjoying the flashing of fireflies each evening. There are only a small number of fireflies, and the flashes are unsynchronized. It is relatively easy to match the successive flashes to each firefly. However, if there were many flies and their flashes were synchronized so that there were alternate periods of dark and light (as happens with several species), it would be very difficult to match the sequence of flashes firefly by firefly. In the previous chapter, I considered the correspondence problem for static textures. In this chapter, I consider the correspondence problem for moving stimuli, primarily in the visual domain, and tracking the erratic movements of fireflies is one of the most difficult problems.

It could be argued that detecting motion is the most important thing animals do. Animals must detect motion when they are stationary and when they are moving. Motion degrades camouflage and crystallizes objects. It protects us from predators and provides prey. At one level, motion perception simply is another kind of texture segmentation. There is a change in the visual field such that one region pops out and is perceived as beginning and ending at different locations in the field. In fact, Julesz (1995) and others list movement as one of the factors leading to texture segmentation. However, in this section, I treat movement in terms of the correspondence problem to emphasize the similarity to the perception of repetition and symmetry.

Two findings from the research on texture perception stand out for me. The first is that both preattentive effortless perceiving and attentive "scrutinizing" perceiving are found for visual textures and repeating noise segments. It is not clear whether these two impressions imply that there are two distinct and nonoverlapping processes or if it means that several processes necessarily are active simultaneously, another example of multiresolution.

The same problem of the multiplicity of processes is also central here. To foreshadow the discussion, there appear to be multiple stimulus dimensions and multiple perceptual processes that affect the perception of motion (e.g., texture, shading, distance, timing). Moreover, it seems that the perceptual processes are so intertwined that the dominant one is a function of the overall context.

The second finding is the "hardening" of the percept. For repeating noise stimuli, as the number of repetitions increases, the competing noise disappears, the perceived tone:noise ratio "explodes," and the overall sound becomes treated as a unit. For visual textures, the Glass patterns illustrate that above a certain level of internal coherence, segregation becomes unambiguous. We can imagine a similar hardening for motion. Suppose we start with an array of dots moving in random directions and distances. Progressively, we constrain the movement of a subset of those dots so that they move in the same direction. At a certain level of constraint in terms of the variation of motion, that subset reaches a degree of internal coherence such that the subset is seen moving together as a unified surface (and may even induce a reverse-direction movement in the other dots).

This chapter discusses the classic research on apparent motion with one or a small number of discrete visual elements that move together, then moves to more complex configurations involving the movement of many elements, and finally considers recent research that employs stimuli that create second-order movement.

Visual Apparent Movement

It is difficult to come up with an adequate perceptual definition of motion because the simple physical definition of change in distance across time does not adequately portray how we perceive motion. Distance, time, and velocity are all perceptually related, so it is not clear which ones are independent and could be used to derive the others. We could argue that motion is perceived directly, or we could argue that motion is perceived in terms of the objective definition of a distance change across time. Real motion occurs when objects change position continuously across intermediate points over time. Apparent motion occurs when objects change position in discrete jumps over time; the object disappears from one position and reappears at another. Given the appropriate combinations of step size and time intervals between steps, the discontinuous motion is seen as continuous (e.g., neon signs and motion pictures). It may appear that studying apparent motion is a dead end because physical motion is normally continuous. Yet, being able to extrapolate the trajectory of animals that are alternately hidden by trees and exposed in a forest environment must have been a very important survival tool.

Up to the late 1800s, motion was thought to be perceived by tracking one's own eye movements. But even at that time, it was known that motion was perceived when the eye did not move. Exner (1875) provided convincing evidence that motion was a distinct perceptual quality, and not a derivative of static views spread across space and time. Exner produced two slightly displaced sparks, separated by a short time interval. The critical outcome occurred when the sparks were so close spatially that both sparks were always seen together (they could not be separated by any type of eye movement). Even in this case, there was a clear perception of a single spark moving back and forth between locations at intermediate time intervals. To demonstrate that these apparent movements were not due to small, nonperceptible eye movements, Wertheimer (1912) constructed an apparatus that created two out-of-phase motions, for example a red light moving left-right-left and simultaneously a green light moving right-left-right. Observers saw both motions, and Wertheimer argued that the eye could not move in both directions at once.

One-Dot Apparent Movement

The Gestalt psychologists used apparent motion to denounce what they claimed was the orthodox sensation + experience theory of perceiving. Actually, the Gestalt psychologists had constructed a straw man, as no theorist adhered to the viewpoint that perception emerged only from the compounding of sensations. The positive outcome was that extensive research was undertaken to map out the optimal space-time relationships characterizing apparent motion.

In the simplest case of apparent motion, a single target at position x_1 is flashed at time t_1, and a second target is flashed at position x_2 at time t_2. The basic case occurs when the targets are identical in the two frames and are either brighter or darker than the background. Given the appropriate interval $(t_2 - t_1)$, the target seems to move from x_1 to x_2, regardless of whether the target is brighter or darker than the background. The outcomes are more complex if the two targets differ, and those will be discussed later.

Now consider the cases in which the targets are continuously alternated. Korte (1915) summarized experiments that incorporated three factors: (1) the discriminability of two lights; (2) the distance between the lights; and (3) the time interval between the onset of each light. Korte originally used the time interval between the offset of the first light and the onset of the second, but the results are simpler to interpret if the timing between the onscts is used. (This differs from hearing, in which the offset-to-onset interval determines some types of organization, as discussed in chapter 9; Bregman, Ahad, Crum, & O'Reilly, 2000.) The important law here is that the onset-to-onset interval is directly proportional to the spatial distance. In order to create the appearance of smooth motion, as the separation between the targets is increased, then the onset interval must also be increased, and conversely, as the interval is increased, then the distance must be increased. For each individual, there usually is a wide tolerance for perceiving smooth motion. The onset differences for smooth motion can range up to a factor of five, so that the perceived velocity of the movement can vary greatly. Korte's "laws" should be considered only as gross generalities (Kolers, 1972).

Apparent motion occurs even between physically different stimuli. Cavanagh, Arguin, and Grunau (1989) reported that subjects saw motion between two stimuli defined by any combination of attributes such as brightness, color, texture, relative motion, or depth. For example, a green light will gradually change into a yellow light and vice versa along the movement path. But if a green light alternates with a red light (i.e., an opponent pair of colors) there is a binary switch at an intermediate point, and similarly, a white spot on a gray background flows into a black spot on the same gray background (i.e., a contrast reversal) by changing from white to black at an intermediate point.

Apparent motion also occurs between two stimuli with different physical shapes. Moreover, the optimal onset-to-onset interval for movement depends on the separation only and does not vary among diverse pairs of different shapes. Some examples, taken from Kolers (1972), that provide illustrations of the "plasticity" of contour are shown in figure 5.1. These examples illustrate the "sensibleness" of the perceived motion, even though the smooth motions that occur may disregard nearest-neighbor movement or occur between quite different shapes. The trajectory of the movement can be influenced by the stimuli as well as surrounding context. Shepard and Zare (1983) first created a sequence consisting of alternating single black dots and found the optimal onset difference for the straight-line movement between the dots. Then they inserted a flashed curved gray arc connecting the first and second dots so that the sequence was dot-arc-dot. Instead of the direct straight-line motion between the two black dots, the perceived movement followed the path of the arc, and the optimal onset difference increased due to the extra length of the arc.

Apparent Motion and the Correspondence Problem

As soon as we construct patterns made up of multiple dots, the problem of the best correspondence between the dots in the two images emerges. The local information in each view does not specify the correspondence. If we assume a one-to-one match of the dots in the two views, the number of possible matches is equal to the factorial of the number of dots (if the one-to-one restriction is dropped, then the number of matches equals 2^n). For

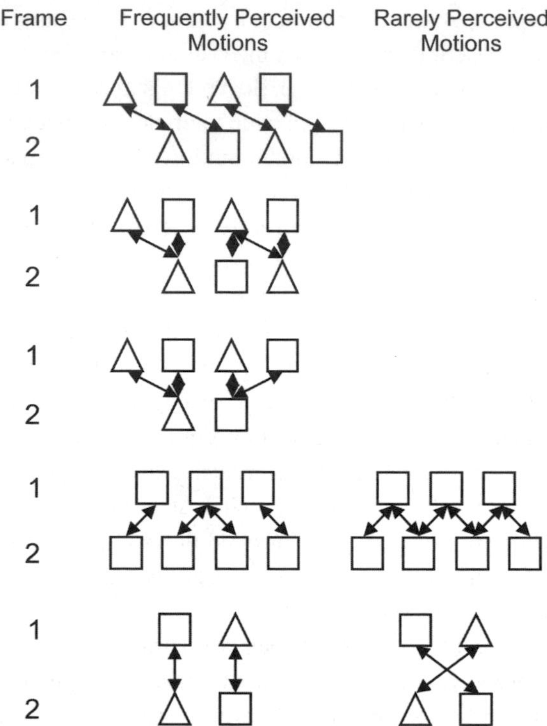

Figure 5.1. Illustrations of frequently and rarely perceived apparent movements. The alternating images are shown in the two rows, and the double-headed arrows indicate the back-and-forth movements. Movements that cross each other are rarely perceived, even if the alternative movement requires objects to change shape. Adapted from *Aspects of Motion Perception*, by P. A. Kolers, 1972, Oxford, UK: Pergamon Press.

patterns of 2 dots there are only 2 possible matches, and for patterns of 4 dots there are 24 possible matches, while for 10 dots the number of possible matches explodes to over 3 million. Even for relatively simple dot patterns, the number of possible matches makes an exhaustive search for the best correspondences among the dots in the two images beyond comprehension. The visual system must relentlessly prune out unlikely matches until only a few likely candidates remain. I consider some of these heuristics later.

Let us start with the simple configuration based on four dots positioned at the fixed corners of an imaginary square.[1] The two dots along one diagonal

1. Instances of apparent motion in which the successive locations of each point are determined probabilistically are discussed later.

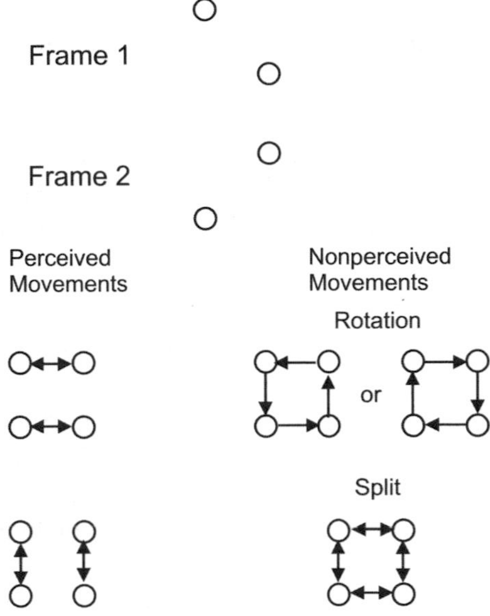

Figure 5.2. The movement "quartet." Frame 1 and Frame 2 are alternated. Horizontal and vertical movements predominate, even though the two movements for each are out of phase (the left-to-right movement of one pair of dots occurs simultaneously with the right-to-left movement of the other pair). Adapted from *Dynamic Neural Field Theory for Motion Perception*, by M. A. Giese, 1999. Boston: Kluwer Academic.

are alternated with the two dots along the other diagonal, termed the *motion quartet* by Giese (1999). There are two simple apparent motions in which both dots simultaneously undergo either horizontal or vertical motion, as illustrated in figure 5.2. Two other possible types of apparent motion that are rarely perceived also are shown in figure 5.2: (1) motions in a clockwise or a counterclockwise direction, and (2) motions in which each dot appears to split and to move in two directions.

Even this simple configuration demonstrates some of the fundamental aspects of apparent movement:

1. The perceived motion tends to switch between horizontal and vertical motion (and may switch to perceiving the two pairs of dots simply alternating without movement at all). Given that the stimulus presentation is inherently ambiguous and underdetermined, continuous viewing nearly always leads to the emergence of alternative percepts. Attneave (1971) termed these configurations *multistable*. We can operationally define the strength of each organization by measuring the percentage of time it occurs within an interval or by the probability that it is the initial perception.

It is unlikely that these perceptual shifts are due simply to the satiation and consequent reduction of firing rates of stimulated cells. Moving one's eyes, shifting attention to a different part of the visual object, or imagining a different percept often instigates switches. Leopold and Logothetics (1999) provocatively suggested that the switches are an active attempt to try out different perceptual solutions to avoid local minima that represent nonoptimal percepts. These attempts would be directed by nonsensory parts of the cortex (Areas V4 and higher levels of the cortex; see chapter 2).

2. The perceived motion often is determined by spatial proximity. We can alter the imaginary square by varying the height and width to create narrow horizontal rectangles or tall vertical rectangles. The perceived motion occurs between the closest pairs of dots. In this simple case, correspondence is based on proximity. Of course, in more complex configurations, the nearest-neighbor correspondence may create a false solution (as illustrated for the Glass patterns in chapter 4), but proximity might be considered to be the first and most frequent heuristic employed. The heuristic for the nearest-neighbor match is roughly equivalent to a preference for the slowest movement, and therefore this preference can be understood as representing gradual and continuous movements that occur most frequently in the environment.

3. The perceived motion is the one that makes each of the individual motions as similar as possible. This heuristic has the effect of minimizing changes to the configuration of the points. If the points are understood as lying on the contours of an implicit object, this heuristic can be understood as being a preference for assuming rigid objects, and such a preference would match the ubiquity of rigid objects in the natural environment.

4. The perceived motion rarely involves one dot splitting into two parts (e.g., the split motion in figure 5.2 never occurs). Again, this heuristic makes good naturalistic sense because nearly all objects maintain their integrity over time, and only in rare cases do objects split into parts or fuse together. Dawson (1991) detailed the interrelations among heuristics 2, 3, and 4.

5. The perceived motion rarely involves crossing paths that could result in collisions. Kolers (1972) constructed a slightly different array, also shown in figure 5.1, which placed a noncollision path in conflict with motion between different shapes. Viewers invariably saw the noncollision path.

6. Pantle and Picciano (1976) made use of a simple three-dot linear array that was originally used by the Gestalt psychologist Ternus. In the traditional sequence, three dots in a horizontal row are flashed together, followed by three identical dots offset to the right. The perceived motion turned out to be a function of the timing between the two flashes. If the onset of the second stimulus immediately followed the offset of the first, then only the outer dot was perceived to move. The middle two dots remained stationary. However, if the onset of the second stimulus was delayed, then the entire row of three dots was perceived to have shifted to the right. Both

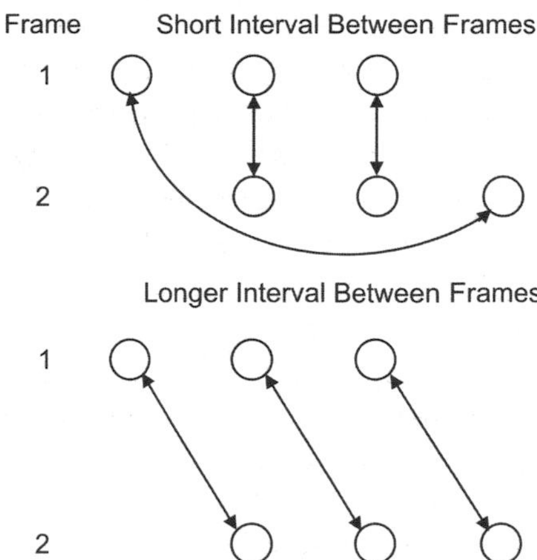

Figure 5.3. The two perceived movements in the Ternus display. The double-ended arrows represent the back-and-forth motion as the frames are alternated.

outcomes are shown in figure 5.3. The perception of group movement also occurred if the two stimuli were presented to different eyes. The three-dot shift, which is perceived at all but the shortest time intervals, makes each of the dots move in exactly the same way.

7. The perceived motion can be influenced by prior movements within the display. Antis and Ramachandran (1987) primed either horizontal or vertical perceived motion by initially displaying one of the two movements. The perceived motion follows the direction of the priming movement; it is as if the dots do not want to change direction. It is interesting to note that it is only the direction of the priming motion that influences the apparent motion; speed or distance do not. The visual system expects objects to move in rather consistent paths and not to change direction quickly or erratically.

8. The perceived motion can be influenced by the perceptions from prior trials, a phenomenon termed *hysteresis*. Imagine starting with a narrow horizontal rectangle so that the perceived motion is vertical (along the short dimension). If that rectangle is gradually changed over time so that it becomes tall and vertical, observers will continue to perceive vertical motion far beyond the height-to-length ratio that would normally bring about a shift to horizontal motion. Conversely, starting with a tall vertical rectangle yielding horizontal motion will bring about horizontal movement even for narrow horizontal rectangles. Hysteresis can be understood as a type of priming, in which the visual (and auditory) system expects to see one kind of motion and will cling to that percept even if an alternative perception would usually be preferred if that stimulus configuration were presented in isolation.

9. Motions in distant parts of the array can determine the perceived motion within a small region. Ramachandran and Antis (1983) presented multiple rectangles in one visual array and alternated the diagonal pairs of dots of each rectangles (like Frame 1 and Frame 2 at the top of figure 5.2) at the same time. They found that the normal oscillations between horizontal and vertical apparent motion occurred at the same time, so that at any instant the same kind of motion occurred in all rectangles. If the orientation of the rectangles differed in two parts of the field, then all rectangles still oscillated together, even though that might require a different perceptual shift in each of the two fields. These outcomes illustrate global processes for resolving motion ambiguity, because there are no reasons that all the rectangles ought to shift at the same time, particularly if they are at different orientations. The authors point out that stick-figure Necker cubes that undergo spontaneous reversals do not synchronize their shifts. The above synchronization may be restricted to configurations that are not perceived as three-dimensional figures.

To summarize, two principles stand out: (1) match two points in nearby spatial positions, and (2) match pairs of points that could have undergone the same smooth motion. Surprisingly, shape, color, or brightness similarity do not influence apparent motion to any degree. Watamaniuk, McKee, and Grzywacz (1995) argued that over time, less ambiguous motion correspondence gradually spreads across connected units, replacing more ambiguous possibilities.

Configural Effects

All these studies suggest that there are linkages between the motions of the individual elements, but they do not make those connections critical to solving the correspondence problem. The group motion can be understood as the correspondence that makes each dot movement identical, without arguing that the motion depends on the figural properties. The next three approaches do postulate that the integration of the perceived motions of individual elements within a global figure is based on an overall scene description.

Yuille and Grzywacz (1998) hypothesized that observers segment the moving points by how well they match real motions in the physical world including translation, rotation, rigid motion in three dimensions, pure expansion, and differential motions at boundaries (see Zanker, 1993, 1995). In effect, observers calculate likelihood ratios: which physical motion most probably generated the perceived movements. The initial step would be the derivation of the velocity and direction of the image points. The local movement measurements feed modules that group similar movements

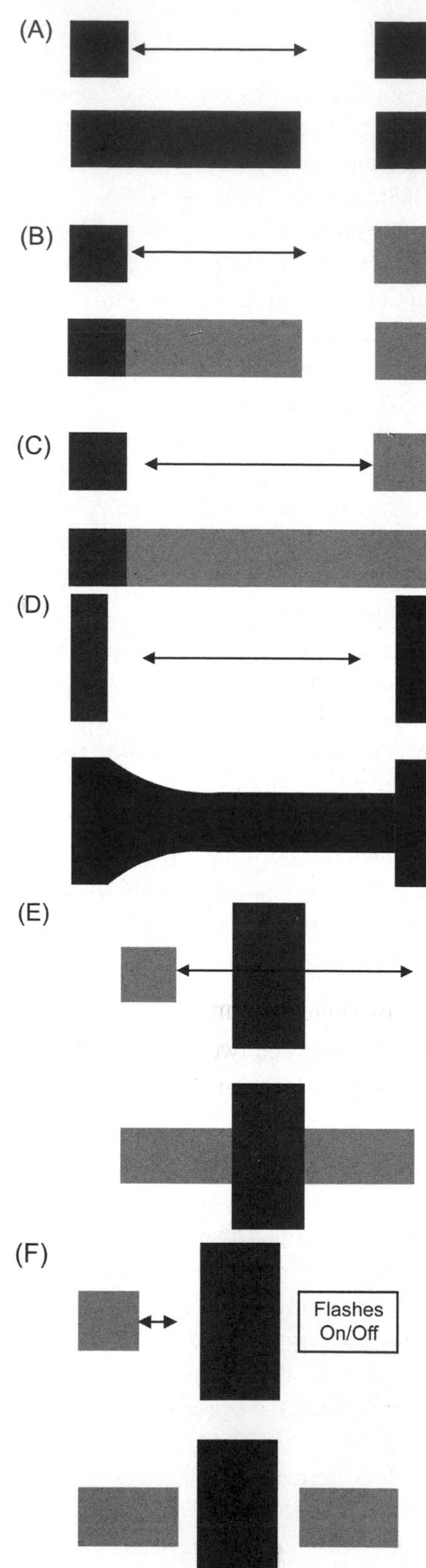

Figure 5.4. Configural motions demonstrating the interplay of the parsing and correspondence stages in apparent movement. In each display, the two rows portray the alternating images. The arrow in the top row illustrates the perceived motion that connects those two images (A). For example, in (A) a black rectangle grows out of the black square on the left, in (B) a gray rectangle grows out of the black square on the left, and in (C) a gray rectangle grows out of the gray square on the right. Adapted from "The Role of Parsing in High-Level Motion Processing," by Tse, P, Cavanagh, P., and Nakayama, K.,1998, in T. Watanabe (Ed.), *Computational Neurobiological, and Psychophysical Perspectives* (pp. 249–266). Cambridge, MA: MIT Press.

(The two frames are alternated in exactly the same way as in the classic apparent motion presentations.) Even though the two stimuli are presented discretely, the perception is that the elongated rectangle appears to grow out of the contiguous square (figure 5.4A) even if the extension is the brightness of the opposite square (figure 5.4B). If the elongated rectangle touches both squares, then the rectangle appears to grow out of both if the squares are identical or grows out of the one with the same brightness if the squares differ (figure 5.4C).

In the second type of configuration, two different rectangles are shown in frame 1, and then a connected combination of the two shapes is shown in frame 2. The perceived motion goes along the smoothest contours and tends to parse the figures along concave contours (figure 5.4D). In the third type of configuration, the first frame contains a small square and an elongated vertical rectangle. In one variant, the second frame contains an elongated horizontal rectangle that appears to go behind the original vertical rectangle (figure 5.4E). The perception here is a smooth extension of the original square into a horizontal rectangle that proceeds behind the vertical rectangle. If the two frames alternate, the horizontal rectangle appears to extend and contract. In the other variant, the second view contains two horizontal rectangles that do not touch the vertical rectangle (figure 5.4F). The perception here is quite different: the original square seems to extend to the right but is not part of the right rectangle, and the right rectangle flashes on and off. The parsing module guesses that the right square represents a brand-new object because it does not butt up against the vertical rectangle. It is not part of the apparent motion of the original left square (a similar auditory outcome is presented below).

Using the same type of stimuli, Holcombe (2003) demonstrated that the sudden onset of a visual stimulus could be interpreted as a morphing motion, as found by Tse et al. (1998) above, but it also could be interpreted as the disappearance of a shape in the foreground. Several examples are shown in figure 5.5. If we simply compare figures 5.5A, 5.5B, and 5.5C, in 5.5A only 27% of observers see the small gray square morph into the gray rectangle, but in 5.5C nearly all observers perceive a morphing motion. Figure 5.5A is consistent with the black rectangle disappearing, exposing the hidden part of the gray rectangle, but that cannot occur in figure 5.5C. Figure 5.5B is an intermediate case because the gray segment overlapping the black rectangle provides an ambiguous cue to occlusion. Similarly, in 5.5D and 5.5E, the small textured rectangle could occlude a central segment of the black-and-white gradient in 5.5D, but the texture background in 5.5E makes occlusion unlikely.

Tse et al. (1998) and Holcombe (2003) argued, successfully in my opinion, that these results blur any distinction between the parsing and matching

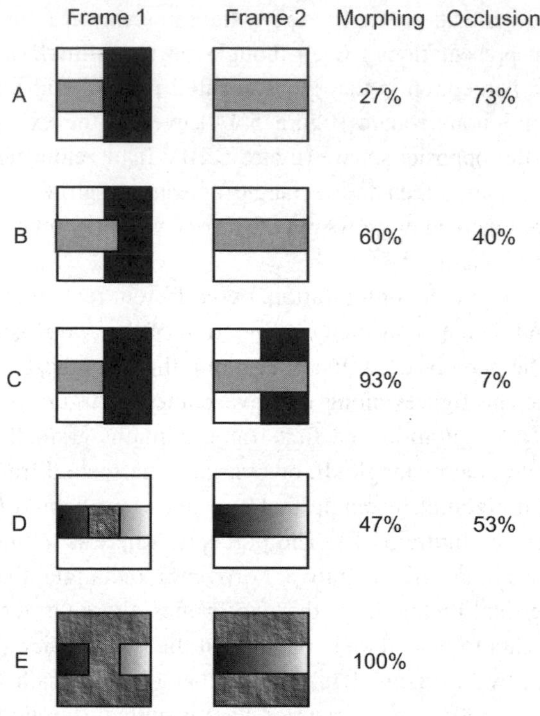

Figure 5.5. The perception of occlusion as opposed to morphing in shape depends on the likelihood that occlusion of the horizontal rectangle could occur. Frames 1 and 2 are alternated. Adapted from "Occlusion Cues Resolve Sudden Onsets Into Morphing or Line Motion, Disocclusion and Sudden Materialization," by A. Holcombe, 2003, *Journal of Vision, 3*, 562–572.

stages and that the perceived motion reflects the most likely interpretation. The perceived motion "makes sense" of the parsed shapes in the two views. Dawson (1991) presented a similar view that the basic function of visual systems is to identify objects in the world, and that motion perception tracks those identified objects.

Parallel Outcomes in Hearing

Auditory Induction and Visual Apparent Motion

One compelling parallel outcome has been termed *auditory induction* (R. M. Warren, 1999). If we present a tone, a silent interval, and then the identical tone again, the perception is of two tones separated by a silent interval, that is, the correct percept. However, if we present the tone, a loud noise signal that contains the frequency of the tone, and then the same tone again, two perceptions can result as a function of the timing of the first tone, noise, and second tone.

First, if the first tone ends at the onset of the noise and the second tone begins immediately after the noise ends, there is an illusion that the tone has continued within the noise. It is as if the auditory system decided that the noise simply drowned out the tone based on the fact that the tone occurred until the noise began and reappeared immediately after the noise ended, and that the noise contained the frequency of the tone. The tone captures its frequency within the noise, and as a result the noise sounds subtly different. This perception seems perfectly analogous to the visual example shown in figure 5.4E (except for the occlusion due to the vertical rectangle). Visual objects are hidden; sounds are drowned out. Auditory induction is not limited to constant tones: Listeners hear frequency glides and connected speech in noise.

Second, if the first tone ends slightly before the onset of the noise so that there is a silent interval between them, and the second tone starts slightly after the noise ends again, producing another short silent interval, there is no illusion: Listeners hear a tone-noise-tone sequence. It is as if the auditory system decided on the basis of the intervening silences that there were really three discrete and unconnected sounds. This second outcome seems perfectly analogous to the visual example in figure 5.4F, in which apparent motion does not occur.

Bregman (1990) has suggested that these auditory outcomes can be understood in terms of an *old + new* heuristic. If a sound undergoes a rapid change and then reverts back to the original sound, the auditory system interprets that change as being due to the onset and offset of a new additional sound rather than being a rapid change away from and then back to the original. This perception occurs only if the components of the original sound still are found in the changed sound. This auditory heuristic rests on the physical fact that environmental sounds normally do not change rapidly and is no different in kind from the visual heuristic that rests on the physical fact that objects normally do not change direction dramatically (Antis & Ramachandran, 1987). Here, the old + new heuristic becomes the most plausible description of the events because the old stimulus abuts on both sides (in space or in time) of the occluding stimulus.

Interleaved Auditory Melodies and Visual Transparency

One type of stimulus used to study transparency makes use of two superimposed black-and-white gratings oriented at different angles that construct a visual plaid. Each grating can be characterized by its frequency (i.e., the number of alternating black-and-white line cycles per visual degree), the contrast between the white and black bands, and its orientation with respect to vertical. As described in the chapter 1, if the grating moves within an aperture, the motion path is ambiguous because it is impossible to judge movement along the axis of the grating. Normally, observers judge that the grating is moving strictly perpendicular to the grating.

If each grating (at different orientations) moves perpendicularly, there are two perceptual outcomes. In the first, both gratings are seen to move coherently in the same direction toward the intersection of constraints (see figure 1.2); the two gratings appear to be at the same depth. In the second, the two gratings are seen as two separate transparent surfaces moving relative to each other; one surface is perceived as being in front of the other.

The experimental question is, under what conditions are the individual motions incorporated into a single coherent surface or segmented into two (or more) coherent surfaces in depth that appear to be sliding across each other (Stoner & Albright, 1994)? In general, transparent perceptions occur when the two gratings have different spatial frequencies, different velocities, different brightness contrasts, and when the difference in orientation is greater than 100°, as shown in figure 5.6. (Differences in the colors of the gratings and differences in perceived depth also increase the probability of transparent motion.) These outcomes are explained in terms of a proposed two-stage mechanism. There is an initial stage that abstracts the local velocity information from each grating separately (Yuille & Grzywacz, 1998) and a second stage that integrates the local outputs using some form of population coding. If combining the local information yields one central peak, coherence occurs. In contrast, if combining the local information yields a bimodal peak, then transparency occurs.

To summarize the important point, if the two gratings are similar, move at the same velocity, and differ in orientation by 90° or less, the perception is of one coherent sheet. Otherwise, differences in the gratings or orientations lead to the perception of one transparent surface on top of another.

A second, more common, type of transparency occurs when the foreground surface does not give off any light itself but simply attenuates the background surface by its transmission fraction: The overall illumination decreases, but the contrast between the parts of the background does not change. Transparency occurs when the ratio of C to A equals the ratio of D to B, and occlusion occurs when A = B = C (Beck, 1982; Metelli, 1974; see figure 5.7). For transparency, the perceived order in depth of the three surfaces is ambiguous, but for occlusion the perceived order in depth is obvious. Stone, Watson, and Milligan (1990) varied the brightness of region A and demonstrated that brightness configurations that normally lead to the perception of transparency for static displays also enhance the perception of two or more sliding surfaces for moving plaid displays. These outcomes suggest that coherence-transparency-occlusion judgments can be

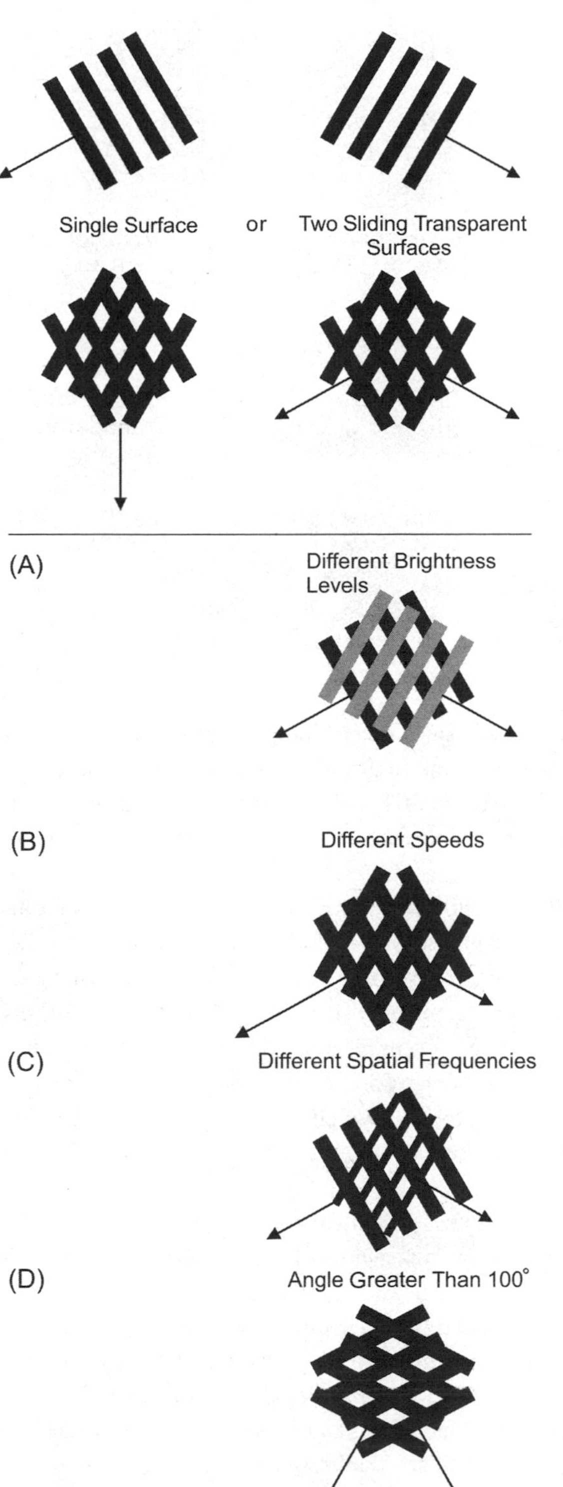

Figure 5.6. If two black-and-white gratings move independently, it is possible to perceive the two gratings forming a single surface and moving in the direction of the intersection of constraints or to see each grating as being a separate surface and sliding past each other. The sliding perception is likely if the two gratings are different in brightness or color (A), move at different speeds (B), have different spatial frequencies (C), or have an angular difference greater than 100° (D).

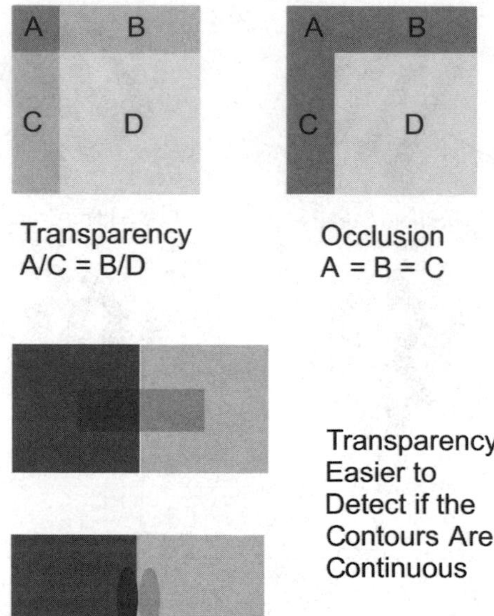

Figure 5.7. The brightness ratios between different surfaces determine whether the surfaces are perceived as transparent (i.e., equal ratios) or whether one surface is perceived as occluding and covering another.

influenced by knowledge of the rules determining images formed in natural settings. This is essentially the same argument made by Yuille and Grzywacz (1998), as well as Tse et al. (1998). Strictly computational models do not capture the implicit knowledge about how natural events are organized.

The auditory parallel to moving plaids, or generally to coherent-incoherent visual stimuli, are interleaved melodies in which one takes two well-known tunes (e.g., "Mary Had a Little Lamb" and "London Bridge") and alternates the notes, keeping an equal time interval between the onsets of each pair of adjacent notes (coming from different melodies). The experimental question is what conditions lead to the perception of one coherent but meaningless melody and which ones lead to the perception of the two separate melodies, exactly the identical question asked about plaids.

If the sound quality of the notes is identical and the notes come from the same scale region so that it is impossible to isolate the notes of each melody by pitch, it is extremely difficult to pick out each melody. The similarity in pitch creates one coherent tonal sequence that does not resemble either melody. If the notes of one melody are progressively raised in pitch until there is no overlap in the notes of each melody, the two melodies separate to form separate coherent melodies, and it becomes easy to identify either one (Dowling, 1973; Hartmann & Johnson, 1991). Furthermore, Bey and McAdams (2003) showed that differences in the timbre between the notes of the interleaved melodies can also lead to the perception of the interleaved melody (in that work, one melody was interleaved with a random string of notes).

Thus, when the two gratings and two melodies have the same frequency content, the perception is coherent. Making the frequencies different brings about the split into two surfaces or two melodies. The visual models mentioned above have an explicit second stage that either "decides" to integrate the motions to produce coherence or decides to keep the motions separate to produce sliding transparency. Presumably, auditory models should have a similar second stage to decide if the pitch sequence should remain integrated or split when there is partial overlap of frequencies, but such a model has not been formulated. Probably such a second stage for both hearing and seeing would be Bayesian, reflecting knowledge and experience about natural events.

van Noorden's Frequency-Time Relationship for Auditory Streaming and Korte's Space-Time Relationship for Visual Apparent Motion

Korte's "law" summarizes the necessary relationship between the distance between two lights and the onset interval required to perceive smooth apparent motion. To review, as the distance between the lights increases, the onset interval must be simultaneously increased to maintain the perception of apparent motion. In pioneering work, van Noorden (1975) alternated two tones (as in apparent motion) and varied the frequency ratio and the onset interval between the two tones. Two perceptions could result. In the first, the two tones appeared to alternate coherently, sounding like a musical trill. In the second, the two tones split apart and appeared to form separate pitch streams. It was possible to attend to one stream or the other, but it proved impossible to attend to both at the same time. One consequence was that it was very difficult to keep the two tones in registration; the notes in the streams seemed to occur simultaneously.

Van Noorden found that the transition between the perception of one coherent alternating sequence of two tones and the perception of two separate sequences, one of higher-pitched tones and one of lower-pitched tones, was an inverse function of the frequency ratio between the tones and the onset-to-onset timing of the tones, essentially the number of tones per second. If the tones are presented at a moderately fast rate so that the onset interval is 200 ms (5 tones per second), the sequence breaks into two streams if the frequency ratio of the tones is 2 or greater, an octave apart. But as the onset interval decreases to 100 ms (10 tones per second), the necessary frequency ratio is only 1.25, 4 musical steps apart. Even though the default percept is that of a coherent two-tone pattern, Bregman (1990) pointed out that the split is obligatory; the notes form two streams even if the listener is trying to hear the two tones together.

In making judgments about apparent motion and auditory segregation, the auditory and visual perceptual systems metaphorically are asking whether the two stimuli could have come from the same object. For both systems, the expectation is that objects change slowly. Thus, if the interval between the two stimuli is relatively short, and yet the physical separation or frequency difference is large, the perceptual systems judge that the two stimuli come from different objects. Two lights are seen flashing alternately without connecting movement, and two tones are heard as coming from different sources.

Auditory and Visual Hysteresis

Hysteresis refers to the tendency to stick with the initial percept even as the stimulus changes greatly. The same effect found for apparent visual movement occurs for the alternating tone sequences used by van Noorden (1975). In some of the continuous tonal sequences, the frequencies of the two tones gradually became more different. Listeners heard a coherent sequence at frequency ratios that would normally result in two streams; conversely, if the frequencies of tones were gradually made more similar, listeners heard two streams at frequency ratios that would normally lead to a coherent sequence.

Theories of Motion Perception

Apparent Motion of Rigid Arrays

Over the last 25 years, the consensus has been that there is no single motion detection system. Originally, the notion was that there were two systems. The first captured small quick movements of complicated patterns in one eye based on global matches, while the second captured longer slower movements of simple figures based on feature matches that could be integrated across the two eyes.[2] Although such a dichotomy has proven inadequate, the basic concept of two or more systems still seems sound. In what follows, I begin by discussing the types of experimental results that lead to the short/long motion distinction, and then discuss how this notion has evolved in the past 10 years.

2. The term *feature* is used rather loosely. Features are defined by the context. Convex or concave would be a feature in a mixed set of figures, but not if all the figures were convex or concave.

Braddick (1974) originally proposed the small-distance versus long-distance distinction. Braddick and others used white-and-black random dot patterns similar to those used originally by Julesz to study texture differences. Typically, the random dot patterns were built from square matrices in which 50% of the cells were filled with black dots (e.g., 288 dots in a 24×24 matrix). Two such patterns are alternated at the same spatial position: One dot pattern contains the original array of dots, and the second dot pattern is modified in some way.

1. The dots in the cells of one small region of the array are reversed by chance. Thus, each black cell would have a 0.50 probability of shifting to white, and each white cell would have a .50 probability of shifting to black. If two such patterns are presented sequentially, the small region seems to flicker or glitter, but there is no perception of movement.
2. The dots in the cells of one small region are shifted by a certain amount (a 4×3 rectangle is shifted five columns to the right). The black-and-white pattern in the rectangle remains fixed and overwrites the original pattern in the target columns. This leaves the cells in the original rectangle empty, and they are filled randomly. Here, if the two patterns are presented sequentially, the small rectangle seems to move to the right. The visual system must be performing a global comparison between the two arrays, because the rectangle cannot be seen in either static view.
3. The dots in the cells of one small region are shifted by a certain amount (as in number 2) and then the black and white cells are reversed. If the two patterns are presented sequentially, the perceived movement is from the second pattern to the first; the perception is the reverse of the actual temporal sequence.

All three of these possibilities are shown in figure 5.8.

To see that a small region has been shifted laterally (or vertically) as in numbers 2 or 3, the correspondences in the dot patterning within the region must be recognized in the two different arrays. The perceptual problem is that after the shift of the small region, there may be several similar regions in the array that can act as incorrect matches. We can conceptualize this process as having two steps. The first step isolates the local correspondences between the dots in the two arrays: Each cell in the first array has a list of all the possible brightness matches in the second array. Somehow, the indeterminacy of these matches must be resolved in order to see motion. The second step searches for sets of connected cells with identical correspondences (e.g., correspondences equal to two steps to the right) and groups those cells to create the perception of coherent movement. This grouping process will inevitably misallocate cells, and there are many examples in which a true

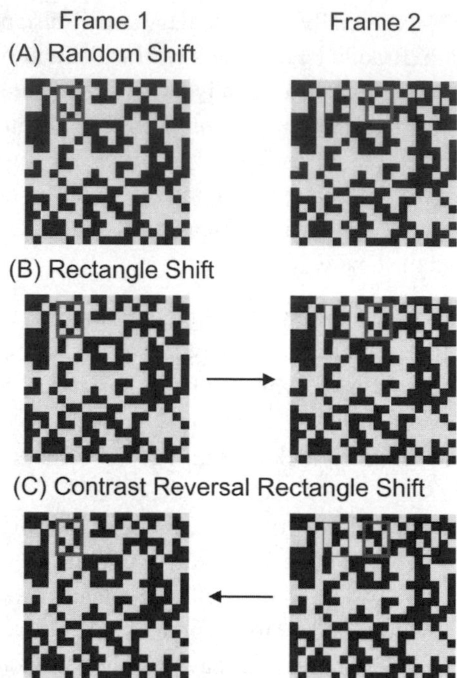

Figure 5.8. Rigid movement: The black-and-white squares within two small 4 row × 3 column rectangles change between frame 1 and frame 2. In frame 1, the rectangle in the cell in the upper left corner is located at row 2, column 5 (enclosed by a thick outline). In frame 2, the rectangle shifts five columns to the right so that the upper left cell is located at row 2, column 10 (the initial position is enclosed by a thin outline and the new position by a thick outline). In (A), the black-and-white squares in the two rectangles randomly change between frame 1 and frame 2: No movement is seen. In (B), the left rectangle in frame 1 is shifted five columns to the right in frame 2, and the black-and-white squares in the original position are changed randomly: Left-to-right movement is seen. In (C), the left rectangle in Frame 1 is shifted five columns to the right, and the brightness of every square is reversed: The rectangle appears to move to the left, reversing the temporal sequence.

coherent movement captures incoherent movements. Julesz and Hesse (1970) termed this a global process that resolves the ambiguities of the local process of cell correspondence and argued that the capture process demonstrates a cooperative system for movement in which the elements are bound by nonlinear excitatory and inhibitory forces.

Braddick (1974) argued for a separate short-term global motion detection system based on several experimental outcomes. First, there is a limit to the allowable displacement. This displacement, which has been termed d_{max}, is a function of several variables: retinal position, size, and density of the dots. Lappin and Bell (1976) found that subjects performed better with larger arrays and Baddeley and Tirpathy (1998) suggested the perception of movement was based on the fraction of dots that moved, so that the detection of motion appears to be a global operation on the whole pattern, and not a local operation founded on the perceived motion of just several dots. If the displacement is beyond d_{max}, the target region does not appear to move. Instead, the dots within the region appear to oscillate independently in different directions, being the chance pairing of noncorresponding dots. Second, there is a limit to the onset-to-onset interval. In Braddick's experiment, if that interval was greater than 50 ms, the perception of motion was diminished. Moreover, there was no relationship between displacement and time as found for the apparent movement of single figures. Third, apparent movement does not occur if the first array is presented to one eye and the second array is presented to the other eye. In contrast, apparent movement of single figures will occur for the same alternating eye sequence.

I will return to the difficulties of the short-long distance distinction. However, I do believe that there is a real distinction between short-distance perception based on spatial correlation and long-distance perception based on the identification and correspondence of features, and that the short-long distinction is very similar to the pitch-feature distinction discussed for the perception of repeated noises in chapter 4. A segment of auditory noise is just like a random dot pattern.

Apparent Motion of Nonrigid Arrays

Another type of visual stimulus used to study motion detection is similar to the seemingly unconnected movements of the fireflies. A random array of dots is shown in the initial frame. In the next (and successive) frames, each dot moves to a new position. The direction and distance of movement could be randomly determined for each dot, or the direction and distance of movement could be constrained for a subset of the dots. For example, 10% of the dots would move vertically in each frame. The observer's task is to identify the direction of the coherent subset of dots.

This paradigm is similar to but more complicated than the random dot arrays described in the previous section. In those experiments, all of the dots that shifted from frame to frame formed a connected vertical or horizontal rectangle so that each dot moved identically. Here, the dots constrained to move in one direction are usually scattered throughout the entire field, and each can move a different distance. Moreover, different dots will move in the target direction on successive frames. Any single dot has a limited lifetime, so that it can move in one direction only for very few steps. This restriction disallows observers from tracking the movement of a single dot. The movements shown in figure 5.9 illustrate these constraints. In the two frames shown, 4 of the 10 dots move to the right. But only dots F and

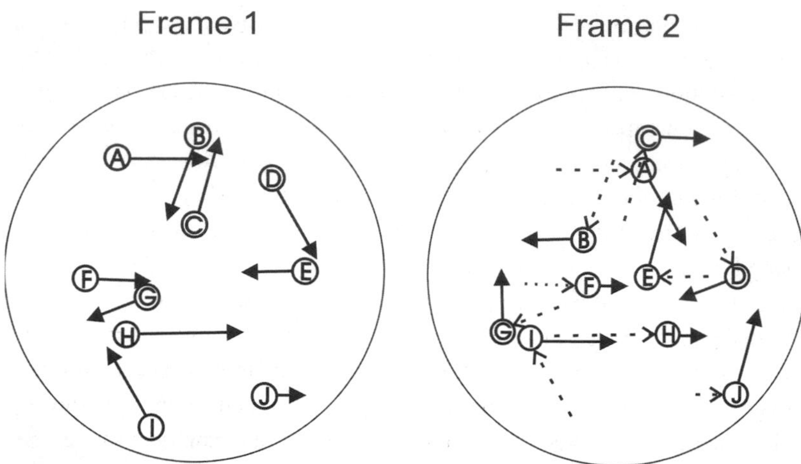

Figure 5.9. Nonrigid movement: Each dot moves independently. Some dots continue in the same direction (although the velocity may change), while others change direction and velocity. The movements of the dots from frame 1 to frame 2 are shown as dotted arrows ending at the starting position in frame 2.

H move rightward in both frames, and the number of rightward movements of those dots would be restricted by the limited lifetime constraint. Thus, the observer must integrate the variable local movements of dots across the entire field, and the cooperative effects described for the identical movements of the dots within rectangles are not likely to occur.

In the majority of previous experiments, all the dots were identical and the independent variable was the percentage of dots that moved coherently in one direction. If all the dots moved in random directions and distances, the observer would see a swarm of dots moving incoherently on the screen. This is the same perception found by Braddick (1974) when the displacement of the displaced rectangular region was greater than d_{max}. However, if the percentage of coherent dots is as low as 5%, observers will perceive the coherent direction. Moreover, the observers report that the movement of the coherent dots creates the perception of a unified surface. It is remarkable that the visual system can perceive coherent motion from such a proportionally small signal. Braddick (1995) pointed out that this paradigm can be conceptualized as a masking experiment in which the coherent movement signal dots are being masked by the incoherent masking dots. This makes the signal-to-noise ratio, as conceptualized for auditory experiments using a decibel measure, 20 log (0.05/0.95) = –25.6 dB, equal to the best performance in detecting a pure tone in noise.

Using alert monkeys trained to judge the direction of the coherent dots, researchers (Britten, Shadlen, Newsome, Celebrini, & Movshon, 1996; Britten, Shadlen, Newsome, & Movshon, 1992) compared the accuracy of the judgments to the actual response of individual units in the monkeys' MT cortical region. First, they measured the directional selectivity of a cell. Then they presented random arrays for 2 s with differing percentages of coherent dots moving either in the preferred direction of that cell or in the opposite direction. The number of spikes to dot motion from the cell was recorded in the preferred and nonpreferred directions of the cell. We can think of this as a signal-to-noise problem, with the signal being the number of spikes to movement in the preferred direction and noise being the number of spikes to movement in the nonpreferred direction. If a monkey adopts the strategy of responding in the preferred direction if the total number of spikes exceeds a certain number (the traditional criterion assumed in signal detection theory), then performance will improve to the point that the distribution of spikes generated by movements in the preferred and nonpreferred directions do not overlap.

The distribution of the number of spikes overlaps when the percentage of dots undergoing correlated movement is less than 1%, but there is a clear split when as few as 3% of the dots move coherently in the preferred direction, and the percentage of correct responses approaches 100% if 12.8% of the dots move coherently, as depicted in figure 5.10. The major effect is that the number of responses to motion in the preferred direction increases dramatically, but there is also a small decrease in the number of responses to motion in the nonpreferred direction. If we compare the actual pointing performance of the monkey to that of a single neuron based on the strategy of responding if the number of spikes exceeds a criterion number, sometimes the monkey is better, but sometimes the neuron is better. Why is the monkey not better than a single neuron? The monkey should be able to integrate responses from many neurons with different directional sensitivities to improve discrimination. One answer lies in the fact that the responses of all the neurons that respond to the movement are somewhat correlated (estimated to be about +0.12), so that simply combining the outputs does not provide independent estimates. In fact, including the responses of neurons tuned to a different direction is likely to reduce accuracy.

A second point concerns the neural code. As presented in chapter 1, the relevant neural code must depend on the time course of the event. When presented with a 2 s stimulus (each frame lasted for 45 ms), the timing of the individual steps is somewhat irrelevant, and the number of spikes may be a sufficient statistic to yield optimal discrimination. However, if the stimulus is presented for 1/20 of the time, 100 ms, the behavioral discrimination is reduced by about one third, while the neural discrimination based on the number of spikes declines dramatically. In these cases, it is likely that information about the correlated movements of clusters of dots could be contained in the neural signal by means of the timing between individual spikes. Even for random motion sequences, Bair and Koch (1996) have

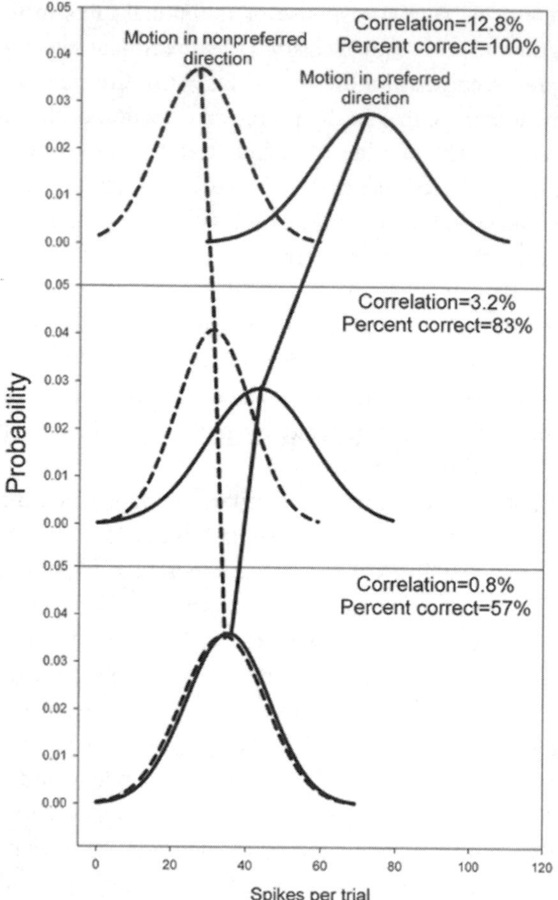

Figure 5.10. The discriminability of nonrigid motion in the preferred (solid curve) and nonpreferred direction (dashed curve) of a neuron in the MT (V5) of an awake monkey. The probability distributions diverge sharply as the percentage of dots moving in the same direction increases. Adapted from "The Analysis of Visual Motion: A Comparison of Neural and Psychophysical Performance," by K. H. Britten, M. N. Shadlen, W. T. Newsome, and J. A. Movshon, 1992, *Journal of Neuroscience, 12*, 4745–4765.

shown that that there can be a remarkable similarity in the timing between spikes for each repetition of the sequence.

Croner and Albright (1997) investigated whether color or brightness cues increased the detectability of the coherent moving dots. The results for the control conditions in which all of the dots were the same color were similar to those of previous experiments: The percentage of coherent dots necessary for motion detection was about 5%. If all of the coherent signal dots were one color and all of the incoherent masking dots were a different color, this percentage was reduced to approximately 1%. The problem here, as pointed out by H.-C. O. Li and Kingdom (2001), is that all of the coherent dots were one color and all of the incoherent masking dots were another color (say 1% red, 99% green). Even when the dots were not moving, it was possible to attend to the coherent ones. H.-C. O. Li and Kingdom constructed 50% red-50% green dot configurations in which a small percentage (e.g., 3%) of the red or green dots moved coherently. In these cases, the coherent and masking dots were of the same sort: for example, 3% of the red dots moved coherently, while 47% of the red dots and 50% of the green dots moved incoherently. In these configurations, color or brightness cues did not improve the detection of the coherently moving dots. Unless it is possible to attend to one feature beforehand, the authors argued that the motion detection system will integrate movement across color and luminance differences without first segregating the dots by feature. In fact, motion-detecting neurons in the middle temporal visual area respond to directional motion defined by any feature, a property termed *form-cue invariance*. The motion signals from all features are combined and summed by a motion detector. In a real environment with unknown multicolored objects, the best strategy would be to integrate coherent motion from all possible features.

In the extreme case, Watamaniuk et al. (1995) investigated the ability to detect a single dot moving in a relatively coherent trajectory embedded among dots in random motion. In each successive frame, the target dot moved in one direction while all the other dots moved in different random directions, including the direction of the target dot. Thus it would be impossible to detect the target dot within a small number of frames because other dots could have randomly mimicked that identical motion. Watamaniuk et al. argued that motion detection is based on an interconnected network of adjacent similarly oriented lower-level detectors. The idea is that the firing of one such detector leads to an excitation signal to other adjacent detectors that makes them easier to fire. The facilitation inherent in the network acts to smooth out random motion and maintain the original track of the dot (the detection of motion in gentle arcs equals that for straight lines). This is the same effect hypothesized to account for contour formation in chapter 4. Here again is the notion of cooperative systems that act to integrate noisy data and that reflect the natural physics of the world, where objects tend to go straight or bend in gentle arcs.

Overall, the important observation is that the perception of coherent surfaces occurs even if only a small fraction (or one) of the dots are moving coherently in the same direction. Moreover, the motion can be based on any differentiating feature. One question is the degree to which attention and task requirements can affect motion detection. One possible answer is that the initial stages of sensory processing are changed so that the actual data sent to the motion detection mechanism produced are different. A second possible answer would be that the initial stages are obligatory, being based on neural connections, so that the same data are always created. Attention shifts could occur in the motion detection mechanism, possibly created by higher-level cortical feedback, and determine the phenomenal nature of the surfaces and objects specified by the motion. There is recent evidence that, in fact, cognitive mechanisms may interact with motion detection mechanisms. The basic finding is that the strength of the neural response in the parts of the dorsal cortex thought to be involved in motion detection depends on the focus of attention of the observer. For example, Beauchamp, Cox, and DeYoe (1997) constructed a complex stimulus in which different regions simultaneously changed brightness, color, or the direction of coherent dot movement. The neural response was greatest when the observers made judgments about the movement direction and were attenuated when the observers made judgments about the nonmovement properties.

Motion Aftereffects

Aftereffects demonstrate that movement can be perceived without any physical movement at all. If you stare at a waterfall for about 30 s and then shift your gaze to a stationary region, you will find that the region appears to move in the reverse direction at roughly the same speed as the waterfall. (Aristotle was the first person to report motion aftereffects, but he reported incorrectly that the stationary region seemed to move in the same direction as the waterfall.)

We expect that any neural encoding unit would lose its sensitivity after long periods of stimulation and firing. This loss in sensitivity will alter the overall response to subsequent stimuli compared to the response without the adapting stimulus, and the resulting change is a way to probe the operation of that perceptual system. At the simplest level, the existence of an aftereffect is taken as evidence for neural encoding units selective for a particular property.

If aftereffects were simply due to the loss of sensitivity of neurons within the visual (or auditory) systems, then I do not believe they would be of much interest to anyone but sensory physiologists. However, aftereffects can be affected by the segregation of the elements into surfaces, as well as by attention. Aftereffects are not obligatory; the manner and strength of the aftereffect is a reflection of both the lower- and higher-level organizations of the pathways. Moreover, recent analyses suggest that aftereffects are not simply physiological flaws but that they can be thought of as adaptations that tune perceptual systems to different stimulus probabilities to maximize information transmission.

To review, neurons sensitive to motion direction are found in the primary visual area V1 stemming from the magnocellular pathways that are insensitive to color and stationary contours, but that make strong transient firing responses to moving contours. The V1 neurons project to the middle temporal visual area and then onto the medial superior temporal area. For the higher regions, the general rule is that the size of the receptive field increases and the selectivity for complex motion patterns increases. The basic conception is that the direction-sensitive neurons in V1 with small receptive fields extract the local motion signals autonomously, and those local motion signals are integrated in the temporal areas to form objects and surfaces.

On this basis, models for motion aftereffects are composed of two parts. The first is adaptation in the first-stage local motion detectors. Barlow and Hill (1963) measured the firing rate to rotating random dot patterns in the rabbit retina. They found that the rate decreased over a period of about 20 s. After the pattern was removed, the firing rate dropped below its baseline and gradually recovered over a period of about 30 s.

The second part is competitive comparison between the local motion detectors in a second stage of analysis. Motion aftereffects occur when the unadapted detectors override the adapted detectors. Often the comparison is between opposing motion detectors so that the aftereffect is reversed motion, but that is not always the case. The motion aftereffects seem due to the drop in responsiveness of the adapted neurons. There is little change in the unadapted neurons.

Motion Integration

Vidnyanszky, Blaser, and Papathomas (2002) summarized interesting research illustrating how the segmentation of random dot movements into one surface or two transparent surfaces affects the motion aftereffect. If there is a pattern of moving dots, the local direction of movements determines whether we perceive one coherent surface or two transparent surfaces moving relative to one another (similar to the two possible perceptions resulting from the movement of two gratings shown in figure 5.6). The motion aftereffects are particularly interesting in the latter case because there are two adapting directions at each point in space, and so we might expect that the motion aftereffect would also be in two directions. But that is not the outcome due to the integration of motion from all directions.

Consider the prototypical case: coherent motion of all of the dots to the right, creating the perception of a single surface moving to the right (figure 5.11A). That motion would adapt and reduce the firing rates of the rightward-direction neurons. When followed by a static dot pattern, the normal balance in the firing rates between the leftward and rightward neurons that yield no motion would have been disrupted. The leftward neurons

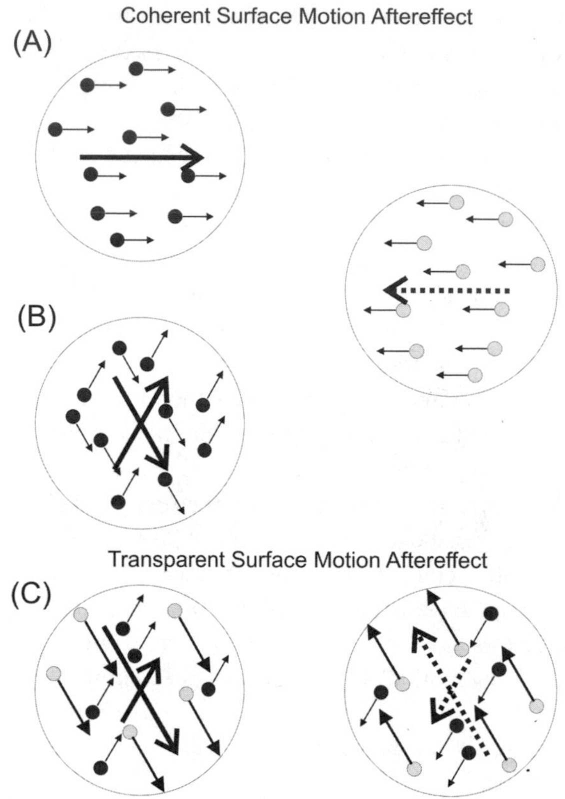

Figure 5.11. The motion aftereffects arise from the integrated motion in the adapting stimulus. For that reason, the two motions in (B) combine to generate only a single motion aftereffect direction that is opposite to the pooled movement in the stimulus. There are two motion aftereffect directions if the stimulus motions are perceived to be on different surfaces. Different velocities between the gray and black dots, as in (C), can yield those two motion aftereffects in different directions and velocities. Adapted from "Motion Integration During Motion Aftereffects," by Z. Vidnyanszky, E. Blaser, and T. V. Papathomas, 2002, *Trends in Cognitive Science, 6*, 157–161.

would be firing at a higher rate and all the static dots would appear to move to the left.

Now consider the prototypical case for motion in two directions: 50% of the dots scattered throughout the array move up to the right, and the remaining 50% move down to the right (figure 5.11B). When followed by a static dot pattern, there is only a single motion directly to the left (as for figure 5.11A) and not two motion aftereffects. Vidnyanszky et al. (2002) argued that, as stated in the paragraph above, there are two motion directions at each spatial point. But those motions are integrated to yield a direct rightward movement so that the motion aftereffect is to the left.

Transparency aftereffects do occur if the adapting stimulus affects two independent sets of direction-sensitive neurons. For example, transparency aftereffects occur if the two motions appear to be two surfaces at different distances, or if one motion is at a very slow speed and the second at a very fast speed, as illustrated in figure 5.11C (Van de Smagt, Verstraten, & van de Grind, 1999). The important point is that the balance between opposite-motion-direction neurons is not sufficient to explain motion aftereffects.

Optimal Coding

It is easy to think of aftereffects as design flaws in perceptual systems, but Wainwright (1999) and Clifford, Wenderoth, and Spehar (2000) suggested that aftereffects can be seen as a model for the tuning of perceptual systems to the probabilities of occurrences of events in the world. To maximize information transmission for any dimension (e.g., motion, direction, orientation, color), perceptual systems should match their sensitivity to the probability of occurrence of the values along each dimension so that each output occurs equally often (see figure 3.5).

In the case of motion aftereffects here, there is a strong signal with little noise. The optimal information strategy is to reduce sensitivity to the adapting stimulus so that more of the dynamic range of the neuron's firing rate can be used for other events. A person comes to these experiments with a long history of viewing motions in different directions. We can assume that over time, all directions occurred equally often, so that the optimal prior sensitivity would be flat across directions. The experimental adapting conditions slightly increase the probabilities of motion in one or two directions. In order to continue to maximize information transmission, this should lead to a decrease in the sensitivity to motion in those directions and create a motion aftereffect if the subject is presented with a stationary pattern. The predicted change in sensitivity has been found by Hosoya et al. (2005) in retinal cells as described in chapter 2.

First Order (Fourier) and Second-Order (Non-Fourier) Motion Patterns

Visual Second-Order Patterns

The distinction between short- and long-distance motion perception has become blurred. In general, the fact that motion is perceived for discrete presentations implies that the visual system integrates over spatial distances and temporal intervals so that the empirical outcomes that led to the conclusion that there are two different limits would suggest that there are two kinds of space-time processes. But Cavanagh and Mather (1989) argued that there are not two different limits; instead, short- and long-distance motion perception exist on a continuum and the previous distinction based on d_{max} rests on the confounding of stimulus properties with distance. There would be only one system whose output reflects the spatial and temporal properties of the stimulus.

Cavanagh and Mather (1989) suggested another type of dichotomy in motion processing that occurs between first- and second-order patterns (sometimes termed Fourier and non-Fourier patterns). First-order statistics refer to spatial and temporal variations in intensity or wavelength. Put simply, two areas have different first-order statistics if they differ in average brightness or color. Black-and-white gratings can be described in terms of the intensity variation across space and so are first-order stimuli. Second-order statistics, as used here, are derived from the first-order characteristics and refer to differences in the variation of brightness (i.e., contrast) or color across space. It is the contrast that is the important perceptual quantity, as described in chapter 1, here, and in chapter 6.

A single point in space cannot be defined in terms of its contrast. Local contrast must be defined in terms of the set of points within that region, and the variability in local contrast across the entire field generates one possible second-order description of the field. Suppose we construct a rectangle composed of randomly arranged black squares (–1 reflectance) and white squares (+1 reflectance) adjacent to a similar rectangle composed of dark gray (–0.50 reflectance) and light gray (+0.50 reflectance) squares. The average brightness is identical, but the contrast within the rectangles varies, a second-order statistic. From the results in chapter 4 (figure 4.1), the two rectangles will effortlessly segment apart even though the average brightness is identical. This implies that there must be visual processes that can discriminate contrast differences.

From the results in the first part of this chapter, we know that motion perception occurs for first-order differences. The empirical question then becomes whether there is motion perception for pure second-order differences (i.e., no first-order differences). Chubb and Sperling (1988) created one type of image sequence making use of drifting sinusoid waves in which there was no net directional energy that could stimulate first-order detectors. They termed such sequences *drift balanced* because the first-order luminance changes were equal in each direction.[3] Technically, for drift-balanced

3. Even though a stimulus might be drift balanced, it is possible that a localized Fourier motion detector might be strongly excited (e.g., if not centered on a receptive field). To avoid this possibility, Chubb and Sperling (1988) defined microbalanced stimuli such that a microbalanced stimulus is drift balanced when viewed through any separable space-time filter (window). In essence, if the stimulus is space-time separable as defined in chapter 2, then it is microbalanced.

stimuli, the expected power of a sinusoid drifting in one direction is equal to the expected power of a sinusoid of the identical frequency drifting in the opposite direction (Chubb & Sperling, 1988). If movement is based on the power of the Fourier components, then movement in either direction should be equally probable because there is equal power in each direction. But the perceived motion direction is not ambiguous, as described below.

One type of drift-balanced stimulus is based on contrast-modulated noise. We start with a two-dimensional array composed of random black or white squares and modulate the contrast among the squares within each column. In the simple example shown in figure 5.12, a square wave modulates the random array by changing the black-and-white squares into dark gray/light gray squares. Five rightward steps are shown in figure 5.12. For the actual stimuli used in experiments, a sinusoidal wave modulates (i.e., multiplies the brightness) the elements in the arrays so that the contrast

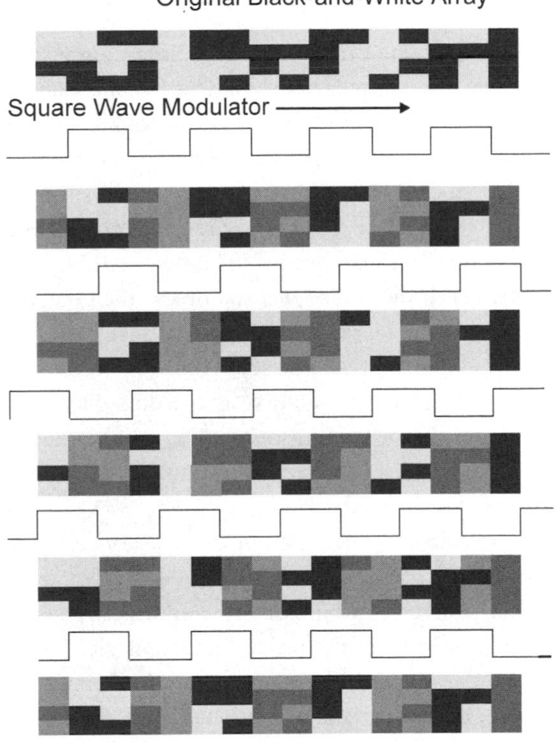

Figure 5.12. Simplified second-order motion. As the square wave travels to the right, it progressively changes the contrast of columns in the two-dimensional array. At the high point of the square wave, the black-and-white contrast is maximum; at the low point, the contrast is greatly reduced. The perception is that of contrast bands moving from left to right.

varies from white and black when the amplitude of the sinusoid is +1, to dark gray/light gray (sinusoid amplitude equals 1/2), to equal grays (sinusoid amplitude equals 0), to light gray/dark gray (sinusoid amplitude equals −1/2), to black and white when the sinusoid amplitude is −1.

If the square wave or sinusoidal wave moves horizontally left to right while the array remains constant, there is clear perception of motion in one direction across the array.

Why is this pure second-order motion? In every column of the array, the average luminance is equal, roughly halfway between white and black. The moving square or sinusoidal wave does not change that average; it only changes the contrast. There is no change in the first-order average brightness of the columns to detect. Moreover, the modulating waves are drift balanced; the first-order energy in each direction is equal. Furthermore, the original array was generated randomly; the correlation between any pair of columns is zero; and after multiplying each column by a constant based on the height of the sinusoid, the correlations are still zero. We perceive the motion of the sinusoid "carried" by the change in contrast, a pure second-order effect.

A second type of second-order motion is more complex. Imagine that each dot in the array reverses polarity from white to black and back again at a rate equal to the amplitude of a horizontal sinusoidal wave. The sinusoid will create a grating defined by the rate of reversals–rapid reversals at the sinusoid peaks (90° and 270°) and slow reversals at the sinusoid zero points (0° and 180°). For example, one dot might reverse 5 times per second and the adjacent dot at 4.9 times per second. The dots will be reversing out of phase with each other. If the sinusoid is stationary, the perception is that of a periodic vertical grating defined by the rate of reversal of the flickering dots. As in the first example, if the sinusoid is shifted horizontally, there is a distinct impression of horizontal motion as the dots change their rates of flashing. Although each dot remains stationary, the average luminance is always zero, and the contrast within each column does not change. We perceive the motion of the sinusoid.

A third type of second-order pattern consists once again of a two-dimensional array composed of randomly placed white and black squares. If each column of squares is progressively contrast-reversed (each square in the column is switched from white to black and vice versa), there is a strong perception of movement. Six successive reversals are shown in figure 5.13. Again, each dot remains stationary, the average luminance is always zero, and the contrast within each column does not change.

Before continuing, it is worthwhile asking whether the study of second-order patterns has any validity for understanding a visual system that evolved in response to natural events. Several times previously I have argued that perceptual outcomes mirror the physical changes underlying important

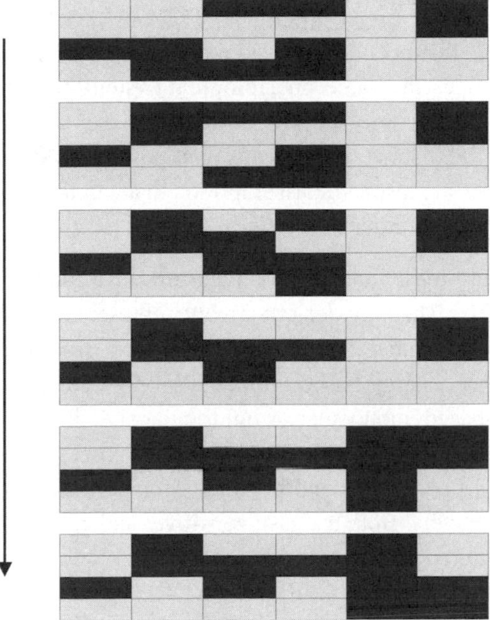

Figure 5.13. Contrast-reversing arrays. At successive time points, the black-and-white squares in next column reverse brightness levels. The previous column does not reverse back to its original pattern. A column-width band appears to move to the right.

objects and events necessary for survival. Those physical changes then become the initial stimuli to probe perceptual processing under the assumption that the perceptual systems have evolved to pick up that type of information. It is true that contrast-modulated drift patterns do not occur naturally. Almost always, the first- and second-order textures would move together: the random dot array and the sinusoidal modulator shift simultaneously. However, H. R. Wilson (1994) has shown that second-order processing is necessary to perceive "illusionary" contours that may separate two textures. For this reason, what is learned about second-order perceiving of moving patterns probably is quite relevant to the issue of texture segmentation.

The importance of the first- and second-order pattern issue lies in formulating how many physiological mechanisms, and what kind, are necessary to account for the varieties of motion perception. For first-order moving patterns such as gratings, dots, and so on, the perception of motion is generally understood to be in terms of spatial-temporal correlation detectors. These detectors are picking up a change in luminance, a first-order property, across a specific distance in a specific time interval. But, purely second-order patterns do not have luminance changes that could be registered by such receptors. Given that people perceive movement in pure second-order patterns, two issues emerge:

1. Are there distinct channels and mechanisms for second-order perception or does the same physiological system perceive both types of motion?
2. If there are distinct mechanisms, is it possible to develop neural models based on reasonable assumptions that can account for the perception of second order motion?

In answering these questions, I make use of a model by Z.-L. Lu and Sperling (2001). Their model effectively represents a redirection and redefinition of the original dichotomy proposed by Braddick (1974) between short-range, fast, energy-based, monocular-only detection and long-range, slow, feature-based, monocular or interocular (i.e., alternating between the two eyes) presentation. Braddick's short-range process splits to become Lu and Sperling's first and second processes for first-order and second-order patterns respectively. Both are fast, sensitive, and primarily monocular, although not limited to short distances. Braddick's long-range process becomes Lu and Sperling's third process: slow, insensitive, monocular or interocular, and able to compute motion from a wide variety of features and stimuli. This third process can be influenced by attention, but the first and second processes cannot.

Underpinning all of this research is an elaborated neural circuit model based on the original model of Reichardt (1961) that essentially computes a spatial autocorrelation. The elaborated model consists of two simple oriented cortical neurons whose receptive fields are separated by some retinal distance. Each neuron is assumed to change its output based on the frequency/orientation and intensity of the light reaching its retinal position. In the elaboration shown in figure 5.14, the receptive fields at the two locations are connected symmetrically (i.e., mirror images) so that the output can signal movement in either direction. The output of each of the visual fields is delayed (Δt), and then multiplied by the direct output of the other field at time t. The multiplication is always between t + delay and t. This multiplication creates a temporal autocorrelation based on the firing pattern at t + delay and t. There are multiple delay lines, as described in chapter 4, to detect different speeds. Two delay lines (Δt_1 and Δt_2) are shown in figure 5.14 between cells A and B. Finally, the two results are subtracted from each other to indicate leftward (a positive sum) or rightward (a negative sum) movement, as illustrated in figure 5.14. Such a circuit will fire maximally if a bright dot or oriented bar moves from the retinal position of the first neuron to the retinal position of the second neuron (or vice versa) in the delay interval. I assume that there are a multitude of such energy detectors, each tuned to a particular spatiotemporal frequency and spatial

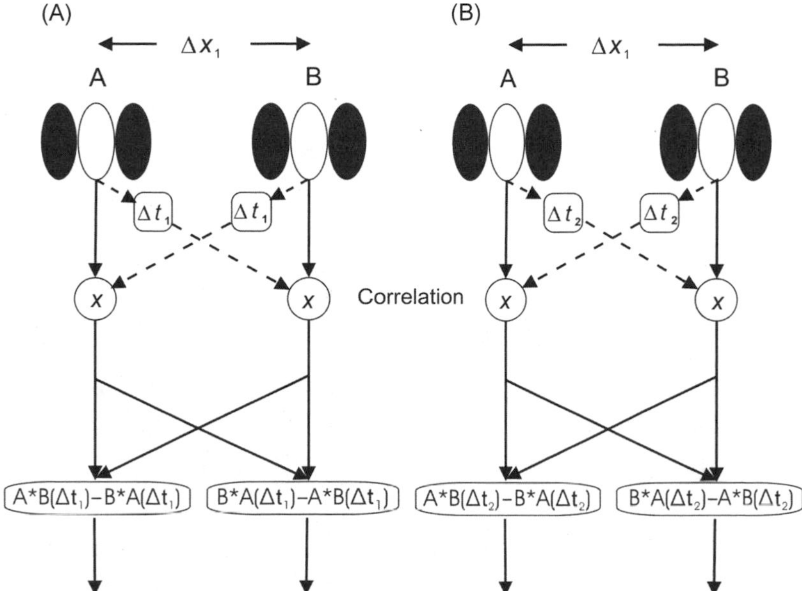

Figure 5.14. A motion energy detector. The excitation from two receptors A and B are correlated to determine the direction and speed of movement. The outputs from each receptor are time delayed for progressively longer times along different delay lines and correlated to the direct output of the other receptor to determine the movement speed. In (A), the outputs from A and B are delayed for Δt_1 and compared to the direct outputs from B and A respectively. In (B), the outputs are delayed by Δt_2. The value of Δt that maximizes the correlation is an indicant of the speed of the movement. Adapted from "Three-Systems Theory of Human Visual Motion Perception: Review and Update," by Z.-L. Lu and G. Sperling, 2001, *Journal of the Optical Society of America, A, 18*, 2331–2370.

distance. Z.-L. Lu and Sperling (2001) termed this unit a *motion energy detector*. The integration of the outputs of all these units is assumed to somehow lead to the perceived motion.

To determine if the detection of first- and second-order motion is based on energy detection by means of a motion correlator, as illustrated in figure 5.14, or by the detection of image features, Z.-L. Lu and Sperling (2001) made use of two important properties of the proposed motion energy detectors. The first property is termed *pseudolinearity*: If a stimulus is composed of several component sine waves of different temporal frequencies, then the output of a motion energy detector is the sum of the responses to individual inputs. The second property is that static displays result in zero output.

The key trick in Lu and Sperling's technique is to add a static sinusoidal wave termed the *pedestal* to motion stimuli assumed to be detected by first- or second-order energy detectors. The addition of the pedestal changes the

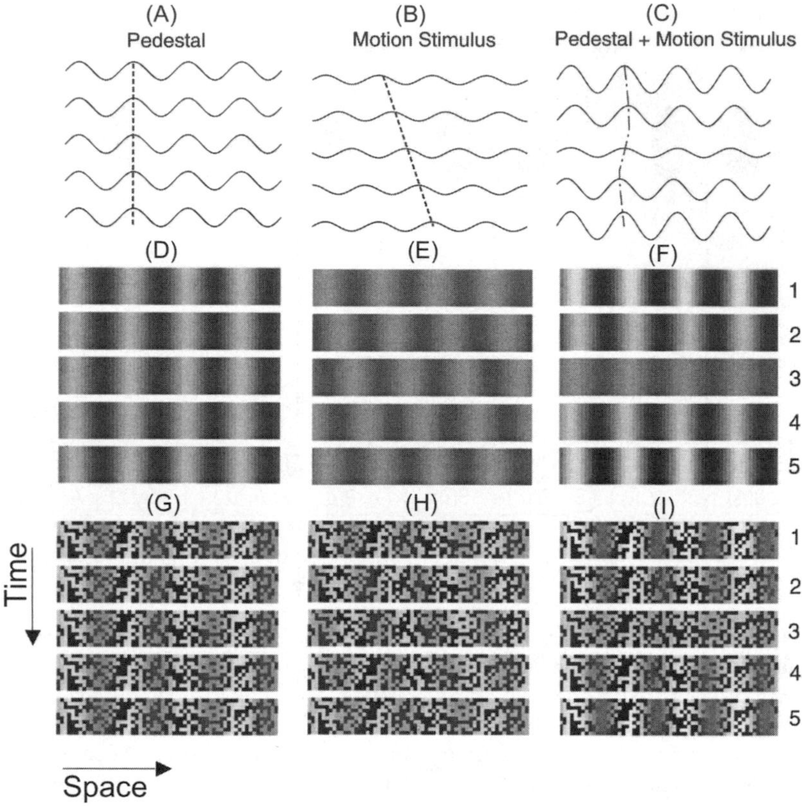

Figure 5.15. The addition of a constant sinusoidal wave (i.e., the pedestal) provides a way to determine if motion perception is due to motion energy detection. From "Three-Systems Theory of Human Visual Motion Perception: Review and Update," by Z.-L. Lu and G. Sperling, 2001, *Journal of the Optical Society of America, A, 18*, 2331–2370. Copyright 2001 by the Optical Society of America. Reprinted with permission.

motion of a moving luminance or contrast grating. The dark and light bands of the grating oscillate back and forth, and this effect is purely due to the addition of the pedestal energy (figure 5.15).

First, if the detection systems for first-order or second-order patterns are based on energy detection, then the addition of the pedestal should have no effect on the perception of motion, because a static wave does not change the output. A moving luminance grating will appear to move to the right even if the pedestal is added. (This outcome does not tell us if there are one or two systems; it simply tells us if the systems can detect energy.)

Second, if the detection systems for first-order or second-order patterns are based on the detection of features such as light or dark peaks, zero crossings, or valleys, then the addition of the pedestal should result in the perception of oscillation only, and observers should be unable to detect the direction of motion.

For all types of first-order stimuli that involve changes in luminance, there were no effects resulting from the addition of the pedestal. On this basis, Lu and Sperling argue that a motion energy detector is responsible for the perception of first-order motion. For simple grating stimuli, observers are able to detect motion up to temporal frequencies of 12 Hz (i.e., 12 periods of a sinusoidal, or square wave, grating pass a single point per second).

However, for second-order patterns, the motion energy detectors as shown in figure 5.14 would not be able to signal movement. The leftward and rightward outputs would always be equal because there is no net lightness change (only the contrast changes). Yet observers do see second-order motion. The temporal limits are exactly the same as for first-order patterns, roughly 12 Hz, and there is no effect resulting from adding a pedestal. This led Lu and Sperling to make the supposition that second-order patterns could be detected by a modified version of the motion energy detector. In the modified version, preceding the motion energy detector there would be a spatial filter, a temporal band-pass filter limiting the response to lower frequencies followed by a full-wave rectifier. The full-wave rectifier makes all of the outputs positive, so that they sum to equal two times the individual output. A grating from white (+1) to black (−1) sums to 2, but a grating from light gray (+1/2) to dark gray (−1/2) sums to 1. This makes different contrasts, with the identical average luminance that previously summed to the same zero value now summing to a different value.[4] This is a LNL model of the sort hypothesized to account for the perception of second-order texture patterns in chapter 4 (figure 5.16).

The identical temporal limits for first- and second-order patterns led Lu and Sperling to make a second supposition, namely that there are separate detectors for first-order and second-order patterns that travel along parallel circuits, but which ultimately converge. To test this, Lu and Sperling created combination patterns to test whether first- and second-order motions in opposite directions would cancel each other and if first- and second-order motions in the same direction but different phases would cancel each other. The results indicated that phase did not affect the detection of motion, but the patterns moving in opposite directions did cancel each other. This led the authors to hypothesize that first- and second-order motion is first calculated in independent parallel processes (lack of phase effect) but then combined and summed (opposite directions cancel).

4. If we assume that neural signals are made positive, we are effectively calculating the range of the values. Alternately, if we assume that the neural signals are made positive by squaring the values, we are effectively calculating the variance.

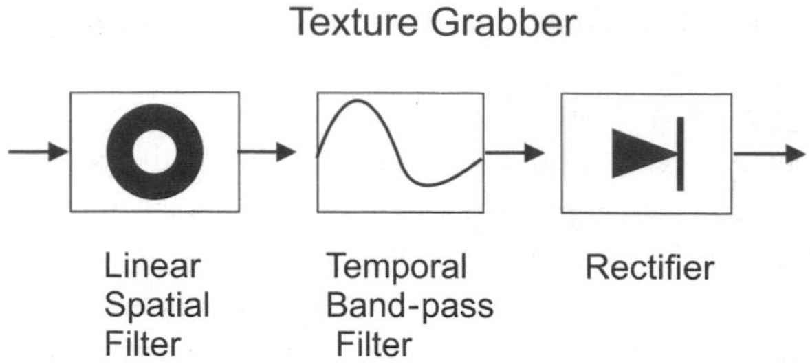

Texture Grabber

Linear Spatial Filter

Temporal Band-pass Filter

Rectifier

Figure 5.16. Texture grabber to detect second-order movement. The texture is detected by a linear spatial filter (e.g., a center-surround or a frequency × orientation Gabor filter) within a temporal frequency band. The variation in contrast of the texture measured by the filter is either full-wave rectified or squared to convert increases and decreases in contrast into excitations. Adapted from "Three-Systems Theory of Human Visual Motion Perception: Review and Update," by Z.-L. Lu and G. Sperling, 2001, *Journal of the Optical Society of America, A, 18*, 2331–2370.

To further assess the similarity between first- and second-order systems, Lu and Sperling presented the frame sequences either entirely to one eye, or alternately to the left and right eyes. For both the first- and second-order patterns, observers were unable to detect energy motion if the frames were presented alternately to each eye. However, there was some evidence that motion could be detected for interocular presentation by a feature detection system that is inherently slower and less efficient.

To sum up at this point, Lu and Sperling contended that first- and second-order patterns are encoded by parallel energy detection processes. The difference is that the perception of motion of second-order patterns requires that there is some transformation of the neural code so that decreases in firing rates (i.e., negative outputs) are recoded into increases in firing rates. The authors hypothesized a rectifier to make negatives into positives, but squaring the outputs to remove negatives would also.

Lu and Sperling also constructed a stimulus pattern that could not be detected using either a first- or second-order detection system. In this pattern, random dots move up and down within columns. The percentage of dots moving upward and downward within a column varies horizontally according to a sinusoidal function. At the peaks of the sinusoidal all the dots move in one direction, while at the zero points an equal number of dots move upward and downward (see figure 5.17). To perceive motion as the horizontal sinusoidal is shifted laterally, the observer must detect that the differential vertical up-down movements drift horizontally. First- and second-order energy detectors would not pick this motion because there is no consistent change in luminance or contrast. Lu and Sperling term these *motion-modulation stimuli*.

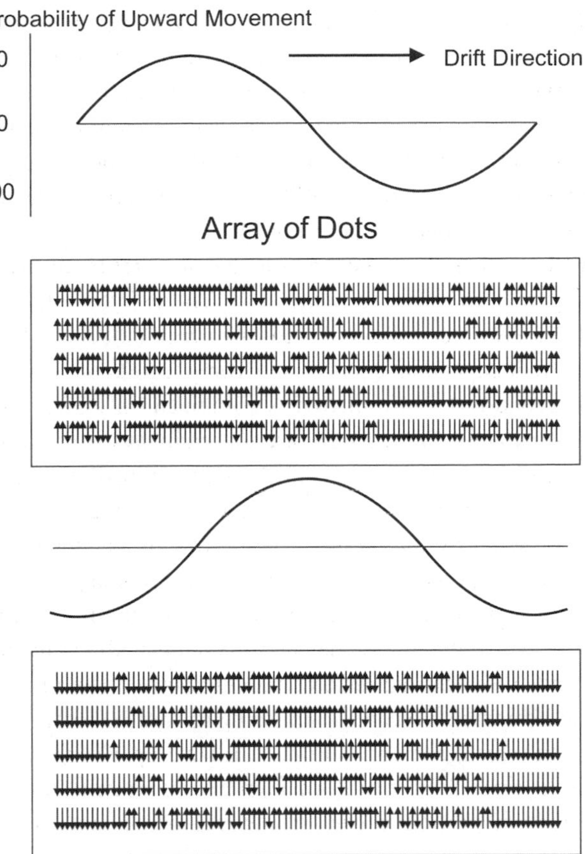

Figure 5.17. Motion-modulated stimuli. Dots scattered throughout the array undergo up-and-down motion determined by the amplitude of the sinusoidal wave. As the sinusoidal wave moves toward the right, the dots change their up-and-down motion. Motion-modulated stimuli cannot be detected by the combination of a texture grabber and a motion energy detector. Adapted from "Three-Systems Theory of Human Visual Motion Perception: Review and Update," by Z.-L. Lu and G. Sperling, 2001, *Journal of the Optical Society of America, A, 18*, 2331–2370.

The results for motion-modulated stimuli are nearly the direct opposite of those for luminance (first-order) and contrast-modulated (second-order) stimuli. First, the sensitivity for these stimuli is much less. Observers can detect motion of the drifting sinusoid only up to 3-6 Hz, instead of the 12 Hz found for the other types of patterns. In other words, if the sinusoidal wave drifts above 6 Hz, the observer merely sees random motions. Second, observers could not perceive motion when the pedestal was added. As described above, the masking effect of the pedestal implies that an energy detection system was not used and that the motion was detected by means of features in the displays. Third, monocular and interocular presentation was essentially the same. The feature-tracking system can make use of single-eye and alternate-eye sequences equally well. Locations of the features in space are marked, while the background is unmarked. Moreover, it seems that the binocular feature tracking system is indifferent to the type of variation (this resembles the finding of Kolers, 1972, about shape indifference for apparent movement and that of Stoner and Albright, 1994, about feature indifference for transparency perception).

Taken all together, these outcomes lead to a representation of the motion detection system, as shown in figure 5.18. On the left are the pathways for first- and second-order patterns based on energy detection. For each pathway, there are independent connections from the left and right eyes, and the first- and second-order information is combined only after each has been computed separately. On the right are the pathways for feature detection. There are no energy detectors, and the extraction of features can occur within one eye or between eyes. At a subsequent stage of processing, the features abstracted by the motion energy system and those found by the feature extraction processes are combined. At this point, the observer can weight the importance of each feature to achieve the final perception.

The synthesis of the motion-detecting systems with the feature-detecting systems binds the local motion to a moving object. The first- and second-order systems create "objectless" movement, and the feature salience system based on selective attention in Z.-L. Lu and Sperling's (2001) model is where the different kinds of information are integrated. The same kind of hypothesized integration occurs in several processes. In Julesz's final model, textons merely attract attention to discontinuities, and attention shifted to that location is necessary to identify the differences. In Stoner and Albright's (1994) experiments on transparency, neurons in the visual system respond to any kind of motion, so that it is necessary to hypothesize a mechanism to integrate the motion of surface with the properties of the surfaces themselves.

Up to this point, I have considered lateral movement and how the perception of coherent movement is synonymous with the perception of a figure, either a surface or an object. Even for the perception of objectless second-order motion, there are proposed mechanisms that bind that motion to features of objects. In an interesting demonstration, S.-H. Lee and Blake (1999) showed that the correlated timing of local motions can give rise to the perception of figural areas, that is, objects. This is an important demonstration because none of the motion energy detector models can explain the outcome, and because it reinforces the view that the fine structure of the firing pattern of individual cells underlies motion and object perception.

Lee and Blake made use of two similar stimulus configurations. In the first, the array was composed of roughly 700 little Gabor patches. Each patch looked like a striped circle, and the stripes were pointing in random

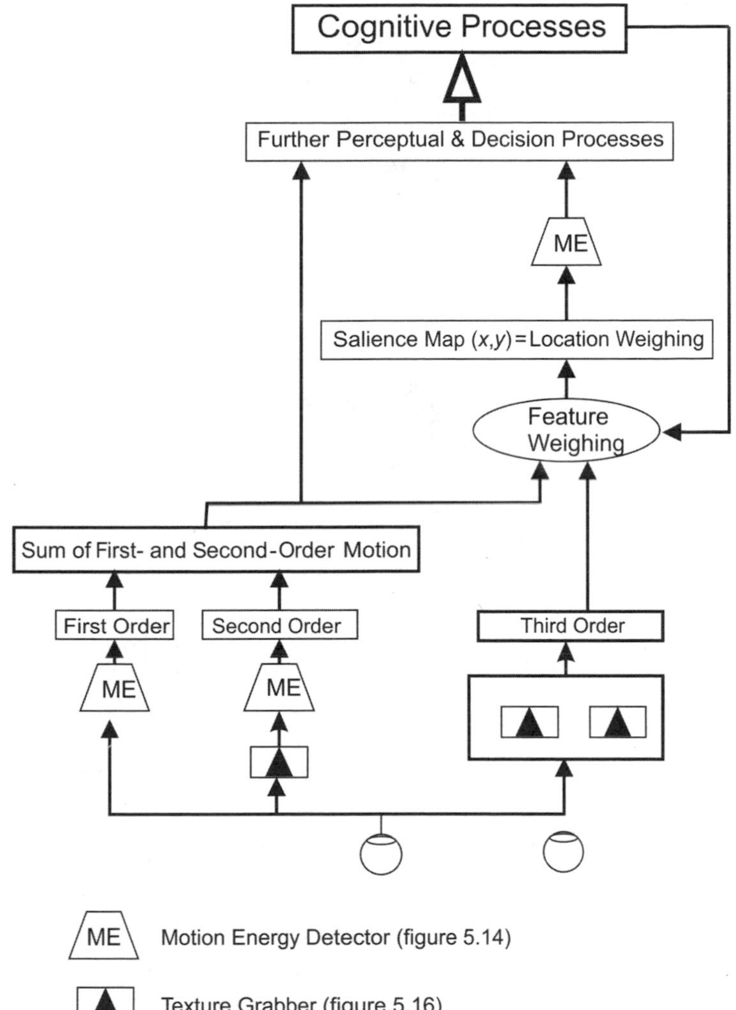

Figure 5.18. The model proposed by Z.-L. Lu and Sperling (2001) that contains three parallel channels to detect movement. From "Three-Systems Theory of Human Visual Motion Perception: Review and Update," by Z.-L. Lu and G. Sperling, 2001, *Journal of the Optical Society of America, A, 18*, 2331–2370. Copyright 2001 by the Optical Society of America. Reprinted with permission.

orientations. Each patch could move only in an orthogonal (i.e., perpendicular) direction to its stripes (see figure 5.19A). Every patch moved 100 times per second, and Lee and Blake varied the probability that a patch reversed direction or continued in the same direction. If the probability was 0.5, each patch had an equal chance of reversing or continuing its direction (an average of 50 reversals per second) so that the motion was highly irregular, while if the probability was 0.2, each patch tended to continue in the

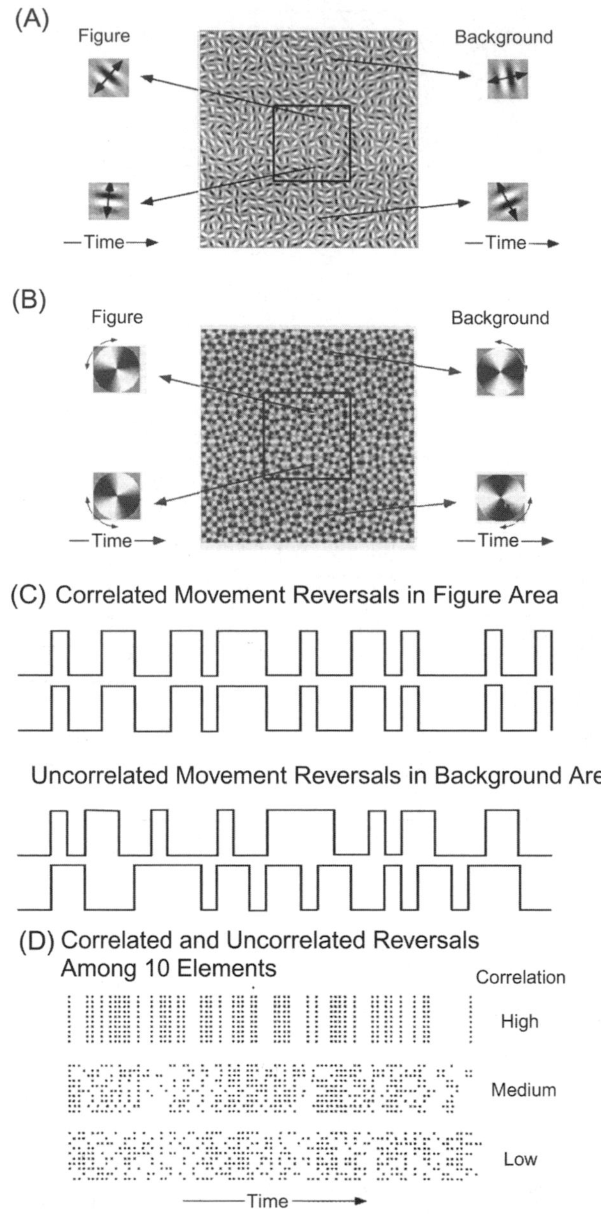

Figure 5.19. Detection of synchronous reversals and rotations. The Gabor patches and windmills are sketched in (A) and (B) respectively. The double-ended arrows illustrate the reversing motions. Perfectly correlated reversals are illustrated in the first part of (C). The vertical lines depict each reversal, and the length of the horizontal lines depicts the time spent in one direction. Uncorrelated reversals are illustrated in the second part of (C). Each reversal is depicted by a dot in (D). The reversals are shown for 10 elements; the correlation among the elements ranges from high to low. Adapted from "Visual Form Created Solely From Temporal Structure," by S.-H. Lee and R. Blake, 1999, *Science, 284*, 1165–1168.

same direction with few reversals. In the figure region of the array, the patches tended to change their direction of movement at the same time, as illustrated in (C); Lee and Blake varied the predictability of the direction reversals among the patches so that at one end nearly all the patches changed direction at the same time (high correlation in D), while at the other end a simple majority of patches changed direction at the same time. In the nonfigure region, each patch changed direction independently of all others, according to the overall reversal probability. Remember that the orientation of the stripes is random and the process starts randomly (see figure 5.19). Thus, the figure cannot be identified by motion in any single direction. Even for two patches with the same orientation of stripes within the figure region, those two patches might be moving in opposite directions. The only thing that characterizes the figure region is that there is a synchronous change in direction for each patch, not a common direction. Performance was much better than chance even if the degree of internal predictability within the figure region was relatively low.

The second array demonstrated that rotational synchrony also provided a means to identify a figure region. Instead of laterally moving Gabor patches, Lee and Blake constructed little "windmills" that rotated either clockwise or counterclockwise (figure 5.19B). As above, the reversals in direction for the windmills within the figure region were correlated, while the reversals in direction for the windmills in the nonfigure region occurred independently. In the exact same way as above, direction of rotation provided no cue to identify the figure region; only the correlated change in direction could define the figure. Here too, observers were able to identify the figure region.

Lee and Blake argued that to perceive the figure based on correlated synchronous reversals, the visual system must: (a) register with high accuracy the times at which the changes in velocity occur for a set of spatially distributed points; (b) correlate the times of these changes over neighboring regions throughout the array; and (c) identify boundaries marked by sharp transitions in correlations among local elements. The authors rightfully claimed that current visual models do not incorporate these steps and tend to minimize the importance of the temporal structure. (This work also is relevant to work on grouping and segregation, discussed in chapter 9.)

Watson and Humphreys (1999) illustrated an interesting difference between linear and rotational motion. In their work, letters (H, T, X, and O) were either stationary, rotated around their center points, or translated vertically. The observer's task was to search for a specific letter. If the target letter was rotated, it was easy to detect that letter if the other letters were stationary, or translated vertically up or down. However, if the target letter was rotated, say clockwise, and the nontarget letters were rotated counterclockwise, it was much harder to detect the target letter. This outcome is quite different from that for linear motion. If the target letter moved upward and the nontarget letters moved downward, it was easy to detect the target. Watson and Humphreys concluded that segmenting the array on the basis of rotation is very difficult, in contrast to segmenting the array on the basis of linear motion. Previous research of Julesz and Hesse (1970) supports these results. Julesz and Hesse constructed an array (roughly 80 × 60) of 4,800 "needles" that rotated around their center points. If the target and nontarget needles rotated at the same speed in different directions, observers could not perceive the target region. However, if the needles rotated at different speeds, regardless of direction, the array segmented into different regions.

The authors suggested an explanation based on the organization of local elements into one or more surfaces. If elements with different motions form separate surfaces, then detection is made easier because the observer can attend to one surface. If the local motions do not create different surfaces, the observer must scan every element, so that detection becomes much harder. From this perspective, they hypothesized that the rotation of individual letters (or any small shape) does not give rise to the perception of a surface, and that accounts for the poor performance.

I think what connects the research of S.-H. Lee and Blake (1999) to that of Watson and Humphreys (1999) and Julesz and Hesse (1970) is that rotation direction does not lead to segregation. In Lee and Blake, segmentation was due to synchrony; in Watson and Humpheys, segmentation was due to different kinds of movement; in Julesz and Hesse, segmentation was due to rotation speed. If differences in rotational motion do not give rise to a set of surfaces such that each surface corresponds to one motion (a failure of the Gestalt principle of common fate), it demonstrates that visual attention is not simply afloat in space but is necessarily attached to continuous surfaces. This is the same argument made by Wandell (1995) in chapter 1 that we perceive motion with respect to dense surface representations.

Auditory Second-Order Patterns

Huddleston and DeYoe (2003) have developed an analogy to second-order vision patterns by equating movement through pitch with movement through space. Suppose we start with a set of 10 to 12 tones that range from 300 to 10000 Hz. If we present each tone separately, one after the other, then we would have the equivalent of a first-order visual stimulus, and we would expect that it would be trivial for listeners to determine if the tones were increasing or decreasing in pitch. Now suppose we conceptually start at Time 0 presenting all of the tones at once, but some of the tones are on and some are off. As illustrated in figure 5.20, tones 1, 2, 3, 5, 8, and 10 are on and 4, 6, 7, and 9 are off. Now at each successive time point, we switch the next highest tone on-to-off or off-to-on. As shown in figure 5.20, at

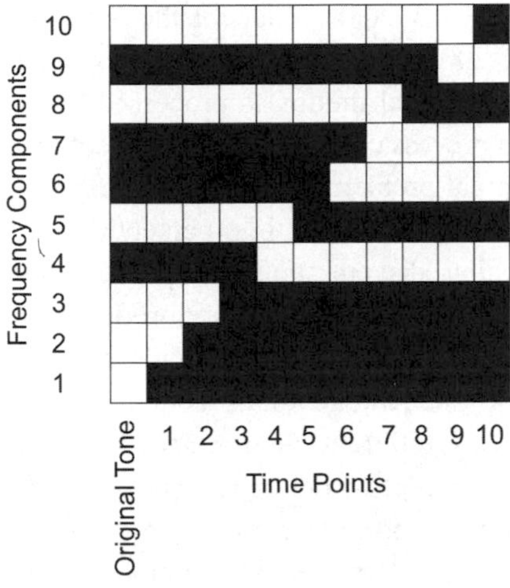

Figure 5.20. Second-order auditory sequences. At successive time points, one frequency component either is turned from on to off or from off to on. For example, at time point 5 the fifth frequency component that had been presented during the first four periods is turned off, and that component remains silent for the rest of the sequence.

Time 1, Tone 1 is turned off, at Time 2, Tone 2 is turned off, at Time 3, Tone 3 is turned off, at Time 4, Tone 4 is turned on, and so forth. Across all of the steps, there will be no net change of energy, analogous to second-order visual patterns.[5] Listeners were able to detect whether the change in tonal components created an ascending or descending change. However, they were unable to do so at faster presentation rates at which first-order patterns were easily identified. This type of stimulus is almost identical to that used by Kubovy and Jordan (1979), described in chapter 4, in which the phases of the component tones were changed one after the other.

Summary

I believe that Cavanagh and Mather (1989) provided a very useful summary. They argued that all motion processing starts with local spatial-temporal comparators based on the Reichardt model or variants described in this chapter. The comparators operate throughout the visual field in parallel, at several spatial and temporal scales, and at many directions and can be modified by context. Although I have presented the three-process model (Z.-L. Lu & Sperling, 2001), it is still unclear whether there are three distinct parallel mechanisms based on the spatial-temporal comparators or

5. This auditory stimulus is exactly analogous to Demonstration 3, "Traveling contrast reversal of a random bar pattern," in Chubb and Sperling (1988). Chubb and Sperling pointed out that the standard nonlinear filter such as full- or half-wave rectification does not explain the perception of motion. They argued that a time-dependent linear transformation such as differentiation is necessary.

whether one or two branching mechanisms can account for the outcomes (for example, Bertone and Faubert, 2003, argued that complex second-order processing such as radial and rotational motion is processed by the same hard-wired mechanisms used to process complex first-order motion).

I have been struck by how perceptual problems seem to flow together. The changes in stimulus configurations and resulting perceptions are gradual and continuous. Neither falls into discontinuous categories. Noise transforms into structure, texture segregation blurs into motion detection, and both are determined by contrast. What seems to be underlying all of this is the correspondence problem. The stimulation at the eye or ear is underdetermined: It can represent many different environmental objects. General-purpose receptors, specialized receptive fields, and physiological "calculators," along with the expectations and intentions of the perceiver, determine what is perceived. Even if each determinant is dichotomous, the resultant perceptions will not fall into exclusive categories. What we hear and see will be continuous, encompassing the range of possibilities.

6

Gain Control and External and Internal Noise

Up to this point, I have discussed how noise can become structured to yield the perception of something. This chapter concerns the more common notion that noise is energy that disrupts perception. The first issue is how to measure internal physiological noise, and how to compare internal noise to the normal levels of external background noise. The second issue is how perceptual systems adapt to the immense variation in environmental energy (on the order of 10^8 units) compared to the much smaller variation in receptor firing rate (on the order of 10^2). It is this mismatch that has led to the development of various mechanisms, termed *gain controls*, to shift the response rate of neurons to represent the variation in intensity (the contrast) around the mean intensity. The third issue is how to measure the efficiency of observers in perceiving auditory and visual stimuli embedded in internal and external noise.

Internal Noise

Dark Noise

The classic experiment of Hecht, Schlaer, and Pirenne (1942) attempted to measure the absolute visual threshold. Prior to that, there was general agreement that the threshold for seeing a dim light against a dark background was remarkably low; estimates ranged from 10 to 50 quanta at the retina. Hecht et al. set out to measure the minimum amount of light, so they performed a series of preliminary experiments to determine the important experimental parameters (e.g., duration of dark adaptation, retinal location, size, duration, and wavelength of the light source) that would lead to an estimate of the minimum number of quanta necessary to see. Cornsweet (1970) beautifully summarized this work. Hecht et al. estimated that under the optimum conditions, humans could see as few as 5–9 absorbed quanta. Due to reflection off the cornea and absorption in the eye itself, roughly 100 quanta are necessary to yield the 5–9 quanta at the retina that excite retinal cells. (These values are for light presented off-center in the eye where the rod density is highest. The minimum number of quanta is roughly five times greater for light presented to the cone fovea.) These quanta were spread over a spatial summation region in the retina composed of about 300 rods, so that it seemed that one quantum is sufficient to trigger a receptor. This assumption was confirmed by electrophysiological recordings showing that neural responses could be recorded due to the absorption of a single quanta of light (Baylor, Lamb, & Yau, 1979).

Absolute thresholds always are defined statistically—60% detection here. Hecht et al. (1942) attempted to identify any source that could lead to variation in the subject's response. Was it due to variation in the light or in the subject? From a decision theory perspective, we can assume that subjects report seeing the dim light when the number of spikes in the trial interval exceeds some fixed number. But, on any trial, the number of quanta actually emitted by the light source can vary; the emitted quanta may not reach the retina; and any quanta reaching the retina may not stimulate a cell. Whatever the criteria, there are going to be instances when the number of spikes does not reach criterion when the stimulus was presented, and conversely there are going to be instances when the variability of the firing patterns within the visual system generates the required number of spikes even when the dim light is not presented. Hecht et al. concluded that any variation in the detection of the light flash was due to the inherent variability of the light source itself and resulting variability in quanta absorbed by the retinal receptors, rather than some internal biological or cognitive randomness. The finding that spontaneous firings of the retinal cells that could result in a false detection of light are amazingly infrequent supports this conclusion. It has been estimated that the firing of rods in the primate eye yielding a false alarm due to the spontaneous transformations of rhodopsin is less than one every 100–160 s (Aho, Donner, Hyden, Larsen, & Reuter, 1988; Lamb, 1987).

Nonetheless, a completely dark-adapted human observer will see flickering specks and flashes that occur randomly in a dark field. Barlow (1956) termed the lightness level resulting from the spontaneous firing *dark noise* and conceptualized that it operated in the same way as any physical light. Thus, the effective background for perceiving is the actual background light (however dim) plus the dark noise, and together they set limits for the detection of dim light flashes. In a decision theory coneption, observers must set their criteria in terms of the variability of the signal and noise (i.e., together. Then physical motion modules calculate which physical motion would best account for those movements. The grouping module and physical motion model module interact to yield the most likely perceptual representation of the movements.

Consider rotation. Points at different distances from the center of a surface move at different rates and trajectories. The grouping module would tend to place all dots at the same distance together based on the common movement (velocity and trajectory direction), and the physical motion module would interpret those movements as implying a rigid rotation. This leads to the perceptual illusion of coherent motion (motion capture), even though the motion of each dot is different. Wagemans, Van Gool, Swinnen, and Van Horebeek (1993) similarly argued that the perception of lower-order regularities between pairs of individual elements is supported by higher-order structures defined between pairs of pair-wise groupings of elements and so on upward, involving larger numbers of elements but fewer structures.

Tse, Cavanagh, and Kakayama (1998) made explicit the two steps implicitly involved in the typical apparent motion stimuli that alternate between images. The first step is to identify the "something" in each image, termed the *parsing step*, and the second step is to match the "somethings" in the two images, termed the *correspondence step*. In the traditional experiment, because the two stimuli are nonoverlapping (one stimulus appears and then disappears at one location, to reappear at a distant location), the parsing step is automatic and unambiguous, and the strongest correspondence cue simply is spatial proximity, as detailed above. However, if a different shape in the second image that shares part of the same contour replaces the shape in the first image, the perceptual problem is to determine what are the figures in each image. The shared contour creates the ambiguity in the parsing step, because there is not sufficient information in the views to yield the two independent but overlapping or abutting objects. The inability to solve the parsing step should stop the processing, because the correspondence step needs units to proceed. The authors argue that the visual system has evolved rules for resolving these ambiguities in the parsing step, and that these rules follow the ecological constraints found for real objects. These rules must make use of both views (i.e., the space-time representation) in order to determine the way in which one shape could transform into a second.

Tse et al. (1998) present several configurations to demonstrate the action of higher-level process in solving the apparent motion, as illustrated in figure 5.4. In the first type of configuration (figures 5.4A, 5.4B, and 5.4C), the first frame contains two simple square objects and the second frame contains an elongated rectangle, along with one of the original squares.

a signal-to-noise ratio), and Barlow argued that the conclusions of Hecht et al. (1942) should be modified to include the biological variability of dark noise as well as other sources of noise such as intrinsic stimulus variability (see above), receptor sampling errors, randomness of neural responses, loss of information during transmission through cortical centers, and lack of precision in cognitive processes. Following Barlow's approach, research has been aimed at describing and quantifying the various noise sources and ultimately deriving a figure of merit, *perceptual efficiency*, to describe the overall performance.

It is worthwhile to characterize two kinds of noise. The term *additive noise* signifies a constant level of noise that is independent of the level of the signal. The resulting signal is the sum of the actual signal + the noise. Additive noise can be overcome by increasing the level of the signal to the point at which the signal-to-noise ratio, $(S + N)/N$, sustains a desired performance. This is possible because N is assumed to be independent of the signal level. The term *multiplicative noise* signifies a noise whose power is proportional to the signal power ($N = kS$). For multiplicative noise, increasing (or decreasing) the signal power simultaneously increases (or decreases) the noise power so that the signal-to-noise ratio, $(S + N)/N = (S + kS)/kS = (1 + k)/k$, does not change. We can infer the type of noise by changes in performance. If performance increases directly with increases in brightness or contrast, we assume that the noise is additive. The fact that we cannot detect images with weak contrasts suggests that the internal noise is additive. In contrast, if performance is independent of contrast, then we assume that the noise is multiplicative. For example, if a square wave grating is masked by visual noise, once a critical level of the contrast is reached, further increases do not improve performance. We attribute this lack of improvement to the fact that the noise increases proportionally with the contrast. (This distinction between additive and multiplicative noise was discussed in chapter 3 with respect to optimizing information transmission.) Both internal and external noise can be additive or multiplicative.

Detecting Changes in Illumination

Based on Barlow's (1956) thinking, we can imagine dark noise as being independent of input noise that is added to the signal, that is, independent of the intensity of the signal. The amplitude of dark noise has been termed *equivalent input noise*. Suppose we measure the threshold for a simple visual (or auditory) stimulus with no background noise, say the threshold for a small bright disk. We then increase the background illumination and continue to measure the threshold for the small disk as a function of the background illumination. The threshold will remain relatively constant up to some background level because here the internal noise, being greater than the weak external noise due to the dim background, determines the threshold. It is dark light that creates the noise that limits sensitivity in this range (Hecht et al., 1942). Beyond that point, the threshold will begin to increase as a function of the background level. Here, the external noise is greater than the internal noise, so that the external noise will determine the threshold. The noise level at the "knee" in the threshold curve is an estimate of the point at which the internal and external background noise are equal, and that level becomes the estimate of the equivalent input noise (see figure 6.1). Above that level, the total noise is now the sum of the external noise (N) and the equivalent input noise (N_{eq}).

If we continue to increase the illumination of the background, the threshold now increases as the square root of the background illumination.

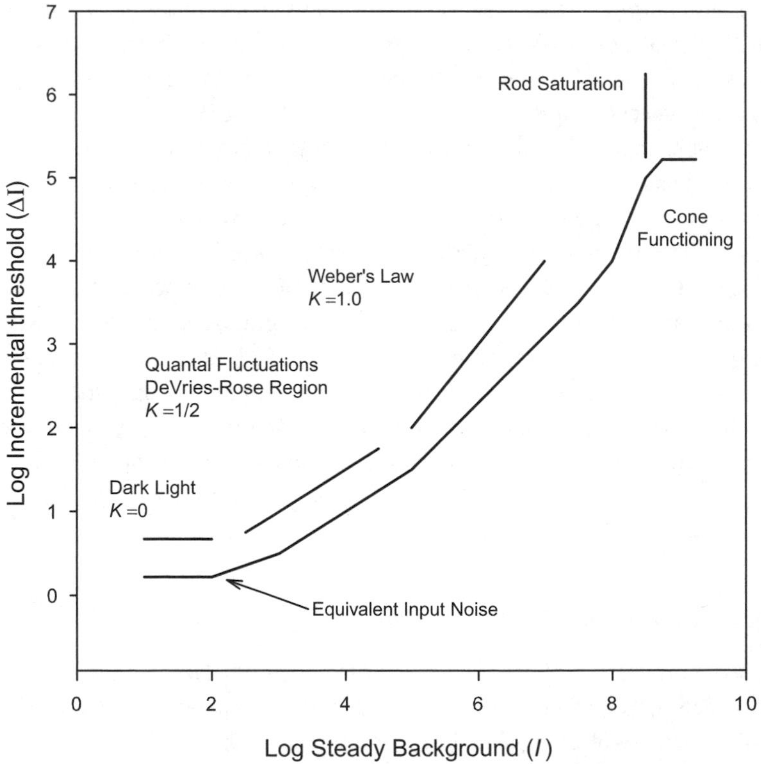

Figure 6.1. The threshold for a small disk as a function of the intensity of a steady background. The theoretical slopes for the DeVries-Rose region ($K = 1/2$) and the Weber region ($K = 1$) are shown as short straight lines. The *equivalent input noise* is found at the elbow between the flat initial region and the DeVries-Rose region. Adapted from "Visual Adaptation and Retinal Gain Controls," by R. Shapley and C. Enroth, 1984, *Progress in Retinal Research, 3*, 263–346.

In this range, sensitivity would be limited by the quantal fluctuations in the target and background illumination that are relatively large relative to the average illumination.[1] The observer has to detect when the increment in firing rate due to the target disk is significantly greater than the variability in firing rate due to inherent fluctuations in the brightness of the background. Suppose the observer tries to keep the signal-to-noise ratio constant (i.e., responds that the target is present if the firing rate is a multiple of the variability, analogous to a z-score, or responds at a constant likelihood ratio). Then the increment in signal strength for detection will have to grow in proportion to the standard deviation of the background noise, which is a function of the square root of the illumination. This loss in sensitivity is strictly due to the variation in the stimulus.

At still higher illumination levels, the threshold becomes proportional to the background; it is a constant times the background illumination. Thus, contrast (the ratio of the illumination of the stimulus compared to the background) sensitivity is constant and Weber's law holds true. This is the goal of perceptual adaptation: perceptual invariance of reflectance across different illuminations. Finally, at the highest illuminations, the threshold increases more rapidly than Weber's law predicts. At this illumination, the firing rate of the rods saturate, and the threshold increases as the square of the background illumination.

We can do a similar experiment to determine the value of the squared contrast of the grating that yields a given level of performance for different values of external contrast noise (analogous to the brightness of the target for different backgrounds). To do this, we construct a random noise with a given contrast and then vary the contrast of the grating added to the noise until observers achieve the desired performance level. The results of such an experiment closely resemble the outcome for detecting an increment in brightness (as in Figure 6.1):

1. The threshold is constant for low noise levels. At these levels, the external noise is small relative to the observer's internal noise (termed *contrast equivalent noise*) so that increases in the contrast of the external noise do not affect the threshold.
2. There is a linear increase in c^2 (the contrast power) at higher noise levels. At these values, the contrast of the external noise is greater than the contrast equivalent noise, so that increases in the contrast of the external noise directly affect the threshold. The noise level at the transition point between the constant and linear segments is the contrast invariant noise (N_{eq}).

1. At this illumination level, quanta are emitted according to a Poisson process in which the mean equals the variance. This has been termed the *de Vries-Rose region*.

For the detection of spatial gratings in dynamic noise, the observer's equivalent input noise at most spatiotemporal frequencies mainly reflects the inability to capture or make use of all the quanta coming from the image, *photon noise*. Across a fourfold range of luminances (10,000), just a small fraction of the corneal quanta (1–10%) are actually encoded and used perceptually. Only at very low spatiotemporal frequencies, when the image is essentially constant, does the neural noise become predominant. This suggests that our simple model should incorporate a filter that reflects the frequency selectivity of the pathway.

We can put all of this together in a basic model of the human observer detecting a grating embedded in noise, shown in figure 6.2. Z-L. Lu and Dosher (1999) termed these sorts of models *noisy linear amplifiers* (perfect linear amplification with additive noise). If we track the figure from input to output, an external noise and the signal (in terms of the contrast of the image squared, c^2) controlled by the experimenter are summed together. We use c^2 (contrast power or variance) because the variance of the sum of independent components is simply the sum of the individual components, and that makes the theoretical development easier. (We could use the variance to model the contrast necessary for the perception of second-order movement in chapter 5.) The signal + external noise first passes through a template (e.g., a spatial frequency filter) that restricts the processing to just part of the energy reaching the observer. The filtered signal + external noise

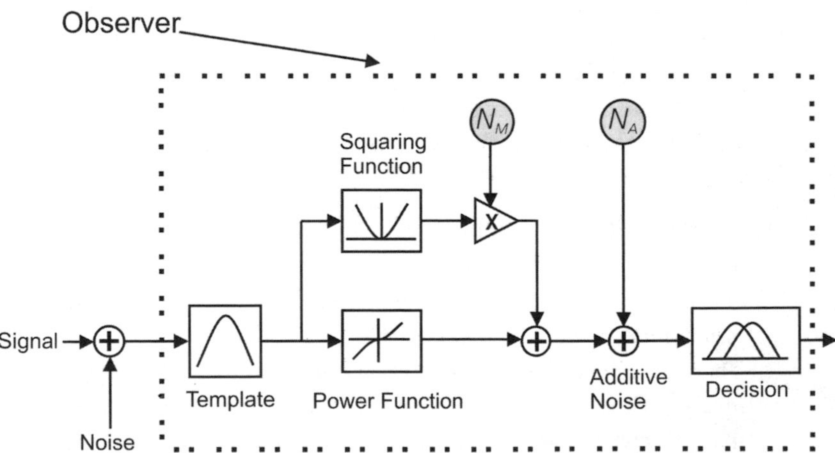

Figure 6.2. A model of noisy linear amplifiers (perfect linear amplification with additive noise). The input signal is squared, multiplied by the input multiplicative noise fraction (N_M) and then added back to the signal path. In similar fashion, the additive noise (N_A) is added to the signal path. From "Characterizing Human Perceptual Inefficiencies With Equivalent Internal Noise," by Z.-L. Lu and B. A. Dosher, 1999, *Journal of the Optical Society of America, A, 16*, 764–778. Copyright 1999 by the Optical Society of America. Reprinted with permission.

is further transformed in two ways. First, an expansive nonlinear power function accentuates the higher intensities. Second, the input is squared, multiplied by the internal multiplicative noise fraction, and added to the transformed signal. Finally, additive equivalent input noise independent of the signal also is added so that the effective stimulus becomes

transformed input signal + external noise + independent multiplicative equivalent input noise + independent additive equivalent input noise

and that stimulus is used to make a decision about the presence or absence of the signal. The basic model assumes that the calculation-decision process is independent of the stimulus.

Researchers (Gold, Bennett, & Sekular, 1999; R. W. Li, Levi, & Klein, 2004; Z.-L. Lu & Dosher, 2004) used such a model to investigate whether practice reduced the equivalent input noise or increased the efficiency of

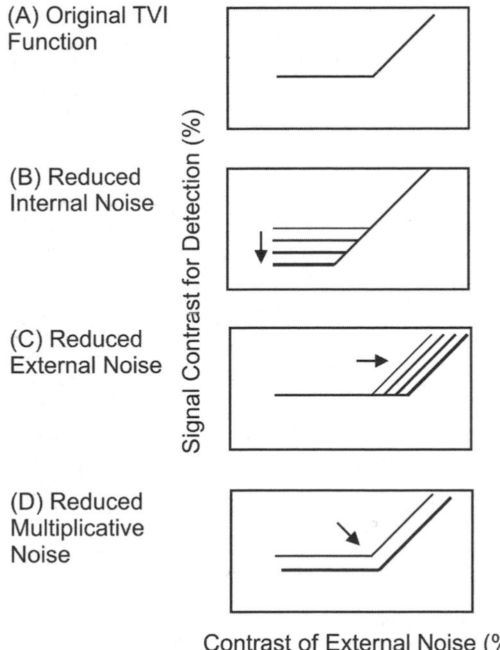

Figure 6.3. The basic threshold versus external noise function (threshold versus intensity, TVI) consists of two segments (A). The flat segment is due to the equivalent internal noise, and the sloping segment is due to the effect of the external contrast noise. Representations of the effects of reduced internal (B), external (C), and multiplicative noise (D) are depicted by the darkening line segments and by the direction of the arrow. Adapted from "Perceptual Learning Retunes the Perceptual Template in Foveal Orientation Identification," by Z.-L. Lu and B. A. Dosher, 2004, *Journal of Vision, 4*, 44–56.

the decision process as pictured in figure 6.3. The magnitude and type of effect of the practice depended on the specific neural pathways and task. In general, both factors were important. Practice allowed the observers to reduce the internal additive noise to some degree and to retune the perceptual template to more completely exclude the external noise.

Adaptation and Gain Control in General

As described previously, the auditory and visual systems face an immensely wide range of natural intensities, on the order of 10^8 to 10^{10}, from moonlight to sunlight and from the softest sound to the loudest (see table 6.1).

Table 6.1 The Dynamic Range of the Auditory and Visual Systems.

Intensity (log units)	Sound Pressure Level (dB SPL)	Audition (watts/m2)	Luminance of White Paper in	Vision (log cd/m2)	Retinal Functioning	
8	200					
7	190	Normal Atmospheric Pressure		Retinal Damage possible		
6	180					
5	170		Sunlight		Photopic	
4	160					
3	150			Best Acuity		
2	140		Indoor lighting		Color Vision	
1	130	Threshold of pain		Rod Saturation begins		
0	120	Rock Band				
−1	110		Moonlight		Mesotopic	
−2	100	Subway passing				
−3	90		Starlight	Cone		
−4	80	Loud Radio		Threshold		
−5	70	Average Conversation		Poor Acuity	Scotopic	No color vision
−6	60					
−7	50	Average Residence		Threshold		
−8	40					
−9	30					
−10	20	Quiet whisper				
−11	10					
−12	0	Threshold				

The firing rates of individual neurons rates go from their minimum to maximum firing rates within a narrow band of intensities around 10^2 and therefore cannot track that variation. The auditory and visual systems have evolved similar strategies to cope with this problem in two ways.

1. Both the auditory and visual systems are composed of two classes of receptors. The auditory system contains low-threshold neurons that reach their maximum firing rate at relatively low intensities and less numerous high-threshold neurons that respond to the highest intensities. In the same manner, the visual system contains rods that respond to the lowest three to four logarithmic units, and less numerous higher-sensitivity cones that respond to the higher intensities.
2. Both the auditory and visual systems have built-in mechanical and neural gain control mechanisms. The gain controls adjust the sensitivity of cells so that they do not saturate except at the highest intensities. As the background level changes over a range of 10^6 to 10^7 (six or seven logarithm units), the steady-state response rate changes very little, and the number of spikes necessary to signal a change in intensity is relatively constant. The gain control increases the amplification of the incoming energy when the level is low, so that the signal will be more intense than the internal noise, and decreases the amplification when the level is high, so that the signal intensity does not exceed the sensory firing capacity, to preclude "saturation clipping."
3. Both (1) and (2) deal with the adaptation to mean intensity. But the visual system also has evolved a type of gain control based on the contrast of the illumination, independent of the mean illumination.

The fundamental problem for both looking and listening is to partial out overall changes in intensity (i.e., brightness and loudness) from changes that signify the properties of objects: surface reflectance and contrast and the auditory frequency spectrum. What is invariant in vision across different brightness levels is the percentage of reflected light and the ratio of the reflectance between different surfaces (i.e., contrast). What is invariant in audition across different loudness levels is the ratio of the intensities of the different frequency partials (i.e., the contrast among the partials, although this does change, as is discussed in chapter 8). This implies that it is the average illumination and average sound pressure that should be controlled in order for the two perceptual systems to isolate contrast in its most general sense.

Adaptation and Gain Control in the Visual System

In the visual system, there are two kinds of gain control. At the periphery, there is gain control for the overall intensity of the light. At the cortical level, there is gain control for contrast. As discussed in chapter 2, cortical cells do not fire well to constant levels of light and respond maximally to ratios of intensities. To some degree, these two processes are in opposition. As the prevailing illumination increases during sunrise, the visual system becomes less sensitive to light, and the moon and stars disappear. But at the same time, the black print on a white page becomes more discriminable: The increased sensitivity to contrast goes along with the decreased overall sensitivity to light (Hood & Finkelstein, 1986). Moreover, adaptations to the changes in light intensity modify the ways that the visual system reacts to the spatial and temporal variations in the incoming light, although the mechanisms are still unclear.

At the Retina

Obviously, the retina cannot see, but without understanding retinal functioning, no complete model of visual processing is possible. To say that an outcome is determined by retinal processing or lower-level processing is to argue that perceptual outcomes can be mainly understood without additional assumptions about cortical processes and judgments.

The basic perceptual experiment is to detect an increase or decrease in luminance of a small stimulus centered on a background. The luminance of the background varies across a wide range, and one might expect that due to rate saturation of individual neurons there would be a value of the background luminance at which any change in the central stimulus could not be detected. Yet that is not what happens, as shown in figure 6.1. Thus, the problem is to understand how the retinal mechanisms get around the limitations that would be imposed by rate saturation. At higher illuminations, detection follows Weber's ratio: Changes in illumination are exactly compensated by changes in sensitivity. Discrimination becomes based only on contrast (the difference in illumination divided by the illumination) and not illumination per se.

At this point, it is worthwhile to formally define contrast. For the traditional stimulus configuration, the background stimulus is a uniform disk or bar, and the test stimulus (i.e., the object) is a brighter luminance presented once each trial somewhere within the background. The contrast ratio is the difference between the luminance of the object (L_o) and the luminance of the background (L_b) divided by the luminance of the background. Because the important issue is the minimum brightness contrast, experimentally L_o is the level that is detected on a specified percentage of the trials. This becomes the familiar Weber's ratio:

$$C = (L_o - L_b)/L_b. \tag{6.1}$$

To the extent that Weber's ratio is constant at different background levels, it reflects the invariance of contrast across changes in illumination.

Suppose we have a background that has reflectance R_b illuminated by light I_b, so that the luminance is $R_b \times I_b$. We then select objects of different reflectances (R_o) and place each of them on top of the background so that the same light I_b illuminates them. For any object, the contrast ratio becomes:

$$C = (R_o \times I_b - R_b \times I_b)/R_b \times I_b. \tag{6.2}$$

The illumination I_b can be cancelled out of the numerator and denominator, leaving only reflectances:

$$C = (R_o - R_b)/R_b. \tag{6.3}$$

The contrast is independent of illumination.

For a periodic spatial pattern such as a spatial grating, the brightness oscillates across the visual field. The observer's task is to detect the orientation of the oscillation (e.g., horizontal or vertical), and the experimental variable is the difference between the highest and lowest luminance (i.e., the depth of the oscillation). Here the contrast ratio is defined by the difference in luminance divided by the sum of the highest and lowest luminance or, equivalently, by the difference in reflectance divided by the average reflectance:

$$\mathrm{C} = (\mathrm{L}_{max} - \mathrm{L}_{min})/(\mathrm{L}_{max} + \mathrm{L}_{min}) \tag{6.4}$$

$$C = (L_{\mathrm{max}} - L_{\mathrm{min}})/2L_{\mathrm{avg}} \tag{6.5}$$

or by replacing L with $R \times I$:

$$C = (R_{\mathrm{max}} - R_{\mathrm{min}})/2 \times R_{\mathrm{avg}}. \tag{6.6}$$

At the retinal level, discussions of gain control revolve around two types of stimuli. The first stems from a tradition of presenting a steady nonperiodic stimulus against a background of varying intensity and plotting the threshold versus intensity (TVI) plots of the stimulus as a function of the background intensity, as in figure 6.1. The second stems from a more recent tradition of presenting periodic stimuli in which the brightness of a small disk oscillates between white and black as a sinusoidal wave at different frequencies.

Nonperiodic Stimuli

To test nonperiodic stimuli, a small test flash is pulsed against a continuous uniform background, and the independent variable is the luminance of the background. The test flash and the background either begin at the same time or the test flash is delayed for varying amounts of time.

For experiments in which the flash and background start simultaneously, the firing rates of the cat's retinal ganglion cells clearly reflect the effect of the gain control, as illustrated in figure 6.4. At each background luminance,

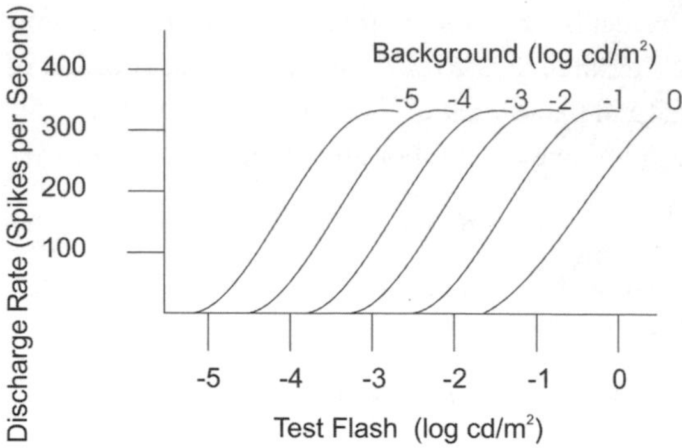

Figure 6.4. Stimulus-response curves from an on-center cell that illustrates gain control for illumination. The change in firing rate (from 0 to more than 300 spikes per second) remains identical across a 10^5 illumination range of the background. Adapted from "The Control of Visual Sensitivity: Receptoral and Postreceptoral Processes," by J. Walraven, C. Enroth-Cugell, D. C. Hood, D. I. A. MacLeod, and J. Schnapf, 1990, in L. Spillman and J. S. Werner (Eds.), *Visual Perception: The Neurophysiological Foundations* (pp. 53–101). New York: Academic.

the cell's firing rate ranges from 0 to more than 300 spikes per second. The firing rate does not saturate, and the firing rate has the maximum sensitivity (i.e., steepest slope) in the middle of the luminance of each background, even across a luminance range of 10^5. A gain control mechanism moves the stimulus-response curve to the right for each increase in the luminance of the background.

For experiments in which the brief test flash is started at different times relative to the onset of the background light, Crawford (1947) measured the threshold for the test light, the amount of light relative to the background light required to detect the test light (it will be plotted as the logarithm of the incremental light). Overall, the results showed that the threshold for the test light was highest when the onsets were identical and that the threshold decreased if the test light was delayed by 200–1,000 ms relative to the onset of the background light. If the test light was delayed by more than 1 s, the threshold decreased even further (Adelson, 1982). Figure 6.5 displays the incremental thresholds as a function of the delay of the test light. The decrease in threshold as a function of the onset delay has been termed the *background-onset effect*.

The important point is that the incremental threshold for the test light presented at the onset of the background is greater than when the test light is delayed, particularly at the higher background levels. For both cone (fovea) and rod vision, there is a rapid decrease in the incremental threshold during the first 200 ms, followed by a slower decrease over several seconds. Adelson (1982) suggested that two adaptation processes are working

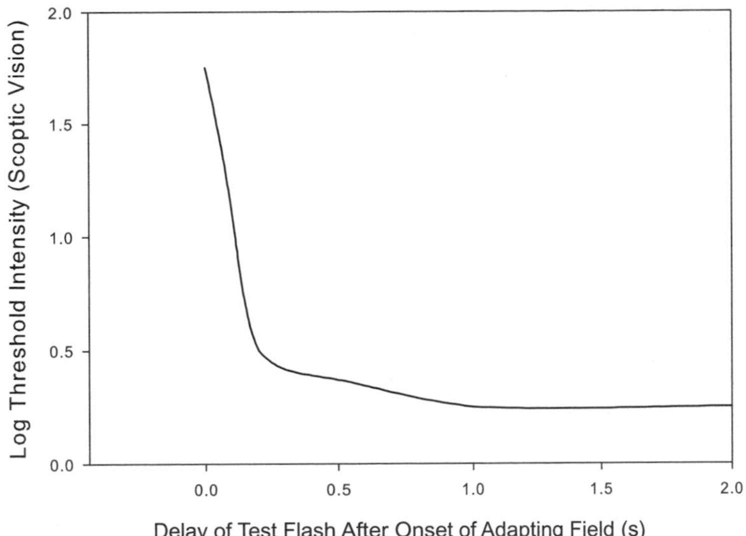

Figure 6.5. The threshold to detect an intensity increment decreases as the test flash is delayed. There is an additional decrease of about .2 log units, not shown in the figure, for delays up to one minute. Adapted from "Sensitivity to Light," by D. Hood and M. A. Finkelstein, 1986, in K. R. Boff, L. Kaufman, and J. P. Thomas (Eds.), *Handbook of Perception and Human Performance: Vol. 1. Sensory Processes and Perception* (pp. 5-1 to 5-64). New York: John Wiley.

here. When the background light is first turned on, the firing rate of the rods saturates, so that the incremental test light is difficult to perceive. During the first 200 ms there is a rapid adaptation process that acts like a gain control. It divides the background light by a constant to reduce the firing rates and thereby eliminates the saturation. Then a slow adaptation process extending even over 30 s acts like a subtractive process.

A general model of gain control to explain light adaptation (Graham & Hood, 1992; Hood & Finkelstein, 1986) incorporates three processes:

1. A static nonlinearity between intensity and neural response rate. The nonlinearity is assumed to be constant, that is, to start at the light onset and remain at the same level for the duration of the light. The static nonlinearity is a fundamental part of the transformation of the incident illumination into firing rates.
2. A multiplicative or divisive process that increases with time.
3. A subtractive process that increases with time. The multiplicative and subtractive processes act together to reduce the firing rate due to the background to a level that allows the firing rates of the ganglion cells to track changes in luminance.

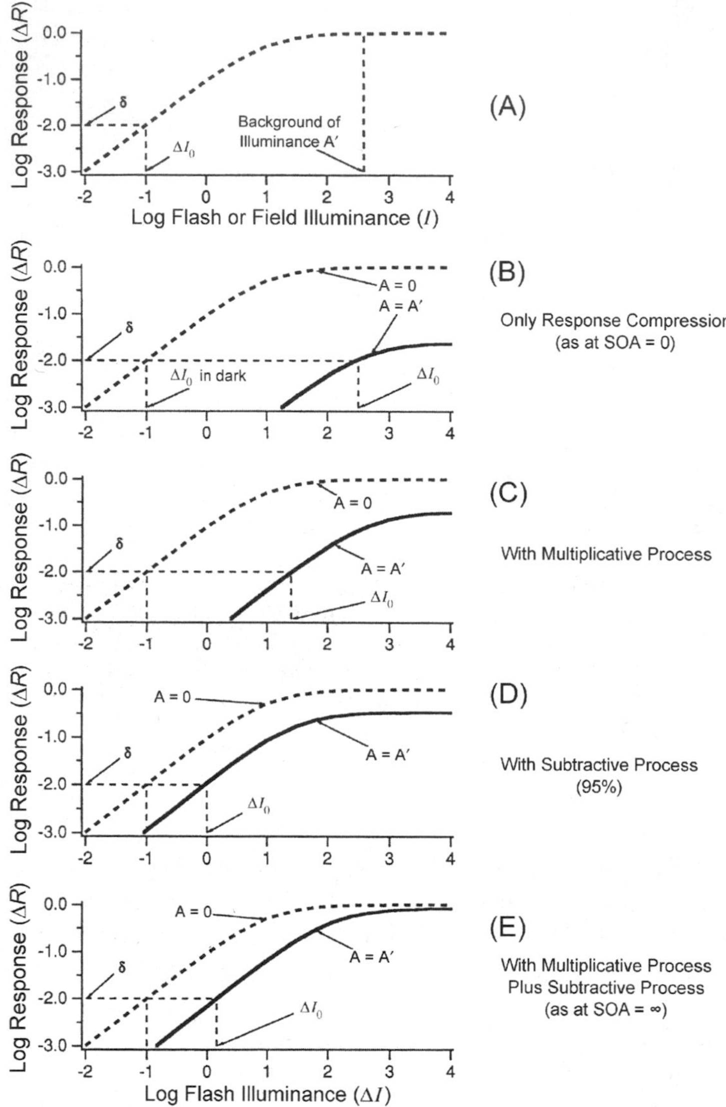

Figure 6.6. Model of multiplicative and additive gain control for light adaptation. From "Modeling the Dynamics of Light Adaptation: The Merging of Two Traditions," by N. Graham and D. C. Hood, 1992, *Vision Research, 12*(7), 1373–1393. Copyright 1992 by Elsevier Science Ltd. Reprinted with permission.

The five panels in figure 6.6 illustrate the hypothesized excitation of retinal cells.

Figure 6.6A depicts the hypothesized nonlinear static function (i.e., starting at light onset) relating the dark-adapted neural response to the background light intensity. At low intensities, the response grows at the same rate as the intensity (a slope of 1 in log/log coordinates). Then as the intensity increases, the response growth slows, and at even higher intensities the response becomes constant because the neurons have saturated at their highest possible firing rate. This type of stimulus-response function can be modeled by a simple exponential function or by an equation introduced by Naka and Rushton (1966):

$$R = [I/(I + I_s)]R_{max}. \tag{6.7}$$

R is the response change from the totally dark-adapted level, I_s is termed the *semisaturation constant* at which the response reaches its half-maximum level, and R_{max} is the maximum firing rate of the cell. Above the semisaturation level, although the light can increase by several orders of magnitude, the neural response can increase only by a factor of two. The contrast gain (Weber's ratio for the threshold for seeing a test flash) will decrease as a function of the level of the background light.

Assume that the test flash is perceivable when the response to the test flash plus background light exceeds the response to the background light alone by a criterion number of spikes. In the figures, an increase in R of one unit from –3.0 to –2.0 log units (ΔI_o) leads to the detection of the test light (δ).

In Figure 6.6B, assume that the background light intensity has been increased to 2.5 units so that the background itself creates a high firing rate. To detect the increase in the intensity of the test light, we still need to increase R by 1 log unit. (Note that in figure 6.6A the x axis represents the background illuminance, but in figures 6.6B–E, the x axis represents the incremental illuminance due to the test flash.) The solid line in figure 6.6B shows the hypothetical incremental change in firing rate due to test flash at different intensities against the 2.5 unit background:

$$\begin{aligned}\text{Incremental response} = {} & R(\text{flash intensity} + 2.5 \text{ unit background}) \\ & - R(2.5 \text{ unit background}).\end{aligned} \tag{6.8}$$

To create a 1-unit change in the response rate requires a very large increment in the test flash intensity, about 4.5 log units (–2 to +2.5) as opposed to the 1 log unit against a black background (a 3.5 log unit increase beyond that necessary for detection against a black background). In general, there is little effect on the detection threshold due to low background levels. But even moderately intense background fields can come close to maxing out the response range and dramatically reduce the ability to signify increments by increasing the response rate to saturation levels. Without some reduction in sensitivity, the visual system would be blind to any increments.

If we present the brighter background before the test flash, the multiplicative and subtractive processes kick in and enormously reduce the negative effect of the background, as shown in figures 6.6C–E. The effect of the multiplicative process is shown in figure 6.6C. The basic notion underlying this process is that both the background and test flash illuminations are effectively reduced by multiplying both illuminations by a fraction $m(a)$ between 0 and 1, assumed to be determined by the overall illumination. The background becomes $m(a) \times I_b$, the test flash becomes $m(a) \times I_f$, and the (background + flash) becomes $m(a)(I_f + I_b)$. This type of mechanism has been called von Kries adaptation, cellular adaptation, pigment depletion, or the dark glasses hypothesis, and is discussed further in chapter 7. Since the multiplicative adaptation acts on both the background and test flash, it is as if there was a neutral density filter in front of the stimulus, much like dark glasses (or like closing down the pupil). The decrease in the background illumination acts to reduce the threshold because the background intensity is reduced, but at the same time the decrease in the test flash acts to increase the threshold because the test flash intensity also is reduced. The multiplicative adaptation recovers some of the response range, as shown by the leftward shift of the response curve; for a fraction of 0.1 the shift is roughly 1 log unit. Moreover, the dynamic range of the response is increased: there is roughly a 1 log unit increase in the range of firing rates.

The operation of the subtractive mechanism is illustrated in figure 6.6D. The subtractive process is assumed to decrease the intensity of long-duration lights by removing some of the signal. The subtractive process does not affect lights presented for brief periods, so it will not affect the test flash. The effective intensity of the background is $I_b - s(I_b)$, where s is the subtractive constant that is a function of the background intensity; the intensity of the test flash remains I_f. The function in figure 6.6D illustrates the outcomes if the subtractive process removes 95% of the background light. There is a great deal of recovery of the response function, and the difference between the subtractive function and the original dark background function is relatively constant across all the background illuminations.

If the multiplicative and subtractive processes are combined (as in figure 6.6E), the effective background becomes $m(a)[I_b - s(I_b)]$ and the effective test flash becomes $m(a)I_f$. The combination of the two mechanisms removes the effect of the background illumination at higher intensities where the response reaches the asymptote at the no-background firing rate, but does not completely compensate at the lowest intensities.

Kortum and Geisler (1995) suggested that the multiplicative constant is inversely proportional to the background illumination, particularly at the higher intensities. Thus the multiplicative processes create the constant Weber ratio. In contrast, the subtractive constant is fixed (at higher illuminations) so that the subtractive mechanism only reduces the Weber ratio.

These mechanisms are illustrated in a different way for a flashed stimulus presented against a fixed background in figure 6.7. The two dashed lines represent the response rate if there is no gain control. The bottom line

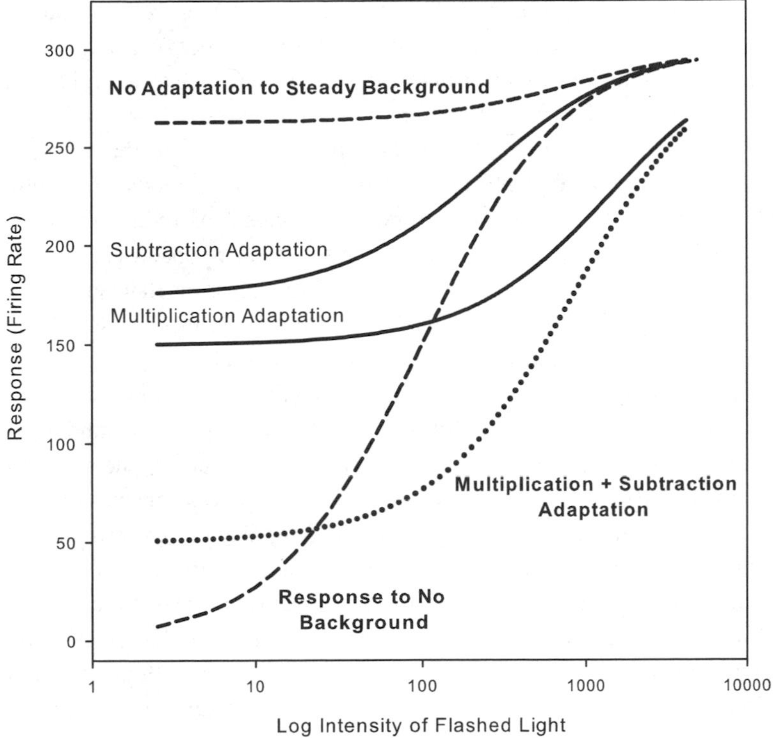

Figure 6.7. The effect of the multiplicative and additive gain controls on the detection of a flashing stimulus. The basic equation is based on a generalized Naka-Rushton equation (6.7):

$$R(I) = R_{\max}\,[m_a(I - s)]^n/[m_a(I - s)]^n + I_s^{\,n}$$

In this figure, the subtraction constant is assumed to affect both the flash and the background. In contrast, the subtractive gain control in figure 6.6 is assumed to affect only the background because of the presumed delay after onset for the subtractive gain to function. In the figure, the maximum response rate $R_{\max} = 300$, the background = 700, the multiplication gain constant $m_a = 0.143$, the subtraction constant $s = 560$, and the semisaturation constant $I_s = 100$. The exponent $n = 1$. Adapted from "Adaptation Mechanisms in Spatial Vision. II. Flash Thresholds and Background Adaptation," by P. T. Kortum and W. S. Geisler, 1995, *Vision Research, 35*, 1595–1609.

depicts the response rate to the flashed light if there was no background, and the top line depicts the response rate to the flashed light in front of a steady 700 td (troland) background light. The two solid-line curves represent the response rate if there was multiplication or subtraction gain for a light flashed against the 700 td background. The single dotted line depicts the response rate if there was both multiplication and subtraction gain. If there was no adaptation at all, the dynamic range in firing rates to the flashed light would be minimal. However, the multiplicative + subtractive adaptation processes reduce the response rate to the background light to such a degree that the dynamic range increases by as much as fivefold compared to the range if there were no adaptation processes.

To summarize, background illumination uses up most of the ability of neurons to signal increments in intensity. Over time periods of roughly 200–300 ms, multiplicative and subtractive mechanisms reduce the firing rate to the background so that a larger part of the response range can be used to signal changes in intensity. The multiplicative mechanism affects both the background and target, while the subtractive mechanism affects only the background, at least within a limited time span.

A real example of the effects of multiplicative and subtractive mechanisms can be found in recordings of ganglion cells in the mudpuppy (Makous, 1997, taken from Werblin, 1974). In this example, the surround appeared to have a subtractive effect on the response to a flickering stimulus confined to the center mechanism of the ganglion cell. Experimentally, the flicker was continuous, and the surround was alternately on and off. Figure 6.8A shows that the alternation of the surround over time reduces the overall rate of response but, most important, the oscillation in output voltage generated by the flicker does not change. The membrane potential is plotted in figure 6.8B in terms of the intensity of the surround. Again, the important point is that the response function to the flicker with the surround on has the same slope and is merely shifted to the right. I would argue that this effect is mainly due to subtractive adaptation because the response to the flicker does not change at the different background intensities.

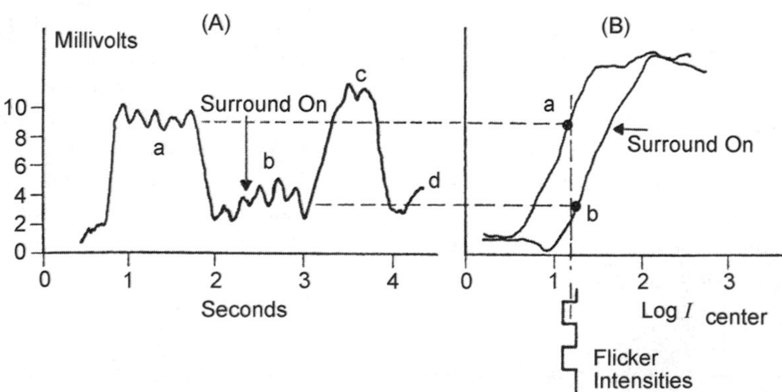

Figure 6.8. The surround acts as a subtractive gain control in bipolar cells. The gain control maintains the response to the flicker modulation in spite of the increase in background intensity. From "Control of Retinal Sensitivity. II. Lateral Interactions at the Outer Plexiform Layer," by F. S. Werblin, 1974, *Journal of General Physiology, 63*, 62–87. Copyright 1974 by the *Journal of General Physiology*. Reprinted with permission.

Makous (1997) pointed out how difficult it is to go from physiological or perceptual data to psychophysical models. The sequencing of the nonlinear transformation, multiplicative mechanisms, and subtractive mechanisms can be modeled in different ways and still yield the same simulated results. Makous concluded that the major gain control for the cones over the normal range of illumination comes from the subtractive mechanism that precedes the nonlinear response compression. At greater illuminations, multiplicative mechanisms may dominate, and at the highest illuminations the bleaching of the cone pigments is the main factor reducing the firing rates. The bleaching of the cones reduces the probability of absorption so that the effective illumination remains constant at the higher-intensity backgrounds.

Periodic Stimuli

Experiments that have investigated adaptation to periodic stimuli have used two kinds of stimuli: (1) a disk in which the luminance undergoes sinusoidal modulation across time, and the observer reports whether the light appears to flicker or remain constantly visible; and (2) a stationary spatial grating, and the observer reports whether the white-and-black spatial pattern is perceivable or looks a uniform gray. We set a given spatial frequency or a temporal frequency and overall illuminance and then vary the depth of the modulation until the variation is perceptible. The dependent measure is the difference between the peak and average illuminance (or for sinusoidal stimuli, one half the difference between the maximum and minimum intensity) of the periodic stimulus that is detectable. The results, shown in figure 6.9, illustratc that at low levels of illuminance the temporal threshold (the ability to see the flicker) is poorest at the lower frequencies, but as the illuminance increases, there is no difference in thresholds among the temporal frequencies. This termed the *high-temporal-frequency linearity* or *envelope* by Graham and Hood (1992).

The results in figure 6.9 also illustrate the transitions between the different sensitivity regimes. At the higher temporal frequencies, there is a linear region where the sensitivity for temporal modulation does not depend on overall steady illuminance. At lower temporal frequencies, there is a region where the threshold increases as the square root of the illuminance ($K = 1/2$), where the quantal variation in the illuminance is thought to determine sensitivity (the DeVries-Rose regime). At still higher illuminances, the threshold increases according to Weber's ratio ($K = 1.0$). It is within the Weber region that the ratio of reflectances, the requirement for object constancy, is independent of illumination.

As the illumination increases, the visual system comes to resemble a band-pass filter: The maximum sensitivity occurs at the middle spatial frequencies and the attenuation of the higher temporal frequencies is

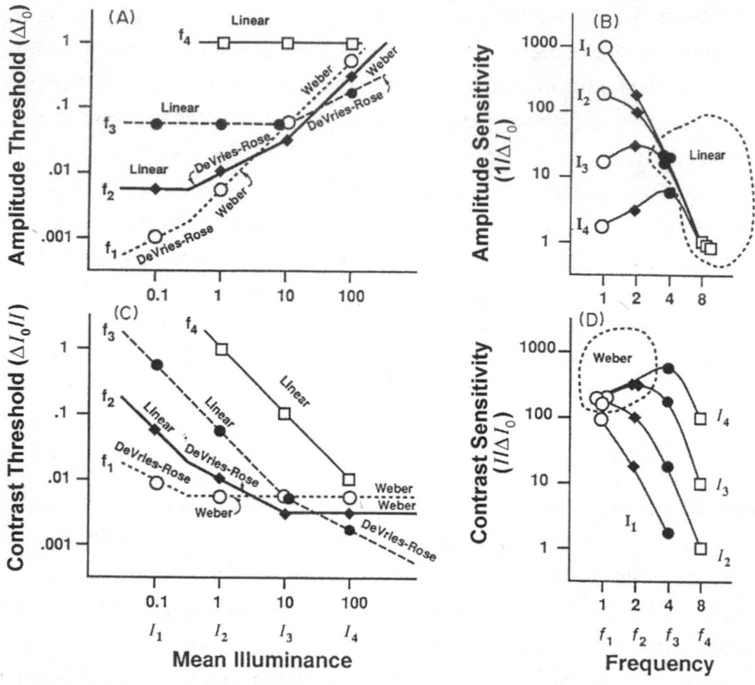

Figure 6.9. The visibility of the flickering of sinusoidal stimuli as a function of luminance and frequency. The observer's task was to judge whether the stimulus flickered or appeared to be a constant gray. From "Modeling the Dynamics of Light Adaptation: The Merging of Two Traditions," by N. Graham and D. C. Hood, 1992, *Vision Research, 12*(7), 1373–1393. Copyright 1992 by Elsevier Science Ltd. Reproduced with permission.

reduced. The visual system is metaphorically faster, responding to rapid spatial and temporal transients.

Loftus and Harley (2005) argued that the commonsense observation that it is easier to recognize a face when it is close than when it is far away is due to the attenuation of the higher spatial frequencies. As the face (or any other visual image) recedes, the spatial frequencies used to characterize that image increase inversely proportionally to distance. Thus, the lower, coarser frequencies that are necessary to identify objects become higher frequencies that are subject to visual attenuation. It is the resulting blurring that makes identification difficult and suggests that eyewitness testimony at long distances is problematic.

Contrast Gain Control

As argued previously, it is intensity contrasts rather than average intensities that are the important perceptual variables. For example, it is variation in contrast that defines the boundaries between objects. Retinal gain control is adaptation due to the average intensity of the background illumination. In analogous fashion, contrast gain control is adaptation due to the average contrast of the background illumination, that is, the variance of the background. For both types of gain control, the visual system adjusts its sensitivity so that the background illumination and contrast become metaphorically the null values. Changes in the firing rate occur only to variation above or below the null values. Without intensity and contrast gain control, the average illumination and contrast of the background would use up much of the dynamic range. Both types of gain control recover that range.

There are several issues. First, the response to one value of contrast should be invariant in the face of differences in light intensity. If the ratio of reflectances between two surfaces is 9:1, then illuminances of 900:100, 90:10, or 9:1 should create the same neural response. Only the contrast should determine the response, not the illumination.

Second, the ratio of responses to other properties of two objects should be invariant of the contrast. For example, the neural response to different orientations should be equivalent in spite of differences in the contrast. Here is the problem. For simple cortical cells, at low contrast levels the response is determined both by the stimulus contrast and by how closely the stimulus matches the selectivity of the cell due to spatial location, orientation, and frequency (i.e., the spatial-temporal receptive fields; see figures 2.6 and 2.9). But as the contrast increases for any constant illumination, the firing rate of all neurons increases until the cells are firing at their saturation rate. An 80:20 reflectance grating would tend to saturate the firing rate, while a 55:45 grating would not. If this were allowed to happen, it would be impossible to discriminate among stimuli at higher contrasts. The contrast gain control must reduce the saturation firing rate due to high levels of contrast so that selectivity is independent of contrast. It has been suggested that it is the nonclassical receptive fields that produce the contrast gain control. As shown in chapter 3 (figure 3.15), stimulation of the nonclassical receptive fields increases the sparseness of the response of cortical cells to natural stimuli, and the same process is hypothesized to account for the contrast gain control.

Third, based on the concepts underlying efficient information transmission (see chapter 3, figure 3.5), the firing rate for different contrasts should reflect the range of contrasts found within the environment.

Gain Control Due to Background Contrast

W. S. Geisler and Albrecht (1992) made use of a stationary counterphase grating to demonstrate that the background contrast acts as a multiplicative gain control, that is, the response rate shifts to the right, as illustrated in figure 6.6. Cortical cells give only a steady maintained response to constant illumination, so that it is necessary to modulate the stimulus in time to measure the cell's contrast response (in normal activity, the eye constantly would pass over different objects that would inherently change the firing rate). A spatial counterphase white-and-black grating varies the contrast at one temporal frequency. The variation in contrast is shown for four cycles of white-and-black bands at 1 Hz in figure 6.10A. Starting at 0.0 s, all the bands are gray, a point of zero contrast. At 0.25 s, the bands alternate white to black, the point of maximum contrast. At 0.50 s, another point of zero contrast occurs. At 0.75 s, the contrast again reaches its maximum albeit reversed, and at 1.0 s all the bands return to being equally bright. Thus, the contrast between adjacent regions continuously changes and reverses.

The counterphase grating that served as the background contrast was centered on the receptive field of a simple cortical cell. To recall, these cells are characterized by an opposing center-surround organization. Because the grating reversed polarity at the temporal frequency rate, the output of the cell was effectively zero for all counterphase contrasts. The authors then superimposed a drifting grating (exactly like the ones used to modulate the contrast for second-order motion discussed in

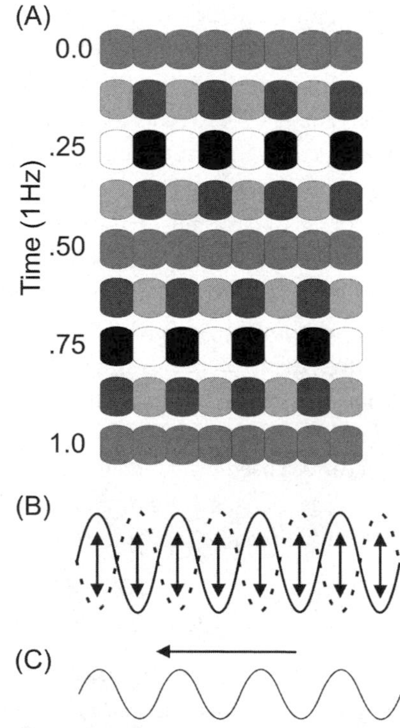

Figure 6.10. A demonstration of contrast gain in the visual system. A stationary counterphase grating is illustrated in (A). The contrast ratio between the grating bars varies from 0, to +1, to 0, to –1, back to 0. A common representation is shown in (B): the double arrows portraying the reversing brightness regions. A drifting sinusoidal grating was superimposed on a stationary counterphase grating at the same spatial and temporal frequency (in C). As the contrast of the counterphase grating increased, the response to the drifting grating shifted to the right, but still maintained a relatively high firing rate (D). The contrast response shift occurred within 200 ms. Adapted from "Cortical Neurons: Isolation of Contrast Gain Control," by W. S. Geisler and D. G. Albrecht, 1992, *Vision Research, 32*, 1409–1410.

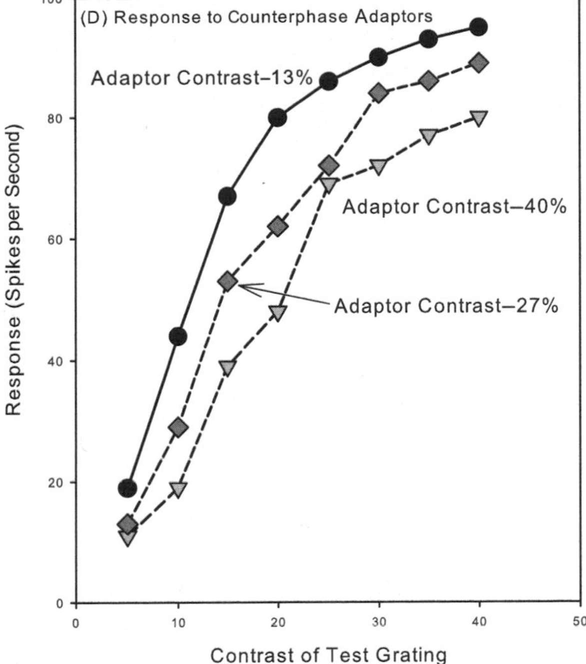

Figure 6.10. Continued

chapter 5) that did stimulate the cell and measured the response to the drifting grating. As the contrast of the counterphase grating was increased, the response to the drifting test grating was shifted to the right, suggesting a multiplicative contrast-gain mechanism. These results are shown in figure 6.10.

Independence of Contrast and Illumination

Walraven, Enroth-Cugell, Hood, MacLeod, and Schnapf (1990) summarized data from cells in the cat's optic nerve, demonstrating that the response to counterphase gratings at different levels of contrast is independent of the mean illumination. Counterphase gratings are ideal stimuli for these experiments because it is possible to independently vary the average luminance as well as the contrast between the light and dark bands (essentially, the mean and variance). The response rate at each level of contrast (ranging from 1 to 100%) was nearly identical over a 100-fold range in retinal illumination. Thus, the contrast gain control achieves the goal of tuning only to contrast, not to illumination.

As discussed toward the beginning of this chapter, the results of experiments delaying the onset of a uniform test disk relative to the onset of the background illumination suggested that there is a slow and a fast illumination adaptation process. S. Brown and Masland (2001) have proposed that there is also a fast (100 ms) contrast gain adaptation for small retinal areas and a slow (tens of seconds) contrast gain adaptation for large retinal areas. For both types, an increase in the contrast decreased the sensitivity of retinal ganglion cells (i.e., lower firing rates), and a decrease in contrast increased sensitivity. The fast adaptation seems suited to detecting the contrast changes due to head or object movements. The slower adaptation seems suited to adapting to large but slowly evolving environmental changes such as moving into a fog. Burton (2002) has found the same duality for adaptation in houseflies.

Independence of Contrast and Receptive Field Selectivity

We have argued that the visual (and auditory) system represents the values of perceptual dimensions (e.g., orientation, speed of motion, temporal modulation of lights or sounds) by the relative response among individual cells or distinct groups of cells with different receptive field selectivities. The confounding problem, as mentioned above, is that as the contrast ratio increases for visual and auditory stimuli, the response rate of neural cells with different receptive fields can increase to such a degree that the firing rate of every cell saturates. It then becomes impossible to discriminate among the values of any other perceptual dimension. What is necessary is a mechanism that allows the response to, for example, orientation to be independent of contrast.

The proposed models that preserve selectivity in the face of contrast saturation make use of divisive (or equivalently multiplicative) feedback to reduce the overall firing rate and to maintain the response selectivity. A typical model, proposed by H. R. Wilson and Humanski (1993), is shown in figure 6.11.

In these models, the outputs of all cells are determined by the fit of the stimulus to the cell's orientation-spatial frequency receptive field. At this point, the models diverge to some degree according to how the outputs are treated. However, for all models the outputs of cells in the local area are summed together. This sum is then fed back before the filtering due to the receptive field and divides the input to the cell. The feedback mechanism is not instantaneous and takes anywhere from 100 to 200 ms to reduce the initial firing rate to the normalized rate. Usually, the feedback sum is assumed to decay exponentially over time so that outputs in the past are discounted (see Olzak & Thomas, 2003, for evidence that such a model can account for the masking effects of gratings at different orientations).

Consider a concrete example. Suppose there are two cells with different receptive fields such that the stimulus generates firing rates with a ratio of

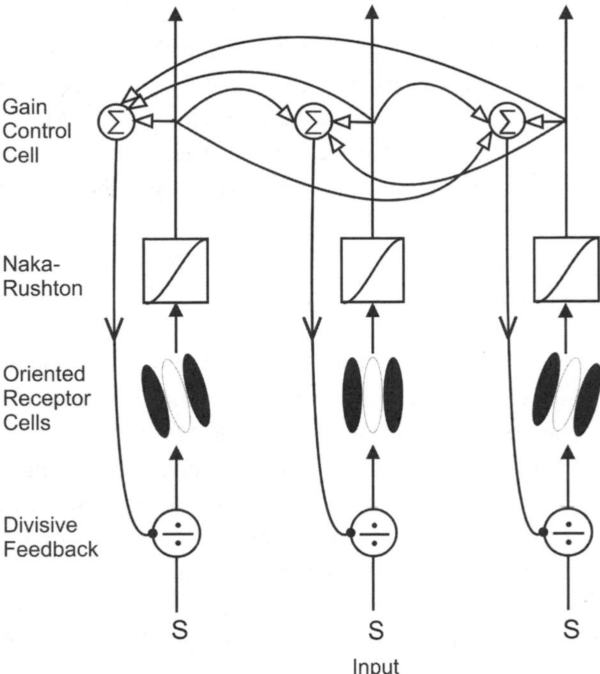

Figure 6.11. A simplified model of a contrast gain control using the weighted sum of outputs as the divisive feedback. The output of each oriented receptive field cell is first transformed by a Naka-Rushton-type nonlinearity. The transformed output is then weighted and combined in the gain control unit (Σ) with the weighted outputs of surrounding cells. A set of three outputs for each cell is shown in the figure. The output of the control unit generates a recurrent inhibitory signal that divides the input to each cell. In the actual simulation done by H. R. Wilson et al. (1997), there were 12 oriented receptor cells (15° spacing) at each retinal location. Adapted from "Spatial Frequency Control and Contrast Gain Control," by H. R. Wilson and R. Humanski, 1993, *Vision Research, 33*, 1133–1149.

3:1. As the contrast increases, the firing rates would go from 3:1 to 6:2, to 9:3 so that the ratio does not change, but eventually at higher contrast levels the firing rates of each cell would increase to the saturation level. The firing rate ratio of 3:1 would at best be reduced and possibly even be equalized so that the discrimination would be lost. However, if the divisive feedback is based on the average firing rates, then the outputs become 3/2:1/2, 6/4:2/4, 9/6:3/6, and so on. The individual firing rates are reduced to a low level so that the 3:1 ratio is maintained across all intensity levels.

There have been several demonstrations that feedback gain control can preserve receptive field selectivity. H. R. Wilson and Humanski (1993) simulated the effects of such a dividing feedback gain control on the response to a 0° degree grating at 40% contrast. In the absence of any gain control, a fully saturated response occurs from –30° to +30° and there was even a strong response to orthogonal gratings. However, with the proposed gain control included, the response was centered on 0° and the maximum firing rate was well within the saturation limits. Carandini, Heeger, and Movshon (1997) have shown that such feedback maintains the relative firing rates between stimuli differing in orientation, and spatial frequency as the contrast increases.

Gain Control in the Auditory System

In the auditory world, stimuli tend to be short in duration and intermittent, and the frequency components of nearly all sounds have relatively low frequencies generated by the physical vibration of object surfaces. The construction of the cochlea yields a one-dimensional array of hair cells with differing characteristic frequencies lying along the basilar membrane. It is the motion of the basilar membrane traveling along its length that stimulates hair cells with different characteristic frequencies.

I described two kinds of visual gain control. The first was illumination gain control based on the adaptation of individual cells. For the cone system, adaptation is a function of photochemical depletion. The second was contrast gain control that leads to the conservation of spatial-temporal selectivity at higher contrast levels. Contrast gain control is presumed to operate by divisive feedback from neighboring cells in the two-dimensional spatial array.

What should we expect for auditory gain control with the knowledge that the auditory perceptual system is faced with the same problems? Clearly there needs to be some type of gain control for the intensity of the sound pressure. Given the physiology of the auditory system, this gain control could be accomplished partly through the mechanical action of the basilar membrane, partly through some sort of depletion mechanism similar to that for cones, and partly through the distribution of hair cells with different thresholds. I would argue that it is equally necessary to have some sort of contrast gain control to preserve frequency selectivity. By analogy to the visual system, this could be accomplished by divisive feedback from cells with similar characteristic frequency tunings.

At the Basilar Membrane

The deflections at the basilar membrane are very compressive and essentially instantaneous. For the chinchilla, the response of the basilar membrane near the stapes is shown for high frequencies in figure 6.12. For frequencies above 9000 Hz, while the intensity of tones increases by 80 dB (10,000 times), the response of the basilar membrane increases only about tenfold (figure 6.12A). If there was no compression and the response of the basilar mem-

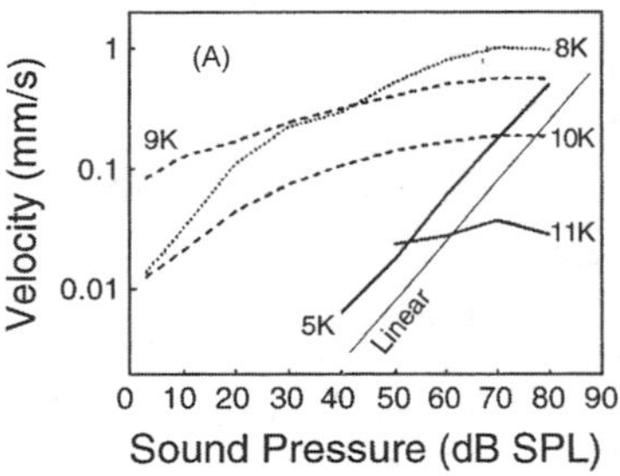

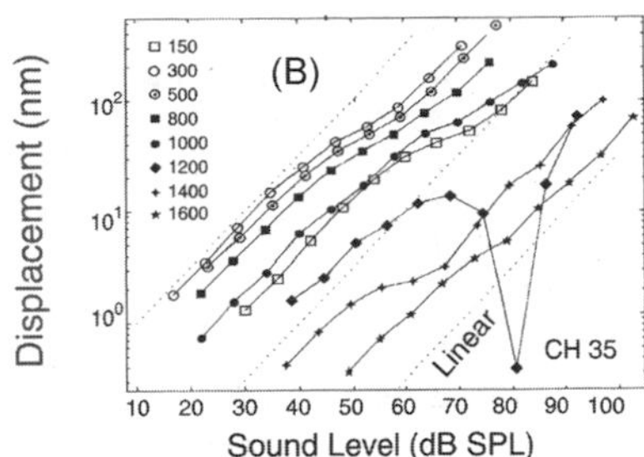

Figure 6.12. Displacement of the cochlea partition for different frequencies. For higher frequencies processed near the stapes (A), there is a great deal of compression. For lower frequencies processed toward the apical end (B), there is less compression. At the apical end, the growth in displacement is linearly related to sound pressure level. Adapted from *From Sound to Synapse: Physiology of the Mammalian Ear*, by C. D. Geisler, 1998, New York: Oxford University Press.

brane was linear, the higher sound pressure levels would create displacements that would destroy the membrane itself. The compression is less for lower frequencies that would excite the membrane at the apical end (figure 6.12B). But the apical sections respond only to low-frequency components of stimuli, and these components all cause temporal synchronization of the neural discharges. Hence, stimulus-waveform information is faithfully preserved even if the auditory nerve fibers' average discharge rates become saturated (see figure 2.21). The mechanisms by which this occurs are not entirely clear, but clearly involve the outer (apparently nonencoding) hair cells in some manner.

At higher intensities, the basilar membrane excitation is broader and presumably stimulates a greater number of hair cells. It is difficult to understand how the spread of excitation on the basilar membrane and the resulting excitation of different numbers of hair cells caused by a pure tone presented at different intensities still results in sensations of a pure tone at each of those intensities. Possibly a form of population coding involving divisive feedback (figure 6.11) is used.

At the Hair Cells

Each hair cell seems to have a built-in gain control. For a typical high-spontaneous-firing-rate hair cell with a characteristic frequency of 6900 Hz tone, in spite of the 60 dB difference (1,000-fold) in intensity, the onset firing rate increases only by a factor of 3, and the steady-state firing rate increases only by a factor of 2.

The level of neurotransmitter in the hair cells' immediately available reservoirs can explain why the steady-state rate is relatively constant across

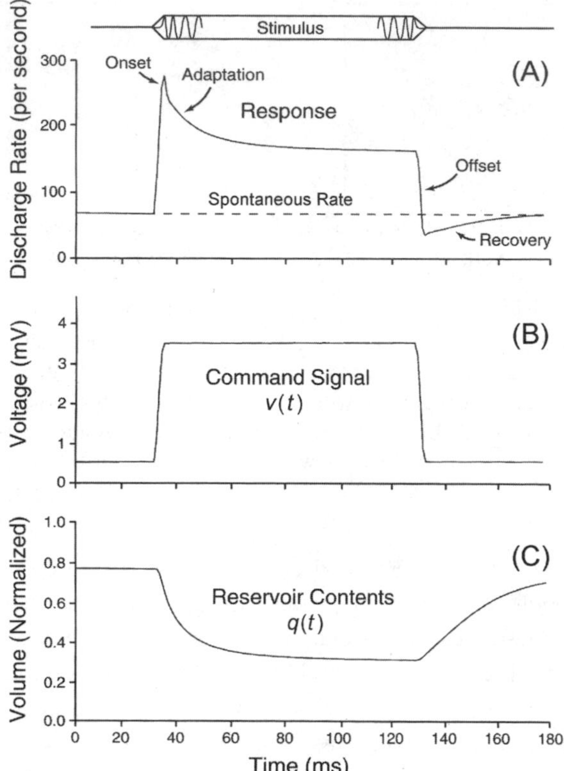

Figure 6.13. The output of the reservoir when stimulated by a constant medium-intensity tone. The reservoir contents [$q(t)$] in (C) gradually diminish over the duration of the tone and then recover after the tone offset. The command signal (i.e., the membrane potential) in (B) is constant over the duration of the tone. The firing rate in (A) shows an initial-onset burst and then gradually declines, matching the decline in the reservoir contents. At the offset of the tone, the firing rate falls below baseline and then recovers. From *From Sound to Synapse: Physiology of the Mammalian Ear*, by C. D. Geisler, 1998, New York: Oxford University Press. Copyright 1998 by C. D. Geisler. Reprinted with permission.

the large change in intensity. In a simplified version of the model, the probability of a nerve fiber discharge as a function of time is:

$$\Pr(t) = q(t) * v(t) \tag{6.9}$$

where $q(t)$ stands for the reservoir level at time t and $v(t)$ stands for the hair cells' membrane potential related to the stimulus waveform.

When the reservoir is full the maximum firing rate occurs, but when the reservoir is only partially full the same stimulus causes a lower firing rate, since the reservoir level is assumed to multiply the receptor's generator potential to arrive at the firing rate probabilities. It has been illustrated

(C. D. Geisler, 1998; C. D. Geisler & Greenberg, 1986) how the model works, as shown in figure 6.13. The fluid can be replenished only so quickly, which limits the maximum firing rate of the cell. On this basis, both the auditory hair cell and visual cone gain control are due to chemical depletion.

Gain Control Due to Background Noise

If a tone is presented against a broad frequency-constant background noise, the effect of the noise is to shift the response curve to the tone. The noise increases the baseline response and reduces the firing rate at saturation. But more important, the noise increases the intensity at which the firing rate saturates. This shift can be easily seen in figure 6.14 for cells with different

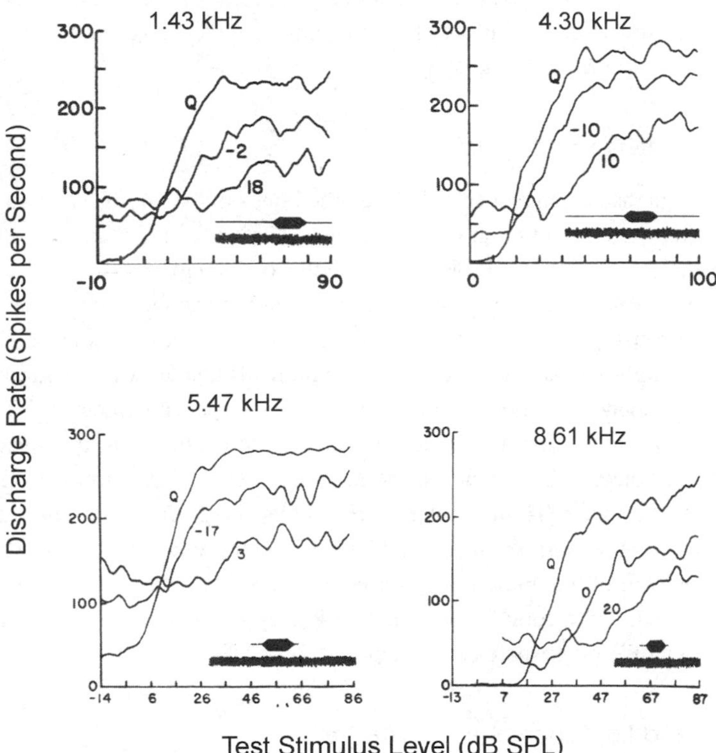

Figure 6.14. The effect of continuous broadband background noise on the response of four auditory cells. The tone is pulsed against the background, as shown by the small insets. The baseline is no background (Q), and the strength of the background increases by 20 dB for all the neurons. From "Effects of Continuous Noise Backgrounds on Rate Response of Auditory Nerve Fibers in Cat," by J. A. Costalupes, E. D. Young, and D. J. Gibson, 1984, *Journal of Neurophysiology, 51*, 1326–1344. Copyright 1984 by the American Physiological Society. Reprinted with permission.

characteristic frequencies. The shift in intensity can be as much as 1 to 1, such that each 1 dB increase in the background noise causes a 1 dB increase in the saturating intensity. The firing rates of the four cells clearly shift to the right, indicating multiplicative and subtractive gain control as the background noise increases.

The proposed mechanism for the effect of the noise is feedback from the descending corticofugal pathways.[2] In particular, the olivocochlear bundle in the auditory brainstem (superior olivary complex) projects back to the hair cells in the cochlea. The functions of the olivocochlear bundle are not fully understood, but it is suppressive in nature, providing divisive feedback. If a tone is masked by noise in the same ear, presenting noise to the other ear increases the response to the tone by activating the crossed olivocochlear bundle (Dolan & Nuttall, 1989). It would be a slow feedback on the order of 100 ms, but that could be quite functional in a noisy environment, where the noise would be expected to keep the same spectral characteristics (and thus the same basilar membrane excitation) over long periods of time (compared to the feedback delay).

Acoustic Reflex in the Middle Ear

At high intensities, the muscles holding the bones in the middle ear contract, stiffening the connection among the bones. The stiffening attenuates sound frequencies below about 1000 Hz by a factor of 1/10 to 1/100. The reflex is rather slow and, surprisingly, adapts to long-duration sounds. In all probability, the acoustic reflex is of minor importance in terms of gain control. However, the high-intensity low-frequency components tend to severely mask the higher-frequency components that are critical for speech perception.[3] Thus, the acoustic reflex could serve to enhance the perception and identification of sound objects that depend on the higher-frequency spectrum (see Gygi, Kidd, & Watson, 2004, in chapter 8). From this perspective, it resembles the pupillary contraction for high illuminances. While reducing the size of the pupil does limit the amount of light energy reaching the retina, the importance of that contraction for light and dark adaptation is minimal. The more important effect is to increase the depth of the field that is in focus.

High- and Low-Spontaneous-Rate Cells

The compression at the basilar membrane and the depletion at the hair cells are mechanisms to circumvent response saturation. Another mechanism

2. An extensive review of corticofugal modulation in the auditory system is found in Suga and Ma (2003).

3. The acoustic reflex is also triggered by mastication so that its function may be to reduce internal sounds that could mask external signals.

depends on having two (or possibly three) different types of auditory nerve fibers to cover the entire intensity range (Frisina, 2001). By splitting the intensity range, there will always be a set of nerve fibers that is not saturated (and not below threshold). The high-spontaneous-rate fibers (more than about 15 spikes per second) would cover the lowest intensity range from 0 to 20 or 30 dB Sound Pressure Level (SPL) (at the characteristic frequency of the fiber). These fibers (roughly 85% of the neurons) have a low threshold but limited range. The low-spontaneous-rate fibers (0.5–15 spikes per second) would cover from 20 to 80 dB, and the very-low-spontaneous-rate fibers (less than 0.5 spikes per second) would cover the highest intensities. The latter fibers have a high threshold but wide dynamic range. Sumner, Lopez-Poveda, O'Mard, and Meddis (2002) suggested that the difference among the types of hair cells is attributable to the rate of release of neurotransmitter described above.

Let me try to summarize at this point. Keep in mind that the auditory world is one of discontinuities, so that adaptive processes that extend over several seconds or minutes (as in vision) are likely to be unhelpful. Looked at this way, the auditory system would have a hierarchical gain-control system. The mechanical compressive action of the basilar membrane acts instantaneously, followed by very rapid (~5 ms) chemical depletion in the hair cells. Then there is the slower feedback system based on the olivocochlear bundle, which seems to have been adapted to serve as a mechanism to prevent overload due to background noise. Although experiments show that the lack of the olivocochlear bundle does not seem to have very strong effects on signal detection (and hence on survival in the wild), its very existence suggests that it must be having some effect. Finally, there is the acoustic reflex operating over a longer time span, which acts to maintain the selectivity to higher frequencies that would have been masked by high-intensity low frequencies. All of these processes are assumed to act on the three types of spontaneous-rate neurons.

Summary of Adaptation and Gain Control

Fairhall, Lewen, Bialek, and de Ruyter van Steveninck (2001) pointed out that any adaptation or gain control system must be multilayered. Features of the acoustic and visual arrays evolve along different time scales from milliseconds to seconds, so that information about these changes also must be collected along equivalent time scales and transmitted along parallel channels. Moreover, as a sensory cell changes its response rate due to adaptation, there is a potential problem of ambiguity because the auditory and visual centers would not know what the current response rate signified. There is a need for information about the actual context in order to interpret the spike train. For a fly, Fairhall et al. found that following a shift in stimulus contrast, the initial change normalized the timing of individual spikes in terms of the stimulus variance within 1 s. Now the same firing rate encodes a different variability in the input. Spike timings over longer intervals appear to code the properties of the stimulus ensembles, and changes over still longer intervals code changes in the ensembles. We should expect such a multilevel system to exist for hearing and seeing.

Efficiency and Noise in Auditory and Visual Processing

Up to this point, I have discussed the concept of internal noise and how it limits discrimination and identification. Typically, these experiments have presented a simple uniform disk against a uniform background. But that is obviously not the normal environment in which we need to identify auditory and visual objects. The fundamental problem is that all perceiving takes place in the midst of statistical variation (e.g., detection of a breast tumor from X-ray images, detecting the sound of a predator among rustling leaves). Given the limited resolution of the auditory and visual systems, the information available to human observers is not complete and is often based on restricted sampling and confined to low-frequency components. In an environment in which the noise can take on a wide range of values, any input could have come from a set of possible objects (or no object at all). Thus, any decision can be made only statistically, and, as discussed in chapter 2, Bayes' theorem provides a disciplined procedure to evaluate the probabilities of different objects. Consider the simple case in which the observer has to decide whether a signal was presented in background noise ($S + N$) or the background noise (N) was presented alone. Bayes' theorem argues that the decision should be made of the basis of the ratio of the posterior probabilities: likelihoods (the ratio of the conditional probabilities of the $S + N$ given the input to the conditional probability of N given the input) × the ratio of the a priori probabilities of $S + N$ to N:

$$\Pr(S + N|\text{input})/\Pr(N|\text{input}) \times \Pr(S + N)/\Pr(N). \tag{6.10}$$

In what follows, I discuss the theory behind the experiments in terms of measuring the efficiency of humans as observers and compare detection and identification in a variety of fixed and random backgrounds.

To create a measure of the performance possible for an ideal detector, the likelihoods are calculated by cross-correlating the input with a template of the signal. To be concrete, suppose the detection problem is to determine if a light gray square was presented at a known location in a random noise visual field.[4] The $S + N$ input would be the image of the square embedded in the random noise; the N input would be the random noise only. The template would be the representation of the gray square at the known location. For a yes-no detection task, if the cross-correlation, pixel by pixel, between the input and the template is greater than some criterion value a, the ideal detector would judge that the light gray square was present. For a two-alternative forced choice (2AFC) in which the $S + N$ is presented in one interval and the N is presented in the other interval, the ideal detector would choose the interval with the higher cross-correlation between the input and template. Given the variability of the noise, performance will not be perfect: There will be trials in which the noise image will yield the higher cross-correlation.

These outcomes give us the maximum performance for the given signal and noise. Such an ideal detector has none of the obvious human limitations: internal noise, physiological degradations of the input, imperfect knowledge of the template, imperfect memory, and attention lapses. The performance of the ideal detector provides a normative baseline, and much of the research described below attempts to pinpoint discrepancies between performance of the ideal detector and that of human detectors.

Input Transformations

Internal Noise

Nearly all performance models assume that there is internal noise that adds variability to the input. As described below, the relative power of the internal and external noise can be assessed by the consistency of the observer's responses to identical inputs across trials. The template and cross-correlation calculation are assumed to be invariant, so that different responses to the identical physical input are assumed to be due to internal noise. The internal noise is the limiting factor for trial-by-trial prediction.

Matched-Filter Models

Matched-filter models transform the input stimulus based on the known physiological transformation of the peripheral auditory and visual systems. For all models, the template is transformed in the identical fashion as the input.

There are two general classes of models. In the simpler of the two, the filter is based purely on the psychophysics of the ear or eye. For the ear, the

4. A more realistic task would be to detect an unknown object at one of several locations, such as a kayak (S) crossing the path of your boat on a foggy (N) Maine morning.

intensity of the component frequencies is normalized in terms of their thresholds, and combined in terms of the width of their critical bands. For the eye, termed a *nonwhitening model*, two properties are usually included in the filter. The first is a band-pass contrast sensitivity filter that peaks at about 2 cycles/deg and essentially drops to zero at about 10 cycles/deg (see figure 6.9). The second is an eccentricity filter that mimics the decrease in retinal sensitivity away from the fovea. For the nonwhitening model, the filtering is assumed to be fixed and does not depend on the statistics of the background.

In the more complex of the two models, termed a *prewhitening model* for visual scenes, the statistics of the noise background partially determine the filter. We know from the analysis of auditory and visual natural scenes that the variability in power falls off at higher frequencies according to the $1/f^2$ relationship. We also know that maximum information transmission occurs when the power at every frequency is equal, the "bathtub" distribution (figure 3.7). Therefore, one plausible prewhitening filter would divide the power at each frequency by $1/f^2$, to make the power at all higher frequencies equal. Such a prewhitening filter would eliminate any intrinsic correlation in the noise and would equalize the autocorrelation at all temporal and spatial separations.[5] The correlation in amplitude between adjacent time points (t_i and t_{i+1}) and adjacent pixels (x_i and x_{i+1}) would equal the correlation between points separated by any interval or distance. Regardless of the filter chosen, the optimal signal detection method would be based on the cross-correlation of the transformed (i.e., prewhitened) stimulus with a prewhitened representation of the template.

Template Representations: Classification Images

The model of the ideal detector assumes a perfectly accurate template for the expected signal. This obviously is unrealistic. We can estimate the observer's template by a method that is analogous to that used to identify the space-time receptive field of a cell. What we are doing intuitively is to measure the influence of each frequency or pixel of the external noise on the observer's responses.[6] If the signal could be A or B, the template will be proportional to the average of the external noise of all trials on which the observer responds A, and the negative template will be proportional to the average of the external noise of all trials in which the observer responds

5. The autocorrelation occurs because of the limited sampling power of the nervous system. The higher-frequency components that create rapid shifts in amplitude are reduced in power so what remains are only the slow changes in amplitude. These slow changes generate the autocorrelation.

6. Although I have written these sections with parallel auditory and visual explanations, the majority of the research has used visual presentation.

B. Murray, Bennett, and Sekular (2002) showed that for the 2AFC procedure the best estimate of the observer's template is gotten by:

$$(N_{AA} + N_{BA}) - (N_{AB} + \mathrm{N}_{BB}) \tag{6.11}$$

or by rearranging the terms:

$$(N_{AA} - N_{AB}) - (N_{BB} - N_{BA}) \tag{6.12}$$

where N_{AA} is the average external noise for signal A and response A and N_{AB} is the average external noise for signal A and response B.

The classification image comes from the difference between the external noise fields for correct and incorrect responses for each signal (equation 6.12).

Imagine that A is a brighter object ↔ and B is the same shape but rotated 90° (↔). The observer will mistake ↔ for ↕ when the random noise field makes the horizontal line forming ↔ look dark and vertical line forming ↕ look bright. The observer will mistake ↕ for ↔ when the reverse occurs. The pixels along the horizontal and vertical lines will have the maximum effect on the observer's response. The template for ↕ should be a positive contrast 0° line and a negative contrast 90° line. The template for ↔ should be the reverse. The difference between the two templates is the best classification image.

The observer's actual template calculated from the above equations will, in all probability, differ from the ideal, and the cross-correlation between the ideal and the derived template is a measure of the accuracy of the perceptual template, termed *selection efficiency*. The selection efficiency sets an upper bound to performance, much as reliability does for validity.

Visual Processing

The maximum possible performance, given an ideal detector, makes it possible to measure the efficiency of the human observer in different contexts. There are two issues here. First, we need to determine the maximum performance based on different matching filters. Second, we need to determine whether the performance of the human observer allows us to determine which filtering model is more likely to be correct.

From a signal detection theory perspective, usual performance measure (d') is equal to:

$$d' = (X_{s+n} - X_n)/[1/2(\sigma^2_{s+n} + \sigma^2_n]^{1/2}. \tag{6.13}$$

For both nonprewhitening and prewhitening matched filter models, the cross-correlation between the transformed stimulus and transformed template is the statistic that optimizes performance. Therefore, d' becomes the difference between the filtered average cross-correlation when $S + N$ is presented and the filtered average cross-correlation when N only is presented, and the variances of the $S + N$ and N become the filtered autocorrelations of the $S + N$ and N trials.

For the simple two-alternative forced-choice task, d' can be calculated for the ideal detector empirically by generating a series of trials using examples of $S + N$ and N stimuli. The cross-correlations are calculated for each interval, and the ideal detector would then automatically select the interval with the highest cross-correlation. Given the variability in the noise, the ideal detector will make errors. The percentage correct then can be converted into d' for the two alternative case by the simple formula:

$$d'_{\text{ideal detector}} = 2^{1/2} \times Z \text{ score of percentage correct for ideal detector.} \tag{6.14}$$

We convert the percentage correct to d' because the percentage correct will be a function of the number of alternatives, but d' will not.

To calculate the performance for each possible matching filter, we would filter the $S + N$ and N stimuli as well as the template using each of the filters, and calculate the resulting d's for an ideal detector. To calculate human performance, we would run the observer through the same trials and calculate the resulting d'. Comparing the performance of human observers to that of the ideal detector for each filter should suggest which filter the observers use.

Finally, we can create an efficiency measure for the human observer either by comparing the energy required by the ideal detector and human observer to obtain the same d' values, or by comparing the d' values for the human and ideal detector at one signal and noise level. The assumption is that the human always calculates the cross-correlation correctly and then always chooses the interval with the higher cross-correlation. Thus, the reason that human performance is poorer than that achievable by the ideal detector is that the input has been degraded in some way or that the template of the expected stimulus is not optimum. If we could specify the actual input and template exactly, then we should be able to predict human performance trial by trial.

It must be kept in mind that the predicted performance for the ideal detector for both visual and auditory detection is only as good as the assumptions that generate it. There are many possible assumptions about the nature of a detection task. Furthermore, as discussed in chapter 1, we should be careful about proposing what the perceptual systems evolved to do.

Researchers (Ahumada & Beard, 1997; Beard & Ahumada, 1999; Eckstein, Ahumada, & Watson, 1997) performed a series of experiments to measure the sources of internal noise by using four different backgrounds. All the experiments used a forced-choice procedure: the $S + N$ was in one of two or four locations.

The authors proposed that the four backgrounds create a hierarchy in which it is possible to hypothesize that decrements in performance (i.e., reductions in human efficiency) are due to additional sources of noise. For the ideal detector, *d′* will be equal to:

$$d'_{\text{ideal detector}} = (E_o/N_o)^{1/2} \tag{6.16}$$

where E_o equals the signal contrast energy and N_o equals the pixel noise variance (I use S_e^2 to represent the external noise variance in human experiments).

Uniform Background

The uniform background was a constant gray luminance. The luminance was changed across trials so that the average value equaled that for the other conditions. Compared to an ideal detector, we can postulate at least two factors that might impair human performance. The first factor is additive internal observer noise due to fluctuations in neural firing (termed $S^2{}_i$). The internal noise corresponds to equivalent input noise, discussed at the beginning of this chapter. The second factor is an internal template that is not perfectly matched to the signal. The correlation between the internal template and the signal (essentially pixel by pixel) represents the sampling efficiency (*SE*). Given these two factors that can degrade performance, we can represent the expected *d′* as:

$$d' = (E_o \times SE)^{1/2}/(S^2{}_i + S^2{}_e)^{1/2}. \tag{6.17}$$

The signal contrast energy is degraded by the sampling efficiency and the noise variance becomes the sum of the observer's internal noise and the external noise. The noise variances are independent and therefore add.

Fixed Structured Background

The background was identical at each location across all trials. In some experiments the background was taken from medical images and in others it was a random dot matrix. Surprisingly, the performance for the ideal detector in a fixed background should be no different from that for a uniform background. Remember that the best strategy is to correlate the stimulus at each location to the template and then choose the location with the highest cross-correlation. Since the background is identical at all locations, performance using the cross-correlation strategy should be identical for any type of fixed background.

In spite of the prediction from the ideal detector model, a high-contrast fixed background such as a sine wave grating does degrade human performance. The authors hypothesized that the fixed, structured background introduces another source of variability due to the contrast gain control, S^2_{cgc}. The contrast gain control is presumed to divide the responses to the signal at each spatial frequency by the average contrast and thereby introduce added variability. The S^2_{cgc} is conceptually the amount of external noise that must be added to a uniform background to make that performance equal to that for a fixed structured background.

We can represent the predicted d' as:

$$d' = (E_o \times SE)^{1/2}/(S^2_i + S^2_e + S^2_{cgc})^{1/2}. \quad (6.18)$$

Fixed-Trial Structured Background

The structured background was identical at each location for every trial, but the background changed on each trial. For the ideal detector, changing the background on every trial should not affect performance for the same reason described above. The background at each location is still identical. But changing the background on every trial does reduce the efficiency of human observers. We can speculate that when the background is fixed across trials and observers are given feedback, observers can build up an accurate template. Such recalibration of the template would not be possible if the background is shifted on every trial.

We would predict that d' should decrease due to the variance introduced by the changed background (S^2_{bg}):

$$d' = (E_o \times SE)^{1/2}/(S^2_i + S^2_e + S^2_{cgc} + S^2_{bg})^{1/2}. \quad (6.19)$$

Random-Trial Structured Background

The background differed at each location for every trial. For the ideal detector, the random variation of the background will clearly reduce performance. As described previously, the optimum strategy is to construct a filter that removes the noise correlation and then cross-correlate the filtered stimulus with the filtered template. If the background differs at each location, the ideal detector must create a different prewhitening filter for each location and then choose the location in which the cross-correlation is highest.

The random background clearly degrades human performance, and we can represent the predicted reduction in d' by adding another variance due to the random background variation (S^2_{rbv}):

$$d' = (E_o \times SE)^{1/2}/(S^2_i + S^2_e + S^2_{cgc} + S^2_{bg} + S^2_{rbv})^{1/2}. \quad (6.20)$$

By combining the results of three studies (Ahumada & Beard, 1997; Beard & Ahumada, 1999; Eckstein et al., 1997), a rather consistant picture emerges. The detection performance in terms of d' for three background conditions as a function of the signal contrast energy is schematically presented in figure 6.15. There are two graphs. In the first the added noise energy is relatively small, and in the second the added noise energy is several times greater.

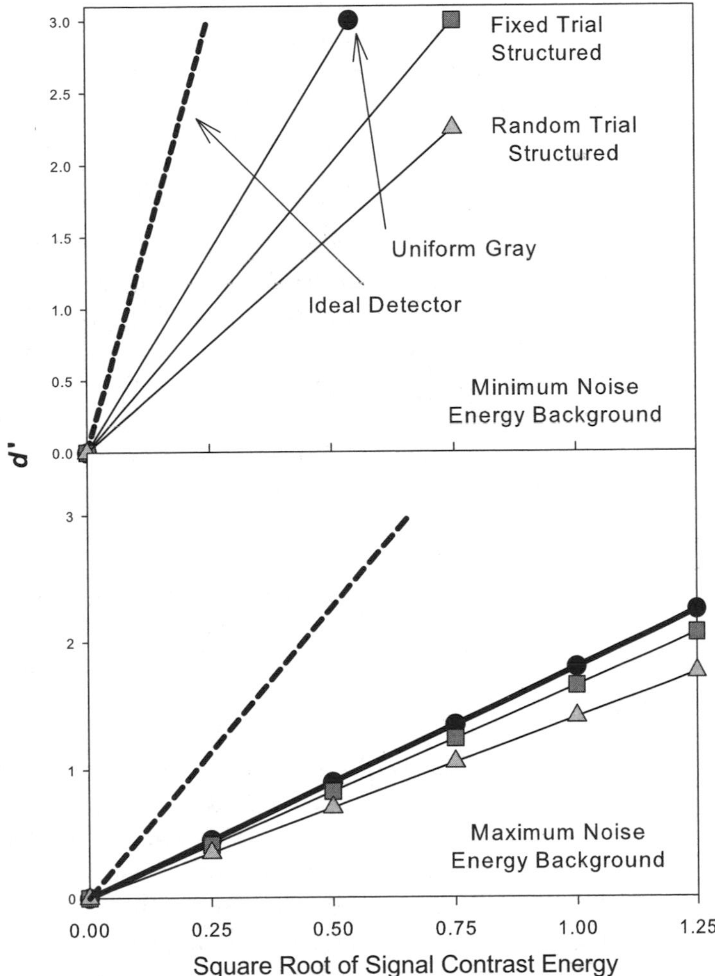

Figure 6.15. The average performance for detecting a signal in three different medical backgrounds (X-ray coronary angiograms). The signal was presented in one of four locations (4AFC). Five levels of signal contrast were used to determine the effect on detection of signal strength. The results are shown for the minimum and maximum amount of presented background noise energy. The ideal detector values are calculated from $d'_{\text{ideal}} = (E_o/N_o)^{1/2}$ (equation 6.16 in text). Adapted from "Visual Signal Detection in Structured Backgrounds. II. Effects of Contrast Gain Control, Background Variations, and White Noise," by M. P. Eckstein, A. J. Ahumada, and A. B. Watson, 1997, *Journal of the Optical Society of America, A, 14*(9), 2406–2419.

At all conditions, detection was best with a uniform gray background. Detection was intermediate with the fixed-trial backgrounds, and poorest with the random-trial structured backgrounds.

1. As would be expected, detection improved as the stimulus contrast increased and degraded as the background contrast increased.
2. The effect of the external noise was to reduce the differences between the background conditions. The task was made more difficult, and observers could not make use of the repeated-trial structured background to detect the signal. At the maximum noise energy background, there was no difference between the fixed trial and random trial background.

Across the three experiments, rough estimates for the overall efficiency for the uniform background, the fixed-trial structured background, and the random-trial structured background conditions were 20–30%, 10%, and 0.05–1% respectively. Eckstein et al. (1997) estimated that the sampling efficiency (i.e., the correlation between signal and the observer's template) in the uniform background was about 0.30, which dropped to 0.16 in the structured backgrounds. They further estimated that the equivalent internal noise and the equivalent contrast gain noise were about equal and roughly one half of the equivalent background variation noise. These values for the sampling efficiencies are much greater than those found by Simpson, Falkenberg, and Manhilov (2003) for drifting gratings. In that work, the sampling efficiency was about 1%. Simpson et al. (2003) suggested that observers were using representations based on slowly moving gratings regardless of the actual speed of the grating.

In similar work, Burgess (1999) investigated the ability of observers to detect signals in non-Gaussian background noise that is more representative of backgrounds in natural scenes. One type of noise maintained the positive correlations found in natural objects (adjacent pixels are likely to have the same value, creating low-frequency spatial frequencies), but the other type of noise created negative low-frequency correlations, so that adjacent pixels were likely to generate regions of reversed brightness (creating high spatial frequencies). Burgess found that observers were able to compensate for the positive low-frequency noise correlations but were unable to compensate for the negative low-frequency correlations when the signal was a set of small discrete blobs. This finding supports the contention that the visual system prewhitens the image to remove local positive correlations found in scenes but is unable to compensate for background correlations that do not occur naturally.

Efficiency and Noise in Auditory Processing

Ideal Detector Models

The optimal decision rules are identical for hearing and seeing. Both senses must segment and identify objects against a varying noisy background.[7]

Imagine that the background noise is passed through a low-pass filter such as an amplifier or headphone. The amplitude of this filtered output changes slowly because the rapid changes due to the high frequencies have been removed. The amplitudes of two noise values close together in time will be similar, so that we can approximate the noise to a high degree from a finite set of individual points. Sampling theorems prove that it is possible to exactly reconstruct a waveform that is limited to frequencies less than W by the amplitude of a set of discrete, equally spaced intervals at times $1/2W$, $2/2W$, $3/2W$, and so on. For a signal limited to 500 Hz, the points would be separated by 1 ms and the representation would be based on 1,000 points/s.

First, if the signal is known exactly (SKE), the ideal detector will know the true value of the amplitude at each of the $2WT$ sample points. If the signal + noise and the noise are normally distributed, and the variance of the noise and signal + noise distributions are equal, then the performance of the ideal detector can be expressed in terms of d':

$$d' = (2E_s/N_0)^{1/2}. \tag{6.21}$$

where E_s is the signal energy and N_0 is the noise power density. The noise power density is actually energy: the power in a one-cycle band per second × seconds. N_0 is a very useful measurement because it determines the ability of listeners to hear a signal embedded in noise.

Second, if the signal is one from a set of m orthogonal signals, typically two assumptions are made: (1) the signals are uncorrelated with each other, and (2) all possible signals have the same energy. D. M. Green and Swets (1966) demonstrated that as the uncertainty increases due to more possible waveforms, the energy of any waveform must be increased to achieve the same performance. Specifically, the energy must be increased approximately as the logarithm of the number of alternatives. For this reason, after the uncertainty has increased beyond a small value, large changes in the uncertainty can be balanced by relatively small changes in the signal intensity.

Efficiency of Human Detectors

The measure of efficiency is the ratio of the actual performance to the ideal performance, $d'_{\text{ideal}} = (2E_s/N_0)^{1/2}$. Keeping in mind that the measure of

7. This treatment of the ideal detector closely follows that of D. M. Green and Swets (1966).

efficiency depends critically on the assumptions about the ideal detector, the ratio of actual performance to ideal performance usually ranges from 0.25 to 0.50 based on the published papers collected in Swets (1964). But there are exceptions where the efficiency drops to 1% or less. Several studies have pointed out that the particular characteristics of the noise masker can drastically affect performance. For example, Isabelle and Colburn (1991) used ten different narrow-band noise maskers in a simple pure-tone (500 Hz sinusoidal wave) detection task. Across the three subjects, for one noise sample the percentages of hits [Pr(saying Signal|Signal)] and false alarms [Pr(saying Signal|Noise)] were (22%, 22%), (20%, 25%), and (65%, 22%), yielding *d′* values of 0.0, –0,16, and 1.0 respectively. However, for a different noise sample the percentages were (92%, 90%), (92%, 85%), and (95%, 52%), yielding *d′* values of 0.12, 0.60, and 1.35. For still another noise sample, the hits and false alarms were (95%, 10%), (95%, 28%), and (98%, 40%), yielding *d′* values of 2.92, 2.22, and 2.30. These outcomes clearly demonstrate that each noise produces a different perception: The first noise makes it seem that the signal was never presented; the second noise makes it seem that the signal was always presented; and the third noise makes it easy to detect when the signal was presented. There also seems to be a subject × noise interaction. The first subject does relatively poorly with the first two noises, but was the best with the third noise. Siegel and Colburn (1989) presented similar results.

Internal and External Noise

The fact that equivalent noise samples yield remarkably diverse performances implies that there striking differences in the external noise and the fact that equivalent listeners give different responses to the same stimulus implies that there also are striking differences in the amount of internal noise. The problem is to develop strategies that will allow us to measure the two kinds of noise.

D. M. Green (1964) advocated a quasi-molecular approach in which each noise sample is presented several times to measure the internal noise. For example, Spiegel and Green (1981) used a clever technique for estimating internal and external noise. In a two-alternative forced-choice procedure, they presented two different noise samples (no signal at all) and asked listeners to pick the signal interval. The same pair of noises was repeated many times and the percentage of times the listener picked the same noise sample was calculated. If the listener's choice was random, 50/50, then we can argue that it was all internal noise because there was no discrimination between the two samples. Conversely, if the listener's response was highly consistent, say 85/15, then we can argue that the internal noise was low and performance was determined by the external noise (i.e., the variation between samples). Spiegel and Green found that the percentages ranged between 65% and 75% depending on the particular pair of noise samples, and that value indicated that the internal and external noise were approximately equal. In a visual detection task, Murray et al. (2002) found that the percentages ranged between 68% and 76%, so they also estimated that the internal and external noise power was roughly equal. Isabelle and Colburn (1991) and Siegel and Colburn (1989), using a different analysis, found internal/external noise ratios that ranged from 0.5 to 2.5, with an average about 1. However, we cannot partition the internal noise into those components due to the stochastic nature of neural transmission, fluctuations in the subject's criterion, or the subject's attentiveness. Similarly, we cannot partition the external noise into its components.

Fixed (Frozen) and Random Noise

Pfafflin and colleagues (Pfafflin, 1968; Pfafflin & Mathews, 1966) investigated whether detection and identification were better with a fixed unvarying noise masker than with a noise masker that changed on every trial in two studies, using a two-alternative forced-choice procedure. (This is analogous to the fixed structured background [frozen noise] and fixed-trial structured noise conditions used by Eckstein et al., 1997). In the first study, a sinusoidal tone was masked by 1 of 12 different noises in one interval, and only a noise was presented in the second interval. On some trials, the same noise was presented in both intervals (e.g., $S + N_1$ versus N_1), while in other trials the noise in the two intervals differed (e.g., $S + N_1$ versus N_2). The detection of the tone signal was slightly better when the noise in both intervals was identical, but the difference was not large (compare this outcome to figure 6.15). (In another study, listeners could correctly determine if the noise in the two intervals was the same or different in about 80% of the trials.)

The second study consisted of three stages. In the first, the two intervals in every forced-choice trial used the same noise, but the 12 noises were randomly presented across trials. The authors then selected the noises that produced the poorest performance and presented blocks of trials with exactly the same noise on every trial (e.g., $S + N_9$ versus N_9 for every trial). Detection of the tone signal was much better in the blocked second stage for both two-alternative forced-choice tasks and simple yes-no tasks (was the tone signal presented or not). Clearly, listeners are gaining information about the noises that could be used to improve performance.

In an experiment to measure the difference threshold for intensity, Buus (1990) compared tones, frozen noise, and random noise. On every trial, the sound in one of the intervals was incremented by ΔI, and listeners had to identify that interval. The sounds were a 3000 Hz tone, a frozen noise sample that was presented for the entire block of trials, or a random noise sample that changed on every trial. The difference threshold was smaller for the frozen noise than for the random noise only when the noise had a narrow bandwidth, and here the difference thresholds resembled those for the tones.

In sum, the performance gain from frozen noise is small. This conclusion differs from the visual results, where fixed structured noise produced significantly better detection.

Profile Analyses and Comodulation Masking Release in Audition

We know that the basilar membrane performs a pseudo-Fourier analysis of the incoming sound wave: Each auditory nerve transmits a range of frequencies, and the auditory cortex is organized along isofrequency contours. These physiological facts, along with the observation that for many tasks performance appears to be based on the energy in a narrow band of frequencies, led to the conceptualization that perception was a function of *critical bands*. Energy within any band was integrated, and only the energy within a band determined masking effectiveness. Energy in critical bands that were far removed from the frequency of the signal was supposed to have little effect on performance. Below I consider two kinds of experiments that demonstrate that performance can be determined by the pattern of energy at widely different frequencies and not solely by the energy in nearby critical bands. Each type of experiment is related to later chapters: profile analysis is related to the perception of timbre (chapter 8) and comodulation release is related to the formation of auditory objects (chapter 9).

Profile Analysis

In the typical profile analysis task, the standard stimulus is composed of 10 to 20 sinusoidal components widely separated in frequency. Each component is exactly equal in amplitude. The profile stimulus is exactly the same as the standard except that the amplitude of only one of the components is increased. In a two-alternative forced-choice task, the listener must identify the profile stimulus as opposed to the standard. Two factors seem to make this a very difficult task. First, the incremental frequency component is buried among the other components, and in some cases listeners will not know which of the components will be increased in amplitude. Second, the overall intensity of the standard and profile stimuli can differ within a trial. Thus, the profile stimulus is not necessarily the louder of the two, so that listeners must make their judgments in terms of the quality of the sounds.

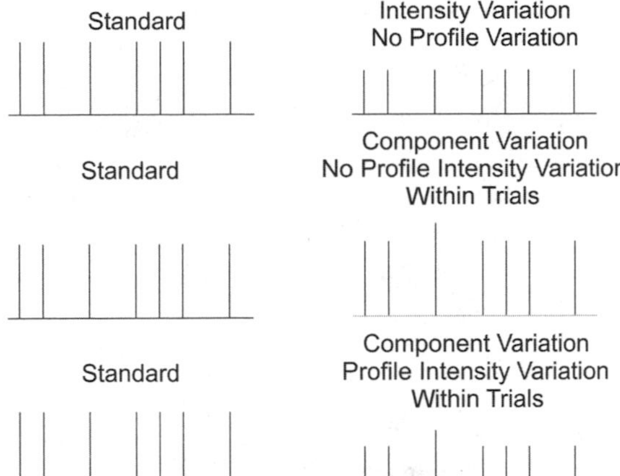

Figure 6.16. Three possible comparisons between the standard and profile stimulus are sketched. In the first, all of the components of the profile are changed in intensity by the same amount so that the profile is constant and flat. In the second, one frequency component is incremented but the remaining components do not change. The intensity is changed between trials, but the intensity always is identical for the components of the standard and profile stimuli, except for the target frequency. In the third, the intensity variation occurs within a single trial: The intensity of all component frequencies within the profile stimulus is increased or decreased, and then the target frequency is incremented.

As shown in figure 6.16, the incremented component actually may be less intense than that component in the standard if all the components are reduced in intensity.

To do this task, the listener must be able to compare the relative intensities at different frequencies. What is surprising is that some listeners find the task easy, and the difference threshold is no worse and is usually better than the difference threshold for a single isolated tone (D. M. Green, 1988). Listeners are extraordinarily sensitive to the shape (amplitude envelope) of the spectrum. What I find impressive is that listeners do so well given that the stimuli are quite unrepresentative of natural sounds, in which overall changes in intensity tend to increase the relative amplitudes of the higher frequencies. For naturally produced sounds, the amplitudes of the frequency components do not vary independently. D. M. Green (1993) summarized some of the important findings based on the experiment by D. M. Green, Kidd, and Pickardi (1983) shown in figure 6.17. There were four conditions:

1. A single 1000 Hz tone was presented in each interval, and listeners judged which of the intervals contained the more intense tone. The intensities were the same in both intervals (except for the increment, of course), but the intensity varied from trial to trial.

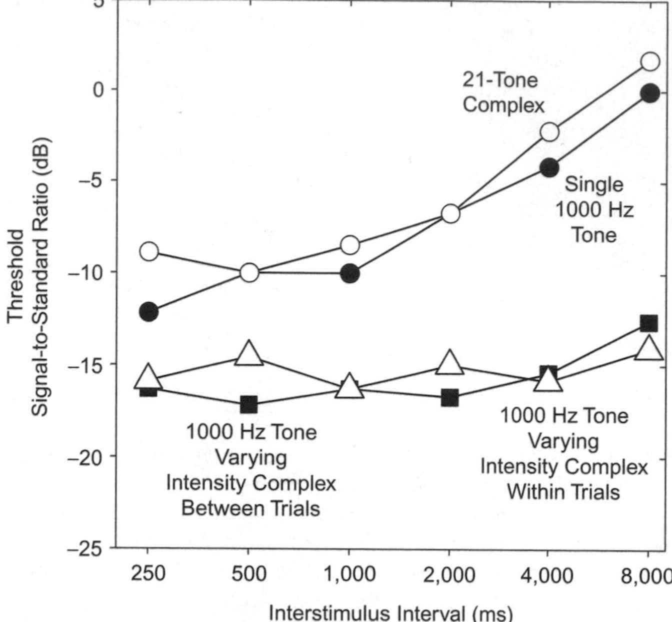

Figure 6.17. Results from profile analysis experiments demonstrating the difference between traditional intensity threshold measurement and intensity threshold measurement as a sound quality judgment within tonal complexes. The filled circles represent the results for a 1000 Hz tone with intensity variation between trials. The open circles represent the results for a 21-tone complex with intensity variation between trials. The filled squares represent the results for the increment of a single tone with intensity variation between trials. The larger open triangles represent the results for the increment of a single tone with intensity variation within trials (see figure 6.16). Adapted from "Auditory Intensity Discrimination," by D. M. Green, 1993, in W. A. Yost, A. N. Popper, and R. R. Fay (Eds.), *Human Psychophysics* (Vol. 3, pp.13–55). New York: Springer-Verlag.

2. The same 1000 Hz tone was combined with 20 other tones to create a 21-tone standard complex. To create the profile stimulus, all 21 tones were incremented. Listeners judged which interval contained the louder complex tone. As in (1), the base intensities for the standard and profile stimulus were identical, but the base intensity varied from trial to trial.
3. Only the 1000 Hz tone embedded in the 21-tone profile stimulus, as in (2), was incremented in amplitude. As in (1) and (2), the base intensities of the standard and profile were the same on each trial, so that the profile stimulus would be slightly louder. The base intensities varied from trial to trial.
4. Only the 1000 Hz tone embedded in the 21-tone complex was incremented, as in (3). Here, however, the overall intensity varied within a

trial, so that either the standard or profile could be the louder sound. Listeners would need to judge differences in the spectral shape (i.e., a comparison of the relative amplitudes of the components), disregarding loudness, to perform the discrimination.

D. M. Green (1993) argued that there are two important findings. First, the difference thresholds for (3) and (4) did not differ and were less than those for (1) and (2). In spite of the fact that only 1 of 21 tone components changed, subjects were able to discriminate intensity changes within the complex better than when only the single component changed in isolation. An increment of only 1 dB (12%) was perceivable. D. M. Green (1988) argued that listeners create a verbal description of the spectral profile (e.g., rough, smooth, sharp). It is this derivative judgment that is used to compare the standard and profile, not the remembered loudness of individual components.

Second, the difference threshold for conditions (1) and (2) in which listeners are making direct judgments of loudness increased as the two intervals between the two sounds got longer, while the difference threshold for conditions (3) and (4) did not. This finding supports the contention that listeners are making qualitative judgments about spectral shape, reducing those judgments to simple verbal terms, and remembering those terms. The verbal terms would be immune to memory loss. It is not clear to me how the verbal description provides a means to compare the intervals. I would suspect that the verbal description provides a tag to re-create an auditory image of the sound in the first interval and that complex sounds provide several kinds of perceptual properties that can be employed retrospectively by listeners to detect the profile.

It is interesting to note that as the number of components increases, the difference threshold tends to decrease. As long as 100 Hz or so separates the components, it does not much matter whether they are "compactly or widely positioned around the incremented frequency. Listeners are making their judgments based on the overall profile and not on the local region of the incremented frequency.

Let me summarize at this point. The results here demonstrate that listeners are more able to detect increments in the amplitude of one component when it is embedded in a tonal complex than to detect the identical increment if that component is presented alone. Our proposed explanation is Gestalt-like: The spectral shape of the tonal components creates a timbre quality, and listeners compare the timbre of the standard to the profile to make their judgments. If this is true, then we should be able to make discrimination more difficult if we can strip away the surrounding components to force listeners to make their judgments only on the loudness of the one target frequency.

One way to strip away the surrounding components and make them form a separate auditory source is to manipulate the temporal properties of the components. The most powerful acoustic cue for the fusion of component sounds is onset asynchrony (see chapter 9). In nearly all instances, if frequency components start at the same instant, they are perceived as coming from the same object. On this basis, we would expect that if the target component started before or after the remaining components, it would be treated as a separate entity, and performance would then mimic that of a single component presented alone. D. M. Green and Dai (1992) found that leads and lags as small as 10 ms disrupted detection (this is slightly shorter than the 20–30 ms delay that causes components to split apart in other tasks discussed in chapter 9). Hill and Bailey (2002) attempted to create a separate stream by presenting the target component to one ear and the flanking components to the other ear (termed *dichotic presentation*). If the target and flanking components were synchronous, dichotic presentation was only slightly worse. If the components were presented asynchronously, detection was much worse, but there was no added decrease due to dichotic presentation. Onset asynchrony between two sounds is a much stronger basis for the formation of two sounds than is different spatial locations (also discussed in chapter 9).

A second way to strip away the surrounding components is by means of coherent amplitude modulation. There are several possibilities: (a) the target component is modulated, but the nontarget components are not (or the reverse); or (b) all the components are modulated, but the target component is modulated out of phase to the other components. For all of these conditions, the detection of the increment in intensity is impaired.

Comodulation Masking Release

The fundamental lesson from profile analysis research is that the acoustic signal is typically treated as representing a single source and that listeners attend to the entire spectrum. Isolating individual components leads to degradation in the ability to detect the amplitude change of those components.

We can also demonstrate that the acoustic signal with a coherent temporal pattern is treated as a single source from the reverse direction. Suppose we have a target masked by noise. How can we make that target more discriminable? If adding more tonal components to form a coherent spectral shape makes one tonal target more discriminable, then, paradoxically, adding noise that combines with the masking noise to form a coherent noise source also should make the target more detectable. The trick is to amplitude modulate both the original masking noise and the added noise, identically in frequency, phase, and depth, to make the coherent noise into a source. The coherent noise source now seems separate from the target.

Hall, Grose, and Fernandes (1984) were the first to demonstrate that amplitude modulation of a noise masker could lead to unmasking. Listeners were trying to detect a 1000 Hz tone in a noise masker. The first part of the experiment replicated previous work. As the bandwidth of the noise increased, the detectability of the tone decreased and then remained constant after the bandwidth exceeded 130 Hz. This result confirmed the view that only noise within a critical band surrounding the tone affected performance. Then Hall et al. slowly amplitude modulated the noise masker. The unexpected result was that the tonal signal was easier to detect in the modulated noise (the tone could be 1/10 the amplitude as before [20 dB softer] and still be detected) and that as the noise bandwidth increased, the signal became even easier to detect.

Hall et al. (1984) provided another demonstration of masking release. The initial condition was similar to that above: a 1000 Hz tone target and a masking noise 100 Hz wide centered on 1000 Hz. In the second part, a second nonoverlapping noise band 100 Hz wide at a different center frequency also was presented (e.g., 750–850 Hz). If the two noise bands were amplitude modulated coherently, the detectability of the tone increased up to 10 dB. The second noise band could be separated by as much as an octave (500 or 2000 Hz) and still improve detection. In general, the most important factor determining the amount of masking release was the number of comodulated masker bands: The amount of release increased with the number of masker bands as long as the bands occurred in regions that excited different critical bands. The release was maximized if the modulation rate was low and the depth of modulation was high.

The temporal modulation properties of the masker bands are critical (Hall & Grose, 1990). Suppose we start with the typical demonstration of comodulation release, comparing the detectability of a tone masked by narrow-band noise (figure 6.18A) to the same tone masked by a set of noise bands that undergo coherent amplitude modulation (figure 6.18B). The tone in the latter case may still be detected if it is 20 dB less than when presented in one noise band. Now, we add two more masker bands that fall between the tonal target and the two nearest noise bands, but these new bands are modulated at a different rate than the other masker bands (figure 6.18C). The interpolated bands dramatically degrade the detectability and the threshold falls nearly back to the case in which there are no comodulated masker bands. The coherent amplitude modulation creates the perceptual cue that all the noise comes from one source and that leads to the noise being segregated from the tone (which is not being modulated). The two new interpolated noise bands presumably do not segregate with the other noise bands and, being just two bands, probably do not form a second noise object. The interpolated bands are adjacent to the noise band "on top of" the tone, so that they weaken the tendency for the noise band directly

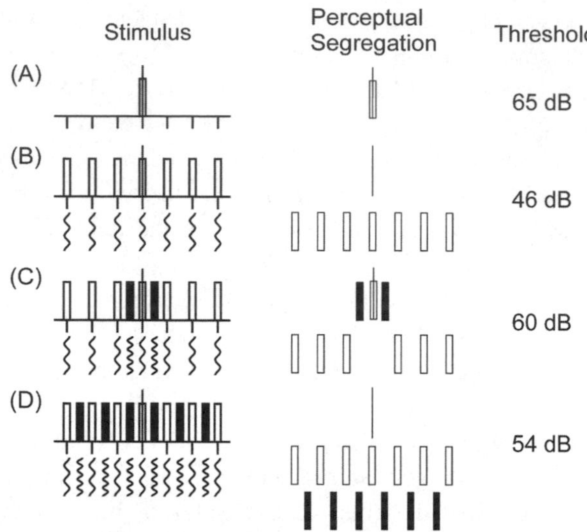

Figure 6.18. The magnitude of comodulation release depends on the degree to which the noise forms a separate perceptual entity. The simple detection experiment is illustrated in (A). A tone (narrow line) is embedded in the middle of a noise band (narrow rectangle). The basic comodulation release experiment is illustrated in (B). All of the noise bands are modulated coherently (wiggly lines under noise bands) and the tone is much easier to detect (by 20 dB). The interference of deviant bands is illustrated in (C). The two deviant noise bands (modulated at different rate) disrupt the segregation of the noise bands, and the tone remains embedded in the deviant plus the original noise bands. The formation of the deviant noise bands into a perceptual entity is illustrated in (D). Adding more deviant bands at that modulation frequency and depth makes it easier to detect the tone. Three sounds emerge. Adapted from "Comodulation Masking Release and Auditory Grouping," by J. W. Hall and J. H. Grose, 1990, *Journal of the Acoustical Society of America, 88*, 119–125.

masking the tone to segregate with the comodulated bands. Perceptually, there are two sounds: the tone masked by three noise bands and the six remaining coherently modulated bands. If we add additional noise bands that match the modulation of the deviant bands (figure 6.18D), that creates a stronger tendency for the deviant bands to form their own noise source and a stronger tendency for the noise band at the tone frequency to rejoin the coherently modulated bands. Perceptually, there now are three sounds: the coherently modulated deviant noise bands, all the original coherently modulated noise bands, and the tone target. The detectability of the tone increases due to the greater degree of comodulation masking release.

Another temporal factor that determines the degree of masking release is the onset of the noise bands. Paralleling the outcomes for profile analysis, if the onsets of the surrounding noise bands are not synchronous with the onset of tonal noise band (greater than 50 ms), the degree of masking release is reduced (Grose & Hall, 1993).

In sum, the masking release is greatest when the bands are perceived to form one (or more) noise sources based on the onset synchrony of noise bands with the same amplitude modulation envelopes. This really does not tell us why it is easier to detect the tonal target. It might simply be that the tone is more easily heard in the amplitude dips of the noise bands. If the two noise bands are comodulated, the sum has distinct intervals in which the masking noise is very weak. But if the noise bands are uncorrelated, the sum does not have such distinct intervals of low intensity. However, a dip explanation does not explain why onset asynchrony affects the size of the release.

Summary

At least two major issues have been covered here. First, how does noise, both internal and external, affect detection and identification performance? Second, how does the nervous system compensate for the limited firing range of individual receptors in the face of the enormous range of environmental input?

The material presented here reinforces the contentions presented in chapter 1 that perceiving is inherently contextual and depends on processes at both multiple spatial and temporal time scales. The effect of noise and the processes underlying gain control depend on the specifics of the actual stimulus presented and its internal correlational structure and temporal variation, as well as the context of the experiment and the statistics of the natural world. It is tempting to conceptualize the resulting efficiency in terms of maximizing information transmission.

7

The Perception of Quality: Visual Color

Color and Timbre

The correspondences between looking and listening are often slippery, with several possible matches at each stage in the process of perceiving. Here is another of those choice points. The reflected light is a joint function of the illumination and the surface reflectance of an object, and the emitted sound is a joint function of the source energy (corresponding to the illumination) and the overlapping resonances (corresponding to the surface reflectance) of an object. All the nervous system has is the rate of firing of the different receptor cells, but the firing of any single one is completely ambiguous.

The firing rates of the retinal cells and the cochlear cells are probabilistic. A medium-wavelength cone (colloquially called a green cone) can be excited (although at a lower probability) by light energy at nearly every visible wavelength, and a hair cell with a characteristic frequency of 1000 Hz can be excited (although at a lower probability) by a range of frequencies around 1000 Hz. The ratios of firings among the three cone systems and the ratios among the different hair cells can lead to an accurate interpretation of the energy reaching the receptor, but the ambiguity between the frequency distribution of the energy source and that of the reflectance and resonances remains. Nonetheless, the nervous system must interpret the firing pattern and make a best guess about the properties of the object.

There are several possibilities when comparing seeing and hearing. The first matches color to pitch. We specify a color by its frequency and we similarly specify pitch by its frequency. Moreover, color and pitch are the classic examples of secondary perceptual attributes: The perceiver creates color and pitch; they are not inherent in the frequency of the energy. Galileo, Locke, and others first advanced this distinction between a primary and secondary attribute. Newton's famous expression was, "For the rays, to speak properly, are not coloured. In them there is nothing else than a certain power, and disposition to stir up a sensation of this or that colour" and we can generalize that "vibrations to speak properly are pitchless." If we follow this possibility, we could describe the particular characteristics of the color space and the pitch space and describe any correspondences between the two spaces. The emphasis would be on the perceptual properties of the qualities themselves without reference to the sources carrying the color or pitches. It would be the perception of the proximal excitation only.

I prefer the second, which matches color contrast to timbre contrast for two reasons. The first is that one overarching theme of this book is that the perceptual variables are those of contrast, not those of individual magnitudes. As described above, any single auditory or visual perception is ambiguous. We can create many visual stimuli that lead to the same firing pattern using different combinations of illumination and surface reflectance, and similarly we theoretically could create many auditory stimuli that create the same firing pattern by different combinations of source frequency and filter resonance. However, if we can assume that the illumination is roughly constant and that the source frequencies are similarly constant, then the contrasts among different regions of the visual scene or among different sounds can lead to an estimate of the properties of the object.

Another reason for my preference for the second match is my belief that color and timbre are source attributes and therefore are properties of objects. The goal is to describe the perceptual and cognitive processes that allow us to recover the "true" color (i.e., the fixed surface reflectance of an object) and timbre (i.e., the fixed resonances of an object) in spite of variations in the source (or any other environmental factor). The first step would be to describe the source-filter models underlying the creation of colored objects and sound objects and describe any correspondences between the two models. The second step would be to point out the equivalences in the perceptual process yielding color and timbre.

A basic question is, why should perceptual systems perceive one property independently of others? Why should there be presumably independent neural pathways for location, shape, color, pitch, and brightness? Why does the auditory system construct timbre instead of merely constructing the pitch? Moreover, why does it seem perfectly natural to describe visual objects in terms of their color and sound sources (and not merely individual sounds) in terms of their timbres so that comparative statements like "he sounds just like Johnny Cash" are so easily understood? The same question can be posed in terms of any other property. Conceptually, it is possible to have sensory systems in which the perceptual representation is a gestalt, not analyzable into separable properties. My answer would be that such properties provide independent ways to break auditory and visual scenes into objects. For visual scenes, the constancy of one such property allows viewers to segment the visual scene into objects; for example, viewers can link together the surfaces of a single object based on color constancy in spite of changes in shape due to motion. I would argue that the usefulness of timbre is identical: It allows the perceiver to segment the auditory world into objects in spite of the variation in individual sounds due to pitch or loudness. Color and timbre help create the coherence of objects in a changing world.

Both color and timbre are defined by exclusion. Kaiser and Boynton (1996, p. 315) defined chromatic color: "chromatic color is that aspect of visual perception by which observers distinguish differences between equally bright, structure-free fields of view of identical size and shape." The American National Standards Institute (1973, p. 56) definition of timbre is, "the quality of sound by which a listener can tell that two sounds of the same loudness and pitch are dissimilar." The equivalence of the two definitions is obvious: Each tells us that color or timbre is defined by discrimination, but neither tells us what color or timbre is. There is a difference; color is defined as an act of perception while timbre is defined in terms of a sound quality. This has led timbre to be conceptualized as one acoustically measurable property such that each note of an instrument or singing voice, as well as each spoken sound of one voice, would be characterized by a single value of that property. This viewpoint has been reinforced by the inability to create models of instruments that sound correct across pitch.

Yet I think that this definition of timbre is misguided. The usefulness of timbre is identical to the usefulness of color: It specifies the inherent resonant properties and thereby allows the perceiver to segment the world into objects. What is important about timbre is that it is in some way unchanged across changes in loudness and pitch, so that the listener can track the trajectory of that object. Similarly, what is important about color is that in some way it is unchanged across changes in illumination. Thus, I believe that both color and timbre are the result of perceptual acts.

On this basis, the appropriate conceptualization for color is that of the ratios of absorption (or firing rates) of the rods and three types of cones to adjacent surfaces. (There is no doubt that the firing rates of each type of cone are transformed into firing rates of opponent color neurons, so that the resulting firing pattern is based on ratios. But in what follows I stay at the level of the cones, which makes the presentation easier.) Each colored surface would be characterized by a set of ratios of absorption. Under any fixed illumination, differences in those ratios would create the perception of edges that delimit objects. Under varying illumination, it is the constancy of the ratios that creates the perception of a single color. By analogy, the appropriate conceptualization for sounds would be the set of ratios of the firing rates across the hair cells due to the different frequency components. At one fixed source frequency, differences in those ratios characterize the timbre of instruments and voices. At varying source frequencies, it is the constancy of the ratios that creates the perception of a one-sound object.

Although I have organized this book in terms of the equivalence of color (this chapter) and timbre (chapter 8), the equivalence fails in several ways. First, visual source energy usually is constant across the scene. There may be shadows, localized frequency filtering due to dust, or reflections from one object onto another, but the most likely bet is that the source is constant. Moreover, although the shape of the frequency distribution of energy does change across increases or decreases in intensity, the distributions can be transformed into each other. This relative constancy is not true for sound objects. The source energy does not change in any simple way at different frequencies as the intensity is increased or decreased. Consider a violin: The source of sound is the vibration of the string. Bowing produces a different set of source vibrations than plucking, and the position, duration, and intensity of bowing and plucking also affect the pattern of source vibrations. Moreover, the resonances may be changed by changing the length of the tube for wind instruments or lengthening the vocal tract while singing. Perhaps this is where the analogy fails: We can look for color in reflectance and disregard illumination, but we must listen for timbre in both the source and resonances. The construction of object properties is harder for listening.

A second place where the analogy between seeing and hearing fails is the existence of visual metamers and the lack of equivalent auditory metamers. The visual system is composed of four types of receptors—rods and three types of cones—and the principle of invariance appears to be almost certainly true. Thus, no matter what hue excites a cone, that cone signals its own particular hue. At normal illumination levels, any hue can be matched by a combination of three other hues (i.e., metamers). Cornsweet (1970) gave an elegant presentation illustrating how the number of independent receptor types equals the number of hues necessary to create metamer matches. Color appearance models (see review in Fairchild, 1998) attempt to predict hue matches under different illumination sources by independently scaling the excitations in the three cone systems. In contrast, the auditory system is composed of roughly 2,000 inner hair receptor cells. The principle of invariance also is certainly true for the hair cells. As found for cones, each hair cell will respond to a range of frequencies so that a single tone will create multiple firings (i.e., there is no such thing physiologically as a pure tone or pure color). Following Cornsweet's presentation, the number of tones required to create an auditory metamer would be equal to the number of hair cells excited by the single tone. Although it is still theoretically possible to create exact matches, practically it is impossible.

Why do we have only three cones that yield metamers and yet have 2,000 hair cells that do not? Why not have only three hair cells or many more different kinds of cones? I think the reason has to do with the differences between visual and auditory information. As is described in more detail below, the visual sources and filters are characterized as being smooth and continuous across wavelengths. Thus we can integrate the energy across a wide band of frequencies and still have an adequate representation of the stimulus. In contrast, the auditory sources and filters are characterized as having energy and resonances at discrete wavelengths. Thus, we cannot integrate energy across a wide band of frequencies because we need finer resolution to distinguish among sounds.

I believe that it is our naive realism view of the world as well as language that misleads us here. We think that there are invariant colors and sounds, and language reifies that conceptualization. We think that other people agree with our use of color categories, and that reinforces our faith that color is an inherent property of objects. It is only color illusions that convince us that the perception of color depends on our inferences about illumination and about surrounding colors. Perceived color is thus a second-order calculation based on the relative ratios of absorption in different parts of the field. Moreover, our interpretation of an object's color is determined by our simultaneous interpretation of geometric shape, depth, and orientation, and our interpretation of an object's sound is determined by our simultaneous interpretation of distance, the acoustics of the surround, and the acoustics of any background sound. Color and timbre perception must be conceptualized as being part of the general problem of figure-ground segmentation that constructs objects.

Jameson and Hurvich (1989) made an additional point. Our auditory and visual systems have evolved to give perceptual information about the invariants of objects but also about the particular characteristics of each instance. We do perceive variations in timbre due to sore throats, physical exhaustion, aging, or emotion, and we do perceive variations in color due to shadows, fading, dust particles, or time of day. Jameson and Hurvich further pointed out that the color of some objects (e.g., haystacks and concrete) arises only after we have identified the object. On top of this, we can vary the mode of perceiving. We can be analytical and discriminate up to physiological limitations or we can be global or categorical and merely assign objects to discrete categories when fine-grain differences are unimportant.

Visual Worlds

Modeling the Light Reaching the Eye

Light reaches the eye directly from the source, such as the sun or a lamp, and indirectly from the reflectance of the direct light by materials. The reflected light is the basis for perceiving objects. We can identify two basic classes of reflection, that arising from the air-surface interface and that arising from the body interface. In addition to direct reflections created by the source and object, there are reflections caused by one-step, two-step, or greater mutual reflections created by other objects. It is implicitly assumed that the body reflection is independent of the type of illumination. In commonsense fashion, when we talk about color constancy we are thinking about body reflection caused by pigments embedded in the surfaces of objects.

Air-Surface Reflection (Specular Reflection)

Air-surface reflection is created by the surface properties of the material and is the only type of reflection from metals. For a very smooth material, the reflection is specular or mirrorlike in that the surface produces a clear virtual image of the environment. As the surface becomes rougher, the image from the reflection changes from shiny to glossy to satinlike and becomes blurred and diffuse for very rough materials.

The critical assumption is that at least some of the specular reflected light has the same distribution of energy at each wavelength as the incident light; that is, the specular reflection is constant for all wavelengths and therefore will take on the color of the illumination. The specular reflection will be concentrated in one direction, depending on both the relative position of illuminating light and the viewing angle. The specular reflection by itself cannot be a reliable source of information about object color. However, the assumption that the reflection is a constant fraction at all wavelengths provides a way to isolate the body reflection signifying object color from the combined specular and body reflection that reaches the eye.[1]

Air-Body Reflection

Not all light is reflected at the surface. Some of it penetrates the surface and is then scattered due to reflections and refractions by embedded colorant

1. Some butterflies camouflage themselves by means of a surface metallic sheen that reflects all of the incident light (Parker, 1999).

particles. Some of the reflected light is reabsorbed by the surface while the remaining light reemerges from the surface. The spectral absorption properties of the embedded particles determine the fraction of the incident illumination that emerges at each wavelength. Because the embedded particles are assumed to be randomly distributed, the reflected light also is assumed to be similar in all directions. Body reflectance predominates in materials such as clay, plaster, and concrete, but in general reflected light is a combination of specular and body reflection. Both specular and body reflections are illustrated in figure 7.1A.

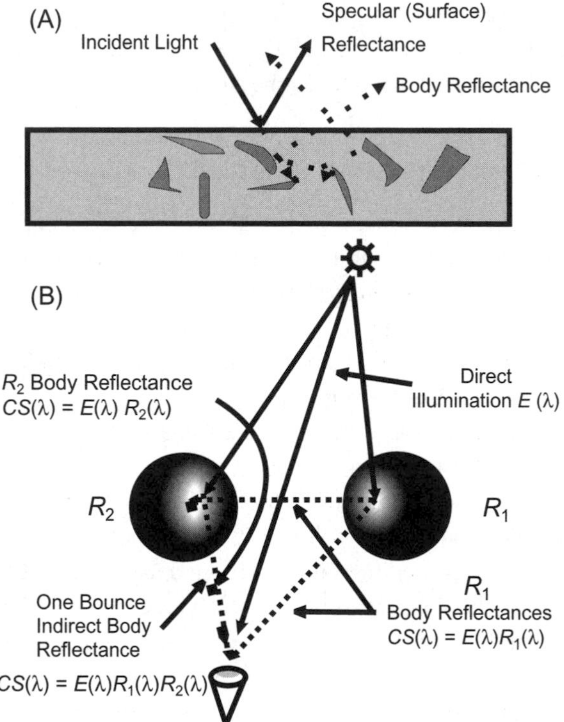

Figure 7.1. (A) The directional specular reflectance occurs at the air-surface interface. The body reflectance is the result of the light penetrating the surface, being reflected by the colored particles (possibly being reflected several times), and ultimately being reflected back into the air. The body reflectance is diffuse, and is assumed to be equal in all directions. (B) The light reaching the eye due to body reflectance is the sum of the direct reflectances and the indirect bounce reflectances. $E(\lambda)$ is the spectral power distribution of the incident illuminant, $R(\lambda)$ is the spectral distribution of the reflectances, so that $CS(\lambda)$ is the spectral power distribution of the illumination reaching the eye. (The specular reflectances are not drawn for clarity.) Abbr.: CS, Color Signal.

Indirect Illumination Causing Specular or Body Reflection

Indirect illumination comes from reflection off another object. Surprisingly, although the second (and higher) reflections are rarely noticed, indirect illumination can account for up to 15% of the illumination on an object. Every possible kind of indirect illumination can occur: specular or spectral reflection off one object can in turn produce specular or spectral reflection off the second object. Although we could consider every "bounce," a one-bounce model seems adequate in most situations. A model of direct, body reflectance and one-bounce body reflection is shown in figure 7.1B.

Lambert Reflection Model

The assumption that spectral reflection is the same in all directions because the pigment particles are uniformly distributed is termed the *Lambert reflection model.* (The Lambert model will fail if the surface is pitted so that the light reaching the observer will change as a function of viewing direction; Nayar & Oren, 1995.) What this assumption allows us to do is to decompose the surface reflection into (1) a specular spatial component dependent on the shape of the object, the source angle, and the viewing direction; and (2) an independent spectral reflection component dependent only on the properties of the particles and not on the shape of the object, its orientation to the light source, or the viewing angle. Empirical measurements indicate that a spatial-spectral decomposition is representative of a wide range of materials: The spectral power of the different frequencies reflected by an object at different viewing angles is linearly related, so that only brightness changes at the different viewing directions (H.-C. Lee, Breneman, & Schulte, 1990).

The Lambert model of reflection allows us to simplify composite illumination due to direct and indirect illumination by considering the composite as coming from but one source. The single source is simply the weighted average of the indirect and direct illumination.

Simplified World Models: Flat-World and Shape-World Models

All world models make simplifying assumptions; otherwise the source-filter indeterminacy would make predictions impossible. Two assumptions are found for all models: (1) the illumination is due to a single point of light that is angled toward and distant from the surface, and (2) each surface point projects to one retinal location.

Shape World

To achieve a realistic world model, we need to include three-dimensional objects that create shadows, indirect reflections, and specular reflections. The relationships between the surfaces and reflectances are complex, and there are two simplifications that are commonly employed (L. T. Maloney, 1999).

1. *Geometry-reflectance separability*. A change in viewing conditions is assumed merely to scale by a constant the surface reflectance function.
2. *Diffuse-specular superposition*. Some surfaces do not satisfy the geometric-reflectance separability assumption when considered in terms of the sum of the specular and spectral reflectance. However, the separability assumption may be satisfied if the specular and spectral (diffuse) reflectances are considered separately. If this is true, there will be different geometric functions for the two types of reflectances, and the light reaching the observer is some mix of the two.

Flat World

To simplify the computational problems in recovering the color of objects, some models further assume what L. T. Maloney (1999) termed the *flat-world environment*. The flat-world model reduces a three-dimensional world to a flat two-dimensional plane. The observer is viewing a world painted onto a flat sheet with all areas equidistant from the observer. The scene is illuminated by one source; all the light reaching the viewer comes from the direct body reflection of the pigments. There are no specular reflections and no indirect reflections from other objects. Moreover, due to the flat-field assumption, there are no shadows created by obscuring objects. Stimuli that create these assumptions are colloquially termed *Mondrian stimuli*: They are coplanar patchwork patterns of different hues resembling paintings by the Dutch artist Piet Mondrian (figure 7.2). Troost (1998) was skeptical that such Mondrian patterns reach the level of complexity that leads observers to directly perceive surface color. He suggested that the hues are perceived as free-floating colors not belonging to any surface. The observer reasons about what the colors ought to be, rather than perceiving the surface colors directly.

It should be kept in mind that the above models are essentially pointwise. They are designed only to depict physical energy processes that can be explained by characteristics of material at one point. But the visual world also has surface effects that can only be defined on a finite patch of surface, for example wood grain or texture. In addition to surface effects, there are environmental effects that cannot be explained by any description

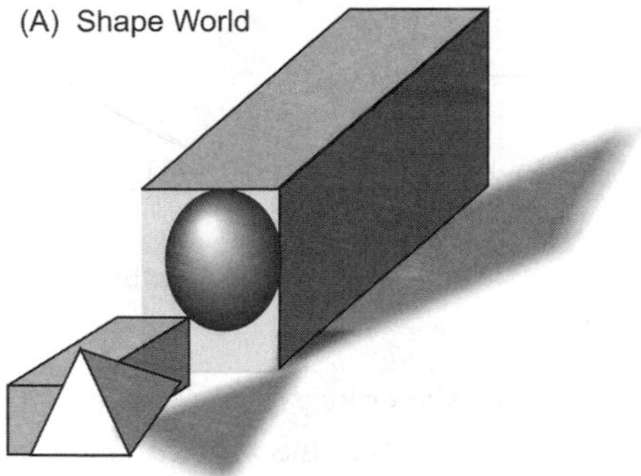

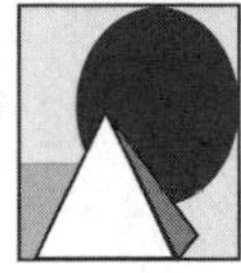

Figure 7.2. The shape world is three-dimensional, containing shadows and specular reflectances (A). The flat world reduces the shape world to a two-dimensional array (B). The flat world retains diffuse body reflectance and occlusion, but not shadows or specular reflections.

of an object but also require the consideration of surrounding elements. For example, the perception of wetness comes from the darkening of one area coupled with another area that reflects more light. It seems to me that the concept of multiresolution can be extended to color; the interpretation of color occurs at several spatial resolutions at once. Moreover, we need to conceptualize color constancy as based on heuristics that make use of several cues at once. In some circumstances, the local scene will determine the color, while in other circumstances the global scene will determine the color. Again, it is our language that deceives us into thinking that there is an invariant color out there.

Computational Models for Color Constancy

Computational models have two basic parts. The first is the image equation, which calculates the color signal reaching the retina from the physical properties of the scene, an energy description. The second converts the color signal into the firing rates of the three cone systems based on the spectral absorption curve of each cone type, a physiological description (Hurlbert, 1998).[2]

2. The number of ways to describe the light stimulus and the resulting physiological and perceptual effects is bewildering. Here I make one distinction, between a description of the light in terms of physical properties (energy–irradiance and radiance in watts) that are independent of the human vision system (termed *radiometry*) and a description in terms of its visual effectiveness (*colorimetry* and *photometry*). Photometry reduces that light stimulus to one number that estimates its visual effectiveness (essentially brightness–luminance). Colorimetry reduces the light stimulus to three numbers that estimate its effects on the three cone receptors.

Color Image Equation

In general:

Color signal (CS) [λ(wavelength) × (position on surface)]
= direct irradiance + reflected body irradiance
+ reflected specular irradiance + indirect body irradiance
+ indirect specular irradiance.

In a generalized three-dimensional world, the color signal reaching the eye depends on the angles between the light source, the surface, and the viewer's eye. I am not including those terms because all color constancy models assume a two-dimensional world with Lambertian reflectance in which those terms disappear.

1. Direct irradiance can be represented as $E(\lambda,x)$ so that it depends on the wavelength λ and the surface position x.
2. Reflected body irradiance is direct irradiance filtered by body reflectance R_b (R_b is a function of wavelength and surface position).

$$\text{Reflected body irradiance } CS(\lambda,x) = [E(\lambda,x)][R_b(\lambda,x)]. \tag{7.1}$$

3. Reflected specular irradiance is direct irradiance filtered by specular reflectance R_s (R_s is a function of wavelength and surface position, like R_b). The body and specular irradiances have parallel equations:

$$\text{Reflected specular irradiance } CS(\lambda,x) = [E(\lambda,x)][R_s(\lambda,x)]. \tag{7.2}$$

4. The indirect body + indirect specular irradiance coming from point x is based on the sum of the irradiance from all other points y that reflect onto x; the reflectances from all points y are treated as a second direct irradiance. This second direct irradiance is multiplied by the reflected and specular coefficients at x to yield the indirect irradiance (to the eye). The intensity and spatial frequencies of the one-bounce irradiance from y to x is going to depend on the physical geometry between x and each y, [$\alpha(x,y)$] as well as the total irradiance reflectance at each y, $E(\lambda,y)[R_b(\lambda,y) + R_s(\lambda,y)]$. The sum of the irradiance reflectances from all y to x (i.e., the indirect part of the color signal) is therefore:

$$\begin{aligned}&\text{Indirect body + indirect specular irradiance}\\&= \Sigma[\alpha(x,y)E(\lambda,y)][R_b(\lambda,y) + R_s(\lambda,y)].\end{aligned} \tag{7.3}$$

Combining the four sources described above, we obtain a complete description of the image. But, as stated above, all models of color constancy make further simplifications based on Lambertian reflections in a flat world. Namely, surfaces are flat, there are no specular reflections, and there are no mutual indirect reflections. Moreover, only one light source is assumed, so that the surface irradiation E can be separated into spectral and spatial components: Every wavelength will change in the same way at different spatial points. (We could simplify further and assume that the irradiance is constant across space, so that the irradiance becomes simply $[E(\lambda)]$.)

$$CS(\lambda,x) = [E(\lambda,x)][R_b(\lambda,x)]. \tag{7.4}$$

Now the color constancy problem becomes decomposing the contribution of the E (irradiance) and ρ_b (body reflectance) components at every point in space.

Cone Absorption

For the simplified image equation, the light hitting the receptors equals the product of the irradiance and body reflection taken at individual wavelengths. But the three cones in the human eye do not sample the irradiance at each wavelength separately. Instead, by the principle of invariance, the firing rate of any cone is based on the light intensity absorbed across the perceivable wavelengths; the output of any cone is going to be the sum of the firings that would be produced by absorbed light energy at each wavelength. For any cone, the spectral absorption curve gives the probability that it will absorb irradiance at any wavelength. Thus, to convert the irradiance into firing rates, we integrate and combine the excitation over the cone's spectral sensitivity:

$$\begin{aligned}\text{Excitation cone M} &= \Sigma[S_m(\lambda)][CS(\lambda,x)] \\ &= \Sigma[S_m(\lambda)][E(\lambda,x)][R_b(\lambda,x)]. \end{aligned} \tag{7.5}$$

The function $S_m(\lambda)$ represents the spectral sensitivity of cone M (middle wavelengths) and there would be two other equations for the long-wavelength (S_L) and short-wavelength (S_S) cones.

To return to understanding color constancy, the starting point would be the set of equations for cone excitations. We can define color constancy simply as the apparent invariance in color appearance of objects upon changes in irradiance. Color constancy is nowhere close to perfect; in fact, it could be legitimately argued that it does not occur in humans. If constancy did occur, then we would not have to include illumination in predicting color matches. The reflectances combined with the spectral sensitivities of the cones would suffice. But two objects may look matched in color using one light source but look mismatched using another. Colors are not independent of irradiance. These kinds of matches and mismatches are even worse for surfaces with irregular reflectances.

The computational problem is that information is coded in only three cone systems. Therefore, there are theoretically many solutions to any set of cone excitations (i.e., metamers). What proverbially saves the day is that the possible set of illuminant functions is relatively smooth and regular and, similarly, the possible sets of surface reflectance functions are relatively smooth and regular. If observers can make use of those, a priori physical regularities, estimates of the surface color are likely to be close to right.

Linear Models

Constancy models make the assumption that both the spectral body reflectance and spectral irradiance functions can be represented by the linear sum of a small number of basis functions, because both functions usually are smooth and regular. We start with a set of distributions from naturally occurring objects and illuminants. The mathematical goal is to derive a set of decorrelated functions such that multiplying each function by a constant and then adding them together can replicate any one of the distributions. Obviously, different constants would be utilized to replicate a specific distribution. This process is nearly identical to the derivation of basis functions for cortical cells found in chapter 3. There the basis functions were modeled by Gabor functions. Here, the basis functions are continuous and change smoothly and regularly across wavelengths. The implicit idea both here and in chapter 3 is that these distributions should somehow be related to visual features and channels.

Although the number of basis functions necessary to adequately characterize body reflection and the illuminants probably depends on the specific set of objects and sources, research has suggested that three functions, $E_1(\lambda)$, $E_2(\lambda)$, and $E_3(\lambda)$, may be sufficient to approximate all daylight distributions (Judd, MacAdam, & Wyszecki, 1964; Wyszecki & Stiles, 1982) and other broadband illuminations (L. T. Maloney, 1986). Moreover, several different analyses have shown that three functions, $R_1(\lambda)$, $R_2(\lambda)$, and $R_3(\lambda)$, may be sufficient to characterize some surface reflection functions, but typically seven or more functions are necessary (Parkkinen, Hallikainen, & Jaaskelainen, 1989; Vrhel, Gershon, & Iwan, 1994). Thus, the equations for illumination and body reflectance would be of the same form (here we are assuming three basis functions, although in most real cases there will be different numbers of equations for the illumination and body reflectances):

$$\text{Illumination } E(\lambda) = \varepsilon_1 E_1(\lambda) + \varepsilon_2 E_2(\lambda) + \varepsilon_3 E_3(\lambda) \quad (7.6a)$$

$$\text{Reflectance } R_b(\lambda) = \alpha R_1(\lambda) + \beta R_2(\lambda) + \gamma R_3(\lambda). \quad (7.6b)$$

Examples of basis functions for daylight irradiance are shown in figure 7.3. What this means is that we can approximate the light reflecting off objects and reaching the observer's eye in terms of linear functions.

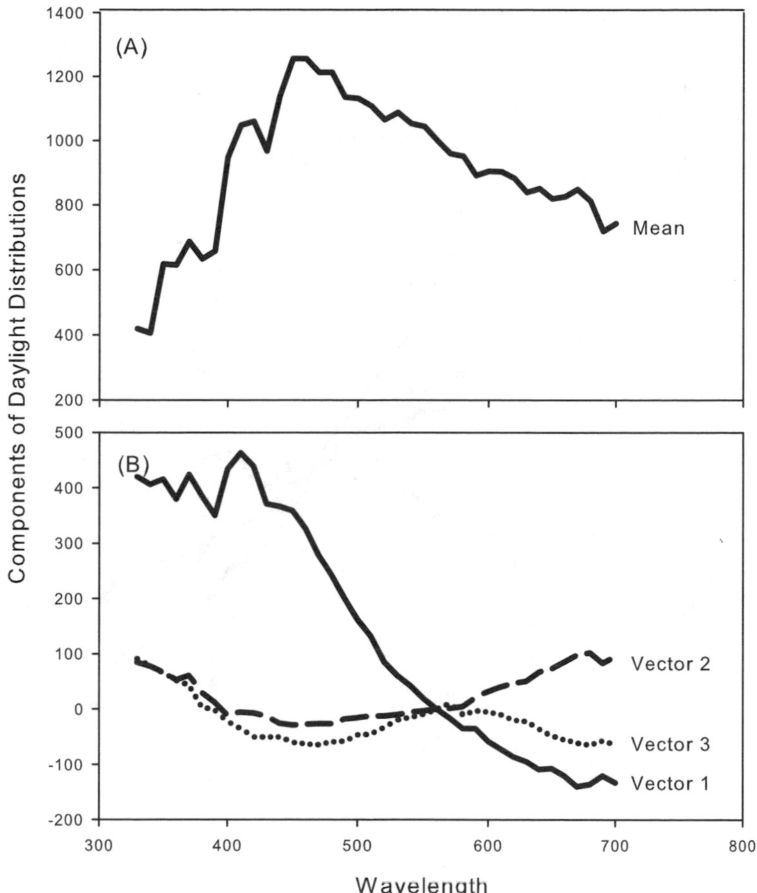

Figure 7.3. The average daylight irradiance is drawn in (A). A wide variety of daylight spectral distributions can be re-created by the sum of three independent vectors, shown in (B). By combining the three vectors in different proportions, it is possible to simulate the irradiance spectral distribution for different kinds of daylight (shown in (C)). Adapted from "Spectral Distribution of Typical Daylight as a Function of Correlated Color Temperature," by D. B. Judd, D. L. MacAdam, and G. Wyszecki, 1964, *Journal of the Optical Society of America, 54*, 1031–1040.

Each basis function is independent of spatial location; the values for each function depend only on wavelength. To adjust for changes in illumination or reflectance at different spatial points in the scene, the weights for the individual basis functions are changed. Thus, at one illumination $\varepsilon_1 = \varepsilon_2 = \varepsilon_3$, but at another one $\varepsilon_1 = .75$, $\varepsilon_2 = .25$, and $\varepsilon_3 = 0$. Identical types of variation will occur for reflectance. To solve the color constancy problem, we would derive the coefficients for the reflectance function, α, β, and γ.

To make this more concrete, suppose that there are three basis functions for both illumination and body reflectance to match the trichromatic color

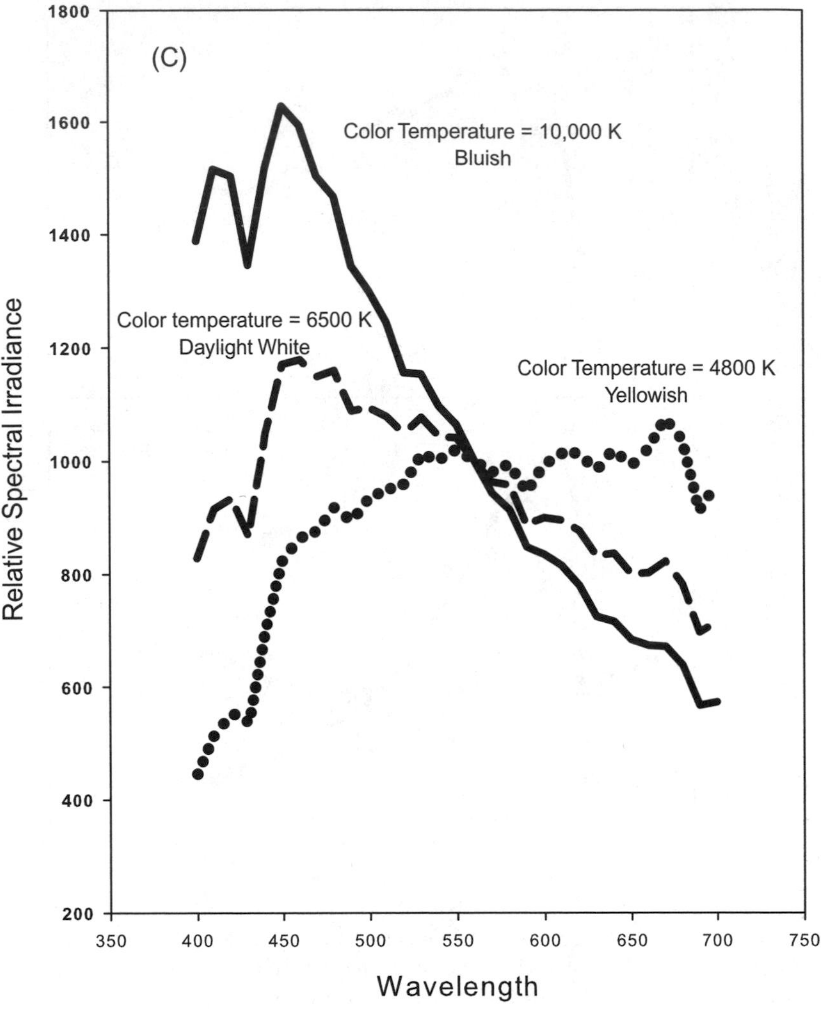

Figure 7.3. Continued

visual system. Moreover, suppose that the illumination and surface are completely uniform so that light excitation and body reflectance are constant at every point.

We can simplify equation 7.5 because of our uniform assumptions, so that

$$\text{Excitation cone M} = \Sigma[S_m(\lambda)][CS(\lambda,x)] = \Sigma[S_m(\lambda)][E(\lambda,x)][R_b(\lambda,x)]$$

becomes

$$\text{Excitation cone M} = \Sigma[S_m(\lambda)][CS(\lambda)] = \Sigma[S_m(\lambda)][E(\lambda)][R_b(\lambda)]. \quad (7.7)$$

Now we can substitute equation 7.6a for $[E(\lambda)]$ and equation 7.6b for $[R_b(\lambda)]$ to create the rather complex equation:

$$\text{Excitation cone M} = \Sigma[S_m(\lambda)][\varepsilon_1 E_1(\lambda) + \varepsilon_2 E_2(\lambda) + \varepsilon_3 E_3(\lambda)][\alpha R_1(\lambda) + \beta R_2(\lambda) + \gamma R_3(\lambda)]. \quad (7.8)$$

The basis functions for illumination multiplied by the basis functions for reflectance create the excitation for each cone system at each wavelength. The excitation is multiplied by the absorption curve to yield the firing rate. There would be analogous equations for the two other cones.

To estimate the surface color, we need to derive the surface descriptors α, β, and γ. But to estimate the color, the observer simultaneously must figure out the illumination. The difficulty is that there are more unknowns than data points. There are three unknowns for the illumination (one value for each of the three basis functions), and there are three unknowns for the body reflectance (one value for each basis function). However, there are only three known values, one for the excitation of each cone system. The indeterminacy problem gets worse if more basis functions are needed to model reflectance or if the surface is not uniform. Now, the indeterminacy occurs at each point. All color models basically begin with three equations like equation 7.8, one for each cone system. Each model described below makes slightly different simplifying assumptions to achieve a solution.

Before considering specific color models, it is worthwhile to consider the advantage of thinking about color constancy in terms of the linear sums of excitation and reflectance basis functions. Linear models represent a priori hypotheses about the likely set of inputs and, to the extent that the visual system has evolved to pick up those likely inputs, the perceptual inference problem becomes more tractable. Given that the illumination can be described with three basis functions, then we can calculate the relative amounts of each illumination basis function from the excitation of the three cones. Similarly, given that the reflectances of most objects can be adequately described with three basis functions, we can calculate the relative amounts of each reflectance basis function from the excitation of the three cones. We are replacing the direct calculation of the continuous illumination and reflectance functions with the calculation of the relative amounts of the respective basis functions.

Moreover, to the extent that the basis functions appear to be analogous to physiological or perceptual functions, we can argue indirectly that the basis functions underlie color constancy. For example, three basis functions have been found to represent surface reflectance for a set of Munsell colors (Cohen, 1964). The first function is relatively flat across the wavelengths. The second function contrasts green with red, while the third function contrasts yellow mainly with blue and less strongly with red. Each basis function has one more reversal, mimicking basis functions described previously. Thus, the three basis functions bear a resemblance to the single additive and two types of opponent cells found in the lateral geniculate. It is possible to make a too-strong analogy here. The resemblances are not perfect, and several attempts to model surface reflectances have required five to eight basis functions to adequately represent the spectral reflectance. A better way of thinking about the correspondences is in terms of decorrelating responses. In chapter 3, I argued that on-off cells and the Gabor-like receptor fields found in V1 could be thought of as a physiological mechanism to remove redundancies in the visual image. The same argument works here: The opponent cells remove the correlation in firing rates among the three cones, so that there should be no surprise that the basis functions calculated to minimize the intercorrelations look like the opponent cells.

The linear bases for artificial illuminations are more complicated. Fluorescent lights, in particular, introduce high-amplitude spikes so that the basis functions cannot be smooth as found for daylight conditions, but must contain peaks at different wavelengths to reconstruct the spectral distribution as pictured in figure 7.4A. Romero, Garcia-Beltran, and Hernandez-Andres (1997) found that four to seven multiple-peaked bases were necessary to represent a wider range of artificial and natural illuminants. The first three bases are shown in figure 7.4B.The increased number of required bases makes the indeterminacy worse.

It is also the case that visual scenes obey the $1/f^{\alpha}$ amplitude frequency distribution discussed previously. Parraga, Brelstaff, Troscianko, and Moorhead (1998) measured the amplitude of the luminance at different spatial frequencies for natural scenes. They defined two measures: (a) *Luminance* was defined as the sum of excitations from the long- and middle-wavelength cones $L + M$; and (b) *chrominance* was defined as the difference between the long- and middle-wavelength cones divided by the sum to remove shadows:

$$\text{Chrominance} = (L - M)/(L + M). \tag{7.9}$$

Both luminance and chrominance followed the $1/f$ function, and the slope was close to 1. Over the set of natural scenes, there was more luminance energy at lower spatial frequencies and higher chrominance energy at higher spatial frequencies. Surprisingly, this is just the opposite of human sensitivity curves: Humans are more sensitive to chrominance at low frequencies and luminance at higher spatial frequencies. The authors offer several explanations why the visual system is not more sensitive to higher-frequency chrominance: (a) chrominance is more important at low frequencies to segment objects (e.g., berries against leaves), and fine-grain variation in chrominance is unimportant; and (b) there is a great deal of chromatic optic blurring at higher frequencies that makes higher-frequency information useless.

Figure 7.7. In the asymmetric color-matching task, the standard and test colors were mounted on the back wall. The gradient projector (G) created a blue-to-yellow gradient on the back wall using two bulbs. The observer's task was to make the standard and test color look the same by manipulating the blue, green, and red beams of the adjustable projector. Adapted from "Color Constancy in the Nearly Natural Image. I. Asymmetric Matches," by D. H. Brainard, W. A. Brunt, and J. M. Speigle, 1997, *Journal of the Optical Society of America, A, 14*, 2091–2110.

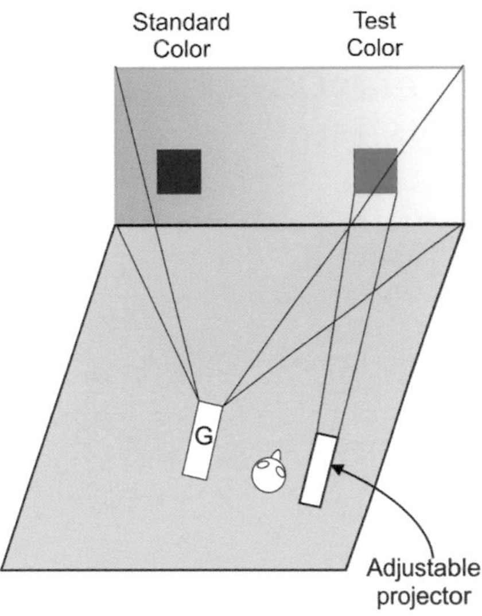

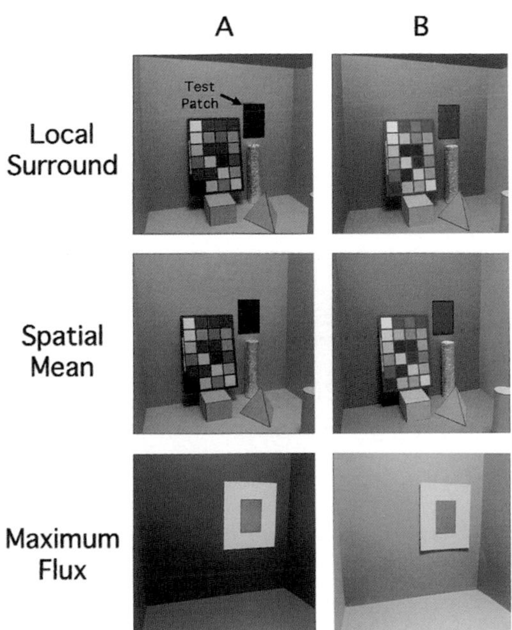

Figure 7.8. The experimental room used by Kraft and Brainard (1999). There was a hidden adjustable projector (like that in figure 7.7) that the participant used to make the test patch in the (B) conditions look achromatic. The three views shown in (A) used the neutral illuminant. In the three views in (B), the local surround used an orange-red illuminant; the spatial mean used a pale red illuminant; and the maximum flux used a yellow illuminant. From "Mechanisms of Color Constancy Under Nearly Natural Viewing," by J. M. Kraft and D. H. Brainard, 1999, *Proceedings of the National Academy of Science, 96*, 307–312. Copyright 1999 by the National Academy of Science. Reprinted with permission.

(A)
Scene:Daylight
Specular:Daylight

(B)
Scene: Daylight
Specular: Incandescent

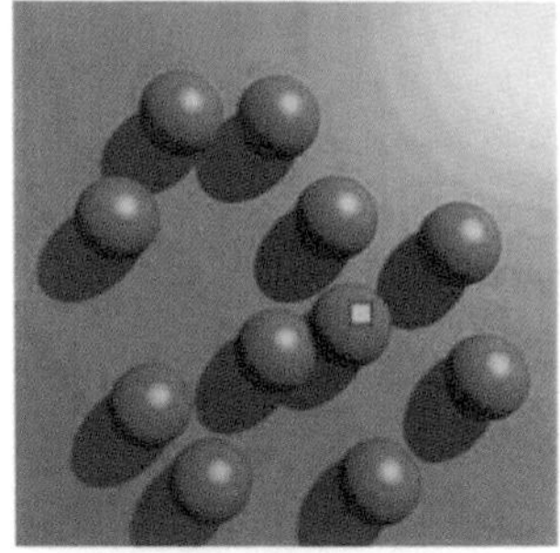

(C)
Scene: Incandescent
Specular: Daylight

(D)
Scene:Incandescent
Specular: Incandescent

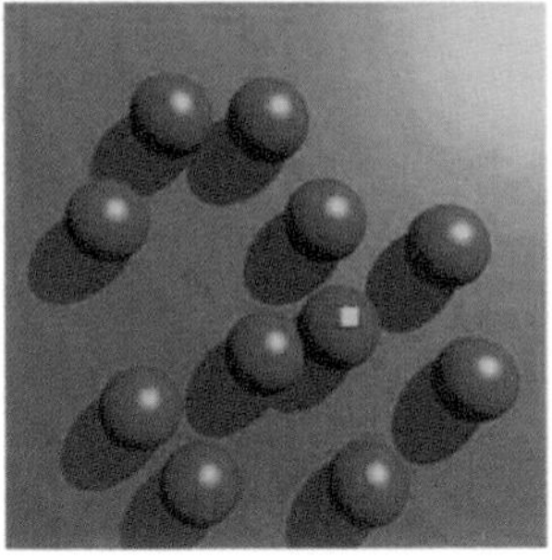

Figure 7.9. The effect of specular and surface reflections on color constancy was investigated using a cue conflict paradigm. Two illuminants were used: standard daylight (D65) and incandescent A. In two conditions (A and D), the specular and surface reflections were based on the same illuminant, but in two conditions (B and C), the surface and specular reflections were based on different illuminants. Participants were asked to adjust the small green squares shown in the figure to appear achromatic. From "Illuminant Cues in Surface Color Perception: Tests of Three Candidate Cues," by J. N. Yang and L. T. Maloney, 2001, *Vision Research, 41*, 2581–2600. Copyright 2001 by Elsevier Science Ltd. Reprinted with permission.

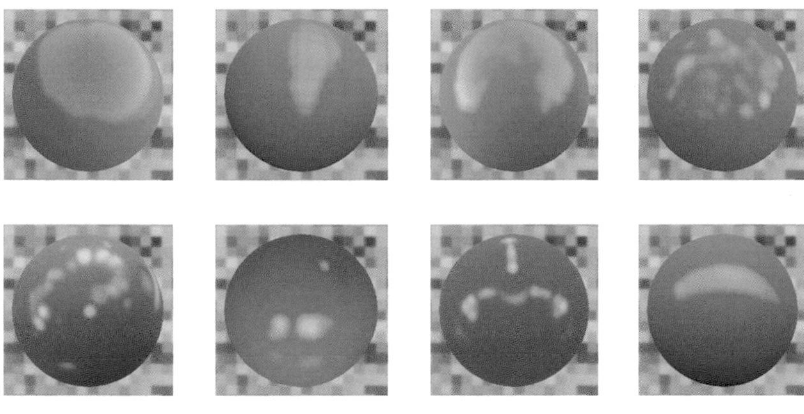

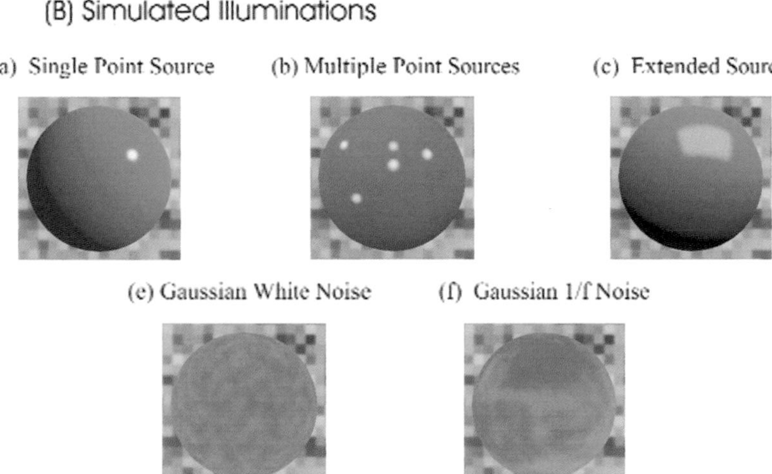

Figure 7.10. The perception of surface gloss and roughness depends on the properties of the illumination. In all examples, the surface reflectance of the spheres is the same. The perception of surface characteristics is best with real-life illuminations (A) and gets much poorer as the simulated illumination deviates from what is normally expected (B). From "Real-World Illumination and the Perception of Surface Reflectance Properties," by R. W. Fleming, R. O. Dror, and E. W. Adelson, 2003, *Journal of Vision, 3*, 347–368. Copyright 2003 by AVRO. Reprinted with permission.

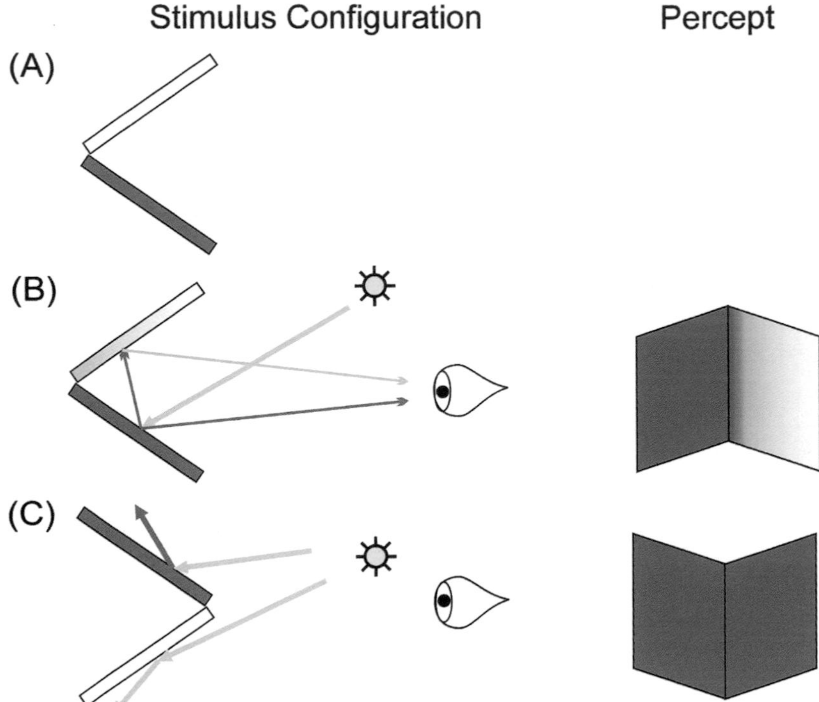

Figure 7.11. The stimulus was a card folded in half, one side painted magenta and the other painted white (A). If an incandescent light aimed at the magenta side illuminated the card, the light reflected from the magenta side onto the white side created a magenta gradient from desaturated magenta to white (B). Observers judged the inside corner of the white side as pale pink. If the appearance of the card was reversed so that it appeared to be convex, observers then judged the white side as being deep magenta instead of pale pink (C). As illustrated in (C), if the card really was convex, there could not be a one-bounce reflection from the magenta side. Adapted from "Perception of Three-Dimensional Shape Influences Colour Perception Through Mutual Illumination," by M. G. Bloj, D. Kersten, and A. C. Hurlbert, 1999, *Nature, 402*, 877–879.

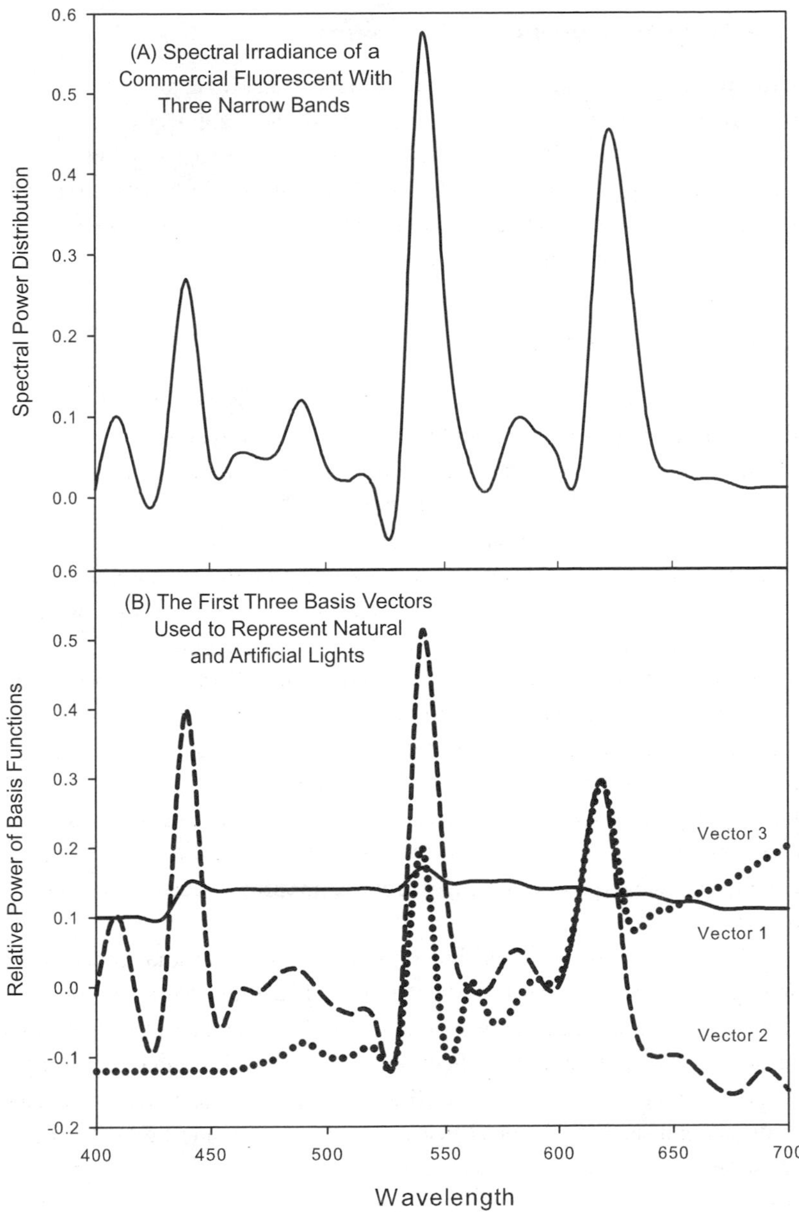

Figure 7.4. The spectral power distributions of fluorescent lights is peaky. There are several frequencies at which there are large increments in the relative power, illustrated in (A). If the basis functions are derived from a set of irradiance distributions that include smooth natural daylights (as in figure 7.3) and peaky artificial lights, the resulting bases also contain peaks, and more than three bases are necessary to closely simulate the irradiance distributions illustrated in (B). Adapted from "Linear Bases for Representation of Natural and Artificial Illuminants," by J. Romero, A. Garcia-Beltran, and J. Hernandez-Andres, 1997, *Journal of the Optical Society of America, A, 14*, 1007–1014.

Simplifying Assumptions and Constraints

Even if we restrict the illumination and reflectance to a small number of basis functions, further simplifications or constraints are necessary to solve for the surface color. The constraints are used to calculate the illumination, which in turn allows for the calculation of the reflectance. Some of the constraints represent possible perceptual mechanisms, while others seem motivated more by computational possibilities.

Shape-World Algorithms

1. The first type of algorithm assumes that the observer can identify the illumination directly (e.g., by looking at it). Alternately, the observer could identify a perfectly reflecting surface or a white surface and make use of those surfaces to identify the illumination. (Obviously, this assumption could be used for flat-world models as well.)

2. The second type of algorithm makes use of the separability of the specular and diffuse body reflection. The reflected light from any surface is always a combination of two kinds of reflectance, although we do not know the proportions of the two types. The specular reflection is assumed to equal the spectral power distribution of the illuminant and to vary as a function of viewing angle. The diffuse reflection is assumed to be a linear function of the spectral reflectance of the object and to be independent of viewing angle. If there are two objects, each with a combination of surface and specular reflection, and if there are multiple views to get different amounts of each type of reflection, then it is possible to abstract the surface reflectance.

3. The third type of algorithm makes use of the mutual reflectances among surfaces to derive the illumination. The illumination hitting one surface is reflected according to the spectral reflectance (R) of the first surface $[E(\lambda)R_1(\lambda)]$ and that reflection becomes the illumination hitting a second surface, where it is reflected according to the spectral reflectance of the second surface $[E(\lambda)R_1(\lambda)R_2(\lambda)]$, as diagrammed in figure 7.1. Funt, Drew, and Ho (1991) demonstrated that it is possible to derive an iterative solution.

Flat-World Algorithms

Reference Surfaces The first class of solutions assumes that there are reference surfaces that allow the observer to calculate the illumination. In all such solutions, the illumination is assumed to be constant across the scene.

First, as long as the number of cones, reflectance functions, and illumination functions are equal, then only one reference point is necessary. The reference point pins down the lighting matrix so that the unknown weighting of the illumination basis functions in equation 7.6a can be determined. Once that is done, the number of unknown weightings of the surface reflectance basis functions will be equal to the number of known cone excitations (as required by the assumptions), and the surface color can be recovered.

Second, a further assumption about a fixed reference point is termed the gray-world algorithm: the mean intrinsic color of a scene is a specific gray. If the single reference point is replaced by the weighted average of the excitation across the entire scene, then the averaged light becomes the spectral distribution of the illuminant. Buchsbaum (1980, p. 24) stated, “It seems that arbitrary natural everyday scenes composed of dozens of color subfields, usually none highly saturated, will have a certain almost fixed spatial reflectance average. It is reasonable that this average will be some medium gray.” D’Zmura and Lennie (1986, p. 1667) made the identical claim: “thus space averaged light from most natural scenes will bear chromaticity that closely approximates that of the illuminant.”

While the weighted average does not need to be gray, it does need to be known, so that the algorithm explicitly makes a strong claim about the physical environment. Clearly we can question whether models that require reference surfaces are useful models for human vision. To the extent that any variation in the mean intrinsic color is small relative to changes in illumination, then the gray-world assumption has heuristic value.

Multiple Views The above solutions assume that there is a single view under a single unknown illumination. D’Zmura and Iverson (1993a, 1993b) pointed out that in more natural situations, observers have access to multiple views of the object surfaces and that often the illumination may change between successive views or that one view may include a change of illumination. As long as the observer can maintain correspondence of the surfaces across the views, it is possible to derive the surface reflectances. There are sets of constraints among the number of basis functions, receptors, and views that are necessary. For example, for illuminants that can be represented by three basis functions, a visual system with three cones, given three views, can solve for reflectance functions with up to eight basis functions.

For scenes that include a change in illumination, absorption in the three cone systems based on one illumination will be highly correlated to the absorption based on the second illumination. As argued above, the two sets of absorption rates would allow the observer to recover the illuminants and surface reflectances.

Color Appearance Models and Color Constancy

I now shift orientation and consider models and experiments in which observers attempt to match the surface colors viewed under different illuminations, termed *asymmetric color matching*. For any stimulus, we can calculate the expected number of absorptions for each of the three cones by multiplying the illumination by the surface reflectance by the respective spectral absorption curve [i.e., $E(\lambda)R(\lambda)S_s(\lambda)$, $E(\lambda)R(\lambda)S_m(\lambda)$, and $E(\lambda)R(\lambda)S_l(\lambda)$].

First, color constancy will be perfect if the surface reflectance of the match color is identical to the standard color. Therefore, the number of cone absorptions will differ between the standard and test because the illumination is different.

Second, color constancy will be zero if the reflectance of the test color multiplied by the test illumination by the absorption curve yields the same number of cone absorptions as the standard stimulus. In this case, observers are unable to abstract the reflectance from the light energy reaching the eye.

Consider a simple example of achromatic asymmetric matching. The standard gray might have a reflectance of .40 and be illuminated by 10,000 units. The test gray would have variable reflectance and be illuminated by 40,000 units. The subject would be asked to adjust the test gray so that it matched the standard gray. If the subject displayed perfect constancy, then the reflectance of the test gray would be set at .40, even though the excitation from the test gray is four times greater than that from the standard gray. If the subject displayed zero constancy, then the reflectance would be set at .10, so that the amount of excitation from the two grays would be equal (right now I am not considering any effects due to the receptor absorption curves). Reflectance values between .10 and .40 represent intermediate degrees of constancy.

Now consider a more representative chromatic case, but still use simplified discrete frequency illumination and reflectance functions. The standard illumination projects 10,000 units at 550 nm and 10,000 units at 600 nm. The standard color reflects .40 of illumination at 550 nm and .20 of the illumination at 600 nm, thereby reflecting 4,000 units at 550 nm and 2,000 units at 600 nm. The test illumination projects 15,000 units at 550 nm, and 5,000 units at 600 nm. The observer's task is to select a test color that matches the standard color. Following the identical logic as above, if the subject displayed perfect constancy, the reflectance of the test color would match that of the standard color (e.g., .40 and .20), so that the excitation reaching the eye would be different (4,000 vs. 6,000 units at 550 nm and 2,000 vs. 1,000 units at 600 nm). If the subject displayed zero constancy, the excitations due to the standard and test color would be made equal, so that the reflectance of the test color would be .267 at 550 nm to generate 4,000 units and .40 at 600 nm to generate 2,000 units.

Thus, color constancy is not matching the number of cone absorptions. Color appearance and constancy is the outcome of a higher-level estimate of the surface reflectance from the properties of the entire scene.

How Good Is Color Constancy?

It is clear that there are many potential visual cues that could be used to recover the surface reflectance. We would expect observers to make use of any single cue or any combination of cues that work best in a given situation. There is not going to be a smoking gun. Moreover, the experimental outcome that one cue does not affect constancy in one context does not mean that it will not affect constancy in another context. The models described above give some of the possible cues that could be used: (1) local context, (2) global context, (3) specular reflectance, (4) mutual reflections among three-dimensional shapes, (5) shadows, and (6) multiple views due to changes in illumination or scene motion.

Several complex issues are embedded in the achievement of even rough constancy. The first complexity is that the above cues are so interrelated that it may be impossible to disentangle them. For example, how are the shadows, possibly due to three-dimensional shapes, distinguished from illumination changes without first determining that there are three-dimensional shapes, since the perception of those shapes is due to the perception of the shadows? Or how could we make use of mutual reflectances to deduce the individual surface reflectances without knowing something about the individual reflectances that enable us to detect the mutual reflectances?

A second complexity is what I call *belongingness* (further discussed in chapter 9). Which colors in the scene are perceived as being attached to objects and which colors are seen as floating in space? Fairchild (1998) has arranged five possibilities to summarize these differences:

1. Glow color: The color belongs to an object.
2. Illumination color: Color is due to the illuminant and not the object.
3. Surface color: Color is due to light reflected off the object surface.
4. Volume color: Color belongs to a volume or bulk of a more or less uniform or transparent object such as sea or fog.
5. Film color: Color is perceived within an aperture with no connection to an object; perceived at the depth of the aperture.

Another aspect of belongingness concerns which parts are perceived as related to other parts, and which parts are seen as being unrelated. Fairchild (1998) defined unrelated colors as those perceived to belong to an object seen in isolation from other colors while related colors are those perceived to belong to an object seen in relation to other colors. Some color phenomena occur only for related colors—the perception of brown occurs only when orange is placed against a white background. Related colors have perceptual properties such as lightness and saturation that do not exist for unrelated colors.

Observers do make asymmetric color matches based on both the nearby and distant color context. L. T. Maloney (1999) suggested that the problem be broken into two parts. First, identify the possible alternative adaptation effects due to different ways of integrating and perceiving the overall context. For example, are they limited to nearby regions or do they encompass the entire scene? Second, discover the factors that determine the choice of the adaptation scheme. Each adaptation scheme is fixed physiologically, but the choice of scheme is a function of the observer's intentional state, biases, and so on.

Visual Frameworks for Estimating Color Constancy

Gilchrist et al. (1999) presented a perceptual model for the judgment of achromatic lightness (black to white) that explicitly considers the trade-off between local and global constancy. The excitation reaching the eye is the product of the illumination striking the object, reflectance of the shade of gray used, and the percentage of the reflected light that is absorbed or deflected by the atmosphere (e.g., haze). In fact, the ratio between the highest and lowest illumination (1 billion to one) can be much greater than the ratio between the highest and lowest reflectance (30:1). Any excitation can be perceived as any shade of gray, depending on its context within the visual image.

To me, the important concept is thinking that the visual scene is composed of frameworks, groups of surfaces that belong to each other and that are perceived as being illuminated by a common source. Observers can make use of alternative sets of frameworks that may split the scene into disjoint areas, into a hierarchy, or into intersecting areas. In all cases, however, the largest framework encompasses the entire visual field and is termed the *global framework*. Any partition of the global field is termed a *local framework*, so that any part of the scene will be a member of one or more local frameworks and the global framework. The formation of the local frameworks is not based simply on location but on the classical Gestalt principles of grouping and figure-ground articulation. Thus, regions that appear to be coplanar, that appear to move in the same direction, or that change lightness together, and so on, can form a local framework.

The judgment of lightness then becomes a weighted average of the perceived lightness from each of the local frameworks and the global framework. Gilchrist et al. (1999) focused on instances of one local and one global framework. In the cases considered, constancy will be poor to the extent that the observer attends to the global framework, while constancy will be better to the extent that the observer attends to the local framework. Consider a concrete example that is similar to those used for assessing color constancy. A set of five achromatic squares from white to black is suspended from the ceiling. The squares are illuminated with a bright light that is roughly 30 times brighter than the light illuminating the back wall. If the observers focus exclusively on the local framework created by the five adjacent coplanar squares, then constancy should be nearly perfect. However, if they focus on the global framework created by the dimmer back wall, then all of the squares ought to be perceived as nearly white, since each square is lighter than the background. The results indicated a compromise: 30% local and 70% global (see figure 7.5). The balance between local and global weighting could be changed by varying the stimulus characteristics: Increasing the number of squares and scrambling them into a Mondrian pattern increases the importance of the local framework.

Wishart, Frisby, and Buckley (1997) and Adelson (1993) showed how manipulating the perceived coplanar regions can affect the allocation between local and global frameworks, as illustrated in figure 7.6. The squares A and B are the same reflectance, but A is the darkest square in its row

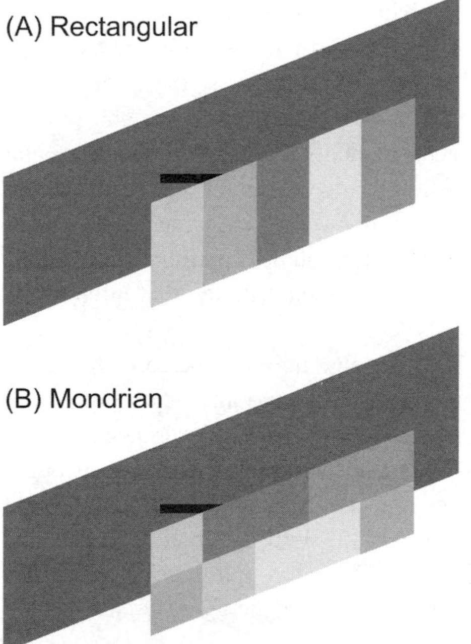

Figure 7.5. If a surface composed of relatively bright rectangles is floated in front of a darker, larger background, observers can attend and make judgments with respect either to the local brighter surface framework or to the global darker background framework. The rectangles could be presented in a simple rectangular array (A) or in a more complex Mondrian organization (B). Adapted from "An Anchoring Theory of Lightness Perception," by A. Gilchrist et al., 1999, *Psychological Review, 106*, 795–834.

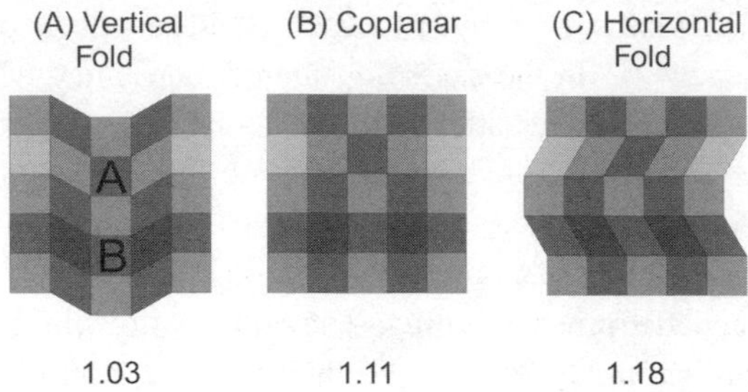

Perceived Brightness Ratio B/A

Figure 7.6. Lightness judgments are affected by local frameworks. In all three configurations, the reflectance of (A) and (B) are identical. If the configuration looks flat, (B) looks slightly brighter than (A). If the configuration is redrawn so that it looks like there is a vertical fold, (A) and (B) now seem to be coplanar and appear to have equal brightness. In contrast, if the configuration is redrawn so that it looks like there is a horizontal fold, the brightness difference between (A) and (B) appears to be greater. In this case, (A) and (B) are judged in terms of the brightness values within its own row, and that magnifies the contrast due to the surrounding squares. Adapted from "The Role of 3-D Surface Slope on a Lightness/Brightness Effect," by K. A. Wishart, J. P. Frisby, and D. Buckley, 1997, *Vision Research, 37*, 467–473.

while B is the lightest square in its row. When the checkerboard pattern is perceived as flat, the global framework is strengthened, and constancy increases; B is judged as slightly brighter than A. This difference could be due to the local contrast among the squares. If the checkerboard pattern is vertically ridged so that A and B appear to be coplanar, the local vertical column framework predominates; A and B appear equally bright. In contrast, if the checkerboard pattern is horizontally ridged, the local horizontal row framework predominates; B is judged much brighter than A. Wishart et al. demonstrated that as the horizontal framework is strengthened by accentuating the perceived depth, the change in brightness mainly occurs for B. The authors suggested that B is perceived as shaded, and that inference is strengthened as the depth increases.

Anderson and Winawer (2005) argued that lightness perception is critically determined by the segmentation of the image into depth layers, not simply into two-dimensional frameworks. The critical variable was the contrast between the object boundary and the varying "filmy" surround. With a darker surround, the target objects appeared white, as if visible through a dark, partially transparent cloud. With a lighter surround, the identical target objects appeared black, visible through light clouds. Viewers interpreted the differences in the surrounds as being differences in the amount of light transmitted through the transparent layer in front of the objects, and that changed their perception of the lightness of the targets.

What this all means is that lightness and color constancy is always a compromise among competing alternative percepts. To the degree that an experiment can closely simulate all of the information in naturally occurring scenes, the results will be close to those found naturally. Of course that does not mean the color constancy will be perfect, but at least we will have information about the upper limits.

Von Kreis Adaptation

Von Kreis (1970) offered the first method to compensate for changes in illumination. Von Kreis's coefficient law seems most relevant for simple center-surround configurations in which we use the surround to compensate for the center. The basic notion is that the effective amount of absorption in a specific spatial region for each cone system must be scaled by the overall absorptions of that cone system only. The compensation for the surround illumination is done independently for each cone system: The absorptions in one cone system do not affect the scaling in the other cone systems. The coefficients act as a type of gain control.

There is one simple equation for each cone system:

$$L_m = L_{\text{region}}/L_{\text{surround}} \tag{7.10}$$

where L_m is the postadaptation brightness (essentially absorption) for the M cones based on the independent adaptation in each cone system to the surround illumination. There are similar equations for the L cones and S cones.

For complex scenes, the natural generalization is to scale the absorption for each cone system by some type of averaging of the absorption in that system across the scene. The averaging could be a simple average, or the geometric mean taken across the scene. Alternately, the scale factor could be the inverse of response for the whitest part of the scene $= 1/L_{\text{white}} = 1/L_{\text{max}}$.

The assumption is that there is a white patch for each cone system that reflects all the illumination for that system, but there does not have to be a pure white patch. In effect, if there is a perfectly reflecting surface, the visual system will make use of that surface to recover the illumination and thereby scale the cone excitations independently.

To test the degree to which the von Kreis algorithm represents color matching, we calculate the scaled *L*, *M*, and *S* cone absorptions for the perceptual matches under two different illuminations assuming a white patch. Remember that color constancy means that the number of absorptions will not be the same under the two illuminations. The question is whether the von Kreis correction makes the adjusted absorptions equal.

1. Calculate the scaled absorptions for the standard color a under illumination 1:

$$L_{a1} = L_a/L_{max1} \quad (7.11a)$$

$$M_{a1} = M_a/M_{max1} \quad (7.11b)$$

$$S_{a1} = S_a/S_{max1}. \quad (7.11c)$$

   L, M, and S absorptions are calculated from the known spectral reflectance of the standard color multiplied by the absorption curves of each cone, and L_{max1}, M_{max1}, and S_{max1} come from the maximum response (the white region) in the scene multiplied by the absorption curves.
2. Calculate the scaled absorptions for the match color b chosen under the second illumination by the same procedure:

$$L_{b2} = L_b/L_{max2} \quad (7.12a)$$

$$M_{b2} = M_b/M_{max2} \quad (7.12b)$$

$$S_{b2} = S_b/S_{max2}. \quad (7.12c)$$

3. The error of estimate is the difference between the two predicted absorption measures:

$$L_{a1} - L_{b2} = L_a/L_{max1} - L_b/L_{max2} \quad (7.13a)$$

$$M_{a1} - M_{b2} = M_b/M_{max2} - M_a/M_{max1} \quad (7.13b)$$

$$S_{a1} - S_{b2} = S_a/S_{max1} - S_b/S_{max2}. \quad (7.13c)$$

If there is no error, then the absorptions in different illuminations are linearly related and the y intercept should be zero. Wandell (1995) concluded that von Kreis is a good start toward explaining constancy.

Land (1986) argued that the color of an object is determined by the lightness (i.e., the perceptual reflectance of a surface) values in the three receptor channels.[3] Land demonstrated that changing the relative brightness of three narrow-band lights did not change the colors of the flat patchwork Mondrian colors in spite of changing the relative amounts of excitation in the three receptor systems (termed *retinex* to emphasize the retina-to-cortex connection). In Land's model, for any channel the lightness of a surface is relative to the

3. Brightness refers to perceiving a surface viewed in isolation, for example through an aperture, so that the surface appears to float in space. Lightness refers to perceiving a surface relative to other surfaces, so that it appears to be a reflective solid surface.

light reflected by all surfaces in the scene. The color at every point is therefore based on the relative excitations in the three cone systems scaled by the space-averaged responses to each system. (In contrast, the orthodox view is that the color is determined by the ratio of the cone excitations at one point in space.) The lightness correction in Land's model and von Kries's model are the same except for slight differences in the way the scaling factor is calculated.

It is clear that the color of surfaces does depend on the surrounding colors, so that some sort of normalization or scaling must occur. The questions that remain unanswered are how the normalization takes place and in what spectral channels, and to what degree a simple scaling of the channels accounts for color constancy.

Asymmetric Chromatic Matching

Due to the difficulty of providing observers with an adequate set of matching colors, and the relative ease of creating systems that allow observers to change the illumination, a different procedure to measure color constancy has emerged. In one experimental procedure, the standard color and a different test color are placed at different positions along the back wall of the experimental chamber. Brainard, Brunt, and Speigle (1997) found that the degree of color constancy was relatively independent of the test color chosen. Both the standard and test colors are illuminated by a fixed ambient illumination common to the entire chamber, and in addition the test color is also illuminated by independent illuminants that produce a blue-to-yellow gradient on the back wall. At this point, the standard and test colors will look different. The observer is given control of a hidden projector that projects only onto the test color with independent control of the intensity of red, green, and blue beams (see figure 7.7). The observer's task is to vary the intensity of these beams so that the standard and test colors appear to be the same. To the observer, it looks like the color of the test patch is changing, although in reality it is the change in illumination that produces the change in appearance.

To achieve color constancy, the observer has to figure out how the standard color would appear under the test color illumination (it will look different due to the extra illumination) and adjust the projector so that the test color matches that estimated appearance. One strategy is as follows:

1. Estimate the illumination on the standard color. This could be done from the gray background color of the chamber: The gray will reflect all frequencies of the illuminant equally.
2. Estimate the reflectance of the standard color based on the illumination that has just been estimated from the gray background.
3. Estimate the illumination on the test patch created by the extra gradient illumination from the reflection off the back wall.

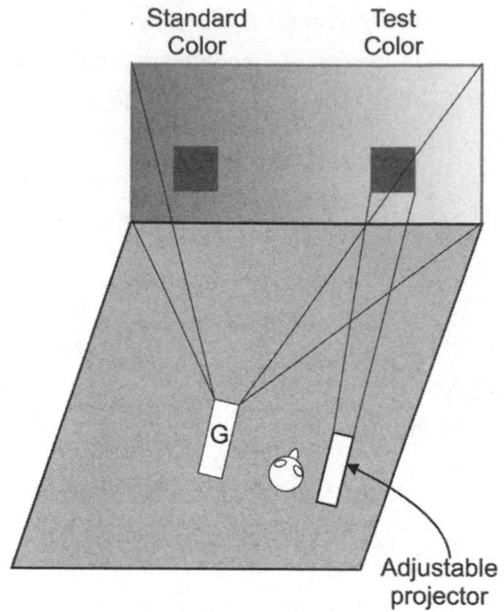

Figure 7.7. In the asymmetric color-matching task, the standard and test colors were mounted on the back wall. The gradient projector (G) created a blue-to-yellow gradient on the back wall using two bulbs. The observer's task was to make the standard and test color look the same by manipulating the blue, green, and red beams of the adjustable projector. Adapted from "Color Constancy in the Nearly Natural Image. I. Asymmetric Matches," by D. H. Brainard, W. A. Brunt, and J. M. Speigle, 1997, *Journal of the Optical Society of America, A, 14*, 2091–2110. See color insert.

4. Imagine how the standard color would look under the test illumination.
5. Adjust the projector to make the test patch match what the standard color would have looked like under the original illumination.

Based on this logic, color constancy is calculated from: (A) the reflected light from the standard color under the ambient illumination; (B) the reflected light from the test color patch that is perceived to match the standard color using the ambient + test + adjusted projector illumination; and (C) the reflection of the standard color patch at the test patch location under the ambient + test illumination. If there is perfect color constancy, then the reflected light from the standard color at the location of the test color patch (C) should equal the observer's adjusted test color match (B). The degree of constancy can then be measured as:

1 – [(standard color/test illumination C) – (test color/adjusted illumination B)/(standard color/test illumination C) – (standard color/ambient illumination A)].

Constancy is equal to 1 when the adjusted (using the projector) test color patch would create the same retinal excitation as the standard color under the test illumination and is equal to 0 when the adjusted test color patch produces the same retinal excitation as the standard color under the ambient illumination.[4] Using this procedure, the average constancy is about .60.

4. Brainard et al. (1997) converted the reflected light at the three conditions into coordinates in a color space and measured the absolute differences in that space.

In another type of asymmetric matching procedure, the test patch is achromatic, somewhere between white and black seen under normal daylight. Since achromatic colors (i.e., the grays) reflect all spectral wavelengths equally (termed *spectrally nonselective*), their reflected light will match the spectral properties of the illuminant. If the illuminant has more energy in the reds, then the achromatic patch will look reddish. The matching task requires the observer to use the adjustable projection colorimeter to add spectral energy to make the test patch look gray (again). The observer must adjust the colorimeter so that the reflected light from the achromatic patch, now based on the sum of the ambient and adjustable colorimeter spectral energies, would equal the reflectance of gray under normal daylight illumination (Brainard, 1998). To do so, the observer must use the reflected light from the standard patch and background to estimate the ambient illumination in order to adjust the colorimeter.

A good starting point is experiments by Kraft and Brainard (1999) that made use of a highly realistic visual scene and that attempted to tease apart the contributions of various cues that have been hypothesized to account for color constancy. Observers looked into a test chamber that contained a flat panel composed of 24 different colored squares, a tube wrapped in tinfoil that could produce specular reflection and thereby illuminate other parts of the scene by means of interreflections, and three-dimensional cube and pyramid shapes constructed from gray cardboard that could provide shadow cues (see figure 7.8). One wall of the chamber was covered with the same cardboard as used to construct the cube and pyramid. The dark gray test patch hung on the back wall. In all of the experiments, the observer's task was to make the test patch look gray by manipulating the red, green, and blue beams of a hidden projector.

The purpose of the experiment was to determine the relative importance of the various cues postulated to account for constancy. Prior to the actual experiment, Kraft and Brainard (1999) determined the maximum degree of constancy achievable in the "rich" test chamber and the minimum degree of constancy achievable when all cues were removed. The authors first maximized the cues for constancy. The experimental chamber was lined with the same gray background for the neutral illuminant and for the orange-red test illuminant. These combinations made the test patch look dark gray for the neutral illumination, but orange-red for the second illumination. In this case, observers easily adjusted the test patch to look gray under the orange-red illuminant. The constancy index was 0.83, a remarkably high value. Kraft and Brainard then minimized the cues by removing all the objects (only the test patch remained) and comparing one condition in which the background was gray with a neutral illumination to a second condition in which the background was blue with an orange-red illumination (i.e., the patch still looked orange-red). Here the local illumination from the

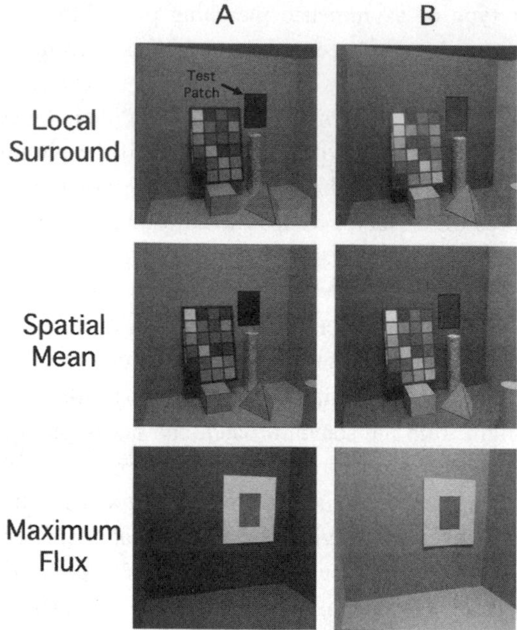

Figure 7.8. The experimental room used by Kraft and Brainard (1999). There was a hidden adjustable projector (like that in figure 7.7) that the participant used to make the test patch in the (B) conditions look achromatic. The three views shown in (A) used the neutral illuminant. In the three views in (B), the local surround used an orange-red illuminant; the spatial mean used a pale red illuminant; and the maximum flux used a yellow illuminant. From "Mechanisms of Color Constancy Under Nearly Natural Viewing," by J. M. Kraft and D. H. Brainard, 1999, *Proceedings of the National Academy of Science, 96*, 307–312. Copyright 1999 by the National Academy of Science. Reprinted with permission. See color insert.

background was identical (both looked black because the blue background reflected very little of the orange-red illumination) and there were no other objects in the scene that could provide spectral cues. In this minimum configuration, constancy was close to 0, averaging 0.11. The authors speculated that the residual constancy was due to mutual reflections among the parts of the chamber.

The first part of the actual experiment investigated the role of local contrast in color constancy. The logic is based on von Kreis's adaptation: For each cone system separately, the excitation from the test patch is divided by the excitation of that system from the local surround. If the illumination over the patch and surround changes (e.g., more green energy), then more energy will be reflected in the green region by both the test and surround, but the ratio of reflected light between the test patch and surround will stay the same. Moreover, the ratios between the three pairs of cones between the test and surround will also remain the same. Thus, the constancy of relative ratios should lead to color constancy.

Kraft and Brainard (1999) equalized the local surround by using different combinations of illumination and surface reflectance. The logic of the experiments is that if we illuminate a gray paper with two different illuminants but somehow balance the excitation due to illumination × reflectance, observers will not be able to achieve color constancy because they cannot untangle the illumination from the surface reflectance. In the first combination, the background wall was gray cardboard, and the illumination in the entire chamber was a neutral light producing a uniform reflectance spectrum (figure 7.8, local surround A). In the second combination, the background wall was blue and the illumination in the entire chamber was orange-red, which also produced a neutral uniform reflectance spectrum from the back wall (local surround B). Thus, the reflection from the back wall surrounding the test patch was identical in the two conditions, although the light reflected from the test patch and all of the other surfaces in the chamber differed. (Note that the difference between the local surround condition and the minimizing control condition described in the above paragraph is the inclusion of the colored surfaces and objects in the local surround condition. In both conditions, the local surround is matched.) If the local surround is the only cue for constancy, then equalizing the local surround should eliminate any constancy. But if the local surround is but one of several cues and if observers can use the more orange appearance of other objects in the chamber to infer the illuminant, then constancy should simply decrease. In fact, constancy did decrease to roughly 0.50, although this is still relatively good.

The second part of the experiment investigated the role of the global surround. The notion parallels that for the local surround, but here the three cone responses to the test patch are compared to the three cone responses averaged across the entire scene. On this basis, Kraft and Brainard (1999) compared neutral illumination of the chamber (spatial mean A) to pale red illumination that equated the average cone responses across the entire scene (spatial mean B). In this condition, if subjects are judging the test patch in terms of the entire scene, then constancy should be zero, but if they are making use of other cues, then constancy should simply decrease. The constancy did decrease to 0.40, demonstrating that a difference in the global surround is not the sole mechanism for constancy.

The third part of the experiment investigated the role of absorption from the most intense region of the scene, the white areas described previously. In one condition, the yellow frame was illuminated by a neutral light (maximum flux A), while in the second condition a magenta frame was illuminated by a yellow light (maximum flux B). For both conditions, the background was the identical dark gray cardboard, and all the other surfaces and objects were removed. The light reflected from the frames created the maximum number of absorptions in each cone system. Even though the region of greatest intensity was the same under both illuminations, observers were able to make use of reflections off the walls, and color constancy was roughly 0.30.

What this experiment demonstrates is that there is no single cue for color constancy. Cues will be evaluated in specific situations, and judgments will be made on the basis of cue reliability and validity as well as a priori expectations. Delahunt and Brainard (2004) provided a caution to this conclusion. Observers did not have more accurate color constancy if the illumination changes matched those that occur naturally (more bluish or more yellow) than they did when illumination changes did not match (more greenish or more reddish).

A second experiment (Yang & Maloney, 2001) came to the same conclusion that there are multiple cues that can be used to achieve constancy. Yang and Maloney investigated whether observers exploit specular and background cues to make inferences about illumination. As described above, constancy models propose that observers first estimate the illumination and then derive the surface reflectance. The illumination can be estimated from the surface or specular reflections. The specular reflections can come from single highlights or can be part of a surface's overall reflection. If reflections from one or more highlights can be found in the visual scene, then those reflections are assumed to act like a mirror, so that the illumination can be estimated directly. However, as Yang and Maloney pointed out, usually it is not easy to pick out neutral highlights: They are not always the brightest points because they may be due to a distant source or they may not be spectrally neutral, being due to metallic reflections from materials such as gold or copper.

In instances where there are not perceivable highlights, the spectral reflectance from a surface reaching the viewer can be modeled as the sum of a perfectly matte surface (Lambertian) and a neutral mirror. The surface and specular reflections are intermixed, and the relative amounts of the two types of reflection vary with viewing position and light source position. Thus, it may be possible to infer the purely specular reflection at one viewing location.

In general terms, the authors used a cue conflict paradigm. They measured the achromatic match under two cue conditions, C_1 and C_2, and a mixed condition that altered one cue value from C_1 to C_2. The importance of the altered cue was measured by the extent that the achromatic setting moved toward C_2 (obviously, the converse conditions must also be utilized to measure any asymmetries). To be specific, in the uniform conditions C_1 and C_2, both surface and specular reflections were based on one illuminant, either normal daylight (D65) or incandescent lighting (A). In the conflict conditions, the surface reflectance was based on one of the illuminants, and the specular reflectance was based on the other illuminant.

The stimuli resembled billiard balls resting on a flat surface. All the billiard balls were blue-green and the surface was a darker gray. The stimuli were presented stereoscopically so that the billiard balls appeared in depth (see figure 7.9). The test patch was located tangentially to the tops of the billiard balls. This is an important point, and I will return to it later.

In the first set of experiments, the illumination of the balls was varied. For stimuli with 10 or more balls, there was marked asymmetry in the effects of the illuminants. Starting with the incandescent illuminant A, but

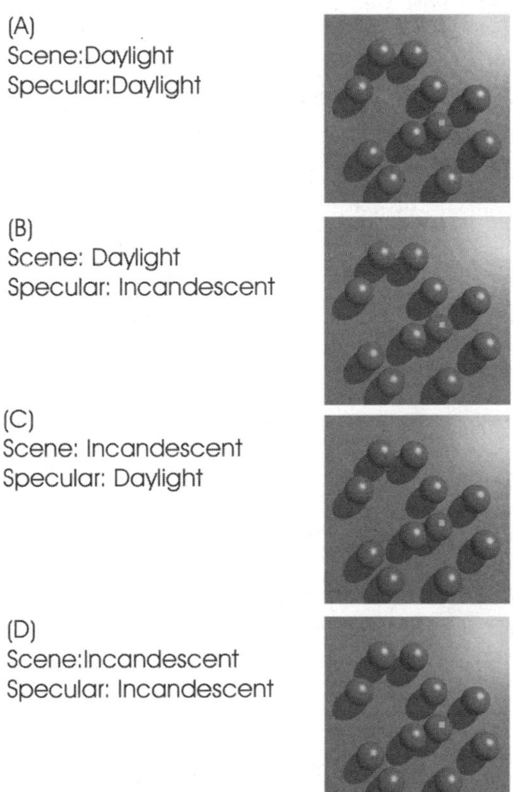

Figure 7.9. The effect of specular and surface reflections on color constancy was investigated using a cue conflict paradigm. Two illuminants were used: standard daylight (D65) and incandescent A. In two conditions (A and D), the specular and surface reflections were based on the same illuminant, but in two conditions (B and C), the surface and specular reflections were based on different illuminants. Participants were asked to adjust the small green squares shown in the figure to appear achromatic. From "Illuminant Cues in Surface Color Perception: Tests of Three Candidate Cues," by J. N. Yang and L. T. Maloney, 2001, *Vision Research, 41*, 2581–2600. Copyright 2001 by Elsevier Science Ltd. Reprinted with permission. See color insert.

moving the specular reflectance toward daylight (D65), there was a large shift in the achromatic judgments. The converse is not true: If the specular reflectance moved toward illuminant A, there was only a small shift. It is surprising to note that if each ball was represented by a different matte reflectance, there was no effect of the change in illumination. The effect was restricted to instances in which there were at least six identical balls. In the second set of experiments, the illumination of the background was varied. Here, there were no effects of the perturbation of the illumination.

These results reinforce the notion that color perception is the result of many simultaneously presented cues and that the visual system is somehow evaluating the validity of each cue to arrive at a single percept. Here, (a) daylight is given more weight than incandescent light; and (b) there must be several identical specular highlights before they affect color judgments; but (c) multiple specular highlights from different matte surfaces are discounted because they probably signal a nonuniform illuminant. The change in the illumination of the background did not affect color judgments if the test patch appeared to float on top of the background. If, however, the test patch was localized on the background (in preliminary experimentation), then all of the results reversed: (a) there was little effect of the specular cues, and (b) the strongest effect was due to the background changes.

Fleming, Dror, and Adelson (2003) proposed that observers have a tacit knowledge of the illumination properties found in the real world and tend to discount illuminations that violate those prior expectations (as suggested by Yang and Maloney, 2001, previously). The underlying notion is that all types of illumination share the same statistical properties and that allows the visual system to derive the surface roughness and reflectance of objects even in the absence of context. Actually, Fleming et al. made even a stronger assertion. Namely, the partitioning of the illumination and the reflectance is readily accomplished because observers expect the illumination to have certain properties. Given those properties, the surface reflectance can be easily calculated. For real illuminations, there is an extremely wide dynamic range (2,000:1, discussed in chapter 3), and the vast majority of pixels on the surface of the object are much darker than the few brightest pixels. The brightest pixels tend to be clumped together, creating local extended highlights from the specular reflectance. This clumping yields a $1/f$ function for brightness that accounts for the majority of light that is reflected from the surface. The clumped illumination creates the perception of a directional source that in turn creates highlights with extended edges organized into regular shapes. Simply having bright pixels is not sufficient for the perception of surface features. As shown in figure 7.10, the real-life illuminations create extended glossy regions that allow the perception of the specular reflectance and surface roughness. Even though the simulated illuminations may have the same distribution of pixel values, the perception of

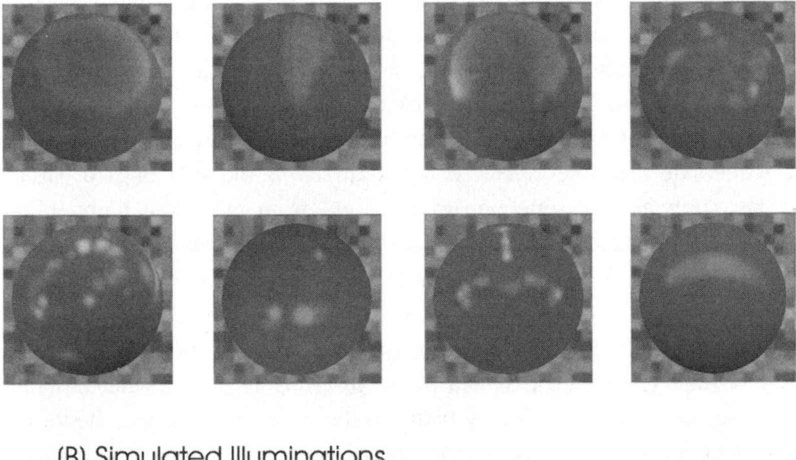

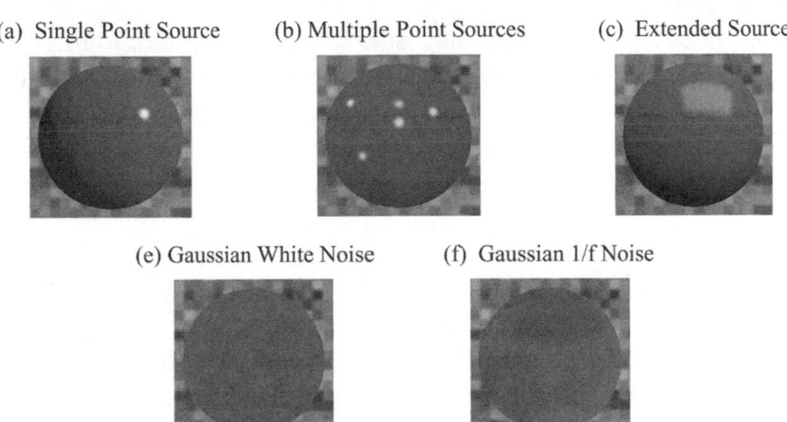

Figure 7.10. The perception of surface gloss and roughness depends on the properties of the illumination. In all examples, the surface reflectance of the spheres is the same. The perception of surface characteristics is best with real-life illuminations (A) and gets much poorer as the simulated illumination deviates from what is normally expected (B). From "Real-World Illumination and the Perception of Surface Reflectance Properties," by R. W. Fleming, R. O. Dror, and E. W. Adelson, 2003, *Journal of Vision, 3*, 347–368. Copyright 2003 by AVRO. Reprinted with permission. See color insert.

the surface is much poorer. The sphere loses its gloss using the pink noise illumination, and looks like a semitransparent globe with an internal light using the white noise illumination. It is the higher-order correlations that are important.

A clever experiment by Bloj, Kersten, and Hurlbert (1999) demonstrated yet another factor that determines our perception of color, namely the effects of mutual reflections among object surfaces. The authors made use of a folded card. One side of the fold was painted magenta, and the second side of the fold was painted white. The light source was pointed toward the red half of the card. Physically the card was folded inwardly so that the magenta side reflected light onto the white side (and vice versa) and the light reflected from the white side took on a pinkish color gradient caused by the mutual reflection, as depicted in figure 7.11. The light reflected from the white side therefore can be conceptualized as the sum of two parts: (1) the purely neutral reflection of the light from the white paint, plus (2) the neutral reflection of the magenta-tinged light due to the one-bounce mutual reflection. By the same token, the light reaching the observer from the magenta side of the card is the sum of the direct reflection from the magenta paint plus the one-bounce neutral reflection from the white side being re-reflected by the magenta paint, resulting in a somewhat desaturated magenta. Two of the many paths to the observer's eye are shown in figure 7.11: the direct reflection from the magenta side and the one bounce from magenta to white.

Observers reported that the white side of the card appeared to be only slightly pink (they selected the match from a set of colors ranging from

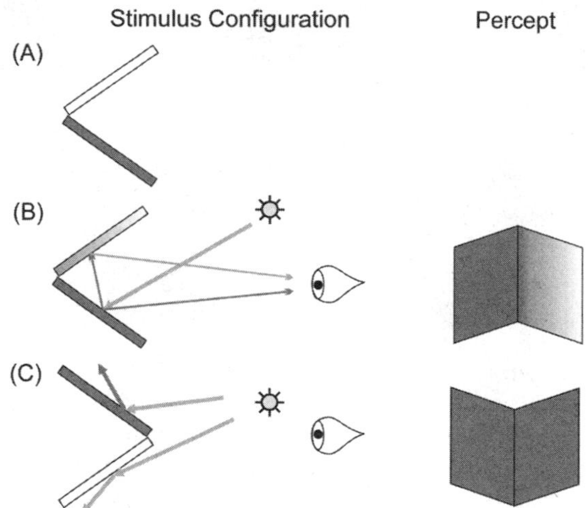

Figure 7.11. The stimulus was a card folded in half, one side painted magenta and the other painted white (A). If an incandescent light aimed at the magenta side illuminated the card, the light reflected from the magenta side onto the white side created a magenta gradient from desaturated magenta to white (B). Observers judged the inside corner of the white side as pale pink. If the appearance of the card was reversed so that it appeared to be convex, observers then judged the white side as being deep magenta instead of pale pink (C). As illustrated in (C), if the card really was convex, there could not be a one-bounce reflection from the magenta side. Adapted from "Perception of Three-Dimensional Shape Influences Colour Perception Through Mutual Illumination," by M. G. Bloj, D. Kersten, and A. C. Hurlbert, 1999, *Nature, 402*, 877–879. See color insert.

magenta to white). Then Bloj et al. (1999) made use of a pseudoscope to invert the folded card: It now appeared to be folded away from the observer, that is, the corner was closest to the observer and the magenta and white sides reversed. The physical reflections were still identical, but now the magenta component of the white surface could not have been caused by mutual reflection because the corner seemed to face the observer. The magenta appearance could have been caused only by the inherent surface reflection of the white surface. The mutual reflections were still present but could not be perceptually interpreted as such. Observers now judged the white surface as being a far more saturated magenta. Our inferences about the three-dimensional characteristics of scenes affect our perception of color.

Doerschner, Boyaci, and Maloney (2004) have generalized these results by demonstrating that observers can compensate for different angles between interreflecting surfaces. The authors systematically varied the angle between a light gray test patch surface and an orange cube. As the angle between the test patch and the orange cube increased, the amount of secondary illumination reaching the test patch decreased. Observers tended to underestimate the added orange illumination when the secondary illumination was most intense at the smaller angles. Beyond 120°, observers were unable to detect changes in the secondary illumination at all. Doerschner et al. (2004) concluded that color is not a local phenomenon but is contingent on the global geometry and lighting.

Summary

At the beginning of the section "How Good Is Color Constancy?" I listed six possible cues to estimating illumination. Each of the cues can be and is used depending on the visual scene. It is tempting to ascribe some cues to local retinal processes and others to more central cognitive processes. Local contrast is thought to be based on von Kreis scaling, and in fact such scaling works very well for simple scenes with a center-surround spatial configuration. But even such a seemingly automatic physiological process can be discounted. Even though the physical illumination was identical, Yang and Maloney (2001) found that the background illumination affected color appearance only when the test patch was perceived to be in the same plane as the background, not when the test patch was perceived to be in a different plane. These results further support the conceptualization of Gilchrist et al. (1999) and Anderson and Winawar (2005) that the visual system segments the scene into different frameworks and that different weighting systems for the possible color cues may be employed in each frame or depth plane.

There is clearly a chicken-and-egg problem here. Many of the cues to color depend on the segmentation of the scene into occluding surfaces, and yet the construction of those surfaces depends on the ability to distinguish changes in illumination from changes in surface reflectance. I take all this to mean that the goal of the visual perceptual system (and the auditory perceptual system also) is to create a coherent representation of the physical world. Thus, expectations about surfaces and illuminations that could arise from inherent physiological processes or from a priori probabilities built up from experience are necessary to eliminate ambiguity. It seems to me that a reasonable way of conceptualizing all of this is that the visual system combines the cues in terms of the reliability of the cue in that context. (This is the same conclusion found for cues from different modalities discussed in chapter 9.) For example, the results of Yang and Maloney (2001) suggest that observers do not consider the specular cues to be reliable until more than six objects show the identical specular reflectance.

Opponent Processing

Very early in the visual pathway, the three cone signals are recoded into two parallel spectrally opponent channels that relay chromatic information to the visual cortex. In the first channel, the excitations from the long-wavelength (red) and medium-wavelength (green) cones are placed in opposition so that a balanced mixture of red and green sums to zero, yielding a percept of yellow. In the second channel, the excitations from the L and M cones are added, and are placed in opposition to the excitations from the short-wavelength (blue) cones. There is a third channel that combines the outputs of all three cones to yield an achromatic excitation. The two chromatic pathways seem to reflect the evolution of the cone systems. The S cones evolved first, followed by the joint evolution of the M and L cones. The evolution of the M and L cones in primates is hypothesized to aid in the detection of colored fruit in a green forest background (Dominy & Lucas, 2001).

All opponent cells have a center-surround spatial configuration. What is surprising is that the center is linked to only one cone by means of the midget ganglion cells (say, one S cone), but the surround is a blend of both M and L cones. Moreover, the relative frequency of the M and L cones in the surround is variable. Again surprisingly, there seems to be a wide distribution in the relative number of M and L cones across individuals. The range may be as great as 4:1, and this can account for the variability of the distribution of the M and L cones to the surround. The opponent processing is restricted to the fovea, where there is a one-to-one connection between a cone and midget ganglion cell, and disappears in the periphery, where many cones converge on each midget ganglion cell (see reviews by Lennie, 2003; Packer & Williams, 2003).

Why is there opponent processing? One possibility is that the M and L cones and the opponent pathways evolved to match the spectral distribution of natural scenes. If this is the case, then the spectral responses of the opponent pathways should be correlated to the basis functions for natural scenes. Ruderman, Cronin, and Chiao (1998) and Wachler, Lee, and Sejnowski (2001), although using different statistical methodologies, argued that the independent basis functions do have the same structure as the opponent channels. Ruderman et al. first converted the spectral distribution at each central region of the scene into the output of the L, M, and S cone systems by multiplying the distribution by the cone sensitivity functions. The outputs of all cone systems were highly correlated due to overall changes in light intensity, and the correlation between the L and M cones was highest. Using a principal components analysis to decorrelate the image, Ruderman et al. found three principal axes: (a) an achromatic luminance dimension; (b) a yellow-blue opponent direction; and (c) a red-green opponent direction. These three directions were uncorrelated to spatial position so that cone responses can be thought of as arising from three superimposed processes. Wachler et al. made use of independent component analyses to calculate basis functions that are independent but not necessarily orthogonal (as in the principal components analyses used by Ruderman et al.). Some of the basis functions were achromatic, while the chromatic basis functions tended to display color opponency but not be orthogonal.

On the whole, there is a reasonable match between the opponent color channels and the spectral properties of natural scenes. The opponent channels decorrelate the M and L cone absorptions, and there is a set of linear functions that resemble opponent color functions that effectively decorrelate the spectral distribution of natural scenes. Thus, these chromatic basis functions seem to serve the same purpose as the basis functions described in chapters 2 and 3 that match the receptive fields of V1 cortical neurons. The chromatic basis functions decorrelate the outputs of the two cones in the same way that the basis functions in V1 decorrelate the outputs of spatially adjacent receptors. Both types of basis functions can yield sparse coding that maximizes mutual information.

It seems to me that the issue of whether the opponent color channels are somehow optimized for information transmission is still unresolved. The match between the color channels and the linear functions will of course depend on the set of scenes analyzed.

Summary

Although the emphasis of this chapter has been on how a source filter can be used to understand the spectral distribution of the light reaching the eye, the perceptual outcomes demonstrate that the spectral distribution can explain only a part of color constancy and color appearance. Our experience of color is affected by activity at several neural levels and ultimately probably depends on the activity of several cortical areas (Gegenfurtner, 2003). Cortical cells may respond only to specific colors, and there are large differences in the frequency bandwidth. There is little functional segregation: Cortical color cells that are highly selective for specific colors can be selective or nonselective to other properties such as orientation.

One principle that underlies the research findings here and in all previous (and future) chapters is that our understanding of the scene controls our perceptions. Visual and auditory scenes are segmented into frameworks and objects, and that segmentation gives rise to our guesses about and estimates of texture, motion, brightness, and color. The segmentation may be due to innate physiological processes, Bayesian-like experience, or the observer's purposes.

8

The Perception of Quality: Auditory Timbre

I analyzed color perception using the source-filter model, and I will use the same model to analyze the production and perception of sound quality.[1] However, the source-filter model for sound and that for color are marked by several important differences. In describing the source-filter model for color, I made use of several simplifying properties. First, the spectral distribution (wavelength variation) of nearly all sources and reflectances are rather smooth and continuous. Second, the variation in the spectral distributions, especially for natural sources (i.e., daybreak to nightfall), is continuous, so that the distributions can be represented by a set of linear functions. Third, there are but three broad color channels, so that only three numbers represent the entire neural excitation. Fourth, I assumed strict independence between the spectral distributions of the light source and surface reflectance and nearly all of the computational and perceptual models underlying color constancy assume that the first step is estimating the illumination, and then using that estimate to derive the surface reflection (i.e., the color). Fifth, computational models have assumed that the colored scene is constant over time.

My analysis of the perception of timbre cannot make use of any of these simplifications. First and second, the sources and filters of nearly all sound-producing objects are marked by discrete source frequencies and discrete filter-resonant frequencies. Moreover, the changes in both the source and

1. I use the term *timbre* interchangeably with the phrase *sound quality*. The use of the term *timbre* to distinguish between sounds has a history of at least 300 years. In the last 100 years it has referred almost exclusively to an attribute of the sound of musical instruments. Here I use it to describe all types of sounds.

filter frequencies are not smooth across frequencies, due to the physical properties of the objects. A set of linear functions does not seem possible. Third, there are many auditory frequency channels, defined by the responsiveness of individual hair cells and their summation into critical bands. To a large degree, the intensity pattern of the resulting frequency channels determines sound quality. For example, "bright" sounds have relatively more energy at higher frequencies. Fourth, there are instances in which the source and filter frequency distributions are not independent. For example, in singing there is simultaneous variation in the vocal fold vibrations and mouth position to produce a particular vowel at a pitch, and for reed instruments the filter resonances support specific source frequencies by means of air pressure feedback. There are cases in which the filter is fixed, (e.g., the wooden body of a violin), but even here the wood and air resonances of the body can affect the vibrations of the source string. Fifth, sounds have onsets and offsets, and the attack and decay temporal profiles provide critical information about the sound source.

At a more metaphorical level, I think that the conceptualization of sound quality differs from that for visual quality. Sound quality has no fixed referents, and the descriptors for sound quality are often ambiguous. Descriptions are based on multiple acoustic properties, some based on the overall spectrum and some based on the temporal pattern of the sound. In contrast, the descriptors for color seem universal using the primary colors blue, green, red, and yellow (Buchsbaum & Bloch, 2002). There are several color description systems but all make use of just a small number of color specifications. For example, the Munsell system uses hue, lightness, and saturation.

There is another fundamental difference between color and timbre. Color, on the whole, does not uniquely signify objects. Even though color allows us to segment the visual scene into surfaces and edges, many different objects occur within the same narrow color range, and most objects can be different colors. I would argue that pitch is analogous to color in this respect. Many sound sources occur within the same narrow pitch range, and most sources can occur at different pitches. Of course, the specific color or pitch undoubtedly aids recognition and identification. Yet voices, instruments, and many environmental sources are multipitched, so that some consistent property of the sound (what I will call timbre) becomes the only way to identify those objects across pitch. Although timbre is technically defined as a sound quality at one frequency and intensity (American National Standards Institute, 1973), I think it is more natural to conceptualize timbre as belonging to and inherent in an object, in spite of changes in the sound due to frequency and intensity variation. When we hear a sound, our natural tendency is to identify the sound-producing object, not to describe qualities of that sound. What this means is that timbre exists at several levels: (a) describing the differences between sounds that are composed of a broad band of frequencies and do not have a clear pitch, such as sawing or scraping; (b) describing the differences between sounds at one frequency and intensity, that is, the ANSI (1973) definition; (c) describing and identifying sources across different frequencies and intensities, such as a clarinet as opposed to a saxophone; (d) describing and identifying source categories across different sources, frequency, and intensity, for instance, sopranos as opposed to mezzo-sopranos, woodwind instruments as opposed to brass instruments. For (c) and (d), timbre must be reconceptualized as a sound transformation that allows us to predict an object's sound at different frequencies and thereby allows us to track objects in the environment. We might characterize (a) and (b) as a proximal description of sound quality, and (c) and (d) as a distal description of objects.

I am not ready to abandon timbre as an empty concept even though the term is used in so many ways, like the term *appearance*, that it means whatever we wish. Moreover, because sound production results in so many acoustical properties, there may not be any fixed set of acoustic cues that allow us to identify the same object in real environments with overlapping, competing sounds of other objects. Perhaps the only possibility is to list the possible acoustic variables and transformations, and then identify the subset used at different times (this is the same conclusion we reached for the cues to color).

In spite of this perceptual and conceptual inexactness, we still have the basic perceptual issues. We presume that the goals of the auditory and visual systems are identical: Namely, to construct a coherent representation of objects in the external world. These objects will have inherent properties, and perceptual systems should be tuned to pick up those properties. At this point, we cannot distinguish between innate and learned mechanisms, or the degree to which recognition is a purely inferential process, but that does not matter.

Sound Production: The Source-Filter Model

Let us start by comparing the source-filter model for seeing to that for hearing. For seeing (color), the source was the energy of the illuminant at different frequencies; the filter was the reflectance of the surface at those frequencies; and we multiplied the illumination by the reflectance to predict the light reaching the eye. The assumption was that the light at all frequencies reached the eye at the same time. For hearing (timbre), the model is more complex. First, we need energy to excite the source. What makes this complicated is that different ways of exciting the source (e.g., hitting, plucking, or bowing a string) can change the vibration pattern of the source. Second, there may be large timing differences between the amplitudes of the vibrations at different frequencies throughout the sound. We still multiply the source by the filter, but due to the temporal evolution of the amplitudes of the component vibration, that multiplication must be done separately at every time point across the duration of the sound (i.e., frequency and time are nonseparable). It is this change in the vibration pattern that can be critical for object identification.

Vibratory Modes

If we excite a material by striking it, vibrating it, blowing across it, bending or twisting it, and then stop the excitation, the material may begin to vibrate at one or more of its natural resonant frequencies. There are two physical properties that yield continuing vibrations:

1. The material must possess a stiffness or springlike property that provides a restoring force when the material is displaced from equilibrium. At least for small displacements, nearly all materials obey Hooke's law that the restoring force is proportional to displacement x, $F = -Kx$. Hooke's law is correct only at small displacements. At longer displacements, springlike materials tend to become harder so that the restoring force increases. This nonlinearity in the restoring force at those longer displacements can change the natural frequencies of the vibration modes.

2. The material must possess sufficient inertia so that the return motion overshoots the equilibrium point. The overshoot displacement in turn creates a restoring force in the direction of the original displacement that recharges the motion. The overshoots create a continuing vibration that eventually dies out due to friction (although the vibration frequency remains the same throughout the decay, an important property).

For materials that satisfy properties (1) and (2), the amplitude of the movement across time for every single vibratory pattern will resemble the motion of a sinusoidal wave and is termed *simple harmonic motion*. In nearly all vibratory systems, any source excitation will create several vibratory modes, each at a different frequency. Each such vibratory mode will have a distinct motion and can be characterized by its resonant frequency and by its damping or quality factor. The resonant frequency of each mode is simply the frequency at which the amplitude of vibration is highest. The material itself will determine the possible frequencies of vibration. For strings under tension, the resonant frequency of the first vibration mode (termed the *fundamental frequency*) is equal to:

$$F = 1/(2\pi)[K(\text{tension})/M(\text{mass of the string})]^{1/2}. \qquad (8.1)$$

In all cases, the vibration frequency of the mode will equal the excitation frequency. If the excitation frequency equals the resonant frequency (say 100 Hz), the amplitude of vibration mode will be greatest. If we excite the string at slightly different frequencies, the decrease in amplitude is determined by (1) the difference between the natural resonant frequency of the string and the driving frequency, and (2) the damping of the vibration mode. The damping, or inversely the quality factor (Q), of each vibration mode is a measure of its sharpness of tuning and resulting temporal response. For a heavily damped vibration mode (i.e., low Q), the amplitude of vibration is relatively constant across the frequency of the excitation, and the amplitude of the vibratory mode will rapidly track increases or decreases in the excitation amplitude. For a lightly damped mode, (i.e., high Q), the amplitude of vibration mode is high if the excitation vibration is at the resonant frequency, but low at surrounding frequencies. Here the amplitude of the vibration mode lags behind increases or decreases in the amplitude of the excitation vibration.[2]

In simple terms, energy is first applied to the source (plucking a guitar string, blowing into a trumpet mouthpiece). The energy generates a set of component vibration modes of the source, and each such mode can be characterized by its resonant frequency and damping. Because each mode may have a different amount of dampening, some modes will rapidly reach their maximum amplitude, while other modes will reach their maximum at a later time. An additional factor is that the source vibration may have an initial period of noise due to the time and energy it takes to get the vibration started. For example, a stable clarinet or trumpet mouthpiece source vibration requires feedback due to the pressure pulses returning from the end of the instrument. Until this happens, there may be only a turbulent airflow.

So what we have is a set of source vibrations that have different onset timings and amplitudes. These source vibrations then excite the filter, which may contain a multitude of vibration modes, each also with different damping. Each time-varying vibration mode of the source can excite one or more damped modes of the filter, so that the acoustic output is the product of two or more time-varying vibrations. Each excitation can hit different sets of source and filter vibration modes, so that we should not expect a single acoustical property that can characterize an instrument, voice, or sound-producing object across its typical pitch and amplitude range. The changing source-filter coupling precludes a single acoustical correlate that can predict the ease of identifying sounds or that can describe sound timbre. The perceptual problem therefore is constructing transformations

2. The quality factor (Q) is defined as the characteristic frequency (F_{cf}) divided by the bandwidth (BW): $Q = F_{cf} / BW$). The band-pass characteristics of cells in the auditory and visual cortex were discussed in chapter 2.

of sound quality between different pitches and loudness that can be used to identify objects.

String and Percussion Instruments: Vibrations in Strings and Plates

Vibrations of Strings

Suppose we pluck a string at the midway point. When we release the string there will be two traveling waves, one moving toward each end of the string. At the ends, each wave will be reflected back toward the middle of the string. If the reflections continue, the wave pattern along the string can become stationary. If we view the motion from the side, the individual points of the string oscillate up and down, but the wave profile does not move laterally. The original traveling waves have summed to produce a standing wave. The overall motion of the string is complex (although each point simply moves up and down in sinusoidal motion), because the motion is actually the sum of several simple harmonic motions. The simplest harmonic motion is the up-and-down movement of the string as a whole. The second harmonic motion occurs when the string effectively splits into two parts, and each half undergoes an up-and-down motion out of phase with each other. The frequency of each of these vibrations is twice the frequency of the motion of the string as a whole. The motion of all of the higher harmonics can be understood in exactly the same fashion. The string breaks up into more and more subunits; the vibratory frequency of each subunit is the number of subunits times the frequency of the fundamental vibration (F_0, $2F_0$, $3F_0$, $4F_0$, $5F_0 \ldots$).[3]

The fundamental frequency of the string is determined by its physical construction and the amount of tension (equation 8.1). It is not determined by how the string is excited. However, the position and the manner of excitation do determine the relative amplitudes of the vibration modes. The maximum amplitude of a resonance mode occurs when the point of excitation occurs at an antinode (a point of maximum displacement), and the minimum amplitude occurs when the point of excitation occurs at a node (a stationary point). Thus, if the string is excited at the center point, the first up-and-down resonance will be maximized because that is the point of maximum movement, but the second resonance will be minimized because that is the point of zero movement separating the vibration of the two halves of the string. In general, the overall amplitude of the vibration

3. By convention, F_0 is termed the *fundamental*, $2F_0$ the *second harmonic* (F_0 being the first harmonic), $3F_0$ the *third harmonic*, and so on. If the vibration modes are not related by integers (e.g., the vibration modes found for 2-dimensional wooden violin plates), the vibration modes are termed *partials*.

mode is proportional to the relative amplitude of the mode at the point of excitation.

Strings can be bowed, plucked, or struck. The manner of excitation affects the amplitudes of the resonance modes. For bowing and striking with a heavy mass, the amplitudes of the harmonics fall off at the rate of $1/n$ (n is the harmonic number). For plucking, the amplitudes of the harmonics fall off more rapidly, at the rate of $1/n^2$. Each particular manner of excitation has unique effects. Plucking a string makes the frequency of the higher harmonics slightly sharp relative to the lower harmonics. In contrast, bowing maintains the integer ratios among the harmonics, but the slip-stick process of the string against the bow creates a great deal of frequency jitter that varies coherently among the harmonics. Moreover, the bow may scrape the string during the initiation of the stable slip-stick process, creating noise. Performers can create frequency variation, termed *vibrato*, during the steady-state part of a tone by rolling a finger to change the effective length of the string. In a stringed instrument, the frequency variation due to vibrato can alter the output from the sound body resonances so that there is both frequency and amplitude variation. The damping and the rate of decay of strings are determined by the physical construction of the string and its connection to the supports. The decay of the vibration is due to the frictional effect of the motion through the air (viscous drag) and due to the internal friction within the string itself.

Before considering the vibration modes of more complex plates and surfaces, which follow the same basic principles found for strings, it is worthwhile to emphasize that the resonant frequencies and temporal amplitude patterns of the vibratory modes are going to be the perceptual information that we can use to discover the physical properties and identify objects. In some instances, it may be the onset timing of the modes that is most predictive, while in other instances it may be the steady-state amplitudes. Moreover, the best cue may change for the same object at different pitches, contexts, and so on.

Two-Dimensional Plates

When a string is excited, the vibratory pattern is the sum of the vibration modes. In a similar fashion, when excited, the vibratory pattern of a continuous plate (the soundboard of a piano, the wooden top and bottom plates of a violin, the stretched skin of a drumhead) is the sum of its characteristic modes. The important difference, however, is that for a complex surface like the top plate of a violin, there are no simple integer relationships among the resonant frequencies. Moreover, there are so many modes with nearly overlapping frequencies, particularly at higher frequencies, that there are resonant frequency regions rather than discrete resonant frequencies found for strings. Nevertheless, each of the vibration modes of a plate has great similarity to those found for vibrating strings. The two-dimensionality of plates merely allows new spatial patterns of vibrations to occur.

For a uniform string, the motion for the lowest resonant frequency is an up-down motion of the string as a whole. Similarly, the motion for the first mode of a uniform plate is an up-down motion of the plate as a whole (figure 8.1A). For a string, the motion for the second vibration mode consists of the out-of-phase motion of the two halves, and the maximum amplitude occurs at the midpoint of each half; there is a null point at the center of the string. This, again, is the same motion found for the second mode of a plate: The plate vibrates in two out-of-phase sections at the same frequency; there is a single null line (figure 8.1B). Because the plate has two dimensions, there is one vibratory mode that divides the plate into two vibratory regions along the length and one that divides the plate along the width. It is quite possible to have the length and width vibratory mode simultaneously. The third string mode consists of three out-of-phase vibrations; the third plate modes consist of three out-of-phase motions in regions of the plate. The nodal lines (zero amplitude) can run along either the width or length (figure 8.1C). Standing waves for each vibratory mode along one dimension of the plate are independent of the standing waves along the other dimension. Given the two dimensions of the plate, there also are vibration modes that are twisting motions along the diagonals (figure 8.1D). If the membrane is not uniform (e.g., wooden plates of a violin then some of the vibration modes can extend for long distance. An example of such a third vibration mode is shown in figure 8.1E.

As found for vibrating strings, the position and manner of excitation determine the relative amplitudes of the vibration modes. Any vibratory mode can be stilled by either (1) exciting the plate, say by hitting it with a narrow hammer, at a null region; or (2) mechanically restricting the displacement at a region of maximum amplitude (antinode).

Source (String Vibration)-Filter (Sound Body) Model

Strings are not good sound radiators; the periodic physical motion creates a compression wave in front of the string and a rarefaction wave in back, and they effectively cancel each other. The string must transfer its vibration energy to the sound body and the shape of the violin body has evolved to increase that transfer to maximize the sound output power. As described above, each of the string vibrations can excite one or more of the sound body vibration modes. Depending on the match between the vibration frequencies of the string and sound body, some of the string vibrations are effectively amplified and others are effectively nulled, and the spectral

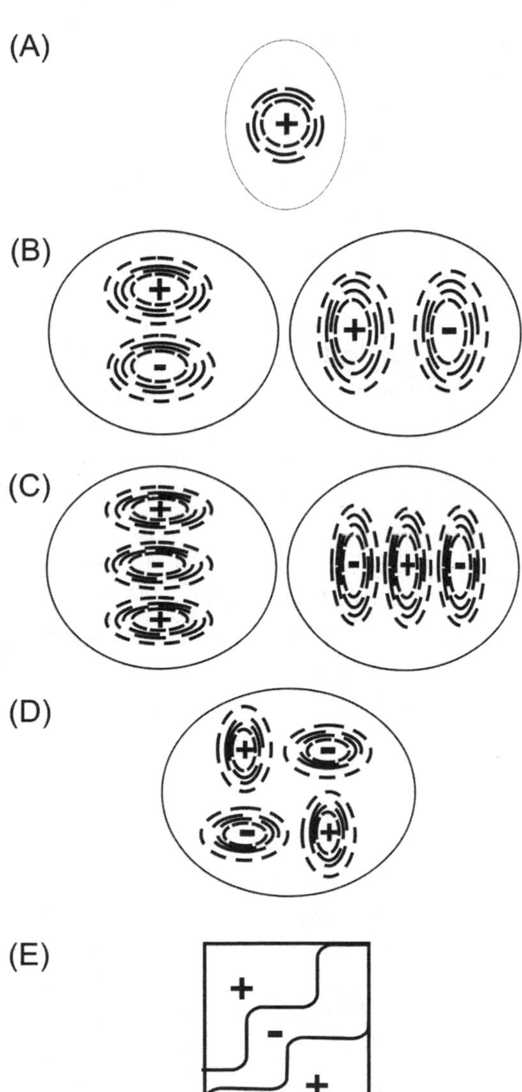

Figure 8.1. The vibration modes found on a two-dimensional plate. Different driving frequencies give rise to different patterns of nodal lines. See text for a full description.

output will vary from note to note. A good sound body is shaped so that its strongest vibration modes fall at the frequencies of musical notes.

Wind Instruments: Air Vibration Within Hollow Tubes

We can imagine the vibration of a string as the up-down movement of individual masses along that string and the vibration of a plate as the up-down motion of individual regions of the plate, and we can imagine the vibration modes of a hollow tube as the motion of slugs of air within that tube (Benade, 1960). The vibration modes of strings and plates are standing waves that result from the summation of traveling waves reflected from the ends of the strings and plates. The same is true for the vibratory modes of a hollow tube. The excitation at one end of the tube produces regions of higher pressure (compressions) and regions of lower pressure (rarefactions) that travel down the tube and are reflected back up the tube at the other end. At a closed end, compression and rarefaction are reflected back as compression and rarefaction respectively (it is an antinode); at an open end, compression is reflected back as rarefaction and vice versa (it is a node). It takes four trips up and down the pipe to complete one cycle, so that the wavelength of the first vibratory mode (i.e., the fundamental) is four times the pipe length. The traveling waves sum to produce a standing wave within the tube.

For a tube open at one end, the stronger vibration modes can occur only at the odd vibration modes (i.e., $3F_0$, $5F_0$, $7F_0$, $9F_0$) because there must be zero net pressure at the open end and maximum pressure variation at the closed end. However, if the open end of the tube is flared out to create a cone, then all vibratory modes are possible.

Source Excitation

For brass instruments, the player's tensed lips inject puffs of air when the oscillating air pressure at the mouthpiece is at a maximum. For woodwind instruments, the reed acts to inject air puffs when the oscillating air pressure at the mouthpiece is at a maximum (the lips and mouthpiece are antinodes—regions of maximum pressure variation). The feedback from the reflected pressure wave is critically important to stabilize the lip vibrations for the brass instruments and to open and close the reed mouthpiece for the woodwinds. However, it may take several round trips before the reflections build up to the point that the lip reed vibrations become stable. During that initiation time there are often variations in pitch and inharmonic blips of energy.

Changing lip tension and the amplitude of the blowing pressure varies the frequency spectrum of the airflow entering the instrument. When the instrumentalist is blowing softly, the lips and reed will oscillate gently. The air is never completely shut off, and the input is almost purely sinusoidal. As the pressure is increased, the lips and reed will undergo large movements. The air may not be completely shut off though, and the amplitudes of the higher harmonics increase. Finally, at the highest blowing pressures, the lips and reed snap shut and stop the airflow for up to 50% of the cycle.

The overall result is that the relative amplitude of the higher harmonics increases as the wind instruments are played louder. If the amplitude of the fundamental is increased 3-fold, then the amplitudes of the second and third harmonics may increase 8-fold and 27-fold.

Filter (Sound Body)

For the brass instruments, the mouthpiece and bell make the hollow tube a more usable instrument. The mouthpiece more closely couples the player's lip vibrations to the reflected pressure waves. The purpose of the flaring bell is to allow the sound energy at higher frequencies to radiate more completely out of the hollow tube (a megaphone acts like a bell). Without the bell, most of the energy is reflected back up the tube due to the difference in air pressure in the tubing and in the atmosphere; with a bell, nearly all of the energy above 1500 Hz is propagated to the listener. The bell reflects the low-frequency energy back up the tubing so that the damping increases. The increased damping makes the onset of the lower-frequency vibration modes more rapid (less than 20 ms), slower for the middle vibration modes (40–60 ms), and still slower for the higher-frequency vibration modes. One final effect of the bell is to change the spatial radiation of the sound. The lower frequencies tend to cling to the bell and are propagated in all directions, while the higher frequencies are beamed directly ahead.

For the woodwind instruments, the pattern of open holes changes the effective length of the hollow tube and also changes the radiation pattern of the sound. The lower-frequency waves are reflected back up the tube at the highest one or two open holes so that the lower-frequency energy can only escape from those open holes. In contrast, the higher-frequency waves penetrate down the entire instrument and radiate from all the open holes. What this means is that within the instrument tubing, the lower-frequency waves have far more energy. But this does not mean that the radiated sound is dominated by the low-frequency energy because the energy at higher frequencies is more efficiently radiated into the air. There is a "treble" boost. At lower frequency, the odd harmonics are stronger, but at higher frequencies the odd and even harmonics become equal in strength. The woodwinds have a pattern of attack times similar to that of the brasses: The lower-vibration modes reach maximum in 15–30 ms and the higher modes reach maximum 10–20 ms later.

Woodwinds have register holes that, when opened, reduce the amplitude at the lowest vibration mode. This makes it easier for the player to excite the higher-frequency vibration modes. The spectrum of the radiated sound differs between registers; at the higher registers, the pattern of the harmonics is variable.

Percussion Instruments and Impact Sounds

The wide range of complex and nonperiodic sounds for the percussion instruments follows the same vibration principles described above. All such instruments have many periodic vibration modes, and all complex vibrations can be understood as the summation of the vibration of the individual modes. The amplitude of each mode resulting from striking the instrument depends on the point of excitation (like that for a vibrating string), the area of the impact, and the strength of the excitation. For steel drums, multiple notes are created on the concave surface by pounding the location of each note to a different shape and thickness and then heat treating the entire surface. The excitation of a single note at one location excites many other notes and that gives the drums their unique sound.

On the whole, the attack times for percussion instruments are short; there is little or no steady state; and the decay times for each mode will be exponential although different. What this means is that the percentage of reduction of energy for each mode within each time period will be constant. If the energy decays to 50% within the first 50 ms, then it will decay another 50% from 50 to 100 ms (to 1/4), another 50% from 100 to 150 ms (to 1/8), and so on. Again, on the whole the higher-frequency vibration modes decay more rapidly because they involve more frequent and severe bending that creates greater internal friction.

Speaking and Singing: Air Vibrations Within Nonuniform Hollow Tubes

The voice is our most expressive instrument; it creates human interaction. But fundamentally, the voice is no different from any other instrument. The air expelled through the vocal folds creates the source vibration. The source vibration is coupled to the vocal tract, composed of the mouth, lips, tongue, and nose. The vocal tract acts as the sound body filter that selectively amplifies the spectrum of the source vibration. The resulting sound is then radiated from the mouth and nose.

Source Excitation

The vibration of the vocal cords creates the frequency spectrum of the source excitation. The speaker controls the vibration frequency of the vocal cords by varying the tension of the cords. The speaker can also control the spectrum of the source by varying the lung pressure. At low pressures, the flow pattern is weak, continuous, and sinusoidal; at higher pressures, the cords can remain closed for up to 70% of the period. The source becomes a series of air puffs. The similarities to other instruments should be obvious. The tension on the vocal cords controls the vibration frequency (stringed instruments). The oscillation of the vocal cords resembles the oscillations of a reed mouthpiece (clarinet) or the tensioned lips (trumpet). At greater source intensities, there is a relative increase in the strength of the higher harmonics due to the harmonic content of the air puffs. This is the same change found for the brass and woodwind instruments, and also for higher bowing pressures due to the narrower kink in the string brought about by stronger stick friction.

Vocal Tract Filter

We approximated the filter of the woodwind and brass instruments by a single hollow tube. If we do that with the vocal tract (and assume a constant diameter), it resembles a realistic configuration only for a neutral vowel sound. A better model of the vocal tract filter approximates the vocal tract as two (or more) uniform, cascaded tubes of different cross sections. The lengths and diameters of the tubes are variable and under the control of the speaker. A two-tube model and a more complex four-tube model are shown in figure 8.2.

The positions of the tongue, teeth, and jaw create the resonant cavities that generate the resonances of the vocal tract. The positions for the three vowels shown in figure 8.3 span the vowel space and are termed the *cardinal vowels*: /i/, tongue as far forward and as high as possible; /u/, tongue as far back and as high as possible; and /a/, tongue as far back and as low as

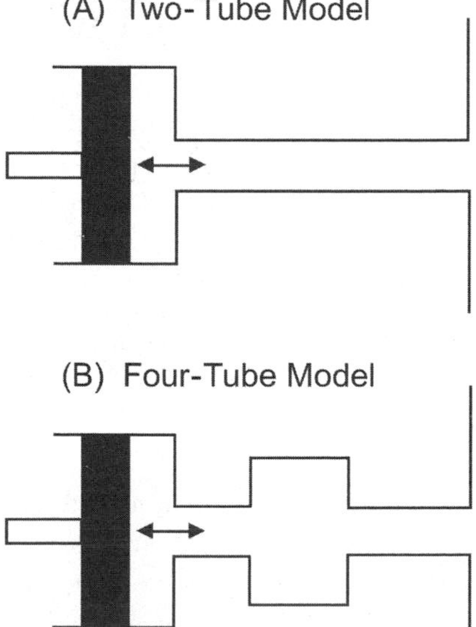

Figure 8.2. Two-tube and four-tube models for speech production. In order to produce different vowels, the sizes of the sections are varied to change the resonant frequencies.

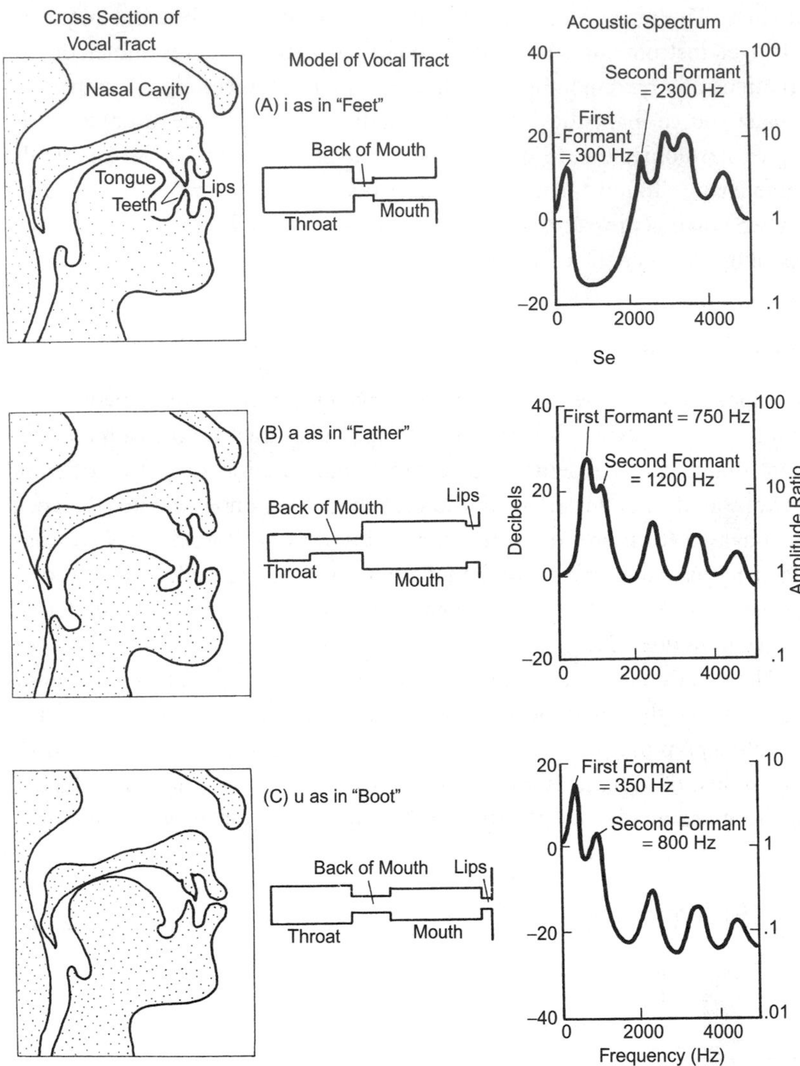

Figure 8.3. The articulatory process: the positions of the tongue, lips, teeth, and jaw create the resonant cavities that create the resonances of the vocal tract. Those resonances can be calculated on the basis of the size and shape of the cavities, and the theoretical acoustic spectrum for each vowel is shown in the right column. Adapted from *Language and Communication*, by G. A. Miller, 1981, San Francisco: Freeman.

possible. Traditionally, the cardinal vowels have been thought to underlie speaker normalization. Listeners use those vowels to correct for speaker differences due to the size of the vocal tract, speaking rate, accent and dialect, and so on. But in all likelihood, vowels are not recognized by the frequencies of their resonances but by the ongoing speech signal that is

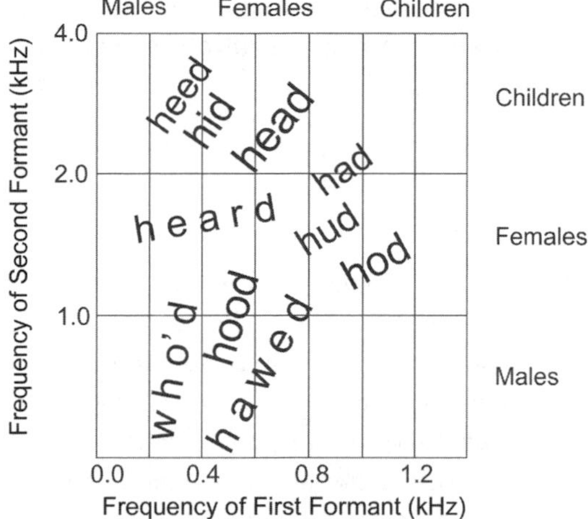

Figure 8.4. The range of frequencies for the first and second formants. The keywords contain each vowel. The frequencies of the two formants for adult males fall at the lower frequencies, the frequencies for females in the middle frequencies, and those for children at the higher frequencies. Adapted from "Control Methods Used in a Study of Vowels," by G. E. Peterson and H. E. Barney, 1952, *Journal of the Acoustical Society of America, 24*, 175–184.

interleaving and overlapping the acoustic signals for consonants and vowels in running speech. In fact, it may be best to think of the speech signal as being composed of two interleaved components, one for consonants and one for vowels. The flexibility of the vocal tract as opposed to the rigid construction of tubelike instruments allows singers to move their vocal tract resonances around to match the pitch of the sung vowels (Joliveau, Smith, & Wolfe, 2004). The first and second resonances for all the vowels are plotted against one another in figure 8.4.

The model for vowels assumes that the excitation occurred at the closed end of the two-tube model. If the excitation is applied forward of the point of constriction (as for the fricative consonant /s/), there are frequencies of maximum sound transmission (poles) but also frequencies of zero sound transmission (zeros). Often, the poles and zero are close in frequency and effectively balance each other; at other times the pole and zero frequencies differ, leading to increased sound radiation at the poles and decreased sound radiation at the zeros. For the fricative /s/, there is a zero at 3400 Hz and a pole at 6500 Hz in the spectra of /s/ in *sect* and *salve*. If the turbulent source is applied at the juncture of the two tubes as in /f/, the poles are the same but the zeros occur at multiples of the length of the larger-diameter tube. This makes the poles and zeros line up, and the resulting spectra are nearly uniform.

There is a large degree of coupling among the connecting tubes, so that it is a mistake to associate a specific vowel to a particular resonance of a particular vocal cavity. The pattern of the vibration modes is a characteristic of the system as a whole. Any given vowel could be produced by different arrangements of the cavity lengths.

Perceptual Cues

When I consider the various types of vibrating objects that create multiple, yet correlated, acoustic cues, the similarities between visual color perception leading to object recognition and auditory timbre perception leading to object recognition seem even more strained. The source vibratory modes (i.e., excitation) are not continuous across frequency and change as a function of the many factors detailed above. In many cases, the sound body vibration modes (i.e., the filter) are discrete and nonuniform across frequency. Those modes may be fixed by physical construction, such as that of a violin sound body, but in other cases the modes can be varied as when speaking or singing. Perhaps we could argue that in contrast to visually abstracting out the illumination source to identify the independent color reflectance filter, the simultaneous perception of the excitation source and sound body filter is necessary to identify auditory objects.

Still another difference is the phenomenology of the visual and auditory worlds. Our experience is that visual objects are stable, metaphorically either present or not present. Although there may be small differences in the time to detect surface reflectance across the spectrum when illumination begins, no perceptual model makes use of that information. Our experience of auditory objects is that they are events: They emerge against a background of unstructured acoustical energy, continue for various durations, and then fade into silence.[4] Much of our knowledge about an auditory object comes from changes in the sound over time. It is those changes in the amplitude of the vibratory modes due to the damping and coupling among the modes that give us information about the (resonant) properties of the object producing the sound.

Below I describe some of the time-varying and steady-state characteristics of the radiated sound that could be used to infer the properties of the object. Remember that these characteristics are interrelated, not a set of independent cues. Research to the present suggests that the changes in amplitude of the individual vibration modes over the duration of the sound

4. Speech is characterized by the smoothly changing F_0 and formant frequencies that occur in consonant-vowel or vowel-consonant transitions and a looser rhythmic structure. Classical western instrumental music is characterized by discrete pitch changes that occur abruptly between notes and a rather strict metric rhythm.

(termed the *amplitude envelopes*) are the critical acoustic information. (Sometimes the term amplitude envelope refers to amplitude of the entire sound and not the amplitudes of individual frequencies.)

However, before summarizing the evolving spectral envelope, it is worth considering the usefulness of pitch, loudness, and noisiness as perceptual cues. All give information about the size and physical construction of the object. Yet although pitch, loudness, and noisiness may be useful for the categorization of sounds, they seem restricted in their ability to allow the identification of specific objects. For example, the fundamental frequency of the vocal fold vibration is the most important cue for identifying male, female, and child speakers, and the pitch range and variation in loudness can provide additional information about the age and size of the source. But neither pitch nor loudness uniquely specifies an individual. Helmholtz (1877) describes the seamless transition between noise and tones (and that was part of the argument in chapter 1). Sound sources can be understood to fall somewhere on that continuum. At one extreme, the sound is all noise, for example snare drums, fan noise, gurgling of fluids, and computer noise; at the other extreme, the sound is the superposition only of sinusoidal waves. Most sources fall between the ends: Flutes are characterized by a steady noise due to blowing across the mouthpiece opening; voices may be characterized by breathiness due to incomplete closure of the vocal folds; and other sources may be characterized by an initial noisy sound that evolves into a stronger pitch sound such as the initial metallic sounds for struck triangles and the initial scratchy bowing sounds before the bow catches the string and generates a musical note. But, again, noisiness seems restricted to identifying types of sounds.

Although the amplitude envelope changes smoothly, we can operationally define three parts: (1) the onset, (2) the steady state, and (3) the decay. For each part, the goal is to derive acoustic properties that correlate with the perceived qualities of the sounds.

The Onset of the Sound

The rise or attack time from the initiation of excitation until the sound reaches its maximum amplitude is determined by the manner of excitation and the damping of the vibration modes. If the damping is similar for all the modes, then the attack time for all the frequency components is similar and the amplitudes increase synchronously. If the damping differs, then the attack times of the components will differ, and the amplitudes of the components can follow significantly different trajectories. In spite of the possible differences in onset among the frequency components, the onset duration usually is measured by the time it takes for the entire sound to increase from its initiation to its maximum amplitude.

The Steady State at Maximum Amplitude

In reality, the sound at maximum intensity is not steady at all. There are dynamic changes in the frequency and amplitude of the vibration modes due to unstable physical processes as well as the performer's intentions. We can derive measures that reflect both the average and dynamic properties in the steady-state segment.

1. The most commonly used average property of the steady state is the spectral centroid, a measure of the energy distribution among the frequency components. A simple way of computing the spectral centroid is the weighted average of the amplitudes of the components:

$$\text{Spectral centroid frequency} = \sum a_i f_i / \sum a_i \qquad (8.2)$$

where a_i and f_i are the amplitudes and frequencies of each harmonic or partial of the sound.

While the spectral centroid captures the balance point of the amplitudes, it is incomplete because many different spectral distributions will yield the same frequency. For example, a sound with equal amplitudes at 400, 500, and 600 Hz will have the same centroid as a sound with equal amplitudes at 100, 500, and 900 Hz. Moreover, a sound with equal amplitude at every frequency component can have the same centroid as another sound with drastically unequal amplitudes at the component frequencies. For these reasons, several other measures have been used.

2. The irregularity in amplitude among the spectral components is another way to characterize the steady state. For example, the relative strength of odd and even harmonics defines different types of horns, and an extreme jaggedness of amplitudes indicates a complex resonance structure such as that found for stringed instruments. In addition, variation in the frequency ratios among the components can distinguish between continuously driven instruments (bowed strings, wind instruments, and voices) and impulsive instruments (piano, plucked strings). J. C. Brown (1996) found that for continuously driven instruments, the components were phase-locked and the frequencies occurred at nearly integer ratios. For impulsive instruments, the components were not related by integer ratios. After the impulse, each vibration mode decayed independently, and differences in damping caused the frequencies to deviate out of an integer relationship.

3. The spectral spread of the amplitudes of the harmonics is yet another measure. Suppose we have two sounds with components at 100, 500, and 900 Hz. For the first sound the amplitudes are 1, 4, and 1, while for the second sound the amplitudes are 4, 1, and 4. The energy is spread more widely for the second sound, and the two sounds, in spite of identical centroids (500 Hz) and spectral irregularity, will sound different.

4. The variation in the frequency of the spectral centroid is one measure of the dynamic properties of the steady state. The frequency of the spectral centroid can be determined at different time points and the variance of those values calculated. The variation in the frequency of the spectral centroid probably is due to correlated frequency variation among the harmonics. The source frequency variation will also change the amplitude of the harmonics as the source frequencies move in and out of the sound body resonances.

5. The frequency of the spectral components may change independently so that the frequency of the spectral centroid is not affected. Nevertheless, the variation of the components gives sounds a warm quality that is missing in synthesized instruments. To quantify this variation, we can measure the frequency variation of each component and average those variances in some way.

Decay From the End of the Steady State to Inaudibility

There are significant acoustic differences in decay time among materials. A struck metal bar will decay far more slowly than a struck clay bar. Moreover, spectral components may decay at different rates. For percussion and stringed instruments (including the piano), the higher-frequency components decay more rapidly due to increased friction, so that the sound quality becomes purer as it decays and softens.

Although the vast majority of research has made use of single sounds, that is clearly unrepresentative of natural occurrences. The onset, steady state, and decay are useful for describing single sounds, but we live in an evolving auditory world with overlapping sounds. Given that several sources may sound alike at times, it may be that the consistency or change in sound quality at different pitches and amplitudes is necessary to identify the source. This is the same indeterminacy discussed for color, and computational models needing multiple views to derive surface color are analogous to arguing that several sounds are needed to derive the source.

Furthermore, sources have different rhythms and timings. Some sources produce continuous sounds (sawing); others oscillate in intensity (motorcycle engines); and others are simply a sequence of short discrete sounds (faucet dripping, footsteps). The change in the rhythm of the sounds indicates whether we have repaired the drip or made it worse. The extent of the overlap of the offset of one sound and the onset of the next sound is still another cue to source identity. The degree of overlap is going to be a function of the damping of the decay and the following onset (and a function of the reverberation of the environment).

What can we take away from this? First, there are a large number of possible acoustic cues that are not independent due to the interlocking of the source and filter in sound production. These cues are not invariant and will change across method of excitation, pitch, duration, intensity, and tempo. In addition, performers may vary the sound quality by excitation technique, intonation, or expressive emphasis. Second, there are no pure cues—all cues exist within a context defined by all the other cues. In exactly the same way, there are no pure colors; every color exists within a context.

What are the perceptual consequences to the listener of the multiple interactive cues? First, no single cue uniquely determines object identification. Any single cue will afford some level of performance, and multiple cues will produce better performance than any specific cue. Cues are redundant and substitutable due to production interactions. This redundancy makes performance robust. Listeners rarely make horrible errors, and performance will degrade gracefully in noisy conditions. Second, the effectiveness and importance of any cue will depend on the context, and the level of performance will depend on the context and the task. Listeners should learn to make use of whatever cues lead to best performance for a specific set of objects in a specific context. Comparisons between humans and machines are ambiguous; in some cases humans outperform machines, and in others the reverse occurs (J. C. Brown, 1999; J. C. Brown, Houix, & McAdams, 2001). There is no evidence that listeners can identify and then make use of the most invariant or most stable cues. Again, this conclusion is identical to that for color vision (Kraft & Brainard, 1999).

All of the above is going to make it difficult to summarize research findings; any one finding will be the result of one context out of many possible ones. It is important to keep in mind the differences between visual color experiments and auditory timbre experiments. In the color experiments, the subject's task was to adjust the hue of the test color to equal that of the standard. Unfortunately, such a matching task is impossible in timbre experiments because the many hair cell receptors would require the subject to manipulate a huge number of frequencies. Thus, what we find are experiments that employ multidimensional scaling techniques to isolate the acoustic properties that determine the perceived differences between two sounds or experiments that investigate the ability to identify which instrument, speaker, singer, or natural object produced a given sound.

Timbre as a Sound Quality

Multidimensional Scaling

I start with scaling experiments that attempt to uncover the perceptual dimensions and their acoustic correlates that underlie differences in sound timbre. With rare exceptions, the typical similarity judgment experiment induces listeners to treat the stimuli as acoustic sounds, not as objects. The dimensional space rarely shows object categories.

McAdams, Winsberg, Donnadieu, DeSoete, and Krimphoff (1995) used an extended version of multidimensional scaling that yielded a common Euclidean dimensional space for all simulated instrumental sounds, a value for the specificity for each sound, and a grouping of subjects into classes with similar response profiles. The grouping of the subjects into a small number of classes is a compromise between treating all subjects as being equivalent and treating each subject as having a unique profile. By comparing the groups, it is possible to determine if there is a relationship between the subject's musical background (or any biographical category) and the utilization of the different acoustical properties in judging timbre similarity.

The 18 stimuli were synthesized electronically. Twelve stimuli imitated traditional instruments and six were designed to imitate hybrid instruments, such as a trumpar, designed to capture the perceptual characteristics of a trumpet and a guitar. The duration of the majority of stimuli was about 500 ms, although several were 1,000 ms. The instructions were made deliberately vague and listeners simply were told to judge the similarity between each pair of sounds.

The best solution required three common dimensions and a specificity for each instrument. A representation of the instruments in the three-dimensional space is shown in figure 8.5.

The position of the instruments along the first dimension was correlated with the attack or rise time of the sounds. Struck or impulsive instruments with short rise times fell at one end of the continuum, while wind instruments with longer rise times fell at the other end. We do not actually compare the attack time of two instruments in making such similarity judgments. What we compare is the perceptual consequences of the differences in the acoustic wave due to the differences in attack times. Instruments with short rise times may have an initial impact sound composed of many frequencies that reach their maximums within a short time span. (A short-impulse excitation such as plucking a string has energy at all frequencies and will set in motion all the vibration modes of the filter at the same time.) There may be an emergent pitch as the higher-frequency resonance modes decay more rapidly. In contrast, instruments with longer rise times may have an attack in which the component frequencies reach their maximums along different time courses, creating an evolving quality.

The position of the instruments along the second dimension was correlated with the spectral centroid of the sounds, essentially a measure of the amount of energy in the higher frequencies (perceptual brightness). Finally, the position of the sounds along the third dimension was correlated with the spectral flux of the harmonics. Spectral flux is a measure of the similarity (i.e., correlation) of the amplitude spectra of the harmonics at adjacent time

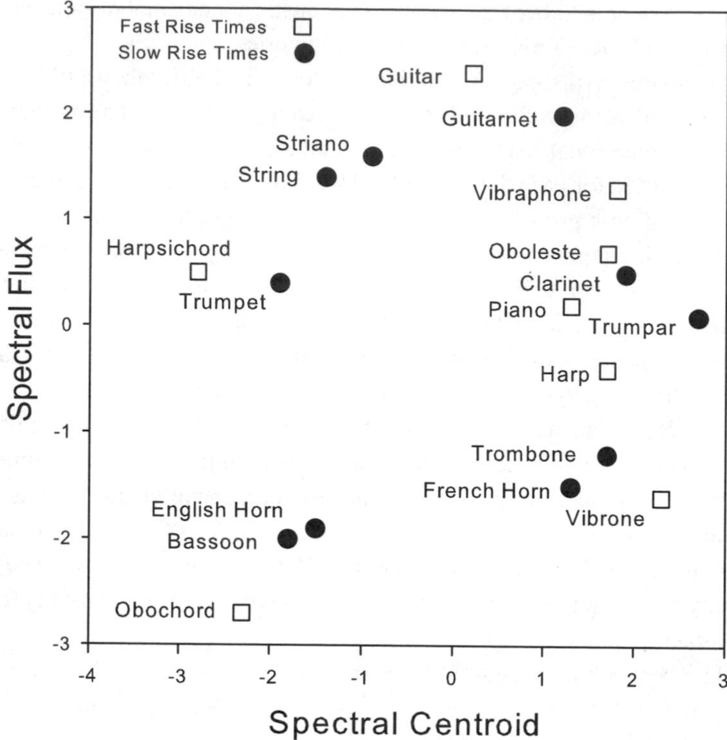

Figure 8.5. The multidimensional space for the set of simulated real and hybrid instruments used by McAdams et al. (1995). The first dimension was attack time; differences in attack time formed two categories, represented by squares (fast) and circles (slow) and the two categories would be at opposite ends of the first dimension. The second dimension (x axis) was the frequency of the spectral centroid, and the third dimension (y axis) was a measure of the spectral flux. The six hybrid instruments in the figure are: trumpar, trumpet-guitar; oboleste, oboe-celeste; striano, bowed string-piano; vibrone, vibraphone-trombone; obochord, oboe-harpsichord; guitarnet, guitar-clarinet. Adapted from "Perceptual Scaling of Synthesized Musical Timbres: Common Dimensions, Specificities, and Latent Subject Classes," by S. McAdams, S. Winsberg, S. Donnadieu, G. DeSoete, & J. Krimphoff, 1995, *Psychological Research, 58*, 177–192.

points. The amplitude spectrum at one time point is a list of the amplitudes of perhaps 10 to 12 harmonics. The amplitude spectra are determined for time windows t_0, t_1, t_2, and so on. The correlation between the amplitudes of those 10 to 12 harmonics is calculated at t_0 and t_1, at t_1 and t_2, and so on. The spectral flux is the average of those correlations and will be high when the relative amplitudes of the harmonics are constant across time. The third dimension separates the woodwind instruments (constant amplitude of each harmonic) from the brass instruments (variable amplitude of each harmonic). The fit of the acoustic representation for the spectral flux was weakest (the trumpet is obviously misplaced). The majority of subjects (60%) weighted each of the three common dimensions equally. The remaining listeners either weighted attack time most heavily or weighted spectral centroid and spectral flux equally. Musical background did not differentiate the listeners.

The degree of specificity was not predictable from instrument class, and the hybrid instruments did not differ from the simulated instruments. The authors suggested that two types of sound qualities determine specificity: (1) qualities that vary in degree, such as raspiness, inharmonicity, or hollowness; and (2) qualities that are discrete, such as presence of a thud or damped offset.

Subsequently, Marozeau, de Cheveigne, McAdams, and Winsberg (2003) investigated whether the dimensional representation of sound quality was equivalent at different notes. There were two major conditions. In the first, listeners judged the difference between two instruments playing the same note. Three different notes within one octave were used in separate experiments. In the second, listeners judged the difference between two instruments playing different notes, the maximum note difference being slightly less than an octave. The similarity judgments were quite consistent across conditions. First, the three perceptual dimensions derived in all conditions were identical. The first was a measure of attack time (termed *impulsiveness* here); the second was a measure of the spectral centroid; and the third dimension was spectral spread. Thus, the first two dimensions are identical to those found by McAdams et al. (1995). The third dimension found by McAdams et al. correlated with spectral flux in contrast to spectral spread, but we would expect some differences as a function of the particular instruments used. Second, if both instruments played the same note, the spatial arrangement of the instruments at the three different notes tended to be similar. When the notes played by the two instruments differed by 11 semitones, there were significant shifts for roughly half of the instruments, as shown in figure 8.6.

The results of McAdams et al. (1995) and Marozeau et al. (2003) demonstrate that the dissimilarity in the perceived sound quality between two instrumental notes can be represented by the temporal and spectral acoustic properties of the sounds. The research outcomes reviewed below suggest that differences in attack time and the frequency of the spectral centroid consistently covary with perceptual judgments, but that differences in other acoustic measures such as spectral flux or spectral spread affect judgments only in specific contexts determined by the individual sounds themselves.

Spectral Differences

Every scaling experiment has found that the predominant factor in judged similarity is differences in the amplitudes of the component frequencies,

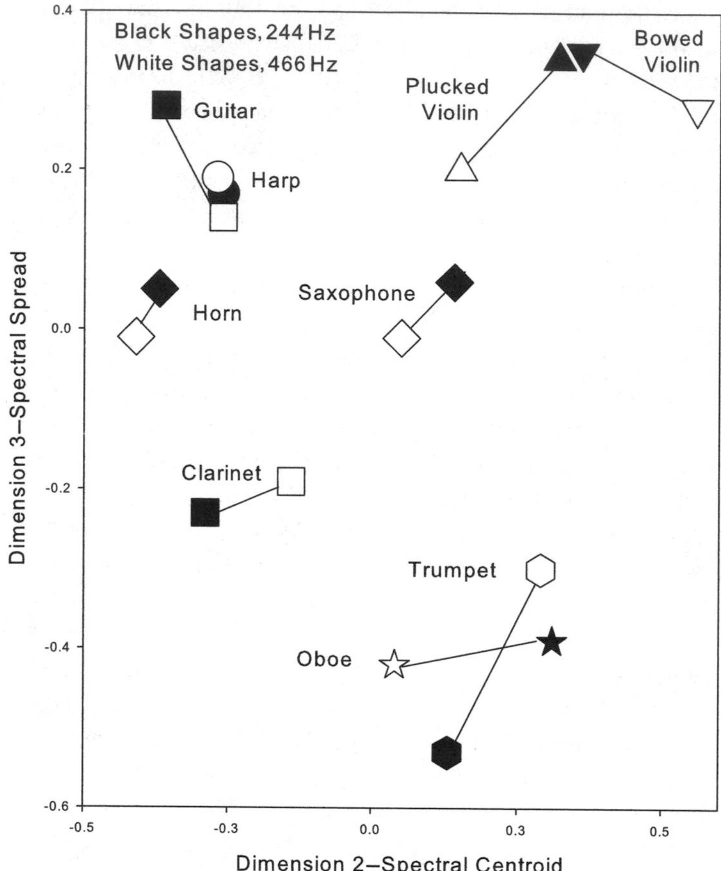

Figure 8.6. The multidimensional representation for the instruments used by Marozeau et al. (2003). The two notes from each instrument were separated by 11 semitones. The first dimension, not shown, was attack time, which separated the guitar, harp, and plucked violin (short attack time) from the rest of the instruments. The second and third dimensions were spectral centroid and spectral spread. Data courtesy of Dr. Jeremy Marozeau.

typically measured by the frequency of the spectral centroid. (It should be kept in mind that the centroid is a weighted average, and many different combinations could have the identical centroid frequency.) For both real and simulated instrumental sounds (Lakatos, 2000; Wedin & Goude, 1972), complex tones (Plomp, 1975), and simulated sonar signals (Howard, 1977), the difference in the frequency of the spectral centroid was the most important factor in judged dissimilarity.

For speaking and singing, the spectral centroid predicts the similarity between the same vowel spoken or sung by different individuals and also predicts the similarity between different vowels spoken or sung by the same individual (Bloothooft & Plomp, 1988). Erickson (2003) asked experienced choral directors and musically untrained listeners to judge the similarity among sung vowels at different pitches. The judges were supposed to disregard the pitch differences and base their judgments solely on the differences in voice quality. Nonetheless, judges were unable to disregard pitch, and pitch differences were the first dimension. The second dimension was based on the spectral centroid. The centroid predicted the perceived dissimilarity between singers in different voice classes even at the ends of the singing range where there was only a small number of harmonics.

In prior work, Grey and Gordon (1978) exchanged the relative maximum amplitudes of the harmonics between instruments (i.e., the spectral shapes) but did not change the attack and decay timings. Such an exchange is shown in figure 8.7. Similarity judgments were obtained and compared to those for the original unaltered notes. The pairs of notes that exchanged spectral shape did swap positions on the spectral envelope dimension. The notes did not swap position on the temporal dimensions because, in fact, the temporal characteristics were unchanged. The correlation between the acoustic exchange and perceptual swap supports the contention that spectral shape is a predominant factor in similarity judgments.

J. C. Brown (1999) investigated a different question: Can differences in the spectrum predict how accurately listeners distinguish between oboes and saxophones? To do so, Brown collected short segments of oboe and saxophone sounds from different sources, and listeners categorized each segment. This is in contrast to previous work that used but one fixed note

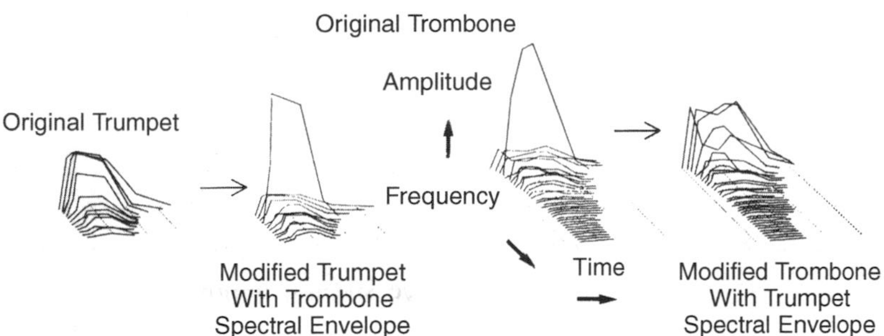

Figure 8.7. Exchange of spectral envelopes between the trumpet (far left) and trombone (third from left) to form the modified trumpet (second from left) and trombone (far right). Note that only the common harmonics trade peak amplitude values; hence, the original frequency bandwidths (number of harmonics) are retained. Adapted from *Listening: An Introduction to the Perception of Auditory Events*, by S. Handel, 1989, Cambridge, MA: MIT Press.

for each instrument. The results indicated that listeners were quite accurate, roughly 85% to 90% correct.

Using the same sounds, human performance was compared to a classification model that used only spectral information. The classification model compared each test sound to a set of prototypical spectra for both the oboe and saxophone. To derive prototypical instruments, Brown (1999) used oboe and saxophone passages (about 1 min in length) to derive an overall spectral envelope averaged across notes. The overall envelope portrays the sets of overlapping sound body resonances that amplify the excitation in different frequency ranges. These overlapping resonances are termed *formants*, and a formant in the 800–1000 Hz range would amplify the fourth harmonic of 200–250 Hz excitations, the third harmonic of 300–333 Hz excitations, and the second harmonic of 400–500 Hz excitations and 800–1000 Hz fundamental excitations. Thus, across a set of notes, there would be consistent energy in the 800–1000 Hz range and that formant would be part of the signature of a particular instrument.

To measure the performance of the computer model, the short segments presented to the listeners were partitioned into 23 ms windows, and the spectral envelopes of the windows were compared to the prototypical envelopes. The computer model then calculated the likelihood that the segment was played by the oboe or by the saxophone. Overall, the computer was better than human listeners at identifying the oboe but equal at identifying the saxophone. The success of the computer model demonstrates that the spectra information was sufficient to distinguish between the two instruments, but of course it does not unambiguously demonstrate that human listeners are making use of the same information.

In subsequent work, J. C. Brown et al. (2001) used four wind instruments, oboe, saxophone, clarinet, and flute. The results were similar to the previous work: human and computer identification were roughly identical. For the computer model, the most effective spectral information was the shape of the spectrum due to overlapping resonances or the jaggedness of the spectrum measured by the variation in the amplitudes of the harmonics. A detailed spectral envelope description yielded better performance than just the frequency of the spectral centroid, which is based on only one number.

Two studies illustrate that the spectral envelope can be used to discriminate among natural events. Freed (1990) investigated whether listeners could judge the hardness of mallets when they struck aluminum cooking pots. The mallets were made of metal, wood, rubber, cloth-covered wood, felt, and felt-covered rubber. The judges based their ratings on the spectra. Mallets were judged as hard if the sound energy initially was concentrated at higher frequencies and then shifted to lower frequencies over time (about 300 ms). As can be imagined easily, the harder mallets created a louder sound, which also affected the hardness judgments. X. Li, Logan, and

Pastore (1991) investigated whether listeners could judge gender by the sounds of walking. Males and females used shoes with leather soles and solid synthetic heels and walked naturally across a hardwood stage. Listeners judged the walkers to be male if there was more low-frequency and less high-frequency energy, based on the belief that males were taller and heavier and had bigger shoes. This is a somewhat incorrect belief, as the size of the person will not directly affect the vibration of the hardwood floor. Shoe size, however, will affect the floor resonances, as bigger shoes will tend to still higher-frequency vibration modes.

Onset (Attack Time) Differences

Lakatos (2000) used three sets of instruments: a pitched set contained wind, string, and pianolike instruments; a percussion set containing drums, cymbals, marimbas, and vibraphones; and a combination set that included a subset of the pitched and percussion instruments. For each set, one dimension was highly correlated with the rise times of the instruments. For the pitched instruments, the struck piano, harp, and harpsichord with short rise times differed from the other instruments, while for the percussion instruments the bowed cymbal and bowed vibraphone with long rise times differed from the other instruments. If those instruments are excluded, being of a somewhat different type, rise time no longer affects the similarity judgments. As argued above, the method of excitation and resulting rise time are unimportant in themselves; they are indicants that the rapid excitation created a perceptible impulse transient made up of nonharmonic frequencies. (A very rapid-impact excitation contains energy at all frequencies.)

Spectral Envelope Variation

The initial work demonstrating the importance of the temporal properties of the spectral envelope was that of Grey (1977). He created rather short-duration simulated instrumental sounds (roughly 300 ms) that consisted mainly of the attack and decay portions. Two of the three dimensions appeared to be based on the temporal evolution of the sounds. The first temporal dimension was characterized by the synchrony of the higher-frequency harmonics—the harmonics of woodwinds started and decayed at the same time, while the upper harmonics of strings had different patterns of attack and decay. The second temporal dimension was characterized by the quality of the initial attack—reed woodwinds had low-amplitude high-frequency inharmonic energy (due to stabilizing the reed vibration), while brass instruments had dominant lower harmonics. These sounds were really like chirps, so that we might expect that the temporal characteristics would be dominant. Grey stated that longer notes yielded different multidimensional spatial configurations in which those temporal dimensions did not emerge.

Another measure of spectral flux essentially refers to the change in the shape of the spectral envelope over time. This change could be due to variations in the source excitation, different damping of the filter's resonance modes (see Freed, 1990, described above), or a performer's use of vibrato, which creates both frequency and amplitude modulations. Such variation is easily perceived, and McAdams, Beauchamp, Meneguzzi (1999) demonstrated that listeners consistently discriminated between simulated instrumental sounds that contained normal spectral flux and those in which the flux was eliminated by making the ratios among pairs of harmonics constant across the sound duration. Moreover, Horner, Beauchamp, and So (2004) found that for instruments with high levels of spectral flux, it was difficult to detect added random alterations in the amplitude of the harmonics (an expected outcome from a signal detection perspective).

However, spectral flux does not emerge consistently in the multidimensional solutions. For example, a measure of spectral variation was found to weakly correlate to the third dimension by McAdams et al. (1995), but such a measure was not found by Lakatos (2000) using sets of stimuli that might be expected to show that variation. Erickson (2003), using classically trained mezzo-soprano and soprano singers, found that rate of vibrato was weakly correlated to a third dimension for experienced choral directors, but not for inexperienced judges. The reason for this inconsistency may be the scaling method itself. The scaling procedure tries to find the minimum number of dimensions to account for the judged similarity, and the predominant importance of the onset timing and the spectral centroid may hide the effect of spectral flux.

In an identification task, Kendall (1986) completely eliminated the possibility of any spectral flux. Kendall isolated one cycle and then repeated that cycle continuously for the entire duration of the steady-state component. He found that identification of instruments was poorer for the single-cycle simulations than for the natural instrument. It appears that spectral flux is important for recognizing an instrument (or discriminating among simulated sounds) but not as relevant for judging similarity between sounds.

Individual Differences

In nearly all work to date, the differences between untrained and trained listeners (e.g., musicians, classical singers, choral directors) have been small and variable. For example, Lakatos (2000), using the same statistical procedure as McAdams et al. (1995), did not find any effects of musical experience. Erickson (2003) found that when untrained listeners and choral directors judged the similarity between sung vowels of classical singers, the first two dimensions were identical: pitch and frequency of the spectral centroid. The choral directors did, however, also use the vibrato frequency to judge similarity.

I would argue that the lack of effect due to experience is due to the task itself. Regardless of experience, all subjects were judging the difference in terms of acoustic differences and not in terms of the source or musical implications. Only two sounds were presented at one time, and the pairs were presented in a random order. Listeners were instructed to judge the difference between the sounds and not commit the stimulus error of judging the difference between the sources. This outcome can be contrasted to the typical results comparing untrained and trained listeners in tasks involving musical tonality. In such tasks, untrained listeners make their judgments in terms of the difference in pitch, while trained listeners make their judgments in terms of the musical intervals. Thus, untrained listeners are treating pitch and timbre differences acoustically, while explicit training allows trained listeners to treat intervals as entities (Krumhansl, 2000).

The effect of musical training on identification and discrimination tasks has also been small (e.g., Brown et al., 2001). Erickson, Perry, and Handel (2001) found that experienced singers were only slightly more accurate in detecting which of three vowels sung at different pitches was produced by the "oddball" singer. Moreover, this difference disappeared when the range in pitches exceeded one octave. In similar fashion, Lutfi, Oh, Storm, and Alexander (2005) found no differences among practiced listeners, musicians, and nonmusicians in distinguishing between actual and synthesized impact sounds.

Timbre as a Source Variable

We would expect that there would be a close coupling between the physical properties of objects and the acoustical properties of the resulting sounds and that that coupling should enable the listener to identify the source. This emphasis on identifying the source of a sound may result in different ways of listening than when a subject is listening for the quality or the meaning of the sound. Of course, the source itself can have inherent meaning: something to run toward or run away from, for example.

Moreover, we would expect the context, the prior probabilities of different sounds, higher-level cognitive factors such as memory and attention, and individual differences among the listeners to be important factors in determining the ability to identify the source. Although there seem to be consistent acoustic properties that correlate with similarity judgments, this does not seem to be the case for source identification. Listeners will judge widely different sounds as coming from the same event (e.g., walking) or coming from the same source (e.g., singing or piano notes). It may be that there is an acoustical invariant that occurs only for every sound from one source, but I doubt that. I prefer to think that listeners develop transformations or trajectories that link the sounds at different frequencies, intensities, and sound qualities that are produced by one source or type of action.

If this conceptualization is correct, then any invariants will not be found at a single pitch and loudness. Moreover, it is unclear whether the sound qualities found at one note using multidimensional scaling are useful for source identification. Some temporal properties such as onset time would be useful because they would characterize different classes of instruments across the playing range. Other spectral properties such as the frequency centroid or spectral spread would not be useful because they can change dramatically across the playing range. Right now, the answer is unknown.

Single Events

Many studies have investigated the identification of objects, including instruments, speakers, and environmental events. Performance varies dramatically depending on the objects, the stimulus presentation conditions, listeners' prior knowledge about the possible objects, and so on. On the whole, identification is reasonably good, although it is quite difficult to assess the relative effects of any the above factors. Listeners will make use of whatever acoustic properties make the sounds most discriminable in the experimental context.

Gaver (1993) suggested a way of organizing environmental events in terms of physical actions. The three major categories are: (1) vibrating objects due to impacts, scraping, or other physical actions; (2) aerodynamic sounds due to explosions or continuous excitation; and (3) liquid sounds due to dripping or splashing. Although this hierarchy does not necessarily separate events in terms of their acoustic properties, we would expect a strong relation between the physical events and their acoustic properties. There is not a perfect correspondence between this classification and the acoustic properties, particularly with respect to rhythmic patterning, but this hierarchy does have heuristic value.

The research on timbre as a sound quality suggested that the acoustic properties could be organized into one class dealing with the temporal properties, particularly onset time, and a second class dealing with the spectral properties. Such a split will prove useful in this section, as long as we expand our conception of the temporal properties to include rhythmic patterning within individual sounds as well as between sounds and as long as we expand our conception of the spectral properties to include noise.

Rhythmic patterning usually gives information about the actions that generated the sound, and the spectral properties usually give information about the object material.

Rhythmic Patterning

Vanderveer (1979) recorded events like hammering, finger snapping, crumpling paper, whistling, and walking up and down stairs and asked listeners to group similar sounds. She concluded that the most salient acoustic determinants of similarity were: (a) the temporal patterning of the sounds, including repetitive sounds such as hammering, continuous rough sounds of saws, the crackling of shuffling cards, and repeated ringing sounds that decrease in amplitude such as a spoon bouncing off a teacup; and (b) spectral properties due to the resonance, size, and physical characteristics of particular objects, surfaces, and substances, such as metal, paper, and things with a rough texture. Temporal patterning can distinguish different actions on the same material, such as crumpling versus ripping paper, while the spectral properties can distinguish the same action on different materials, such as banging a block of metal or of wood.[5]

W. H. J. Warren and Verbrugge (1984) demonstrated that time-varying spectral patterning provides the information needed to distinguish between bouncing objects and breaking objects. Actually, each piece of a broken bottle bounces, so the difference is between one bouncing object and the many bouncing pieces of the broken object. The acoustic information for bouncing is that the spectral content is identical for each impact, although the sound will decrease in intensity and the interval between impacts will shorten. The acoustic information for breaking is a set of overlapping bouncing sequences in which each sequence represents one broken piece, and each one has a different damped pattern. The sounds coming from each piece will alternate in seemingly random fashion. W. H. J. Warren and Verbrugge found that bouncing was perceived when the successive sounds had the same spectral content and that breaking was perceived when the successive sounds had distinct spectral properties signifying the multiple pieces of a broken object.

Spectral Properties

One approach to determine which spectral properties underlie the identification of environmental sounds is to filter the sounds into frequency bands

5. Listeners can be misled, particularly by the tempo of the sounds. Listeners expect women to walk faster than men (X. Li et al., 1991) and men to clap more slowly than women (Repp, 1987). Neither belief is correct.

and measure identification performance using only those frequencies. Gygi et al. (2004) chose 70 different sounds and used six different band-pass filters (150–300, 300–600, 600–1200, 1200–2400, 2400–4800, and 4800–9600 Hz). On the whole, identification was better using the 1200–2400 Hz and 2400–4800 Hz filters. But there were many sounds that did not follow this pattern, and for each sound, the energy in each band did not predict which bands led to the best identification.

Gygi et al. (2004) then investigated whether the amplitude variation within a frequency band influenced the ability to identify the sounds. To do this, first the amplitude envelope for the band was calculated. This envelope then multiplied a segment of noise to create a sound that had the identical amplitude envelope but a flat uniform frequency spectrum. There were two conditions. In the first, the amplitude envelope was determined for the sound as a whole, and that envelope multiplied a wide-band noise segment. In the second, the amplitude envelope was calculated for the frequencies within each of the six band-pass filters. Those amplitudes then multiplied segments of equivalent band-pass noise, and finally all of the six amplitude-modulated noise segments were summed together. In this condition, there will be some frequency information due to the segments of band-pass noise. The identification performance was surprisingly good. Experienced listeners were able to identify 46% of the sounds using the single overall envelope. Across two days of testing, inexperienced listeners improved from 13% to 23% for the single envelope and from 36% to 66% for the sum of six envelopes. The sounds that improved most across days were inharmonic sounds with strong temporal patterning (e.g., helicopter, gallop) and the sounds that were identified better with the six filter envelopes were those with strong harmonic components (e.g., bird, dog). Thus, the temporal variation of the amplitude, even without frequency information, was sufficient to identify sound sources and events. Listeners' experience was critical, presumably because they learn to abstract the crucial temporal variation.

It is clear from these results that we cannot simply talk about environmental objects and events. They must be broken into subclasses along acoustic dimensions (e.g., harmonic versus inharmonic; strength of temporal structure), or on the basis of the nature of sound production as outlined by Gaver (1993) above, because listeners presumably have some a priori ideas of the possible causes of a sound. Alternately, the objects and events can be classified on the basis of "semantic" or expressive features.

Obviously, we would expect the acoustic properties and event-related properties to covary. The research by Vanderveer (1979), X. Li et al. (1991) and W. H. J. Warren and Verbrugge (1984) described above supports this assertion. Several more recent studies further confirm that spectral properties can be used to identify actions and the material properties of objects.

1. Lakatos, McAdams, and Causse (1997) attempted to determine the acoustic properties that enabled listeners to distinguish the width:height ratios of metal and wooden bars of constant length. Hitting the center of the metal bars with a steel hammer and the center of the wooden bars with a hard resin hammer generated the sounds. The listener's task was to identify the presentation order of two bars from a visual schematic of the exact width and height of the two bars.

The percentage correct was used as a measure of similarity, and the resulting multidimensional space contained two dimensions for the metal bars but only one for the wooden bars. The first dimension, for both the metal and wooden bars, correlated with the width:height ratios, and the second dimension, for the metal bars, correlated with the spectral centroid of the struck bar. Lakatos et al. (1997) then attempted to find the acoustic cues that correlated with the width:height ratios. As described at the beginning of the chapter, extended surfaces such as bars and plates can vibrate independently in several ways: by bending along the width and height axes as well as twisting along the length axis. The bending frequency in one plane is determined by the width; the bending frequency in the other plane is determined by the height; and the frequency of the twisting vibration is determined by the width:height ratio. The lowest frequency of the twisting vibration and the difference in the lowest frequencies of two bending vibrations were highly correlated to the width:height ratios for the metal bars. The correlations were lower for the wooden bars because the twisting vibrations were weak or missing due to the irregularity and higher damping of the wood. In sum, there are spectral properties that can be used to identify whether the sound came from a block with a low width:height ratio, or with a high ratio.

2. Subsequently, Kunkler-Peck and Turvey (2000) investigated whether inexperienced listeners could independently identify the length and width of thin struck steel, wood, and Plexiglas plates. The plates were squares (48 cm per side), slightly taller rectangles (height 60 cm, width 36 cm), or very tall rectangles (height 90 cm, width 25.4 cm). After the plate was struck, the listeners judged one of the two dimensions. For both the steel and wood plates, the judgments were linearly related to the actual size, although they were not very accurate. For example, the listeners judged the length of the very tall rectangle to be less than 50 cm even though it was about 90 cm. For the Plexiglas plates, the length and width judgments did not vary much, possibly due to the greater damping of the Plexiglas.

Kunkler-Peck and Turvey (2000) calculated the frequency of the vibration modes of the plates and found that the frequency of the first three even modes correlated most closely with the judgments of perceived length. The correlations were nearly identical for the three modes, suggesting that there was redundant information and that the listeners could attend to only one and still do as well.

One interesting phenomenon that occurs with struck objects is that the resulting sound becomes split into two parts, one representing the striking object and the second representing the struck object. In Freed (1990), the hardness of the struck pots did not affect the listener's judgments of the hardness of the mallets. Thus it appears that the listeners did split the impact sound. This type of split in vision has been termed *phenomenal scission* or *double representation.* The paradigmatic case is transparency where a surface is perceived as the superposition of two surfaces, the upper one being transparent. The perception of transparency discussed in chapter 5 was based on the relations among the reflectances of the involved surfaces and possibly some figural characteristics such as orientation. In the auditory domain, the aim is to discover the heuristics listeners use to split the impact sound into the part that builds the acoustic properties of the striking body and the remaining part that builds the acoustic properties of the struck one.[6] I can suggest several possibilities to split the acoustic wave: (a) slight differences in the onset and rise times of the frequency components associated with the striking and struck object; (b) differences in the decay of the frequency components of the two objects due to unequal damping; or (c) large differences in the frequencies of the vibrations of the two objects. As detailed in chapter 9, differences in onset time usually are the dominating acoustic cue for object segregation, and that is probably true here also.

3. We have all experienced the change in sound produced when we pour a liquid into a bottle. There is a continuous whooshing gurgling sound, and, as the bottle becomes full, the pitch center of the sound increases. The pitch is due to air vibrations within the empty part of the bottle, a tube closed at one end by the water and open at the other. The frequency of the lowest vibration (the fundamental) is roughly

$$F = \text{speed of air}/(4 \times \text{length of tube}). \tag{8.3}$$

Cabe and Pittinger (2000) found that listeners could easily judge by sound alone if a bottle (in this case a trash barrel) was filling (increasing frequency), emptying (decreasing frequency), or remaining at the same level. Moreover, when participants could control the water flow, they were able by means of the sound to stop the flow at a comfortable drinking level or at the brim, although the latter judgment was more accurate. The fact that brim filling was more accurate suggests that the rapid change in the fundamental frequency near the brim was the most useful acoustic cue.

6. This is one example of the general issue of auditory scene analysis and is covered in chapter 9.

Let me summarize at this point. The evidence is overwhelming that listeners can use auditory properties to identify a wide variety of events and objects. There seems to be enough information in the waveform to allow judgments about a wide variety of physical attributes of the source of an auditory event. It is tempting to attribute the acoustic dimensions to different classes of receptor cells. The attack time dimension could be traced to cells that have different frequency sweep rates and different sweep directions (see figure 2.25). The spectral frequency dimension could be traced to auditory cortical cells discussed in chapter 2, which have multiple interleaved excitation and inhibition regions (e.g., M. L. Sutter et al., 1999). The spectral frequency variation dimension could be traced to cells that are sensitive to amplitude and frequency modulation (L. Li et al., 2002) or differences in spectral distributions (Barbour & Wang, 2003). The combination of such cells can account for the importance of the distribution of spectral components during the attack and steady parts of the sound. However, I do not believe correlating perceptual features to cells whose receptive fields seem to match those features is a useful approach to understanding timbre (or any other perceptual outcome). The receptive fields of cells are extremely labile and change dramatically in different contexts, as discussed in chapter 2. Carried to an extreme, every feature would demand a unique receptive field. I believe that the perceptual features arise from the interaction of cells with all types of receptive fields.

The evidence also is overwhelming that the experience and capability of the listener will determine the level of performance. The acoustic and cognitive factors are not wholly separable. These sounds have meaning; they seem to have some sort of psychological structure, if not exactly a grammar and syntax, which can affect identification. Below I consider some of the cognitive factors in more detail.

Cognitive Factors

Although it would make identification much easier if each event or source had a unique sound, that is not the case. Ballas (1993) investigated one half of this ambiguity, namely that several sources can produce the same sound, which he termed *causal uncertainty*. Ballas uses the example of a click-click sound that could have been generated by a ballpoint pen, a light switch, a camera, or certain types of staplers. If a sound can come from many possible sources, then it seems obvious that it should be harder to identify the actual source. To measure the causal uncertainty, Ballas and colleagues used information theory to measure the uncertainty of the distribution of responses to one stimulus (as described in chapter 3). The first step was to develop a set of categories such that each category represented similar events. One category could be impact sounds, another water sounds, a third rubbing sounds, and so on (as in Gaver, 1993, above). Then the responses of all the listeners to one sound were put in the appropriate categories. If all listeners describe the sound as the same type of event, then all responses will fall in one category, and the uncertainty will be zero. If all of the descriptions are of different types of events and occur equally in all the different categories, the uncertainty will be the maximum value possible. Simply put, causal uncertainty is an indicant of how many different events could have produced the sound. The measure of causal uncertainty was highly correlated to the mean time it took to identify the sound, and several acoustic features (e.g., presence of harmonics) also were correlated to identification time. Thus, both the causal uncertainty and presence of specific acoustic features influence identification.

Ballas (1993) used several methods to assess the effect of familiarity. First, based on a written description (not the sound itself), listeners rated their familiarity with the object. Second, to measure the a priori probability that the sound occurred in the natural environment, participants were asked to report the first sound they heard when a timer randomly activated. On the whole, there is a weak relationship between ecological frequency (method 2) and causal uncertainty. If a sound occurs frequently, we might expect listeners to have more chances to discover the relevant acoustic cues. One possible reason for the weak relationship is that most of the sounds that occurred frequently were background sounds (air in heating ducts) that listeners normally do not pay attention to.

Ballas (1993) concluded that identification is best conceptualized as arising from information in different domains, rather than arising from a single measure of some sort. The maximum prediction of the identification time included four types of data: (1) temporal acoustic properties (similar spectral bursts in noncontinuous sounds); (2) spectral acoustic properties (average frequency of spectrum); (3) amplitude envelope (ratio of burst duration to total duration); and (4) ecological (frequency of occurrence). This is the same "no smoking gun" conclusion coming from experiments on color constancy.

Source Constancy: Multiple Sounds From One Source

There is hardly any cross-referencing between the research on timbre as a sound quality and the research on source identification, even though both kinds of studies arrive at nearly the same temporal and spectral properties. The research on timbre quality has emphasized human sounds (e.g., musical instruments, speaking and singing voices) that can be produced at widely different fundamental frequencies and amplitudes. The research on source identification has concentrated on the identification of a single sound (even if the sound was a set of discrete impacts, e.g., walking) that is relatively consistent. That was why I characterized causal uncertainty as dealing with one half of the ambiguity problem.

The other half of the ambiguity problem is the identification of an event or source that can create many different sounds. This is another constancy problem akin to visual shape or size constancy. Let me try to match auditory source constancy to the discussion of color constancy. Brainard et al. (1997) hypothesized that viewers essentially estimated what the standard color would look like under the test illumination and then tried to create a match. I imagine that listeners would listen to a sound at one frequency or intensity and then try to estimate what that source would sound like at a different frequency or intensity. To provide a visual analogy, although facial pictures of babies and adults are obviously different (possibly corresponding to timbres at different F_0s), Pittinger, Shaw, and Mark (1979) have shown that people can match baby pictures to adult pictures based on an understanding of normal growth curves. The auditory equivalent would be some form of acoustic transformation understood by the listener to provide a way to predict the sound quality of one note from that of another played by the same instrument or voice.[7] Thus, listeners may judge two instrumental notes as sounding very different and yet maintain that the same instrument produced them. What makes this auditory task much more complex than a comparable task for faces, in which one spatial transformation is postulated, is that each instrument and voice changes acoustically and perceptually in different ways. As the source frequency changes, it excites different source filter resonances. There is no reference sound. It is therefore unlikely that there is an acoustic feature, however complex, that characterizes all the notes of any instrument. At best, there may be invariant features within restricted pitch ranges due to a fixed set of resonances, but those features will transform over larger ranges as new resonances begin to radiate sound. It is these transformations that simultaneously create inclusion and exclusion from source categories.

To some extent, the experiments on water filling and identifying the sizes of struck objects do attack this issue, but the variation in sounds are relatively small. Erickson et al. (2001) recorded two mezzo-sopranos and two sopranos singing the vowel /a/ on pitches ranging from A_3 to A_5, a two-octave range. Three-note sequences were constructed from these notes such that one singer sang two notes and one of the three other singers sang the third note (termed the *oddball note*). Therefore, the oddball note could have been sung by a different singer from the same voice class or from one of the two singers in the other voice class. Both experienced choral directors and inexperienced listeners attempted to identify the oddball note. The ability to

7. The same issue arises for natural events—earthquakes of different intensities, walking at different speeds, and so on.

identify the oddball note dramatically varied as a function of the pitch range. If the two notes sung by one singer were adjacent in pitch (G_4 and B_4), then both the experienced and inexperienced participants were able to identify the oddball stimulus. If the notes were separated by more than an octave (C_4 and F_5), performance was only slightly better than chance. Finally, if the notes were separated by two octaves (A_3 and A_5), performance was actually worse than chance. Both the experienced and inexperienced listeners invariably chose the stimulus that was most different in pitch. What this tells us is that there is no invariant timbre associated with a singing voice because timbre changes with pitch; generally, the larger the separation in pitch, the larger the difference in timbre and the resulting lack of ability to detect source identity. This makes intuitive sense because the same set of harmonics are used to create the sense of pitch and timbre.

Assume that vocal (and instrumental) source timbre is based on our ability to derive a transformation that allows us to predict the sound at different pitches. Then our ability to derive such transformations should improve if we are exposed to a larger, "richer" set of notes. If the change in timbre varies from note to note and includes register breaks, then we might need all of the possible notes to create the transformation. Paradoxically then, if we construct sequences in which one singer sang five notes and a different singer sang one note, listeners should be better able to identify the oddball note, even though the task is more complex and chance performance would be worse (16% to 33%). In fact, Erickson and Perry (2003) found that performance for six-note sequences with one oddball note was almost always absolutely better than for three-note sequences with one oddball note in spite of the added complexity. Performance was nearly perfect if the oddball singer came from the other voice category.[8]

Handel and Erickson (2001, 2004) have done analogous experiments with instruments. In the first (Handel & Erickson, 2001), two different pitch notes were presented. Sometimes they were played by the same wind instrument and sometimes they were played by different instruments. The listener's task was simply to judge whether the same or different instruments played them. As long as the pitch difference was an octave or less, listeners were accurate. If the pitch difference was greater than an octave, listeners invariably judged that the instruments were different. In the second, Handel and Erickson (2004) used a three-note sequence with one oddball note (exactly the same task as above). If the two instruments were both woodwinds (clarinet and English horn), then listeners always judged

8. The idea that the number of exemplars necessary to derive the source timbre is a function of the complexity of the source resonances is similar to the idea that the number of views necessary to derive surface reflectance depends on the number of linear basis functions required to match the reflectance spectrum (D'Zmura & Iverson, 1993a).

the oddball note to be the one most different in pitch, exactly the same result found for the singers. In contrast, if the two instruments were clarinet or English horn and trumpet (i.e., different instrument classes), then listeners were able to identify the oddball note.

From these results, it seems that source constancy is built up by developing a sense of how the sounds from one source will change across pitch. For difficult discriminations such as between singing voices or woodwind instruments, listeners need a fine-grain auditory image of the timbre at each pitch to detect the oddball note, and that requires many notes to be able to derive the necessary detailed trajectory of each source. We can imagine that given only two notes, the listener will accept a wide range of sounds as possibly coming from the same source. As the number of given notes increases, the added information about the timbre transformations allows the listener to restrict the range of possible sounds. For easier discriminations, such as between a woodwind and brass instrument that sound widely different, listeners do not need a detailed trajectory, so that a broadly tuned one based on just a few notes will suffice.

Poulim-Charronnat, Bigand, Madurell, Vieillard, and McAdams (2004) have investigated a different issue. Suppose we present a musical passage using one sound source (e.g., a piano) and then present the same or a different passage using a second source (e.g., a clarinet). Will listeners be able to generalize across the two timbres and discriminate between the two passages? On the surface, it seems that it should be an easy kind of constancy, particularly for Western classical music, which mainly revolves around harmonic structure. Yet Poulim-Charronnat et al. found that the discrimination task was surprisingly difficult if one source was a solo piano and the second source was an orchestra. Even skilled musicians were unable to do better than roughly 65–70% correct when the timbre changed for passages from a Liszt symphony. The same listeners were able to achieve an accuracy of 90% if the timbre did not change. The poor performance when the timbre changed could be due to the large difference in the sources and resulting timbre. It is easy to predict that performance will vary as a function of the difference in the source timbres, and in fact this provides a converging operation on the results from the multidimensional scaling experiments.

Summary

Of all the chapters, this is the one I feel most uncomfortable about. There does not seem to be a consistent thread running through all of these results except for the fact that listeners can and do identify objects and properties of objects by their sound quality alone. The acoustic measures that correlate with the perceptual judgments tend to change from experiment to experiment, often are not clearly connected to the sound production process, and much of the time do not seem intuitive to me. Maybe that should be expected because of the complexity of the stimuli due to the large number of vibration modes of the source and filter and the number of unique receptor cells, and because listeners will make use of any acoustic property that works in a context.

A recent approach to source identification, termed *physically inspired modeling*, may provide a systematic way to investigate the perception of simple rigid objects. Physically inspired modeling makes use of the vibration wave equations for the motions of simple bars to synthesize the sounds of those objects. The advantage of this approach is that it allows the experimenter to vary the parameters of the vibration modes (e.g., the decay rates) and thereby isolate the properties that listeners actually use to identify the objects. For example, Lutfi (2001) synthesized the sound of freely vibrating hollow and solid bars and required listeners to distinguish between the two types. The first vibration mode of hollow bars decays more quickly, is louder, and has a lower frequency than the first mode of solid bars. Some listeners used decay and frequency while others used only frequency to make their judgments. By comparing the wave equations to discrimination, Lutfi was able to show that the limits of human sensitivity (i.e., internal noise) can account for the errors made as the intrinsic acoustic relationships are perturbed.

Moreover, I have equated color constancy with the ability to predict sound quality at one pitch and loudness from the sound quality of the same object at a different pitch and loudness. At least at a superficial level, that seems to be a correct analogy. To achieve color constancy, the observer must remove the effects of the change in illumination to capture the unchanging surface reflectance. To achieve sound source constancy, the listener must remove the effects of changes in pitch and loudness to capture the source resonances. But the source filter resonances change at different excitation frequencies so that the listener can be, in effect, faced with a different sound object when the excitation frequencies are widely different. Without sounds at intermediate frequencies to characterize the connecting transformation, it would be impossible to judge whether two sounds come from the same object. Perhaps the analogy holds within overlapping frequency ranges of about one octave where the source filters are fairly constant.

9

Auditory and Visual Segmentation

I heard Dr. Fritz Heider, the famous Gestalt psychologist, say, "The job of psychologists is to pierce the veil of the obvious." The organization and segmentation of the auditory and visual worlds into objects and sources is so obvious, so commonplace, and so effortless that the problem of how this organization was accomplished went unnoticed until the Gestalt psychologists made it central to visual perceptual theory. But it still took another 80 years before the pioneering work of Bregman (1990) made auditory figure-ground organization central to auditory perceptual theory.

The essential problem for the visual system is to segment the retinal mosaic composed of independent receptors into enclosed objects with continuous surfaces. The outputs of the receptors can be grouped in an infinite number of ways. We cannot simply argue that we organize it the way it is, because we do not know how it is. We are restricted to the information on the retina, the proximal information. From that, we construct our best guess about the environment, the distal world. The proximal information must provide at least a provisional representation of the distal environment; otherwise useful perception would not occur at all. But there are ambiguities that must be resolved. The continuous surfaces often are partially covered by other surfaces, so that the reflected light reaching the observer consists of fragments of varying shapes and sizes that must be assigned to objects. Moreover, we cannot perceive the entire perceptual field at once. The objects have to be constructed by shifting attention to different regions and then knitting the fragments together. This is simply the aperture and correspondence problem posed once again. The aperture is determined by span of attention, while the correspondence problem is to determine which fragments go with which other fragments.

Similarly, the essential problem for the auditory system is to segment the acoustic wave into auditory sources. The auditory world consists of coherent objects whose sounds usually change slowly and continuously over time. But the sounds from individual objects may be masked or mixed up with sounds from other objects, so that the pressure wave reaching the listener is the blend of all the ongoing sounds. The proximal information, though, is the independent outputs of the hair cells tuned to different frequencies. These outputs can be grouped in innumerable ways to create different distal sources, exactly like the outputs of the retinal cells, which can be grouped to create different objects. Moreover, there are the same kinds of attention limits. It is difficult to attend to all the frequency components at any instant, and there are limits to our ability to integrate sound fragments over time. Here the aperture is determined by our perceptual ability to hear only the present sound, and by memory limitations. The correspondence problem is to determine which frequency components go with which other components.

In many ways, this chapter connects and sometimes contrasts many of the concepts in previous chapters.

1. Sensations belong to things. There is a remarkably strong tendency to hear the world in terms of sources that change only slowly and to hear and see the world in terms of rigid objects.

2. Structure and noise are end points. We have argued that perception is the abstraction of structure from ongoing change and that abstraction must occur in real time, often based on sparse representations.

3. Perceptual processes exist at many levels simultaneously. Grouping begins with the sensory elements, which are combined into intermediate features or elements, and finally combined into objects. None of the levels are fixed or invariant, and all depend on the overall context. The problem is to find the appropriate "grain" that maximizes structure.

4. Perceptual processes are tuned to the physical processes that create the sensory structure. There are two possibilities. The first argues that the segmentation and grouping of sensory fragments is the outcome of evolutionary processes that have created automatic processes that function without attention. These processes take advantage of the physical invariants that create auditory and visual sensation. This is the view advanced by Shepard (1981), which he termed *psychophysical complementarity*. The second possibility argues that grouping is the end result of perceptual expectations (i.e., likelihoods) generated through experiences that are being constantly upgraded by new information. The preferred interpretation is the one that has the highest probability of being correct (e.g., W. S. Geisler et al., 2001, in chapter 4). This is Helmholtz's concept of unconscious inference: at first, perception is figuring out which real-world object most likely produced the proximal sensations, but those perceptual processes

become "telescoped" with experience so that the problem-solving component becomes automatic and lost to consciousness. Both kinds of perceptual processes act to limit the large number of ways of configuring the sensory field to a small set of possibilities that can be tested by the perceiver. We can combine the two approaches by arguing that distal stimuli that are biologically important or result from frequent physical processes will have high likelihoods of occurring. These processes may not all point to the same organization, creating a need for rules that declare the "winner."

Another way of framing this issue is in terms of what van der Helm (2000) termed *viewpoint-independent* and *viewpoint-dependent processes*. This difference is best illustrated by an example. Suppose the proximal stimulus is simply a small black circle. Many objects could produce such a circle: a three-dimensional sphere, a flat circle, a three-dimensional cylinder, an ellipse slanted in depth, and so on (see figure 3.1). The sphere will produce a proximal circle from all viewpoints; that distal stimulus is viewpoint independent. In contrast, the circle, cylinder, and ellipse will produce a proximal circle only from one accidental viewpoint; those distal stimuli are viewpoint dependent. Rock (1983) proposed that perceivers make their judgments assuming that the proximal stimulus did not arise from a unique (i.e., unlikely) position of the distal stimuli. That is, perceivers avoid interpretations that are based on accidental viewpoints or coincidental arrangements. From this perspective, viewers would guess that a sphere produced the circle.[1] For a second example, consider a straight-line proximal stimulus. A straight edge will produce a straight proximal stimulus from all viewpoints, but a curved edge will produce it only from one accidental viewpoint. Therefore, the best guess would be that a distal straight line produced the proximal straight line.

Let me suggest a hearing example based on coincidental timing. In chapter 5, I discussed auditory induction effects. If a sound is temporarily masked by a louder sound that contains the same frequency components, the softer sound is heard to continue during the duration of the louder masking sound. It would be a low-probability coincidence if the softer sound ended at the instant that the louder sound began and then restarted at the same instant that the louder sound ended. It is much more likely that the softer sound was continuous so that there would be no silences between the softer and louder masker, regardless of the timing of the masker.

5. Perceptual processes are equivalent for all senses. A unifying theme is that both the auditory and visual systems analyze the sensory input into frequency channels. The outputs of these channels may be combined in diverse ways and thereby create many alternative descriptions of the structure.

1. Alternately, viewers might see just a flat dot because it would lack highlights and shadows that nearly always occur with a sphere.

For a first approximation, we can say that it is the cross-frequency correlations for both hearing and seeing that generate the perception of structure, and it is probably at this level that the correspondences between the two are clearest. We can also understand the grouping in terms of redundancy reduction (Barlow, 1981). Channels that are correlated can be combined, leaving independent channels that maximize mutual information.

Contributions of the Gestalt Psychologists

As described in earlier chapters, the Gestalt psychologists embraced the notion of psychophysical isomorphism. What we see is due to the operation of field forces on the visual cortex, which organizes the sensory fragments into continuous objects (see figure 9.1). The sensory fragments create attractive and repulsive forces, and the field forces link fragments together

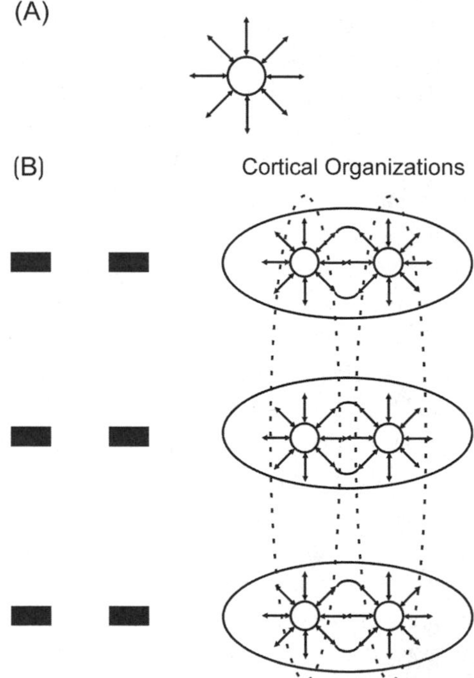

Figure 9.1. Every cortical point, if excited, generates an electrical field that diminishes with distance (A). The particular stimulus configuration determines the polarity. The proximal stimulus creates the excitation pattern and resulting field forces. The field forces can combine to generate a larger unified field that determines the organization (B). In this case, the stronger fields between nearer cortical units lead to the perceptual grouping by rows (solid-line ellipses) instead of the alternate grouping by columns (dotted-line ellipses).

phenomenally. The isomorphism is between the cortical structure resulting from the interacting field forces and our percept.

One problem with this explanation is that the field forces are not strictly deterministic, so that many alternative organizations are possible. What was hypothesized was that the fields acted to minimize the cortical current thereby generating the simplest, most coherent organization. This is the concept of *prägnanz*. The metaphor was a soap bubble that equalized surface tension while enclosing the maximum volume with the minimum surface area. Unfortunately, prägnanz is a very slippery concept because it is not clear whether it refers to specific figures in the field, to the entire field itself, to some mathematical code definition of simplicity, or merely to a statistical likelihood (van der Helm, 2000). Even though counterexamples can be found for any precise definition, we can use it as a useful guiding principle.

The Gestalt psychologists used the concept of prägnanz to uncover the laws of organization, or more appropriately the principles of organization. If you believe in psychophysical isomorphism, these principles are reflections of the actions of the field forces themselves. Perceptual and physiological prägnanz are one and the same (isomorphic, in Gestalt terminology).

The principles of organization were induced using simple visual pictures that isolated one principle while "zeroing out" other principles. The visual principles include the classic ones found in all textbooks (see figure 9.2):

1. Similarity: Elements that are similar in physical attributes (e.g., shape, size, loudness, timbre, brightness, etc.) tend to be grouped together.
2. Proximity: Elements that are close together in space or time, or are located within a common spatial region, tend to be grouped together. Furthermore, elements that are "slurred together" in sound or joined together on one perceived surface tend to be grouped together, termed *element connectedness* (Palmer, 1994).
3. Continuity: Elements that appear to follow each other in the same direction tend to be grouped together.
4. Common fate: Elements that move together tend to be grouped together ("birds of a feather flock together"). Although common fate is usually illustrated in terms of motion, it can be applied to a wide variety of coherent changes. For example, Sekuler and Bennett (2001) started with a checkerboard pattern of random luminances. They then modulated the intensity of one vertical or horizontal linear segment out of phase with the modulation of the rest of the checkerboard (figure 9.3). The modulation rates ranged from about 2 to 9 Hz so that the modulation was clearly visible. The squares in the linear

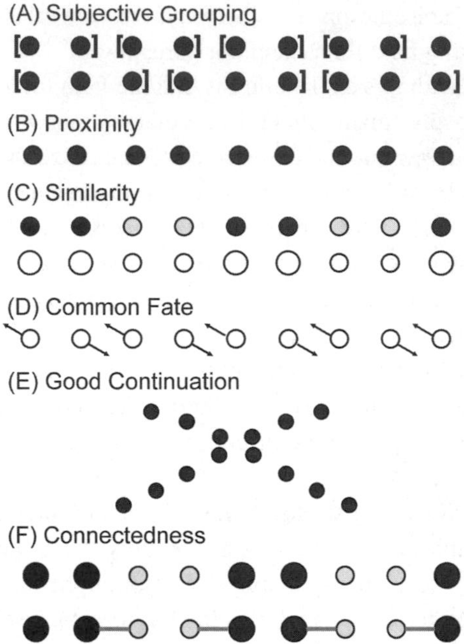

Figure 9.2. Examples of the classic Gestalt grouping principles. A sequence of equally spaced dots will be subjectively grouped into groups of two or three, depending on the spacing between the dots (A). Dots can be grouped into pairs on the basis of physical proximity (B), similarity in brightness, size, or another feature (C), common fate in movement (D), or good continuation along smooth trajectories (E). Dots will tend to be grouped if they are connected in some way, even though they differ in size and brightness (F). All of these Gestalt principles also apply to sounds. For example, a sequence of isochronous sounds will be grouped into twos or threes (subjective rhythms). The term *subjective* was chosen because there was no physical property to account for the grouping. It was an unfortunate choice because all of these groupings are subjective: Elements merely follow each other in space and time.

target segments increased in luminance at the same time as the remaining part of the checkerboard decreased, and vice versa. The out-of-phase modulations segmented the elements in the linear segment from the rest of the checkerboard and permitted the observers to determine if the linear target region was horizontal or vertical. In similar fashion, Alais, Blake, and Lee (1998) found that correlated contrast changes, even in opposite directions, bind Gabor-like black-and-white patterns together. Another example of common fate is coherent amplitude or frequency modulation. If parts of an auditory or visual scene undergo correlated changes (e.g., musical vibrato), it is likely that those parts will be combined into one object.

5. Temporal synchrony: Elements that undergo simultaneous and coherent changes in time are grouped together (e.g., S.-H. Lee & Blake,

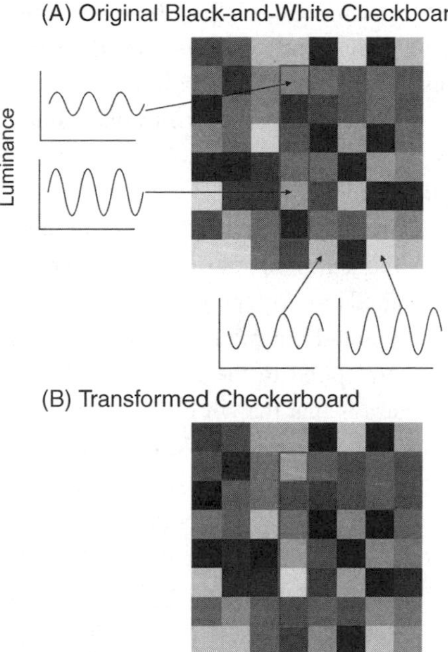

Figure 9.3. One example of common fate is coherent temporal modulation. The six target cells in a vertical array are modulated in phase, but 180° out of phase with all of the background cells. The original black-and-white checkerboard (A) is shown transformed in (B). The vertical target increases in brightness, while the remaining squares in the checkerboard decrease in brightness. In the experimental checkerboards, the amplitude of modulation was a constant proportion of the squares' average luminance, as illustrated. This made the luminance ratios of the squares within the target and within the background constant across time. Adapted from "Generalized Common Fate: Grouping by Common Luminance Changes," by A. B. Sekuler and J. P. Bennett, 2001, *Psychological Science, 12*, 437–444.

1999, discussed in chapter 5). The most obvious principle is that of synchronous onset and offset. Parts of a visual scene that appear and disappear at the same time are likely to come from one object, and parts of the acoustic wave that start and stop at the same instant are likely to have been created by one source. In fact, as described later in this chapter, onset synchrony is the most important cue for auditory grouping (surprisingly, offset synchrony is not that important). I used explanations based on temporal synchrony in chapter 6 to explain some of the results coming from experiments on profile analysis and comodulation masking release. (Temporal synchrony may be considered an instance of common fate, but due to its importance it is worth treating separately.)

6. Symmetry and closure: Elements that form symmetrical and enclosed objects tend to be grouped together.

There is no doubt that the Gestalt psychologists posed the problem of grouping an ambiguous image into objects. Similarly, there is no doubt that the pictorial demonstrations "work." But a fundamental issue is how to take the simple pictures and make use of them to understand the normal complexity of everyday scenes.

There are several problems.

1. The elements are not clearly defined. They are obviously the dots and lines in the Gestalt demonstrations, but discrete elements may not exist at all for time-varying sounds or for spatially varying but continuous visual surfaces. (It has been pointed out many times that the silences we hear in speech often do not correspond to the times that there is no physical energy.) The Gestalt mantra is that the whole is different from the sum of the parts, or, to put it another way, the whole determines the meaning of the parts. But the whole has to emerge from the interaction of the parts; it cannot exist otherwise. Auditory and visual organization is a two-way relationship: parts create wholes, while the whole defines the parts.

2. Because the elements are not clearly defined, it is always uncertain how to apply the principles of organization. Which parts of the scene should be compared for similarity, and which parts undergo common direction? Furthermore, the spatial and temporal region within which the principles apply is indeterminate. Suppose a row of equally spaced circles spanning about .5 m was drawn on a wall. Viewed up close, the circles would probably group into twos or threes. But viewed from afar, all the circles would probably group together.

3. The principles of organization seem most appropriate for one-shot auditory and visual stimuli: a single short auditory stimulus or a single static drawing. But everyday perceiving is about sounds and views that are constantly evolving. We can imagine that time is broken into nonoverlapping intervals, grouping occurs within each interval, and that cohesion between intervals is accomplished by using the same principles used to group the elements within intervals. Alternately, we can rephrase the static principles of grouping into dynamic ones that reflect change over time. For example, common fate might group elements that undergo correlated changes across time. This would group together the back-and-forth motion of two balls connected by a spring even though the balls move out of phase.

4. In the same way that it is uncertain how to apply the principles of organization, it is uncertain when to apply those principles. Assume, for simplicity, that the auditory and visual worlds are relatively static. The physical processes underlying the source-filter production model structure the acoustic and visual energy. Furthermore, assume that the auditory and visual systems first partition the sensory energy into a set of elements that become the basis for the grouping processes. There has to be something to group. This partitioning is simply the result of straightforward physiological

processes (e.g., basilar membrane vibration, retinal on-off cells). At this point, we only have the stuff, the elements of perception, and not the units, the things. The organizing principles cash in on the resulting regularities. The Gestalt psychologists tacitly assumed that grouping occurs as an obligatory first step in perceiving the scene and then these groups are used to determine depth, shape, color, and brightness. More recent research has suggested that this is an overly simplified view and that the grouping of elements often occurs after other processes are completed. The organizing principles are based on perceived properties—lightness, depth, synchrony, loudness, and so on—not on the measured physical energy. What this means is that grouping takes place only after auditory and visual processes have normalized the scene, compensating for extraneous noise, variations in intensity and luminance, and shadows due to other surfaces, among other factors. The gain controls discussed in chapter 6 that normalize lightness and contrast variation buttress this possibility.

Principles of Auditory Grouping

The acoustic properties of sound sources provide logical starting points to evolve heuristics (i.e., rules that usually work) for segregating the acoustic wave. Nearly all sound-producing objects that we hear are relatively small and close. Many environmental sounds (e.g., wind, crackling of footsteps in leaves, impacts, dragging sounds, cars, air conditioning, keyboard strokes) arise from a broad set of frequency components. Some very important sounds for human listeners, such as speech, and the sounds of most Western musical instruments vibrate at discrete frequencies that are multiples of a low-frequency fundamental. The frequencies often oscillate around a base frequency (frequency modulation), and many sounds undergo variation in overall loudness (amplitude modulation). Now the perceptual problem becomes one of assigning sets of frequencies that vary over time to different sources.

The heuristics would therefore be based on the temporal and frequency relationships among those components that are correlated over time and location. In most natural situations, different acoustic properties will support the same organization, so that we cannot measure the relative contributions of each cue. To do so, we need to make the cues conflict. For example, we could present frequencies of 100, 300, and 500 Hz to one ear and frequency components of 200, 400, and 600 Hz to the other ear. If harmonic relationships dominate, then listeners will hear one complex tone with a fundamental frequency of 100 Hz; all the frequency components will fuse. If lateral position dominates, then listeners will hear a 100 Hz complex tone in one ear and a 200 Hz complex tone in the other ear.

Acoustic Cues for Grouping

Harmonicity

One characteristic of voiced speech and most musical instruments is that the partials occur at integer multiples of the fundamental (the lowest repetition rate) frequency (when the partials occur at multiples, they are termed *harmonics*). The regularity of the frequencies yields a coherent percept of a single tone; the higher harmonics are not heard separately. Two complex harmonic tones with different fundamental frequencies tend to split into two sounds even if the difference in the fundamental frequency is small.

To "hear out" one of the harmonics, it is necessary to either mistune, increase the intensity of that harmonic, or direct attention to that harmonic by playing that harmonic alone before presentation of the entire sound (Darwin & Carlyon, 1995). It is relatively easy to hear a single mistuned harmonic (the second harmonic in the sound 100, 203, 300, 400, and 500 Hz), particularly for lower frequencies. A mistuning of only 2% is sufficient for the harmonic to emerge. The mistuned harmonic is heard as a separate entity, but it also is still heard as part of the complex and therefore slightly changes the pitch of the complex. If the mistuning is increased beyond 8%, that harmonic is heard as completely separate, so that it no longer affects the pitch of the complex.

Auditory physiological mechanisms that detect harmonic relationships have been hypothesized many times. The harmonic sieves suggested by Goldstein (1973) and Terhardt (1974) are based on the assumption that there are stored spectral templates that provide representations of harmonic series coming from all possible harmonics. Shamma and Klein (2000) have proposed a model based on coincidence detectors (i.e., neural spike synchrony) among auditory neurons phase-locked to harmonically related characteristic frequencies (described in chapter 2). Because this model depends on phase-locking, it can account for the poorer ability to detect the mistuned harmonic at higher harmonics at frequencies where phase-locking weakens.

Onset and Offset Asynchrony

Probably the most important cue for sound source segregation is onset timing. Using dense harmonic complexes like those used in profile analysis (chapter 6), if all but one component are synchronous, listeners can detect differences in onset times of the remaining component as little as 0.6–2 ms. Surprisingly, there is little difference whether the single component was started before or was delayed relative to the complex (Zera & Green, 1993). However, if all of the components of the complex do not start at the same time, the difficulty of detecting an additional change was much harder, particularly if the changed component was delayed (20–60 ms). It is much more difficult to detect offset asynchrony; components that continue beyond the complex can be detected with offsets between 2 and 10 ms, while components that end before the complex require offsets greater than 20 ms. In these experiments, listeners did not report whether they heard one sound or two, but simply judged which of two sounds contained the asynchronous component. It is quite possible that these judgments were based on qualitative timbre differences.

Typically, the necessary onset asynchrony to create the perception of two natural sounds is on the order of 30 ms, which is much longer than the times used above. Rasch (1978) found that the typical asynchrony among instruments in ensembles was also in the 30 ms range, being between 20 and 50 ms. The sounds for nearly all instruments are more complex than those used in the experiments above: The onsets of the harmonics are not synchronous and the amplitude envelope of each harmonic differs. Thus, the 30 ms value must represent a compromise between sensory limitations, the inherent variation among harmonics of a single source, and the low probability that two different sources will start within 30 ms of each other.

If the onset of one harmonic precedes that of other harmonics, the initial harmonic is heard to continue separately in the complex, and the complex tone is heard without the asynchronous harmonic. The auditory system metaphorically assumes that the early-starting harmonic is continuous and the other harmonics represent a new sound. This is an example of what Bregman (1993) termed the *old + new heuristic*. Suppose sound A "turns into" sound B. The components of A found in B are assumed to be continuations of A. The remaining parts of B are then treated as a new sound, so that B is treated as the sum (or mixture) of an old sound A and a new one (B – A).

Another example of the operation of the old + new heuristic occurs if a soft tone alternates with a louder sound. In this case, listeners report hearing one continuous soft tone with a second intermittent soft tone, not a soft tone alternating with a loud tone. The old + new heuristic was discussed in chapter 5 with respect to auditory induction and at the beginning of this chapter with respect to coincidental proximal stimuli. There, I pointed out the resemblance between hearing a nonexistent tone continuing in noise and seeing a surface continuing behind an occluding surface.

Frequency Modulation

As the fundamental frequency of a complex harmonic tone changes, all of its harmonics change frequency coherently in direction and time (the percentage change of each harmonic and the ratios among the harmonics remain the same). Since we would not expect two different sources to undergo the identical frequency modulation at the same time, coherent frequency modulation could be an important cue to source segregation. The experimental evidence suggests that coherent frequency modulation found in voice and instrumental vibrato aids in the formation of a single sound (Chowning, 1980; McAdams, 1984) and that vibrato applied to a vowel masked by noise makes that vowel more discriminable (Summerfield & Culling, 1992).

Suppose we present two complex sounds with slightly different fundamental frequencies (e.g., interleaved harmonics such as 100, 110, 200, 220, 300, 330 . . . Hz). With no modulation, there is no sense of distinct pitches due to the interleaving of the harmonics. Different modulation rates make the two sounds easier to segregate, but there is little evidence that difference in the rate or degree of frequency modulation aids in the segregation of different sources. Most probably, the differences in frequency modulation reinforce the perception of separate pitches by increasing the perception of harmonicity among the frequency components of each source. If frequency modulation affects segregation indirectly by increasing the sense of pitch and timbre for harmonic sounds and not by the perception of the modulation itself, then we might expect that frequency modulation of inharmonic sounds would not lead to segregation. That, in fact, is the case: Listeners cannot even determine if two nonharmonic tones (1100 and 1925 Hz) are being modulated in phase or out of phase (Carlyon, 2000).

In sum, these results suggest that frequency modulation per se is not an independent cue for segregation. Suppose we have a sound composed of harmonic components. If the components are frequency modulated coherently, then the components always remain harmonically related. But if the components are modulated out of phase, they will become nonharmonic at points and, as described above, the auditory system is very sensitive to such mistuned sounds. Thus, frequency modulation may affect the grouping of components indirectly by affecting the harmonic relationships rather than by the direct effect of the modulation.

Amplitude Modulation

Any physical process that affects the amplitude of one harmonic or partial is likely to simultaneously affect the amplitude of all components. Using identical logic as for frequency modulation, we would not expect two sound sources to undergo identical loudness variation. The outcomes here parallel those for frequency modulation. Two tones can be made to cohere into one complex tone by applying the same amplitude modulation (8–10 Hz) to both (von Bekesy, 1963). Moreover, the results from comodulation masking release (discussed in chapter 6) demonstrate that two noise bands that are modulated coherently tend to form a single unit and therefore create less masking than if the bands were modulated incoherently.

Spatial Location

Intuitively, we would expect that spatial position would be an important cue for grouping. After all, nearly all sound sources we deal with are relatively small and localized in space. In reality though, location is only a weak factor in determining grouping. We can suggest two possible reasons. First, the perceived direction of sound waves can be misleading or even impossible to determine: Sound waves can bounce off walls or obstacles or come through openings such as windows (I find it impossible to localize an outside sound while inside a house). In enclosed environments, most of the power comes from reflected sound that lacks directionality. Second, spatial position must be derived from the comparison of the sound across the two ears. But at each ear the first step is the analysis of the sound wave into frequency components. This implies that to create sources based on spatial position, the auditory system must calculate the position of each component separately, and that might be difficult and time consuming for pressure waves with many components.

If we actually do the experiment proposed at the beginning of this section in which we present different the harmonics of one frequency to separate ears, harmonicity dominates and a single tone is heard. It does not matter how the harmonics are split; the percept is one tone. Moreover, although it is possible to segregate a single harmonic from other harmonics by mistuning, onset asynchrony, or modulation, it is impossible to separate a single harmonic by changing the interaural timing delay.

Although location has only minimal effect for single sounds, spatial location does affect segregation for sequences of sounds after the pressure wave has been segregated by means of other cues. Suppose there are two sentences spoken with different fundamental frequencies and also presented with different interaural timings representing different locations. Now there are two correlated cues for grouping: pitch and location. Now, if we swap the fundamental frequency of a single word, that word remains grouped according to location. It does not shift to the other location due to the change in pitch. This is in contrast to the presentation of single sounds where harmonic relationships dominate location. Darwin (1997) suggested that these results can be understood if we imagine that there are two grouping stages. In the first, the frequency components are grouped on the basis of onsets and harmonic relationships. In the second, over time groups of frequencies with coherent relationships are placed in different subjective locations based on interaural differences.

Frequency

The above cues seem more relevant to the grouping of simultaneous frequency components in a single sound than to grouping successive sounds as found in music. The question here is whether the series of sounds comes from one source or whether the series results from the interleaving of sounds from different sources. The basic methodology is to continuously recycle a small number of sounds and measure whether the listener hears all the sounds as coming from one source or whether the sounds appear to break into separate ongoing sound sequences, often termed *streams*, such that each stream seems to come from a different source. As Bregman (1990) has argued, the default percept is that of one stream, and switching the percept to that of different streams is cumulative and gradual over repetitions.

In a classic set of experiments, van Noorden (1975) presented sequences at different presentation rates that simply alternated two pure tones at different frequencies (also discussed in chapter 5). Listeners reported simply whether they heard the two tones alternate like a trill or whether the notes formed a low-note sequence and a separate high-note sequence. These sequences place temporal proximity (adjacent notes) in conflict with frequency similarity (alternate notes of the same frequency).

The results demonstrated an inverse relationship between rate and frequency ratio. Increasing either the presentation rate or the frequency separation (or both) increases the probability of hearing the two tones as separate streams. Conversely, decreasing the rate or frequency separation increases the probability of hearing the tones as forming a single coherent stream. At intermediate values of rate or frequency separation, the tendency to hear the tones as forming one or two streams can be affected by the listener's attention. Bregman et al. (2000) have shown that it is not the rate per se that affects grouping; it is the gap between the offset of one note and the onset of the next one in the same frequency region, the temporal separation. The tendency to form a coherent stream can be enhanced by connecting the low- and high-frequency tone by a frequency glide between the two tones.

Bregman (1990) made an extremely important distinction about the asymmetry in auditory grouping from the results of van Noorden's experiment. It always is possible to attend to either tone at all presentation rates as long as the frequency separation between the low and high tones allows them to be discriminated apart. In contrast, it is impossible to maintain the perception of a single alternating sequence once the combination of frequency separation and presentation rate reach a certain point. There is an obligatory split into low and high tone streams. On this basis and others, Bregman argued that we have primitive segregation processes that operate preattentively on all sounds to create tentative guesses about the environmental sources. These guesses are then evaluated against what we learned about the probability of those sources occurring and what we learned about how well those cues predict the external sources. In essence, we are calculating the posterior probabilities. Sometimes our expectations about the probabilities of sources and messages are so strong that we misperceive the signal, hearing our own names or a close friend speaking.

If we construct more complex sequences composed of alternating high- and low-frequency notes and present them at a rapid presentation rate, stream segregation will occur. One stream will be composed of the low-frequency tones and the second of the high-frequency tones. If this occurs, it is possible to attend to either the low or high tones, but listeners are unable to attend to both streams at once. Often, attention seems to shift spontaneously between the two streams. Because of this, listeners are unable to report the order of the tones in the overall sequence, although they can correctly report the order in each stream. For example, suppose we create the repeating sequence A3B2C1A3B2C1 . . . in which A, B, and C are low-frequency tones forming one stream, and 1, 2, and 3 are high-frequency tones forming the second stream. Listeners can report the order within each stream (e.g., A-B-C-A-B-C as opposed to A-C-B-A-C-B and 3-2-1-3-2-1 as opposed to 1-2-3-1-2-3; the dashes represent the silent intervals between elements within each stream created by the formation of the other stream). But listeners cannot correctly interleave the two streams. They cannot report whether the sequence was A3B2C1, A2B1C3, or A1B3C2. This inability to keep the two streams in correct registration occurs whether the streaming was due to frequency, intensity, timbre, or location (Bregman, 1990).

The preattentive formation of one or two streams caused by frequency separation and presentation rate has allowed composers to create the illusion of two simultaneous melodies being played on an instrument that can play only one note at a time, like the flute. Two melodies written in different octaves are intermixed so that the low- and high-pitched tones alternate. Due to the rapid frequency shifts, the low- and high-pitched melodies are heard separately, in parallel. This has been term *pseudopolyphony, virtual polyphony*, or *compound melodic line.* In contrast, composers may want to create the illusion of one virtual instrument, fusing the voices in a chorus or the violins in an orchestra, which will not be precisely in tune. In this case, all of the individual voices should start together and undergo parallel frequency changes that keep the harmonic relationships among the sources constant.

As described briefly above, harmonicity, onset-offset synchrony, frequency modulation, amplitude modulation, and spatial location are very likely to be redundant in natural situations. It is hard to imagine an instance in which the harmonic and nonharmonic components of one sound source are undergoing different frequency or amplitude modulations. Likewise, even though there are asynchronous onsets due to the physical processes involved in creating vibrations (e.g., the higher harmonics of a bowed violin start before the lower harmonics), these differences are likely to be small relative to the onset differences between different sources. If we consider Barlow's (2001) contention that sensory systems should focus on the redundancy that specifies objects, the underlying neural representation might be based on a small set of neural mechanisms that pick up and capitalize on the correlated acoustic features in the signal.

Ranking the Importance of the Cues

In order to rank the possible grouping cues, it is necessary to uncorrelate the normally redundant ones. Several experiments have placed the cues to segregation in conflict: Using one cue, such as frequency, leads to one organization, while using a second cue, such as synchrony, leads to another organization. It is important to keep these results in perspective. The outcomes may be specific to a task or to a set of background conditions that are not yet understood. Auditory and visual grouping always occurs in a context.

Turgeon (2000) made use of a masking paradigm in which one rhythmic target was masked by a second rhythmic masker. The rhythmic targets were constructed by varying the timing between the repeated onsets of short 48 ms tones or noise bursts. The masking rhythms were an irregular set of sounds, identical to those of the target rhythms, interspersed among the target rhythm sounds. Together the target and masking rhythms produced an irregular rhythm that precluded identifying the target rhythm. This methodology is very similar to that used to produce interleaved melodies, discussed in chapter 5, and interspersing random noise bands to study comodulation masking release, discussed in chapter 6.

The original rhythm would become perceivable again if the interspersed masking sounds could be induced to form a separate stream. To induce this stream, flanking sounds in different frequency regions were presented concurrently with the interspersed masking sounds. If the masking and flanking sounds fused into a complex sound with a different timbre, it would make the target easier to hear and the strength of the streaming could be measured by the ability to detect the target rhythm. In several experiments, Turgeon (2000) varied the temporal, spectral, or spatial relationships among the masking and flanking sounds and determined which acoustic properties governed streaming by measuring the ease of detecting the target rhythm. For example, the masking sounds and flanker sounds

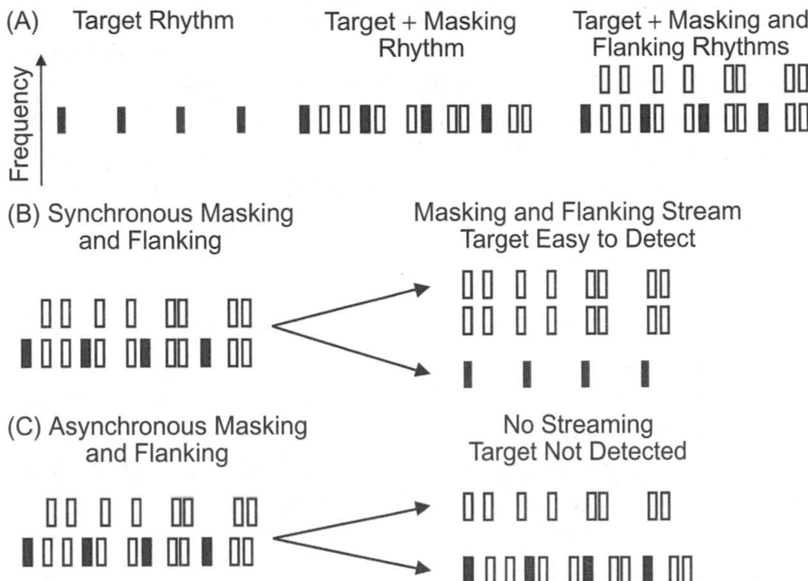

Figure 9.4. The procedure used by Turgeon (2000) to investigate the strength of cues for object segregation. The masking rhythm, at the same frequency as the target rhythm, is combined with the target rhythm. The flanking rhythm, at a different frequency, is added to potentially induce the masking rhythm to stream, thereby making the target rhythm easy to detect (analogous to comodulation masking release) (A). For example, if the noise bursts or tones of the masking and flanking rhythms are synchronous, streaming occurs and the target is detected (B). If the noise bursts or tones are not synchronous, streaming does not occur. The target and masking rhythms remain grouped, forming an irregular rhythm in which the target is difficult to detect (C). Adapted from *Cross-Spectral Auditory Grouping Using the Paradigm of Rhythmic Masking Release*, by M. Turgeon, 2000, unpublished doctoral dissertation, McGill University, Montreal.

might be presented synchronously, but the masking sounds would be presented to the left ear while the flanking sounds would be presented to the right ear. If temporal synchrony dominates streaming, then the masking and flanking sounds should fuse into a stream, and listeners should be able to detect the original rhythm. If spatial direction dominates, then the masking and flanking sounds will not fuse, and the listener should not be able to detect the rhythm (figure 9.4). All the experiments followed this logic.

In this paradigm, temporal synchrony dominates. If the masking and flanking sounds are synchronous, then noise burst sounds will fuse even if they are widely separated in frequency, have uncorrelated amplitude modulation, and are presented to different ears. The identical result holds for tones: synchrony will dominate inharmonic relationships and presentation to different ears. As the asynchrony increases to 20–40 ms, the other cues become more important and can create fusion of the masking and flanking sounds by acting together even if the onsets are asynchronous. Basically, these cues act in an additive manner, so that it is more likely that the masking and flanking sounds will fuse if they have identical amplitude modulation and similar frequencies, and are presented to the same ear. If the masking and flanking sounds share only one or two of these characteristics, they are less likely to fuse.

These results occurred for sequences of about 30 identical 48 ms duration sounds. The probability that two different sources will start synchronously 30 times in a row or lag behind another one by a fixed duration 30 times in a row must be incredibly small. But onset synchrony may be less important for single sounds or sequences of longer-duration sounds. The validity of a cue from a Bayesian perspective, and whether listeners actually make use of that cue, will depend on the overall context.

Summary

1. In natural scenes, it is rare that all the cues to grouping suggest the identical segmentation. Listeners must sift through alternative organizations to select one. Auditory grouping is optimized problem solving.

2. The cues that listeners use to choose their best organization are a grab bag. Some are invariant for all types of sounds, while others are tuned to one type of sound (e.g., speech) and may be localized in specific regions of the auditory cortex, and still others are further detailed to segment specific sounds like bird songs, particular voices, or heart murmurs. Listeners can attend to different aspects of the auditory signal. Moreover, some may be preattentive and obligatory, while others may be based on learned properties, and still others may be based on a combination of the two.

3. Grouping is not all or none. The cues may be contradictory or indeterminate, so that a clear segregation does not happen.The grouping will be ambiguous and weak, so that alternations occur. In Turgeon (2000), listeners perceived only weak fusion between the masking and flanking sounds when the onset asynchrony was in the middle range—10–20 ms.

4. Grouping may evolve over time. I argue that visual grouping is originally based on the physical properties of the elements but that over time the grouping shifts to the perceived properties that are context dependent. Although this has not been proposed explicitly for hearing, I expect that similar transformations occur. (Although you cannot continue to inspect a sound the way you can a visual scene, the ongoing context allows for reinterpretations.) This is similar to the transition from grouping by frequency

to grouping by perceived position described above for speech sentences (Darwin, 1997).

Principles of Visual Grouping

Uniform Connectedness

Palmer (1994) proposed that the basic units in the visual field are enclosed regions defined by edges or contours with similar properties such as color, texture, or lightness. Each such region is presumed to arise from detecting places of discontinuity at abrupt-contrast edges by oriented cells in V1. This type of organization is termed *uniform connectedness* because each region has a relatively uniform surface. Palmer made two supporting arguments. First, there needs to be something to group, the stuff for perceiving. Second, the surfaces of objects in the real world are likely to be relatively uniform, rigid, self-contained, and undergo the same transformations across time. Therefore, organization by uniform connectedness matches the properties of real objects and maximizes the probability that subsequent groupings using these elements will be correct.

Uniform connectedness completely organizes the entire scene, everything in sight. In figure 9.5, it is easy to see that each lighter and darker region is organized by uniform connectedness but also easy to miss the point that the gray region also is organized into an element by the same process. Now the entire scene is organized into elements. But there is no way to determine which elements go with each other. Nearly all of the elements touch each other, and any set of them could be grouped together by proximity or what Palmer (1994) termed *element connectedness*. What is needed now is a process that creates the figure elements and separates them from the ground elements so that the grouping principles can create higher-order figural units.

Figure-Ground Articulation

Rubin (1921) first described the phenomenological differences between the "thing-like" figure regions and the "shapeless" ground. Probably the most important point is that the edges and contours that separate the figure from the ground are perceived to belong to the figure. At a boundary between two regions of uniform connectedness, the boundary appears to enclose the figure region, and the ground region appears to extend behind the figure. Physically, the edge would belong to the object in front. As we interpret the ambiguous scene in figure 9.6 in different ways, the boundary will always

Figure 9.5. The principle of uniform connectedness first breaks the visual scene into enclosed regions. The problem now is grouping the discrete regions into objects (e.g., whether the two small triangles are part of a larger triangle and whether the two rectangular segments are connected) and creating the figure-ground relationships. We perceive the two large light gray areas as forming a continuous ground, but again, that is an inference.

stay with the figure; the boundary shifts from being part of the white rectangle in front of the black rectangle to being a hole in the black rectangle in front of a white continuous background. The boundary shifts as a unit; it does not break apart.[2]

The principles for determining which regions become the figure include the following:

1. Surroundedness: Any region completely surrounded by another usually is perceived as the figure in front of the surrounding ground. (Unless, as illustrated in figure 9.6, it is perceived as a hole in an object, the choice between figure and hole being determined by other cues.)
2. Size: The smaller region usually is perceived as the figure. It is more likely that a smaller object will occlude part of a larger one than the reverse.
3. Contrast: Within a surrounded region, the area with the highest contrast to the background usually is perceived to be the figure.

2. The same perceptual phenomenon is found for auditory induction. The tone (i.e., the figure) appears to continue through the noise masker, and the frequency components common to the tone and masker belong to the tone.

Figure 9.6. The contour stays with the figure. It is the white edges of the smaller rectangle or the edges of the gap in the larger black square.

4. Convexity: Convex figures usually are usually perceived as the figure.
5. Symmetry: Symmetrical regions usually are perceived as the figure.
6. Parallelness: Regions with parallel sides usually are perceived as the figure.

Convexity seems to be the strongest shape principle and will dominate the others if two or more organizations are in conflict. Symmetry may be detectable only after the figural elements are determined by other principles. But the principles for figure-ground organization suffer the same weaknesses as those for grouping. Both sets of principles work for explaining simple illustrations in which the other principles are absent or balanced. But it is extremely difficult to determine how and where to apply these principles for complex scenes and to predict figure-ground organization when each principle would lead to a different solution. What is important is the realization that without some designation of which regions compose the figures, perceptual grouping cannot proceed.

At this point, I have broken up the visual scene into uniform regions and have specified which of those regions are the figure elements that undergo further organization into superordinate regions. What I have not done is consider the ways that the uniform regions could be split into smaller subregions or complex objects into parts. By the same token, I have not considered how the fragments occluded by other regions can be combined to represent objects.

Parsing a Uniform Region Into Parts

Feldman and Singh (2005), starting from the mathematical definition of information (discussed in chapter 3), proved that the information value of a contour is directly proportional to the magnitude of the curvature. Moreover, negative-curvature points carry greater information than equivalent positive-curvature points. Negative curvature is associated with boundaries between objects, while positive curvature is associated with one object only.

When two objects meet or overlap, the overall contour (i.e., the outline of the combined shape) contains concave regions; there are surface discontinuities. Singh and Hoffman (2001) proposed that the natural dividing points occur at the maximum curvature of the concave edge, what they call points of negative minima. Examples are shown in figure 9.7.

This rule can help explain one curious aspect of figure-ground organization. If we take a simple black region with a complex boundary between the two regions and pull the regions apart, the identical boundary looks quite different when attached to the two parts (figure 9.8). In fact, it is often difficult to see that the two parts can be fitted back together. If we apply the negative minima rule, the boundary will split into different parts in the two objects, and that makes it difficult to imagine them as identical. Moreover, the negative minimum rule can help explain why it is easier to detect visual symmetry than visual repetition. Symmetrical objects have the identical placement of minimum points, so that the parts determined by the minima on the left-side and right-side contour lines will be identical. In contrast, objects formed by repeating a shape will not have identical minimum points on the two sides, so that it will be difficult to detect the repetition.

Although the minima rule defines the possible part boundaries, the rule by itself does not predict which parts will, in fact, be formed. To do that,

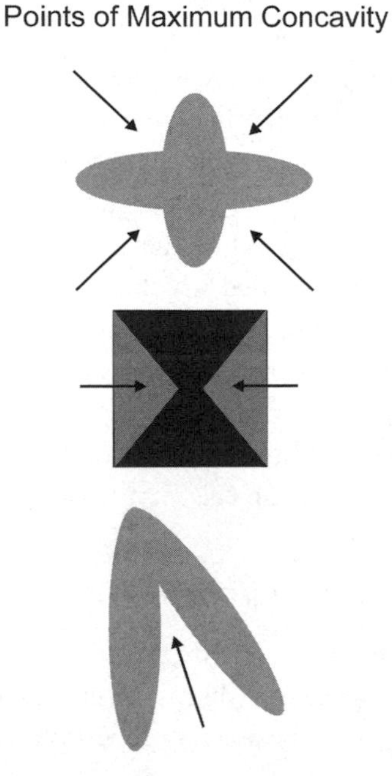

Figure 9.7. Singh and Hoffman (2001) proposed that the natural splitting or dividing points of complex objects occur at points of maximum concavity. In each of the three examples, arrows point to the points of maximum negativity. Adapted from "Part-Based Representations of Visual Shape and Implications for Visual Cognition," by M. Singh and D. D. Hoffman, 2001, in T. F. Shipley and P. J. Kellman (Eds.), *From Fragments to Objects: Segmentation and Grouping in Vision* (pp. 401–459). Amsterdam: Elsevier-Science B.V.

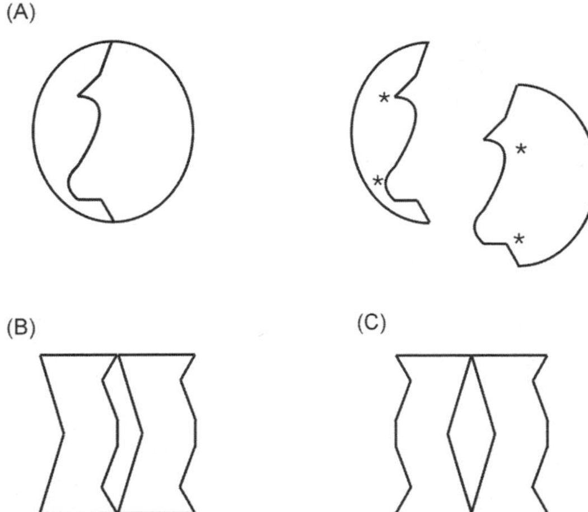

Figure 9.8. If we split a simple object into two irregular parts, the matching sides do not seem to fit back together. Singh and Hoffman (2001) argued that this difficulty occurs because the points of maximum concavity (shown by *) do not coincide (A). A similar argument is used to explain why repetition symmetry (B) is harder to perceive than reflection symmetry (C). Adapted from "Part-Based Representations of Visual Shape and Implications for Visual Cognition," by M. Singh and D. D. Hoffman, 2001, in T. F. Shipley and P. J. Kellman (Eds.), *From Fragments to Objects: Segmentation and Grouping in Vision* (pp. 401–459). Amsterdam: ElsevierScience B.V.

Singh and Hoffman (2001) proposed other principles that predict (again, all other things being equal) what parts will emerge. Imagine cut lines connecting two points on the contour that split the object into two parts. The authors suggested that the goal is to create the lowest number of parts such that each part does not have a negative minimum. If one part does have a negative minimum following a cut, that part should be further divided. The best cut lines to meet this goal (a) have at least one end point at a negative minimum; and (b) cross an axis of local symmetry. Local symmetry is a weak form of symmetry that allows the axis of symmetry to be curved and to occur only in a small region of the figure. Examples are shown in figure 9.9.

Singh and Hoffman (2001) offered the possibility that the choice of which side of a contour is figure and which side is ground is partly based on how the two sides can be broken into parts. Roughly, the idea is that the side in which the parts are more salient due to sharper negative minima becomes the figure and captures the boundary. Thus the figure ground decision is competitive and occurs after comparing both alternatives.[3]

3. We can translate the negative minima rule into sound in terms of loudness. In reverberant environments, a sound rarely decays before another sound starts. According to the negative minima principle, the ongoing sound would be split at points where the increases in loudness would be most rapid.

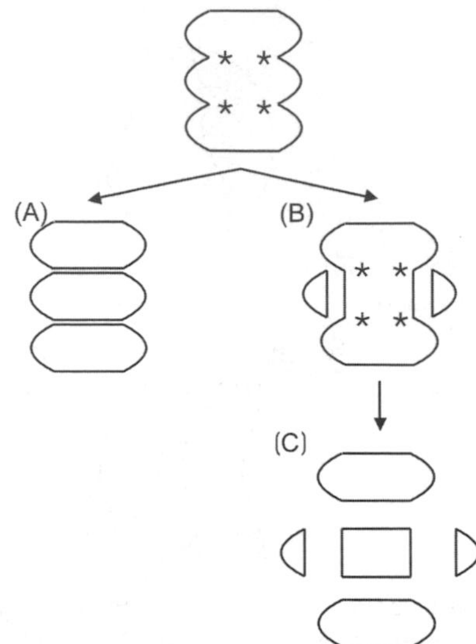

Figure 9.9. Objects are split at points of maximum concavity (shown by *). If a split results in no points of maximum concavity, no further split will occur (A). If a potential split still results in parts with points of maximum concavity (B), those parts are further split until there are no such points (C). Adapted from "Part-Based Representations of Visual Shape and Implications for Visual Cognition," by M. Singh and D. D. Hoffman, 2001, in T. F. Shipley and P. J. Kellman (Eds.), *From Fragments to Objects: Segmentation and Grouping in Vision* (pp. 401–459). Amsterdam: ElsevierScience B.V.

Combining Parts Across Occlusions

The rules underlying the cutting apart of parts of a region do not tell us whether these parts are objects by themselves or if the parts are a portion of a larger object that has been occluded by a smaller nearer object. When an object is occluded, the effect is to create a gap in its edges so that the problem facing the perceiver is whether to close the gap behind the occluding object to create one object from two or more parts or to perceive each part as a separate object. Consider the two cases shown in figure 9.10. In (A), a rectangular shape creates the gap with a different luminance than the ellipse-like surrounding regions. If the two regions of the ellipse are completed, observers do not actually see the closure because there is no energy that could represent that closure. This type of closure is termed *amodal interpolation*. In (B), the ellipse and the rectangle have the same luminance, so that the missing region of the ellipse has the same luminance as the occluding region. If the rectangle is seen in front, this is another example of amodal completion of the ellipse. If the ellipse is seen in front, then the rectangle shape acts to camouflage the contour of the ellipse. To perceive the edges of the ellipse, the observer creates an illusionary contrast contour. This type of closure is termed *modal interpolation*. (The reverse is true for the rectangle shape: If the ellipse is seen in front, then the completion of the rectangle is amodal; if the rectangle is seen in front, then the closure of the rectangle is modal.) Although amodal and modal interpolation have been traditionally thought to be identical, Singh (2004) has shown that amodal interpolation yields sharper corners than modal interpolation.

(A) Amodal Completion

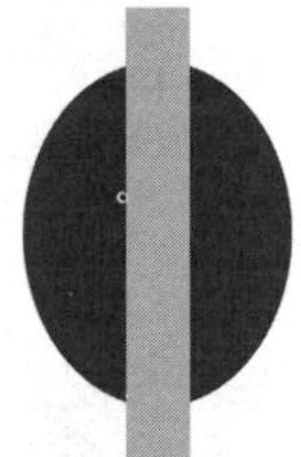

(B) Modal Completion

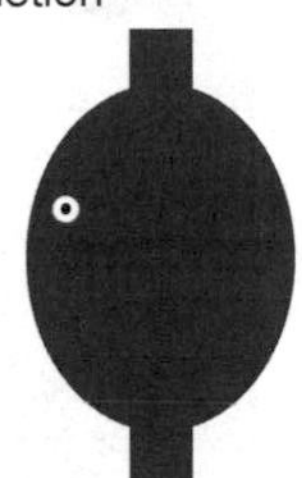

Figure 9.10. Amodal completion occurs if there is no visual energy that could close a gap. This is illustrated in (A): the black region required to close the ellipse is hidden by the rectangle. (Of course, the two regions on either side of the rectangle could be perceived as separate figures; a completed ellipse is but one possible percept.) Modal completion occurs if the visual energy to close the gap is available to the observer (B). Adapted from "Modal and Amodal Completion Generate Different Shapes," by M. Singh, 2004, *Psychological Science, 15*, 454–459.

In real environments, edges can represent different properties. An edge can mark the boundaries of an object or the intersection of two surfaces. But an edge can also represent a change in illumination by a shadow line, or a change in the surface reflectance or texture. Of greatest importance here are edges that signify occlusion, where a surface ends or continues behind another surface. Kellman, Guttman, and Wickens (2001) suggested that while shadow edges are based on discontinuities of one or possibly two properties, occlusion edges are marked by several simultaneous discontinuities such as color, lightness, texture, and motion. Another way to identify occluding edges is in terms of the shape of the edge junctions. Occlusions are invariably signaled by T junctions (see figure 9.11). The defining characteristic of a T junction is that one contour stops at an edge of a smooth second continuing contour. The continuing contour is seen in front, covering the stopped contour, and owns the entire contour. Although it is termed a T junction, the occlusion is seen regardless of the orientation of the two parts.

In sound, edges can be translated as rapid spectral or amplitude changes that can also represent different properties. An edge can mark the boundaries of an object, a louder sound heard against a quieter background, the intersection of two sounds, or the replacement or masking of one by another. But a rapid spectral or amplitude sound edge also can represent a change in illumination such as removing a shadow when the listener (or the sound source) moves out from behind an absorbing or reflecting object such as a wall.

Kellman and Shipley (1991) argued that an edge is perceived to continue behind an occluding surface and join a second edge if the two can be

(A) T Junctions Signifying Occlusions

(B) Y Junctions Signifying an Inside or Outside Corner

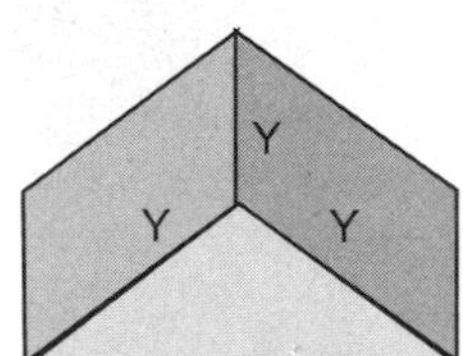

Figure 9.11. T junctions signify occlusion. The two surfaces at T junctions can meet at any angle (A). Other types of junctions signify different surface relationships (B).

connected by a smooth curved line that contains only one bend less than 90°. The smooth curve would start at the end point of one line (matching the slope of the line at that point) and without bending more than 90° join the second line at its slope. Intuitively, this is the general Gestalt principle of good continuation: The inferred connecting line changes direction slowly. Kellman and Shipley (1991) termed this constraint *relatability*. They further argued that relatability determines if the edges get connected regardless of whether the split regions are similar in luminance, color, or texture. The results of Ciocca and Bregman (1987) suggest a similar rule in audition.

Interesting cases occur when complex figures are homogeneous, as shown in figure 9.12. Even though these figures have uniform surfaces and do not have T junctions that signal occlusion, they are usually seen as a single object with multiple parts or as a pair of overlapping objects (termed *self-splitting objects*). Each of the figures possesses negative minima (concavities) to mark points where the figure could be split into parts. The perceptual decision between parts or overlapping objects would then be based on relatability.

For the first two figures (A1 and A2), the possible interpolated contours that match up the disconnected edges satisfy the smooth monotonic relatability constraint, so that they would likely be seen as two overlapping objects. For the third (A3), the relatability constraint is violated, and it is unlikely that the darker left and right regions would be connected. For the self-splitting objects, the first figure (B1) is ambiguous; the ellipses oscillate so that each one is sometimes seen in front of the other. The

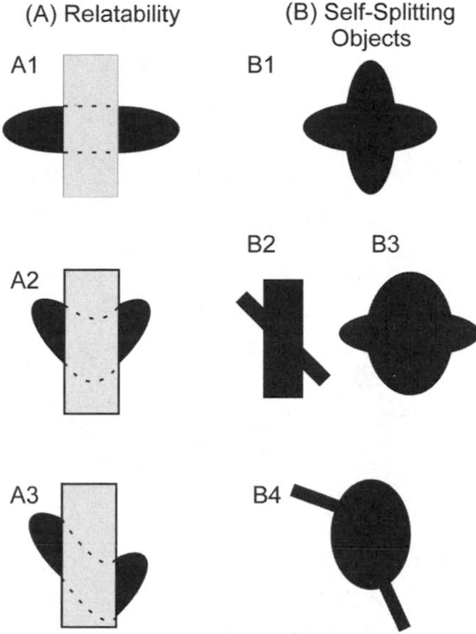

Figure 9.12. The relatability constraint can be used to predict when two surfaces are perceived as continuous and when they are perceived as separate objects. The constraint is satisfied in A1 and A2 because the connecting lines bend less than 90° and the two gray partial ellipses are perceived as forming one continuous object. The constraint is violated in A3, and the two gray regions are perceived as parts of different objects. For self-splitting objects, the "fatter" object is usually seen in front (B2 and B3). If the two possible objects are equal (B1), the perception is unstable and oscillates. If the parts violate the relatability constraint, each region is perceived separately (B4).

second and third figures are not ambiguous. The thick bar (B2) or blob (B3) is seen in front of the thin bar or tail. There is a strong tendency to make the interpolated edge as short as possible, so that the fatter region is seen in front of the thinner region (Petter, 1956). If, in fact, the perceptual decision about which is in front and which is behind is made on the basis of the length of the interpolated edges, then interpolation must precede the depth ordering. For the fourth figure (B4), the relatability constraint is violated, and it is perceived as a single object with several parts.

The concepts of edge interpolation can be extended to surfaces that extend behind an occluding surface. As shown in figure 9.13, the gray circles in the occluding rectangle are seen as part of the complex surface (behind the rectangle) if they fall within the interpolated complex surface. But the identical rightmost gray spot is seen as being on the rectangle because it falls outside the interpolated surface of the occluded shape. Similarly, the black spots are seen as being on the rectangle because they do match the brightness of the occluded surface, while the white spots are seen as holes to the white background.

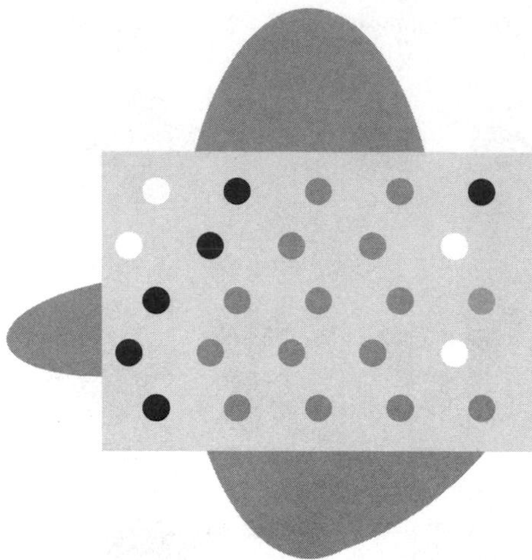

Figure 9.13. The perception of "holed" surfaces occluding other surfaces can be understood in terms of the inferred contour of the occluded surface. The gray circles (except for the gray circle in the middle, far right) come from the occluded shape. The black circles are on the rectangular surface, and the white circles are open holes to the white background. The gray circle in the middle, far right, also appears to be on the rectangle because it is beyond the inferred contour of the occluded shape. Adapted from "Geometric and Neural Models of Object Perception," by P. J. Kellman, S. E. Guttman, and T. D. Wickens, 2001, in T. F. Shipley and P. J. Kellman (Eds.), *From Fragments to Objects: Segmentation and Grouping in Vision* (Vol. 130, pp. 183–245). Amsterdam: Elsevier Science B.V.

When Does Grouping Occur?

Vision

Suppose a trapezoid outline is flashed on a screen and the task is to judge the shape. Was it: (1) a trapezoid perpendicular to the line of sight; or (2) a different shape, say a square, presented at an angle so that the nearer side projects a larger image? The proximal sensation at the eye is ambiguous. To make a decision about the distal shape requires a prior decision about its orientation. Rock (1997) has termed this sort of sequential process *indirect perception*. We can test the degree to which the perceived shape was determined by the perceived orientation experimentally by varying the quality of the depth information. Suppose a square is presented at 45°. Minimizing the depth information should shift the judgments toward the trapezoid, while maximizing the information should shift the judgments toward the square.

Rock and colleagues used a similar approach to argue that grouping is not determined directly by the proximal sensations, but is determined indirectly from perceived proximity and similarity, a distal judgment based on a distal inference. In the first of these experiments, Rock and Brosgole (1964) started with an array of luminous beads connected by invisible strings. The beads were placed in a right-angle vertical-horizontal array perpendicular to the observer so that the distance between lights in a column was clearly less than the distance between lights in a row (figure 9.14A). As expected, the organization was by columns. Then the authors changed the orientation of the array so that the objective distance between the lights in a row became less than the objective distance between lights in a column (see figure 9.14B). Rock and Brosgole created this transformation by rotating the array (which also affected the distance between columns and the size of the proximal images of the beads). But the same transformation could have been done by changing the distance between the beads in the frontal plane without rotation (which would not affect the size of the images). Both possibilities are shown in figure 9.14A. If the observers viewed the display binocularly with good depth information, the observers compensated for the proximal convergence of the lights in a row due to the perceived increased depth caused by the rotation: The observers organized

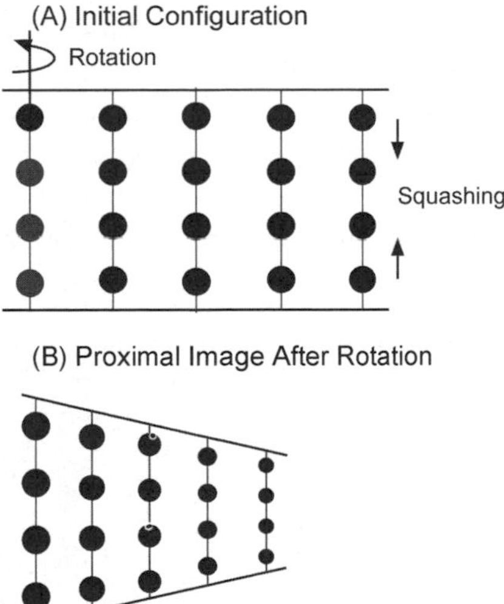

Figure 9.14. The initial array of beads is shown in (A). The beads are placed so that organization into columns is predominant. The proximal image (B) could have resulted from a rotation of the array at one end or by squashing the other end (depicted by arrows in A). If observers perceived the array in depth, column organization was maintained for greater rotational angles; if observers did not perceive the array as being rotated but as a flat trapezoid in the frontal plane, row organization became predominant when the proximal distances favored row organization. Adapted from "Grouping Based on Phenomenal Proximity," by I. Rock and L. Brosgole, 1964, *Journal of Experimental Psychology, 67*, 531–538.

by columns even when the distances between the beads favored row organization (i.e., at the observer's eye, the distance between the beads in a row was less than the distance between beads in a column). In contrast, if the observers viewed the display with one eye and poor depth information so that they were more likely to perceive the array as being squashed, the grouping shifted to organization by rows at the angle at which the proximal distances favored the row organization. In both cases then, the perceived proximity inferred from the perceived orientation of the surface (in depth, or not in depth) was the basis for grouping.

In a similar experiment, Rock, Nijhawan, Palmer, and Tudor (1992) demonstrated that it was perceived lightness, not the proximal luminance, that determined grouping. In the control condition, there were five columns, each with four squares of equal reflectance (see figure 9.15A). In the baseline condition, the three left columns had a greater reflectance (68.4%) than the two on the right (17.6%), and observers obviously grouped the three left columns together. In the experimental condition (B), the authors placed a translucent plastic strip over the central column so that the reflectance of the center column equaled the two on the right (to 17.6%). Following the same logic as before, if the observers grouped on the basis of the physical energy reaching their eyes, they would group the central column with the two on the right. However, they continued to group the middle column with the two on the left. The observers first compensated for the effect of the filter, and then grouped on the basis of perceived lightness. They were able to compensate for the darkening effect of the filter because the filter extended the entire length of the column and simultaneously darkened the background and boundary. The grouping was indirect, following the adjustment for the

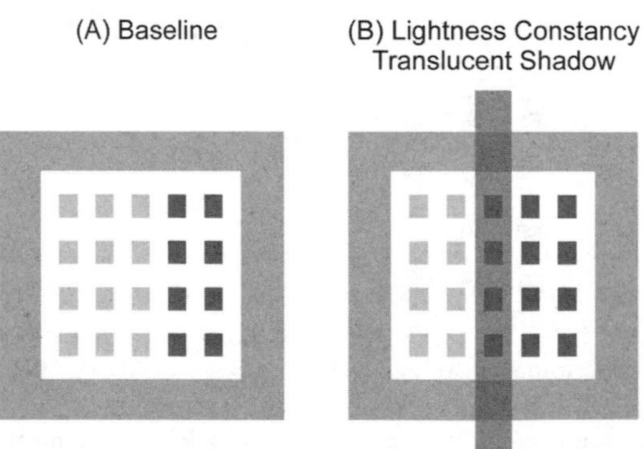

Figure 9.15. Perceived lightness, not proximal lightness, determines organization. Observers were able to compensate for the translucent shadow shown in (B), and judged the middle column to group with the two left-most columns. Adapted from "Grouping Based on Phenomenal Similarity of Achromatic Color," by I. Rock, R. Nijhawan, S. E. Palmer, and L. Tudor, 1992, *Perception, 21*, 779–789.

filter inferred from the background change (this is similar to the strategy proposed in chapter 7 for asymmetric color matching).

Schulz and Sanocki (2003) have demonstrated that proximal (retinal) and constancy grouping coexist but have different time courses. In fact, Rock (1997) proposed that initially there is lower-level literal perception corresponding to the retinal stimulation. If that is inadequate for some reason, the literal perception is replaced by what he termed a *higher-order world* or *constancy mode*. Usually, the transition from the literal to the world mode is irresistible, although the literal mode may bias the world-mode judgment and although it is still possible to make literal-mode judgments. To make this concrete, although observers grouped by reflectance in the experiment described above (Rock et al., 1992), it is very likely that they would be able to group the columns by luminance if asked.

In the later experiment (Schulz & Sanocki, 2003), the exposure time of a grid similar to that used by Rock et al. (1992) was varied from 200 to 2,000 ms. At the shortest exposure time, nearly all choices were based on luminance matching (88%). In contrast, at the longest exposure time nearly all matches were based on reflectance (83%). Schulz and Sanocki proposed that retinal matching is performed in the earliest cortical regions (V1 or V2) and that reflectance matching is carried out in V4.

These sorts of results parallel those discussed in chapter 1 with respect to the perceived motion of spatial gratings through an aperture. Recall that the initial percept is roughly toward the average of the motion of the two gratings (i.e., the additive vector direction), what we would call the proximal percept. This percept is replaced by a perception that is based on the intersection of the lines of constraint, what we would call constancy or world mode. The vector average still biased the intersection of constraint judgments toward the additive vector direction.

Audition

The issue of when grouping occurs has not been explicitly discussed with respect to stream segregation. As described above, the default percept is one of coherence and that it takes several repetitions before streams arise if several sounds are recycled continuously (Bregman, 1990). Thus, there is a shift from proximal to distal perceiving.

It is also likely that the overall context determines segregation. We can imagine the following experiment. We start with a stationary tone with a spoken-vowel spectrum of harmonic components and add energy at one frequency. (A natural vowel would not work because it changes its pitch and spectral content over time.) If the resulting sound were presented for a short duration, we would then expect the listener to report a funny-sounding sound. This outcome would be analogous to retinal or proximal visual processing. On one hand, if the sound was presented for a longer duration or embedded in normal speaking, we might expect that stream segregation based on the listener's knowledge of spoken language to occur, so that the listener would hear two sounds: the original steady vowel tone plus the added harmonic. On the other hand, if the sound was embedded in other nonspeech sounds, we might not expect the sound to break into two parts. Each of these outcomes would be analogous to reflectance or world-mode processing. It is much like interpreting "I3" as a B in text and as 13 in a string of numbers.

How Auditory and Visual Proximal Stimulation Combine to Form One Distal Object

Most real-life scenes we encounter have both auditory and visual inputs. The problem, therefore, is to decide whether the inputs come from the same object or from different objects. We know from the above material that the de facto assumptions are that sounds come from one object, and that the light comes from one continuous smooth surface (Wandell, 1995). By analogy, we would expect the de facto assumption here to be that each distinct auditory sound comes from one distinct visual object, the *unity assumption*. If the working assumption is that the inputs come from one object, then it is useful to combine the information in some way from both senses because neither the auditory nor visual system is powerful enough to produce the correct distal object under all conditions (Ernst & Bulthoff, 2004). When the auditory and visual proximal sensations are complementary and reinforce the one-object assumption, there may be enhancement of the response so that weak stimuli from each modality generate a strong response when combined. When there is conflict between the auditory and visual proximal sensations (e.g., spatial position for ventriloquism), to maintain the unity assumption observers can disregard one source as error, or they can integrate the information to create a compromise percept that may split the differences equally or be biased toward the proximal stimulation from one of the modalities (Partan & Marler, 1999; Welch, 1999).[4] Alternately, if the proximal information is too discrepant, observers can decide that the auditory and visual inputs come from different objects. In what follows below, I first describe the optimal way to combine discrepant auditory and visual information. Then, under the general rubric of the unity assumption, I describe

4. When there are multiple sound sources, some visible and some not (e.g., an orchestra), the correspondence problem of matching sounds to objects occurs. My guess is that a crude correspondence is based on spatial location, but that the correct correspondence is solved by correlated changes in the auditory and visual inputs (e.g., correlated changes in finger plus bow placement and instrumental notes, correlated movements of lips and the sound of one's name).

experiments using discrepant temporal or spatial inputs that reveal how observers integrate information to arrive at their judgments.

Optimally Combining Auditory and Visual Information

The best way to combine information from the two senses depends on the listener's goal. If the goal is to maximize the reliability of the judgments, then from a Bayesian viewpoint, we should weight the information from each modality on the basis of its reliability (or equivalently, its variability). This strategy produces the estimate with the lowest variance (the maximum likelihood estimate). If the cues are equally reliable, then the best solution is simply to average the two, but if one of the cues is more reliable, then that cue should be weighted more heavily. We can write this out in equation form:

$$\text{Judgment} = \text{weight}_{\text{auditory}} \times \text{input}_{\text{auditory}} + \text{weight}_{\text{visual}} \times \text{input}_{\text{visual}}. \quad (9.1)$$

The weights are proportional to 1/variance of the cue, so that the auditory weight is

$$w_{\text{auditory}} = (1/\sigma^2{}_a)/[(1/\sigma^2{}_a) + (1/\sigma^2{}_v)] \quad (9.2)$$

where $\sigma^2{}_a$ is the variance of the auditory cue and $\sigma^2{}_v$ is the variance of the visual cue. The visual weight would have the same form, substituting the variance of the visual cue for the variance of the auditory cue in the numerator.

In general, the weight for any cue will be equal to the inverse of its variance divided by the sum of the inverses of all other cues:

$$W_i = 1/\sigma^2{}_i/\Sigma 1/\sigma^2{}_i. \quad (9.3)$$

If we define the reliability of a cue as the inverse of its variance $1/\sigma^2{}_i$, then the reliability of the integrated information is simply the sum of the individual reliabilities:

$$\text{Reliability} = \Sigma(1/\sigma^2{}_i). \quad (9.4)$$

For auditory plus visual presentation, the reliability will be:

$$1/\sigma_A{}^2 + 1/\sigma_V{}^2 = \sigma_A{}^2\sigma_V{}^2/(\sigma_A{}^2 + \sigma_V{}^2). \quad (9.5)$$

The joint reliability will always be greater than the reliability of either input, and the gain will be greatest when the reliabilities are equal.

The majority of the research described below does not attempt to directly measure the reliabilities or determine how closely the results fit the Bayesian model. Instead, the research attempts to discover which is the dominant modality when the temporal and spatial information is discrepant, and to determine when the percept shifts from a single object to separate auditory and visual objects. Other research explicitly varies the reliabilities by adding noise to one or both of the modalities. In those experiments, the experimental question is to what degree observers change their weighting to reflect those reliabilities.

Unity Assumption

The majority of studies use one auditory and visual input, so the unity assumption is that the discrepant auditory and visual sensations come from the same object. If there are multiple objects, then the unity assumption might be rephrased as a source-object assumption, namely that each distinct sound in the overall mixture comes from a distinct object in, or a distinct part of, the visual scene.

It is easy to miss the difficulty of determining if the proximal stimuli come from the same object. Consider spatial position: The natural way to encode the position of an object is in terms of a frame of reference (a set of axes) that matches the structure of the sense organ. For hearing, the natural frame of reference for spatial direction must be the head-centered position due to the comparisons of the signal at the two ears. In contrast, for seeing, the natural frame of reference must be retinal-centered due to the topographical organization of the retina and visual cortex. If the eyes are not looking straight ahead, there needs to be a superordinate reference frame to coordinate the two (Pouget, Deneve, & Duhamel, 2002).

The de facto assumption is the unity assumption (Welch, 1999), and the two most important properties that determine its strength are the degree of perceived temporal synchrony between the auditory and visual inputs and the degree to which the inputs appear to come from the identical spatial location. Imagine that either the temporal or spatial properties are made progressively discrepant. Initially, the input from one modality would be dominant, and the perception of the input from the other modality would shift toward the dominant modality. Eventually, the discrepancy would be so great that the unity assumption would fail and the inputs would be perceived independently. If both the temporal and spatial inputs were made discrepant, the strength of the unity assumption would depend jointly on the degree of perceived temporal synchrony and spatial location equivalence. There is a trade-off here. Perceived temporal synchrony can balance widely different perceived spatial locations and vice versa. Nonetheless, there should be values of temporal asynchronies or spatial separations beyond which the unity assumption becomes improbable. Although I discuss the temporal and spatial factors separately below, in any real-life situation both will determine the percept.

Another factor that affects the unity assumption is the "compellingness" of the stimulation and the familiarity with the distal objects themselves.

Jackson (1953) found that the sound of a steam kettle coupled with the sight of a spatially offset but silent puff of steam produced a greater bias than the sound of a bell coupled with the sight of a spatially offset but inert bell. However, the results using familiar stimuli may result from observers responding on the basis of what they know about the objects, rather than what they perceive.

Perceived Onset Synchrony

The critical property for the perception of one or more auditory streams was onset synchrony. Onset asynchronies as short as 30 ms were sufficient to lead to the perception of two complex sounds. On that basis, we might expect that perceived onset synchrony of the auditory and visual input would be a critical property for perceiving one object. Lewkowicz (2000) summarized developmental results that propose that all types of multimodal temporal perception (e.g., temporal rate and rhythm) emerge in hierarchical fashion from the fundamental property of temporal synchrony.

The perception of synchrony between auditory and visual inputs poses a more complicated problem than that between two auditory or two visual events because the speed of light is so much faster than the speed of sound. Even at 10 m, a light stimulus will reach the observer 30 ms before a sound stimulus. Any difference in arrival time is compensated to some degree by the faster mechanical processing of the sound at the cochlea. In cats, it takes about 13 ms for an auditory stimulus to activate neurons in the superior colliculus that receive inputs from different modalities, as opposed to about 65–100 ms for a visual stimulus to activate the same neurons due to the slower chemical processing of light energy at the retina (Stein & Meredith, 1993). In humans, the P1 evoked response potential occurs about 75 ms after onset for auditory stimuli and about 100 ms after onset for visual stimuli (Andreassi & Greco, 1975). Balancing the speed and processing differences, it is estimated that the onset of the neural signals will be synchronous only when the object is roughly 10 m away (Poppel, 1988).

Although there is some controversy about whether the perception of synchrony is based on the excitation of individual multimodal cells or the simultaneous excitation of unimodal cells, the underlying conception is that of a temporal integration window. If the activity patterns resulting from the two inputs overlap within such a window, synchrony will be perceived. It is important to keep two things in mind. First, it is the activity pattern due to the inputs that is critical, not the physical onsets or the latencies to activate the neurons. The window can be quite long. Second, do not think that there are discrete nonoverlapping windows. There must be "rolling" overlapping windows (e.g., 0–200, 5–205, 10–210 ms, etc.). If the output from the integration windows depends on the amount of simultaneous activation, then any pair of inputs will generate different output excitations, depending on the amount of temporal overlap of the pair.[5]

Why then do we perceive simultaneity at most distances? One possibility is that there is a long temporal integration window. Based on single-cell recordings, if the auditory and visual neural signals occur within 100 ms of each other, that input will be sufficient to fire neural cells that integrate firings in different modalities (Meredith, Clemo, & Stein, 1987). This implies that the source of the auditory and visual stimulus energy could be +/– 30 m or more from each other, based on the overlap of activation patterns (Meredith et al., 1987). Sugita and Suzuki (2003) have suggested an alternative to a wide integration duration, namely that the integration region shifts as a function of the perceived distance of the source. In their task, observers judged whether an LED light source positioned from 1 to 50 m in front of them was presented before or after a burst of white noise presented by headphones. They found that when the LEDs were 1 m away, the noise needed to be delayed by 5 ms to be perceived as synchronous, but if the LEDs were 40 m away, the noise had to be delayed by 106 ms to be perceived as synchronous. The participants thus expected the sound to occur later relative to the light as the distance increased. There are huge but stable individual differences in this sort of task. With 17 participants, the range of synchrony judgments was 170 ms (Stone et al., 2001).

Perceived Rhythmic Synchrony (Temporal Ventriloquism)

In the research described below, the auditory input is a series of discrete short tones while the visual input may be a continuous light or a series of discrete short light flashes. Here, the onset of a visual target is perceived to occur at the onset of a sound even if the timings are quite different. This illusionary percept has been termed *temporal ventriloquism* to create a parallel to the classical term *spatial ventriloquism*, in which a sound is perceived to come from the spatial location of the visual object.[6]

One type of temporal ventriloquism occurs when the amplitude modulation of a tone induces an illusionary modulation of a light. For example, if a single visual flash is presented simultaneously with two or more short auditory beeps, the light flash appears to oscillate on and off two times (Shams, Kamitani, & Shimojo, 2000). The oscillation occurs even if the beep onset is delayed by 70 ms, but disappears if the onset delay is 100 ms or more.

5. This is yet another example of a population code, analogous to those for orientation or auditory frequency. The perceptual information is found in the distribution of the responses, not the magnitude of any single output.

6. For temporal ventriloquism, the observer's task is to judge the occurrence or rhythm of an event. For spatial ventriloquism, the observer's task is to judge the location of an event.

These timings are consistent with the temporal integration window described above.

Recanzone (2003) has further demonstrated the auditory capture of temporal patterns. In the baseline conditions, a standard series of four lights or four tones was presented at the rate of four elements per second. Then a comparison series was presented at rates between 3.5 and 4.5 elements per second, and the participants indicated whether the rate of the second sequence was faster or slower than the standard. Participants could judge differences in auditory rate far better than differences in visual rate (i.e., the difference threshold for auditory rate was smaller).

The interesting conditions involved the simultaneous presentation of the auditory and visual sequences. In the standard sequences, the auditory and visual stimuli were always presented synchronously at four elements per second. In the comparison sequences, the auditory and visual stimuli were presented at different rates (see figure 9.16). Here, the participants were told to ignore either the auditory or visual sequence and make their judgments of rate only on the basis of the other. On those trials in which listeners were told to attend to the auditory sequence and ignore the visual sequence, listeners were able to ignore the visual sequence and based their judgments solely on the rate of the auditory sequence. In contrast, on those trials in which listeners were told to attend to the visual sequence and ignore the auditory sequence, they were unable to do so. The rate of the supposedly ignored auditory sequence determined their judgments of visual rate. In other words, the timing of the visual lights was perceived to be equal to that of the supposedly ignored auditory stimuli. The arrows in figure 9.16 depict these two outcomes. There were, however, rate limits; if the auditory stimuli were presented at twice the rate of the visual stimuli (8/s versus 4/s) there was no visual capture: Observers were able to accurately judge the visual rate.

These results confirm previous work demonstrating auditory "driving" of the perceived visual flashing rate. For example, Shipley (1964) required participants to adjust the rate of the auditory stimulus so that it appeared just different than the rate of the visual stimulus. If the rate of the flashing light was set at 10 Hz, the mismatch was not detected until the auditory rate decreased to 7 Hz or increased to 22 Hz. Based on these results and those of Recanzone (2003) described above, it appears that the auditory stimulus can drive the visual rate from one-half to two times the actual flashing rate of the visual input.

All of these experiments used nonmeaningful stimuli, so that it is impossible to determine whether the participants perceived the tones and lights as coming from a single object or not, or whether the strength of the illusion depended on the compellingness of the connection between the auditory and visual inputs. My guess is that auditory driving occurs

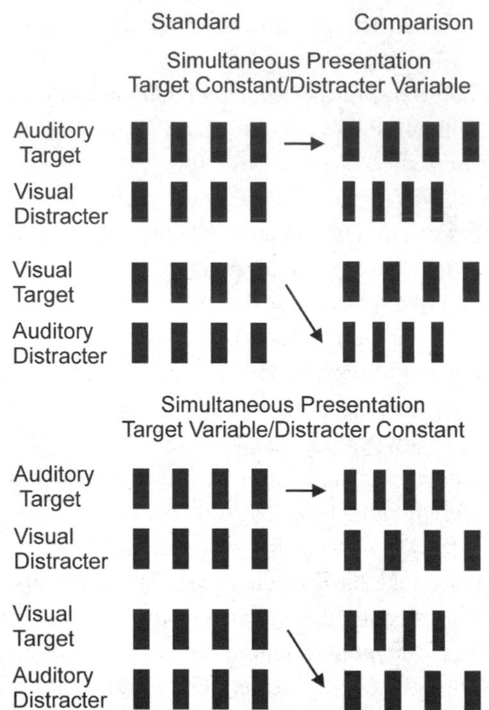

Figure 9.16. Recanzone (2003) used two simultaneous presentation conditions. In both conditions, participants were able to ignore the visual sequences and judge differences in the presentation rate between the standard and comparison auditory sequences. But participants could not ignore the presentation rate of the auditory sequence when required to judge the visual presentation rate. Participants ended up judging the presentation rate of the standard visual rate (4/s) against the rate of the comparison auditory sequence. Adapted from "Auditory Influences on Visual Temporal Rate Perception," by G. H. Recanzone, 2003, *Journal of Neurophysiology, 89*, 1079–1093.

independently of the compellingness of the perceived unity because the sizes of the effects do not change if the tones and lights are separated by more than 90°. Auditory driving appears to be preattentive and obligatory. In contrast, as described below, the magnitude of spatial ventriloquism with real-life objects does depend on the magnitude of the discrepant spatial location and previously formed cognitive expectations.

Perceived Spatial Location (Spatial Ventriloquism)

The second factor that determines the strength of the unity assumption is the difference in the perceived spatial location of the auditory and visual inputs. To maintain the unity assumption as the perceived auditory and visual locations become more discrepant, observers must shift their perception of the location of one or both of the sources to make them coincident. Nearly always, visual-spatial location information dominates auditory spatial location information when the two conflict.[7] As for temporal ventriloquism, I will consider only the immediate effects of the spatial conflict, and will not consider long-term adaptation that may be due to cognitive interpretations.

Slutsky and Recanzone (2001) investigated the temporal and spatial dependency of spatial bias using a bare-bones stimulus consisting of a single LED and one loudspeaker (200 ms noise burst or 1000 Hz tone). In the first experiment, the LED and speaker were directly in front of the participant. The experimental variable was the amount of onset asynchrony between the LED and speaker necessary to produce the perception that the two did not start or end at the same time. The participants perceived illusionary synchrony between the light and tone as long as the light did not lead the tone by more than 150 ms or as long as the tone did not lead the light by more than 100 ms. Thus, participants were more likely to judge that the two were simultaneous if the light preceded the tone. Onset disparities beyond these limits, particularly if the tone preceded the LED, eliminated the illusion of synchrony.

In the second experiment, the LED remained in front of the participant but the tone was offset in 4° increments to the left or right and was presented 0, 50, 100, 150, or 250 ms after the onset of the LED. The participant's task was to judge whether the tone and LED were presented at the same location, disregarding temporal differences. Two regions were found, illustrated in figure 9.17.

1. For the spatial offsets of 0° and +4/–4°, the tone and LED were invariably judged to be at the same position up to about a 50 ms offset asynchrony. At longer onset disparities, there was a slight shift to perceiving the tone and LED at different positions.
2. For the spatial offsets of +8/–8° and +12/–12°, the tone and LED were nearly always judged as being at different positions, and there was no effect of the onset disparity.

These results demonstrate that spatial ventriloquism will occur for a tone and light as long as the temporal and spatial disparities stay within certain bounds. Because this stimulus configuration was designed to minimize the perception of unity, I would guess that the limiting disparities found here, roughly 50–100 ms and 6°, are minimums. As the connection between the auditory and visual stimulation becomes more compelling

7. I originally used the term *capture* here, but that is incorrect. The perceived location is invariably a compromise between the auditory and visual positions. Rarely is the auditory + visual stimulus perceived at the exact visual position.

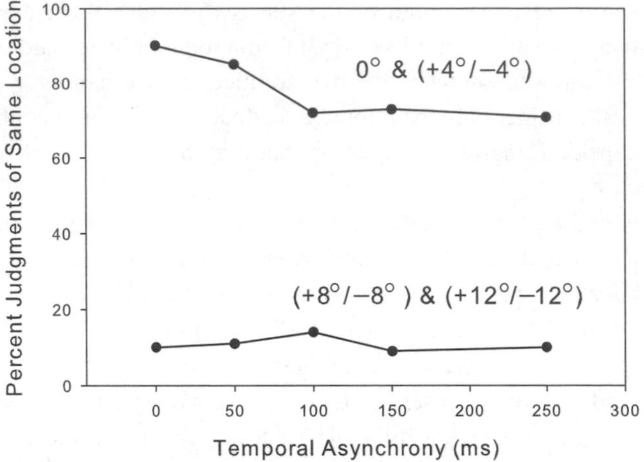

Figure 9.17. Perceived location and onset asynchrony jointly determine spatial ventriloquism. Using a single LED and one loudspeaker (short noise burst or 1000 Hz tone), the light and sound were perceived to come from the same position as long as the actual spatial discrepancy was less than 4° regardless of the temporal asynchrony. In similar fashion, the light and sound were perceived to come from different positions as long as the actual spatial discrepancy was greater than 8° regardless of the temporal asynchrony. Adapted from "Temporal and Spatial Dependency of the Ventriloquism Effect," by D. A. Slutsky and G. H. Recanzone, 2001, *NeuroReport, 12*, 7–10.

(e.g., a speaking face), spatial ventriloquism will occur at far greater temporal disparities and spatial discrepancies.[8]

Ventriloquism can serve the useful purpose of separating two intermixed auditory messages. Driver (1996) created a particularly clever demonstration of this. Participants had to shadow (verbally repeat the words of) one message composed of random words that was presented interleaved with another random word message spoken by the same voice coming from one loudspeaker. Only the visual lip movements on one television corresponding to the target speech sounds specified the relevant message. In the control condition, the loudspeaker and video monitor displaying the lip movements were presented at the same spatial position. In the experimental condition, the video monitor was spatially offset so that the lip movements came from a different location (sketched in figure 9.18). The surprising outcome was that performance was better in the experimental condition in which the spoken words and lip movements were spatially offset.

8. These outcomes resemble those for the formation of auditory streams. Even though onset asynchrony was the most important cue for auditory segregation, other factors would determine segregation if the onset asynchrony was ambiguous (10–20 ms), not long enough to dominate. Here, spatial disparity was the most important cue for visual capture, and temporal disparity was only important if the spatial disparity was ambiguous.

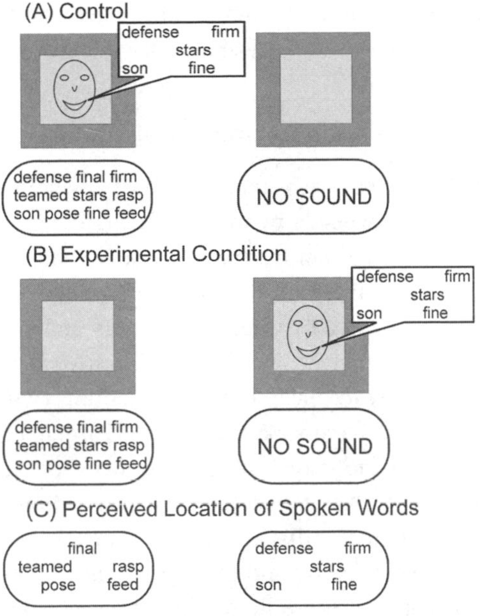

Figure 9.18. In the control condition (A), the talker, shown on the television in front of the participant, makes lip movements corresponding to one of the interleaved messages (in rectangle) composed of random words. The two random interleaved messages are presented through one loudspeaker (rounded rectangle) and all words seem to come from that television. The offset television is blank and there is no sound from that direction. In the experimental condition (B), the talker is shown on the offset television, but the loudspeaker in front of the participant presents all the spoken words. But, as shown in (C), the participant perceives the words corresponding to the lip movements as coming from the offset television (spatial ventriloquism), while the nonmouthed words still appear to come from the television in front (C). Adapted from "Enhancement of Selective Listening by Illusionary Mislocation of Speech Sounds Due to Lip-Reading," by J. Driver, 1996, *Nature, 381*, 66–68.

Driver argued that the better shadowing of the target words was due to spatial ventriloquism. When the visual display was displaced, the target sounds were pulled away from the distracter sounds by the matching lip movements. This illusory spatial separation between the target and distracter sounds helped the selective listening, in exactly same fashion as when the two auditory messages truly would come from different directions (or different frequencies). The ventriloquism could only happen after the joint auditory-visual perceptual system had already worked out to some extent which sounds matched the synchronous lip movements (and so should migrate toward them), and which sounds did not match (and so should be left behind). After this matching problem has been solved, presumably without direct attention, the perceptual system can facilitate attention to different points in the joint auditory-visual space. These results imply that spatial ventriloquism, binding of the target words to the lip movements, can take place before auditory spatial selection is fully completed.

Compellingness of the Auditory and Visual Stimuli

Throughout, I have argued that perceptual processes are tuned to physical processes and outcomes, whether by means of field forces, cortical receptive field organizations, or Bayesian learning. Thus, we should expect that the degree of temporal and spatial ventriloquism will depend on the observer's a priori belief in the connection between the auditory and visual stimuli.

Dixon and Spitz (1980) investigated the ability to detect auditory and visual temporal asynchrony for meaningful events: films (with a sound track) of a speaking face and a hammer hitting a peg. Participants hit a key that progressively increased the temporal disparity between the visual images and the sound track until they perceived asynchrony. Participants were far more tolerant of the temporal disparities if the sound preceded the visual image. People clearly expect to see the action producing the sound to occur before hearing the sound and are more able to detect timing offsets when this occurs. The same asymmetry between visual leading and auditory leading found above (50 ms) was more than doubled here (about 120 ms). Participants were more tolerant of disparities for the speaking faces, particularly if the sound preceded the image. This probably is due to the fact that movements of the facial muscles normally precede the actual production of sound. (The same natural disparity occurs for musical instruments; it takes 50–100 ms after blowing or bowing for the sound to reach its maximum amplitude.) Thus, there is a natural disparity that varies across speech sounds so that it would be harder to perceive the added disparity against the naturally occurring variation.

Researchers (Jack & Thurlow, 1973; Thurlow & Jack, 1973) used "talking" puppets. If the puppets were shown with appropriate mouth movements, particularly of the lower jaw, the visual bias was very strong even if the eyes and nose of the puppet were removed. But without mouth movements, the visual bias was reduced by 50%. The perception of ventriloquism occurred even if the timing of the mouth movements and speech sounds were clearly out of sync. The bias was greatly reduced only if the sound was delayed by 200 ms or more. Subsequently, D. H. Warren, Welch, and McCarthy (1981) varied the meaningfulness of the visual input. If the visual stimulus was a moving mouth synchronous with the voice, there was a strong visual bias. However, if the visual stimulus was a steady light, the visual bias was weak.

Another way to measure the degree of spatial bias for realistic stimuli makes use of a pointing response. Suppose that a silent television displaying a speaking face is located in front of the participant, and the voice is presented through a loudspeaker 15° left of the midline of the participant. In the control condition, either the television or the speaker is used, and the participants are asked to point to each one. This ensures that the two can be localized correctly. Then the television and speaker are used together, and the participants are asked to point to the perceived location of the voice and to the perceived location of the face. The bias measure is the shift in position divided by the distance between the visual and auditory stimulus. If the voice is localized 5° to the left, the visual bias is 33%; if the face is localized 3° to the left, the auditory bias is 20%. If the sum of the two bias measures equals 100%, the visual and auditory stimuli are perceived to be located at the same point. If the sum is less than 100%, the two stimuli are perceived to move toward each other but are still perceived in different locations.

Using a measure of bias, Jackson (1953) varied the spatial separation of a picture of a steaming kettle and the sound of the steam escaping. At horizontal separations of 30°, 60°, and 90°, the visual bias was 97%, 62%, and 37% respectively. Bermant and Welch (1976) varied the spatial separation of simultaneous lights and tones. At horizontal separations of 10°, 20°, and 30°, the visual bias was 57%, 17%, and 12%. Jack and Thurlow (1973) used a speaking puppet with varying horizontal and vertical separations. The visual bias was greater for vertical discrepancies (up to 50°) than for horizontal displacements (up to 30°), which is understandable given that it is harder to locate sounds vertically than horizontally. (If the sound is at the midline, there is no time delay or intensity difference cues, so that the vertical position must be determined from timbre differences due to the shape of the outer ear.) In sum, visual bias is greater when it is likely that the auditory and visual stimuli come from the same object.

Summary of Temporal and Spatial Ventriloquism

These results illustrate that the perception of a unified object from inputs from several modalities depends on temporal, spatial, and cognitive expectations. There are trading relationships in which one correlated physical property (say, onset synchrony) can compensate for a discrepant physical property (say, spatial location) or in which a cognitive expectation can balance a physical discrepancy. Such trading relationships imply that the properties and expectations are functionally equivalent, even though they are of different sorts. It may be that temporal ventriloquism is more obligatory, but since the published research uses such a diverse set of conditions, it is difficult to draw firm conclusions.

Reliability of the Auditory and Visual Cues

The results from the ventriloquism experiments demonstrate that the auditory and visual information is jointly used to make perceptual inferences. There was an auditory bias for temporal discrepancies and a visual bias for spatial discrepancies. This has led to the view that the biases are due to an inherent appropriateness of hearing for timing and seeing for space. An alternate view is that these results reflect that the resolution for timing variations is better for hearing and the resolution for spatial variations is better for seeing. The following results suggest that the resolution view rather than the appropriateness view is correct by demonstrating that the degree of bias is correlated to resolution.

In a spatial discrepancy paradigm, Battaglia, Jacobs, and Aslin (2003) varied the reliability of the visual information by adding random-noise pixels that reduced the discriminability of the location of an auditory-visual "bump." They found that participants tended to use the auditory location more (reducing the visual bias), but there still was a visual bias. This is one of many more examples of perceptual conservatism, in which perceivers do not make optimal use of information. The conservatism may be the outcome of not "updating" the weights appropriately and trying to avoid making egregious errors such as locating the source outside of the visual and auditory location cues.

In contrast, Alais and Burr (2004) found that observers integrated auditory and visual information in nearly optimal fashion. They varied the discriminability of the location of a visual blob by manipulating the blurriness (i.e., the variability) of the image. If the blurriness of the visual image was low (so that the blob was easily localized), the reliability of the visual information was 5–10 times better than the reliability of the auditory localization information, and in this case the observers showed a high degree of visual bias. However, if the blurriness of the visual image was high (so that the blob was poorly localized), the reliability of the visual information was poorer than that of the auditory information, and in this case the observers showed an auditory location bias. If the reliabilities were roughly equal, there was no bias.

Heron, Whitaker, and McGraw (2004) systematically varied the resolution of auditory and visual information in a bouncing stimulus. The auditory signal was a white noise burst that signaled the bounce, and the visual signal was a reversal in the direction of movement of a blob on a computer screen. Making the noise signal occur when the blob was at a different location than the reversal point created the discrepant information. Changing the duration from a short click to a longer swooshing sound decreased the auditory resolution, and increasing the diameter of the blob decreased the visual resolution. If the resolution of either the auditory or visual signal was high, then the resolution of the other signal did not affect the judgments. But if the resolution of either signal was intermediate, the resolution of the other signal affected the bias. Increasing the auditory resolution led to a stronger auditory bias and vice versa. There was a reciprocal shift based on the reliability of each signal.

It is unknown how observers estimate the variability of the sensory information. Do observers have to learn in conscious fashion, or would the spread of excitation across a population of cells derive the variability automatically? As argued in chapter 6, adaptation to changes in sensory arrays are multifaceted. Fairhall et al. (2001) found that adaptation to changes in the input variability occurred within 1 s for the fly and that speed suggests that updating occurs automatically. Nonetheless, observers still can attend to one modality voluntarily and thereby override any biasing toward the modality with the greater precision.

McGurk Effect

Speaking brings forth both visual and acoustic information concerning the articulatory production of speech sounds. We have argued that people will normally assume that the auditory and visual information represent the same activity or event (e.g., the sight of a swinging hammer and the sound of its impact). Moreover, we have argued when there is conflict, the most sensitive modality will dominate the percept.

When we come to speech, the role of vision is less clear. The visual information comes from three sources: (1) lip modulation; (2) maximum lip velocity; and (3) maximum lip amplitude (Summerfield, 1991). Lip reading is very difficult. Summerfield (1991) estimated that there are about 12 distinct visual configurations, so that about 63% of speech sounds are invisible to sight. Nonetheless, visual articulation information can be very helpful in difficult, noisy conditions. Improvements as much as 50% have been reported (Sumby & Pollack, 1954). Furthermore, Munhall, Jones, Callans, Kuratate, and Vatikiotis-Bateson (2004) found that rhythmic head movements were correlated with the pitch (fundamental frequency) and amplitude of the speaker's voice and that visual information could improve performance by 100% over that possible using auditory information only. The large improvement with visual input argues that speech perception is inherently multimodal and that the perceptual goal is identifying the articulatory gestures that underlie both the auditory and visual outputs (Rosenblum, 2004).

A striking illusion that has been used to study temporal and spatial ventriloquism has been termed the *McGurk effect* (MacDonald & McGurk, 1978; McGurk & MacDonald, 1976). Participants are shown a person saying simple consonant-vowel syllables coupled with an acoustic recording of the same type of syllable. In some cases, the acoustic and visual information conflicted, yet few adults perceived the conflict. The participants perceived one of the two syllables that were actually presented, or they perceived a syllable that was not presented at all, or they perceived a composite sound based on the two syllables. For example, if an acoustic [ba] was synchronized with a visual [ga], the majority of listeners reported [da]. However, if the presentation was reversed—an acoustic [ga] and visual [ba]—the listeners reported [ga] or [b'ga]. These two outcomes can be understood in terms of the visual information. The articulation of [ba] requires closing the lips entirely, but the visual display of [ga] does not show a complete lip closure. For this reason, in the first outcome participants do not characterize the syllable as [ba]; instead, they report a different stop consonant [da] that does not require complete lip closure. Complete lip closure is possible for stop consonants like [ga] articulated at the back of the mouth. For this reason, in the second outcome the visual lip closure shown for [ba] could have occurred for [ga], so that participants reported [ga] or the combination [b'ga].[9] The outcomes are relatively consistent across a wide range of temporal asynchronies. Within an asynchrony range of about +/−300 ms, performance is equivalent (Massaro, Cohen, & Smeele, 1996). This is a much wider range than found for other types of stimuli.

The discovery of the McGurk effect has led to a series of experiments investigating the limits of the illusion. On one hand, K. P. Green, Kuhl, Meltzoff, and Stevens (1991) investigated whether the McGurk effect would occur if the visual image came from a female talker while the auditory signal came from a male talker, and vice versa. Surprisingly, the results were the same regardless of whether the visual and auditory stimuli came from two individuals of the same gender (male 1/male 2 or female 1/female 2) or from two individuals of different genders (e.g., male 1/female 2). The authors interpreted this to mean that the speech signal is normalized to remove information about the voice characteristics of individuals before the auditory and visual information are combined. On the other hand, Walker, Bruce, and O'Malley (1995) found that familiarity with the speakers did affect the magnitude of the effect. For unfamiliar faces, there was no difference in the magnitude of the McGurk effect for congruent (same face and speaker male 1/male 1), incongruent same gender (different face and speaker but same gender, male 1/male 2) and different gender (necessarily incongruent, male 1/female 2). Thus, these outcomes replicate those above. But for familiar faces (known lecturers at the university), there were fewer McGurk responses for the incongruent presentations.

9. If the syllable is presented only in the auditory or visual modality, the identification of the syllable is essentially perfect. The McGurk errors are not due to lack of discrimination.

Listeners were more likely to report the correct auditory syllable for the familiar faces than for the unfamiliar faces. (Walker et al. concluded that people are able to use specific knowledge about familiar faces to correct for the auditory-visual mismatch. People were not able to correct for the mismatch on the basis of familiar voices. It might be the case, however, that truly distinguishable voice timbres might also be able to minimize the McGurk errors.

There are differences in the strength of the McGurk effect across languages and cultures. In general, the McGurk effect is stronger for foreign than for native speech stimuli (Sekiyama & Tohkura, 1993). This outcome makes sense in terms of the results of Walker et al. (1995) just described; specific knowledge about facial visual motion tends to reduce the magnitude of the illusion. Thus, lack of knowledge about facial movements commonly occurring in a foreign language should accentuate the illusion. Furthermore, Sekiyama (1997) has investigated whether the cultural tendency of Chinese and Japanese listeners to avoid looking at the face of a person they are talking with would reduce the illusion. This in fact was the case, for both Japanese and American language stimuli. The native Chinese speakers were less likely than both Japanese and American speakers to integrate the visual information and therefore more likely to perceive the auditory syllable correctly. Sekiyama (1997) also pointed out that Chinese is a tonal language, so that visual information is less valuable, which may reinforce the weaker use of visual information for speech perception.

Summary

I would argue that the similarity in the organizational principles for hearing and seeing, as well as the functional equivalence of the auditory and visual inputs for identifying objects and events in the world, supports the arguments made in chapter 1 that the principles of perceiving are identical for all modalities. I would further argue that the correspondence between the organizational principles is not merely coincidental, but a fundamental consequence of environmental properties. Objects are composed of correlated properties that occur in space and time, and are separated by edges. For this reason, perceiving is inherently multimodal, but not inherently equivalent.[10]

10. There are many anecdotes that reflect the premise that perception is multimodal. A colleague reported that a salesman admitted that when he was trying to sell a high-definition television, he switched to a high-quality audio system. The improved audio seemed to make the picture better. Conversely, there is a widely circulated, but uncorroborated, story that when participants were asked to judge television picture quality, their judgments were actually based on the sound quality of the sets and not the screen resolution.

It is difficult to create sensory substitutions that work. Gibson (1966, p. 54) quoted Hornbostel: "it matters little through which sense I realize that in the dark I have blundered into a pigsty." Yet I wonder if that is true. The research here suggests that each sense contributes a different perspective on the external world.

10

Summing Up

Perceiving is the construction of meaningful objects in the world. All such objects exist in a common spatiotemporal framework. All perceptual acts must also occur in the same framework, and that implies that there will be fundamental equivalences in hearing and seeing. There are no significant differences in hearing spoken language, musical passages, footsteps, labored breathing, or emotional sighs, in seeing woodgrain, the steepness of a rock face, birds struggling to maintain a V-shaped migration flight, or facial expressions.

Griffiths and Warren (2004) proposed four principles of object analysis that I would argue apply equally to hearing and seeing. The first, mentioned in chapter 1, is that object analysis deals with information that corresponds to objects in the sensory world. Spectral-space-time receptive fields that are limited by inverse resolution constraints filter the auditory and visual sensory energy. Metaphorically, receptive fields respond to edges that simultaneously bound objects and separate them from the rest of the sensory world. Moreover, the receptive fields for both senses can be understood in terms of maximizing mutual information. The receptive fields decorrelate the sensory energy to create a sparse representation of independent components.

The second principle, also mentioned in chapter 1, is that object analysis deals with information that corresponds to the segregation of objects and the construction of figure-ground relationships. As described in chapters 4, 5, and 9, what I might call a set of generalized Gestalt organizational principles can be applied to both auditory and visual organization. The same principles work in both domains because objects exist in a common space-time framework.

The third principle is that object analysis deals with information that allows for the identification of the same object in different sensory experiences within the same modality. This is the correspondence problem: the ability to track individual fireflies, detect first- and second-degree motion, perceive the same color in different illuminations, recognize the same face at different ages, and predict what an instrument or singer will sound like at a different pitch. The sensory world is composed of objects with correlated redundant features, and those objects change in predictable ways. The coherence of the perceptual world depends on our ability to detect that redundancy and predictability. If the sensory world were not predictable, then the statistics in the sensory world would be meaningless, and perceiving as we know it would not even exist.

These first three principles deal with object perception within a single sense, and the argument here is that there is little difference between auditory and visual object perception. The fourth principle proposed by Griffiths and Warren (2004) is that object analysis deals with cross-modal information, information that fuses auditory and visual information about the same object. The outcomes described in chapter 9 make it clear that perceivers normally assume that auditory and visual stimulation comes from a single source (i.e., the unity assumption) and that people often make illusionary judgments based on that assumption. The McGurk effect is one such illusion. Auditory and visual information is not processed independently, and in some cases I believe that joint processing is obligatory (e.g., temporal ventriloquism).

I think that the very existence of illusions makes a stronger point. Nearly all of our perceptual experiences involve more than one sense, and the "reasonableness" of the illusions requires the substitutability of the auditory for the visual information and vice versa. In order to be substitutable, both types of information must exist within a common frame of reference, and the perceiver must infer that all of the sensory stimulation arises from the same object. The concept of substitutability has been investigated most extensively in speech perception, where any articulatory gesture simultaneously produces visual facial movements and auditory speech sounds. As discussed previously, visual movement information can dramatically improve speech intelligibility from one speaker, particularly when the speech signal is buried in noise (Sumby & Pollack, 1954). Lachs and Pisoni (2004) demonstrated that observers could match visual facial movements to speech sounds of speakers. The observers could not make the match if the faces were static or if the speech sounds were reversed in time. Thus, it is the correlation across time between the auditory and visual information that allows observers to determine if the speech sounds came from the same speaker whose face is moving.

Nelken (2004) made a different argument for the primacy of object perception in the auditory system. Nelken summarized neural results which demonstrate that auditory neurons in A1 match their responses to the time course of the stimulation. It is only when simple single stimuli are presented that the spectral-temporal receptive fields are separable. The receptive fields can change dramatically at different time scales, when the stimuli are embedded in different backgrounds, and so on. The auditory cortex has a large adaptive and plastic capacity, and Nelken speculated that the role of the auditory cortex is to integrate acoustic features into auditory streams or objects. This integration can extend over different time spans and is sensitive to the statistics of the environment.

Albright and Stoner (2002) made a similar argument for contextual effects in vision. They point out that the "meaning" of any local region can be understood only in terms of the information in other regions. Of special importance is information revealing surface occlusion or lighting conditions that underlie depth ordering, figure-ground segregation, and color perception. As described at many points here, the response of individual cells is not invariant but depends on the response of neurons whose receptive fields encode distant retinal points (e.g., Vinje & Gallant, 2002). Although not discussed explicitly, there must be contextual temporal effects also. The interpretation of movement within a short time frame would often be ambiguous without the context provided by prior, contemporaneous, and subsequent information, as in the moving light displays pioneered by Johansson (1973).

If we continue to think about the auditory and visual systems in terms of the question "How does it work?" then we will trapped into conceptualizing hearing and seeing as very different processes, as expressed in table 1.1. But if we transform the question into "What are the auditory and visual systems designed to do?" the essential equivalence becomes apparent. Both are designed to identify objects, mostly the same object, within a common space-time framework. From this perspective, the neurological and perceptual commonalities and interactions are to be expected.

References

Adelson, E. H. (1982). Saturation and adaptation in the rod system. *Vision Research, 22*, 1299–1312.

Adelson, E. H. (1993). Perceptual organization and the judgment of lightness. *Science, 262*, 2042–2044.

Aho, A. C., Donner, K., Hyden, C., Larsen, L. O., & Reuter, T. (1988). Low retinal noise in animals with low body-temperature allows high visual sensitivity. *Nature, 334*, 348–350.

Ahumada, A. J., & Beard, B. (1997). Image discrimination models predict detection in fixed but not random noise. *Journal of the Optical Society of America, A, 14*(9), 2471–2477.

Alais, D., Blake, R., & Lee, S.-H. (1998). Visual features that vary together over time group together space. *Nature Neuroscience, 1*(2), 160–164.

Alais, D., & Burr, D. (2004). The ventriloquist effects from near-optimal bimodal integration. *Current Biology, 14*, 257–262.

Albright, T. D., & Stoner, G. R. (2002). Contextual influences on visual processing. In W. M. Cowan (Ed.), *Annual revue of neuroscience* (Vol. 25, pp. 339–379). Palo Alto, CA: Annual Reviews.

Allport, F. H. (1955). *Theories of perception and the concept of structure*. New York: Wiley.

Altmann, C. F., Bulthoff, H. H., & Kourtzi, Z. (2003). Perceptual organization of local elements into global shapes in the human visual cortex. *Current Biology, 13*, 342–349.

American National Standards Institute. (1973). *Psychoacoustical terminology. S3.20*. New York: Author.

Anderson, B. L., & Winawer, J. (2005). Image segmentation and lightness perception. *Nature, 434*, 79–83.

Andreassi, J., & Greco, J. (1975). Effects of bisensory stimulation on reaction time and the evoked potential. *Physiological Psychology, 3*, 189–194.

Antis, S. M., & Ramachandran, V. S. (1987). Visual inertia in apparent motion. *Vision Research, 27*, 755–764.

Atick, J. J. (1992). Could information theory provide an ecological theory of sensory processing? *Network, 3*, 213–251.

Attias, H., & Schreiner, C. E. (1998). Temporal low-order statistics of natural sounds. In M. C. Mozer, M. Jordan, M. Kearns, & S. Solla (Eds.), *Advances in neural information processing systems* (pp. 27–33). Cambridge, MA: MIT Press.

Attneave, F. (1971). Multistability in perception. *Scientific American, 255*, 62–71.

Baddeley, R., & Tirpathy, S. P. (1998). Insights into motion perception by observer modeling. *Journal of the Optical Society of America, A, 15*(2), 289–296.

Bair, W., & Koch, C. (1996). Temporal precision of spike trains in extrastriate cortex of behaving macaque monkey. *Neural Computation, 8*, 1184–1202.

Balboa, R., Tyler, C. W., & Grzywacz, N. M. (2001). Occlusions contribute to scaling in natural images. *Vision Research, 41*, 955–964.

Ballas, J. A. (1993). Common factors in the identification of an assortment of brief everyday sounds. *Journal of Experimental Psychology: Human Perception and Performance, 19*(2), 250–267.

Barbour, D. L., & Wang, X. (2003). Contrast tuning in auditory cortex. *Science, 299*, 1073–1075.

Barlow, H. B. (1956). Retinal noise and absolute threshold. *Journal of the Optical Society of America, A, 46*, 634–639.

Barlow, H. B. (1981). Critical limiting factors in the design of the eye and visual cortex (the Ferrier lecture, 1980). *Proceedings of the Royal Society, B, 212*, 1–34.

Barlow, H. B. (1990). Conditions for versatile learning, Helmholtz's unconscious inference, and the task of perception. *Vision Research, 30*(11), 1561–1571.

Barlow, H. B. (2001). Redundancy reduction revisited. *Network: Computation in Neural Systems, 12*, 241–253.

Barlow, H. B., & Hill, R. M. (1963). Evidence for a physiological explanation for the waterfall phenomenon and figural aftereffects. *Nature, 200*, 1345–1347.

Battaglia, P., Jacobs, R. A., & Aslin, R. N. (2003). Bayesian integration of visual and auditory signal for spatial location. *Journal of the Optical Society of America, A, 20*(7), 1391–1397.

Baylor, D. A., Lamb, T. D., & Yau, K.-W. (1979). Responses of retinal rods to single photons. *Journal of Physiology, 288*, 613–634.

Beard, B., & Ahumada, A. J. (1999). Detection in fixed and random noise in foveal and parafoveal vision explained by template learning. *Journal of the Optical Society of America, A, 16*(3), 755–763.

Beauchamp, M. S., Cox, R. W., & DeYoe, E. A. (1997). Graded effects of spatial and featural attention on human area MT and associated motion processing areas. *Journal of Neurophysiology, 78*, 516–520.

Beck, J. (1966). Effect of orientation and shape similarity on perceptual grouping. *Perception and Psychophysics, 1*, 300–302.

Beck, J. (1982). Textural segmentation. In J. Beck (Ed.), *Organization and representation in perception* (pp. 285–317). Hillsdale, NJ: Erlbaum.

Bell, A. J., & Sejnowski, T. J. (1997). The "independent components" of natural scenes are edge filters. *Vision Research, 37*, 3327–3338.

Ben Shahar, O., & Zucker, S. W. (2004). Sensitivity to curvatures in orientation-based texture segmentation. *Vision Research, 44*, 257–277.

Benade, A. H. (1960). *Horn, strings, and harmony*. Garden City, NY: Anchor.

Bergen, J. R. (1991). Theories of visual texture perception. In D. Regan (Ed.), *Spatial vision* (pp. 114–134). Houndmills Basingstoke, UK: Macmillan.

Bergen, J. R., & Landy, M. S. (1991). Computational modeling of visual texture segregation. In M. S. Landy & J. A. Movshon (Eds.), *Computational models of visual processing* (pp. 253–271). Cambridge, MA: MIT Press.

Bermant, R. I., & Welch, R. B. (1976). The effect of degree of visual-auditory stimulus separation and eye position upon the spatial interaction of vision and audition. *Perceptual and Motor Skills, 43*, 487–493.

Bertone, A., & Faubert, J. (2003). How is complex second-order motion processed? *Vision Research, 43*, 2591–2601.

Bey, C., & McAdams, S. (2003). Postrecognition of interleaved melodies as an indirect measure of auditory stream formation. *Journal of Experimental Psychology: Human Perception and Performance, 29*, 267–279.

Billock, V. A., Cunningham, D. W., Havig, P. R., & Tsou, B. H. (2001). Perception of spatiotemporal random fractals: An extension of colorimetric methods to the study of dynamic textures. *Journal of the Optical Society of America, A, 18*, 2404–2413.

Bloj, M. G., Kersten, D., & Hurlbert, A. C. (1999). Perception of three-dimensional shape influences colour perception through mutual illumination. *Nature, 402*, 877–879.

Bloothooft, G., & Plomp, R. (1988). The timbre of sung vowels. *Journal of the Acoustical Society of America, 84*, 847–860.

Borst, A., & Theunissen, F. E. (1999). Information theory and neural coding. *Nature Neuroscience, 2*, 947–957.

Braddick, O. J. (1995). Seeing motion signals in noise. *Current Biology, 5*, 7–9.

Braddick, O. J. (1974). A short-range process in apparent motion. *Vision Research, 14*, 519–526.

Brainard, D. H. (1998). Color constancy in the nearly natural image. II. Achromatic loci. *Journal of the Optical Society of America, A, 15*, 307–325.

Brainard, D. H., Brunt, W. A., & Speigle, J. M. (1997). Color constancy in the nearly natural image. I. Asymmetric matches. *Journal of the Optical Society of America, A, 14*, 2091–2110.

Bregman, A. S. (1990). *Auditory scene analysis: The organization of sound.* Cambridge, MA: MIT Press.

Bregman, A. S. (1993). Auditory scene analysis: Hearing in complex environments. In S. McAdams & E. Bigand (Eds.), *Thinking in sound.* Oxford: Oxford Scientific.

Bregman, A. S., Ahad, P. A., Crum, P. A. C., & O'Reilly, J. (2000). Effects of time intervals and tone durations on auditory stream segregation. *Perception and Psychophysics, 62*, 626–636.

Bregman, A. S., & Dannenbring, G. L. (1977). Auditory continuity and amplitude edges. *Canadian Journal of Psychology, 31*, 151–159.

Britten, K. H., Shadlen, M. N., Newsome, W. T., Celebrini, S., & Movshon, J. A. (1996). A relationship between behavioral choice and the visual responses of neurons in macaque MT. *Visual Neuroscience, 13*, 87–100.

Britten, K. H., Shadlen, M. N., Newsome, W. T., & Movshon, J. A. (1992). The analysis of visual motion: A comparison of neural and psychophysical performance. *Journal of Neuroscience, 12*, 4745–4765.

Brown, J. C. (1996). Frequency ratios of spectral components of musical sounds. *Journal of the Acoustical Society of America, 99*, 1210–1218.

Brown, J. C. (1999). Computer identification of musical instruments using pattern recognition with cepstral coefficients as features. *Journal of the Acoustical Society of America, 105*, 1933–1941.

Brown, J. C., Houix, O., & McAdams, S. (2001). Feature dependence in the automatic identification of musical woodwind instruments. *Journal of the Acoustical Society of America, 109*, 1064–1072.

Brown, S., & Masland, R. H. (2001). Spatial scale and cellular substrate of contrast adaptation by retinal ganglion cells. *Nature Neuroscience, 4*(1), 44–51.

Buchsbaum, G. (1980). A spatial processor model for object color perception. *Journal of the Franklin Institute, 310*, 1–26.

Buchsbaum, G., & Bloch, O. (2002). Color categories revealed by non-negative factorization of Munsell color spectra. *Vision Research, 42*, 559–563.

Buracas, G. T., & Albright, T. D. (1999). Gauging sensory representations in the brain. *Trends in Neuroscience, 22*, 303–309.

Burgess, A. E. (1999). Visual signal detection with two component noise: Low pass spectrum effects. *Journal of the Optical Society of America, A, 16*, 694–704.

Burton, G. J. (2002). Long-term light adaptation in photoreceptors of the housefly, *Musca domestica. Journal of Comparative Physiology, A, 188*, 527–538.

Burton, G. J., & Moorhead, I. R. (1987). Color and spatial structure in natural scenes. *Applied Optics, 26*, 157–170.

Buus, S. (1990). Level discrimination of frozen and random noise. *Journal of the Acoustical Society of America, 87*, 2643–2654.

Cabe, P. A., & Pittinger, J. B. (2000). Human sensitivity to acoustic information from vessel filling. *Journal of Experimental Psychology: Human Perception and Performance, 26*, 313–324.

Caelli, T. (1981). *Visual perception*. Oxford: Pergamon.

Carandini, M., Heeger, D. J., & Movshon, J. A. (1997). Linearity and normalization in simple cells of the macaque primary visual cortex. *Journal of Neurophysiology, 17*, 8621–8644.

Cariani, P. A. (1999). Neural timing nets for auditory computation. In S. Greenberg & M. Slaney (Eds.), *Computational models of auditory function* (pp. 235–249). Amsterdam: IOS Press.

Carlyon, R. P. (2000). Detecting coherent and incoherent frequency modulation. *Hearing Research, 140*, 173–188.

Cavanagh, P., Arguin, M., & Grunau, v., M. (1989). Interattribute apparent motion. *Vision Research, 29*, 1197–1204.

Cavanagh, P., & Mather, G. (1989). Motion: The long and short of it. *Spatial Vision, 4*, 103–129.

Chowning, J. M. (1980). Computer synthesis of the singing voice. In *Sound generation in winds, strings, computers* (Vol. Publ. No. 29, pp. 4–13. Kungl. Musicaliska Akademien). Stockholm: Royal Swedish Academy of Music.

Chubb, C., & Sperling, G. S. (1988). Drift-balanced random stimuli: A general basis for studying non-Fourier motion perception. *Journal of the Optical Society of America, A, 5*, 1986–2006.

Ciocca, V., & Bregman, A. S. (1987). Perceived continuity of gliding and steady state tones through interrupted noise. *Perception and Psychophysics, 42*, 476–484.

Clifford, C. W. G., Wenderoth, P., & Spehar, B. (2000). A functional angle on some after-effects in cortical vision. *Proceedings of the Royal Society, B, 267*, 1705–1710.

Cohen, J. (1964). Dependency of the spectral reflectance curves of the Munsell color chips. *Psychonomic Science, 1*, 367–270.

Cornsweet, T. (1970). *Visual perception*. New York: Academic Press.

Costalupes, J. A., Young, E. D., & Gibson, D. J. (1984). Effects of continuous noise backgrounds on rate response of auditory nerve fibers in cat. *Journal of Neurophysiology, 51*, 1326–1344.

Crawford, B. H. (1947). Visual adaptation in relation to brief conditioning stimuli. *Proceedings of the Royal Society of London, B, 134*, 283–302.

Croner, L. J., & Albright, T. D. (1997). Image segmentation enhances discrimination of motion in visual noise. *Vision Research, 37*, 1415–1427.

Croner, L. J., & Albright, T. D. (1999). Seeing the big picture: Integrating of image cues in the primate visual system. *Neuron, 24*, 777–789.

Cusack, R., & Carlyon, R. P. (2004). Auditory perceptual organization inside and outside the laboratory. In J. G. Neuhoff (Ed.), *Ecological psychoacoustics* (pp. 15–48). San Diego: Elsevier Academic.

Cutting, J. E. (1978). Generation of synthetic male and female walkers through manipulation of a biomechanical invariant. *Perception, 7*, 393–405.

Dakin, S. C., & Bex, P. J. (2002). Summation of global orientation structure: Seeing the Glass or the window. *Vision Research, 42*, 2013–2020.

Dan, Y., Atick, J. J., & Reid, R. C. (1996). Efficient coding of natural scenes in the lateral geniculate nucleus: Experimental test of a computational theory. *Journal of Neuroscience, 16*, 3351–3362.

Darwin, C. J. (1997). Auditory grouping. *Trends in Cognitive Science, 1*, 327–333.

Darwin, C. J., & Carlyon, R. P. (1995). Auditory grouping. In B. C. J. Moore (Ed.), *Hearing* (2nd ed., pp. 387–424). San Diego: Academic Press.

Das, A., & Gilbert, C. D. (1997). Distortions of visuotopic map match orientation singularities in primary visual cortex. *Nature, 387*, 594–598.

Das, A., & Gilbert, C. D. (1999). Topography of contextual modulations mediated by short-range interactions in primary visual cortex. *Nature, 399*, 655–661.

Daugman, J. (1985). Uncertainty relation for resolution in space, spatial frequency and orientation optimized by two-dimensional visual cortical filters. *Journal of the Optical Society of America, A, 2*, 1160–1169.

Dawson, M. R. (1991). The how and why of what went where in apparent motion: Modeling solutions to the motion correspondence problem. *Psychological Review, 98*, 569–603.

Dayan, P., & Abbott, L. F. (2001). *Theoretical neuroscience: Computational and mathematical modeling of neural systems*. Cambridge, MA: MIT Press.

De Valois, R., & De Valois, K. K. (1988). *Spatial vision*. New York: Oxford University Press.

DeAngelis, G. C., Ohzawa, I., & Freeman, R. D. (1995). Receptive-field dynamics in the central visual pathways. *Trends in Neuroscience, 18*, 451–458.

DeCharms, R. C., Blake, D. T., & Merzenich, M. M. (1998). Optimizing sound features for cortical neurons. *Science, 280*, 1439–1444.

DeCharms, R. C., & Zador, A. (2000). Neural representation and the cortical code. *Annual Review of Neuroscience, 23*, 613–647.

DeCoensel, B., Botteldooren, D., & De Muer, T. (2003). 1/f Noise in rural and urban soundscapes. *Acta Acustica United with Acustica, 89*, 287–295.

Delahunt, P. B., & Brainard, D. H. (2004). Does human color constancy incorporate the statistical regularity of natural daylight. *Journal of Vision, 4*, 57–81.

Depireaux, D. A., Simon, J. Z., Klein, D. J., & Shamma, S. A. (2001). Spectrotemporal response field characterization with dynamic ripples in ferret primary auditory cortex. *Journal of Neurophysiology, 85*, 1220–1234.

Derrington, A. M., & Webb, B. S. (2004). Visual system: How is the retina wired up to the cortex? *Current Biology, 14*, R14–R15.

Dittrich, W. H. (1993). Action categories and the perception of biological motion. *Perception, 22*, 15–22.

Dixon, N. F., & Spitz, L. (1980). The detection of auditory visual desynchrony. *Perception, 9*, 719–721.

Doerschner, K., Boyaci, H., & Maloney, L. T. (2004). Human observers compensate for secondary illumination originating in nearby chromatic surfaces. *Journal of Vision, 4*, 92–105.

Dolan, D. F., & Nuttall, A. L. (1989). Inner ear responses to tonal stimulation in the presence of broadband noise. *Journal of the Acoustical Society of America, 86*, 1007–1012.

Dominy, N., & Lucas, P. W. (2001). Ecological importance of trichromatic vision to primates. *Nature, 410*, 363–366.

Dong, D. W., & Atick, J. J. (1995). Statistics of natural time-varying images. *Network: Computation in Neural Systems, 6*, 345–358.

Dowling, W. J. (1973). The perception of interleaved melodies. *Cognitive Psychology, 5*, 322–337.

Driver, J. (1996). Enhancement of selective listening by illusionary mislocation of speech sounds due to lip-reading. *Nature, 381*, 66–68.

D'Zmura, M., & Iverson, G. (1993a). Color constancy I: Basic theory of two-stage recovery of spectral descriptions for lights and surfaces. *Journal of the Optical Society of America, A, 10*, 2148–2165.

D'Zmura, M., & Iverson, G. (1993b). Color constancy II: Results for two stage linear recovery of spectral descriptions for lights and surfaces. *Journal of the Optical Society of America, A, 10*, 2166–2180.

D'Zmura, M., & Lennie, P. (1986). Mechanisms of color constancy. *Journal of the Optical Society of America, A, 3*, 1662–1672.

Eckstein, M. P., Ahumada, A. J., & Watson, A. B. (1997). Visual signal detection in structured backgrounds. II. Effects of contrast gain control, background variations, and white noise. *Journal of the Optical Society of America, A, 14*(9), 2406–2419.

Eggermont, J. J. (2001). Between sound and perception: Reviewing the search for a neural code. *Hearing Research, 157*, 1–42.

Elder, J. H., & Sachs, A. J. (2004). Psychophysical receptive fields of edge detection mechanisms. *Vision Research, 44*, 795–813.

Elhilali, M., Fritz, J. B., Klein, D. J., Simon, J. Z., & Shamma, S. A. (2004). Dynamics of precise spike timing in primary auditory cortex. *Journal of Neuroscience, 24*, 1159–1172.

Erickson, M. L. (2003). Dissimilarity and the classification of female singing voices: A preliminary study. *Journal of Voice, 17*, 195–206.

Erickson, M. L., Perry, S. R., & Handel, S. (2001). Discrimination functions: Can they be used to classify singing voices? *Journal of Voice, 15*, 492–502.

Erickson, M. L., & Perry, S. R. (2003). Can listeners hear who is singing? A comparison of three-note and six-note discrimination tasks. *Journal of Voice, 17*, 353–369.

Ernst, M. O., & Bulthoff, H. H. (2004). Merging the senses into a robust percept. *Trends in Cognitive Science, 8*, 162–169.

Exner, S. (1875). Ueber das Sehen von Bewegungen und die Theorie des zusammengesetzen Augues. *Sitzungsberichte Akademie Wissenschaft Wien, 72*, 156–170.

Fairchild, M. D. (1998). *Color appearance models*. Reading, MA: Addison-Wesley.

Fairhall, A. L., Lewen, G. D., Bialek, W., & de Ruyter van Steveninck, R. R. (2001). Efficiency and ambiguity in an adaptive neural code. *Nature, 412*, 787–792.

Feldman, J., & Singh, M. (2005). Information along contours and object boundaries. *Psychological Review, 112*, 243–252.

Ferster, D., & Miller, K. D. (2000). Neural mechanisms of orientation selectivity in the visual cortex. *Annual Review of Neuroscience, 23*, 441–471.

Field, D. J. (1987). Relations between the statistics of natural images and the response properties of cortical cells. *Journal of the Optical Society of America, A, 4*, 2379–2394.

Field, D. J. (1994). What is the goal of sensory coding? *Neural Computation, 6*, 559–601.

Fitzpatrick, D. (2000). Seeing beyond the receptive field in primary visual cortex. *Current Opinion in Neurobiology, 10*, 438–443.

Fleming, R. W., Dror, R. O., & Adelson, E. W. (2003). Real-world illumination and the perception of surface reflectance properties. *Journal of Vision, 3*, 347–368.

Foldiak, P., & Young, M. P. (1995). Sparse coding in the primate cortex. In M. A. Arbib (Ed.), *The handbook of brain theory and neural networks* (pp. 895–898). Cambridge, MA: MIT Press.

Fox, E. (1983). *In the beginning: A new English rendition of the Book of Genesis* (E. Fox, Trans.). New York: Schocken.

Freed, D. (1990). Auditory correlates of perceived mallet hardness for a set of recorded percussive sound events. *Journal of the Acoustical Society of America, 87*, 311–322.

Frisina, R. D. (2001). Subcortical neural coding mechanisms for auditory temporal processing. *Hearing Research, 158*, 1–27.

Friston, K. (2002). Beyond phrenology: What can neuroimaging tell us about distributed circuitry? In W. M. Cowan (Ed.), *Annual review of neuroscience* (Vol. 25, pp. 221–250). Palo Alto, CA: Annual Reviews.

Fritz, J., Shamma, S., Elhilali, M., & Klein, D. (2003). Rapid task-related plasticity of spectrotemporal receptive fields in primary auditory cortex. *Nature Neuroscience, 6*(11), 1216–1223.

Funt, B., Drew, M., & Ho, J. (1991). Color constancy from mutual reflection. *International Journal of Computer Vision, 6*, 5–24.

Gabor, D. (1946). Theory of communication. *Journal of IEEE, London, 93*(III), 429–457.

Gallant, J. L. (2000). The neural representation of shape. In Karen K. De Valois (Ed.), *Seeing* (2nd ed., pp. 311–334). San Diego: Academic Press.

Gallant, J. L., Braun, J., & Van Essen, D. C. (1993). Selectivity for polar hyperbolic, and cartesian gratings in Macaque visual cortex. *Science, 259*, 100–103.

Gardner, M. (1978). White and brown music, fractal curves and one over f fluctuations. *Scientific American, 238*, 16–32.

Garner, W. R. (1962). *Uncertainty and structure as psychological concepts*. New York: John Wiley.

Gaver, W. W. (1993). What in the world do we hear?: An ecological approach to auditory event perception. *Ecological Psychology, 5*, 1–29.

Gegenfurtner, K. R. (2003). Cortical mechanisms of colour vision. *Nature Reviews: Neuroscience, 4*, 563–572.

Gegenfurtner, K. R., & Sharpe, L. T. (Eds.). (1999). *Color vision: From genes to perception*. Cambridge, UK: Cambridge University Press.

Gehr, D. D., Komiya, H., & Eggermont, J. J. (2000). Neuronal responses in cat primary auditory cortex to natural and altered species-specific calls. *Hearing Research, 150*, 27–42.

Geisler, C. D. (1998). *From sound to synapse: Physiology of the mammalian ear.* New York: Oxford University Press.

Geisler, C. D., & Greenberg, S. (1986). A two-stage nonlinear cochlear model possesses automatic gain control. *Journal of the Acoustical Society of America, 80*, 1359–1363.

Geisler, W. S., & Albrecht, D. G. (1992). Cortical neurons: Isolation of contrast gain control. *Vision Research, 32*, 1409–1410.

Geisler, W. S., Perry, J. S., Super, B. J., & Gallogly, D. P. (2001). Edge co-occurrence in natural images predicts contour grouping performance. *Vision Research, 41*, 711–724.

Gibson, J. J. (1966). *The senses considered as perceptual systems.* Boston: Houghton Mifflin.

Giese, M. A. (1999). *Dynamic neural field theory for motion perception.* Boston: Kluwer Academic.

Gilchrist, A., Kossyfidis, C., Bonato, F., Agotini, T., Cataliotti, J., Li, X., et al. (1999). An anchoring theory of lightness perception. *Psychological Review, 106*, 795–834.

Gilden, D. L., Schmuckler, M. A., & Clayton, K. (1993). The perception of natural contour. *Psychological Review, 100*, 460–478.

Glass, L. (1969). Moire effect from random dots. *Nature, 223*, 578–580.

Glass, L., & Switkes, E. (1976). Pattern recognition in humans: Correlations which cannot be perceived. *Perception, 5*, 67–72.

Gold, J., Bennett, J. P., & Sekular, A. B. (1999). Signal but not noise changes with perceptual learning. *Nature, 402*, 176–178.

Goldstein, J. L. (1973). An optimum processor theory for the central formation of the pitch of complex tones. *Journal of the Acoustical Society of America, 54*, 1496–1516.

Gorea, A. (1995). Visual texture. In T. V. Papathomas (Ed.), *Early vision and beyond* (pp. 55–57). Cambridge, MA: MIT Press.

Graham, N., & Hood, D. C. (1992). Modeling the dynamics of light adaptation: The merging of two traditions. *Vision Research, 12*(7), 1373–1393.

Green, B. F. J., Wolf, A. K., & White, B. W. (1957). The detection of statistically defined patterns in a matrix of dots. *American Journal of Psychology, 72*, 503–520.

Green, D. M. (1964). Consistency of auditory detection judgments. *Psychological Review, 71*, 392–407.

Green, D. M. (1988). *Profile analysis: Auditory intensity discrimination.* New York: Oxford University Press.

Green, D. M. (1993). Auditory intensity discrimination. In W. A. Yost, A. N. Popper, & R. R. Fay (Eds.), *Human psychophysics* (Vol. 3, pp.13–55). New York: Springer-Verlag.

Green, D. M., & Dai, H. (1992). Temporal relations in profile comparisons. In Y. Cazals, L. Demany, & K. Horner (Eds.), *Auditory physiology and perception* (pp. 471–478). New York: Pergamon.

Green, D. M., Kidd, G. Jr., & Pickardi, M. C. (1983). Successive and simultaneous comparison in auditory intensity discrimination. *Journal of the Acoustical Society of America, 73*(2), 639–643.

Green, D. M., & Swets, J. A. (1966). *Signal detection theory and psychophysics.* New York: John Wiley.

Green, K. P., Kuhl, P. K., Meltzoff, A. N., & Stevens, E. B. (1991). Integrating speech information across talkers, gender, and sensory modality: Female faces and male voices in the McGurk effect. *Perception and Psychophysics, 50*(6), 524–536.

Greenspan, N. S. (2001). You can't have it all. *Nature, 409*, 137.

Grey, J. M. (1977). Multidimensional perceptual scaling of musical timbres. *Journal of the Acoustical Society of America, 61*, 1270–1277.

Grey, J. M., & Gordon, J. W. (1978). Perceptual effects of spectral modifications on musical timbres. *Journal of the Acoustical Society of America, 63*(5), 1493–1500.

Griffiths, T. D., & Warren, J. D. (2004). What is an auditory object? *Nature Reviews: Neuroscience, 5*, 887–892.

Griffiths, T. D., Warren, J. D., Scott, S., Nelken, I., & King, A. J. (2004). Cortical processing of complex sound: A way forward? *Trends in Neuroscience, 27*, 181–185.

Grose, J. H., & Hall, J. W. I. (1993). Comodulation masking release: Is comodulation sufficient? *Journal of the Acoustical Society of America, 93*, 2892–2902.

Guttman, N., & Julesz, B. (1963). Lower limits of auditory periodicity analysis. *Journal of the Acoustical Society of America, 35*, 610.

Gygi, B., Kidd, G. R., & Watson, C. S. (2004). Spectral-temporal factors in the identification of environmental sounds. *Journal of the Acoustical Society of America, 115*, 1252–1265.

Hall, J. W. I., & Grose, J. H. (1990). Comodulation masking release and auditory grouping. *Journal of the Acoustical Society of America, 88*, 119–125.

Hall, J. W. I., Grose, J. H., & Fernandes, M. A. (1984). Detection in noise by spectrotemporal pattern analysis. *Journal of the Acoustical Society of America, 76*, 50–56.

Handel, S. (1989). *Listening: An introduction to the perception of auditory events.* Cambridge, MA: MIT Press.

Handel, S., & Erickson, M. L. (2001). A rule of thumb: The bandwidth for timbre invariance is one octave. *Music Perception, 19*, 121–126.

Handel, S., & Erickson, M. L. (2004). Sound source identification: The possible role of timbre transformations. *Music Perception, 21*, 587–610.

Handel, S., & Patterson, R. D. (2000). The perceptual tone/noise ratio of merged iterated rippled noises with octave, harmonic, and nonharmonic delay ratios. *Journal of the Acoustical Society of America, 108*, 692–695.

Harper, N. S., & McAlpine, D. (2004). Optimal neural population coding of an auditory spatial cue. *Science, 430*, 682–686.

Hartline, H. K. (1940). The receptive fields of optic nerve fibers. *American Journal of Physiology, 130*, 690–699.

Hartmann, W. M. (1998). *Signals, sound, and sensation.* New York: Springer-Verlag.

Hartmann, W. M., & Johnson, D. (1991). Stream segregation and peripheral channeling. *Music Perception, 9*, 155–184.

Hateren, J. H. v. (1993). Spatiotemporal contrast sensitivity of early vision. *Vision Research, 33*, 257–267.

Hateren, J. H. v., & Ruderman, D. L. (1998). Independent component analysis of natural image sequences yields spatio-temporal filters similar to simple cells in primary visual cortex. *Proceedings of the Royal Society of London, B, 265*, 2315–2320.

Hecht, S., Schlaer, S., & Pirenne, M. H. (1942). Energy, quanta, and vision. *Journal of General Physiology, 25*, 819–840.

Helmholtz, H. L. (1867). *Handbuch der physiologischen Optik.* Leipzig: L. Voss.

Helmholtz, H. L. (1877). *On the sensations of tone*. New York: Dover.

Heron, J., Whitaker, D., & McGraw, P. V. (2004). Sensory uncertainty governs the extent of audio-visual interaction. *Vision Research, 44*, 2875–2884.

Hess, R., & Field, D. (1999). Integration of contours: New insights. *Trends in Cognitive Science, 3*, 480–486.

Hilgetag, C.-C., O'Neill, M. A., & Young, M. P. (2000). Hierarchical organization of macaque and cat cortical systems explored with a novel network processor. *Philosophical Transactions of the Royal Society of London, B, 355*, 71–89.

Hill, N. I., & Bailey, P. J. (2002). A comparison of the effects of differences in temporal gating and ear of presentation on profile discrimination. *Perception, 31*, 1395–1402.

Hochberg, J. (1964). *Perception*. Englewood Cliffs, NJ: Prentice-Hall.

Hochberg, J. (1982). How big is a stimulus? In J. Beck (Ed.), *Organization and representation in perception* (pp. 191–217). Hillsdale, NJ: Erlbaum.

Hodgson, M., Rempel, R., & Kennedy, S. (1999). Measurement and prediction of typical speech and background noise levels in university classrooms during lectures. *Journal of the Acoustical Society of America, 105*, 226–232.

Hoffman, D. D. (1998). *Visual intelligence: How we create what we see*. New York: W.W. Norton.

Holcombe, A. (2003). Occlusion cues resolve sudden onsets into morphing or line motion, disocclusion and sudden materialization. *Journal of Vision, 3*, 562–572.

Hood, D., & Finkelstein, M. A. (1986). Sensitivity to light. In K. R. Boff, L. Kaufman, & J. P. Thomas (Eds.), *Handbook of perception and human performance: Vol. 1. Sensory processes and perception* (pp. 5–1 to 5–64). New York: John Wiley.

Horner, A., Beauchamp, J., & So, R. (2004). Detection of random alternations to time-varying musical instrument spectra. *Journal of the Acoustical Society of America, 116*, 1800–1810.

Hosoya, T., Baccus, S. A., & Meister, M. (2005). Dynamic predictive coding by the retina. *Nature, 436*, 71–77.

Howard, J. H. J. (1977). Psychophysical structure of eight complex underwater sounds. *Journal of the Acoustical Society of America, 62*, 149–162.

Hsu, K., & Hsu, A. (1990). Fractal geometry of music. *Proceedings of the Institute of the National Academy of Science, 87*, 938–941.

Huang, L., & Pashler, H. (2002). Symmetry detection and visual attention: A "binary-map" hypothesis. *Vision Research, 42*, 1421–1430.

Hubel, D. H., & Weisel, T. N. (1962). Receptive fields, binocular interaction, and functional architecture in the cat's visual cortex. *Journal of Physiology (London), 160*, 106–154.

Hubel, D. H., & Weisel, T. N. (1968). Receptive fields and functional architecture of monkey striate cortex. *Journal of Physiology (London), 195*, 215–243.

Huddleston, W. E., & DeYoe, E. A. (2003). First-order and second-order spectral "motion" mechanisms in the human auditory system. *Perception, 32*, 1141–1149.

Hurlbert, A. C. (1998). Computational models of color constancy. In V. Walsh & J. Kulikowski (Eds.), *Perceptual constancy* (pp. 283–322). Cambridge, UK: Cambridge University Press.

Hyvärinen, A., & Hoyer, P. O. (2001). A two-layer sparse coding model learns simple and complex cell receptive fields and topography from natural images. *Vision Research, 41*, 2413–2423.

Isabelle, S. K., & Colburn, H. S. (1991). Detection of tones in reproducible narrowband noise. *Journal of the Acoustical Society of America, 89*, 352–359.

Jack, C. E., & Thurlow, W. R. (1973). Effects of degree of visual association and angle of displacement on the "ventriloquism" effect. *Perceptual and Motor Skills, 37*, 967–979.

Jackson, C. V. (1953). Visual factors in auditory localization. *Quarterly Journal of Experimental Psychology, 5*, 52–65.

Jacobs, R. A. (2002). What determines visual cue reliability? *Trends in Cognitive Science, 6*, 345–350.

Jameson, D., & Hurvich, L. M. (1989). Essay concerning color constancy. *Annual Review of Psychology, 40*, 1–22.

Jeffress, A. (1948). A place theory of sound localization. *Journal of Comparative and Physiological Psychology, 61*, 468–486.

Jenkins, B. (1985). Orientational anisotropy in the human visual system. *Perception and Psychophysics, 37*, 125–134.

Johansson, G. (1973). Visual perception of biological motion and a model for its analysis. *Perception and Psychophysics, 14*, 201–211.

Joliveau, E., Smith, J., & Wolfe, J. (2004). Tuning of vocal tract resonance by sopranos. *Nature, 427*, 116.

Jones, J. P., & Palmer, L. A. (1987a). An evaluation of the 2D Gabor filter model of simple receptive fields in cat striate cortex. *Journal of Neurophysiology, 58*, 1233–1258.

Jones, J. P., & Palmer, L. A. (1987b). The two-dimensional spatial structure of simple receptive fields in cat striate cortex. *Journal of Neurophysiology, 58*, 1187–1211.

Judd, D. B., MacAdam, D. L., & Wyszecki, G. (1964). Spectral distribution of typical daylight as a function of correlated color temperature. *Journal of the Optical Society of America, 54*, 1031–1040.

Julesz, B. (1962). Visual pattern discrimination. *IRE Transactions on Information Theory, IT-8*, 84–92.

Julesz, B. (1971). *Foundations of cyclopean perception*. Chicago: University of Chicago Press.

Julesz, B. (1984). Toward an axiomatic theory of preattentive vision. In G. Edelman, W. E. Gall, & W. M. Cowan (Eds.), *Dynamic aspects of neocortical function* (pp. 585–612). New York: Neurosciences Institute.

Julesz, B. (1995). *Dialogues on perception*. Cambridge, MA: MIT Press.

Julesz, B., & Hesse, R. I. (1970). Inability to perceive the direction of rotation movement of line segments. *Nature, 225*, 243–244.

Julesz, B., & Hirsh, I. J. (1972). Visual and auditory perception: An essay of comparison. In E. E. David & P. Denes (Eds.), *Human communication: A unified view* (pp. 283–340). New York: McGraw-Hill.

Kaernbach, C. (1992). On the consistency of tapping to repeated noise. *Journal of the Acoustical Society of America, 92*, 788–793.

Kaiser, P. K., & Boynton, R. M. (1996). *Human color vision* (2nd ed.). Washington, DC: Optical Society of America.

Kanwisher, N., & Wojiciulik, E. (2000). Visual attention: Insights from imaging. *Nature Reviews: Neuroscience, 1*, 91–100.

Kellman, P. J., Guttman, S. E., & Wickens, T. D. (2001). Geometric and neural models of object perception. In T. F. Shipley & P. J. Kellman (Eds.), *From fragments to objects: Segmentation and grouping in vision* (Vol. 130, pp. 183–245). Amsterdam: Elsevier Science B.V.

Kellman, P. J., & Shipley, T. F. (1991). A theory of visual interpolation in object perception. *Cognitive Psychology, 23*, 144–221.

Kendall, R. A. (1986). The role of acoustic signal partitions in listener categorization of musical phrases. *Music Perception, 4*(2), 185–214.

Kersten, D., & Yuille, A. (2003). Bayesian models of object perception. *Current Opinion in Neurobiology, 13*, 150–158.

Knill, D. C., Kersten, D., & Yuille, A. (1996). Introduction: A Bayesian formulation of visual perception. In D. C. Knill & W. Richards (Eds.), *Perception as Bayesian inference* (pp. 1–21). Cambridge, UK: Cambridge University Press.

Kobatake, E., & Tanaka, K. (1994). Neuronal selectivities to complex object features in the ventral visual pathway of the macaque cerebral cortex. *Journal of Neurophysiology, 71*, 856–867.

Kohler, W. (1969). *The task of Gestalt psychology*. Princeton, NJ: Princeton University Press.

Kolers, P. A. (1972). *Aspects of motion perception*. Oxford, UK: Pergamon Press.

Körding, K., Käyser, C., Einhouser, W., & König, P. (2004). How are complex cell properties adapted to the statistics of natural stimuli? *Journal of Neurophysiology, 91*, 206–212.

Korte, A. (1915). Kinematioskopische Untersuchungen. *Zeitschrift für Psychologie, 72*, 194–296.

Kortum, P. T., & Geisler, W. S. (1995). Adaptation mechanisms in spatial vision. II. Flash thresholds and background adaptation. *Vision Research, 35*, 1595–1609.

Kowalski, N., Depireaux, D. A., & Shamma, S. A. (1996). Analysis of dynamic spectra in ferret primary auditory cortex. I. Characteristics of single unit responses to moving ripple spectra. *Journal of Neurophysiology, 76*, 3503–3523.

Kraft, J. M., & Brainard, D. H. (1999). Mechanisms of color constancy under nearly natural viewing. *Proceedings of the National Academy of Science, 96*, 307–312.

Krumhansl, C. L. (2000). Rhythm and pitch in music cognition. *Psychological Bulletin, 126*, 159–179.

Kubovy, M., & Jordan, R. (1979). Tone-segregation by phase: On the phase sensitivity of the single ear. *Journal of the Acoustical Society of America, 66*, 100–106.

Kubovy, M., & Van Valkenburg, D. (2001). Auditory and visual objects. *Cognition, 80*, 97–126.

Kuffler, S. W. (1953). Discharge patterns and functional organization of mammalian retina. *Journal of Neurophysiology, 16*, 37–68.

Kunkler-Peck, A. J., & Turvey, M. T. (2000). Hearing shape. *Journal of Experimental Psychology: Human Perception and Performance, 26*, 279–294.

Lachs, L., & Pisoni, D. B. (2004). Crossmodal source identification in speech perception. *Ecological Psychology, 16*, 159–187.

Lakatos, S. (2000). A common perceptual space for harmonic and percussive timbres. *Perception and Psychophysics, 62*, 1426–1439.

Lakatos, S., McAdams, S., & Causse, R. (1997). The representation of auditory source characteristics: Simple geometric form. *Perception and Psychophysics, 59*, 1180–1190.

Lamb, T. D. (1987). Sources of noise in photoreceptor transduction. *Journal of the Optical Society of America, A, 4*(12), 2295–2299.

Land, E. H. (1986). Recent advances in retinex theory. *Vision Research, 26*, 7–22.

Lappin, J. S., & Bell, H. H. (1976). The detection of coherence in moving random dot patterns. *Vision Research*, 161–168.

Laughlin, S. B. (1981). A simple coding procedure enhances a neuron's information capacity. *Zeitschrift Naturforschung, 36c*, 910–912.

Laughlin, S. B. (2001). Energy as a constraint on the coding and processing of sensory information. *Current Opinion in Neurobiology, 11*, 475–480.

Laurent, G. (2002). Olfactory network dynamics and the coding of multidimensional signals. *Nature Reviews: Neuroscience, 3*, 884–895.

Lee, H.-C., Breneman, E. J., & Schulte, C. P. (1990). Modeling light reflection for computer color vision. *IEEE Transactions on Pattern Analysis and Machine Intelligence, 12*, 402–409.

Lee, S.-H., & Blake, R. (1999). Visual form created solely from temporal structure. *Science, 284*, 1165–1168.

Lennie, P. (2003). The physiology of color vision. In S. K. Shevell (Ed.), *The science of color* (2nd ed., pp. 217–246). Oxford, UK: Elsevier.

Leopold, D. A., & Logothetics, N. K. (1999). Multistable phenomena: Changing views in perception. *Trends in Cognitive Sciences, 3*, 254–264.

LePage, E. L. (2003). The mammalian cochlear map is optimally warped. *Journal of the Acoustical Society of America, 114*, 896–906.

Lettvin, J. Y., Maturana, H. R., McCulloch, W. S., & Pitts, W. H. (1959). What the frog's eye tells the frog's brain. *Proceedings of Institute of Radio Engineering, 47*, 1940–1951.

Levy, I., Hasson, U., & Malach, R. (2004). One picture is worth at least a million neurons. *Current Biology, 14*, 996–1001.

Lewen, G., Bialek, W., & de Ruyter van Steveninck, R. (2001). Neural coding of natural motion stimuli. *Network, 12*, 317–329.

Lewicki, M. S. (2002). Efficient coding of natural sounds. *Nature Neuroscience, 5*, 356–363.

Lewkowicz, D. J. (2000). The development of intersensory temporal perception: An epigenetic systems/limitations view. *Psychological Bulletin, 126*, 281–308.

Li, A., & Zaidi, Q. (2001). Veridicality of three-dimensional shape perception predicted from amplitude spectra of natural textures. *Journal of the Optical Society of America, A, 18*, 2430–2447.

Li, H.-C. O., & Kingdom, F. A. A. (2001). Segregation by color/luminance does not necessarily facilitate motion discrimination in the presence of motion distractors. *Perception and Psychophysics, 63*, 660–675.

Li, L., Lu, T., & Wang, X. (2002). Neural representations of sinusoidal amplitude and frequency modulations in the primary auditory cortex of awake primates. *Journal of Neurophysiology, 87*, 2237–2261.

Li, R. W., Levi, D., & Klein, S. A. (2004). Perceptual learning improves efficiency by re-tuning the decision "template" for position discrimination. *Nature Neuroscience, 7*, 178–183.

Li, X., Logan, R. J., & Pastore, R. E. (1991). Perception of acoustic source characteristics: Walking sounds. *Journal of the Acoustical Society of America, 90*, 3036–3049.

Licklider, J. (1951). A duplex theory of pitch perception. *Experientia, 7*, 128–134.

Limbert, C. (1984). *The perception of repeated noise.* Unpublished doctoral dissertation, Cambridge University, Cambridge.

Loftus, G. R., & Harley, E. (2005). Why is it easier to identify someone close than far away? *Psychonomic Bulletin and Review, 12*, 43–65.

Lu, T., Liang, L., & Wang, X. (2001). Temporal and rate representations of time-varying signals in the auditory cortex of awake primates. *Nature Neuroscience, 4*, 1131–1138.

Lu, T., & Wang, X. (2004). Information content of auditory cortical responses to time-varying acoustic stimuli. *Journal of Neurophysiology, 91*, 301–313.

Lu, Z.-L., & Dosher, B. A. (1999). Characterizing human perceptual inefficiencies with equivalent internal noise. *Journal of the Optical Society of America, A, 16*, 764–778.

Lu, Z.-L., & Dosher, B. A. (2004). Perceptual learning retunes the perceptual template in foveal orientation identification. *Journal of Vision, 4*, 44–56.

Lu, Z.-L., & Sperling, G. (2001). Three-systems theory of human visual motion perception: Review and update. *Journal of the Optical Society of America, A, 18*, 2331–2370.

Lutfi, R. A. (2001). Auditory detection of hollowness. *Journal of the Acoustical Society of America, 110,* 1010–1019.

Lutfi, R. A., Oh, E., Storm, E., & Alexander, J. M. (2005). Classification and identification of recorded and synthesized impact sounds by practiced listeners, musicians, and nonmusicians. *Journal of the Acoustical Society of America, 118*, 393–404.

Lyon, R., & Shamma, S. (1996). Auditory representations of timbre and pitch. In H. L. Hawkins, T. A. McMullen, A. N. Popper, & R. R. Fay (Eds.), *Auditory computation* (Vol. 6, pp. 221–270). New York: Springer-Verlag.

MacDonald, J., & McGurk, H. (1978). Visual influences on speech perception processes. *Perception and Psychophysics, 24*, 253–257.

Machens, C., Wehr, M. S., & Zador, A. M. (2004). Linearity of cortical receptive fields measured with natural sounds. *Journal of Neuroscience, 24*, 1089–1100.

MacKay, D. M. (1965). Visual noise as a tool of research. *Journal of General Psychology, 72*, 181–197.

Makous, W. L. (1997). Fourier models and the loci of adaptation. *Journal of the Optical Society of America, A, 14*, 2323–2345.

Maloney, L. T. (1986). Evaluation of linear models of surface spectral reflectance with small numbers of parameters. *Journal of the Optical Society of America, A, 3*, 1673–1683.

Maloney, L. T. (1999). Physics-based approaches to modeling surface color perception. In K. R. Gegenfurtner & L. T. Sharpe (Eds.), *Color vision: From genes to perception* (pp. 387–416). Cambridge, UK: Cambridge University Press.

Maloney, R. K., Mitchison, G. J., & Barlow, H. B. (1987). Limit to the detection of Glass patterns in the presence of noise. *Journal of the Optical Society of America, A, 4*, 2336–2341.

Marozeau, J., de Cheveigne, A., McAdams, S., & Winsberg, S. (2003). The dependency of timbre on fundamental frequency. *Journal of the Acoustical Society of America, 114*, 2946–2957.

Marquet, P. A. (2002). Of predators, prey, and power laws. *Science, 295*, 2229–2230.

Massaro, D. W., Cohen, M. M., & Smeele, P. M. T. (1996). Perceiving asynchronous and conflicting visual and auditory speech. *Journal of the Acoustical Society of America, 100*, 1777–1786.

Mazer, J. A., Vinje, W. E., McDermott, J., Schiller, P. H., & Gallant, J. L. (2002). Spatial frequency tuning and orientation tuning dynamics in area V1. *Proceedings of the National Academy of Science, 99*, 1645–1650.

McAdams, S. (1984). *Spectral fusion, spectral parsing, and the formation of auditory images.* Unpublished doctoral dissertation, Stanford University, Palo Alto, CA.

McAdams, S., Beauchamp, J. W., & Meneguzzi, S. (1999). Discrimination of musical instrument sounds resynthesized with simplified spectrotemporal parameters. *Journal of the Acoustical Society of America, 105*, 882–897.

McAdams, S., Winsberg, S., Donnadieu, S., DeSoete, G., & Krimphoff, J. (1995). Perceptual scaling of synthesized musical timbres: Common dimensions, specificities, and latent subject classes. *Psychological Research, 58*, 177–192.

McGurk, H., & MacDonald, J. (1976). Hearing lips and seeing voices. *Nature, 264*, 746–748.

Meddis, R., & Hewitt, M. J. (1991). Virtual pitch and phase sensitivity of a computer model of the auditory periphery. I. Pitch identification. *Journal of the Acoustical Society of America, 89*, 2866–2882.

Meredith, M. A., Clemo, H. R., & Stein, B. E. (1987). Determinants of multisensory integration in superior colliculus neurons. I. Temporal factors. *Journal of Neuroscience, 10*, 3215–3229.

Metelli, F. (1974). The perception of transparency. *Scientific American*, 91–97.

Miller, G. A. (1981). *Language and communication.* San Francisco: Freeman.

Munhall, K. G., Jones, J. A., Callans, D. E., Kuratate, T., & Vatikiotis-Bateson, E. (2004). Visual prosody and speech intelligibility. *Psychological Science, 15*, 133–137.

Murray, R. F., Bennett, P. J., & Sekular, A. B. (2002). Optimal methods for calculating classification images: Weighted sums. *Journal of Vision, 2*, 79–104.

Nabelek, A. K., Tucker, F. M., & Letwoski, T. R. (1991). Toleration of background noises: Relationship with patterns of hearing aid use by elderly persons. *Journal of Speech and Hearing Research, 34*, 679–685.

Naka, K.-I., & Rushton, W. A. H. (1966). S-potentials from luminosity units in the retina of fish (Cyprinidae). *Journal of Physiology, 185*, 587–599.

Nakayama, K. (1985). Biological image motion processing: A review. *Vision Research, 25*, 625–660.

Nayar, S., & Oren, M. (1995). Visual appearance of matter surfaces. *Science, 267*, 1153–1156.

Nelken, I. (2002). Feature detection by the auditory cortex. In D. Oertel, A. N. Popper, & R. R. Fay (Eds.), *Integrative functions in the mammalian auditory pathway* (Vol. 15, pp. 358–416). New York: Springer-Verlag.

Nelken, I. (2004). Processing of complex stimuli and natural scenes in the auditory cortex. *Current Opinion in Neurobiology, 14*, 474–480.

Nelken, I., Rotman, Y., & Yosef, O. B. (1999). Responses of auditory-cortex neurons to structural features of natural sounds. *Nature, 397*, 154–157.

Nirenberg, S., Carcieri, S. M., Jacobs, A. L., & Latham, P. E. (2001). Retinal ganglion cells act largely as independent encoders. *Nature, 411*, 698–701.

Nothdurft, H.-C. (1997). Different approaches to the coding of visual segmentation. In M. Jenkin & L. Harris (Eds.), *Computational and psychophysical mechanisms of visual coding* (pp. 20–43). Cambridge, UK: Cambridge University Press.

Oertel, D., Bal, R., Gardner, S. M., Smith, P. H., & Joris, P. X. (2000). Detection of synchrony in the activity of auditory nerve fibers by octopus cells of the mammalian cochlear nucleus. *Proceedings of the National Academy of Science, 97*, 1773–1779.

Ohki, K., Chung, S., Ch'ng, Y. H., Kara, P., & Reid, C. (2005). Functional imaging with cellular resolution reveals precise microarchitecture in visual cortex. *Nature, 433*, 597–603.

Olshausen, B. A. (2002). Sparse codes and spikes. In R. P. N. Rao, B. A. Olshausen, & M. S. Lewicki (Eds.), *Probabilistic models of perception and brain function* (pp. 257–272). Cambridge, MA: MIT Press.

Olshausen, B. A., & Field, D. J. (1996). Emergence of simple-cell receptive field properties by learning a sparse code for natural images. *Nature, 381*, 607–609.

Olshausen, B. A., & Field, D. J. (1998). Sparse coding with an overcomplete basis set: A strategy employed by V1. *Vision Research, 37*, 3311–3325.

Olshausen, B. A., & Field, D. J. (2000). Vision and the coding of natural images. *American Scientist, 88*, 238–245.

Olshausen, B. A., & O'Connor, K. N. (2002). A new window on sound. *Nature Neuroscience, 5*, 292–294.

Olzak, L. A., & Thomas, J. P. (2003). Dual nonlinearities regulate contrast sensitivity in pattern discrimination tasks. *Vision Research, 43*, 1433–1422.

Pack, C. C., & Born, R. T. (2001). Temporal dynamics of a neural solution to the aperture problem in visual area MT of macaque brain. *Nature, 409*, 1040–1042.

Packer, O., & Williams, D. R. (2003). Light, the retinal image, and photoreceptors. In S. K. Shevell (Ed.), *The science of color* (2nd ed., pp. 41–102). Oxford, UK: Elsevier.

Palmer, S. E. (1994). Rethinking perceptual organization: The role of uniform connectedness. *Psychonomic Bulletin and Review, 1*, 29–55.

Palmer, S. E. (1999). *Vision science: Photons to phenomenology*. Cambridge, MA: MIT Press.

Pantle, A. J., & Picciano, L. (1976). A multistable movement display; evidence for two separate motion system in human vision. *Science, 193*, 500–502.

Panzei, S., & Schultz, S. R. (2001). A unified approach to the study of temporal, correlational, and rate coding. *Neural Computation, 13*, 1311–1349.

Paradiso, M. A. (2002). Perceptual and neuronal correspondence in primary visual cortex. *Current Opinion in Neurobiology, 12*, 155–161.

Parker, A. R. (1999). Light-reflection strategies. *American Scientist, 87*, 248–255.

Parkkinen, J. P. S., Hallikainen, J., & Jaaskelainen, T. (1989). Characteristic spectra of munsell colors. *Journal of the Optical Society of America, A, 6*, 318–322.

Parraga, C. A., Brelstaff, G., Troscianko, T., & Moorhead, I. R. (1998). Color and luminance information in natural scenes. *Journal of the Optical Society of America, A, 15*, 563–569.

Parraga, C. A., Troscianko, T., & Tolhurst, D. J. (1999). The human visual system is optimized for processing the spatial information in natural visual images. *Current Biology, 10*, 35–38.

Partan, S., & Marler, P. (1999). Communication goes multimodal. *Science, 283*, 1272–1273.

Patterson, R. D., Handel, S., Yost, W. A., & Datta, A. J. (1996). The relative strength of the tone and noise components in iterated rippled noise. *Journal of the Acoustical Society of America, 100*, 3286–3294.

Perez-Orive, J., Mazor, O., Turner, G. C., Cassenaer, S., Wilson, R., & Laurent, G. (2002). Oscillations and sparsening of the odor representations in the mushroom body. *Science, 297*, 359–365.

Peterson, G. E., & Barney, H. E. (1952). Control methods used in a study of vowels. *Journal of the Acoustical Society of America, 24*, 175–184.

Petter, G. (1956). Nuove ricerche sperimentali sulla totalizzazione percettiva. *Reivista di Psicologia, 50*, 213–227.

Pfafflin, S. M. (1968). Detection of auditory signal in restricted sets of reproducible noise. *Journal of the Acoustical Society of America, 43*, 487–490.

Pfafflin, S. M., & Mathews, M. V. (1966). Detection of auditory signals in reproducible noise. *Journal of the Acoustical Society of America, 39*, 340–345.

Pittinger, J. B., Shaw, R. E., & Mark, L. S. (1979). Perceptual information for the age levels of faces as a higher order invariant of growth. *Journal of Experimental Psychology: Human Perception and Performance, 5*, 478–493.

Pizlo, Z. (2001). Perception viewed as an inverse problem. *Vision Research, 41*, 3145–3161.

Pizlo, Z., Salach-Golyska, M., & Rosenfeld, A. (1997). Curve detection in a noisy image. *Vision Research, 37*(9), 1217–1241.

Plomp, R. (1975). *Aspects of tone sensation*. London: Academic Press.

Pollak, G. D., Burger, M., & Klug, S. (2003). Dissecting the circuitry of the auditory system. *Trends in Neuroscience, 126*, 33–39.

Pollack, I. (1975). Identification of random auditory waveforms. *Journal of the Acoustical Society of America, 58*, 1262–1271.

Poppel, E. (1988). *Mindworks: Time and conscious experience*. New York: Harcourt Brace-Jovanovich.

Pouget, A., Dayan, P., & Zemel, R. (2000). Information processing with population codes. *Nature Reviews: Neuroscience, 1*, 125–132.

Pouget, A., Deneve, S., & Duhamel, J.-R. (2002). A computational perspective on the neural basis of multisensory spatial representations. *Nature Reviews: Neuroscience, 3*, 741–747.

Poulim-Charronnat, B., Bigand, E., Madurell, F., Vieillard, S., & McAdams, S. (2004). Effects of a change in instrumentation on the recognition of musical materials. *Music Perception, 22*, 239–263.

Prazdny, K. (1986). Some new phenomena in the perception of Glass patterns. *Biological Cybernetics, 53*, 153–158.

Purves, D., Lotto, R. B., & Nundy, S. (2002). Why we see what we do. *American Scientist, 90*, 236–243.

Quiroga, R. Q., Reddy, L., Kreiman, G., Koch, C., & Fried, I. (2005). Invariant visual representation by single neurons in the human brain. *Nature, 435*, 1102–1107.

Ramachandran, V. S., & Antis, S. M. (1983). Perceptual organization in moving patterns. *Nature, 304*, 529–531.

Rasch, R. A. (1978). The perception of simultaneous notes such as in polyphonic music. *Acustica, 40*, 22–33.

Rauschecker, J. P., & Tian, B. (2000). Mechanisms and streams for processing of "what" and "where" in auditory cortex. *Proceedings of the National Academy of Science, 97*, 11800–11806.

Raymond, J. E. (2000). Attention modulation of visual motion perception. *Trends in Cognitive Science, 4*, 42–50.

Read, H. L., Winer, J. A., & Schreiner, C. E. (2001). Modular organization of intrinsic connections associated with spectral tuning in cat auditory cortex. *Proceedings of the National Academy of Science, 98*, 8042–8047.

Read, H. L., Winer, J. A., & Schreiner, C. E. (2002). Functional architecture of auditory cortex. *Current Opinion in Neurobiology, 12*, 433–440.

Recanzone, G. H. (2003). Auditory influences on visual temporal rate perception. *Journal of Neurophysiology, 89*, 1079–1093.

Reich, D. S., Mechler, F., & Victor, J. D. (2001). Independent and redundant information in nearby cortical neurons. *Science, 294*, 2566–2568.

Reichardt, W. (1961). Autocorrelation, a principle for the evaluation of sensory information by the central nervous system. In W. A. Rosenblith (Ed.), *Sensory communication* (pp. 303–317). New York: Wiley.

Reinagel, P. (2001). How do visual neurons respond in the real world? *Current Opinion in Neurobiology, 11*, 437–442.

Repp, B. H. (1987). The sound of two hands clapping: An exploratory study. *Journal of the Acoustical Society of America, 81*, 1100–1109.

Rieke, F., Warland, D., de Ruyter van Steveninck, R., & Bialek, W. (1997). *Spikes: Exploring the neural code*. Cambridge, MA: MIT Press.

Rock, I. (1983). *The logic of perception*. Cambridge, MA: MIT Press.

Rock, I. (1997). The concept of indirect perception. In I. Rock (Ed.), *Indirect perception* (pp. 5–15). Cambridge, MA: MIT Press/Bradford Books.

Rock, I., & Brosgole, L. (1964). Grouping based on phenomenal proximity. *Journal of Experimental Psychology, 67*, 531–538.

Rock, I., Nijhawan, R., Palmer, S. E., & Tudor, L. (1992). Grouping based on phenomenal similarity of achromatic color. *Perception, 21*, 779–789.

Rodieck, R. W. (1965). Quantitative analysis of cat retinal ganglion cell response to visual stimuli. *Vision Research, 5*, 583–601.

Romero, J., Garcia-Beltran, A., & Hernandez-Andres, J. (1997). Linear bases for representation of natural and artificial illuminants. *Journal of the Optical Society of America, A, 14*, 1007–1014.

Rose, J. E., Brugge, J. F., Anderson, D. J., & Hind, J. E. (1967). Phase-locked response to low-frequency tones in single auditory nerve fibers of the squirrel monkey. *Journal of Neurophysiology, 30*, 769–793.

Rosenblum, L. D. (2004). Perceiving articulatory events: Lessons for an ecological psychoacoustics. In J. G. Neuhoff (Ed.), *Ecological psychoacoustics* (pp. 219–248). San Diego: Elsevier Academic.

Rubin, E. (1921). *Visuell Wahrgenommene Figuren*. Copenhagen: Gyldendalska.

Ruderman, D. L. (1997). Origins of scaling in natural images. *Vision Research, 37*, 3385–3398.

Ruderman, D. L., Cronin, T. W., & Chiao, C.-C. (1998). Statistics of cone responses to natural images: Implications for visual coding. *Journal of the Optical Society of America, A, 15*, 2036–2045.

Sary, G., Vogels, R., Kovacs, G., & Orban, G. A. (1995). Responses of monkey inferior temporal neurons to luminance, motion, and texture defined gratings. *Journal of Neurophysiology, 73*, 1341–1354.

Schmuckler, M. A., & Gilden, D. L. (1993). Auditory perception of fractal contours. *Journal of Experimental Psychology: Human Perception and Performance, 19*, 641–660.

Schreiner, C. E., Read, H. L., & Sutter, M. L. (2000). Modular organization of frequency integration in primary auditory cortex. *Annual Review of Neuroscience, 23*, 501–529.

Schroder, M. (1991). *Fractals, chaos, power laws*. New York: W.H. Freeman.

Schulz, M., & Sanocki, T. (2003). Time course of perceptual grouping by color. *Psychological Science, 14*, 26–30.

Sekiyama, K. (1997). Cultural and linguistic factors in audiovisual processing: The McGurk effect in Chinese subjects. *Perception and Psychophysics, 59*, 73–80.

Sekiyama, K., & Tohkura, Y. (1993). Inter-language differences in the influence of visual cues in speech perception. *Journal of Phonetics, 21*, 427–444.

Sekuler, A. B., & Bennett, J. P. (2001). Generalized common fate: Grouping by common luminance changes. *Psychological Science, 12*, 437–444.

Sen, K., Theunissen, F. E., & Doupe, A. J. (2001). Feature analysis of natural sounds in the songbird auditory forebrain. *Journal of Neurophysiology, 86*, 1445–1458.

Seu, L., & Ferrera, V. P. (2001). Detection thresholds for spiral Glass patterns. *Vision Research, 41*, 3785–3790.

Shamma, S. (2001). On the role of space and time in auditory processing. *Trends in Cognitive Science, 5*, 340–348.

Shamma, S., & Klein, D. (2000). The case of the missing pitch templates: How harmonic templates emerge in the early auditory system. *Journal of the Acoustical Society of America, 107*, 2631–2644.

Shams, L., Kamitani, Y., & Shimojo, S. (2000). What you see is what you hear. *Nature, 408*, 788.

Shannon, C. E. (1948). A mathematical theory of communication. *Bell System Technical Journal, 27*, 379–423, 623–656.

Shannon, C. E., & Weaver, W. (1949). *The mathematical theory of communication.* Urbana: University of Illinois Press.

Shapley, R. (2000). The receptive fields of visual neurons. In K. K. De Valois (Ed.), *Seeing* (2nd ed., pp. 55–78). San Diego: Academic Press.

Shapley, R., & Enroth, C. (1984). Visual adaptation and retinal gain controls. *Progress in Retinal Research, 3*, 263–346.

Sharon, D., & Grinvold, A. (2002). Dynamics and constancy in cortical spatiotemporal patterns of orientation processing. *Science, 295*, 512–515.

Shepard, R. N. (1981). Psychophysical complementarity. In M. Kubovy & J. R. Pomerantz (Eds.), *Perceptual organization* (pp. 279–341). Hillsdale, NJ: Erlbaum.

Shepard, R. N., & Zare, S. L. (1983). Path-guided apparent motion. *Science, 220*, 632–634.

Shevell, S. K. (Ed.). (2003). *The science of color* (2nd ed.). London: Elsevier.

Shimojo, S., & Shams, L. (2001). Sensory modalities are not separate modalities: Plasticity and interactions. *Current Opinion in Neurobiology, 11*, 505–509.

Shipley, T. F. (1964). Auditory flutter-driving of visual flicker. *Science, 145*, 1328–1330.

Siegel, S. K., & Colburn, H. S. (1989). Binaural processing of noisy stimuli: Internal/external noise ratios for diotic and dichotic stimuli. *Journal of the Acoustical Society of America, 86*, 2122–2128.

Sigala, N., & Logothetics, N. K. (2002). Visual categorization shapes feature selectivity in the primate temporal cortex. *Nature, 415*, 318–320.

Simoncelli, E. P. (2003). Vision and the statistics of the visual environment. *Current Opinion in Neurobiology, 13*, 144–149.

Simoncelli, E. P., Freeman, W. T., Adelson, E. H., & Heeger, D. J. (1992). Shiftable multiscale transforms. *IEEE Transactions on Information Theory, 382*, 587–607.

Simoncelli, E. P., & Olshausen, B. A. (2001). Natural image statistics and neural representation. *Annual Review of Neuroscience, 24*, 1193–1216.

Simpson, W. A., Falkenberg, H. K., & Manhilov, V. (2003). Sampling efficiency and internal noise for motion detection, discrimination, and summation. *Vision Research, 43*, 2125–2132.

Singh, M. (2004). Modal and amodal completion generate different shapes. *Psychological Science, 15*, 454–459.

Singh, M., & Hoffman, D. D. (2001). Part-based representations of visual shape and implications for visual cognition. In T. F. Shipley & P. J. Kellman (Eds.), *From fragments to objects: Segmentation and grouping in vision* (pp. 401–459). Amsterdam: ElsevierScience B.V.

Slutsky, D. A., & Recanzone, G. H. (2001). Temporal and spatial dependency of the ventriloquism effect. *NeuroReport, 12*, 7–10.

Smaragdis, P. (2001). *Redundancy reduction for computational audition: A unifying approach.* Unpublished doctoral dissertation, MIT, Cambridge, MA.

Snowden, R. J. (1998). Texture segregation and visual search: A comparison of the effects of random variations along irrelevant dimensions. *Journal of Experimental Psychology: Human Perception and Performance, 24*, 1354–1367.

Spiegel, M., & Green, D. M. (1981). Two procedures for estimating internal noise. *Journal of the Acoustical Society of America, 70*, 69–73.

Stein, B. E., & Meredith, M. A. (1993). *The merging of the senses*. Cambridge, MA: Bradford/MIT Press.

Stone, J. V., Hunkin, N. M., Porrill, J., Wood, R., Keeler, V., & Beanland, M. (2001). When is now? Perception of simultaneity. *Proceedings of the Royal Society, B, 268*, 31–38.

Stone, L. S., Watson, A. B., & Mulligan, J. B. (1990). Effect of contrast on the perceived direction of a moving plaid. *Vision Research, 30*(7), 1049–1067.

Stoner, G. R., & Albright, T. D. (1994). Visual motion integration: A neurophysiological and psychophysical perspective. In A. T. Smith & R. J. Snowden (Eds.), *Visual detection of motion* (pp. 253–290). London: Academic Press.

Suga, N., & Ma, X. (2003). Multiparametric corticofugal modulation and plasticity in the auditory system. *Nature Reviews: Neuroscience, 4*, 783–794.

Sugita, Y., & Suzuki, Y. (2003). Implicit estimation of sound-arrival time. *Nature, 421*, 911.

Sumby, W. H., & Pollack, I. (1954). Visual contributions to speech intelligibility in noise. *Journal of the Acoustical Society of America, 26*, 212–215.

Summerfield, Q. (1991). Visual perception of phonetic gestures. In I. Mattingly & M. Studdert-Kennedy (Eds.), *Modularity and the motor theory of speech perception* (pp. 117–138). Hillsdale, NJ: Erlbaum.

Summerfield, Q., & Culling, J. (1992). Auditory segregation of competing voices. *Philosophical Transactions of the Royal Society of London. Series B, 336*, 357–366.

Sumner, C. J., Lopez-Poveda, E. A., O'Mard, L. P., & Meddis, R. (2002). A revised model of the inner-hair cell and auditory-nerve complex. *Journal of the Acoustical Society of America, 111*, 2178–2188.

Sutter, A., & Hwang, D. (1999). A comparison of the dynamics of simple (Fourier) and complex (non-Fourier) mechanisms in texture segregation. *Vision Research, 39*, 1943–1962.

Sutter, M. L., Schreiner, C. E., McLean, M., O'Connor, K. N., & Loftus, W. C. (1999). Organization of inhibitory frequency receptive fields in cat primary auditory cortex. *Journal of Neurophysiology, 82*, 2358–2371.

Swets, J. A. (Ed.). (1964). *Signal detection and recognition by human observers*. New York: John Wiley.

Terhardt, E. (1974). Pitch, consonance, and harmony. *Journal of the Acoustical Society of America, 55*, 1061–1069.

Theunissen, F. E., Sen, K., & Doupe, A. J. (2000). Spectral-temporal receptive fields of nonlinear auditory neurons obtained using natural sounds. *Journal of Neuroscience, 20*, 2315–2331.

Thibos, L. N. (2000). Formation and sampling of the retinal image. In K. De Valois (Ed.), *Seeing* (2nd ed., pp. 1–52). San Diego: Academic Press.

Thomson, M. G. A. (1999). Higher-order structure in natural scenes. *Journal of the Optical Society of America, A, 16*, 1549–1553.

Thurlow, W. R., & Jack, C. E. (1973). Certain determinants of the "ventriloquism effect." *Perceptual and Motor Skills, 36*, 1171–1184.

Troost, J. M. (1998). Empirical studies in color constancy. In V. Walsh & J. Kulikowski (Eds.), *Perceptual constancies* (pp. 262–282). Cambridge, UK: Cambridge University Press.

Tse, P., Cavanagh, K., & Nakayama, K. (1998). The role of parsing in high-level motion processing. In T. Watanabe (Ed.), *Computational neurobiological, and psychophysical perspectives* (pp. 249–266). Cambridge, MA: MIT Press.

Turgeon, M. (2000). *Cross-spectral auditory grouping using the paradigm of rhythmic masking release.* Unpublished doctoral dissertation, McGill University, Montreal.

Tyler, C. W. (2004). Theory of texture discrimination based on higher-order perturbations in individual texture samples. *Vision Research, 44*, 2179–2186.

Uttal, W. R. (1975). *An autocorrelation theory of form perception.* Hillsdale, NJ: Erlbaum.

van der Helm, P. A. (2000). Simplicity versus likelihood in visual perception: From surprisals to precisals. *Psychological Bulletin, 126*, 770–800.

Van de Smagt, M. J., Verstraten, F. A., & van de Grind, W. A. (1999). A new transparent motion aftereffect. *Nature Neuroscience, 2*, 595–596.

Van Essen, D. C., Anderson, C. H., & Felleman, D. J. (1992). Information processing in the primate visual system: An integrated systems perspective. *Science, 255*, 419–422.

van Noorden, L. P. A. S. (1975). *Temporal coherence in the perception of tone sequences.* Unpublished doctoral dissertation, Eindhoven University of Technology, Eindhoven.

Vanderveer, N. J. (1979). *Ecological acoustics: Human perception of environmental sounds.* Unpublished doctoral dissertation, Cornell University, Ithaca, NY.

Victor, J. D. (1994). Images, statistics, and textures: Implications of triple correlation uniqueness for texture statistics and the Julesz conjecture: Comment. *Journal of the Optical Society of America, A, 11*, 1680–1684.

Victor, J. D. (2000). How the brain uses time to represent and process visual information. *Brain Research, 886*, 33–46.

Victor, J. D., & Conte, M. M. (2004). Visual working memory for image statistics. *Vision Research, 44*, 541–556.

Vidnyanszky, Z., Blaser, E., & Papathomas, T. V. (2002). Motion integration during motion aftereffects. *Trends in Cognitive Science, 6*, 157–161.

Vinje, W. E., & Gallant, J. L. (2000). Sparse coding and decorrelation in primary visual cortex during natural vision. *Science, 287*, 1273–1276.

Vinje, W. E., & Gallant, J. L. (2002). Natural stimulation of the nonclassical receptive field increases information transmission efficiency in V1. *Journal of Neuroscience, 22*, 2904–2915.

von Bekesy, G. (1963). Three experiments concerned with speech perception. *Journal of the Acoustical Society of America, 35*, 602–606.

von Bekesy, G. (1967). *Sensory inhibition.* Princeton, NJ: Princeton University Press.

von Kreis, J. (1970). Chromatic adaptation. In D. L. MacAdam (Ed.), *Sources of color science* (pp. 109–119). Cambridge, MA: MIT Press.

Voss, R. F., & Clarke, J. (1978). 1/*f* Noise in music: Music from 1/*f* noise. *Journal of the Acoustical Society of America, 63*, 258–263.

Vrhel, M. J., Gershon, R., & Iwan, L. S. (1994). Measurement and analysis of object reflectance spectra. *Color Research and Application, 19*, 4–9.

Wachler, T., Lee, T.-W., & Sejnowski, T. J. (2001). Chromatic structure of natural scenes. *Journal of the Optical Society of America, A, 18*, 65–77.

Wagemans, J., Van Gool, L., Swinnen, V., & Van Horebeek, J. (1993). Higher order structure in regularity detection. *Vision Research, 33*, 1067–1088.

Wagenmakers, E.-J., Farrell, S., & Ratcliff, R. (2004). Estimation and interpretation of $1/f^{\alpha}$ noise in human cognition. *Psychonomic Bulletin and Review, 11*, 579–615.

Wainwright, M. J. (1999). Visual adaptation as optimal information transmission. *Vision Research, 39*, 3960–3974.

Walker, S., Bruce, V., & O'Malley, C. (1995). Facial identity and facial speech processing: Familiar faces and voices in the McGurk effect. *Perception and Psychophysics, 57*, 1124–1133.

Walraven, J., Enroth-Cugell, C., Hood, D. C., MacLeod, D. I. A., & Schnapf, J. (1990). The control of visual sensitivity: Receptoral and postreceptoral processes. In L. Spillman, & J. S. Warner (Eds.), *Visual perception: The neurophysiological foundations* (pp. 53–101). New York: Academic.

Wandell, B. (1995). *Foundations of vision*. Sunderland, MA: Sinauer.

Wang, X., & Kadia, S. (2001). Differential representation of species-specific primate vocalizations in the auditory cortices of marmoset and cat. *Journal of Neurophysiology, 86*, 2616–2620.

Wang, X., Lu, T., Snider, R. K., & Liang, Li. (2005). Sustained firing in auditory cortex evoked by preferred stimuli. *Nature, 435*, 341–346.

Wang, X., Merzenich, M. M., Beitel, R., & Schreiner, C. E. (1995). Representation of a species-specific vocalization in the primary auditory cortex of the common marmoset: Temporal and spectral characteristics. *Journal of Neurophysiology, 74*, 2685–2706.

Warren, D. H., Welch, R. B., & McCarthy, T. J. (1981). The role of "compellingness" in the ventriloquism effect: Implications for transitivity among the spatial senses. *Perception and Psychophysics, 30*, 357–564.

Warren, R. M. (1999). *Auditory perception: A new analysis and synthesis*. New York: Cambridge University Press.

Warren, R. M., & Bashford, J. A. J. (1981). Perception of acoustic iterance: Pitch and infrapitch. *Perception and Psychophysics, 29*, 395–402.

Warren, R. M., Bashford, J. A. J., Cooley, J. M., & Brubaker, B. S. (2001). Detection of acoustic repetition for very long stochastic patterns. *Perception and Psychophysics, 63*, 175–182.

Warren, R. M., Bashford, J. A. J., & Wrightson, J. M. (1980). Infrapitch echo. *Journal of the Acoustical Society of America, 68*, 1301–1305.

Warren, W. H. J., & Verbrugge, R. R. (1984). Auditory perception of breaking and bouncing events. *Journal of Eexperimental Psychology: Human Perception and Performance, 10*, 704–712.

Watamaniuk, S. N. J., McKee, S. P., & Grzywacz, N. M. (1995). Detecting a trajectory embedded in random motion noise. *Vision Research, 35*, 65–77.

Watson, D. G., & Humphreys, G. W. (1999). Segmentation on the basis of linear and local rotational motion: Motion grouping in visual search. *Journal of Experimental Psychology: Human Perception and Performance, 25*, 70–82.

Wedin, L., & Goude, G. (1972). Dimension analysis of the perception of instrumental timbre. *Scandinavian Journal of Psychology, 13*, 228–240.

Wehr, M. S., & Zador, A. (2003). Balanced inhibition underlies tuning and sharpens spike timing in auditory cortex. *Nature, 426*, 442–446.

Weisz, N., Wienbach, C., Hoffmeister, S., & Elbert, T. (2004). Tonotopic organization of the human auditory cortex probed with frequency-modulated tones. *Hearing Research, 19*, 49–58.

Welch, R. B. (1999). Meaning, attention, and the "unity assumption" in the intersensory bias of spatial and temporal perceptions. In T. Aschersleben, T. Bachmann, & J. Musseler (Eds.), *Cognitive contributions to the perception of spatial and temporal events* (pp. 371–387). Amsterdam: Elsevier Science BV.

Werblin, F. S. (1974). Control of retinal sensitivity. II. Lateral interactions at the outer plexiform layer. *Journal of General Physiology, 63*, 62–87.

Wertheimer, M. (1912). Experimentelle Studien uber das Sehen von Bewegung [Experimental studies on the seeing of motion]. *Zeitschrift für Psychologie unter Physiologie der Sinnesorgane, 61*, 161–265.

Whitfield, I. C. (1979). Periodicity, pulse interval and pitch. *Audiology, 18*, 507–512.

Wiegrebe, L., Patterson, R. P., Demany, L., & Carlyon, R. P. (1998). Temporal dynamics of pitch strength in regular interval noises. *Journal of the Acoustical Society of America, 104*, 2307.

Wilson, H. R. (1994). Model of two-dimensional motion perception. In A. T. Smith & R. J. Snowden (Eds.), *Visual detection of motion* (pp. 219–252). London: Academic Press.

Wilson, H. R., & Humanski, R. (1993). Spatial frequency control and contrast gain control. *Vision Research, 33*, 1133–1149.

Wilson, H. R., & Wilkerson, F. (1998). Detection of global structure in Glass patterns: Implications for form vision. *Vision Research, 38*, 2933–2947.

Wilson, H. R., Wilkerson, F., & Assad, W. (1997). Concentric orientation summation in human form vision. *Vision Research, 37*, 2325–2330.

Wilson, J. A., Switkes, E., & De Valois, R. L. (2004). Glass pattern studies of local and global processing of contrast variations. *Vision Research, 44*, 2629–2641.

Wishart, K. A., Frisby, J. P., & Buckley, D. (1997). The role of 3-D surface slope in a lightness/brightness effect. *Vision Research, 37*, 467–473.

Wyszecki, G., & Stiles, W. S. (1982). *Color science: Concepts and methods: Quantitative data and formulae* (2nd ed.). New York: John Wiley.

Yang, J. N., & Maloney, L. T. (2001). Illuminant cues in surface color perception: Tests of three candidate cues. *Vision Research, 41*, 2581–2600.

Yellot, J. I. J. (1993). Implications of triple correlation uniqueness for texture statistics and the Julesz conjecture. *Journal of the Optical Society of America, A, 10*, 777–793.

Yo, C., & Wilson, H. R. (1992). Perceived direction of moving two-dimensional patterns depends on duration, contrast, and eccentricity. *Vision Research, 32*, 135–147.

Yost, W. A., Patterson, R. D., & Sheft, S. (1996). A time domain description for the pitch strength of iterated rippled noise. *Journal of the Acoustical Society of America, 99*, 1066–1078.

Yuille, & Grzywacz. (1998). A theoretical framework for visual motion, in higher-level motion processing. In T. Watanabe (Ed.), *Computational neurobiological, and psychophysical perspectives* (pp. 187–221). Cambridge, MA: MIT Press.

Zanker, J. M. (1993). Theta motion: A paradoxical stimulus to explore higher order motion extraction. *Vision Research, 33*, 553–569.

Zanker, J. M. (1995). Of models and men: Mechanisms of human motion perception. In T. V. Papathomas (Ed.), *Early vision and beyond* (pp. 155–165). Cambridge, MA: MIT Press.

Zatorre, R. J., Bouffard, M., Ahad, P., & Belin, P. (2002). Where is "where" in the human auditory cortex? *Nature Neuroscience, 5*, 905–909.

Zera, J., & Green, D. M. (1993). Detecting temporal asynchrony with asynchronous standards. *Journal of the Acoustical Society of America, 93*, 1571–1579.

Zetzsche, C., Krieger, G., & Wegmann, B. (1999). The atoms of vision: Cartesian or polar. *Journal of the Optical Society of America, A, 16*, 1554–1565.

Index

Boldfaced entries refer to citations in the references